CHINA AND THE RULES-BASED INTERNATIONAL ORDER

CHINA AND THE RULES-BASED INTERNATIONAL ORDER

Globalized Populism and Crisis Response

Pitman B. Potter

UBCPress · Vancouver

Originally printed in Canada.

Printed and bound by CPI Group (UK) Ltd, Croydon, CR0 4YY

UBC Press is an eBOUND Digital Certified publisher. The epub version of this book meets stringent accessibility standards, ensuring it is available to people with diverse needs.

Library and Archives Canada Cataloguing in Publication

Title: China and the rules-based international order : globalized populism and crisis response / Pitman B. Potter.
Names: Potter, Pitman B., author
Description: Includes bibliographical references and index.
Identifiers: Canadiana (print) 20260142212 | Canadiana (ebook) 20260142220 | ISBN 9780774872591 (hardcover) | ISBN 9780774872614 (PDF) | ISBN 9780774872621 (EPUB)
Subjects: LCSH: Xi, Jinping. | LCSH: China – Foreign relations – 21st century. | LCSH: Populism – China. | LCSH: COVID-19 Pandemic, 2020-2023 – Government policy – China. | LCSH: Climatic changes – Government policy – China. | LCSH: Forced migration – Government policy – China.
Classification: LCC DS779.47 .P68 2026 | DDC 327.51—dc23

UBC Press gratefully acknowledges the financial support for our publishing program of the Government of Canada, the Canada Council for the Arts, and the British Columbia Arts Council.

This book has been published with the help of a grant from the Canadian Federation for the Humanities and Social Sciences, through the Scholarly Book Awards, using funds provided by the Social Sciences and Humanities Research Council of Canada, and with the help of the University of British Columbia through the K.D. Srivastava Fund.

UBC Press is situated on the traditional, ancestral, and unceded territory of the xʷməθkʷəy̓əm (Musqueam) people. This land has always been a place of learning for the xʷməθkʷəy̓əm, who have passed on their culture, history, and traditions for millennia, from one generation to the next.

UBC Press
The University of British Columbia
www.ubcpress.ca

Thanks to the Holy One for the gifts of clarity in perception,
wonder in discovery, and compassion in interpretation
that illuminated my work on this book.

Contents

Figures and Tables

FIGURES

TABLES

Acknowledgments

MY WORK ON THIS book began during the COVID-19 pandemic and continued through multiple revisions and much rethinking. Throughout it all, I have benefited from the sage advice and valued encouragement of many University of British Columbia colleagues, particularly Ljiljana Biuković, Timothy Cheek, Timothy McDaniels, and Yves Tiberghien. I would also like to thank the various anonymous reviewers whose comments and suggestions enabled me to improve the work. I am grateful to the Allard School of Law at UBC for its ongoing support and for providing emerit office space and staff assistance. I am grateful to the Emeritus College and the Institute of Asian Research at UBC for their ongoing support for my research and writing. I would also like to thank the East-West Center at the University of Hawai'i at Mānoa (particularly Jeff Fox and Denny Roy) for encouraging my work, and for inviting me to contribute a short piece to its *Asia Pacific Issues* in January 2022. I am also grateful to the Law School at UH Mānoa (particularly Mark Levin) for affording me an opportunity to present an early version of this work in November 2022. My thanks go as well to UBC Press, particularly Randy Schmidt, for consistent support in bringing this book to press. I would most especially like to thank Vicki for her steadfast and patient encouragement for my work on this project.

Abbreviations

ADB	Asian Development Bank
AIDS	Acquired Immunodeficiency Syndrome
ALL	Administrative Litigation Law (PRC)
APEC	Asia Pacific Economic Cooperation (organization)
APFC	Asia Pacific Foundation of Canada
AUKUS	Australia-UK-US security arrangement
BJP	Bharatiya Janata Party
BRI	Belt and Road Initiative (PRC)
CAA	Citizenship Amendment Act (India)
CASS	Chinese Academy of Social Sciences
CBDR	common but differentiated responsibilities
CCDC	Chinese Center for Disease Control and Prevention (PRC)
CCDI	Central Commission for Discipline Inspection (PRC)
CCG	Centre for China and Globalization (ILO)
CCPI	Climate Change Performance Index
CECC	Congressional Executive Commission on China (US)
CERD	Committee on the Elimination of Racial Discrimination (UN)
CESCR	United Nations Committee on Economic, Social and Cultural Rights

CEWC	Central Economic Work Conference (PRC)
CGTN	China Global Television Network
COP	Conference of the Parties to the UNFCCC
CPC	Communist Party of China
CPLAC	Central Political and Legal Affairs Commission (PRC)
CPPCC	Chinese People's Political Consultative Conference
CRRF	Comprehensive Refugee Response Framework
CRS	Congressional Research Service (US)
CSR	Corporate Social Responsibility
DESA	Department of Economic and Social Affairs (UN)
DNI	Office of the Director of National Intelligence (US)
EPL	Environmental Protection Law of the PRC
ESCAP	Economic and Social Commission for Asia and the Pacific (UN)
EU	European Union
ExCom	Executive Committee of UNHCR
FYP	Five-Year Plan
G20	Group of 20, an international forum that brings together the governments and central bank governors of nineteen countries and the European Union
GCM	Global Compact for Safe, Orderly and Regular Migration
GCR	Global Compact on Refugees
GenBank	Genetic Sequence Data Bank (NIH)
GHG	Greenhouse Gas
HIV	Human Immunodeficiency Virus
HRIC	Human Rights in China (organization)
HRW	Human Rights Watch
ICC	International Criminal Court
ICCPR	International Covenant on Civil and Political Rights
ICERD	International Covenant on the Elimination of All Forms of Racial Discrimination
ICESCR	International Covenant on Economic, Social and Cultural Rights
IFI	international financial institution
IIMM	Independent Investigative Mechanism for Myanmar
ILO	International Labour Organization

IMF	International Monetary Fund
IOM	International Organization for Migration
IPCC	Intergovernmental Panel on Climate Change
JAMA	*Journal of the American Medical Association*
LMDC	Like-Minded Developing Countries
LRNA	Law of the PRC on Regional National Autonomy
LSG	Leading Small Group (PRC)
MEE	Ministry of Ecology and Environment (MEE)
MEF	Major Economies Forum
MEP	Ministry of Environmental Protection (PRC)
MFA	Ministry of Foreign Affairs (PRC)
MIPEX	Migrant Integration Policy Index
MOFCOM	Ministry of Commerce (PRC)
MOJ	Ministry of Justice (PRC)
NDC	Nationally Determined Contributions (under the UNFCCC COP process)
NDRC	National Development and Reform Commission (NDRC)
NEAC	National Ethnic Affairs Commission (PRC)
NGO	non-governmental organization
NHC	National Health Commission (PRC)
NIA	National Immigration Administration (PRC)
NIH	National Institutes of Health (US)
NPC	National People's Congress (PRC)
NPR	National Public Radio (US)
NPRI	National Population Register (India)
NRDC	Natural Resources Defense Council
NSL	National Security Law of the PRC
OAS	Organization of American States
OAU	Organization for African Unity
OECD	Organisation for Economic Co-operation and Development
OHCHR	Office of the High Commissioner for Human Rights
PHEIC	Public Health Emergency of International Concern
PRC	People's Republic of China
PSC	Politburo Standing Committee (PRC)
PSUV	United Socialist Party of Venezuela

RLDC	Regionally and Locally Determined Contribution
ROC	Republic of China
SAGO	Scientific Advisory Group for the Origins of Novel Pathogens (WHO)
SARS	Severe Acute Respiratory Syndrome
SCIO	State Council Information Office (PRC)
SCL	State Compensation Law of the PRC
SDG	Sustainable Development Goals
SSPL	State Secrets Protection Law (PRC)
TCM	Traditional Chinese Medicine
UDHR	Universal Declaration of Human Rights
UN	United Nations
UNCTAD	United Nations Conference on Trade and Development
UNDP	United Nations Development Programme
UNEP	United Nations Environment Programme
UNESCO	United Nations Educational, Scientific and Cultural Organization
UNFCCC	United Nations Framework Convention on Climate Change
UNGA	United Nations General Assembly
UNHCR	Office of the United Nations High Commissioner for Refugees
UNHRC	United Nations Human Rights Council
UNIDO	United Nations Industrial Development Organization
UNRISD	UN Research Institute for Social Development
UPR	Universal Periodic Review
WFP	World Food Programme (UN)
WHA	World Health Assembly
WHO	World Health Organization
WIV	Wuhan Institute of Virology

CHINA AND THE RULES-BASED INTERNATIONAL ORDER

Introduction

CHINA'S RELATIONSHIP WITH the rules-based international order has become increasingly conflicted.[1] Long gone are the days when policies of "reform and opening up" associated with Deng Xiaoping signalled a greater possibility of China's acceptance of international standards on democracy, open markets, and human rights.[2] Xi Jinping's regime has, with growing frequency and intensity, challenged the norms and institutions of the rules-based international order.[3] Even his calls for greater study of international law are oriented toward changing its standards to conform more closely to the priorities of the People's Republic of China (PRC).[4]

In response, many of Beijing's erstwhile partners in Europe and North America have begun to reassess their relations with the PRC in light of these new realities. Canada's Indo-Pacific Strategy labelled China "an increasingly disruptive global power."[5] The United States' Integrated Country Strategy for China reiterated former Secretary of State Antony Blinken's caution that China's efforts to reshape the international order "would move us away from the universal values that have sustained so much of the world's progress over the past 75 years," and committed to "defend democracy and freedom of expression, freedom of the press, religion, and the rule of law."[6] In the United Kingdom, the House of Lords' review of the security and trade relationship with China noted that under Xi Jinping, China has become "more assertive and hardened its stance on its territorial integrity and national sovereignty, reacting strongly to what it perceived to be foreign interference in its domestic politics," and called for an integrated China strategy that would respond to tensions and deterioration in the UK-China relationship.[7] Australia's "comprehensive strategic partnership" with China agreed to in 2014 has come under strain due in part to differences on human rights.[8] While the sudden removal of Foreign Minister Qin Gang in July 2023 may exemplify the drawing down of China's "wolf warrior" style of foreign policy belligerence with which Qin was closely aligned,[9] China's relationship with the international order remains fraught[10] – inviting careful consideration of the factors underlying these conflicts.

This book draws on the rich academic and policy literature on populism to help explain China's responses to the rules-based international order,[11] by reference to the global challenges of COVID-19, climate change, and involuntary migration. It examines the foundations of populism, suggesting that in addition to oft-cited material conditions of inequality evident in perceived political neglect, economic dislocation, and ethnic tensions in society, a behavioural dynamic of complexity and alienation is also at play as conditions of complexity generate an alienated failure of confidence in existing norms and institutions for political and socio-economic relations.[12] The book notes the different locations of populism in societies, regimes, and internationally, while cautioning that populism is neither an exclusively left- or right-wing phenomenon. It examines common features of populism focused on opposition to elites, justification through ideologies of grievance, and practical resistance through alternative standards challenging existing arrangements for governance, the economy, and society.[13]

This book suggests that China's long association with populist political rhetoric has continued under Xi Jinping, as Xi's regime directs populist animus outward against the rules-based international order purportedly dominated by liberal governments in Europe and North America. Such "globalized populism"[14] expresses populist features of anti-elitism, grievance ideology, and practical resistance, bolstered by rhetorical markers around sovereignty, development, and human rights.[15] China's populist differences with the rules-based international order are illustrated in this volume by reference to the global crises of COVID-19 where governance questions are particularly acute; climate change where economic policy is particularly involved; and involuntary migration where local communities are particularly affected. The emergence of COVID-19 in China and ensuing debates over its origins and China's responsibility-cum-liability have lent an air of adversarialism to relations between China and the international public health policy system, affecting the content and tone of China's policy responses as examples of "antagonistic populism."[16] By contrast, the impacts of climate change on China through, for example, deglaciation in the Tibetan Plateau with implications for river systems across southern China; climate-driven desertification in the northern grasslands and farmland with implications for China's food supply; and the challenge of reducing carbon dioxide emissions with implications for China's dependency on fossil fuel consumption[17] have contributed to the country's greater participation in the international climate system, albeit conditioned by populist rhetoric and policy practice – an example of "participatory populism." In contrast to China's handling of COVID-19 and climate change, its response to the crisis of involuntary migration[18] has largely tended toward caution and hesitancy, evincing a sense of "passive populism" against the international migration policy system. The book concludes with suggestions for policy responses aimed at encouraging more cooperative relations between China and the international system.

Understanding China's globalized populism is essential to developing policy responses to its international behaviour. Much of the contemporary scholarly and policy literature on PRC foreign affairs speaks to rational actor discourses around national interests.[19] National interests include material factors of wealth and power, but also account for constraints of domestic politics and the effects of ideological perspectives such as Marxism-Leninism and post-colonialism.[20] Yet national interest discourses may not explain the entirety of China's international behaviour, and have their own share of errors and risks.[21] Assessments of China's response to global crises by reference to discourses of populism can augment national interest analysis, adding to rational actor discourse dimensions of subjective perception and reaction. This book offers such an effort, assessing China's globalized populism as a complement to national interest analysis in explaining the country's international behaviour.

This book relies on original documentation, media reporting, international policy analysis, and scholarly discourse to assess China's populist policy and practice on COVID-19, climate change, and migration. Official documents from China, the United States, and other international actors present indispensable evidence on policy orthodoxy.[22] Media reporting provides useful depictions of PRC policy in action, while reporting by international policy institutions provides insight on the impacts of China's globalized populism and responses thereto. Scholarly discourse provides perspectives illuminating the documentary, media, and policy reporting record.

Chapter 1 surveys scholarly work and policy reporting on populism and develops perspectives on the foundations, locations, political orientations, and common features of populism as context for understanding China's globalized populism. Chapter 2 examines China's globalized populism and offers an overview of the global crises of COVID-19, climate change, and involuntary migration against which China's globalized populism is arrayed. Chapter 3 assesses China's response to the COVID-19 crisis as an example of antagonistic populism involving adversarial relations between China and the world health policy system. Chapter 4 examines China's responses to the crisis of climate change as an example of participatory populism by which China's engagement with the world climate policy system is conditioned by populist ambitions. Chapter 5 examines China's responses to the crisis of involuntary migration as an example of passive populism, where resistance to the world migration policy system is expressed largely through inaction. The Conclusion summarizes research findings and suggests policy responses.

This book builds on my two earlier UBC Press books examining China's engagement with the international system. *Assessing Treaty Performance in China* (2014) explained China's performance of trade and human rights treaties by reference to a dynamic of "selective adaptation" by which international legal standards are mediated by local norms and institutions. *Exporting Virtue?* (2021) examined China's efforts to revise international human rights standards to suit the preferences of the ruling regime. This third volume of an informal trilogy on China's engagement with the international order proceeds from the "outside-in" and "inside-out" perspectives in my two previous books[23] to examine root causes of China's conflicted relationship with the international order and the implications for policy response. In the wake of the US withdrawal from international leadership, exemplified by the second Trump administration's decision to withdraw from the Paris climate accord and the World Health Organization, China's international power and influence will only grow.[24] China's increasing prominence in the world warrants efforts to understand its globalized populism and the implications for China's relationship with the international system going forward. This book seeks to build such understanding and invites consideration of a range of possible policy responses for the international community.

1 Considering Globalized Populism

ASSESSING CHINA'S GLOBALIZED populism requires appreciation of the broader contours of populism in the current age. Populism has long been recognized as a subset of popular attitudes focused on tensions between "ordinary people" and "elites" around political, economic, and social conditions.[1] Populism has precursors in eighteenth-century enlightenment calls for popular representation in governance and for legal restraints on the state and the aristocracy.[2] Later, the Industrial Revolution saw populist sentiments respond to disruption associated with industrialization, whether through the nativism of the Know-Nothing Party or the economic populism of William Jennings Bryan in the United States, anarchist movements in Europe, or Marxist-inspired revolutions in Russia, China, and elsewhere.[3] Populism has become increasingly prominent internationally, as populist preferences on governance, economic development, and social relations challenge liberal standards of the international political economy that had become dominant in the post–Cold War era.

This chapter examines the foundations of populism and suggests that existing discourses explaining its origins in terms of inequality and resentment can usefully be augmented by analysis of complexity and alienation. It addresses locations of populism in society, in regimes, and internationally, as well as varying political orientations of populism, cautioning against assumptions that populism is exclusively an expression of regressive or right-wing sentiment. It then portrays common features of populism as opposition to elites, grievance ideologies that justify such opposition, and practical resistance through alternative law and policy practices in politics, economy, and society. This analytical framework provides a foundation for understanding China's globalized populism and its effects on China's relationship with the rules-based international order.

Foundations of Populism

Populism in the current era has been attributed to a range of factors. While much attention is given to resentments over inequality, the dynamic of complexity and alienation also plays a role. Taken together, inequality and complexity exacerbate differences and perceived conflicts between elites and ordinary society, providing a foundation for populist expression.

Inequality and Resentment

Much of the current discussion of social populism focuses on responses to changing material conditions of inequality.[4] This harks back to debates about historian Richard Hofstadter's classic analysis of the relative importance of economic disaffection in the populisms that emerged in the United States during the nineteenth and early twentieth centuries.[5] Conditions of inequality are endemic factors in the material foundations of populism.[6]

Resentment of inequality contributes to the emergence of populism as declining prosperity for working people generates hostility toward existing economic systems and the political actors seen as responsible for them.[7] Perceived betrayal of ordinary people by elites is exemplified by industrial manufacturing declines in the face of globalization, technological change, and economic restructuring that drive workers to take on low-wage service jobs while at the same time increasing incomes for the wealthy.[8] Resentment over such conditions influences populist challenges to neoliberal economic policies and the influence of globalization.[9] Such sentiments extend to populist claims that markets are rigged against ordinary people in favour of established interests.[10]

Yet populism is not simply about reaction to declining material prospects but also involves cultural resentments over perceived inequalities in the distribution of political and socio-economic privilege.[11] Many supporters of populism are themselves members of the very elites that populism purports to target, even while acting out their populism differently.[12] While some prosperous populists may act against their own interests by supporting calls for tax reform, others resist tax policies perceived as threats to their newly attained wealth.[13] Perceptions of "status threat" prod the newly prosperous uncertain about their future prospects to oppose policy arrangements favouring the disadvantaged in political representation, economic opportunity, and social rights.[14] Populist concerns around political representation, economic dislocation, and social mobilization augment general concerns around material inequality.

Complexity and Alienation

Complementing resentment of inequalities in material conditions and institutional arrangements, the dynamic of complexity and alienation also contributes to the emergence of populism. Complexity may be seen as an inherent condition of contemporary life.[15] Populist sentiments suggest efforts to build a sense of shared meaning in the face of unease and disquiet brought on by complexities of economic and technological change.[16]

The dynamic of complexity and alienation is often depicted as involving socio-psychological responses to increased complexity involving multiple contexts, variables, and conditions.[17] In the political realm, complexity is evident in bureaucratic and administrative decisions and their impacts, in procedures for governance, and in the availability of information on government decisions.[18] Complexity in the economy may be found in conflicting measures of prosperity, intricacies in its distribution, and questions about autonomy for economic actors.[19] In the social realm, complexity is evident in matters of socio-cultural identity, in relations among racial and ethnic groups and individuals, and in the movement of people across social and geographic boundaries.[20]

Conditions of complexity often defy common understanding, driving alienation from existing political and socio-economic arrangements. Alienation from complexity involves a lack of confidence in policy practices associated with existing systems, born of mistrust with their workings and anxiety over their consequences and impacts.[21] Complexity and alienation intersect with conditions of inequality in material conditions, as inequalities in status, education, information, and resources contribute to wariness about complex systems of governance, the economy, and society and lack of confidence in their potential to support ordinary people.[22] Failed confidence in government policies, administrative procedures, and government information engenders political alienation.[23] In the economy, distrust in how prosperity is measured emerges from contradictions between the deprivation experienced by many and elite proclamations about generalized prosperity, leading to conclusions about unfairness in the distribution of the benefits of prosperity and generating hostility toward the apparent autonomy of market actors to do as they please.[24] Alienation in social relations reflects distrust in depictions of personal and group identity in multicultural communities, in prescriptions for managing diversity, and in prospects for social and geographic mobility.[25] Populist responses to social complexity may also contribute to the "othering" of differently situated communities.[26] The impacts of complexity and alienation on individuals and groups in society provide points of reference for populist regimes and governance.[27] The dynamic of complexity and alienation also affects institutional change, as changing governance arrangements in law and policy reflect responses to complexity.[28]

Locations of Populism

In response to varied conditions of inequality and complexity in diverse political and socio-economic conditions, populist sentiments emerge in society, are expressed by regimes, and present internationally. Populism finds expression in both social movements and regime governance, and ultimately through globalized populism. Varying locations of populism suggest linkages between social and regime populism, and the expression of regime populism in a globalized context.

Social and Regime Populism

Populism presents in society and at the regime level. Social populism expresses conflict between "ordinary" members of society and political and socio-economic "elites," attitudes about perceived wrongs associated with such conflicts, and behaviours of resistance in response. Social populism may emerge independently in response to local conditions of inequality and complexity but is often instigated or reinforced by political leaders and media discourses that engage and often lead populist attitudes in society to build power and influence.[29] While social populism often emerges in the course of electoral politics, it also involves aspects of performative politics by disaffected members of society.[30]

Regime populism involves deployment of populist ideals, often by authoritarian governing regimes aiming to challenge political rivals and build popular legitimacy.[31] Populist regimes pursue policy statements, law and regulation, and political action purporting to defend the frustrations of ordinary people against elites.[32] Whether in autocratic or democratic systems, regime populism engages with popular attitudes as both a source of influence and a target of opportunity, as regime leaders disseminate populist ideals with regime imprimatur to enlist public support.[33] Newly empowered populist leaders and their supporters quickly morph from proponents of resistance against elite-led government to advocates for the authority of their own regime positions.[34] Regimes may reflect or seek to manipulate populist sentiment in society, as political leaders portray themselves as standing up for ordinary people against corrupt elites domestically and internationally.[35]

Regime populism serves as both an expression and a driver of social populism. Popular receptivity to regime populism may be shaped by underlying concerns around inequality and complexity, some of which precede particular political and policy debates whereas many are nurtured by political actors.[36] Populist leaders – whether autocratic and democratic – recognize that public support is a key element in building political influence, and so attempt to influence the scope and content of popular attitudes through political campaigns, policy debates, and publicity initiatives.[37] Media coverage of populist causes also helps shape public perceptions of the origins and implications of inequality and complexity, the effects on self-interest, and the virtues of regime responses.[38]

Globalized Populism

In a climate of globalization and its disparate impacts on local political, economic, and social conditions, regime populism often turns outward against international systems. While contenders for political leadership may rely on populist calls for resistance to local elites to gain power, once in office they tend to focus their populist rhetoric against international targets.[39] Whereas populist targeting of local elites is often mingled with assertions that they are beholden to (often unspecified) international interests hostile to the ordinary people of local society, once in power populist regimes tend to focus the oppositional dynamic of their rhetoric more directly against international elites and associated global systems on governance, the economy, and society.[40] Regimes embracing globalized populism express hostility to the international order, positing themselves and their societies as unfairly subordinated to systems of international governance and the states that appear to dominate them.[41]

Political Orientations of Populism

Populism presents across a lateral array of left- and right-wing politics and ideology, both in society and in connection with regimes.[42] Much attention has been paid to the recent resurgence of right-wing populism. The 2024 US election saw nearly 77 million voters support the election of Donald Trump, who also won 312 electoral votes (86 more than his rival, Vice

President Kamala Harris, and 42 more than needed to prevail)[43] – this despite Trump's demonstrable disregard for democratic norms of governance, his tolerance – even support – for inequalities in socio-economic conditions, and his ethnocentric contempt for non-whites and international institutions.[44] Trump's 2024 presidential campaign suggested that his populist message remains powerful, despite multiple criminal indictments and civil complaints against him. Populist electoral messaging also helped propel the Republican Party to majorities in the House of Representatives and in the Senate in 2024.[45]

Looking beyond the United States, right-wing populists in Latin America are resurgent.[46] In Europe, right-wing populism has become increasingly evident.[47] In the United Kingdom, a majority (51.9 percent) of voters supported the 2016 populist Brexit referendum on exiting the European Union, and even as aggregate public opinion has generally shifted against Brexit, popular support in favour remains significant.[48] International linkages among right-wing populist groups are becoming more common despite variation in their purposes and membership.[49]

While so-called right-wing populism has attracted much attention of late and remains significant,[50] populism on the left also merits attention, often sharing claims of resistance with rightist counterparts.[51] Populist champions on the right such as the Proud Boys, Oath Keepers, or QAnon stand juxtaposed with populist reform movements on the left such as Occupy Wall Street, Black Lives Matter, and Extinction Rebellion.[52]

For purposes of comparison, rather than focus on spatial metaphors of "right" and "left" whose uncritical application tends to obscure rather than illuminate,[53] populism may be viewed more usefully as operating between "regressive" and "progressive" alternatives.[54] Regressive populism is seen generally as promoting ideals of autocratic leadership, tolerance for economic inequality, and embrace of social exclusion.[55] It often seeks to explain and justify such sentiments by reference to conspiracy theories reinforcing claims of disregard by elites.[56] Regressive populism tends to resist current conditions by espousing policy practices aimed at recapturing a bygone "golden age."[57] It tends to reflect a "sunk-cost" approach that bemoans current conditions as untoward diversions from investment in tradition – the purported value of commitments to practices of a past age having been lost or taken away under current conditions of governance, economy, and society.[58]

Progressive populism, by contrast, is generally considered as supporting governance that is responsive to the popular will, challenging socio-economic inequalities as impediments to prosperity, and promoting social inclusion.[59] Through criticism of existing conditions, it tends to espouse reforms aimed at achieving an idealized future.[60] Progressive populism offers what amounts to an "opportunity cost" critique of socio-economic and political conditions by reference to idealist alternatives that are attainable with political will and popular engagement, and to the lost opportunity of failing to achieve them.[61] Regressive nostalgia for an imagined past and progressive mobilizing for an idealized future each represent populist responses to conditions of inequality and complexity.

Features of Populism: Anti-Elitism, Grievance, and Practical Resistance

Despite variations in material foundations, locations, and political orientations, populism exhibits common features such as opposition to elites, justification through grievance ideology, and practical resistance through pursuit of alternative legal and policy norms and practice. Each of these reflects the influence of underlying foundations of inequality and complexity.

Opposition to elites in social populism often draws on embedded socio-cultural perspectives around the inequality and complexity in society, and the disparate political and socio-economic positions that result.[62] The oppositional dynamic targeting elites reflects resentment of inequalities of political power, economic opportunity, and social position that attend distinctions between elites and ordinary people.[63] Anti-elitism also reflects frustration with the complexities of modern life and the dominance of specialist elites in managing them.[64] Anti-elitism includes anti-establishment sentiments challenging existing governance and regulatory systems.[65] The oppositional dynamic of anti-elitism takes multiple forms and challenges multiple targets – whether these be so-called liberal elites associated with governance, NGOs, and academic institutions involved in progressive policy development and enactment, or so-called corporate elites associated with regressive socio-economic systems.[66]

Social populism also involves ideologies of *grievance* that explain and justify populist opposition to elites and associated systems of governance, economy, and society.[67] Ideologies of grievance may be appreciated as a response to perceptions about abuses of power and advantage by elites to the detriment of ordinary people, and disquiet about conditions of inequality and complexity that permit such abuses.[68] Grievance ideologies target perceived inequalities in political arrangements, whether these involve privileging political elites or offering preferential treatment to minorities and disadvantaged groups in society.[69] They also target perceived unfairness in the complexities of the economy, whether involving privileging capital over labour or providing preferential access to opportunity for minorities and disadvantaged groups.[70] Grievance ideologies are also evident in populist challenges to social arrangements.[71]

Building on the oppositional and explanatory dynamics of anti-elitism and grievance ideology, *practical resistance* in social populism involves embrace of alternative norms and practices challenging perceived failings of existing socio-economic and political arrangements.[72] Practical resistance stems from failed confidence in existing political, economic, and social arrangements, and offers alternative standards. In politics, regressive populists often call for autocratic policies of governance as necessary to combat the influence of indifferent elites and fuelled by grievances against them, while progressives call for more robust democracies to respond to these issues.[73] On the economy, regressive populists often call for policies promoting freedom from government regulation, while progressives call for more intense government oversight to prevent abuses of economic power.[74] On social relations, regressive populists often call for nativist policies on ethnic relations regardless of potential impacts on discrimination and exclusion, while progressives often call for more expansive government scrutiny of social relations to thwart such outcomes.[75] As factors of inequality and complexity erode confidence in existing policies, practical resistance emerges in response, championing alternative standards.[76] Such reordering reflects ideational and discursive linkages with the roots of populism in inequality and complexity, which are used to explain populist challenges to existing arrangements on governance, the economy, and society. Practical resistance in social populism can be expressed through electoral support for sympathetic political actors, direct action through demonstrations, and targeted violence predicated on presumptions of conflict between members of society and the elites they oppose.[77]

Like social populism, regime populism also expresses features of anti-elitism, grievance, and practical resistance. Adopting the oppositional dynamic of social populism, regime populism purports to act on behalf of the "people" to oppose "elites" through repression of domestic foes, or attacks on political and socio-economic rivals elsewhere.[78] Ideologies of grievance that inform social populism may be used to explain and justify regime populism as well, as individual leaders and governing regimes complain of exclusion and disregard by local or international elites.[79] Populist regimes also pursue practical resistance by offering alternative legal and policy norms and practices that challenge existing arrangements.[80] These features of regime populism appear mostly in expressions of globalized populism.

Regimes embracing globalized populism express anti-elitism, grievance, and practical resistance against existing international systems. Some populists express hostility toward liberal perspectives on governance, the economy, and society, responding to the seeming inability of the international system to respond effectively to global challenges.[81] Grievance around international standards associated with globalization is often portrayed in terms of their disregard for local conditions.[82] Dynamics of anti-elitism and grievance ideology respond to conditions of inequality and complexity associated with global elites and the political and socio-economic systems they support. Thus, international elites are challenged as unresponsive to the needs of ordinary people and the countries in which they live, while grievance ideologies around abuses such as colonialism and imperialism are used to explain and justify attacks on international – mostly Western liberal – elites. Such efforts generate practical resistance supporting alternative law and policy practice through international discourses around reforms in global governance, the economy, and society.[83]

Populist features of anti-elitism, grievance, and practical resistance involve a dynamic akin to "resilience."[84] Resilience involves adaptation to difficult or challenging conditions through mental, emotional, and behavioural flexibility and by adjustment to external and internal demands.[85] While often applied in the context of individual psychology, resilience discourse offers insights into how socio-economic and political systems and actors respond to challenges of inequality and complexity.[86] Resilient responses to conditions of inequality may involve efforts by the disadvantaged to adapt to the limitations of inequality even while resisting its effects.[87] Similarly, resilient responses to complexity may involve efforts to adapt to complex conditions while also embracing standards for simplifying political and socio-economic life.[88]

Dynamics of resilience are evident in populist features of anti-elitism, grievance ideology, and practical resistance. Anti-elitism builds populist resilience of ordinary members of society and their enablers and advocates by contrasting common virtues of common sense, authenticity, and trust with the perceived traits of elites such as intellectualism, deceit, and abuse of ordinary people.[89] Grievance ideology builds populist resilience by reinforcing a sense of community and belonging among the aggrieved.[90] Practical resistance extols alternative law and policy practices opposing the inequalities and complexities of socio-economic and political arrangements against which populism reacts, thus building resilience against them.[91] While concepts of resilience are often deployed to explain responses by democracies to the rise of populism,[92] populist movements such as MAGA and Occupy also exemplify resilience by establishing like-minded communities of resistance in response to perceived inequities of the established order.[93] Confronted with conditions of inequality and complexity, societies and regimes build group identities challenging those purportedly responsible for such conditions, develop explanatory mechanisms to justify their opposition, and organize practical resistance offering alternatives to existing systems. These features of populism exude dynamics of resilience.

Assessing Practical Resistance in Globalized Populism

Whereas populist features of opposition to elites and grievance ideology involve mostly rhetorical challenges against elites and the systems they purportedly control, practical resistance has potentially greater impact through its capacity to change application of law and policy over the longer term. Practical resistance in globalized populism involves pursuit of legal and regulatory arrangements on political, economic, and social relations that challenge existing standards. It may usefully be examined by reference to themes of accountability in politics, prosperity in the economy, and community in society. Themes of accountability, prosperity, and community are particularly useful in assessing responses to crises of COVID-19, climate change, and involuntary migration. As protecting the health and safety of the population is a critically important task of government, the political governance theme of accountability is appropriate to depict populist law and policy practices regarding COVID-19. Similarly, the close relationship between environmental conditions and economic well-being invites application of the economic theme of prosperity to law and policy practices regarding climate change. As well, the close relationship between migration and local society invites application of the social theme of community to law and policy practices regarding migration.

In light of existing academic discourses on decision making, operational norms and associated law and policy practices attendant to themes of accountability, prosperity, and community may be examined by reference to functional categories of standards, processes, and actors.[94] Accordingly, the theme of *accountability* may be seen to involve operational norms and associated law and policy practices regarding standards for assessing governance performance, processes for policy regulation, and access for political actors to governance information. The theme of *prosperity* includes operational norms and associated law and policy practices regarding standards for measuring economic change, processes for distributing the benefits of development, and autonomy for economic actors. The theme of *community* includes operational norms and law and policy practices regarding standards for defining identity, processes for managing diversity, and responses to socio-economic and geographic mobility of social actors.

Accountability in Political Relations

The theme of accountability involves basic expectations about the relationship between governing regimes and their subjects.[95] Accountability in populist regimes is often associated with conditions of autocratic and democratic governance.[96] Both involve ideological and political claims to legitimacy.[97] Both regressive and progressive populist regimes have emerged from nominally democratic systems even while challenging the performance of democratic institutions.[98] Regressive populists are viewed as distrusting institutions of democratic governance and working to weaken associated institutions such as courts, regulatory agencies, intelligence services, and the press,[99] whereas progressive populists challenge limits imposed by democratic norms as untoward constraints against reform.[100]

The theme of accountability may usefully be examined according to operational norms on performance, process, and information and the law and policy practices that result.[101] The operational norm of *performance accountability* involves determinations of how government performance should be depicted, while the operational norm of *process accountability* involves preferences regarding underlying procedures, and the operational norm of *information accountability* involves choices over the extent of state control over information. Mindful that accountability around government decisions is dependent in large part on the way government depicts their outcomes, law and policy practices around *performance accountability* involve variation between aspirational descriptions of government performance in terms of ideals, and empirical depictions of performance that can be assessed by outside observers.[102] Practices around *process accountability* involve variation between reliance in instrumentalist legal arrangements enabling government action and support for impartial rule-of-law standards restraining government actions and officials.[103] They reflect tensions between the legitimizing impacts of impartial rule-of-law standards and the requirements of power and politics that invite regimes to use legal forms to achieve policy goals while insulating themselves from legal restraint.[104] Law and policy practices around *information accountability* involve variation

FIGURE 1 Norms and practices on governance accountability

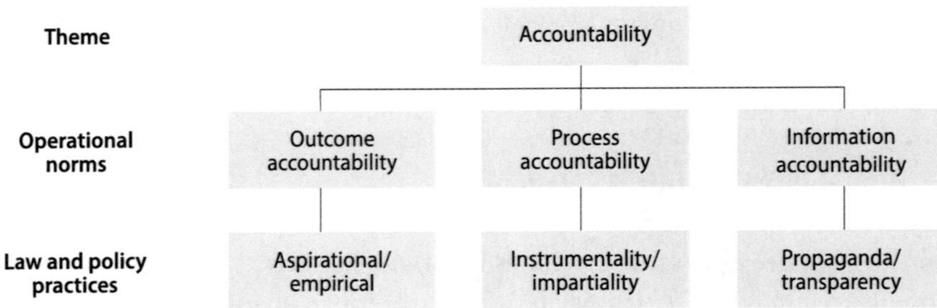

between government propagandizing its preferred information to influence public opinion and transparency processes mandating government releases of information.[105]

Figure 1 depicts the relationships between operational norms of performance, process, and information accountability, and law and policy practices. While the range of possible options for law and policy practice on aspirational or empirical standards for performance accountability, instrumentalism or impartiality in process accountability, and preferences for propaganda or transparency in information accountability fall along a spectrum of alternatives each of which could be documented in detail and associated with other variables, for the purposes of illustration and as used in this study, law and policy alternatives for performance, process, and information accountability are charted as binary dyads.

Equality and Complexity Dimensions of Accountability

Law and policy practices around operational norms of performance, process, and information accountability reflect presumptions about equality and complexity. Practices on accountability reveal general expectations about equality that treat governing elites as agents of the popular will subject to popular supervision, or, alternatively, as superior to ordinary people and hence insulated from supervision.[106] Practices favouring empirical depictions of policy performance, impartial standards binding government processes, and transparency in access to government information each reflect commitments to equality between rulers and ruled. By contrast, law and policy practices favouring aspirational depictions of government performance, instrumentalist processes of governance, or reliance on propaganda to inform the public about policy decisions reflect tolerance for inequality –

whether justified by merit, wealth, class or caste origin, or skills claims about the "best and the brightest."[107] Whereas liberal accountability norms and practice commonly associated with democracies in Europe and North America reflect presumptions about equality, autocratic systems claiming guidance from ideologies such as class struggle and elite meritocracy accept and even champion inequality.[108] Democratic Socialist regimes balance these extremes through efforts to remedy inequalities of opportunity and socio-economic conditions.[109]

Law and policy practices related to performance, process, and information accountability also have implications for complexity. Empirical depictions of policy performance acknowledge the complexities of policy formulation and implementation, whereas aspirational portrayals favour simpler standards for depicting and assessing policy performance.[110] Similarly, support for impartial legal standards binding government processes acknowledges the complexities of the myriad of relationships that dominate the policy process and attempts to respond to them, whereas preferences for instrumentalist standards tend to favour simpler legal and administrative measures focused mainly on empowering power holders.[111] Practices of information accountability favouring transparency or propaganda present similar choices between the complexities of managing the myriad of possible transparency claims and the details of the policies about which information is sought or the relative simplicity of government-managed propaganda efforts.[112]

Law and policy practices around governance accountability can be charted as between aspirational or empirical depictions of governance performance, instrumentalist or impartial standards for governance processes, and propagandist or transparency approaches to governance information disclosure. These in turn can then be assessed in light of their association with varying degrees of tolerance for inequality and acceptance of complexity. Figure 2 illustrates how policy practices associated with operational norms around performance, process, and information accountability reflect differing approaches to inequality and complexity.

Prosperity in Economic Relations

Operational norms and associated law and policy practices related to the theme of prosperity reflect expectations about management of the economy.[113] While populism is sometimes considered to be inconsistent with economic well-being,[114] the influence of populism on economic life may nonetheless be examined by reference to the theme of prosperity involving operational norms involving measurement, distribution, and autonomy.

FIGURE 2 Equality and complexity dimensions of accountability law and policy practice

Policy orientation	Law and policy practice	Operational norm	Law and policy practice	Policy orientation
		EQUALITY		
	←	← →	→	
Tolerance for inequality	Aspirational assessment	*Performance accountability*	Empirical assessment	Support for equality
Tolerance for inequality	Instrumentalism	*Process accountability*	Impartiality	Support for equality
Tolerance for inequality	Propaganda	*Information accountability*	Transparency	Support for equality
		COMPLEXITY		
	←	← →	→	
Preference for simplicity	Aspirational assessment	*Performance accountability*	Empirical assessment	Acceptance of complexity
Preference for simplicity	Instrumentalism	*Process accountability*	Impartiality	Acceptance of complexity
Preference for simplicity	Propaganda	*Information accountability*	Transparency	Acceptance of complexity

Operational norms around prosperity involve questions of how economic development should be measured, to whom its benefits should be distributed, and against what sorts of constraints protected. *Measurement* of prosperity involves basic questions about the standards by which economic development is analyzed and assessed.[115] Law and policy practices related to measurement of prosperity range from reliance on macro-indicators involving aggregated national and regional data such as GDP growth rates, income gains, wealth creation, and the like, to reliance on micro-indicators on localized impacts on socio-economic equity and quality of life.[116] While macro-data on national, regional and even local development are often relied on heavily by policy-makers in measuring prosperity, these do not capture the local impacts of such aspects as gender, income, occupation, family circumstances, housing, and health associated with human rights.[117]

The operational norm of *distribution* of prosperity concerns mainly process questions around determining the identity and functions of beneficiaries of economic development policies.[118] Law and policy practices around distribution of prosperity involve choices between prioritizing business firms with the expectation that society will also benefit, or distributing benefits of prosperity directly to individuals and groups in society.[119] Achievement of development goals through distribution of financial incentives to economic enterprises is embedded in much of the conventional discourse on economic development.[120] Nonetheless, implementation of economic prosperity policies through subsidies, tax breaks, policy lending, and other favourable incentives offered to business enterprises does not necessarily lead to improved prosperity for individuals and groups in society.[121]

The operational norm of *autonomy* of prosperity involves the extent and source of constraints on economic actors.[122] Law and policy practices related to the autonomy dimensions of prosperity reflect choices as to whether the conduct of economic actors should be constrained primarily by market conditions or through state regulation.[123] Thus, practices around autonomy of prosperity reflect priorities regarding autonomy from the state or from the market.

Figure 3 depicts the relationships between operational norms of measurement, distribution, and autonomy of prosperity, and law and policy practices. While the range of possible options for law and policy practice on macro or micro standards for measurement of prosperity, distribution of prosperity to businesses or to individuals and groups in society, and autonomy of prosperity from state or market constraints falls along a spectrum of alternatives each of which could be documented in detail and associated with other variables, for the purposes of illustration and as used in this study law and policy alternatives for measurement, distribution, and autonomy of prosperity are charted as binary dyads.

FIGURE 3 Norms and practices on economic prosperity

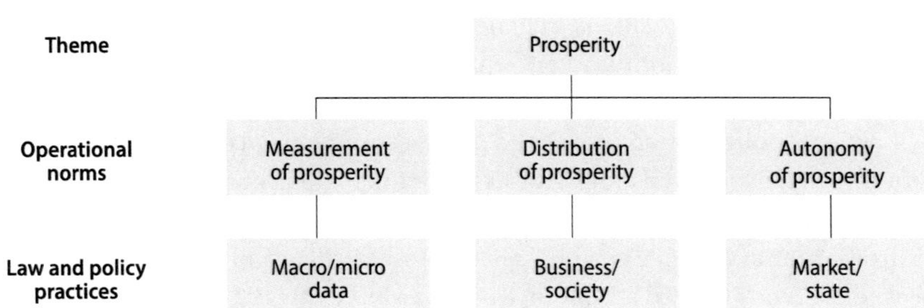

Equality and Complexity Dimensions of Prosperity

As with accountability, law and policy practices on economic prosperity involve expectations about equality and complexity.[124] Practices related to measurement, distribution, and autonomy of prosperity reflect presumptions about equality. Mindful of the cautions urged by scholarly discourses on "critical empiricism" against overreliance on quantitative data to support conclusions about political and socio-economic conditions,[125] preferences for macro or micro measures of prosperity can nonetheless be seen to reflect varying degrees of tolerance for inequality among participants in prosperity. Aggregate indicators such as GDP growth are assumed to benefit different members of society equally regardless of subjective inequalities among them, while localized indicators such as quality-of-life impacts are intended to support remedial responses to subjective difference.[126] Similar presumptions about equality are reflected in law and policy practices related to distribution of prosperity to businesses or society, as expectations that distribution of benefits to business actors will be sufficient to ensure prosperity for society as a whole, with little regard to actual inequalities within society. Progressive commitments to equality tend to focus on the need to overcome inequalities of opportunity, while regressive tolerance for inequality tends to encourage uniform treatment of economic actors regardless of their subjective differences.[127] Distributing economic benefits to business actors in expectation of resulting social benefits reveals tolerance for inequality, such that, absent means or performance testing, economic surpluses distributed through corporate tax breaks and business subsidies supporting health insurance and employment benefits are disconnected from subjective social disparities of wealth and need.[128] Expectations about equality are also reflected in law and policy practice related to autonomy of prosperity – particularly the distinction between autonomy from government control and autonomy from market disciplines.[129] Whereas the state's regulatory authority over the economy permits intervention to ameliorate socio-economic inequalities, reliance on market forces applied equally among disparate economic actors expresses tolerance for inequality among them.

Law and policy practices related to measurement, distribution and autonomy of prosperity also involve expectations about complexity. Reliance on aggregate indicators in the measurement of prosperity tends toward generalization and simplicity, while reliance on localized micro-indicators of prosperity tends toward acceptance of the complexities of economic life and pursuit of efforts to manage them.[130] Practices related to distribution of prosperity also reflect perspectives on complexity, as direct distributions to individuals and groups in society involve complex efforts at design and implementation of such efforts, while distribution to businesses with expectations about trickle-down benefits to society suggests a simpler approach.[131] Similarly, practices related to autonomy of prosperity – particularly the distinction between autonomy from government control and autonomy from market disciplines – are intertwined with expectations about complexity, as the complexities of the market stand in contrast to the appearance of simplicity in state controls over business activity.[132]

FIGURE 4 Equality and complexity dimensions of prosperity law and policy practice

Policy orientation	Law and policy practice	Operational norm	Law and policy practice	Policy orientation
		EQUALITY		
	←	← →	→	
Tolerance for inequality	Reliance on macro-indicators	*Measurement of prosperity*	Reliance on micro-indicators	Support for equality
Tolerance for inequality	Distribution through business firms	*Distribution of prosperity*	Distribution to individuals and groups in society	Support for equality
Tolerance for inequality	Autonomy from the state	*Autonomy of prosperity*	Autonomy from the market	Support for equality
		COMPLEXITY		
	←	← →	→	
Preference for simplicity	Reliance on macro-indicators	*Measurement of prosperity*	Reliance on micro-indicators	Acceptance of complexity
Preference for simplicity	Distribution through business firms	*Distribution of prosperity*	Distribution to individuals and groups in society	Acceptance of complexity
Preference for simplicity	Autonomy from the market	*Autonomy of prosperity*	Autonomy from the state	Acceptance of complexity

Law and policy practices related to prosperity can be charted as between macro- and micro-indicators for measurement, distribution of benefits to business or social sectors, and the autonomy of economic actors from state or market regulation. These in turn can be assessed in light of their association with varying degrees of tolerance for inequality and acceptance of complexity. Figure 4 illustrates how operational norms around prosperity and associated law and policy practices related to measurement, distribution, and autonomy of prosperity reflect varying responses to inequality and complexity.

Community in Social Relations

Operational norms and associated law and policy practices related to the theme of community express general expectations about the social relationships among individuals and groups. Operational norms of identity, diversity, and mobility involve law and policy practices treating identity as inherent or acquired, empowering the respective roles of segregation and integration in responding to conditions of diversity, and assessing socio-economic and geographic mobility in terms of threat or opportunity. *Identity* has much to do with characterizing community membership, such that inherent identity based on family lineage or ethnicity invites different standards for inclusion than identity driven by acquired conditions.[133] Law and policy practices related to identity involve preferences for inherent or acquired determinants of identity – between prioritizing inherent conditions of family and ethnicity and acknowledging acquired attributes such as wealth, skill, and need. *Diversity* involves preferences for community composition and the conditions for inclusion and may be characterized as involving choices between integration and segregation of disparate social groups.[134] Practices related to diversity range from support for including multiple ethnic groups in national society and opposition in favour of mythologies of socio-cultural uniformity. *Mobility* involves both geographic and social dimensions of movement by potential community members.[135] Practices related to mobility involve distinctions between opportunity and threat, such that changes in community membership may be treated as acceptable consequences of people seeking opportunity with associated benefits for society, or, alternatively, as threats to socio-economic stability.

Figure 5 depicts the relationships between operational norms of community identity, diversity, and mobility, and law and policy practices. While the range of possible options for law and policy practice around inherent and acquired identity, segregation and integration in response to community

FIGURE 5 Norms and practices on community in society

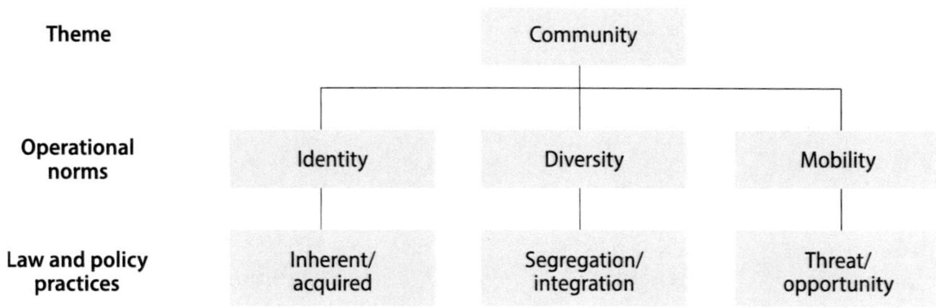

diversity, and considering mobility as threat or opportunity fall along a spectrum of alternatives, each of which could be documented in detail and associated with other variables, for the purposes of illustration and as used in this study alternatives on law and policy alternatives on community identity, diversity, and mobility are charted as binary dyads.

Equality and Complexity Dimensions of Community

As with accountability and prosperity, law and policy practices around community reflect differing expectations about equality and complexity. Norms and practice on community identity, diversity, and mobility involve presumptions about equality.[136] Support for human equality is expressed in law and policy practices related to identity based on acquired rather than inherent attributes.[137] Similarly, practices supporting integration in response to diversity, and supporting mobility as a matter of opportunity rather than threat, reflect presumptions of equality.[138] By contrast, assertions about identity, diversity, and mobility proceeding from tolerance for inequality beget notions of ethnic superiority, opposing integration among social groupings, and resisting social and geographic mobility.[139]

Operational norms around community identity, diversity, and mobility and their associated law and policy practices also reflect differing responses to complexity.[140] Practices favouring the possibilities for acquired identity tend to acknowledge and affirm complexity, as the components and conditions for acquired identity far outstrip single-dimension factors such as ethnicity that inform inherent identity discourse.[141] Similarly, practices supporting integration in response to diversity and supporting mobility as a matter of opportunity tend toward perspectives accepting the value of complexity, in

FIGURE 6 Equality and complexity dimensions of community law and policy practice

Policy orientation	Law and policy practice	Operational norm	Law and policy practice	Policy orientation
		EQUALITY		
	←	← →	→	
Tolerance for inequality	Inherent	*Identity*	Acquired	Support for equality
Tolerance for inequality	Segregation	*Diversity*	Integration	Support for equality
Tolerance for inequality	Threat	*Mobility*	Opportunity	Support for equality
		COMPLEXITY		
	←	← →	→	
Preference for simplicity	Inherent	*Identity*	Acquired	Acceptance of complexity
Preference for simplicity	Segregation	*Diversity*	Integration	Acceptance of complexity
Preference for simplicity	Threat	*Mobility*	Opportunity	Acceptance of complexity

contrast to practices of segregation and threat response grounded in preference for simplicity.[142]

Law and policy practices around community can be charted in relation to preferences for inherent or acquired identity, support for integration or segregation in response to diversity, and expectations of opportunity or threat from geographic and socio-economic mobility. These in turn can be assessed in light of their association with varying degrees of tolerance for inequality and acceptance of complexity. Figure 6 illustrates how operational norms around community and associated practices related to identity, diversity, and mobility reflect differences in relative tolerance for inequality and acceptance of complexity.

Comparison With International Standards

Presumptions on equality and complexity revealed in law and policy practice around operational norms of accountability, prosperity, and community point to issues of commonality and difference with the rules-based international order.[143] Equality dimensions of law and policy practices of globalized populism invite comparison with standards of international law. The rules-based international order tends to embrace equality in governance, the economy, and society. International law favours sovereign equality among states in political relations.[144] The international system also posits the primacy of equality in economic relations of trade and investment.[145] Social equality too is given high priority.[146] While such provisions on formal equality are often challenged by persistence of inequalities in practice, the ideals favouring equality remain a key feature of the liberal rules-based international order.[147] These standards provide points of comparison with populist law and policy preferences.

Law and policy practices around accountability, prosperity, and community also warrant comparison with international standards on complexity. International institutional mechanisms tend to embrace complexity in governance, the economy, and society. Prominent examples include the United Nations system on political relations among states, the World Trade Organization (WTO) and its associated institutions governing international trade and investment, and the UN High Commission on Human Rights (UNHCR) with its mechanisms for protecting individuals and groups in society, all of which adopt highly complex systems and standards.[148] As with assessments on equality, international standards on complexity provide points of comparison with populist law and policy preferences.

THUS, POPULIST PRACTICAL resistance against existing standards for governance accountability, economic prosperity, and social community involve alternative law and policy practices in response to the purported problems with existing standards. These have implications for equality and complexity and stand in comparison with standards of the rules-based international order. Table 1 illustrates the dynamic by which populist law and policy practices emerge from non-confidence in existing standards in governance, the economy, and community.

Conclusion

Populism has come to be recognized as a significant component in discourses on political, economic, and social relations. Foundations of populism involve dynamics of inequality and resentment and complexity and alienation. Populism presents in society and through regimes, which often direct domestic populist sentiments against international systems, engendering features of globalized populism. Populism exhibits diversity in political

TABLE 1 Development of populist law and policy practice

Operational norm	Existing standards	Non-confidence	Practical resistance	Law and policy practice
		ACCOUNTABILITY		
Performance accountability	Existing standards on assessing governance performance	Perceived failures in governance performance	Revised standards on assessing governance performance	Aspirational/ empirical depictions of governance performance
Process accountability	Existing administrative procedures for governance policy process	Perceived failures in governance policy process	Revised procedures for governance policy process	Instrumentalist/ impartial approaches to administrative procedure
Information accountability	Existing standards for reporting on governance policy process	Perceived failures in reporting on governance policy process	Revised arrangements for reporting on governance policy process	Focus on propaganda/ transparency in management of government information
		PROSPERITY		
Measurement of prosperity	Existing standards for measuring prosperity	Perceived failures in measuring conditions of local prosperity	Revised standards for measuring prosperity	Reliance on aggregated macro-/locally informed micro-data
Distribution of prosperity	Existing standards for allocating benefits of prosperity	Perceived failures in allocating benefits of prosperity	Revised standards for allocating benefits of prosperity	Distribution through business/civic actors
Autonomy of prosperity	Existing standards for regulating economic autonomy	Perceived failures on effects of regulation on economic autonomy	Revised standards for economic autonomy	Prioritize autonomy from state regulation/ market discipline

Operational norm	Existing standards	Non-confidence	Practical resistance	Law and policy practice
		COMMUNITY		
Identity in community	Existing standards on socio-cultural identity	Perceived failures in protecting socio-cultural identity	Revised standards on socio-cultural identity	Identity as inherent/ acquired
Diversity in community	Existing standards on socio-cultural relations	Perceived failures in managing socio-cultural diversity	Revised standards on socio-cultural diversity	Segregation/ integration
Mobility in community	Existing standards on movement and status of outsiders	Perceived failures in responding to outsiders	Revised standards on movement and status of outsiders	Mobility as threat/ opportunity

orientation, as evidenced by differences between progressive and regressive populism. Responding to conditions of inequality and complexity, common features of populism involve resilience through opposition to elites and grievance ideology, combined with practical resistance through alternative law and policy practices related to political accountability, economic prosperity, and social community. Law and policy practices emerging from populist practical resistance have implications for equality and complexity and stand in comparison with the standards of the rules-based international order. This framework is useful in analyzing China's globalized populism and its responses to the global crises of COVID-19, climate change, and involuntary migration.

2 China's Globalized Populism and Global Crises

THIS CHAPTER INTRODUCES the fundamental dichotomy in this study, namely, China's globalized populism and the global crises of COVID-19, climate change, and involuntary migration. The globalized populism of the People's Republic of China expresses resistance to international elites, nurturing of grievances against the international establishment, particularly the West, and pursuit of practical resistance to the existing standards of the rules-based international order. These dynamics are expressed through rhetorical markers of sovereignty, development, and human rights. The global crises of COVID-19, climate change, and involuntary migration and the generalized populist responses to them provide context for assessing China's globalized populism in action.

China's Globalized Populism

The discussion of the foundations, locations, political orientations, and features of populism found in Chapter 1 provides essential context for understanding China's globalized populism. Building on the populist legacy of the Communist Party of China (CPC) and challenging domestic and international elites through class struggle and revolution, China has historically supported populist movements and ideologies. Recent years have seen the regime become increasingly active in articulating populist themes in international affairs, asserting hostility to international elites, grievance ideology, and practical resistance in response to international systems.

China's Populist Legacy and the Transition to Globalized Populism

The PRC Party-state has long been associated with ideals of populism.[1] From the slogan "serve the people" adorning entranceways to CPC and government compounds to the provisions of the Party and state constitutions, the regime has grounded its legitimacy in ideals of populism. The CPC's revolutionary struggle had evoked populist resistance to corrupt governance under the Guomindang-led Republic of China (ROC).[2] The early years of the PRC Party-state saw the regime mobilize populist opposition to elites through attacks on so-called counter-revolutionaries (mainly former ROC officials), as well as campaigns against corruption and economic abuses targeting wayward CPC members and a remnant bourgeoisie.[3] Mao Zedong's Cultural Revolution continued the theme, calling for class struggle against political opponents deemed enemies of the people.[4] Mao's populism was also directed outward, through calls for revolutionary struggles of self-determination against colonialism and imperialism.[5] In the early post-Mao period, campaigns against spiritual pollution and bourgeois liberalization also spoke to resistance to international influences.[6]

In recent years, however, as priorities of China's governance have shifted toward goals of wealth and power, space for populism has been severely constrained. The regime has vigorously suppressed organized independent social movements against corruption, unfair labour relations, and deteriorating environmental conditions, even as isolated public protests have been tolerated when unthreatening and consistent with regime policy aims.[7] Xi Jinping's takedown of Bo Xilai in 2012[8] signalled that domestic populism, with its implied challenge to central authority, was incompatible with Xi's rule. Nonetheless, Xi's recent embrace of a "common prosperity" development policy suggests an appreciation that populist appeals remain powerful, as indicated by the recent phenomenon of "Kong Yiji literature" bemoaning the limited prosperity prospects for educated young people.[9] Rising socio-economic inequality has compounded the challenge of securing political support for Xi's regime.[10]

Constraints on domestic populism have not limited China's populist critiques of international actors and systems.[11] In recent years, hostility to purportedly elite liberal states underpinning the rules-based international order has taken on new importance.[12] Regime commentators and social media icons increasingly explain China's ambivalence toward the international order in terms of grievances against international elites and the systems they purportedly control, generating practical resistance through alternative standards and institutional arrangements.[13] Such discourses inform China's national security matters as well.[14] The PRC's emergence as a near-superpower has worked to support its resistance to the international order. China's growing economic might has strengthened efforts to establish alternatives to the existing international trade order.[15] Its emerging strengths in scientific research have led to efforts to create a new international order for science.[16] Pushback from the United States and other liberal systems has served to reinforce China's populist resentment of the international order.[17]

Xi Jinping's leadership role looms large in China's expressions of globalized populism. Xi's evident commitment to personal control over regime policy and politics[18] suggests that support for populist discourse may well be more a matter of political strategy than an expression of personal ideology. Populist tropes were particularly evident in Xi's July 1, 2021, speech at the 100th anniversary of the founding of the CPC (CPC-100).[19] Citing achievements of the Maoist revolution ("Through tenacious struggle, the Party and the Chinese people showed the world that the Chinese people had stood up, and that the time in which the Chinese nation could be bullied and abused by others was gone forever"), Xi continued the call for overcoming oppression against China: "We will never allow any foreign force to bully, oppress, or subjugate us. Anyone who would attempt to do so will find themselves on a collision course with a great wall of steel forged by over 1.4 billion Chinese people." Aside from their potential to garner domestic political support through embrace of nationalism,[20] Xi's frequent assertions of populist features of anti-elitism, grievance, and resistance to general and often unspecified international forces intersects with China's effort to build support among developing economies of the Global South against the liberal international order.[21]

Rhetorical Markers of China's Globalized Populism

China has deployed rhetorical markers of sovereignty, development, and human rights to justify its populist resistance to the international order.[22] These rhetorical markers provide resilience for China's globalized populism against the standards of the international order. Just as anti-elitism lends resilience to opposition against established systems, so too do China's sovereignty claims provide resilience for its globalized populism by insulating PRC law and policy from critique by the established international order. Just as grievance ideology works to justify and provide resilience for populist resistance, so too does China's rhetorical marker of development support challenges against the international order by reference to grievances around the purported failure of the international order to recognize China's development concerns. And just as practical resistance offers legal and policy alternatives that support resilience for populist opposition to the established order, China's law and policy practice on human rights substitutes PRC policy preferences for international standards.

Sovereignty as Resistance to Elites

China's reliance on assertions of nearly absolute sovereignty as a defence to the application of international law[23] expresses populist resistance to international elites and systems and attempts to insulate China from their influences. Xi's remarks at CPC-100 were particularly poignant: "No one should underestimate the resolve, the will, and the ability of the Chinese people to defend their national sovereignty and territorial integrity."[24] This echoed his call at the 2017 CPC's 19th National Congress for reform in global governance under the ideal of a "shared future for humanity," which aimed to increase China's influence while reducing the limits on its sovereignty imposed by the liberal international order.[25] Paradoxically, China's insistence on its own sovereignty does not extend to other countries where Chinese influence operations abound.[26]

Xi's remarks to CPC's 20th National Congress in October 2022 reiterated the idea of Chinese sovereignty: "We have applied a holistic approach to national security. We have steadily improved the leadership, legal, strategy, and policy systems for national security. We have not yielded any ground on matters of principle, and we have resolutely safeguarded China's sovereignty, security, and development interests."[27]

This focus on sovereignty remains a key element in China's norms and practice in international affairs, used to resist efforts to induce China's compliance with international law and policy standards associated with global (mostly Western) elites.

Development and Grievance

Expressing themes of grievance justifying populist anti-elitism, China has cast the West, particularly the United States, as a major impediment to its development – historically through imperialism and neocolonialism and more recently through trade policy, currency controls, and so-called decoupling.[28] Early in his tenure as national and Party leader, Xi expressed grievance that the United States and the West were generally committed to keeping China from realizing its development goals: "Some Western countries absolutely never want to see a socialist China grow strong under the leadership of the Chinese Communist Party" (November 2015). These views have continued in recent years: "Western countries led by the United States have implemented all-around containment, encirclement and suppression of China" (March 2023).[29] Responding to the Australia-UK-US (AUKUS) agreement on nuclear submarines for Australia, Chinese foreign minister Wang Yi referred to the parties as an "Anglo-Saxon clique" (*Angelu Sakexun tuan* // 盎格鲁撒克逊团), adding an ethnic dimension to China's populist response to perceived threats from the West.[30]

Such expressions of grievance explain and justify China's development aims as a virtuous alternative to international economic norms of neoliberalism.[31] Chinese proposals on "South-South cooperation," "regional cooperation," and North-South institutional development mechanisms are embedded with rhetorical markers on development and grievance that position China as a developing economy allied with others in resistance to neoliberal policies of global elites embodied in the International Monetary Fund (IMF), the World Bank, and other international financial institutions (IFIs).[32] China's 2023 proposal on reform of global governance draws on its "initiatives" on global security, development, and civilization that tend to portray the liberal international order as unsupportive of developing economies.[33]

Xi's CPC-100 comments emphasized development concerns: "We must deepen reform and opening up across the board, ground our work in this new stage of development, fully and faithfully apply the new development philosophy, and foster a new pattern of development."[34] Norms of development are fundamental to PRC economic policy discourse, which includes assertions that China's development is threatened by proponents of the liberal international order.[35] The "new development" philosophy speaks to Xi's vision of "common prosperity," prioritizing domestic economic growth over international links.[36] His remarks to CPC's 20th National Congress in October 2022 also addressed development as resistance:

> China is working to achieve modernization for more than 1.4 billion people, a number larger than the combined population of all developed countries in the world today. This is a task of unparalleled difficulty and complexity; it inevitably means that our pathways of development and methods of advancement will be unique. We will, as always, bear China's realities in mind as we address issues, make decisions, and take action.[37]

Xi's references to China's population in comparison with developed countries, his claim to the uniqueness of China's development pathways and methods, and his allusion to China's realities as key to PRC development policy all speak to an effort to justify China's resistance to the rules-based international order. Grievance plays a salient role in this discourse.

Practical Resistance and Human Rights

China's populist posture has included a rhetorical marker on human rights that expresses practical resistance to international standards.[38] The PRC has consistently emphasized that, international standards notwithstanding, human rights protection in China depends on the Party-state's determinations as to national conditions.[39] China's resistance to the liberal international order is particularly evident in the discourse around "Core Socialist Values" endorsed by the Party-state, by which the regime attempts to recast norms associated with liberalism in terms expressing the regime's policy priorities on governance, the economy, and social relations. The regime's purported core values include "national values" of prosperity (富强), democracy (民主), civility (文明), and harmony (和谐); "social values" of freedom (自由), equality (平等), justice (公正), and legal rule (法治); and "individual values" of patriotism (爱国), dedication (敬业), integrity (诚信), and friendship (友善).[40] In an ironic example of "waving the red flag to oppose the red flag" (*da hongqi fan hongqi* // 打红旗反红旗), Mao's political slogan aimed against opponents who cited principles of Marxism to critique Mao's policies,[41] the recitation of Core Socialist Values cites liberal governance norms but interprets them to suit the preferences of the Party-state.[42]

Appropriating terms of prosperity, democracy, civility, and harmony to serve as norms of Party-state governance, the PRC template for "national" values presents prosperity as dependent on direction of the Party-state, democracy as subject to the leadership of the CPC, and civility and harmony as components of regime-controlled stability. Similarly, purportedly "social" values of freedom, equality, justice, and law are adapted to the needs of Party control under constitutional provisions subordinating all legal rights to the supremacy of the Party-state.[43] The Party-state's dominance is underscored by interpretation of so-called individual values of patriotism, dedication, integrity, and friendship as subordinate to Party-led priorities. The dicta of Core Socialist Values have been applied to the legal system as well, facilitating enforcement of Party-state priorities in governance, the economy, and society.[44] Recent criticisms of the prevalence of English in China and internationally speak further to resistance against what is portrayed as an international liberal establishment.[45]

Exemplifying practical resistance to international standards on human rights, China critiqued reports by the UN Committee on the Elimination of Racial Discrimination (CERD) on China's ethnic policies in Xinjiang and other minority areas, suggesting that China was being unfairly singled out and portraying critics as tools of "anti-China forces."[46] China's response to CERD also relied on imagery of international elites intruding on state sovereignty – China's and, by extension, that of other states whose social policies are outside the parameters of international liberal norms. Complaints that CERD criticism of China impinged on China's development and unfairly imposed liberal human rights standards were also evident.

Xi's CPC-100 speech expressed further China's resistance to international arrangements on human rights: "The Party will continue to work with all peace-loving countries and peoples to promote the shared human values of peace, development, fairness, justice, democracy, and freedom."[47] Overlapping somewhat with the Core Socialist Values of Party dominance, Xi's focus on "human values" serves as a proxy for human rights, treating China's rights discourse with its emphasis on CPC dominance, collective rights, and the priority given to certain rights such as development over others such as political expression, as of equal merit with existing international standards on universality and indivisibility of rights and the priority of the individual.[48]

Xi's remarks to CPC's 20th National Congress in October 2022 also underscored China's resistance to international standards on human rights:

> We must firmly stay on the path of socialist political advancement with Chinese characteristics, uphold the unity between Party leadership, the running of the country by the people, and law-based governance, and ensure the principal position of the people, so as to give full expression to their will, protect their rights and interests, and spark their creativity ... We will follow a Chinese path of human rights development, actively participate in global human rights governance, and promote all-around advancement of human rights.[49]

Notwithstanding his generalized language on participation and promotion of international human rights, Xi's comments underscored the primacy of China's conditions, CPC dominance, and China's own path in conceiving and enforcing human rights at home.

TABLE 2 Features of populism and rhetorical markers in China's globalized populism

Features of populism	Rhetorical markers of China's globalized populism
Anti-elitism	*Sovereignty* serves to insulate PRC governance against intrusion from international elites.
Grievance ideology	Complaints about efforts to thwart China's *development* are used to justify opposition to international systems.
Practical resistance	Alternative *human rights* policies challenge application of existing international norms to China.

Reflecting populist features of opposition to elites, grievance ideology, and practical resistance, rhetorical markers on sovereignty, development, and human rights lend resilience to China's opposition to established norms on governance, economic development, and social relations associated with the liberal international order.[50] This is illustrated in Table 2.

WHILE INTERNAL POLITICS and personalities undoubtedly play a role in formulating and implementing foreign policy,[51] the populist features of anti-elitism, grievance, and practical resistance bolstered by rhetorical markers of sovereignty, development, and human rights offer much to explain China's conflicted relationship with the rules-based international order. The Party-state's globalized populism expresses hostility toward international elites through sovereignty claims, grievance over perceived failures to respect the needs of China's development, and practical resistance through alternative policy and legal responses on human rights. Whether as a matter of political strategy to gain influence domestically and internationally or as an expression of genuinely held views, China's globalized populism involves challenges to the existing liberal international order.[52] Such globalized populism not only expresses regime law and policy preferences but also, once formally and repeatedly articulated, constrains regime responses to international events and conditions. This has particular significance for China's responses to the global crises of COVID-19, climate change, and involuntary migration.

Global Crises: Pandemic, Climate, Migration

The interconnected crises of COVID-19, climate change, and involuntary migration provide opportunities for assessing the impact of China's globalized populism on PRC participation in the international community. The scope of these crises is vast, requiring global cooperation among nations and highlighting the significance of China's responses. As well, dilemmas of inequality and complexity underscore the challenges facing global policy response. Populist reactions to the three crises reveal features of anti-elitism, grievance, and practical resistance, offering comparisons with China's crisis response.

Scope

The World Health Organization (WHO) declared COVID-19 a Public Health Emergency of International Concern (PHEIC) on January 30, 2020, and characterized the outbreak as a pandemic on March 11, 2020, some four months after the initial outbreak was detected in Wuhan, China.[53] Three years later, the WHO declared that the public health emergency due to COVID-19 had ended after some 750 million cases of infection and nearly 7 million deaths.[54] As the COVID-19 pandemic raged through 2020 and 2021, hospitalization rates, ICU use, and mortality soared.[55] The emergence of the Omicron variant in November 2021 and the discovery of new Omicron subvariants in 2022 signalled that global responses to the pandemic remained incomplete.[56] As the combination of widespread vaccination and emerging herd immunity began to reduce the frequency and severity of COVID-19 in some areas, experts began to advise on preparations for future novel coronaviruses, even as a new wave of infections in 2023 signalled the persistence of the virus.[57]

As COVID-19 dominated the headlines and the attention of governments, the ongoing crisis of climate change was not far from view. Climate activists warned that the COVID-19 crisis was distracting attention and resources from the all-important climate change struggle.[58] The Intergovernmental Panel on Climate Change (IPCC) has warned repeatedly of severe impacts on natural and human systems from global warming associated with anthropogenic climate change.[59]

A third major crisis of the early twenty-first century involves involuntary migration.[60] Even before the Russian invasion of Ukraine in early 2022, which generated nearly 6 million refugees from the fighting, forced migration emerged as a global crisis, with 117.3 million people forcibly displaced from their homes through mid-2025, among whom were at least 36.4 million refugees.[61] The 2023–25 Gaza war between Israel and Hamas generated a further cohort of involuntary migrants.[62] Israel's 2024 offensive against Hezbollah in Lebanon resulted in at least 346,000 internally displaced persons, with hundreds of thousands seeking refuge in Syria.[63] The vast majority of those fleeing their countries of origin go to developing countries – of the top five destination countries tracked by the Office of the UN High Commissioner for Refugees (UNHCR), Germany is the only developed country listed; the others are Colombia, Turkey, Iran, and Uganda.[64]

The global crises of COVID-19, climate change, and involuntary migration are closely interconnected.[65] Climate change affects human and animal habitats, furthering the interspecies engagement that has contributed to the emergence of multiple corona viruses.[66] Similarly, climate, health, and associated economic factors are key drivers of involuntary migration.[67] The interconnections among COVID-19, climate change, and involuntary migration pose particular challenges for equality and complexity.

Constraints of Inequality and Complexity

Conditions of inequality and complexity discussed in Chapter 1 as foundations for the emergence of populism are no less relevant for understanding the international crises of COVID-19, climate change, and involuntary migration. Global development depends on achieving greater equality of capability to respond to complex challenges in socio-economic relations.[68] Yet disparities of income and well-being continue to be well documented across the world.[69] Inequalities in income and opportunity undermine the general increases in income for the poor that have characterized the recent era of globalization.[70] Complexities of international systems compound the challenge of inequality, as disparities of power and resources among states, organizations, and individuals inhibit access and participation in these processes.[71]

Constraints of inequality affect the impacts of the COVID-19 pandemic, as poorer countries and regions are less able to manage the challenges of containing and treating the virus without outside assistance.[72] As well, complexities of the WHO processes for identifying and responding to public health emergencies challenge the capacity of poorer countries to participate.[73] Inequality and complexity undermine efforts to prepare for future pandemics as resource constraints limit capacity to develop and implement complex prophylactic measures and medical responses.

Inequality and complexity also have a significant effect on impacts of climate change, as predominantly poorer countries and regions bear much of the impact but lack the wherewithal to mitigate or adapt to the complex effects of global warming.[74] Financial and organizational support from international agencies to enable climate change response by poorer economies is constrained by complexities of agency budgets and institutional capacity that depend in turn on the generosity of wealthy donor economies.[75]

Inequality and complexity also affect involuntary migration.[76] Economic and environmental migrants exemplify inequalities between conditions in their places of origin and their destinations, while the UNHCR system for managing involuntary migration involves complexities that are often beyond the capacity of source and recipient countries to resolve.[77] Conditions of war and violence that drive many migrants to take flight are often themselves the product of political upheavals associated with inequalities in complex socio-economic conditions (often intertwined with economic deprivation from climate change).[78] Migrants often face immediate disparities of wealth and opportunity between themselves and the societies of recipient countries, while the complexities of agencies and processes providing aid to involuntary migrants pose additional barriers.[79]

Responses to Global Crises

The crises of pandemic response, climate change, and involuntary migration have generated a range of global governance responses. As multiple waves of COVID-19 infection broke out, the WHO played a central role in disseminating information and proposing policy responses.[80] Early on, global health agencies began preparing to respond to future pandemics.[81] The development of multiple COVID-19 vaccines signalled hope even in the midst of the pandemic.[82] Continued international public health initiatives will no doubt be compromised by the second Trump administration's decision to withdraw the United States from the WHO and cut foreign aid more broadly.[83] International efforts on climate change have continued, despite the US withdrawal from the Paris Agreement on climate change in 2020 during the first Trump administration and the second Trump administration's reversal in 2025 of President Joe Biden's decision to rejoin in 2021.[84] Protecting safe migration and resettlement of migrants has long been a priority for international human rights institutions and policy.[85] Efforts to improve conditions for refugees, including their admission to recipient countries subject to the 1951 Convention Relating to the Status of Refugees and its 1967 Protocol, continue to occupy the UNHCR, while the International Organization for Migration (IOM) tracks refugees as well as other forms of migration.[86] The Global Compacts on migration[87] and refugees[88] offer additional policy guidance. These efforts have elicited populist responses ranging from progressive support to regressive resistance.

Populist Responses

Consistent with the diversity in political orientations of populism discussed in Chapter 1, populist responses to the crises of COVID-19, climate change, and involuntary migration have varied. Regressive populists have often portrayed COVID-19 measures as unwelcome intrusions by global elites on local prerogatives, while progressives have welcomed cooperation with international pandemic control efforts.[89] In response to the challenges of climate change, regressive populists have generally resisted budget efforts supporting renewable energy, green architecture, electric vehicles, and other efforts to reduce energy dependence on fossil fuels, while progressive populists embrace them.[90] Responding to the challenges of involuntary migration, regressive populists have tended to treat this crisis as a threat to local social arrangements, whereas progressive populists tend to view migration as an opportunity for growth and development.[91]

Despite such variation, resistance from regressive populists has been particularly evident in policy discourses on coronavirus infection,[92] climate change,[93] and involuntary migration.[94] Despite wide scientific acceptance of medical truths about pandemic illness,[95] scientific conclusions about climate change,[96] and socio-legal perspectives on involuntary migration,[97] resistance from regressive populists persists. Initiatives around COVID-19 have faced regressive resistance, often articulated in terms of nationalist concerns over protection of local priorities, which entails questions about inequality and complexity in enforcement of international public health standards.[98] Reactions to inequality and complexity are also evident in efforts by authoritarian states to build international standing through simplified distribution of vaccines to poorer countries.[99] Similarly, regressive resistance to climate change initiatives has reflected concerns over inequalities and complexities in the relationship between causation and remediation of climate damage.[100] Regressive resistance to efforts to reduce greenhouse gas emissions under the Kyoto Protocol (1987) has raised similar questions around the emissions reduction targets of the 2015 Paris Agreement.[101]

The crisis of involuntary migration has also seen regressive resistance, as populist antipathy toward outsiders reflects concerns about equality in their legal status and socio-economic conditions and the complexities of international migration standards and processes for their treatment.[102] Regressive populists in Europe have opposed inbound involuntary migration, challenging the European Union to "get a handle on migration."[103] Policy responses from UNHCR and state leaders such as German chancellor Angela Merkel calling for acceptance and compassion have been challenged by regressive resistance denying the legitimacy of refugee claims, marginalizing claimants, and rejecting government supports.[104] The EU's 2023 migration agreement represented a tentative step toward greater control over migration challenges, although human rights groups challenged the initiative as weakening the rights of asylum seekers, refugees, and others.[105] Often, regressives claiming that involuntary migration poses a threat also deny the threats posed by COVID-19 and climate change.[106] Immigration policies in Asia have shown mixed responses to populist influences.[107]

Populist Regime Responses: Anti-Elitism, Grievance, Practical Resistance

As discussed in Chapter 1, globalized populism reveals features associated with social and regime populism around opposition to elites, justification through grievance ideology, and practical resistance through reordering of operational norms and law and policy practices related to accountability, prosperity, and community. These are evident in responses to the global crises of COVID-19, climate change, and involuntary migration by both regressive and progressive populist regimes.[108]

The populist regime in Brazil under Jair Bolsonaro elected in 2019 came to exemplify regressive populism in Latin America, with its economic development policies supporting resource exploitation over environmental concerns and its support for privatization of industry, reduction of corporate taxes, and curtailment of Brazil's generous pension system.[109] Bolsonaro was defeated in national elections in 2022 by former president Luiz Inácio Lula da Silva, although he did not concede defeat and his supporters continued to rally for his reinstatement.[110] Echoing the Trump-inspired attack on the US Capitol building on January 6, 2021, Bolsonaro supporters occupied the Brazilian Congress, Presidential Palace, and Supreme Court buildings in Brasilia on January 8, 2023, only to be repelled by security forces after several hours.[111] Bolsonaro was banned from running for office for eight years by Brazil's Superior Electoral Court for abuse of power and "immoral and appalling lies" in connection with the 2022 election.[112] The Brazilian Congress termed Bolsonaros's post-election activities as "a wilful and premeditated coup attempt."[113] Bolsonaro was convicted of attempting a coup against the state and began a twenty-seven-year prison sentence in November 2025.[114]

Venezuela's Nicolás Maduro exemplifies a hybrid populism involving relatively progressive socio-economic policies combined with illiberal governance.[115] Maduro was appointed president following the death of his mentor, Hugo Chàvez, in March 2013, and won a narrow victory in the presidential election in April.[116] Facing falling oil prices, US sanctions, and regime policy failures, Venezuela struggled with an unprecedented economic and political crisis. Despite possible charges at the International Criminal Court (ICC) for crimes against humanity, and calls by the United States and the multilateral Lima Group for his replacement by opposition leader Juan Guaidó, Maduro continued in power.[117] The easing of US sanctions in 2023 following Maduro's agreement to electoral reforms may relieve the economic crisis somewhat.[118] Maduro was re-elected in 2024, although the poll was widely disputed.[119] The US Trump administration intensified military threats against Maduro and his regime in November–December 2025, and in January 2026 conducted a military raid that saw Maduro captured and brought to the United States to face drug, weapons, and narco-terrorism charges.[120]

In Hungary, Viktor Orbán's populist regime has been termed regressive for its socio-economic policies and illiberal disregard for democracy and the rule of law.[121] Following an earlier term in 1998–2002, Orbán became prime minister again in 2010 after a victory in parliamentary elections by his conservative Fidesz party, and was re-elected in 2018. While emerging from Hungary's liberal tradition, Orbán has embraced nationalist autocracy to cement his hold on power – to the point where the European Parliament labelled Hungary a "hybrid regime of electoral autocracy."[122] Orbán was re-elected to a fourth term as prime minister in April 2022.

In Greece, progressive populist Alexis Tsipras became prime minister following the victory of his Syriza party in parliamentary elections in January 2015.[123] Tsipras became a leading opposition member after losing his parliamentary mandate in 2019 to the New Democracy party led by Kyriakos Mitsotakis.[124] He resigned this position in 2023 after another electoral defeat for Syriza.[125]

In India, regressive populist Narendra Modi became prime minister in 2014 following the parliamentary election victory of his Hindu nationalist Bharatiya Janata Party (BJP), and was re-elected to a second term in 2019.[126] Since his election, India has been portrayed as slipping toward Hindu nationalist autocracy, particularly regarding regime challenges to independence of the legal system.[127] A catastrophic wave of infections, hospitalizations, and deaths swept over India in 2021, challenging Modi's approach to the COVID-19 pandemic and raising questions about his political future.[128] He won re-election in the hotly contested 2024 parliamentary elections but failed to gain a majority, an indication of growing impatience over India's economic difficulties and Modi's Hindu nationalist policies.[129]

Anti-Elitism

Hostility to international elites has been an ongoing feature of populist regimes. Brazil's Bolsonaro evinced resistance to the international health system in the midst of the COVID-19 crisis, calling the WHO a "partisan political organization."[130] Defending his economic development agenda centred on resource exploitation and privatization of industry, he repeatedly expressed themes of resistance to global climate systems associated with global elites.[131] In Venezuela, Maduro challenged international elites embodied by the WHO, noting that US sanctions had prevented Venezuela's payment of COVAX (COVID-19 Vaccines Global Access) fees, and calling out the UN World Food Programme (WFP) for insufficient support for Venezuela's food security challenges.[132] His anti-elitism was evident in his attack on the United States and the European Union for disputing his 2019 election and "waging an imperialist 'world war' against his crisis-stricken nation."[133] Hungary's Orbán has also used hostility toward outside authorities to expand his political power.[134] In Greece Alexis Tsipras challenged the international creditors and business interests on his country's economy, opposing the European Union's market-based economic growth policies and calling for the protection of social well-being through restructuring of Greece's debt.[135] In India, Modi's government expressed hostility toward international standards of governance purportedly driven by the priorities of developed economies.[136]

Grievance

Whether of the progressive or regressive sort, populist regimes have also expressed a range of grievances – including that liberal international governance is insufficiently inclusive of local concerns and conditions, that globalization of commerce insufficiently equitable for developing economies, and that international systems on migration insufficiently responsive to the needs of both source and destination countries.[137] These concerns were evident in responses to international efforts on COVID-19, climate change, and involuntary migration.

On COVID-19, Bolsonaro defended Brazil's lacklustre pandemic response in terms of resentment against WHO standards and internationally influenced domestic political pressures.[138] Venezuela's Maduro expressed grievance against the legacy of US imperialism in the region: "We don't want to go back to the gringo interventions of the 20th century."[139] He charged the United States and its European allies with "illegal blockade [and] aggressions" that hampered his government's efforts to manage the COVID-19 crisis and contributed to Venezuela's challenges of poverty and social inequality.[140] In Hungary, Orbán evinced grievances against political opponents who were purportedly relying on media and culture to oppose his authoritarian rule.[141] Informed by such resentments, he used the pandemic as justification for attacking democratic opponents and securing the power to rule by decree in March 2020,[142] which was replaced by broadly similar powers in May permitted under a "state of health emergency" declaration.[143] Greece's Alexis Tsipras criticized the EU approach to pandemic response as overly dependent on influential pharmaceutical producers,[144] while in India Modi protested that international standards diminished attention to traditional allopathic medicine vis-à-vis conventional pharmaceuticals.[145] Modi's Hindu nationalist vision manifested resentment against international health measures, as he proclaimed the victory of local self-reliance over coronavirus infection.[146]

On climate change, Bolsonaro's development policies in the Amazon were informed by his denial of climate change and couched in terms of grievance against international intrusion, as he demanded "respectful" treatment for Brazil as a condition for remaining in the Paris Agreement.[147] Orbán's grievances against the European Union were in full view when, following a European Council meeting examining EU responses to climate change, he exclaimed, "We survived."[148] Modi, meanwhile, responded to climate change advocates by expressing grievances against the industrialized economies that had contributed so much to climate change, stressing that India did not cause climate change and so should be spared much of the cost of remediation.[149]

On migration policy, Orbán's refusal to join the UN Global Compact on Refugees (GCR) and withdrawal from the Global Compact for Safe, Orderly and Regular Migration (GCM) evinced his sense of grievance against EU immigration policies, which he associated with the "great replacement" agenda excoriated by the far right.[150] Tsipras revealed underlying grievances over the inordinate burden placed on Greece by the recent influx of migrants from the Middle East and Africa in the biggest refugee crisis since the Second World War.[151] In the highly polarized political climate within Greece and in the European Union more broadly during the migrant crisis, Tsipras challenged the "not-in-my-backyard" attitude associated with resistance to immigration.[152] The expression of such grievances has often been augmented by reference to legacies of imperialism and colonialism, echoing critiques levelled against neocolonialism and dependency in the "core-periphery" discourses of decades past.[153]

Practical Resistance

Populist regimes have also expressed practical resistance to the standards of the international system, promoting alternative law and policy practices for engaging international standards on governance, the economy, and social relations.[154] Some populists express impatience with the seeming inability of the international system to respond effectively to global challenges, while others express resentment over expansion of liberal perspectives on governance, the economy, and society.[155] For populist regimes, hostility to liberal international governance standards embodies practical resistance to the purported pro-Western bias of liberal norms such as democracy and rule of law.[156] Resistance to international economic standards often involves criticism of their intrusiveness vis-à-vis local arrangements and failure to ensure equitable prosperity.[157] Resistance to international standards on community relations often focuses on their inattention to the socio-cultural traditions and needs of local settlements.[158]

Examples of practical resistance include Bolsonaro's calls for national autonomy for Brazil in rule making on migration: "The Brazilians and immigrants who live here will be safer under rules that we ourselves make, without external pressure."[159] In Venezuela, Maduro's calls for the United Nations to adopt binding measures recognizing the right to development and funding efforts to overcome poverty and social inequality exemplified practical resistance to existing global standards.[160] Hungary's Orbán expressed practical resistance to EU climate change standards through assertions that international climate rules should not impose on "ordinary people" the costs of taxation measures to fight climate change.[161] He proposed the slogan "Atlanticism, freedom, family, Christianity and sovereignty" as an alternative to EU norms.[162] In Greece, Tsipras called for more equitable distribution of vaccines, support for front-line workers, and debt forgiveness for small businesses, raising practical resistance to the liberal economic standards of the European Union.[163] In India, the Modi government's practical resistance to international standards on migration was evident in the Citizenship Amendment Act (CAA, 2019) and the planned National Population Register (NPRI), whose overt discrimination against Muslims has been extended to immigration policy.[164]

Assessing Practical Resistance: Accountability, Prosperity, Community

As discussed in Chapter 1, populist practical resistance may be usefully examined by reference to governance accountability, economic prosperity, and social community. Pandemic response involves matters of governance accountability in protecting public health, climate change involves policy tensions around climate protection and economic prosperity, and involuntary migration involves conditions of communities in local society.

Accountability and COVID-19

Populist responses to the global crisis of pandemic illness have demonstrated differences in law and policy practice around operational norms on performance, process, and information accountability.[165] Populist responses to the COVID-19 crisis have tended to pursue *performance accountability* largely through efforts to reinforce the appearance of policy success.[166] Populist portrayals of policy performance around pandemic relief have tended to navigate between conflicting tropes of modernization and colonialization associated with the WHO's international standards of health care.[167] Efforts to claim the mantle of modernity have been evident in both aspirational depictions of government efforts as satisfying policy needs, and empirical portrayals of actionable policy success in terms of reductions in infection rates, hospitalization, intensive care unit and emergency room usage, and deaths. Whereas progressive populists may seek credit for modernizing health care through acceptance of international standards on pandemic response, regressive populists have tended to resist the imposition of WHO standards and oversight, engage in outright denial of the disease while downplaying disparate impacts on othered communities of the poor, nonwhite, elderly, and already sick, and embrace libertarian rejection of government policy intervention.[168]

Process accountability in populist law and policy practice during COVID-19 confronts tensions between instrumentalist use of legal terminology to support government power and reliance on impartial rule of law standards limiting government conduct.[169] In practice, this involves choices between regressive reliance on instrumentalist use of law to enforce lockdowns and other social controls and progressive support for impartial rule-of-law standards that restrict state intrusion on personal and property rights.[170]

Information accountability practices reflect tensions between propaganda and transparency on the extent and severity of infection, scope and results of coronavirus testing, and availability and implementation of vaccines.[171] Regressive responses to COVID-19 have tended to pursue propaganda practices related to access to information, combined with resistance to public disclosure through claims around security, confidentiality, privacy, and other barriers.[172] Regressive populist practices on information accountability practices have tended to reflect varying commitments to reliance on science and data, often including "post-truth" architectures involving alternative facts, conspiracy theories, and gnostic-like restrictions limiting access to "hidden knowledge" to privileged audiences.[173] By contrast, progressive commitments to public inquiry about government behaviour have often played out in the context of transparency requirements on retention and disclosure of official information associated with the liberal international order.[174]

Prosperity and Climate Change

Populist responses to the global crisis of climate change are expressed through law and policy practice around norms on measurement, distribution, and autonomy of prosperity. Regressive practices on climate change have tended to reflect preferences for macro-indicators such as GDP growth and aggregate income and wealth in the *measurement* of prosperity, whereas progressive populists have exhibited preferences for micro-indicators such as health care, housing, and living and working conditions associated with the liberal international order.[175] Populist practices related to prosperity in the context of climate change also involve questions regarding the *distribution* of costs and benefits to business or social sector recipients. Progressive law and policy practices related to distribution of prosperity in the context of climate action have tended toward reliance on direct public benefits, while regressive populists have relied more heavily on distribution to business actors with the expectation of indirect benefits to society.[176] Climate change practices also involve the *autonomy* of economic actors in responding to the demands of economic markets or state regulation in climate programming. Populist regimes have tended to pursue contrasting progressive and regressive goals of ensuring social welfare through state regulation or permitting economic actors to attend to market demands regardless of social harm.[177]

Community and Involuntary Migration

Variations in responses to the global crisis of involuntary migration are expressed through law and policy practices related to operational norms of community identity, diversity, and mobility. Aside from the question of legal identity confirmed through bureaucratic processes and documentation, tensions in migration practices related to socio-cultural *identity* have reflected varying approaches to inherent and acquired aspects of identity, with corresponding questions about adaptation and assimilation.[178] Migration law and policy practices related to *diversity* reveal distinctions between policies of segregation emphasizing difference and exclusion, and efforts to build unity and collaboration in society through integration.[179] Migration practices related to *mobility* have entailed differences between regressive denial of rights and conditions of migrants due to concerns about threats to local stability, and progressive support for immigration as a benefit for economic opportunity and in fulfillment of a moral duty to protect.[180] Populist views on involuntary migration have varied between regressive positions asserting inherent features of identity, segregation of diverse groups, and exclusion of outsiders,[181] and progressive respect for norms of identity that transcend ethnicity, integration among different social groups, and welcoming of migrants.[182]

Conclusion

China's globalized populism directs populist resentments outward, away from the PRC's own governance and toward international systems and actors. Populist features of anti-elitism, grievance, and practical resistance are bolstered by rhetorical markers around sovereignty, development, and human rights that lend resilience to China's challenges against international standards. China's globalized populism informs its responses to the global crises of COVID-19, climate change, and involuntary migration. The scope and scale of these crises, together with underlying issues of inequality and complexity, present challenges for international systems in public health, climate, and migration. Populist responses have varied, but reveal common features of anti-elitism, grievance, and practical resistance. Populist practical resistance may usefully be examined by reference to governance accountability, economic prosperity, and social community. This provides perspectives for assessing China's globalized populism. The chapters that follow address in sequence China's response to global crises of COVID-19, climate change, and involuntary migration, in light of PRC policies and practice around political accountability, economic prosperity, and social community.

3 COVID-19
Antagonistic Populism

IN THIS CHAPTER, we examine the responses of the People's Republic of China to the COVID-19 crisis as an example of China's populist resistance to the rules-based international order.[1] The chapter opens with a review of China's experience with COVID-19, from the initial outbreak and reaction to debates over the origins of the pandemic, to China's "Zero-COVID" policy and its aftermath. We then examine China's relationship with the international public health policy system under conditions of inequality and complexity and assesses populist features of anti-elitism and grievance ideology in China's response to COVID-19. In light of the importance of governance accountability for public health policy,[2] this chapter examines China's practical resistance to the international health policy system through alternative law and policy practices related to operational norms on performance, process, and information accountability. China's law and policy practice during the COVID-19 crisis is explained further by reference to rhetorical markers on sovereignty, development, and human rights supporting resilience in China's globalized populism. Controversies over the origins of COVID-19 and Beijing's handling of the crisis lent an air of adversarialism to relationships with the international public health system, making China's COVID-19 response an example of antagonistic populism.

China and the COVID-19 Crisis

China's response to the COVID-19 crisis began with efforts to control people and information linked to the virus. In the course of such efforts, significant tensions emerged between the PRC regime and the international community over questions about the origins of the outbreak and China's response. As the crisis deepened, China's efforts to control the virus intensified through its "Zero-COVID" policy, which was lifted in late 2022.

Outbreak and Reaction

China's initial responses to the COVID-19 crisis have been well documented.[3] December 2019 saw multiple patients presenting with fever and pneumonia at Wuhan hospitals, overwhelming emergency facilities and alarming attending doctors. On December 31, the Wuhan government announced the outbreak while denying evidence of human-to-human transmission. On January 1, 2020, the Huanan Seafood Market, considered the source of the infections, was closed down just as the Hubei Provincial Health Commission ordered genome testing companies, including national leader BGI Group, to stop testing samples from Wuhan and destroy them. Two days later, China's National Health Commission (NHC) prohibited publication of information related to the virus, and ordered labs to transfer their samples to designated institutions or destroy them. The NHC confirmed publicly for the first time on January 20 that the virus could be transmitted between humans (although the World Health Organization had determined as early as January 14 that human-to-human transmission was likely). On January 21, a front-page notice in *People's Daily* (*Renmin ribao* //人民日报) reported on Xi Jinping's important instructions on responses to the virus, followed by the launching of a Leading Small Group (LSG) (*lingdao xiaozu* // 领导小组) under Premier Li Keqiang.[4] Wuhan was placed under lockdown on January 23, confirming the regime's conventional control practices despite considerable hardship suffered by local residents.[5]

The government's initial reaction to reports of a new virus followed a conventional pattern, emphasizing control and suppression of people and information. As Wuhan institutions and doctors relayed information on the virus to the local, provincial, and central authorities, restrictions were imposed on information about the outbreak.[6] Local officials concerned that they would be blamed for the crisis were economical with the truth in their reporting to higher levels, compounding uncertainty and spurring further efforts to control information.[7] The familiar example of ophthalmologist Li Wenliang, who raised the alarm very early on only to punished for "spreading rumours," was matched by the treatment of other doctors and health care workers.[8] Li's death from COVID-19 on February 7, 2020, became a rallying point for many people in China impatient with the government's response. Disillusionment with China's initial response became more apparent.[9] Regime preferences around controlling people and information contributed significantly to increased criticism domestically and abroad.[10] With new waves of infections emerging in 2021–22,[11] the regime continued to grapple with the twin challenges of getting the infection under control and responding to international calls for further investigation.[12]

Debates over the Origins of COVID-19

China's international engagement on COVID-19 was antagonistic almost from the start due to the intensity of disagreements over the question of COVID-19's origins. As the PRC regime continued efforts to control people and information relating to COVID-19, China also faced criticism over the origins of the coronavirus.[13] The debate centred on whether the virus involved natural zoonotic infection between animals and humans or was the result of an event (accidental or planned) at the Wuhan Institute of Virology (WIV). A peer-reviewed study published in March 2020 and cited by the US National Institutes of Health (NIH) concluded that COVID-19 was "not a laboratory construct or a purposefully manipulated construct," in effect refuting the "lab-leak" theory of COVID-19's origins.[14] Yet Germany's intelligence agency concluded in 2020 that a lab leak was in fact the most likely cause of the pandemic.[15] Successive joint China-WHO investigations in 2020 and 2021 concluded that the virus was most likely of zoonotic origins, migrating to humans from bats and other intermediary mammals – such as pangolins sold in Wuhan's live animal markets.[16] With caveats around the need for greater data access, the WHO's 2021 investigation report suggested that the virus likely spread through direct or intermediate zoonotic transmission from small mammals such as bats or pangolins to humans, facilitated by exposure at live products food markets in Wuhan, and that "a laboratory origin of the pandemic was considered to be extremely unlikely."[17] Criticism of the report soon followed as multiple observers noted China's initial refusal to permit entry by WHO virologists participating in the 2021 investigation and criticized China's apparent refusal to provide full access to raw data on the outbreak.[18] The United States launched its own investigation in May that year, which yielded inconclusive results as to whether the virus emerged from a lab or was spread through zoonotic transfer from small mammals to humans.[19] A follow-up report conceded that which of these two possibilities occurred may never be known.[20]

Lab-leak proponents continued to assert the theory's validity, even as China worked assiduously to refute such views.[21] Some observers, including senior Trump administration officials, contended that the virus leaked from the WIV, even suggesting deliberate weaponization of the virus.[22] While the US Office of the Director of National Intelligence (DNI) released an analysis in June 2023 challenging the lab-leak theory, news reports of WIV researchers falling ill with the virus attracted support for the lab-leak theory.[23] In mid-2023, the former director of the Chinese Center for Disease Control and Prevention (CCDC) called for caution in rejecting the lab-leak explanation.[24]

Debates over the origins of the virus continued[25] despite calls to move on from the focus on origins and blame to broader cooperation.[26] While persuasive evidence continued to emerge supporting the zoonotic origins of the virus, questions lingered as to whether this occurred at Wuhan's Huanan live animal market or as a result of humans contracting the disease elsewhere.[27] As new lab findings pointed to zoonotic transfer from raccoon dogs sold illegally at the Huanan market, questions persisted regarding the preservation and publication of data from China on the origins of COVID-19.[28] International observers, including the WHO, called for further investigation requiring China to provide full transparency and data access.[29] While ongoing research tends to point to zoonotic transfer, proponents of the lab-leak theory remained influential.[30] Just before leaving office in 2024, President Joe Biden ordered a further review of COVID-19's origins.[31] The Central Intelligence Agency's new report in 2025, ordered by the Biden administration and released by the second Trump administration, indicated "with low confidence" that a lab leak was the most likely cause of the COVID-19 pandemic.[32] President Trump has endorsed broad-based assertions supporting the lab-leak theory.[33] The WHO's final expert advisory report on COVID-19's origins concluded that, while most data supported zoonotic transfer, the committee was unable to rule out definitively the lab-leak theory due to lack of data from China.[34]

"Zero-COVID" and Its Aftermath

China's most prominent policy response to COVID-19 involved strict enforcement of a "dynamic Zero-COVID" (*dongtai qingling* // 动态清零) policy, under which people were required to undergo regular testing and to show proof of negative test results in order to work, travel, or carry out tasks of daily life, and people with symptoms or who tested positive were subject to strict quarantine.[35] In January 2020, the National Health Commission directed that COVID-19 be included in the PRC Infectious Diseases Law's Class B of infectious diseases (which includes SARS, AIDS, and avian flu) but subject to the stricter isolation and quarantine measures applicable to Class A (which includes plague and cholera), authorizing quarantine and lockdown provisions that served as core content for Zero-COVID.[36] At a press conference in May 2022, WHO director-general Tedros Adhanom Ghebreyesus termed the policy "not sustainable" in light of the capacity of the virus to evolve and generate new variants.[37]

Despite the Zero-COVID policy, outbreaks continued in 2022, with record-high levels of COVID-19 infections being recorded nationally.[38] Outbreaks in Shanghai (April–May 2022) and Chengdu (September 2022) heightened worries about the social and economic impacts of Zero-COVID.[39] The familiar response of increased lockdowns followed.[40] Lockdowns imposed in Xi'an (December 2021),[41] Shenzhen (March 2022),[42] Jilin (March 2022),[43] and Shanghai (March–April 2022)[44] featured some of the harshest anti-COVID measures, confining millions of residents to their homes, cancelling train and air travel, and punishing local officials. Zero-COVID lockdowns left many vulnerable to the emerging Omicron variant, in part due to the uncertain effectiveness of China-made vaccines and a nationalistic reluctance to rely on foreign vaccines that could be more effective.[45] The Zero-COVID approach also challenged social stability as people's patience frayed.[46] COVID crackdowns also hampered economic production, supply chains, and other features of global economic interdependence.[47] The regime's commitment to Zero-COVID was reinforced by fears that the policy's removal would lead to devastating COVID-19 outbreaks.[48] The government's alarm over the Omicron surge in Hong Kong in early 2022 underscored its commitment to Zero-COVID despite concerns about the policy's effects – and effectiveness.[49]

Besides debates over their effectiveness, the quarantine, isolation, and lockdown practices of Zero-COVID had severely repressive effects on society and the economy.[50] A May 2022 Politburo meeting on stabilizing employment called for urgent efforts to stabilize the economy in the wake of COVID-19 even while preserving existing prevention and control measures.[51] This in turn set the tone for an expanded national work conference on employment and the economy chaired by then Vice Premier Han Zheng later in the month that underscored the importance of protecting economic growth and stable employment.[52] After a short postponement nominally due to a COVID-19 surge in Beijing, the annual Central Economic Work Conference (CEWC) held on December 17 reiterated the need to preserve economic stability in the midst of COVID controls: "The meeting stressed better coordinating epidemic prevention and control with economic and social development, urging efforts to optimize epidemic response based on time and situation and focus on the elderly and those with underlying diseases."[53]

Yet Zero-COVID had become so closely associated with Xi Jinping that any revision or dilution of its practices would have posed challenges for his leadership position.[54] Xi had reiterated claims about the importance of Zero-COVID at the 20th National Congress of the CPC in October 2022, clearly suggesting the importance of continued enforcement:

> In responding to the sudden outbreak of COVID-19, we put the people and their lives above all else, worked to prevent both imported cases and domestic resurgences, and tenaciously pursued a dynamic Zero-COVID policy. In launching an all-out people's war to stop the spread of the virus, we have protected the people's health and safety to the greatest extent possible and made tremendously encouraging achievements in both epidemic response and economic and social development.[55]

Nonetheless, growing public dissatisfaction over COVID lockdowns led to a series of public protests in November 2022.[56] Incensed by the death toll from an apartment fire in Urumqi apparently caused by fire exits being locked to enforce Zero-COVID, demonstrations began in Urumqi and quickly spread to Beijing, Shanghai, and elsewhere across China.[57] Protests against Zero-COVID policies quickly morphed into protests against the regime's repression of freedoms of expression and the press.[58] Similar to the Tiananmen Square protests of 1989, the 2022 COVID protests involved more than the stated grievance and reflected general dissatisfaction with the regime's rule, with some even calling for Xi's resignation.[59]

In the wake of popular unrest, along with severe impacts on China's health care facilities and significant effects on China's economy, the regime began signalling a potential revision of Zero-COVID despite concerns that this might lead to further spread of the illness.[60] Following the November demonstrations, COVID restrictions were gradually eased in Beijing and in the provincial capitals of Guangzhou, Shijiazhuang, and Chengdu.[61] On December 7, the State Council's Joint Prevention and Control Mechanism issued a broad notice calling for easing of Zero-COVID policies.[62] Much of the language in the notice supporting the easing of restrictions had appeared previously in official reporting on a Politburo Standing Committee meeting on November 10, albeit combined with a call that "necessary epidemic prevention measures must not be relaxed," which was then diluted in the State Council notice to read, "pay close attention to various prevention and control measures."[63] In addition to easing lockdowns, eliminating testing requirements except in high-risk areas such as care homes, and easing restrictions on isolation of asymptomatic individuals and those with mild symptoms, key elements of the notice called for ensuring access to drugs used in treating COVID-19 symptoms (including anti-virals), increasing vaccinations among the elderly, and expanding detection of illnesses among the elderly that exacerbate COVID symptoms. The notice reflected concerns over the spread of COVID particularly among the elderly in light of their relatively low levels of vaccination, and the relatively low level of protection offered by vaccines produced in China (coupled with continued resistance to importing more effective foreign-made vaccines).[64]

The effective termination of Zero-COVID less than two months after Xi's affirmation of the policy at the 20th National Congress of the CPC seemed an unprecedented challenge to Xi's political leadership.[65] PRC political history offers few direct analogies, although challenges to "reform and opening up" policies associated with Deng Xiaoping and his designated successors Hu Yaobang and Zhao Ziyang following the Tiananmen Square democracy protests in 1989 come to mind.[66] Perhaps a closer analogy involves Mao Zedong (to whom Xi seems rather eager to be compared) and the radical growth policies of the Great Leap Forward (1958–62) that caused untold suffering and privation as upwards of 30 million people starved in the ensuing famine.[67] After the launch of the Great Leap Forward in May 1958, at the second session of the 8th National Congress of the CPC, Mao came under criticism at the Lushan Plenum in July 1959 but held firm in supporting the policy until it was roundly criticized at the Changguanlou meetings in late 1960 to early 1961. Mao made a self-criticism at the conference of seven thousand cadres in January–February 1962 and survived the crisis to lead China for another fourteen years. Xi may well follow Mao's example and survive the effects and sudden demise of Zero-COVID, but the legitimacy of his leadership appeared diminished and his political capital diluted.

As expected, infections increased dramatically following the easing of COVID restrictions.[68] Funeral parlors and crematoria were soon overwhelmed.[69] Nonetheless, the policy shift away from Zero-COVID signalled a transition from suppressing to living with COVID-19.[70] The government attempted to discourage domestic travel during the upcoming Lunar New

Year celebrations to limit the spread of infection, even as it approved the resumption of international travel.[71] Widespread outbreaks in China after the lifting of Zero-COVID have caused international concern about further spread of the virus and the emergence of new variants.[72] Other novel viruses, such as the Langya virus, have also been detected.[73] In late 2023, the outbreak of respiratory illness in China caused alarm, although the authorities were quick to categorize this as a flu variant or other known pathogen rather than a novel coronavirus like COVID-19.[74]

China's Relationship with the Global Public Health System: Inequality and Complexity

China's record in managing COVID-19 operated in the context of relationships with the global public health system that bear the imprint of inequality and complexity. Tensions over perceived inequalities were evident in the priority given to Western medicine over China's rich tradition of endogenous medical practices.[75] Responding to inequalities in the global dominance of Western medicine and associated forces of modernization and colonialism,[76] China accepted the value of modernity in training, equipment, and services as an accepted goal of public health, while resisting the colonialist implications and effects of uncritical and exclusive reliance on Western medicine. Against a backdrop of foreign missionary–led health programs in the late nineteenth and early twentieth centuries, including the famous "Yale-in-China" program (now the Yale-China Association), Mao Zedong's "barefoot doctors" approach had signalled the replacement of the colonial aspects of Western medicine with a localized approach to providing basic medical care.[77] This sentiment continues in the current era.

Features of inequality are also evident in the WHO's standards for public health, which reveal suggestions of modernization and colonialism in the globalization of Western medical practices. The WHO's 13th General Programme of Work (2019–23) set forth ambitious goals of ensuring universal health coverage, better protection from health emergencies, and enjoyment of better health and well-being for one billion more people in each category (the "Triple Billion" targets).[78] Each of these goals involves significant technical detail drawn largely from the Sustainable Development Goals (SDG) adopted by all UN member states, of which the goal on Good Health and Well-Being (SDG 3) has been adopted by China for implementation by 2030.[79] These are presented by the WHO program as assisting countries in strengthening their health care systems by reducing financial hardship to patients through "universal health coverage," building thirteen core capacities designated under the WHO's International Health Regulations, strengthening vaccine capacity to ensure "emergency protection," and strengthening local capacity in sixteen areas of public health, including clean air and water, safe roads, child nutrition, and domestic violence, to support "enjoyment of better health and well-being."

While the goals articulated in the WHO's 13th General Programme of Work exemplify modern standards to which many countries aspire, the program also displays features of inequality and colonial intrusion. The data and record keeping involved in the WHO's implementation of the program impose significant obligations on participating countries, potentially challenging the authority of governments to control access to public health data and records. As the WHO program notes, its implementation requires stronger data collection and monitoring, and the need to understand and address the considerable gaps in public health data that still exist in many parts of the world. Noting that improved data is key to achieving its goals and associated SDGs, the program confirms the WHO's commitment to "supporting and strengthening countries' data capacity and fortifying their ability to use data in driving targeted policy action." While the WHO's emphasis on global standards, voluntariness by participant countries, and collective benefits speak to efforts to overcome local resistance to colonialist intrusion, local ambivalence toward WHO standards persists.[80] These issues are evident in China's conflicted relationship with the WHO – seeking acceptance by the international public health community even while resisting the intrusion of lab audits, data requests, and records oversight. China was not ranked on the Lowy Institute's Global COVID Performance Index due to a lack of data on daily number of tests performed in the country for the entirety of the examined period.[81]

Inequalities in China's relationship with the WHO are evident in China's financial contributions.[82] China's donations to the WHO have grown dramatically in recent years, from approximately US$10.6 million in 2017 to US$57 million in 2020.[83] Yet relative to the size of its economy, such contributions remained modest. China's 2018–19 contribution of US$89 million ranked fifteenth among WHO donors, just above Canada and far below donors such as the United States ($853 million), the United Kingdom ($464 million), and the Bill and Melinda Gates Foundation ($455 million).[84] During 2020–2023, China's contributions remained well below those of the United States, the United Kingdom, and the Gates Foundation.[85] In the wake of the second Trump administration's decision to withdraw from the WHO in

2025,[86] China has stepped up its contributions significantly, pledging $500 million over the subsequent five years.[87] China's conflicted relationship with the WHO is as much about tensions with the organization's key donors as it is about ties to the organization itself. The top donors continue to include liberal democracies such as the United States, the United Kingdom, Germany, Japan, the European Commission, and Norway, all of whom have come into varying degrees of conflict with China in recent years over trade, security, and human rights.[88]

The dynamic of complexity and alienation has also played a role. The rules-based international order undergirding the WHO exemplifies liberal standards of governance accountability that elicit discomfort and failed confidence as to whether liberal governance models are suited to China's national conditions. The complexity of rights-based standards and procedures involved in liberal systems of governance is evident in the range of autonomous advocates and opponents, the scope of their possible legal claims, and the diverse venues on which they rely in the course of notice and comment rule making, legislative investigations and oversight, administrative procedure, and the courts – all of which constrain government action in ways that are anathema to the PRC regime.[89]

In light of these tensions, China has worked to secure greater influence with the WHO's leadership. WHO discourses linking human rights and health are consonant with China's consistent assertions about development as a human right.[90] Despite its own acknowledgment of the close relationship between human rights and health, particularly in discriminatory practices in health care delivery and human rights violations affecting indigenous populations,[91] the WHO has remained largely silent on the public health implications of regime repression in Xinjiang. It has acquiesced to Beijing's resistance to Taiwan's full participation in the WHO.[92] Taiwan was ranked third on the Global COVID Performance Index, which, when compared with the PRC's non-ranking, highlights the contradictions in the WHO's acquiescence to Beijing's insistence on excluding Taiwan from the world health policy community.[93]

The PRC vigorously supported the appointment of WHO directors general Margaret Chan (2006–17) and Tedros Adhanom Ghebreyesus (since 2017), and has been relatively successful in eliciting a wide degree of tolerance for China's authoritarian governance practices – generally and as they relate to public health. Dr. Chan's appointment was supported due to her long-time residence in Hong Kong and her Hong Kong government position as director of health, and she moved quickly to cement the WHO's ties with Beijing.[94] While she oversaw a major report on health and human rights released in 2017, its terms of reference were limited to health issues of women, children, and adolescents, which, although critically important, did not include reference to human rights abuses in China or elsewhere.[95]

Dr. Tedros was prominent in the authoritarian regime of his home country of Ethiopia, where his alleged tolerance for authoritarian denials of health crises such as cholera and for state surveillance of dissidents (often relying on Chinese technology and equipment) seemed to set a tone for his relations with China.[96] And indeed, multiple observers have challenged the WHO's independence under Tedros in investigating the origins of COVID-19 in China.[97] Tedros's walking back of his initial conclusion in favour of zoonotic transfer over lab leaks as the source of the COVID outbreak and calling for further investigation was treated as a betrayal by Beijing.[98]

Thus, China's conflicted relationship the international public health system bears the impact of dynamics of inequality and resentment and complexity and alienation. Its ambivalence toward the international health policy community derives from long-standing historical, structural, and behavioural aspects of the WHO system and seem unlikely to change despite reduced US influence in the wake of the American withdrawal from the WHO altogether. As discussed below, this informs China's populist responses to COVID-19.

China's Populist Response to COVID-19

China's COVID response was undoubtedly driven at first by domestic public health challenges and attendant economic and political issues. However, informed by factors of inequality and resentment and complexity and alienation, China's responses to the COVID-19 emergency also reflected populist features of opposition to elites, justification through grievance, and practical resistance.

Opposition to Elites: Conflicts with the Global Health System

Tensions over China's relationship with the global health system came into sharp relief during the COVID-19 crisis. Resisting the WHO's promotion of Western medicine, China's response to the COVID-19 crisis included reliance on Traditional Chinese Medicine (TCM). Even as China proclaims support for modernization in medical training, equipment, and services, its resistance to uncritical deference to Western medicine is evident in ongoing efforts to promote TCM.[99] The WHO's belated recognition of TCM in 2019 signalled efforts at inclusion, but this was roundly criticized in the scientific community.[100]

China's hostility to international health policy elites intensified over the issue of information disclosure on COVID-19. Just as the SARS crisis in 2003 saw the WHO castigate China for failure to cooperate with ongoing efforts to combat that virus, China's response to COVID-19 has drawn similar criticism.[101] While presenting its cooperation with the WHO as an example of China's global presence and access to modern knowledge associated with global public health standards, the Chinese government has resisted WHO inspections and data requests.[102] It began gradually releasing information and proclaiming its cooperation with the WHO in early 2020.[103] On January 9, 2020, the WHO announced that Chinese authorities had made a preliminary determination of a novel coronavirus. The Chinese Center for Disease Control and Prevention published several viral sequences on January 10, and a full viral sequence was shared with the US National Institutes of Health genetic sequence database (GenBank) on January 11. On January 28, Xi Jinping met with Tedros to discuss a cooperative response, and in February the CCDC and the WHO issued a Joint Mission Report pointing to the zoonotic origins of the virus.[104]

Building on initial cooperation between the CCDC and the WHO, the Chinese government pursued limited engagement with international health institutions through much of 2020. Premier Li Keqiang's May 28 press conference in connection with the annual dual meetings of the National People's Congress (NPC) and the Chinese People's Political Consultative Conference (CPPCC) highlighted efforts to persuade the international community of China's success in responding to the virus through social and economic measures.[105] The SCIO white paper on China's COVID-19 response was issued the following month, largely for international audiences.[106] The WHO praised China's cooperation and transparency, although doubts were raised over whether China had provided full data access.[107]

Nonetheless, pressure for further investigation by the WHO ensued, partially driven by the Trump administration's threat to cut funding and possibly withdraw from the WHO altogether as US electoral politics saw increased blame directed at China for failing to provide full cooperation and data access.[108] A second joint WHO-China investigation was planned for early 2021, by which time strident claims were circulating that the virus had originated in the WIV labs, either accidentally or, according to a minority view, deliberately.[109] In the face of such antagonisms, the WHO's deference to sensibilities of Xi Jinping and the PRC regime in skipping the Greek letter *Xi* (ξ), next in line in the WHO's COVID naming scheme, and naming the new variant of concern "Omicron" reflected an effort to build China's confidence in the WHO's good offices.[110]

China's response to criticism included Xi Jinping's calls to "improve global governance and practice true multilateralism," challenging democracy norms and suggesting that diverse paths to modernization need not include ideals of democratic transformation.[111] China's response also included efforts to promote the superiority of authoritarian governance in responding to the crisis, engaging in "vaccine diplomacy" to strengthen support among developing countries, prodding the World Health Assembly (WHA, the WHO's executive body) to focus attention on control of COVID-19 rather than on its origins, and attacking proposals on investigating the origins of the virus as politically motivated and unfair.[112] Official commentary on Xi's keynote speech to the November 2021 Asia Pacific Economic Cooperation (APEC) conference heralded China's effort to resist US-led pressure by consolidating relations with "countries that have stayed neutral between the US and China, or that have consistently supported China's policies."[113] Such resistance was not confined to foreign countries but included the WHO itself. Foreign Ministry spokesman Zhao Lijian deemed "irresponsible" Tedros's comment in May that the Zero-COVID policy was "unsustainable."[114] In response to a 2022 WHO experts report calling for further investigation, Zhao called the effort politically motivated.[115] Addressing the 20th National Congress of the CPC in October 2022, Xi seemed almost plaintive in claiming that China's international cooperation had won supporters:

> We have demonstrated China's sense of duty as a responsible major country, actively participating in the reform and development of the global governance system and engaging in all-around international cooperation in the fight against COVID-19. All this has seen us win widespread international recognition. China's international influence, appeal, and power to shape have risen markedly.[116]

Yet scientists remain concerned over the absence of adequate access to China's COVID-19 data amid ongoing calls for further investigation.[117]

China's efforts to build international support were mixed with apprehension over policy supervision by the WHO and its supporters on COVID-19.

While the Zero-COVID policy reflected the influence of local economic and political challenges, many of China's responses to COVID-19 were aimed at satisfying an international audience that China was taking meaningful steps to deal with the crisis. As with so many of China's governance initiatives, formal enactments on public health generally and COVID-19 specifically served primarily as opportunities to express the regime's policy ideals. The domestic audience was important, of course, but so was the international public health community, embodied in the WHO and its mostly Western liberal backers. China's conflicts with the international public health policy community are replete with efforts to insulate the country from intrusion by international elites. Its domestic and international efforts attempted to counter perceived elite dominance of the public health legal and regulatory discourse by the WHO and its supporters. Paradoxically, China may enjoy greater influence over the WHO in the wake of the second Trump administration's decision in 2025 to withdraw from the organization a second time.

Grievance: Challenges Against International Critics

As criticism of China's handling of the pandemic grew in frequency and intensity, Beijing's international engagement took a more defensive tack. Resistance against investigation of COVID-19's origins began in early 2020 and continued throughout the crisis.[118] China reiterated its earlier calls for investigation of other possible country sources – particularly the United States for allegedly weaponizing the virus.[119] In July 2021, the WHO proposed further investigation, as Tedros conceded that the conclusions discounting possible laboratory origins of the virus were premature.[120] China rejected the request for further investigation as political and not based on science.[121] A subsequent attempt in 2021 by the WHO to revive its investigation also faced resistance from China.[122] While much of China's response has focused on criticizing the United States, even naming that country as the source of the virus, the European Union has also come in for criticism.[123]

Following the easing of COVID-19 restrictions and the resulting increase in international travel, several countries, including the United States and Canada, imposed testing requirements on airline passengers arriving from China, and the European Union strongly recommended that its member countries do likewise.[124] China challenged such measures as politically motivated and without scientific basis, and vowed retaliation.[125] Its defensive international engagement has remained an obstacle to full cooperation on both the question of origins and the challenges of prevention and treatment.

The PRC joined Russia and others in resisting the terms of a proposed global pandemic treaty that supported international monitoring and review of national systems around pandemic preparedness.[126]

China's growing hostility to international calls for further investigation of the origins of COVID-19 and more complete disclosure of COVID-19 infection and transmission data reflected populist features of grievance against international elites and systems. Attacks on the WHO, the United States, and the European Union for politically motivated critiques of China's COVID-19 response challenged perceived efforts to subjugate China. Having confronted inequality and complexity in the international public health system through opposition to dominance by associated elites, China's ambivalence over international cooperation on investigations of COVID-19's origins was then justified through expressions of grievance ideology. These dimensions of globalized populism set the context for China's practical resistance through legal and regulatory enactments presenting alternatives to the existing standards of the international public health policy community.

Practical Resistance in China's Populist Response to COVID-19

China's populist response to the COVID-19 crisis included practical resistance through domestic legal and regulatory measures presented as alternatives to existing international standards.[127] These efforts affected China's international cooperation, which remained conditional on satisfying domestic law and policy arrangements.

China's regulatory response to the COVID-19 crisis emerged from the legacy of China's previous health crises of HIV/AIDS (ca. 1995–2003) and SARS (Severe Acute Respiratory Syndrome, ca. 2003–05), which generated several important measures on public health.[128] The Infectious Diseases Law (1989, 2004, 2010) contained general provisions on prevention, reporting, and control of infectious diseases, including administrative oversight and legal liabilities for violations.[129] The Regulations on Responding to Public Health Emergencies (2003) contained extensive measures to prevent health emergencies and respond to them when they arise, including provisions on prevention and emergency preparedness, reporting and information release, and emergency management, with accompanying provisions on administrative supervision and legal liabilities.[130] These provisions were reiterated in National Contingency Plan for Public Health Emergencies (2006), which provided detailed rules on the health emergency response system as well as provisions on emergency response and recovery.[131]

In the face of international scrutiny and criticism of its COVID-19 responses, China pursued further regulatory and policy responses to the pandemic.[132] Pursuant to its Vaccine Management Law (2019),[133] China developed multiple COVID-19 vaccines, approving five for emergency use in China and other countries,[134] although cooperation with other countries in the production of vaccines was less successful.[135] Despite concerns about their efficacy, the WHO has encouraged international acceptance of China's COVID-19 vaccines.[136] China's Law on Basic Health Care and Health Promotion (2020) set forth overall terms for administration of the country's health care system, including provisions on basic health services, health care institutions and personnel, medicine supplies, health promotion, funding, and administrative oversight.[137] The State Council Information Office (SCIO) issued a white paper in 2020 summarizing policy responses across the range of government departments and presenting a lengthy defense of China's efforts to respond to the crisis.[138] The Ministry of Justice's "Opinion on Promoting Strictly Regulated, Just, and Civilized Law Enforcement to Provide Forceful Legal Safeguards for Epidemic Prevention and Control Work" (February 24, 2020) provided standards for enforcing lockdowns and other features of China's pandemic response.[139]

As discussed in Chapter 1, protection of public health is an essential responsibility of government, inviting consideration of dynamics of political accountability. China's practical resistance measures may usefully be assessed in light of law and policy practices related to performance, process, and information accountability, in the context of PRC approaches to accountability generally and in comparison with international standards.

Context: Political Accountability in PRC Governance

Discourses of accountability in PRC governance stem from ideological and political conditions.[140] As I discussed in my previous book, the PRC Party-state pursues a governance model of "patrimonial sovereignty" that combines the patrimonialism of Confucianized Marxism-Leninism Mao Zedong Thought with the sovereign authority of the Party-state.[141] This has important implications for performance, process, and information accountability.

Patrimonial Sovereignty

Under Xi Jinping, China has combined a neo-Confucian discourse of authority and obedience with the historical materialism of Marxism-Leninism, by which the Communist Party of China (CPC) is mandated by history to lead the country's transition to modernity.[142] Thus, the Party-state claims authority not by reference to the popular will but based instead on its historical mission of revolutionary transformation and development. Pursuant to the Four Cardinal Principles (*sixiang jiben yuanze* // 四项基本原则),[143] the PRC Party-state has elevated the principle of CPC leadership to a position of dominance, which has taken on even greater importance under the leadership of Xi Jinping.[144] While the PRC regime claims a mantle of legitimacy for its efforts in furthering the people's welfare, the Party-state does not accept accountability to the subjects of its rule, exemplifying the regime's responsibility *for* but not its responsibility *to* the people. This has important implications for regime depictions of policy achievement.

Socialist Rule Through Law

Discussions of political accountability in China often point to supposed constraints imposed by the country's "socialist legal system," which, as many specialist observers have noted, reflects the dominance of Party leadership.[145] The regime's approach to the "socialist law" echoes the thought of Carl Schmitt that the foundation of a legal order lies in formal legal institutions controlled by the state rather than legal norms held in society.[146] While the adage of "ruling the country through law" (*yifa zhiguo* // 依法治国) suggests ideals of the rule of law, the dominance of the CPC in all aspects of the legal system undermines such possibilities.[147] The 2023 revised rules on the work of the State Council reiterated the requirement to submit to CPC leadership.[148] Accountability of individual Party members for corruption or other malfeasance is subject almost entirely to internal CPC supervision through the Central Commission for Discipline Inspection (CCDI).[149] Revised regulations for the CCDI were issued in 2023, providing a range of punishments for such conduct as authoring, reading, or disseminating materials contrary to CPC policies: organizing "secret groups" to split the Party; engaging in factionalism; refusing to implement Party policies; engaging in local protectionism to thwart Party interests; and engaging in disloyalty or dishonesty against the Party.[150] The CCDI system operates separately from the court system, which itself is subject to Party oversight.[151]

Accountability of administrative processes on which so much of the Party-state's rule depends is based on the overall dominance of the CPC over governance and law. The Administrative Litigation Law (ALL; 1990) provided for judicial review of administrative action, but its implementation was less than was hoped for as the courts have consistently ruled in favour of the government.[152] Revisions to the ALL in 2015 and 2017, explained through a Supreme People's Court interpretation in 2018, expanded the scope of ALL review and its provisions on standing to sue, while attempting to strengthen adjudication through expanded case registration and jurisdiction provisions and new rules imposing personal responsibility on agency officials.[153] The Supervision Law (1994, revised 2010 and 2012) provided for administrative oversight of government officials.[154] The State Compensation Law (SCL; 2010, revised 2012 and 2018) permitted compensation awards to individuals and organizations harmed physically or financially by unlawful bureaucratic action.[155] A 2018 State Council circular imposed restrictions on the content and management of regulatory documents in an effort to curtail abuses through stronger judicial oversight.[156] Despite imposing a degree of accountability on government agencies and officials, such measures remain subject to the CPC leadership. China earned a ranking of 94 out of 142 (between Serbia and Tanzania) in the World Justice Project's Rule of Law Index.[157]

Implications for China's COVID-19 Response

Traditional governance practices of the PRC Party-state impacted China's response to COVID-19 by setting the confines of law and policy practice on political accountability. Patrimonial sovereignty insulates the Party-state from review and critique by outsiders. The ideological foundations of Party rule determine the boundaries and potential for law and policy practice. Thus, the terms of reference given to COVID-19 task forces and Leading Small Groups emphasized the unquestioned supremacy of CPC leadership (and by extension the leadership of Xi Jinping). Similarly, policy processes remain under CPC control, subject to socialist rule through law, which itself underscores CPC dominance. Taken together, the interrelated dynamics of patrimonial sovereignty and CPC control were significant for accountability of the Party-state in managing the COVID-19 crisis.

Accountability in China's COVID-19 Response

As discussed in Chapter 1, governance accountability involves operational norms on policy performance, process, and information management. Law and policy practice around performance accountability involves choices between empirical and aspirational depictions of government policy achievements. Process dimensions involve preferences for instrumentalism or impartiality in law and regulation. Information dimensions involve disparities between propaganda and transparency in the state's management of information. These aspects of accountability were evident in China's responses to the COVID-19 crisis, as exemplified particularly by the SCIO's COVID-19 white paper and the Ministry of Justice (MOJ) "Opinion" on COVID-19 law enforcement, both of which articulated standards for performance by a wide range of government departments charged with implementing COVID-19 policies, laws, and regulations.[158]

Performance Accountability: Empiricism/Aspiration

PRC law and policy practice related to performance accountability in the course of the COVID-19 crisis reinforced the importance of aspirational depictions of policy performance. This seems due in large part to the comparative absence of democratic legitimacy for the authority of the PRC Party-state, which instead must rely on claims about policy performance as a foundation for regime legitimacy.[159] China's COVID-19 white paper[160] exemplified an aspirational approach to performance accountability, as indicated by the annotated text provided in Appendix 3A (page 84). The white paper focused almost entirely on steps taken by the regime to contain the virus, with little reliable empirical data on actual effects of such measures. The white paper relied on timetable reconstructions of the COVID-19 crisis and China's response that are disputed by outside observers. The white paper's inclusion of statistical information on caseloads and on recovery and fatality rates was undermined by empirical uncertainties related to the regime's failure to provide full data access to domestic, let alone international, observers.

The white paper was also replete with aspirational conclusions about the regime's care for the people, the people's unified spirit and support, the effectiveness of China's authoritarian governance, and the regime's success in containing the spread of the virus. The foreword to the white paper, for example, proclaimed China's success in "cutting all channels for the transmission of the virus" and claimed that China's notices to the international community were "open, transparent, and responsible," but provided little if any empirical support in the face of significant evidence to the contrary. Section I of the white paper extolled the leadership of the CPC and Xi Jinping in successfully combatting the virus, while Section II praised the virtues of China's authoritarian system in managing the virus; both positions lack empirical support and are subject to considerable analysis to the contrary. Section II also lauded China's provision of "authoritative and detailed" information about COVID-19, but provided little if any empirical evidence to refute ongoing criticisms from the WHO and others. Section III claimed that a "powerful synergy" was formed to combat the virus through CPC-led authoritarian rule, without providing empirical evidence of the success of such synergy or addressing the perspectives of outside experts who doubted the effectiveness of China's authoritarian policies.

The white paper extolled Xi Jinping's calls for the 73rd World Health Assembly to help build a "Global Community of Health for All," underscoring China's efforts to establish alternative processes for international health policy and epitomizing aspirational over empirical features in China's COVID-19 response.[161] While the proposals and measures articulated in Xi's speech to the assembly, as reiterated in the white paper, were presented as commitments to the welfare of the global commons, in fact they underscored China's pursuit of parochial interests and strategic ambitions.

The orientation toward aspirational assessments of policy performance was also evident in the National Health Commission's interpretation of the State Council's Joint Prevention and Control Mechanism's December 7, 2022, notice easing COVID-19 restrictions:

> Since the outbreak of the new corona pneumonia epidemic, the Party Central Committee and the State Council have always put the safety of people's lives and health first, and according to the characteristics of virus mutation and the development of the epidemic, they have adhered to the principle of steadiness and progress, taken small steps and never stopped, and optimized and improved prevention and control measures according to the situation ... [We must] continue to improve the scientific and accurate level of prevention and control, protect people's life, safety and health to the greatest extent, and minimize the impact of the epidemic on people's production and living order and economic and social development.[162]

Thus, as indicated by China's 2020 SCIO COVID-19 white paper and the referenced measures and proposals made by Xi Jinping at the 73rd World Health Assembly, as well as official directives on easing Zero-COVID restrictions, China's pronouncements during the COVID-19 emergency have tended toward an aspirational approach to performance accountability. This stands in contrast to international standards. As a component of the rules-based international order, the WHO supports empirical approaches to performance accountability. The WHO's 2019–23 General Programme of Work[163] includes calls to "support Member States in strengthening national statistical capacity at all levels to ensure good-quality, accessible, timely, reliable, and disaggregated health data, including through, where appropriate, the Health Data Collaborative." The WHO's constitution provides: "The extension to all peoples of the benefits of medical, psychological and related knowledge is essential to the fullest attainment of health."[164] Such WHO principles underscore standards of the rules-based international order favouring empirical law and policy practice in contrast to aspirational preferences in PRC performance accountability.

Process Accountability: Instrumentalism/Impartiality

Policy preferences related to process accountability involve choices between instrumentalist uses of law and regulation for specific policy purposes or reliance on laws of general application applied impartially to all. China's application of its socialist law discourse to the COVID-19 crisis reflected basic PRC practices related to the instrumentalist use through law in furtherance of development goals. Instrumentalist approaches to the rule through law were evident when the Ministry of Justice (MOJ) issued its February 24, 2020, opinion on law enforcement during the pandemic.[165] As indicated by the annotated text of the opinion presented in Appendix 3B (page 90), legal measures on COVID-19 control consistently elevated legal instrumentalism over impartiality. The opinion placed primary emphasis on Party leadership, Xi Jinping's guidance, and coordination of law enforcement in the course of China's pandemic response.[166] The opinion listed operational priorities for enforcing COVID-19 control measures, ranging from raising the position of politics in law enforcement to ensuring strict enforcement of lockdowns, both of which expressed preferences for instrumentalist use of law in pursuit of policy goals rather than impartial application of law. The opinion called for standardized enforcement against opposition and allowing for fair and civilized law enforcement to ensure consistency, but these goals were raised not in in pursuit of impartial application of common legal standards but rather to strengthen the effectiveness of law as an instrument of policy. The opinion also called for innovative law enforcement aimed particularly at education, and persuasion in administrative law measures directed toward achieving policy goals. Additional measures, such as coordinating law enforcement under unified regime authority, strengthening supervision by central authorities, creating a responsibility system for law enforcement for matters like arrest quotas, and raising enforcement safeguards against resistance to COVID-19 control measures, each reflected the instrumentalist use of law to further the policy goals of the central government.

The MOJ opinion suggested that the regime's use of law and regulation to enforce mechanisms and standards for law enforcement should remain in service to the Party-state. Confronting challenges of corruption, abuse of authority, police violence, and other ills, the opinion expressed laudable ideals intended to constrain judicial and law enforcement personnel from abusive conduct. Such standards do not bind the Party-state, however, but rather serve as instruments to enforce the regime's policy goals. The MOJ opinion's fealty to CPC rule was reinforced by the commitment to implement the terms of Xi Jinping's "important" speech and instructions to the CPC Politburo Standing Committee (PSC) three weeks earlier.[167] In that speech, Xi responded to questions concerning his role in the pandemic response, particularly how early he had known about the outbreak and how involved he had been in leading China's response, by recounting his instructions to the PSC on January 7 and January 20 about prevention and control of the pandemic.[168] Key elements of Xi's remarks noted that the COVID-19 crisis was "directly related" to the overall stability of China's economy and society. He instructed Party committees and governments at all levels to uphold the "four consciousnesses" (primarily concerning fealty to political leadership), "four confidences" (in the path, theory, system, and culture of China's CPC-led political culture), and "two maintenances" (bolstering Xi Jinping's core position and the authority and centralized unified leadership of the CPC Central Committee), while conscientiously implementing the decision making and deployment of the Party Central Committee.[169]

Process accountability issues were also evident in the regime's easing of COVID-19 restrictions. In response to popular protests against the restrictions, the CPC's Central Political and Legal Affairs Commission (CPLAC) asserted, "We must resolutely crack down on infiltration and sabotage activities by hostile forces in accordance with the law, resolutely crack down on illegal and criminal acts that disrupt social order and effectively maintain overall social stability,"[170] exemplifying the instrumentalist use of law to further the policy goals of the regime without much regard for the nominal rights of assembly and expression articulated in Article 35 of the PRC Constitution. The State Council's Joint Prevention and Control Mechanism's December 2022 notice made no mention of the popular unrest over Zero-COVID aside from noting the need to "minimize the impact of the epidemic on people's production and living order and economic and social development."[171] Instead, the notice and its interpretation presented the easing of restrictions as a result of continuing efforts by the CPC Central Committee and the State Council to manage the pandemic.[172] Rather than acknowledge the evident impact of public input,[173] regime pronouncements ignored popular responses to COVID-19 measures almost entirely, in favour of depictions of the regime taking the initiative as the basis for the policy change. Yet a comparison of the readout for the November 10 Politburo meeting and the December 7 Joint Prevention and Control Mechanism notice suggests that the question of easing COVID-19 restrictions remained unresolved at the former, only to be resolved after the outbreaks of public unrest.[174]

The Joint Prevention and Control Mechanism's December notice reflected continued reliance on instrumentalist regulatory mechanisms to direct responses to COVID-19.[175] Going beyond instrumentalist directives to government offices, the notice required that

> medical personnel, public security, transportation and logistics, supermarkets, supply assurance, water, electricity and heating and other personnel who ensure basic medical services and the normal operation of society ... do a good job in personal protection, vaccination and health monitoring, ensure normal medical services and basic living materials, water, electricity and heating and other supplies, do their best to maintain normal production and work order, promptly solve the urgent and difficult problems raised by the masses, and effectively meet the basic living needs of the masses during the epidemic handling period.

The range of activities and socio-economic actors covered by the directive was vast – reflecting in part the broad impacts of COVID-19 across the society and economy, but also suggesting the scope of the regime's use of instrumentalist legal measures to manage responses to the pandemic. Even while reiterating its commitment to ruling the country according to law, the regime vigorously opposed civil litigation efforts aimed at securing compensation for COVID-19 victims. After Changsha Funeng, a public interest advocacy non-governmental organization (NGO), indicated a willingness to assist families seeking compensation for the death of loved ones from COVID-19, staff were arrested and tried for "subversion of state power."[176] The tendency toward instrumental over impartial application of law characterized China's approach to process accountability in responding to COVID-19. This contrasts with international standards. International principles on the rule of law emphasize the importance of the impartial application of law.[177] Legal impartiality is underscored by international law principles on equality and non-discrimination,[178] which admit the need for complexity in application. Standards of the rules-based international order favouring impartiality contrast with China's instrumentalist approach to law and regulation in process accountability.

Information Accountability: Propaganda/Transparency

Law and policy practices related to information accountability involve choices between asserting state control over information as propaganda or state release of information in response to transparency. The PRC Party-state has continued to control public access to information in furtherance of the regime's conception of collective interests in stability and security.[179] CPC control of information enables the Party to exercise authority over all aspects of public information.[180] Even modest efforts to support transparency in governance are counterbalanced by concerted efforts to keep governance information from public view. Legal judgments on proceedings challenging government administrative action have been removed from public databases, impending public access to information about governance decisions.[181]

China's National Security Law (NSL, 2015) restricts information considered harmful to national security, a broad category that includes public health information.[182] The State Secrets Protection Law (SSPL; 1989, 2004) prohibits disclosure of a wide array of information, and restricts non-official commentary on scientific matters such as infectious disease (including SARS and COVID-19).[183] The Implementing Regulations for the State Secrets Protection Law (2014) underscore the government's monopoly on controlling information through the establishment of a national State Secrets Bureau with counterpart organs at and above the county level.[184]

While the PRC regime has adopted the term "transparency" (*toumingdu* // 透明度) as an ideal for governance, Party-state practices of patrimonial sovereignty reject the fundamental principle of equality between state and society on which transparency standards are based. Instead, "transparency" has been used as the rubric for discretionary releases of government information rather than a mandated outcome of legal processes initiated by non-governmental actors.[185] In practice this has amounted to appropriation of the word without the associated institutional practice for its enforcement.[186] China's regulations on disclosure of government information, although prefaced in terms of transparency and public access, nonetheless empower governments at all levels to control the disclosure of government information.[187] Under these measures, governments at and above the county level are directed to disclose government information on a wide array of issues, including medical care, only if the matters (1) involve vital public interest; (2) require the broad public's knowledge or participation; (3) involve the workings of administrative organs; or (4) involve other matters that will be made public in accordance with applicable laws and regulations

(Article 9, 10), thus underscoring the discretional authority of government oversight of information releases. While citizens as well as legal persons and other organizations may apply to the State Council and to local governments for release of information, the agency receiving such applications has broad discretion to determine release and may not disclose matters involving state secrets and personal privacy (Articles 13, 14), both of which have been cited as cause for China's control of COVID-19 information.

As well, China's public health laws and regulations impose significant restrictions on exchanges of information. The Infectious Diseases Law (1989, 2004, 2010) requires medical staff to confine their reporting on epidemic outbreaks to the designated administrative channels (Article 30) and prohibits staff from making false reports (Articles 37, 66).[188] The Public Health Emergencies Regulations (2003) contain extensive measures on reporting on health emergencies, prohibiting work units and individuals from falsely reporting emergencies (Article 21) and providing administrative penalties for violation (Article 38, 51).[189] These provisions are reiterated in the National Contingency Plan for Public Health Emergencies (2006), which provides for reporting on health emergencies to government offices (Article 3.3) and references sanctions under the Public Health Emergencies Regulations for punishing violations (Article 5.3).[190]

Despite recognizing that the initial COVID-19 outbreak was mishandled in part through failures of information, legal enactments during the crisis continued to prioritize official reporting and discourage individual initiatives seeking information. The Law on Basic Health Care and Health Promotion (2019) contained extensive provisions on administration of China's health care system, including prohibitions against unauthorized disclosure or distribution of personal health information of citizens (Article 92) and imposed administrative penalties for violations (Articles 102, 106).[191]

As well, the SCIO's 2020 COVID-19 white paper expressed regime preferences on information accountability.[192] As presented in Appendix 3A, the white paper revealed consistent priorities toward strict control over releases of information, establishing regime-controlled news outlets and elevating regime-controlled propaganda over transparency. The regime's approach to information accountability was also evident in efforts to suppress assessments of policy outcomes that conflicted with the regime's preferred narrative. Paragraph 3 of the 2020 MOJ opinion on pandemic law enforcement (presented in Appendix 3B) directed administrative law enforcement agencies at all levels to punish all kinds of illegal acts, such as resisting epidemic prevention and control measures and disturbing social order (the offence that ophthalmologist Li Wenliang was accused of before his death), and called for referral of instances of disinformation and rumours to judicial organs in order to maintain social order. The regime initially cracked down on social media, particularly after public outrage over the punishment of Li Wenliang for his early warnings about the virus that the regime condemned as unauthorized disclosures.[193] Later, it actively promoted social media disinformation on the origins of the virus.[194] Engagement with the media also involved intimidation of local reporters.[195] Following his postings on the impact of the COVID-19 crisis in Wuhan, journalist Li Zehua was investigated for disrupting public order and was subjected to quarantine rather than detention, after which his public statements reflected the extent to which the regime successfully intimidates it critics.[196] Citizen journalist Zhang Zhan was arrested and sentenced to a four-year prison term for "picking quarrels and provoking trouble" for her criticisms of the regime's early handling of the Wuhan outbreak.[197] Citizen journalist Fang Bin was jailed for three years for sharing video footage of the impact of the COVID-19 outbreak in Wuhan.[198]

The regime acted more aggressively in retaliating against establishment critics of its pandemic response. Property tycoon Ren Zhiqiang was detained incommunicado and placed under investigation by the CPC's Central Commission for Discipline Inspection for alleged serious violations of law and discipline in response to his criticisms of the regime's handling of the crisis.[199] Tsinghua University law professor Xu Zhangrun was demoted and banned from teaching, writing, and publishing, and was ultimately placed under house arrest, after he publicly criticized Xi Jinping's handling of the COVID-19 crisis.[200] Another prominent jurist, Xu Zhiyong, co-founder of the New Citizens' Movement, was detained for criticizing Xi's handling of the crisis.[201] Xu suffered harsh conditions during his detention, and was charged with subversion, which under Article 105 of the Criminal Law of the PRC carries a sentence of up to life imprisonment.[202]

China's policy responses to the 2022 upsurge in popular protests against COVID-19 restrictions relied on a familiar model of control over information and repression of unauthorized views – tilting further away from transparency and more toward social control – and continued with crackdowns on social media and cellphone use.[203] Long-standing efforts by the regime to control public information have been applied to internet reporting, to support regime narratives regarding the COVID-19 crisis and suppress contrary views.[204] The State Council's Joint Prevention and Control Mechanism's December 2022 notice easing COVID-19 restrictions required adherence to Party leadership with all the limits on public information that this entailed in light of CPC Document No. 9 and related edicts: "All relevant departments in all localities should further improve their political standing, unify their thinking and actions with the decision-making and deployment of the Party Central Committee."[205]

China's approach to information legitimacy relying on propaganda rather than transparency has contributed to international concerns about insufficient and unreliable data and the need for COVID-19 testing of air travellers from China.[206] Questions about reliability and transparency of data from China resurfaced after the regime reported that nearly sixty thousand people had died during the first month of the upsurge in COVID-19 infection after the easing of restrictions, while knowledgeable observers suggested that the actual number may be much higher as infection and mortality rates are generally underreported.[207] The WHO itself called for greater data transparency in the wake of this surge in infections.[208] Even as some 80 percent of the population was reportedly infected following the easing of Zero-COVID policies, the regime made a vigorous propaganda effort to paint the reopening in a favourable light.[209]

Thus, the PRC regime's law and policy practice related to information accountability has tended to favour propaganda over transparency. Information accountability in the COVID-19 crisis consistently evidenced the regime's control over the issue and content of information on the government's COVID-19 response. Despite its appropriation of transparency discourse, the PRC Party-state has consistently opposed public access to information not approved by the regime. This was reinforced by repression of opposing critical voices. Consistent with the long-standing practices of the PRC Party-state on controlling information, China's approach to information accountability during COVID-19 revealed a continuing commitment to using information as propaganda aimed at preserving the regime's authority.

China's approach to state control over information contrasts with international standards. UNESCO's International Standards for Open Science calls for greater openness in publishing scientific information.[210] The WHO's 2019–23 General Programme of Work commits to supporting systematic and transparent translation of evidence to inform policy and national decision making, promote open reporting of health data by member states and the Secretariat, and support member states' creation of transparent data warehouses for such data.[211] Such transparency provisions reflect international standards on equality in access to information and acceptance of the complexity this entails. International standards on transparency contrast with PRC approaches to information accountability favouring state-controlled propaganda.

CHINA'S COVID-19 RESPONSE revealed the authoritarian governance practices of the PRC Party-state, including assertions that Chinese authoritarianism is more effective than liberal democratic approaches in responding to the crisis.[212] Standards of political accountability were subjected to the authoritarian law and policy norms and practices of the PRC regime, emphasizing accountability to the Party-state.[213]

PRC law and policy practice related to operational norms of performance, process, and information accountability revealed differences with corresponding international standards. Law and policy practices favouring aspirational depictions of policy outcomes contrasted with WHO standards on empirical data-driven policy reporting. PRC preferences for instrumentalist application of law and regulation contrast with international standards on impartiality in the rule of law articulated by the United Nations and the United Nations Development Programme. China's reliance on propaganda in managing information on governance contrasted with international transparency standards associated with the WHO and UNESCO.

Aside from their substantive differences with corresponding international law standards, PRC accountability practices also reflected tensions with ideals on equality and complexity. As suggested in Chapter 1 and illustrated in Figure 2, international standards on empirical performance accountability, impartial processes accountability, and transparency in information accountability reflect policy orientations favouring equality and accepting diversity. These contrast with the acceptance of inequality and resistance to complexity bound up in China's preferences for aspirational performance, instrumentalist process and state-controlled propaganda in information. Paradoxically, even as China's opposition to elites and embrace of grievance ideology speak to resentment of inequality, PRC law and policy practices related to performance, process, and information accountability entrench standards of inequality. Table 3 summarizes conflicts between China's accountability standards and those associated with the rules-based international order.

TABLE 3 Accountability: Comparing China standards with rules-based international order standards

	Performance accountability	Process accountability	Information accountability	Global Health Security Index ranking*
China standards	Aspirational	Instrumentalist	Propaganda	52/195
RBIO standards	Empirical	Impartial	Transparency	N/A

* Global Health Security Index, "2021 GHS Index Country Profile for China," https://ghsindex.org/country/china/.

Rhetorical Markers of China's Globalized Populism in Response to COVID-19

China's responses to COVID-19 have embraced rhetorical markers on sovereignty, development, and human rights. These link China's resistance to the international order with populist features of anti-elitism, grievance ideology, and practical resistance and support resilience in China's globalized populism.

Sovereignty: Safeguarding China's Management and Reporting on COVID-19

The marker of sovereignty in China's globalized populism has been integral to the PRC Party-state's defence of its management and reporting on COVID-19 from international control. China's resistance against the international public health system – particularly the WHO and its liberal state supporters – has been depicted in terms of concerns over protecting its sovereignty against intrusion by international elites. Sovereignty issues came to the fore in China's efforts to defend its domestic health policy initiatives and insulate them from foreign interference, as well as in China's resistance to the colonial dimensions of international investigations and data access regarding COVID-19 origins and responses, and its insistence on excluding Taiwan from WHO processes.

The sovereignty marker was evident in China's official COVID-19 white paper, whose presumptions regarding China's sovereign equality with other members of the international health policy community formed the foundation for China's international cooperation:

> China believes that all countries should make the choice that is right for the interests of all humanity and the well-being of our future generations. Upholding the vision of a global community of shared future, we should support each other and join hands to contain the spread of the virus, and protect the health and well-being of people across the globe.[214]

The white paper's positioning of China as a responsible member of a global community reflected the claims of the Party-state regarding China's status as a sovereign international actor.

More importantly, sovereignty claims were used to insulate China from criticism – opposing the authority of international public health elites and systems as contrary to China's sovereignty. Unfettered by the limits of electoral or performance legitimacy, the regime's sovereignty claims allow it to rely on aspirational depictions of its achievements in relation to COVID-19 without the constraints inherent in empirical depictions. Extolling the supposed virtues of China's "highly efficient" system of Party rule, the white paper averred:

> Under the strong leadership of the CPC Central Committee with Xi Jinping at its core, China has put in place an efficient system under which the central authorities exercise overall command, while local authorities and all sectors follow the leadership and instructions of the central authorities, perform their respective duties, and cooperate with each other. This highly efficient system has made it possible for China to win its all-out people's war against the virus. (Section II.1)

Sovereignty claims were also evident in Xi Jinping's 2020 speech to the WHO that, in calling for international cooperation, also attempted to rebuff ongoing critiques of China's handling of questions regarding the origins of COVID-19 and its problematic responses to international requests for greater access to data on infections and treatment:

> In China, after making painstaking efforts and enormous sacrifice, we have turned the tide on the virus and protected the life and health of our people. All along, we have acted with openness, transparency and responsibility. We have provided information to WHO and relevant countries in a most timely fashion. We have released the genome sequence at the earliest possible time. We have shared control and treatment experience with the world

> without reservation. We have done everything in our power to support and assist countries in need.[215]

Assertions about sovereignty were also embedded in China's calls for multilateralism at the United Nations:

> We need to practice true multilateralism, observe the purposes and principles of the UN Charter and the basic norms governing international relations; respect the sovereignty of all countries and equality among them, big or small; uphold diversity in the world and respect the legitimate development rights of all countries and their own choice of development path; handle world affairs through extensive consultation and advocate greater democracy in international relations. We need to oppose the attempt to seek exclusive, bloc politics under the disguise of multilateralism, or to impose the rules made by a few countries on the wider international community under the pretext of multilateralism.[216]

Thus, Chinese expressions of sovereignty have served as a rhetorical marker supporting resilience for China's populist resistance to the international health system. Sovereignty claims work to insulate China from the obligations and restrictions of the international health system even while deflecting criticism of China's authoritarian governance.

Development: Justifying China's COVID-19 Response

Just as populist grievance serves to explain and justify opposition to elites, so does the rhetorical marker on development serve to justify China's responses to the COVID-19 crisis. The rhetorical marker on development provides resilience for China's resistance to the international health system, couched in terms of justifying the country's responses to COVID-19 and also expressing grievance against efforts to thwart its development. This was evident in the authoritative discourses on the regime's COVID-19 policy process emphasizing the needs of China's development:

> Pandemic prevention and control work has provided important support for the restoration of economic development, ensuring the human, material, and financial resources required for economic construction ... While the pandemic in China is under effective control, the country will promptly resume work and restore its economic production capacity.[217]

China's hostility toward calls for investigation of the origins of COVID-19 was a reaction to perceived threats to China's development veiled in claims about the lab-leak origins of the pandemic:

> To date, China remains the only country that has invited more than once WHO expert groups to conduct joint COVID-19 origins study inside the country, [Ministry of Foreign Affairs spokesperson] Mao [Ning] said. "A laboratory origin of the pandemic was considered to be extremely unlikely" is a science-based, authoritative conclusion reached by the experts of the WHO-China joint mission following their field trips to the lab in Wuhan and in-depth communication with researchers, according to Mao. The conclusion is accurately recorded in the mission's report and has been widely acknowledged by the international community and the science community.[218]

Development issues were also embedded in China's positing of Traditional Chinese Medicine as a viable alternative to Western medicine in light of local conditions:

> From the outset, China's goal in its medical response to COVID-19 has been to improve the patient admission and cure rates and reduce the infection and fatality rates. The infected were treated in dedicated medical facilities where medical specialists from all over the country and all the necessary medical resources were concentrated. Both traditional Chinese medicine and Western medicine were applied.[219]

The development marker was also evident in references to the PRC's socialist rule through law system, which is aimed specifically at supporting China's development.[220] Development markers were evident in the white paper's repeated references (e.g., pages 17, 19–21, 24–26, 28–29, 31, and 45–51) to the regime's efforts to coordinate virus control with China's economic and social development. The white paper's references to the "new development philosophy" championed by Xi Jinping underscored the importance of the rhetorical marker of development in China's populist resistance to international standards on COVID-19. Thus, the populist marker of development is presented as both an expression of grievance against international elites trying to stifle China's development and as justification for China's COVID-19 response, providing a measure of resilience for China's globalized populism.

Human Rights: Conflicting Priorities in China's COVID-19 Response

Human rights issues were at play in China's COVID-19 control measures that prioritized social stability and public health over individual rights, adopting a hierarchical approach to human rights that conflicts with international law. Such priorities were consistent with the orthodoxy set forth in a 2017 SCIO white paper on public health, which, even as it termed public health as an "essential element of human rights," presented human rights as matters of regime management of collective interests pursuant to the development initiatives of the Party-state:

> Health is a precondition for the survival of humanity and the development of human society. The right to health is a basic human right rich in connotations. It is the guarantee for a life with dignity. Everyone is entitled to the highest standard of health, equally available and accessible ... China is a large developing country with 1.3 billion people. The CPC and the Chinese government have always attached great importance to developing the medical and health services, to transforming the development model of the health sector, and to respecting and protecting citizens' right to health. A mechanism based on China's conditions to ensure the people's right to health has been put in place.[221]

China's human rights orthodoxy permits prioritization of some rights over others.[222] Hence, international human rights standards regarding freedom from detention and arbitrary arrest (Article 9 of the International Covenant on Civil and Political Rights [ICCPR]) were routinely ignored under China's Zero-COVID policy. Indeed, China's COVID-19 white paper's heralding of a people-centred approach to managing the pandemic spoke to a relationship of state to society in terms of patrimonial sovereignty rather than enforceable rights.[223] Human rights tensions also arose in conflicts between China and major WHO donors over such matters as mass detention of Uighurs in Xinjiang, harassment and arrests of human rights lawyers in China, and repression in Hong Kong.

The marker of human rights in China's practical resistance to the international health system was particularly evident in China's information control efforts on COVID-19 that contrasted with international standards recognizing access to information as a human right under Resolution 59 of the UN General Assembly adopted in 1946, as well as Article 19 of the Universal Declaration of Human Rights (1948).[224] While the 2020 COVID-19 white paper claims the mantle of transparency in depicting China's handling of information on the pandemic, every example of COVID-19 information has been limited to government releases pursuant to a "tiered news release mechanism," with neither attention nor approval given to civic information channels or requests for information. In supporting China's authoritarian approaches to political and social control, the rhetorical marker on human rights worked to insulate China from human rights criticism and built resilience for its globalized populism.

Thus, rhetorical markers on sovereignty, development, and human rights complemented populist features of anti-elitism, grievance, and practical resistance, providing resilience for China's COVID-19 responses. Rhetoric on sovereignty insulated China from critiques by international elites over its handling of information on COVID-19 and its origins. Development rhetoric justified conditions for China's handling of the crisis and expressed grievance over purported international disregard. The rhetorical marker of human rights offered alternatives to international standards by prioritizing social stability and public health over individual rights. These rhetorical markers of China's globalized populism underscored tensions between China's policy preferences and the standards of the rules-based international order while providing resilience for China's COVID-19 response. The resilience provided by China's rhetorical markers on sovereignty, development, and human rights for PRC law and policy practice on COVID-19 may impede the possibilities for change, with implications for China's ongoing approaches to political accountability generally.

Conclusion

Responding to conditions of inequality and complexity in relations with the international health policy community, China's responses to COVID-19 expressed populist resistance to the rules-based international order. This involved dynamics of opposition to global elites, justification through grievance ideology, and practical resistance through alternative law and policy practices related to governance accountability. Accountability in China's law and policy practice on COVID-19 tended to favour aspirational over empirical assessments, in contrast to international standards favouring empirical measures. Process accountability tended to favour legal instrumentalism over impartial law and regulation, in contrast to international rule-of-law standards. Information accountability tended to subordinate transparency in information access to state propaganda aimed at maintaining stability, in contrast to international standards favouring transparency. China's response to COVID-19 also included rhetorical markers supporting resilience in China's globalized populism, through claims around sovereignty against international assertions related to China's withholding of information and possible responsibility for COVID-19's origins, around development as a legitimate limitation for China's COVID-19 response, and around human rights policies favouring social stability and public health over individual rights. Each of these supported resilience in China's populist resistance to the international public health system. China's responses to COVID-19 reflected adversarial dynamics of its relationship with the international health policy community, suggesting features of antagonistic populism.

Appendix 3A

Annotated Excerpts from the State Council Information Office's June 7, 2020, White Paper "Fighting COVID-19: China in Action"

Below, excerpts from the white paper are followed by comments and interpretation.[225]

Foreword

> **Making people's lives and health its first priority, China adopted extensive, stringent, and thorough containment measures, and has for now succeeded in cutting all channels for the transmission of the virus.**

Comments and interpretation. The white paper's claim that China has cut all channels for transmission of the virus seems wildly aspirational in light of the fact that the Zero-COVID policy enacted because transmission rates were unacceptably high did not come into effect until two years after release of the white paper. After it was implemented, the Zero-COVID containment measures, including artificial intelligence and big data surveillance, also featured crackdowns on dissenters who criticized the government's responses.[226] As well, international observers have noted that China's systems for mass testing, reporting cases, and use of personal protective equipment (PPE) varied considerably from international standards but were publicized nonetheless to bolster the regime's claims of success in managing the virus.[227]

> **Having forged the idea that the world is a global community of shared future, and believing that it must act as a responsible member, China has fought shoulder to shoulder with the rest of the world. In an open, transparent, and responsible manner and in accordance with the law, China gave timely notification to the international community of the onset of a new coronavirus, and shared without reserve its experience in containing the spread of the virus and treating the infected.**

Comments and interpretation. The oft-repeated ideal of "global community of shared future" was used frequently in the regime's international communications to justify China's globalized efforts to revise international governance standards to suit the authoritarian practices of the Party-state.[228] Assertions about international notification in an "open, transparent, and responsible manner" have been contradicted by well-documented conclusions to the contrary.[229] Claims that information disclosure was made "in accordance with the law" sidesteps the fact that China's laws impose significant restrictions on information disclosure.[230] Claims about timely notification to the international community have been contradicted by evidence of repeated delays in responding to international requests for more detailed information on the outbreak and on China's containment efforts.[231]

Section I: China's Fight Against the Pandemic

> **The Communist Party of China (CPC) and the Chinese government have addressed the epidemic as a top priority, and taken swift action. General Secretary Xi Jinping has taken personal command, planned the response, overseen the general situation and acted decisively, pointing the way forward in the fight against the epidemic.**

Comments and interpretation. Respected observers have suggested that, while presented as a virtue, the leadership of the CPC and Xi himself compounded the challenges posed by the pandemic.[232]

Section II.1: Well-Coordinated Prevention, Control, and Treatment

> **Under the strong leadership of the CPC Central Committee with Xi Jinping at its core, China has put in place an efficient system under which the central authorities exercise overall command, while local authorities**

and all sectors follow the leadership and instructions of the central authorities, perform their respective duties, and cooperate with each other. This highly efficient system has made it possible for China to win its all-out people's war against the virus.

Comments and interpretation. Section II of the white paper presented several timetables of events in the course of the pandemic, highlighting China's positive efforts. However, close observers noted that by beginning the timetable on December 27, 2019, the white paper sidestepped the difficult and sensitive questions about the regime's conduct during the initial discovery and response, in effect rewriting the history of the pandemic in China.[233] Efforts to portray China's authoritarian system as particularly efficient in responding to the COVID-19 crisis have been persuasively rebutted by outside specialists.[234]

Section II.4: China Has Released Information in an Open and Transparent Manner as Required by Law

[China] has provided information on COVID-19 in a thoroughly professional and efficient way. It has released authoritative and detailed information as early as possible on a regular basis, thus effectively responding to public concern and building public consensus. Its experience is something other countries can draw on in their fight against the virus.

Comments and interpretation. China's release of information has been widely criticized by multiple observers, including the World Health Organization.[235]

A strict system of information release has been established. **China has released information on COVID-19 in a timely, open and transparent manner as required by law. Strict regulations are in place to see there is no withholding of information, underreporting, or delay in reporting cases of infection. On December 31, 2019, the Wuhan government began to release coronavirus information in accordance with the law, and gradually increased the frequency of release. Since January 21, 2020, the NHC [National Health Commission] has provided daily updates on nationwide cases on its official website and social media platform, and provincial health departments have done the same on local cases. Starting from February 3, the NHC has released the information simultaneously on its English-language website.**

Comments and interpretation. The white paper's reference to a strict system of information release attempted to lend legal legitimacy to the regime's efforts to curtail the flow of information that conflicted with its narratives. Strict regulations preventing withholding, underreporting, and delay in reporting COVID-19 cases were qualified by provisions in the Regulations on Disclosure of Government Information restricting unauthorized release of information.[236] Reference to "transparent" release of information was conditioned by the provisions of the state regulations on disclosure of government information, whose use of transparency rhetoric did not diminish state control over information access.[237] The qualifier "in accordance with the law" spoke not to external accountability involving legal restrictions on government but rather to China's legal restriction on access to information.[238]

> ***A tiered news release mechanism has been formed.* At both national and local levels, a tiered information release mechanism has been formed to circulate authoritative information through various channels and platforms, both onsite and online, in order to address domestic and international concerns on virus control, medical treatment, and scientific research.**

Comments and interpretation. State control over information was underscored by the provisions of the Regulations on Disclosure of Government Information authorizing establishment of local government offices at and above the county level overseeing information disclosure, and the Implementing Regulations for the State Secrets Protection Law (2014) establishing a national State Secrets Bureau with counterpart organs at and above the county level, with concomitant provisions on government control of information.[239]

> **By May 31, the Joint Prevention and Control Mechanism and the Information Office of the State Council had held 161 press conferences during which officials from more than 50 government departments appeared over 490 times and answered more than 1,400 questions from Chinese and foreign media. One hundred and three press conferences had been held in Hubei and 1,050 in the other provinces.**

Comments and interpretation. The reference to numbers of press conferences and official appearances on the pandemic reflected attention to the aggregation of activities rather than their content, underscoring the prevalence of aspirational over empirical features in China's depiction of its COVID-19 achievements. As noted by many observers, press conferences and official appearances often provide little reliable information.[240]

> ***COVID-19–related information is provided through various channels and platforms.*** **The NHC's official Chinese and English websites and its social media platform have special sections where COVID-19–related information is released on a daily basis, including information on relevant policies, progress in China's containment efforts, updates on disease prevention and control, and clarifications that refute rumours.**

Comments and interpretation. This provision underscored the regime's control over information on the pandemic. While daily updates are helpful, many have questioned the reliability of government-controlled information, and the implication that non-official information is little more than rumour reinforces the regime's claimed monopoly on information release.[241]

Section III: Assembling a Powerful Force to Beat the Virus

> **Facing the sudden onslaught of a previously unknown virus, China has put the people's interests first – nothing is more precious than people's lives. It has rapidly mobilized the manpower and resources of the whole nation and done everything possible to protect the lives and health of its people. A powerful synergy has been formed thanks to the following factors: observing the people-centred governance philosophy of the CPC; China's ability to mobilize resources to accomplish major initiatives; its composite national strength built up during more than four decades of reform and opening up, particularly since the 18th National Congress of the CPC held in November 2012; remarkable achievements in modernizing governance; two defining values of Chinese culture – solidarity and mutual assistance; and the profound love of the Chinese people for their family and their country.**

Comments and interpretation. The white paper's references to "China's ability to mobilize resources," China's "composite national strength," and "achievements in modernizing governance" spoke to China's authoritarian governance model as a preferable alternative to liberal democracy, a matter disputed by experts.[242]

Section IV: Building a Global Community of Health for All

> **On May 18, [Xi Jinping] addressed the opening of the 73rd World Health Assembly, calling for a joint effort on the part of all countries to overcome the virus and build a global community of health for all. Six proposals were put forward: to do everything we can for COVID-19 control and treatment, to support the WHO in leading the global response, to provide greater support for Africa, to strengthen global governance in public health, to restore economic and social development, and to strengthen international cooperation.**

Comments and interpretation. Xi Jinping's speech to the 73d World Health Assembly emphasized aspirational policy plans presented in part as a distraction from ongoing calls for further WHO investigation into the origins of the virus, and in contrast to the conduct of the Trump administration, which was threatening to withdraw WHO funding.[243] Xi's proposal on COVID-19 control and treatment included calls for global research on the source of the virus and WHO leadership in global response. In light of China's resistance to investigation of its own responsibility, this seemed like an effort to shift attention from China to other possible sources.[244] In light of multiple reports on popular dissatisfaction with and resistance to China's Belt and Road Initiative activities in Africa,[245] Xi's call for greater support for Africa's battle against COVID-19 appeared aimed at diluting the impact of such concerns. His proposal on strengthening global governance on public health echoed China's repeated efforts to "reform" the rules-based international order to suit the authoritarian imperative of the PRC Party-state.[246]

Appendix 3B

Annotated Excerpts from the Ministry of Justice's February 24, 2020, "Opinion on Promoting Strictly Regulated, Just, and Civilized Law Enforcement to Provide Forceful Legal Safeguards for Epidemic Prevention and Control Work"

Below, excerpts from the opinion are followed by comments and interpretations.[247]

> 1. **Raise the position of politics (*zhengzhi zhanwei* // 政治站位) [mainly through political guidance in law enforcement], echoing the references to the "four consciousnesses," "four self-confidences," and "two maintenances" in Xi's February 4, 2020, speech on strengthening work in COVID-19 prevention and control.**[248]

Comments and interpretation. Raising the position of politics in legal affairs echoed the provisions of the 4th Plenum of the 18th CPC Congress to the effect that Party leadership is fundamental to the socialist rule through law.[249] The CPC's "Plan for the Construction of a China Under the Rule of Law (2020–2025)" (CPC Law Construction Five-Year Plan) noted the importance of Party leadership over legislation, enforcement, adjudication, and compliance.[250] These were echoed in the Ministry of Justice's opinion on COVID-19 response and worked to pressure local officials to echo the regime's conclusions on the origins, transmission, and control of the virus.

> 2. **Persist in strict (*yange* // 严格) law enforcement [with a focus on upholding regime lockdowns and information control].**

Comments and interpretation. In addition to reflecting provisions of the 4th Plenum of the 18th Central Committee and the CPC Law Construction Five-Year Plan, the call for strict law enforcement over lockdowns and information control echoes Xi Jinping's 2018 speech to the first session of the Central Commission on Comprehensively Ruling the Country According to Law, in which he prioritized "scientific legislation, strict law enforcement, fair justice, and popular legal compliance."[251] This echoes long-standing PRC formalism in justifying authoritarian controls in the name of law enforcement.

3. **Persist in standardized (*guifan* // 规范) law enforcement [with the focus being on public health and COVID-related laws and regulations, such that enforcement efforts are grounded in existing measures] to ensure that law enforcement acts are well founded and documented, and that administrative law enforcement decisions are lawful and effective.**

Comments and interpretation. Standardization in public security enforcement during the COVID-19 pandemic has been linked explicitly with "cracking down on resistance to epidemic prevention and control measures, attacks on medical personnel, production and sale of fake and inferior protective materials and other serious illegal and criminal activities, effectively maintaining social stability during the outbreak for the safe, and restoring orderly production."[252] Such measures were aimed at limiting the discretion of local officials and strengthening central control over COVID-19 response policies.

4. **Persist in fair (*gongzheng* // 公正) law enforcement [such that enforcement efforts are consistent and grounded in existing laws and regulations, avoid arbitrary punishments, and enforce consistency].**

Comments and interpretation. Fairness in law enforcement involved primarily instrumentalist efforts to standardize judicial decision making and has often been linked to efforts to reduce corruption among judicial officials.[253]

5. **Persist in civilized (*wenming* // 文明) law enforcement [with a focus on promoting respectful cooperation with administrative agencies and] give full consideration (*chongfen kaolü* // 充分考虑) [to public sentiment during the pandemic so as not to inflame public opinion (*bimian yinfa shehui yuqing* // 避免引发社会舆情)].**

Comments and interpretation. Civilized law enforcement combines instrumentalist reliance on formal law texts with efforts to reduce abusive police violence and educate the public on the role of law in pandemic enforcement.[254] The provisions reveal the regime's concern over public unrest in response to the pandemic and the regime's control methods. Provisions for strict (*yange* // 严格), standardized (*guifan* // 规范), fair (*gongzheng* // 公正), and civilized (*wenming* // 文明) law enforcement echo provisions in the 4th Plenum of the 18th Central Committee and subsequent documents and plans underscoring CPC dominance over China's socialist legal system generally and centralized control over local COVID-19 policy responses.[255]

6. **Innovative law enforcement methods (*chuangxin zhifa fangshi* // 创新执法方式) [including improving service by administrative law enforcement agencies, expanding online services, and timely licensing].**

Comments and interpretation. Under the 2021–25 CPC Central Committee/State Council Provisional Outline on Establishment of Lawful Governance, innovative law enforcement has particular application to administrative law enforcement, through reliance on education and persuasion in law enforcement, and the use of guidance cases.[256]

7. **Strengthen coordination of law enforcement (*jiaqiang zhifa xietiao* // 加强执法协调) [in part by empowering agencies at the next highest level to oversee cooperation among subordinate offices].**

Comments and interpretation. Coordination in law enforcement is subject to the authority of the Administrative Law Enforcement Coordination and Supervision Bureau in the Ministry of Justice.[257] These provisions revealed once again the regime's commitment to strengthening central control over local COVID-19 control efforts.

8. **Strengthen law enforcement supervision (*zhifa jiandu* // 执法监督) [to strengthen inter-agency coordination, manage administrative law enforcement disputes, and curb "illegal law enforcement activities" (weifa zhifa xingwei // 违法执法行为)].**

Comments and interpretation. Provisions on law enforcement supervision were detailed in the Supervision Law of the PRC (2018), enacted to govern activities of the CPC National Supervision Commission.[258] Efforts to centralize control over local COVID-19 policy efforts were again evident.

9. **Strict responsibilities (*yange zeren* // 严格责任) for law enforcement [outlining a responsibility system for law enforcement aimed at**

strengthening accountability through imposition of Party discipline and criminal penalties against abusers].

Comments and interpretation. Responsibility systems have long been a feature of law enforcement in the PRC. These have mostly involved arrest quotas. In the case of COVID-19 (echoing the terms of the SCIO's 2020 COVID-19 white paper), law enforcement was aimed at maintaining social order and stability. The Ministry of Justice opinion presented the responsibility system as aimed at overcoming problems of weak law enforcement, unfair law enforcement, and even law enforcement corruption. While provisions for responding to unfair and even corrupt law enforcement are notable, these have been evident in past responsibility systems for law enforcement only to be subordinated to mandates to fulfill arrest quotas to overcome "weak law enforcement."[259]

10. **Raise law enforcement safeguards (*tisheng zhifa baozhang* // 提升执法保障) [including providing sufficient personnel and equipment and protecting law enforcement personal in the course of their work].**

Comments and interpretation. While much of the policy discourse concerning safeguarding law enforcement has focused on corruption and abuse of power,[260] the Ministry of Justice opinion also emphasized the importance of providing personal protective equipment for police engaged in COVID-19 law enforcement efforts, as well as ensuring their personal safety and strengthening the authority of law enforcement officers facing resistance to COVID-19 controls.

4 Climate Change
Participatory Populism

THIS CHAPTER EXAMINES PRC responses to the global crisis of climate change as an expression of China's globalized populism. We begin with a review of China's initial responses to climate change through conventional domestic measures and tentative international cooperation, followed by an examination of China's relationship with the international climate policy system in light of challenges of inequality and complexity. This chapter assesses China's populist response, beginning with features of anti-elitism and grievance ideology. As prosperity is a key dimension in China's responses to climate change,[1] the chapter goes on to examine China's practical resistance to the international climate policy system through alternative law and policy practices around operational norms of measurement, distribution, and autonomy of prosperity. The chapter then examines China's use of rhetorical markers on sovereignty, development, and human rights to build resilience for its populist responses to climate change. In contrast with the antagonistic populism of China's COVID-19 response, PRC responses to climate change evinced greater participation in international efforts, conditioned by populist perspectives.

China's Initial Responses to the Climate Change Crisis

China's dramatic economic growth and accompanying increases in greenhouse gas (GHG) emissions has led to significant policy focus on climate change, particularly in light of the 1992 United Nations Framework

Convention on Climate Change (UNFCCC) and the 2015 Paris Agreement.[2] China's initial responses to climate change discourse combined reliance on conventional domestic measures with limited cooperation on international initiatives.[3] These efforts are intertwined such that domestic arrangements conditioned China's international cooperation, which in turn generated standards and processes for domestic application in China's climate change efforts. Unlike the crisis of COVID-19, in which China's globalized populism was evident in response to immediate and rapidly changing policy challenges under conditions of antagonistic relations with the world health policy system, China's responses to the climate change crisis have involved longer-term participation conditioned by general features and localized rhetorical markers of populism.

Conventional Domestic Measures

In the face of growing appreciation of the challenges of climate change and calls to reduce emissions, China began early on to incorporate climate change into its development policy framework.[4] The 2011 climate change white paper from the State Council Information Office (SCIO) summarized China's responses to climate change, attending to both mitigation and adaptation measures enacted through policy and law and responding to climate change as both a strategy for economic and social development and an "opportunity for economic restructuring and the transformation of its economic development pattern."[5]

Development Plans

The National Climate Change Office was moved to the National Development and Reform Commission (NDRC) in 1998, underscoring the policy linkages between climate change efforts and development planning under the NDRC's authority.[6] The 11th Five-Year Plan (FYP) for 2006–10 included targets on energy efficiency and emissions reductions.[7] This was followed in 2007 by the first National Assessment Report on Climate Change, followed by subsequent assessment reports.[8] The NDRC also issued its first National Plan on Adaptation to Climate Change, focusing on GHG emissions controls, reforms in energy production and conversion, increasing energy efficiency and conservation, and extension of climate change adaptation efforts to industry, agriculture, forestry, and municipal waste.[9]

The 12th FYP (2011–15) gave particular attention to climate change, providing detailed guidance on mitigation and adaptation measures, including reducing energy consumption and promoting energy efficiency, controlling

GHG emission intensity (emissions per unit of GDP), and integrating responses to climate change in broader industrial policy.[10] The 12th FYP was supported in turn by the NDRC's 2013 National Climate Change Adaptation Strategy, which emphasized the importance of climate change policy.[11] Whereas the 2013 strategy focused on adaptation and its "synergy" (*xietong* // 协同) with mitigation, the NDRC's National Plan on Adaptation to Climate Change (2014–20) issued the following year made clear that China should "attach equal importance to adaptation and mitigation" (*jianhuan yu shiying bingzhong* // 减缓与适应并重).[12] And whereas key tasks for the NDRC's 2013 adaptation strategy focused on infrastructure development, managing agricultural impacts of climate change, water and marine resource protection, reforestation, and managing impacts on human health, the 2014 national plan focused more specifically on controlling GHG emissions, improving adaptive capacity, developing regional and pilot projects, strengthening incentives for mitigating climate change such as carbon trading, strengthening scientific and technological support, and general capacity building (primarily in record keeping and public support). The 13th FYP (2016–20) continued the focus on mitigation and adaptation measures, zeroing in on emissions controls, adaptation through rural-urban development planning, infrastructure development, and distribution of production; it also established for the first time a national energy consumption cap.[13]

Issued in March 2021, the 14th FYP (2021–25)[14] presented planned policy initiatives spanning nearly the whole of China's policy agenda, from economic and social conditions to international affairs and security. It focused directly on climate change and pollution.[15] Chapter 38.4 of the plan specified continued action on climate change, identifying goals on achieving peak carbon by 2030 and carbon neutrality by 2060, imposing controls on fossil fuel consumption, prioritizing control of carbon intensity over general carbon emissions (*shishi yi tanqiangdu kongzhi wei zhu, tan paifang zongliang kongzhi wei fu* // 实施以碳强度控制为主、碳排放总量控制为辅),[16] advancing low-carbon transformation of industry, construction, and transportation, increasing controls on GHG emissions, and improving carbon sink capacity. The expansion of green tech and alternative energy has contributed to the decline in China's carbon emissions in the year leading up to May 2025.[17]

Legislation

Despite calls for its completion and enactment, a draft law on responding to climate change remains unfinished.[18] The draft, begun in 2010 under the leadership of the NDRC in collaboration with the Chinese Academy of

Social Sciences (CASS), was completed in 2014 but remains under discussion.[19] The draft purportedly elevates mitigation efforts over adaptation and links climate change with the NDRC's economic and social development planning goals.[20] The priority given mitigation would require expansive socio-economic restructuring, possibly inviting political resistance, such that subsequent policy guidance called for equal attention to mitigation and adaptation.[21] A Climate Change Law was included in the State Council's 2016 legislative work plan, and may yet be enacted pursuant to the 15th Five-Year Plan (2026–30).[22]

Nonetheless, legislative efforts have been important in response to ongoing and seemingly intractable challenges of environmental degradation in the face of China's economic growth, with obvious implications for climate change.[23] China's 1990 Environmental Protection Law (EPL) was revised effective January 1, 2015.[24] The revised law provided unified supervision and management by the State Council administrative department on environmental protection – at the time it was the Ministry of Environmental Protection (MEP; established in 2008), which had grown out of the former State Environmental Protection Agency (established in 1998). Supporting the MEP's authority, a joint opinion of the CPC Central Committee and State Council issued in June 2018 called for unified action by "Party committees and governments at all levels" on air, water, and ground pollution.[25] Of particular importance to climate change, China has enacted several measures to combat air pollution.[26] In addition to the Air Pollution Prevention and Control Law (1987, revised 2000 and 2015), China released action plans for air pollution prevention and control in 2013 and 2018.[27] The 2013 action plan focused on reducing airborne particulate matter and linked air pollution controls with environmental impact assessments. The 2018 action plan, issued shortly after the joint Central Committee/State Council opinion, focused on coordinating air pollution controls with reduction of GHG emissions, further integrating China's air pollution and climate change policies.

Policies on environment protection have also been important. A National Environmental Protection Plan issued in 2011 by the State Council for the 12th FYP period (2011–15) contained national pollution emissions standards, many of which have climate change implications.[28] The plan called for implementation of the "Catalogue for the Guidance of Industrial Structure Adjustment" and the "Catalogue for the Guidance of Eliminating Backward Production Process Equipment and Products in Some Industrial Industries," aimed at curtailing pollution emissions from aging industries.

The plan also targeted atmospheric pollutants and called for specific regional emissions control efforts to implement national standards.

Bureaucratic Competition

Bureaucratic competition between environmental agencies and the NDRC over policy priorities has complicated China's climate change response.[29] A cabinet reshuffle in March 2018 transferred the NDRC's responsibilities for managing greenhouse gases and combatting climate change to the newly formed Ministry of Ecology and Environment (MEE).[30] Reflecting this change, the MEE issued in November 2019 a summary report on China's policies and actions that mirrored the structure and nomenclature of the 2011 SCIO climate white paper, while also asserting its responsibility for climate change policy.[31] The 2019 report addressed familiar issues related to climate change mitigation and adaptation, strengthening planning and institutional systems, including developing a carbon market, strengthening basic capacity, and supporting broad social participation. The MEE's follow-up 2021 report[32] addressed the same general range of issues but added an important introductory chapter on "Strengthening Top-Level Design," underscoring the ministry's claim to a leading role in climate change policy.

Bureaucratic and policy competition between the MEE (and its predecessor agencies) and the NDRC was evident in the formation of Leading Small Groups (LSG) on climate change policy. A National Climate Change Coordinating Group was established in 1990 under the State Meteorological Bureau and then moved to the NDRC in 1998.[33] In 2007, the coordinating group was elevated to LSG status as the National Leading Small Group to Address Climate Change Adaptation and Energy Conservation and Emissions Reduction under the NDRC's administration.[34] Under the rubric "one institution, two brands" (*yige jigou liangkuai paizi* // 一个机构、两块牌子), the new climate change LSG's responsibility for emissions reduction was to accord "to the needs of external work,"[35] suggesting its importance for international cooperation measures on climate change. The LSG was headed by the Premier of the State Council and included officials from the various ministries and commissions under the State Council. All provinces, autonomous regions, and centrally administered cities were directed to set up corresponding groups.

With the transfer of climate change responsibilities to the MEE in 2018, the climate change LSG also became subject to the ministry's authority.[36] The MEE soon established yet another Leading Small Group to oversee preparation of the National Climate Change Adaptation Strategy 2035.[37] The

MEE also issued a set of "Guiding Opinions on Integrating and Strengthening Efforts in Climate Action and Ecological and Environmental Protection" in January 2021, aiming to integrate climate law and policy practice under its leadership.[38] Section VII.2 of the Guiding Opinions noted the ministry's communication and collaboration with other members of the "national leading group for climate change, energy conservation and emission reduction," combining an assertion of MEE leadership with a nod to interagency cooperation.

Despite the MEE's new-found prominence, the NDRC remained a force in China's climate change policy process. A "leaders' group" on carbon peaking and carbon neutrality led by Vice Premier Han Zheng was established under the NDRC in mid-2021.[39] The group included NDRC director He Lifeng, with the MEE playing a more subordinate role. The NDRC's prominent role in overseeing carbon peaking and neutrality matters was confirmed by a 2021 Central Committee/State Council opinion on carbon peaking and neutrality that tasked the NDRC with strengthening overall planning, organizing implementation of an action plan for carbon peaking and a work plan on carbon neutrality, and overseeing implementation, while calling on "all relevant departments" to cooperate on these efforts.[40] The NDRC's subsequent issuance of an "Action Plan" and "Working Guidance" on carbon dioxide peaking and carbon neutrality[41] underscored its claims to a leading role in climate change matters. The continued prominence of the NDRC was also evident in the person of its former vice chair, Xie Zhenhua, who was appointed as China's lead negotiator on international climate talks.

The bureaucratic politics of MEE-NDRC competition that continued to influence China's climate change policies was evident in the lead-up to the 26th Conference of the Parties to the UNFCCC (COP26) in Glasgow, Scotland, in 2021. Even as the MEE issued its January 2021 "Guiding Opinion" on climate change and environmental protection and its June 2021 summary report on China's policies and actions on climate change, the State Council (to which both the NDRC and the MEE report) issued its June 2021 climate white paper, and the NDRC issued its Working Guidance and Action Plan on carbon emissions and carbon neutrality in October. The multiplicity of climate policy statements from different agencies and the questions this raises as to their respective responsibilities and authority was compounded by China's report to COP26 on its Nationally Determined Contributions (NDC) issued in October 2021 without naming a lead issuing agency – unlike the 2015 NDC report to the COP21 sessions in Paris, which was issued by the NDRC.[42] The NDRC's influence on China's 2021 NDC submission was evident as the NDC tracked closely with the NDRC-issued 14th FYP (2021–25) summary of responses to climate change.[43] The NDRC took the lead position over the MEE, Ministry of Foreign Affairs (MFA), and the Ministry of Commerce (MOFCOM) in issuing a joint opinion in early 2022 affirming the establishment and guiding principles of a Leading Small Group for green development in China's Belt and Road Initiative (BRI) infrastructure development program linking China with South and Central Asia, Africa, the Middle East, and Europe.[44] In August 2023, the NDRC declared it would review all policy decisions from State Council ministries (including climate measures), to ensure consistency in national application.[45] This was confirmed in connection with the 2023 Central Economic Work Conference (CEWC).[46]

Formal expressions of policy preferences by often competing government agencies provided important indications of the PRC regime's responses to climate change. Ongoing competition between the NDRC and the MEE reflected the continued involvement of bureaucratic politics in China's conventional domestic responses to climate change. Such factors may impede China's capacity to meet the 1.5°C temperature increase limit set forth in the Paris Agreement.[47] Continued dependence on coal has contributed to China's carbon emissions growing in 2022 at the highest rate in more than a decade.[48] In order to meet energy needs, the government in early 2022 ordered coal supplies to be increased and coal-fired power plants to run at full capacity.[49] Energy shortages driven by drought and severe weather added to the pressure for greater coal production and consumption.[50] In steel production, which accounts for approximately 15 percent of China's total carbon emissions, the government has extended the deadline for peak emissions from 2025 to 2030 to avoid "unbearable economic costs" in meeting carbon emissions requirements.[51] China's climate change policies also face multiple obstacles to performance, as local interests and incentives are often inconsistent with national policy.[52] Questions about effective coordination with local interests were evident in the Communist Party of China (CPC) Central Committee's April 2021 call for unified action on climate change.[53]

Tentative International Cooperation

China's initial responses to the crisis of climate change also involved international cooperation. China ratified the UNFCCC in 1993, signed (1998) and ratified (2002) the Kyoto Protocol operationalizing the UNFCCC, and ratified the 2015 Paris Agreement.[54] As part of its participation in the UNFCCC process, China issued four national communications on climate change through 2023, in order to inform the international community about its climate policy efforts.[55] China has partnered effectively with the UN Environment Programme (UNEP) to support China's domestic environmental protection efforts.[56] Its cooperation with the UNEP extended to commitments on biodiversity as China hosted the 2021 15th Session of the Conference of the Parties to the Convention on Biological Diversity and proclaimed the importance of "pragmatic cooperation" within the framework of the convention.[57] China's international cooperation included support for developing countries.[58] The China Trust Fund, emerging from a framework agreement between China and the UNEP, committed to annual contributions of US$2 million to support environmental capacity building for developing countries in Africa and Asia.[59] Such commitments extended to climate change.

China's tentative international cooperation on climate change was exemplified by its participation at the COP26 meetings in Glasgow in November 2021. The critical importance of the Glasgow meetings was underscored in advance by US government reporting on the security threat posed by climate change and international responses (including China's).[60] China too had come to recognize the national security implications of climate change.[61] In anticipation of COP26, the world's two largest GHG emitters managed to agree on a range of climate commitments. Meeting in Shanghai in April 2021, climate envoys John Kerry and Xie Zhenhua made commitments on emissions reductions and transitioning away from carbon-based industry and energy in order to strengthen implementation of the Paris Agreement and support the COP26 summit in Glasgow.[62] At the Leaders' Summit on Climate convened in Washington, DC, in April 2021, Xi Jinping reiterated commitments to achieve carbon neutrality by 2060 and peak carbon emissions by 2030, as well as to limit increases in coal consumption over the course of the 14th FYP (2021–25) period and phase it down in the 15th FYP (2026–30) period.[63] Xi Jinping's speech to the UN General Assembly in September 2021 repeated these commitments, and included a new pledge to end Chinese financing of coal-fired power plants in developing economies.[64]

Nonetheless, at the G20 meetings held just prior to COP26, China continued to resist pressure to further curtail emissions, prompting the United States and its European allies to pursue alternative plans to seek broader climate commitments from other developing countries.[65] President Biden seized on Xi's failure to appear in person at COP26 as a "big mistake," inviting questions about China's commitment to global climate change efforts and attempting to reclaim US leadership.[66]

China's Relationship with the Global Climate System: Inequality and Complexity

Similarly with China's relationship with the international public health system in the context of COVID-19, Chinese involvement with international institutions and standards on climate change reflected underlying conditions of inequality and complexity that inform populism more broadly. While the antagonistic populism evident in China's responses to COVID-19 was largely absent, its responses to climate change remained conditional on populist expectations. These factors were evident in China's resistance to firm commitments to evolving UN climate standards and in its efforts to adjust global climate targets to suit the conditions of its economic and social development.[67]

Inequality issues have arisen in the context of China's claims regarding conditions of development. China's engagement with the UNFCCC system has long been accompanied by apprehension over the potential for such engagement to thwart China's development. Its ratification of the UNFCCC in 1993 was predicated on asserting China's status as a developing country with comparatively low per capita emissions, and hence subject to the convention's provisions on "common but differentiated responsibilities and respective capabilities" (CBDR).[68] Expressing solidarity with developing economies like India, China had supported the 1997 Kyoto Protocol operationalizing the UNFCCC, subject to the condition that the convention's GHG emissions restrictions would apply only to developed economies and not to developing countries, under the differentiated responsibilities principle.[69] China's continued insistence on differentiating emissions rules for developed and developing economies was widely blamed for the perceived failure of the 2009 Copenhagen climate summit (COP15).[70] Nonetheless, the CBDR principles were reiterated in the 2015 Paris Agreement.[71]

The dynamic of complexity and alienation has also played a role. China's alienation from international climate policy institutions included unease over the complex networks of relationships, standards, and practices among liberal market-oriented economies that embody the liberal international order and dominate global climate change discourse.[72] Moreover, much of PRC policy on state control of the economy can be seen in terms of anxiety and lack of confidence over whether the complexities of economic liberalization will serve China's development goals. In liberal systems, government oversight of the economy where a multiplicity of autonomous economic actors engage in rights-based market activities involves a wide range of regulatory bureaucratic processes that have the potential to challenge regime authority.[73] For many policy drivers in China, including senior officials and their advisers who influence policy initiative, periodic and temporary directives supporting reliance on market measures for certain sectors seldom extend to full market liberalization due to concerns over harmful socio-economic and political consequences associated with liberalization in the West.[74] By contrast, the administrative planning process and bureaucratic supervision, complex though these may be, is more consistent with PRC traditional practice, relying on internal bureaucratic and administrative controls under purportedly unified Party leadership.

Thus, resentment of inequality and alienation from complexity have been evident in China's engagement with the international climate policy system. While China's domestic legislative and regulatory measures were undoubtedly influenced by local environmental concerns and political-bureaucratic manoeuvring, the surfeit of white papers, national plans, guiding opinions, and strategies also reflected efforts to manage international expectations even while conditioning China's commitment to managing climate change on local development needs. This was exemplified by China's participation in the COP26 meetings in Glasgow, which, while significant in and of itself, also saw tensions with the international system in China's proposals and behaviour supporting disparate treatment for developing economies. Wariness of signing on to COP26 proposals supported by the United States and the European Union, association with the group of "Like-Minded Developing Countries" (LMDC), and consistent calls for more financial support from developed economies for climate change efforts in the Global South all suggested the extent of China's populist reaction to conditions of inequality and complexity in the UNFCCC system.

China's Populist Response to the Climate Change Crisis

As with its handling of COVID-19, China's populist responses to the global climate change crisis include features of anti-elitism, grievance, and practical resistance. Unlike the antagonistic features of China's COVID-19 response, however, China's engagement with the international climate policy system tended toward greater participation, conditioned by a populist calculus of China's interests and capacities.

Opposition to Elites: Tensions with the International Climate Policy System

Tensions between China and the international climate policy system were underscored by differences between China's preferred policy positions and the final COP26 agreement at Glasgow.[75] Notwithstanding Xie Zhenhua's efforts to prevent adoption of a firm 1.5°C limit on temperature rise, the final agreement doubled down on the resolution to pursue efforts to limit the temperature increase to 1.5°C, reaffirming the Paris standards on temperature rise but emphasizing the need for the 1.5°C limit.[76] On climate financing, the agreement failed to match China's ambitions on expanding adaptation financing (non-binding goals were provided instead) and establishing a facility to further compensate for loss and damage suffered by developing countries (a "dialogue" was agreed to instead).[77] The 2022 COP27 meetings in Sharm el-Sheikh, Egypt, saw establishment of a Loss and Damage Fund, even as disputes remained over its administration and activities.[78] COP28 opened in Dubai in 2023 with continued attention to loss and damage, but uncertainties remained over contributions from China and other large developing economies.[79] Loss and damage remained a key policy issue in 2024's COP29, although criticisms were raised over the reliability of commitments made by wealthy countries and indeed over the general utility of the COP process itself.[80] COP29 also saw challenges to claims by China and India to be developing countries, in light of the vast disparities with poorer developing countries in Africa.[81]

Table 4 compares China's COP26 positions with those of developed countries central to the international climate policy establishment and reflects the extent of China's resistance. China's COP26 commitments varied significantly from those of the United States, the United Kingdom, and the European Union. With the exception of the Deforestation Pledge, China did not join major COP26 climate pledges. Instead, it offered alternative commitments on net-zero emissions and coal (including a promise to halt investment in coal-fired power plants abroad). China's individual climate commitments combined with rejection of COP26 standards suggest an aversion to being bound by the formal standards of the international climate policy community.[82]

China's populist responses to the international climate policy system and associated global elites were exacerbated further by underlying geopolitical conflicts with the United States.[83] The United States had signed but not ratified the Kyoto Protocol even while committing to meet an emissions reduction target of 7 percent from 1990s levels by 2012 and making a further pledge at the 2009 Copenhagen Climate Summit to reduce emissions by 17 percent below 2005 levels by 2020.[84] The Trump administration's withdrawal from the Paris Agreement created a significant opportunity for China to claim leadership of global climate change efforts.[85] Some observers note the possibility that US-China competition may benefit climate efforts,

TABLE 4 Comparison of COP26 policy positions

COP26 issue[1]	Temperature goal	Methane pledge[2]	Net-zero emissions[3]	Coal pledge[4]	Loss and damage facility[5]
Paris Agreement[6]	Limit global temperature increase to well below 2°C; pursue efforts to limit increase to 1.5°C	COP21 side event[7]	Balance between carbon emissions and removal by second half of the century	Paris temperature goals require the EU and OECD to phase out coal by 2030, China by 2040, and the rest of the world by 2050[8]	–
Country[9]					
China	Accept Paris targets, but policies suggest 3°C increase	No	2060	• Non-signatory • Pledge peak coal use by 2025[10] • Pledge to end investment in international coal power[11] NB: Change in COP26 final agreement re "phase down," not "phase out"	Yes
US	1.5°C	Yes	2050	Yes	Glasgow Dialogue[12]
UK	1.5°C	Yes	2050	Yes	Glasgow Dialogue
Germany	1.5°C	Yes	2045	Yes	Glasgow Dialogue
EU[13]	1.5°C	Yes (co-sponsor)	2050	Yes	Glasgow Dialogue

►

◂

1 UN Climate Change, "World Leaders Kick Start Accelerated Climate Action at COP26," press release, November 2, 2021, https://unfccc.int/news/world-leaders-kick-start-accelerated-climate-action-at-cop26.

2 European Commission, "Joint EU-US Press Release on the Global Methane Pledge," September 18, 2021, https://ec.europa.eu/commission/presscorner/detail/en/IP_21_4785; Phil McKenna and Marianne Lavelle, "Over 100 Nations at COP26 Pledge to Cut Global Methane Emissions by 30 Percent in Less Than a Decade," Inside Climate News, November 2, 2021, https://insideclimatenews.org/news/02112021/global-methane-pledge-cop26/.

3 UN Environment Programme (UNEP), "Emissions Gap Report 2021," October 26, 2021, https://www.unep.org/resources/emissions-gap-report-2021.

4 "Global Coal to Clean Power Transition Statement," November 4, 2021, https://ukcop26.org/global-coal-to-clean-power-transition-statement/.

5 "Warsaw International Mechanism for Loss and Damage Associated with Climate Change Impacts (WIM)," United Nations Climate Change, https://unfccc.int/topics/adaptation-and-resilience/workstreams/loss-and-damage/warsaw-international-mechanism; Damien Carrington, "What Is 'Loss and Damage' and Why Is It Critical for Success at Cop26?" *The Guardian,* November 13, 2021, https://www.theguardian.com/environment/2021/nov/13/what-is-loss-and-damage-and-why-is-it-critical-for-success-at-cop26?CMP=Share_AndroidApp_Other.

6 UN Climate Change, "Key Aspects of the Paris Agreement," https://unfccc.int/process-and-meetings/the-paris-agreement/the-paris-agreement/key-aspects-of-the-paris-agreement; "What's in the Paris Agreement on Climate Change?" *The Economist,* October 29, 2021, https://www.economist.com/interactive/paris-climate-agreement-annotated/?gclid=Cj0KCQiAsqOMBhDFARIsAFBTN3en7seAtunMtJ84ShWr8uk0aIQH9SHWTVWwZUJJdQ5rune_2GfXk6YaAnZKEALw_wcB&gclsrc=aw.ds; David Waskow and Jennifer Morgan, "The Paris Agreement: Turning Point for a Climate Solution," World Resources Institute, December 12, 2015, https://www.wri.org/insights/paris-agreement-turning-point-climate-solution.

7 "COP21 Side Event – Reducing Methane Emissions from Oil & Gas Operations," December 7, 2015, https://www.ccacoalition.org/events/cop21-side-event-reducing-methane-emissions-oil-gas-operations.

8 Marcia Rocha and Bill Hare, *Implications of the Paris Agreement for Coal Use in the Power Sector* (Berlin: Climate Analytics, 2016), https://climateanalytics.org/media/climateanalytics-coalreport_nov2016_1.pdf.

9 Lindsay Maizland, "COP26: Here's What Countries Pledged," Council on Foreign Relations, November 15, 2021, https://www.cfr.org/in-brief/cop26-heres-what-countries-have-pledged; Climate Action Tracker, "Climate Target Update Tracker," https://climateactiontracker.org; Helen Lock, Akindare Okunola, and Kate Nakamura, "COP26: The Biggest Announcements Coming Out of the UN Climate Conference," Global Citizen, November 5, 2021, https://www.globalcitizen.org/en/content/cop26-glasgow-climate-announcements/.

10 Reuters, David Stanway, and Cate Cadell, "President Xi Says China Will Start Cutting Coal Consumption from 2026," *Reuters,* April 22, 2021, https://www.reuters.com/worldchinachinas-xi-says-china-will-phase-down-coal-consumption-over-2026-2030-2021-04-22/.

11 Jennifer Hillman and David Sacks, "Making Sense of China's Pledge to Stop Building Coal-Fired Power Plants Abroad," Council on Foreign Relations, October 4, 2021, https://www.cfr.org/blog/making-sense-chinas-pledge-stop-building-coal-fired-power-plants-abroad.

12 FN UNFCCC, "SB 56: GLASGOW DIALOGUE ON LOSS AND DAMAGE," June 7, 2022, https://www.lossanddamagecollaboration.org/link-page/sb-56-glasgow-dialogue-on-loss-and-damage#:~:text=COP%2026%20established%20the%20Glasgow,Change%20Impacts%20(WIM%20ExCom).

13 European Commission, "EU at COP26 Climate Change Conference," https://ec.europa.eu/info/strategy/priorities-2019-2024/european-green-deal/climate-action-and-green-deal/eu-cop26-climate-change-conference_en; European Commission, "European Climate Law," https://ec.europa.eu/clima/eu-action/european-green-deal/european-climate-law_en.

while others call more explicitly for stronger collaboration.[86] Yet underlying distrust has undermined effective joint efforts.[87] After the United States issued a "Fact Sheet" on China's environmental abuses in September 2020 that highlighted climate emissions, the Ministry of Foreign Affairs excoriated the US withdrawal from the Paris Agreement.[88] US climate envoy John Kerry pressured China to go beyond the 2030 peak emissions commitment, suggesting that the 1.5°C limit on global warming agreed to in the Paris Agreement was itself insufficient and would be impossible to achieve under China's current commitments.[89] US calls at a bilateral climate meeting in Tianjin in September 2021 for China to make deeper emission reductions were rejected.[90] While a surprise US-China agreement at COP26 to strengthen climate cooperation suggested progress, it mainly affirmed the Paris Agreement's emissions targets and promised future bilateral climate cooperation.[91] Efforts to solidify such cooperation through a bilateral working group on reducing greenhouse gases were derailed when China withdrew from all cooperation with the United States in response to the August 2022 visit to Taiwan by the Speaker of the House of Representatives, Nancy Pelosi.[92]

Preparations for the ensuing COP27 meetings in Egypt revealed further tension as John Kerry called for renewed collaboration with China, while his Chinese counterpart urged the United States to "clear barriers" to better cooperation, referring in part to the Pelosi visit to Taiwan.[93] While bilateral talks did indeed resume at the COP27 summit, following an agreement between Xi Jinping and Joe Biden reached just weeks earlier on the sidelines of the G20 meeting in Bali, expectations on concrete results were limited.[94] Prior to his visit to Beijing in mid-2023, Kerry called again for putting disputes aside in search of joint action on climate change in anticipation of COP28 in Dubai, and secured agreement for the United States and China to co-chair the first "local climate summit" attached to COP28.[95] As the Biden administration continued to call for pressure on China to take further action on emissions and climate change, envoys Kerry and Xie concluded a framework agreement on future cooperation in anticipation of the bilateral meeting between Biden and Xi at the APEC summit in November 2023.[96] The agreement raised hopes for resolution of questions such as methane controls, but the all-important issue of fossil fuel reduction (including China's burgeoning reliance on coal) remained largely unaddressed. After the 2024 election of climate change skeptic Donald Trump to the US presidency for a second time, the United States withdrew from the Paris Agreement and from the Loss and Damage Fund agreement finalized at COP27.[97] The United States seemed, in effect, to be yielding to China's leadership over international climate change efforts, whether these concerned COP29's financial commitments to the Loss and Damage Fund or emissions controls more broadly.[98]

Tensions with the international climate policy community were also evident in China's relations with the European Union. While the European Union has pursued a long-term program of climate cooperation with China and in 2021 agreed to joint actions that affirmed China's 2030/2060 pledge,[99] China's refusal to join the EU co-sponsored Global Methane Pledge signified continued alienation.[100]

Grievance: Disregard for China's Conditions

China's participation at COP26 revealed the influence of ideologies of grievance related to perceived disregard for China's needs and conditions. Xi Jinping declined to appear personally or on video for the conference, offering a written submission instead.[101] In his written statement, he repeated prior commitments to curb peak carbon dioxide emissions before 2030 and achieve carbon neutrality by 2060, and reiterated prior positions on developed countries bearing primary responsibility for curbing emissions and providing financial support for emissions reduction measures in developing countries.[102] China's 2021 NDC report, submitted in advance of the COP26 meetings in Glasgow, reiterated demands for developed countries to bear the main responsibility for reducing emissions and declined to revise China's pledged deadline for carbon neutrality from 2060 to 2050 to meet the standards proposed for COP26 in the United Nations' 2021 Emissions Gap Report.[103] China also joined the LMDC group in the lead-up to COP26 in calling for developed countries to contribute financially to climate change remediation and adaptation efforts in developing countries.[104] Paralleling China's 2021 NDC report, the SCIO issued a new climate white paper in October 2021, presenting "new principles" on climate change, emphasizing Xi Jinping's "new development philosophy," calling for green development as essential to sustainability, and promoting a "people-centred" approach, while stressing China's role in maintaining "the unity of developing countries and defending their common interests."[105] The 2021 joint CPC Central Committee and State Council opinion on the new development concept in carbon peaking and neutrality efforts emphasized protecting China's development rights and interests in the UNFCCC process.[106]

China's grievances were evident in chief climate negotiator Xie Zhenhua's resistance to calls from developed countries for stronger climate commitments expressed through more frequent NDC reports, averring that China was pursuing its own detailed and concrete plans on meeting its climate commitments.[107] Xie decried efforts to adjust the Paris Agreement's existing global warming targets of "limiting global temperature increase to well below 2° Celsius, while pursuing efforts to limit the increase to 1.5°C," to a new firm commitment to the 1.5°C limit.[108] Resistance was also evident when China (together with India) imposed a last-minute revision to the COP26 final agreement, changing agreed-on language on accelerating efforts toward the phase-out of unabated coal power and inefficient fossil fuel subsidies, substituting "phase down" for "phase out" on coal.[109] In the lead-up to the 2023 COP28 in Dubai, Xie went even further, decrying rigid commitments to phasing out fossil fuels.[110]

Thus, China's populist response to the international climate policy system involved reactions to challenges of inequality and complexity. This included dynamics of opposition to international elites and the policy systems they purportedly control, and justification through grievances over neglect of China's local conditions. China's populist response also included practical resistance through legal and regulatory standards and practice presenting alternatives to established arrangements.

Practical Resistance in China's Populist Response to the Climate Change Crisis

Complementing populist features of anti-elitism and grievance, China's responses to the climate change crisis involved practical resistance challenging international standards while protecting China's prosperity goals. As its responses to climate change have often been presented in terms of effects on socio-economic conditions, China's practical resistance measures may usefully be assessed in light of operational norms and law and policy practices related to prosperity.[111] These may be viewed in the context of China's evolving development policies more broadly and in light of standards of the rules-based international order.

Context: Prosperity in China's Development

China's policies on economic development have long sought to balance growth and distribution of prosperity. Xi Jinping's recent embrace of "common prosperity" and the discourse of "new development" reflects this tension.

Balancing Growth and Equity in Economic Development

Policy discourse on prosperity in China has attempted to respond to the challenge of balancing economic accumulation with concerns over equity in the distribution of benefits.[112] Acknowledging variation in economic development policy during the Mao years – particularly during the years of hardship and famine in the early 1960s following the Great Leap Forward, regime goals of prosperity were presented largely in terms of equitable allocation of economic benefits. Government control of the planned economy expressed ideological imperatives of class struggle mandating policies promoting workers and peasants against the power of former political and commercial elites.[113] The landmark 3rd Plenum of the 11th CPC Congress (1978) enacted policies of "reform and opening up"[114] aimed at strengthening practices on accumulation ("productive forces") while remaining attentive to class struggle ("relations of production").[115]

Tensions between equity and accumulation continued throughout the post-Mao period, often depicted in terms of the transition from planning to market forces as the basis for economic development.[116] Paramount leader Deng Xiaoping's proclamation that "to get rich is glorious" symbolized acceptance that accumulation would occur unevenly and benefit some sectors and regions before others.[117] Premier Zhao Ziyang's call at the 13th CPC Congress in 1987 for separation of the CPC from enterprise management under the rubric *dang-zheng fenkai* (党政分开) aimed to improve production capacity in support of accumulation.[118] Following the death of CPC General Secretary Hu Yaobang in April 1989 and the ensuing pro-democracy demonstrations at Tiananmen Square and across China, the purge of Zhao Ziyang and other reformers put a damper on economic reform efforts.[119] The subsequently appointed CPC General Secretary Jiang Zemin continued calls for balance between economic equity and accumulation with his discourse on creating a "moderately prosperous society" (*xiaokang shehui* // 小康社会), adopted at the 14th CPC Congress (1992), that would enable market forces to stimulate growth while also attending to equity concerns in the distribution of benefits.[120] Jiang's successor, Hu Jintao, articulated ideals of "scientific development" (*kexue fazhan* // 科学发展 and "harmonious socialist society" (*shehui zhuyi hexie shehui* // 社会主义和谐社会) at the 16th CPC Congress (2007), responding to growing challenges of inequality and corruption, and empowering an emerging private sector even while retaining governmental oversight.[121] Greater reliance on market mechanisms was embraced at the 3rd Plenum of the 18th CPC Congress (2014) under the rubric "let the market play a decisive role in allocating resources and let the government play its functions better."[122] Yet market-oriented practice has remained subject to interpretation and direction by the Party-state, which continued to exert control over economic actors and activities.[123]

Common Prosperity and New Development

Changing approaches to economic prosperity were evident in Xi Jinping's populist vision on "common prosperity" (*gongtong fuyu* // 共同富裕) approved at the 5th Plenum of the 18th CPC Congress in 2015.[124] Ironically, the term had earlier been championed by Xi's disgraced foe Bo Xilai as a populist effort to support more equitable distribution of economic benefits in Chongqing.[125] Responding to the myriad policy challenges of an aging population, inequality, poor social services, and disparities in regional development,[126] Xi's common prosperity policy aimed at reforming income distribution through taxation of higher-income earners while also cracking down on large tech firms and other high-income generators.[127] Pursuant to a five-year plan for "establishing lawful governance," private sector tech and education enterprises would be subjected to increased scrutiny, and ultimately increased state ownership and control.[128] Subject to governing principles of adhering to Xi Jinping's interpretation of rule through law and upholding of Party leadership, the plan called for "optimizing the business environment," mainly through anti-monopoly efforts.[129] While the policy no doubt involved aims to rein in ever-larger and more powerful business interests that competed with the regime for power and influence, the equity dimensions of common prosperity also appealed to popular sentiment on economic dislocation that, unchecked, might lead to populist critiques against the regime itself.

Addressing the 19th CPC Congress in October 2017, Xi noted the distinction between accumulation and equity in his direction that the principal challenge facing Chinese socialism was the "contradiction between unbalanced and inadequate development and the people's ever-growing needs for a better life."[130] The point was reiterated at the 5th Plenum of the 19th CPC Congress in October 2020, with efforts to link the benefits of prosperity more directly with people's welfare under the 14th FYP for 2021–25.[131] Xi summarized these developments in a major article on development issued in July 2021, articulating principles of "new development" that would come to underlie "common prosperity."[132] At the 10th Session of the Central Committee for Financial and Economic Affairs in August 2021, he called specifically for a focus on common prosperity to achieve balanced economic growth.[133] The meeting readout noted the call for more effective efforts to ensure balance between accumulation and equity:

> Rather than being egalitarian or having only a few people prosperous, common prosperity refers to affluence shared by everyone, both in material and cultural terms, and shall be advanced step by step ...
>
> The meeting underlined efforts to properly deal with the relationship between efficiency and fairness, make basic institutional arrangements on income distribution, expand the size of the middle-income group, increase the earnings for the low-income groups, adjust excessive incomes and prohibit illicit income to promote social fairness and justice.[134]

Reflecting these challenges, inconsistencies were evident in balancing pursuit of common prosperity with maintaining economic growth. An SCIO white paper issued in September 2021 depicted China's transition from poverty to relative prosperity as a prelude to ongoing efforts to build common prosperity.[135] But whereas the white paper mentioned common prosperity only once, as a goal for "sustained and healthy economic growth," a major report published just a few weeks earlier by the China Development Research Foundation (associated with the Development Research Center of the State Council) claimed that the policy involved more than simply modifying expectations and measurements of economic growth: "Overall, common prosperity emphasizes universal prosperity, which covers all members of society; comprehensive, common prosperity includes material prosperity and spiritual prosperity, covering all aspects of people's lives."[136] By way of explanation, the publication of the foundation's report was prefaced by the assertion that "continuously improving people's livelihood and well-being and solidly promoting common prosperity is one of the main goals and major tasks of China's economic and social development during the 14th Five-Year Plan period."[137]

The notion of common prosperity also received particular attention in the CPC "Resolution on Chinese History" issued in November 2021: "With unswerving resolve, we will pursue common prosperity for all."[138] Speaking at the December 2021 Central Economic Work Conference, Xi claimed victory in achieving what he termed the goal of the CPC's first centenary of building a "moderately prosperous society," as a prelude to pursuing common prosperity as a second centenary goal.[139] Xi's speech to the conference was published as the lead article of the CPC's theoretical journal *Seeking Truth* (*Qiushi* // 求是) in the lead-up to the 20th CPC Congress.[140] The congress saw Xi elucidate further the importance of common prosperity:

> Chinese modernization is socialist modernization pursued under the leadership of the Communist Party of China. It contains elements that are common to the modernization processes of all countries, but it is more characterized by features that are unique to the Chinese context ...
>
> – *It is the modernization of common prosperity for all.* Achieving common prosperity is a defining feature of socialism with Chinese characteristics and involves a long historical process. The immutable goal of our modernization drive is to meet the people's aspirations for a better life. We will endeavour to maintain and promote social fairness and justice, bring prosperity to all, and prevent polarization.[141]

A joint CPC Central Committee/State Council strategic plan on expanding domestic demand issued in anticipation of the 2022 CEWC reiterated the importance of common prosperity.[142] Xi's speech to a seminar on implementation of the spirit of the 20th CPC Congress in early 2023 presented common prosperity as a foundation for "Chinese-style modernization" (*Zhongguo shi xiandaihua* // 中国式现代化), adopting the vernacular "Chinese characteristics" (*Zhongguo tese* // 中国特色) associated with Deng Xiaoping to shield "common prosperity" from latent disregard or even criticism:

> We have continuously deepened our understanding, created the idea of socialism with Chinese characteristics in the new era, achieved a new leap in the Sinicization of Marxism, and provided a fundamental basis for Chinese-style modernization.[143]

The extent to which common prosperity had become embedded in PRC economic policy discourse was evident in the NDRC's announcement (with the National Data Administration), following the 2023 CEWC, of a five-year implementation plan on supporting common prosperity through development of the digital economy.[144]

Nonetheless, the common prosperity policy faced significant political and bureaucratic obstacles, raising questions as to its effectiveness in supporting China's economic development trajectory.[145] Xi Jinping's remarks to the 2022 CEWC responded to apparent continuing resistance to the policy:

> Comrades attending the meeting said that General Secretary Xi Jinping deeply explained five major theoretical and practical issues such as achieving common prosperity at last year's Central Economic Work Conference, and this time he further resolved doubts, cleaned up the source, and

> gathered consensus around several major issues in next year's economic work, demonstrating our party's confidence and courage in always proceeding from the overall strategic situation and always grasping the main contradictions.[146]

Differences in emphasis between calls for greater equity in socio-economic relations and support for optimizing the business environment suggested that Xi's call for common prosperity was not without its critics.[147] Some observers questioned whether the common prosperity policy would lead to expanded state control over the economy, with the potential to reinforce structures and practices of patronage and corruption.[148] Others criticized the program as China's economy slowed significantly in 2022–23.[149]

In the face of such uncertainty, the vernacular of "common prosperity" has largely given way to references to China's "new development concept" (*xin fazhan linian* // 新发展理念) and "new development paradigm" (*xin fazhan geju* // 新发展格局), which echo the goals of common prosperity but avoid the political sensitivities associated with it. The new development concept focuses on "high-quality development," challenging past preoccupations with GDP growth and addressing structural change, while the new development paradigm focuses on domestic demand-led growth.[150] Interpreting the "spirit" of the 2021 CEWC, Han Wenxiu, a senior official of the Central Committee for Financial and Economic Affairs, gave priority to the new development concept and the new development paradigm as policy themes of immediate application, while treating common prosperity as a longer-term strategic goal.[151] The 2022 CEWC focused on building economic stability and called for strengthening domestic demand as a component of the new development paradigm.[152]

The 2023 CEWC emphasized China's new development concept emphasizing greater equity in economic growth, and new development paradigm emphasizing boosting domestic demand.[153] Xi Jinping's speech to the 2023 CEWC stressed that economic policy in 2024 should "faithfully implement the new development philosophy on all fronts," limiting mention of common prosperity to an oblique reference to the guiding principles of the 20th CPC Congress, which had extolled its virtues.[154] Xi's speech to the December 2024 CEWC linked references to the new development concept and new development paradigm with an emerging emphasis on high-quality development and increasing domestic demand, while eliding specific mention of common prosperity.[155] This was foreordained by the Politburo session that preceded the CEWC itself.[156]

Throughout this period, China's economy faced significant headwinds. The COVID-19 pandemic sharpened contradictions between growth and distribution of prosperity, with emerging concerns about economic stagnation vying with commitments to continue the Zero-COVID policy, which was widely seen as harming the economy.[157] The mortgage crisis of mid-2022, where debtors refused to make mortgage payments on purchased but uncompleted real estate projects, further exacerbated China's economic woes.[158] The prospect of deflation coupled with persistent youth unemployment dimmed hopes for ongoing prosperity.[159] Statistics on China's economy were not released in anticipation of the October 2022 20th CPC Congress, further indication of the political sensitivities surrounding China's faltering economic growth.[160] Areas of concern were indicated in Xi Jinping's speech to the 2023 CEWC emphasizing the importance of economic growth in the post-COVID period, as well as calling for promoting technological innovation, expanding domestic demand, and strengthening core functions and core competitiveness of state enterprises while also promoting private enterprises through market access measures, access to factors of production, and fair law enforcement and protection of rights and interests.[161] In December 2023, just before the 2023 CEWC, Moody's downgraded its credit rating for China's sovereign bonds from stable to negative.[162]

Challenges to China's economic development continued into 2024.[163] Building economic growth was a key theme in anticipation of the 3rd Plenum of the 20th CPC Central Committee in July 2024.[164] In September, the People's Bank of China announced an ambitious set of stimulus measures, including interest rate cuts and reduced borrowing costs for stock market investors.[165] Whether these will be effective or sufficient to reverse China's economic malaise remains to be seen in light of ongoing systemic issues such youth unemployment, disruption in the real estate market, low productivity, and high local government debt.[166] Acknowledging perhaps the persistence of economic inequality despite common prosperity efforts, authoritative commentary on China's 15th FYP underscored the importance of economic equalization goals associated with common prosperity as a component of new development.[167]

Not unlike the situation depicted in Chapter 3 regarding public reactions to China's harsh Zero-COVID policy and the implications for Xi Jinping's leadership, continuing problems in China's economic development posed challenges for Xi's position. In response, China's Ministry of State Security has cracked down on expressions on social media of pessimism about the economy.[168] As well, the policies of the July 2024 3rd Plenum of the 20th

CPC Central Committee emphasized political control over economic growth measures.[169] Following the 2024 CEWC, Xi averred that China's growth rate would expand to 5 percent in 2025 and dismissed prominent economist Gao Shanwen, who had publicly doubted this figure, suggesting that 3 percent was more accurate.[170] China ultimately did report a 5 percent growth rate for 2024 despite public concerns over worsening living standards.[171] This was the lowest growth rate since 1990 (aside from the COVID years), and even this figure has been challenged as overly optimistic.[172]

The challenges for Xi Jinping's leadership were also evident in changing policy perspectives on developing the private sector. Crackdowns on private firms in the midst of the common prosperity policy had seen veiled push-back against Xi Jinping.[173] Nonetheless, efforts to encourage growth in the private economy were evident by mid-2023, albeit met with skepticism.[174] In October 2024, the Ministry of Justice and the NDRC released a draft law for promoting the private economy, although the draft was short on specific measures to promote private enterprises.[175] As Xi has taken personal control over economic reform policies,[176] his political standing will continue to depend on the effectiveness of reforms aimed at building economic growth, maintaining stability, and ensuring equity in China's development.

Implications for China's Climate Change Response

China's policy record on economic development sets the tone for its practical resistance to the international climate policy system through alternative law and policy practices on operational norms of measurement, distribution, and autonomy of prosperity. On measurement of prosperity, law and policy practice in the post-Mao period tended to focus on aggregate macro-data on national and regional performance.[177] On distribution of prosperity, the state enterprise system inherited from the Maoist period provided a mechanism for distribution of prosperity benefits through allocation of education, medical care, housing, food, and other benefits to employees and their families.[178] This changed, however, in the transition from state enterprises (*guoying qiye* // 国营企业) to state-owned enterprises (*guoyou qiye* // 国有企业), which were less a vehicle for socio-economic equity than a means of generating profits to support state budgets.[179] Distribution of prosperity through state-owned business enterprises came to include gradual allowances for independently owned firms.[180] Concerns over distribution of prosperity benefits to society[181] suggest that enterprise-centred distribution mechanisms still had equity challenges. Law and policy practices related to the autonomy of prosperity have tended to turn on debates over the respective roles of state planning and markets.[182] All of this may change in the wake of Xi Jinping's common prosperity policy, which has emphasized greater reliance on local micro-data in measurement of prosperity, support for state-led distribution, and reduction in market autonomy, but which also faces fiscal constraints, obstacles to growth, and bureaucratic incapacity.[183]

Attending to Prosperity in China's Climate Change Response

China's responses to climate change have included practical resistance to international standards through alternative law and policy practices related to measurement, distribution, and autonomy of prosperity. As discussed in Chapter 1, law and policy practices related to measurement of prosperity involve choices between reliance on macro-indicators like GDP growth rates, income gains, wealth, and the like, and reference to micro-indicators on quality-of-life impacts. Law and policy practices related to distribution of prosperity involve choices between prioritizing business firms with the expectation that society will also benefit and allocating benefits of prosperity directly to individuals and groups in society. Law and policy practices related to autonomy of prosperity involve questions as to whether the conduct of economic actors should be subject primarily to market conditions or to regulation by the state. Each of these is evident in China's responses to the climate change crisis.

Measurement of Prosperity: Reliance on Macro- and Micro-Indicators

As a component of the regime's prosperity agenda, China's climate change policies revealed varying degrees of reliance on macro- and micro-indicators in measuring policy effects. In the context of China's responses to climate change, reliance on micro-data is essential to reveal the diverse dimensions of its climate change policies and their impacts on local society and economy, as well as to illuminate the content and origins of changing popular attitudes about climate change.[184] As Yasheng Huang and others have noted, reliance on PRC macro-economic data is often inadequate to capture the details of local socio-economic conditions.[185] Yet micro-data on local socio-economic conditions remains difficult to access for both Chinese and foreign scholars, further increasing reliance on macro-data.[186]

Reliance on macro-indicators in the measurement of economic and social development has been a consistent feature in China's Five-Year Plans. The 12th FYP highlighted climate change as a factor in China's development, but like the 11th FYP, relied nearly entirely on national and regional macro-data in measuring both past achievements and future plans.[187] Aside from depicting its "main economic and social development indicators" in terms of aggregated national data, the 13th FYP[188] presented a range of ambitious goals for "environmental governance and protection initiatives" applied at both the national and regional levels and dependent on aggregate data to measure both the scope of each goal and the indicators of success (Chapter 44, box 17, in the 13th FYP). Similarly, the 13th FYP's depiction of "economical, intensive, and circular resource use initiatives" relied on national measures for energy conservation (Chapter 43, box 16). While reliance on macro-indicators may be tempered somewhat in light of contending political and policy priorities regarding local socio-economic development,[189] the Five-Year Plans nonetheless reveal a consistent orientation toward reliance on aggregated national and regional data over localized micro-data.

Similarly, other climate change policy documents have relied on aggregated national and regional indicators over localized micro-data. China's first national program for climate change adaptation, issued by the NDRC in June 2007, presented aggregate macro-data on national and regional impacts of climate change in China.[190] China's national assessment reports on climate change present aggregate macro-data on national and regional impacts of climate change in the country.[191] Successive reports on different aspects of China's climate change policy have similarly relied on aggregate national and regional macro-data.[192] The 2011 white paper on climate change called for "enhancing statistical and accounting capabilities."[193] This placed primary emphasis on establishing record-keeping facilities at the national and regional levels, signalling recognition of the importance of measurement but still focused on aggregated national and regional macro-data rather than locally informed micro-data. The NDRC's 2013 National Climate Change Adaptation Strategy and 2014 national climate change plan presented national goals measured by aggregated national macro-data, to be implemented at the regional and local levels.[194]

In anticipation of the COP21 meetings in Paris in December 2015, China's NDC submission to the UNFCCC process contained national aggregate commitments on reducing carbon dioxide emissions per unit of GDP, increasing the share of non-fossil fuels in primary energy consumption, and increasing forestation.[195] As well, China's 2015 NDC submission provided aggregate national data installed capacity for hydro, wind, solar, and nuclear power. The document also included commitments to achieve carbon peaking by around 2030, lower CO_2 emissions per unit of GDP to 60–65 percent from 2005 levels, increase the share of non-fossil fuels in primary energy production to around 20 percent, and increase forest stock by 4.5 billion cubic metres over 2005 levels. The NDC commitments included national and regional strategies on climate change, calling for enhanced support for science and technology research and improved statistical and accounting systems for greenhouse gas emissions. All of these measures emphasized reliance on national and regional aggregate data.

China's 2021 NDC submission for the COP26 meetings in Glasgow contained similar emphasis on aggregate macro-data.[196] The submission reviewed China's efforts to improve its institutional system for climate change, including integration with economic and social development planning; progress in controlling GHG emissions; proactive adaptation to climate change in part through implementation of the 2013 National Climate Change Adaptation Strategy; and systemic supports such as a GHG emissions statistics system, funding and policy support, technological support, and social participation. In all these areas, depictions of climate change conditions and changes relied on macro-indicators such as provincial and municipal climate measures and aggregated national and regional data. China's 2021 NDC submission also highlighted national statistics on China's installed capacity of non-fossil fuel energy in 2015–19 (Figure 2 in the submission) and China's renewable energy investment for 2015–19 (Figure 3). The same section presented a case study on clean energy development in Qinghai, which was bolstered by aggregate provincial data on installed capacity and electricity generation, along with national aggregate data on coal consumption and emissions reductions (Figure 4). This pattern of depicting local conditions by reference to aggregate national and regional data continues through section on controlling GHG emissions (Section II.II). References in China's climate change policy guidance to people's livelihoods and well-being are couched in general terms that underscore the focus of China's climate policy statements on macro-indicators based on aggregate national and regional data.

Measurement indicators in China's climate change policies were also evident in the MEE's 2019 and 2021 reports on China's climate change response.[197] As had the 2011 white paper, both the 2019 and 2021 MEE reports called for strengthening statistical reporting on emissions focused on macro-indicators of aggregate national and regional data on climate policies and practices, while also calling for more local measures to mitigate and adapt to climate change. The MEE's January 2021 "Guiding Opinions" on climate action also called for more attention to implementing local regulatory and policy enactments.[198] Yet such attention to local implementation remained informed by aggregated national and regional macro-data. Paralleling the 2021 NDC report for the COP26 meetings in Glasgow, the SCIO issued a new climate white paper in October 2021.[199] Despite references to Xi Jinping's new development discourse calling for greater attention to local human conditions, the white paper focused on aggregated macro-data on climate measures in state economic planning, and national targets such as CO_2 emissions, carbon intensity, and energy consumption. The white paper continued the focus of earlier climate policies on industrial restructuring and expansion of efforts at energy conservation and efficiency, reinforcing the SCIO's 2020 white paper on "Energy in China's New Era," which had relied on aggregate macro-data on energy intensity (consumption per unit of GDP), as well as on social issues like household electricity consumption.[200]

Reliance on macro-indicators was also prevalent in the NDRC's Working Guidance and Action Plan on CO_2 peaking and neutrality issued in anticipation of the COP26 meetings. Both documents were linked with the 14th FYP (2021–25), prepared under the NDRC's direction. The Working Guidance emphasized the importance of integrating CO_2 peaking and carbon neutrality goals into economic and social development plans.[201] The document called for nationwide planning that includes a "whole-of-nation" approach, including "top-level design" to be implemented by CPC and government agencies with allowances for local adaptation, along with efforts to strengthen national standards for statistical monitoring. The NDRC's Action Plan on CO_2 peaking echoed many of the provisions of the Working Guidance, including prioritizing a national, whole-of-nation approach involving top-level design and local implementation.[202] While both the Working Guidance and the Action Plan acknowledged the role of local policy adaptation in implementation of national carbon emissions standards, measurement of climate conditions and responsive efforts relied on aggregated macro-indicators. These priorities continued in the NDRC's 2023 report to the 14th National People's Congress, with its emphasis on "big data" (pages 29 and 46), although implied attention to localized micro-data was evident in the report's call for cracking down on data fraud on carbon emissions (page 64).[203]

Xi Jinping's "new development" discourse may come to support broader reliance on micro-data to determine the impacts of climate change and the content and effect of China's policy response. In presenting policies of new development, Xi questioned reliance on macro-data:

> At a meeting of the Standing Committee of the Central Committee Political Bureau on April 25, 2013, I stressed that local governments should not take national regulatory targets as the baseline for local economic development, nor should they compete with each other to have higher growth rates. I said that we needed to shift the focus to improving the quality and returns of economic growth, to promoting sustained and healthy economic development, and to pursuing genuine rather than inflated GDP growth and achieving high-quality, efficient, and sustainable development.[204]

The new development discourse has seen greater attention to local case studies on climate change, raising the prospect of greater inclusion of local data. Thus, localized case studies on such matters as water conservation in the Yangtze region, forestry practices in Yunnan, grasslands agriculture in Lanzhou and Inner Mongolia, and the Tibet Qinghai Plateau in the14th FYP (Chapter 37.3, Table 14, Chapter 38.4), and carbon intensity reduction targets, carbon markets, and energy conservation in Sichuan, Qinghai, and Beijing-Tianjin-Hebei in China's 2021 COP26 NDC submission (Sections 1.3, 1.4, 2.2) permit consideration of localized data. Aggregated regional data remained the norm for these local case studies, however, even while inviting appreciation of the need for micro-data to depict the impacts of climate change and policy responses on such matters as gender, income level, education, ethnicity, and so on.

Possibilities for such inter-sectoral analysis were evident as well in China's 2021 *Blue Book on Climate Change.*[205] Attention to micro-indicators of prosperity was evident in the Ministry of Finance and State Taxation Administration announcement of August 2023 offering a series of tax policies aimed at supporting micro and small enterprises.[206] As China's climate change policies come to extol a "people-centred" approach, the need for localized micro-data to depict local conditions and socio-economic impacts may come to be accepted more fully.

PRC law and policy practices related to measurement of prosperity contrast with international standards. The United Nations' 2030 Agenda for Sustainable Development (associated with the United Nations Millennium Development Goals) confirms that "quality, accessible, timely and reliable disaggregated data will be needed to help with the measurement of progress and to ensure that no one is left behind."[207] This suggests tensions with China's approach to measuring prosperity.

Distribution of Prosperity: Reliance on Businesses/Civic Actors

China's 2015 NDC submission for COP21 in Paris expressed strong support for implementing climate change policies through incentives for businesses.[208] Section II.K called for increasing financial and policy support through, among other things, exploring new investment and financing mechanisms for enterprises pursuing low-carbon development. Similarly, the NDRC's 2013 National Climate Change Adaptation Strategy[209] called for implementation and improvement in relevant preferential tax policies, and encourages all kinds of market entities to participate in adaptation action (Section 5.3.1). The strategy also called for creation of climate financial markets and development of climate-related service products. (Section 5.3.2). The NDRC's subsequent National Plan on Adaptation to Climate Change (2014–2020)[210] focused on national and regional governmental activities and directives, including the development of "public-private-partnerships" and private sector funding for climate change efforts. The plan called for preferential tax policies and investment subsidies to encourage enterprises with advanced low-carbon technologies to enter the infrastructure and public utilities fields. In each of these pronouncements, economic enterprises were to serve as the primary mechanism for distributing benefits – even when subsidizing consumers (whether individuals and enterprises). Many of the proposals have been implemented, as the banking industry has opened new businesses to promote the green and low-carbon development of entity enterprise, and the steel and energy industries have pursued green transformation and low-carbon development.[211] The emphasis on economic enterprises was also evident in the MEE's 2019 report on China's climate change policies and actions, which noted the provision of quota-based subsidies to enterprises that eliminate hydrofluorocarbons – a major GHG and climate change agent.[212]

Incentivizing enterprises to bring about reform has extended to environmental protection. The joint opinion of the 2018 CPC Central Committee and the State Council on controlling pollution specified the main responsibility of enterprises in environmental governance:

> Promoting co-governance among the whole people. The government, enterprises and the public each do their part and work together; the government actively plays a leading role, enterprises take the initiative to assume the main responsibility for environmental governance, and the public consciously practices green life.[213]

China's white paper on energy issued in December 2020 focused on technology and innovation by enterprises as potential solutions to China's green energy needs under an energy security strategy focused on constraining consumption through reform of the industrial structure.[214]

China's NDC submission for COP26 identified the energy and transportation sectors as receiving climate change subsidies.[215] Financial institutions were to be supported in providing green financing for authorized projects under China's "Guiding Catalogue of Green Industries," and were encouraged to develop green mortgage and guarantee methods and a variety of forms of green credit for business development. Government supports for transforming the energy, industrial production, urban and rural construction, transportation, and agricultural sectors away from carbon reliance are pursued through business regulation. Market-based mechanisms such as carbon trading are also emphasized. The NDC's reliance on distribution of climate change benefits through businesses included finance measures (Section III.3):

> China will promote the development of green low-carbon financial products and services in an orderly manner, prepare monetary policy tools for carbon emission reduction, incorporate green credit into the macro-prudential assessment framework, and guide the banking industry and other financial institutions to provide long-term, low-cost funding for green and low-carbon projects.

The general emphasis of China's climate change policy on the role of business enterprises limited the attention given to social benefits. When China's 2011 climate change white paper suggested that climate change policies would improve people's lives, the benefit was presented as largely indirect:

> During the 11th Five-Year Plan period, China strengthened scientific research in and impact evaluation of climate change, improved relevant laws and policies, and enhanced the capability of key sectors to adapt to climate change, so as to reduce the negative impact of climate change on economic and social development and people's lives.[216]

The State Council's 2011 National Environmental Protection Plan[217] also presented social benefits as indirect outcomes:

> Gradually realize the equalization of basic public services for environmental protection, safeguard the environmental rights and interests of the people, and promote social harmony and stability. (Section II.2, Basic Principles)

Similarly, the NDRC's 2013 National Climate Change Adaptation Strategy reiterated the focus on indirect effects of climate change on society:

> Vigorously promote the construction of ecological civilization, adhere to the people-oriented approach, strengthen scientific and technological support, incorporate the requirements of adapting to climate change into the whole process of China's economic and social development, coordinate and strengthen the adaptation actions of climate-sensitive and fragile areas, regions and groups of people, and comprehensively enhance the awareness of adaptation and the ability of the whole society to adapt. Effectively safeguard public safety, industrial safety, ecological security, and people's production and life security.[218]

China's 2015 NDC submission to COP21 acknowledged the importance of climate change policy for people's livelihoods, but again as a component of the broader benefits of mitigation and adaptation efforts:

> To act on climate change in terms of mitigating greenhouse gas emissions and enhancing climate resilience is driven by China's domestic needs for sustainable development in ensuring its economic security, energy security, ecological security, food security as well as the safety of people's life and property and to achieve sustainable development, but also to deepen participation in global governance, build a community with a shared future for mankind, and promote the common development of all mankind.[219]

While preferences for distribution of prosperity to businesses through subsidies, tax credits and deductions, rebates, and other benefits offer important avenues for climate change mitigation and adaptation, such measures represent a missed opportunity to distribute climate change incentives to individual members of society. With the emergence of the common prosperity policy, official guidance on China's climate change efforts has focused increasingly on more direct benefits for people.[220] The MEE's 2019 report on China's policies and actions on climate change also emphasized the link between climate change policy and the broader goals of economic development and improving people's livelihoods.[221] The SCIO's 2020 white paper on energy emphasized "putting people first" as a guiding principle, and included in its depiction of China's historic achievements a reference to providing "Solid Benefits for People's Lives."[222] In the wake of common prosperity discourse, the SCIO's 2021 white paper on climate change highlighted more specific benefits to individuals and groups in society:

> Taking into full consideration the people's aspiration for a better life, their expectation of a sound eco-environment, and their responsibility for future generations, China is pioneering a new approach that synergizes the efforts to fight climate change, develop the economy, generate employment, eliminate poverty, and protect the environment. It guarantees and improves people's wellbeing through development, strives for social equity and justice in the process of green transition, and increases people's sense of gain, happiness and security. (Section I.3)[223]

China's 2021 NDC submission to COP26 reiterated the linkage between climate change policy and improving people's lives:

> Adhering to a people-centered approach, China will move faster to cultivate green and low-carbon new drivers, establish a sound economic structure for green, low-carbon and circular development, accelerate the construction of a clean, low-carbon and efficient energy sector while ensuring energy security, and encourage simple, moderate, green and low-carbon ways of life. (Introduction, page 2)[224]

Thus, the tension between distribution to economic enterprises or to social actors remains a key feature of China's climate change response. The common prosperity policy may have the effect of encouraging more direct distribution of climate change policy benefits to individuals and groups in society. Whether such efforts and the expectations surrounding the need for direct social benefits from climate change policy continue remains to be seen. The NDRC's 2022 report to the 14th National People's Congress, for example, extolled the role of enterprises and businesses in leading China's development, in the expectation that this would benefit people's lives but with little in the way of direct transfers to civic individuals and groups.[225]

China's law and policy practice related to the distribution of prosperity stands in comparison with international standards. The liberal international order places significant emphasis on distributing climate change subsidies to individuals and civic groups.[226] The UN Guiding Principles on Business and Human Rights suggests that business interests often conflict with protection of individual human rights: "States' international human rights law obligations require that they respect, protect and fulfil the human rights of individuals within their territory and/or jurisdiction. This includes the duty to protect against human rights abuse by third parties, including business enterprises."[227] This emphasis on civic over corporate channels for distribution of prosperity contrasts with PRC preferences for distribution through business entities.

Autonomy of Prosperity: From State/Market

The call for greater reliance on market forces at the 2014 3rd Plenum of the 18th CPC Congress had a significant impact on China's development policies.[228] Yet the long-term implementation of its market-oriented policies has been uneven – caught between the ideals and expectations of their market nomenclature and the challenging reality of their implementation under Party control.[229] Whereas China's 11th and 12th FYPs (covering 2006–10 and 2011–15, respectively) had included mention of market forces,[230] the 13th FYP (2016–20)[231] reflected more completely a new focus on market-oriented development, containing some eighty-seven references to the market and calling in particular for greater reliance on market forces in energy consumption (Chapter 43, Section 7). China's 14th FYP (2021–26),[232] promoted market-oriented policies across a wide range of sectors, including technology and innovation (Section 4), manufacturing (Section 8.4), service (Section 10), infrastructure (Section 11.1), and oil and gas exploration and development (Section 11.3), yet omitted reference to market forces in the specific context of climate change (Section 38.4). The omission was underscored by the preceding section on compensation for ecological protection (Section 38.3), which called for marketization and diversification, while the succeeding section on environmental governance (Section 38.5) called for "marketized trading of pollutant discharge rights, energy use rights, water rights, and carbon emission rights." The FYP also called for markets to support a "market-oriented green technology innovation system," which would include climate change initiatives (Section 39.3).

Aside from the Five-Year Plans, the call for greater reliance on market forces has been evident in climate change policy guidance. The 2011 climate change white paper[233] called for promoting energy conservation through market mechanisms (Section 1.2), while also promoting the "circular economy" through recycling technologies and the market mechanism (Section VII.2.5). The white paper also noted China's efforts to develop a carbon emissions trading market (Section VII.2.7). Similarly, the 2011 National Environmental Protection Plan[234] supported efforts to explore the use of market-oriented means to promote environmental protection (Section 2.2). The plan also called for reliance on market mechanisms in investment projects aiming to fulfill the environmental protection goals of the 12th FYP (Section 7), and called for "professionalization, socialization and marketization of the construction and operation of pollution facilities" (Section 8.6). The plan supported reliance on market-oriented financing mechanisms to promote environmental protection (Section 8.7).

The NDRC's 2013 National Climate Change Adaptation Strategy called for market entities to participate in climate change adaptation action, including financial markets and development of climate-related service products.[235] The strategy called for tax policy reform that would encourage all kinds of market entities to participate in adaptive action (Section 3.1), while also calling for greater participation by financial markets through bonds, insurance, and other measures (Section 3.2). Similarly, the NDRC's National Plan on Adaptation to Climate Change (2014–2020)[236] noted that China's market mechanisms for climate change adaptation needed to be strengthened (*shichanghua jizhi xuyao jinyibu qianghua* // 市场化机制需要进一步强化) (Section I.2). The plan called for reliance on market mechanisms to support technology and innovation on climate change adaptation (Section II.1). The plan devoted considerable attention to the development of carbon emissions trading markets (Chapters II.2, VII.2). Price reforms were encouraged to reflect resource scarcity, market supply and demand, and environmental costs (Section VII.4). Echoing these provisions, the SCIO's 2020 energy white paper called for greater reliance on market forces in the course of deepening reform of the energy system.[237] The SCIO's 2021 white paper on climate policies and actions issued in anticipation of the COP26 meetings emphasized the role of carbon emissions trading markets.[238] China's NDC submission to COP26 promoted its reliance on market mechanisms in the development of carbon emissions trading markets (Section II.1.4); using market mechanisms to support low-carbon development, financial support for climate change mitigation efforts, and innovation in climate change investment and financing (Section II.4.2); and reliance on market-oriented and legal principles in policy-oriented financial institutions (Section III.2.III).[239]

In light of the emerging policy of common prosperity, emphasis on market-oriented policies has changed somewhat. A 2018 Central Committee/State Council opinion on pollution controls noted the role of market forces in only three areas – green technology, carbon trading, and enabling of market actors.[240] The MEE's 2019 summary report contained only limited references to reliance on market forces, confining its treatment of markets mainly to the issue of developing China's carbon emissions trading market.[241] Similarly, the MEE "Guiding Opinions" on climate action issued in January 2021[242] contained but five references to market forces, three of which involved carbon emissions trading, while the others were heavily qualified – touching on "gradually" expanding market coverage in energy and building "relevant" market mechanisms.

This presented a challenge for the NDRC, which has long been associated with market mechanisms in climate change policy even while bearing responsibility for issuing China's FYPs. Born of the former State Planning Commission combined with the State Council's Economic Reform Commission (*Tigaiwei* // 体改委), the NDRC was established to further market-oriented reforms under Premier Zhao Ziyang.[243] While noting the role of the various FYPs for which it has responsibility (referred to directly or by reference to "overall planning"), the NDRC expressed support for increased reliance on markets in its 2013/2014 National Climate Change Adaptation Strategy and action plan:

> <u>2013 National Climate Change Adaptation Strategy</u>
> Implement and improve relevant preferential tax policies, and encourage all kinds of market entities to participate with adaptive action ... Promote the construction of climate financial markets and encourage the development of climate-related service products. (Section V.3)[244]

> <u>2014 National Plan on Adaptation to Climate Change</u>
> Relevant fiscal and taxation, investment, price, and financial policies and mechanisms need to be further innovated, the market-oriented mechanism needs to be further strengthened. (Section I.2.2)[245]

Yet in the wake of common prosperity, the NDRC has come to revisit the function of government in the market-oriented pronouncements of the 3rd Plenum of the 18th CPC Congress in its Working Guidance on CO_2 peaking and carbon neutrality, and its Action Plan on carbon neutrality:

> 2021 Working Guidance
>
> Leveraging the strengths of the government and the market. Both the government and the market have an important role to play. (Section I.2)[246]
>
> 2021 Action Plan
>
> We will give better play to the role of the government by building a new system for mobilizing the nation, and give full play to the role of the market. (Section I.2)[247]

The NDRC's 2023 report to the 14th National People's Congress called for market-oriented approaches to supporting green technology innovation (page 20), but prefaced this by presenting multiple references to market reforms in terms of state oversight over competition, market access, breaking monopolies, and financial supervision (pages 11–12). Much of this was tied to fealty to Xi Jinping. The 14th FYP's "guiding ideology" extolled the importance of Xi Jinping's "new development philosophy" (Chapter I.2), with its emphasis on people-centred development. Acceptance of Xi's leadership was expressed even more fulsomely in the NDRC's "Working Guidance" and "Action Plan" on CO_2 peaking and carbon neutrality issued in anticipation of COP26, both of which used identical language in Section I.1:

> We must follow the guidance of Xi Jinping Thought on Socialism with Chinese Characteristics for a New Era, fully implement the guiding principles from the 19th CPC National Congress and the second through fifth plenary sessions of the 19th CPC Central Committee, and thoroughly apply Xi Jinping's thought on ecological civilization.

Thus, China's law and policy practice on autonomy of prosperity through climate change measures saw an initial emphasis on market forces following the 3rd Plenum of the 18th CPC Congress give way somewhat to renewed support for state planning and regulation under the common prosperity policy. As has been the case for most of the PRC's economic history, the tension between reliance on state plans and protection of market disciplines has been an ongoing feature of the country's prosperity policies in the wake of climate change. This seems unlikely to change in the near term as the bureaucratic interests aligned with policies giving primacy to planning and/or markets remain largely unmoved by political arguments and socio-economic interests aligned with their opponents.

PRC law and policy practice related to autonomy of prosperity from state control or market discipline, respectively, operate in the context of international standards. Reliance on market forces has been a salient feature of the rules-based international order.[248] Nonetheless, the Paris Agreement called for greater reliance on non-market measures:

> 8. Parties recognize the importance of integrated, holistic and balanced non-market approaches being available to Parties to assist in the implementation of their nationally determined contributions, in the context of sustainable development and poverty eradication, in a coordinated and effective manner, including through, inter alia, mitigation, adaptation, finance, technology transfer and capacity-building, as appropriate. These approaches shall aim to:
>
> a) Promote mitigation and adaptation ambition;
> b) Enhance public and private sector participation in the implementation of nationally determined contributions; and
> c) Enable opportunities for coordination across instruments and relevant institutional arrangements.[249]

The Paris Agreement's support for non-market measures suggested a middle path between favouring state oversight and protecting market discipline. The balancing of state control and market discipline, a key feature of China's economic development policies over the past decades, has particular application in PRC responses to climate change.

THUS, CHINA'S LAW and policy practices related to climate change showed general preferences for reliance on aggregated macro-data in measurement of prosperity, distribution of prosperity through business enterprises with indirect benefits for society, and autonomy from state intrusion through greater reliance on market forces. Appendix 4A (page 141) depicts the dominant features of key documents related to China's response to climate change in the context of dimensions of economic prosperity. With the introduction of the common prosperity policy and the broader new development discourse, greater attention has been paid to reliance on micro-data, direct benefits to society, and more autonomy from market forces through state planning, although the long-term viability of this policy remains unclear.

PRC law and policy practice related to operational norms of measurement, distribution, and autonomy of prosperity in response to climate change revealed a mix of commonality and difference with international standards. PRC law and policy practice related to measurement of prosperity has tended toward preference for reliance on national and regional macro-data over localized measurements. Distribution of prosperity has tended to favour business enterprises, with presumed indirect benefits for society at large rather than direct allocations to individuals and groups in society. These two areas of law and policy practice contrast with the standards associated with the rules-based international order (particularly the United Nations' 2030 Agenda for Sustainable Development and the UN Guiding Principles on Business and Human Rights), which tend to favour reliance on local disaggregated micro-data and express caution about reliance on distribution to business enterprises. PRC law and policy practice related to autonomy of prosperity has been more consistent with international standards expressed in the Paris Agreement with respect to balancing the respective roles of markets and state controls, although this depends somewhat on the long-term viability of the common prosperity and new development discourse.

Aside from their substantive comparisons with corresponding international law standards, PRC prosperity practices have been in tension with

TABLE 5 Prosperity: Comparing China standards with rules-based international order standards

	Measurement of prosperity	Distribution of prosperity	Autonomy of prosperity	Climate change performance ranking[1]
China standards	Macro-indicators with recent attention to micro-data	Business enterprises and social benefit	From market discipline and state controls	55/63+EU
RBIO standards	Local disaggregated indicators	Civic individuals and groups	From state controls and from market discipline	N/A

1 Climate Change Performance Index, "China," https://ccpi.org/country/chn/.

international ideals on equality and complexity. As suggested in Chapter 1 and illustrated in Figure 4, international standards on measurement of prosperity through reliance on micro-data, distribution through civic entities, and autonomy from state control reflect policy orientations supporting equality and accepting diversity. These contrast with the acceptance of inequality and resistance to complexity bound up in China's approaches favouring reliance on macro-data in measurement, business entities in distribution, and autonomy from market disciplines. Ironically, while China's opposition to elites and embrace of grievance ideology spoke to resentments over inequality, the PRC's law and policy practices related to the measurement, distribution, and autonomy of prosperity often accepted standards of inequality. Initial contrasts and conflicts, however, have recently been tempered by the new development discourse and policies around common prosperity. Table 5 summarizes contrasts between China's prosperity standards and those associated with the rules-based international order.

Rhetorical Markers of China's Globalized Populism in Response to Climate Change

China's responses to climate change include rhetorical markers on sovereignty, development, and human rights. These link China's responses to climate change with tensions between PRC policy priorities and international standards, while providing resilience for the PRC's globalized populism.

Sovereignty: Safeguarding China's Climate Change Policies

Expressing opposition to elites, China has relied on an expanded discourse of national sovereignty as a basis for resisting imposition of international standards on climate change.[250] Xi Jinping has repeatedly emphasized that China's climate change measures should not be done at the request of others, but on China's own initiative.[251] China's 2021 report on Nationally Determined Contributions under the UNFCCC COP process underscored the autonomy of the state in implementing international climate change standards as a national priority:

> China implements a national strategy to actively respond to climate change, and regards the implementation of its nationally determined contributions as its responsibility to promote the building of a community with a shared future for mankind, and as an important starting point for the construction of ecological civilization and the realization of high-quality development.[252]

Ministry of Foreign Affairs spokesperson Zhao Lijian's depiction of independent efforts on climate change reflected presumptions about China's sovereignty as an independent state:

> China has always been a contributor to global climate governance, a leader in the construction of global ecological civilization, and a doer in the implementation of the Paris Agreement ... As the largest developing country in the world, China will achieve carbon neutrality from the peak of carbon emissions in the shortest possible time, which fully demonstrates China's responsibility as a major country ... In the future, China will continue to independently increase its climate action and make greater contributions to the global response to climate change.[253]

China's participation in the UNFCCC process has underscored its state sovereignty as a precondition for engagement with the international climate policy community.[254] The UNFCCC endorsed state sovereignty as a key principle for climate change efforts: "*Reaffirming* the principle of sovereignty of States in international cooperation to address climate change."[255] China's ongoing discussions with the European Union reflected PRC state sovereignty as a condition for international cooperation on emissions:

> Both sides reaffirmed their commitment to multilateralism and the rules-based international order with the United Nations at its core, and to uphold the UN Charter and international law, including the principles of sovereignty, territorial integrity and inviolability of borders.[256]

Similarly, China's opposition to a request by small island states for an advisory opinion on states' duties on climate change under the International Tribunal for the Law of the Sea (ITLOS) reflected concern that such advisory opinions might jeopardize China's sovereignty over regulation of CO_2 emissions standards, not to mention its territorial claims in the South China Sea.[257]

The marker of sovereignty has also been also evident in law and policy practice protecting autonomy of prosperity from market forces. Sovereignty is intrinsically bound up in state policies on planning and markets, such that reliance on market forces diminishes the control of the state over economic activities and hence stands as a challenge to regime sovereignty. PRC sovereignty claims have reflected China's assertions of state power over the role of planning and markets in coordinating economic policy and climate change measures. Under conditions where international standards vary between emphasizing market disciplines and calling for greater attention to non-market forces, China's rhetorical marker on sovereignty provides resilience for the PRC regime's alternative standards on the relative roles of state regulation and market discipline in responding to climate change.

Development: Justifying China's Climate Change Response

Linked with populist themes of grievance, the rhetorical marker on development serves to justify and lend resilience to China's populist responses to the climate change crisis. Assertions that local development conditions are relevant to both causes of and remedies for climate change generally have been expanded to explain China's climate policies in terms of its own development conditions. The element of grievance extended to the international climate policy system's purported disregard for China's conditions of development. In response to early efforts to combat climate change driven largely by developed economies in Europe and North America, China has consistently held to the view that climate change was the responsibility of advanced industrial economies whose responses should not impinge on poorer countries' right to development.[258]

Assertions about "common but differentiated responsibilities" and collaboration with the Like-Minded Developing Countries group have highlighted the importance of development in China's climate change response. Such views have characterized China's response to international standards on climate change.

> Calling the principle of common but differentiated responsibilities "the cornerstone of global climate governance," [Xi Jinping] said that developed countries need to increase climate ambition and action and make concrete efforts to help developing countries strengthen their capacity and resilience against climate change. Xi urged developed countries to support developing countries in financing, technology and capacity building, and refrain from creating green trade barriers ... "The historical responsibility, development stage, and coping capacity of developed and developing countries are different, and that's why the principle of common but differentiated responsibilities should always be followed," said Xu Huaqing, director of the National Center for Climate Change Strategy and International Cooperation.[259]

Development priorities have also been evident in regime reliance on traditional state-centred economic actors in the distribution of climate change benefits. As discussed above, China's development policies have long emphasized the role of first state-run, then state-owned, and finally quasi-private enterprises as vehicles for distribution of the benefits of development. This has been present in climate policy as well. China's 2021 NDC report noted the integration of climate change with China's social and economic development:

> Both plans [13th FYP (2016) and 14th FYP (2021) state social and economic development plans] have special chapters on energy conservation, emission reduction, and climate change response. In 2016, the State Council promulgated the 13th Five-Year Plan for Energy Conservation and Emission Reduction and the 13th Five-Year Plan for Controlling Greenhouse Gas Emissions. It clarifies the goals, tasks, requirements and division of labor of various departments for energy conservation, emission reduction and control of greenhouse gas emissions. In key areas of energy consumption and carbon emissions, provincial-level local governments have also prepared relevant plans to deploy and implement goals and tasks for energy conservation, emission reduction, and climate change.[260]

The NDRC's 2021 Working Guidance on emissions called for integrating climate measures with economic and social development goals:

> Through the application of systematic thinking, we will strike a balance between development and emissions reduction, between overall and local imperatives, and between short-term and longer-term considerations. Endeavors to peak carbon dioxide emissions and achieve carbon neutrality must be incorporated into the overall economic and social development framework.[261]

The MEE's 2019 climate change report drew similar linkages:

> The Chinese government has always attached great importance to addressing climate change ... It is not only the internal needs to achieve sustainable development but also the due responsibility to promote the development of the community with a shared future for mankind. At the National Conference on Ecological and Environmental Protection, President Xi Jinping

> clearly proposed that we would implement a national strategy for actively addressing climate change.[262]

Links between climate change and development support regime preferences for distribution of development benefits through businesses and enterprises rather than civic individuals and groups, despite international standards favouring the latter. China's NDC submissions to the UNFCCC system in 2015 and 2021 emphasized the role of businesses and enterprises in implementing climate goals and as recipients of government support in this effort.[263] China's national climate change plan (2014–20) similarly underscored the role of private sector partnerships and funding in combatting climate change.[264] While the new development discourse and policies of common prosperity may see emergence of people-centred measures, the long-term effects remain uncertain. Whatever the outcome, the rhetorical marker of development and its linkage with grievance ideology offer a measure of resilience to China's climate change response.

Human Rights: Contending Priorities on People and Development
China's responses to climate change have also resonated with the rhetorical marker on human rights as an element of practical resistance against international standards. Early on, China's resistance to international calls for emissions reductions relied on human rights in food and health as grounds for PRC policy.[265] As well, China has consistently asserted that the human rights are subject to the priority of the right to development:

> China has always taken development as the foundation for human rights and has ensured more effectively the rights to subsistence and development for our people. We have eradicated absolute poverty, once and for all, on our land. We have met the target of poverty reduction set out in the United Nations 2030 Agenda for Sustainable Development 10 years ahead of schedule. We, the over 1.4 billion Chinese people, have achieved moderate prosperity in all respects. We have established the world's largest education, social security, and health care systems. All our people now enjoy more equal access to more fruits and benefits of development.[266]

The SCIO's 2021 white paper on moderate prosperity extolled China's achievement of moderate prosperity as a human rights achievement, in which eco-environmental progress such as protection from climate change are subject to coordination and possible diminution in favour of other rights:

> A moderately prosperous society emphasizes economic, political, cultural, social, and eco-environmental progress to benefit the people. It upholds the basic principle of interdependence and indivisibility of human rights. To advance all human rights and fundamental freedoms in all respects, it protects economic, social, and cultural rights, political and democratic rights, personal rights, personality rights, and property rights.[267]

Yet China has been slow to formally recognize human rights in environmental and climate protection, abstaining from the 2022 UN General Assembly resolution on human rights in the environment.[268] China's submission to COP26 focusing on people-centred policies spoke to the patrimonial dynamic of state responsibility *for* the people rather than the rights-oriented perspective of responsibility *to* them.[269]

Human rights issues have been evident in law and policy practice related to measurement of prosperity in the course of efforts to combat climate change.[270] The NDRC's various Five-Year Plans have consistently emphasized aggregated national data over localized reporting. Similarly, the NDRC's 2007 National Plan on Adaptation to Climate Change emphasized national over local data. While the UNFCCC process for Nationally Determined Contributions might be expected to generate a focus on national data, increased calls for reliance on Regionally and Locally Determined Contributions (RLDCs) pointed to the importance of localized micro-data.[271] Yet China's submissions have been more uniformly oriented toward reliance on aggregated national macro-data. While the MEE's policy reporting and action have been more attentive to local conditions, it has remained constrained by the overarching influence of the NDRC. Reliance on localized data may come further to the fore under Xi Jinping's new development discourse, but this remains to be seen. As well, distribution of prosperity through business enterprises rather than civic groups reflected the regime's human rights priorities in collective over individual rights. Human rights have also been implicated in PRC law and policy practice related to autonomy of prosperity, as this involves the extent of – or limits to – state control over economic actors. In the face of tensions with international standards, China's rhetorical marker on human rights shields the PRC regime's human rights conduct from international criticism, contributing to resilience for China's climate change responses on prosperity.

Thus, China's relationship with the international climate policy system has included rhetorical markers of sovereignty, development, and human rights linking general populist features of anti-elitism, grievance, and practical resistance with China's policy priorities and providing resilience for China's climate change response. The rhetorical marker of sovereignty has been evident in the regime's resistance to imposition of international climate standards, and also in law and policy practice related to autonomy of prosperity leaning toward protecting economic actors from market conditions and disciplines through state controls. The marker of development has been evident in PRC positions on the origins of and remedies for climate change (with associated expressions of grievance), as well as law and policy practices favouring reliance on businesses and enterprises over civic individuals and groups in the distribution of prosperity. The marker of human rights has been evident in China's efforts to prioritize the right to development in climate policy, and also in law and policy practices prioritizing national and collective interests over local and individual conditions in measuring prosperity in the wake of climate change. These rhetorical markers of China's globalized populism underscored tensions between China's policy preferences and the standards of the rules-based international order while providing resilience for China's climate change response. The resilience provided by China's rhetorical markers on sovereignty, development, and human rights for PRC law and policy practice on climate change may impede the possibilities for change, with implications for reform in China's ongoing approaches to economic prosperity generally.

Conclusion

China's responses to the crisis of climate change have involved responses to conditions of inequality and complexity in China's relationship the international climate policy system. China has expressed populist opposition to global elites by challenging the standards and processes of this system. It has expressed themes of grievance ideology in challenging the purported disregard by the international climate policy system of the disparate levels of responsibility for the climate crisis by developed and developing economies. China has pursued practical resistance through alternative law and policy practices related to measurement, distribution, and autonomy of prosperity. China's climate change law and policy practices related to measurement of prosperity have tended toward reliance on macro-data, in comparison with international standards favouring attention to local conditions. PRC law and policy practices related to distribution of prosperity in the course of climate change have tended toward reliance on business enterprises over civic individuals and groups, in comparison with international standards cautioning against abuses of corporate power and privilege. Law and policy practices related to autonomy of prosperity in the context of climate change response have suggested greater reliance on market forces, reflecting the influence of international standards. These policy features may change as Xi Jinping's new development discourse admits to the need to attend to localized micro data, emphasizes the need for direct distribution of prosperity to society, and allows for greater reliance on state planning and regulation to protect against the vagaries of market conditions. China's climate law and policy practices related to prosperity have resonated in turn with rhetorical markers on sovereignty in resisting international climate standards, development as a condition for China's climate change efforts, and human rights priorities on collective over individual needs. These provide resilience for China's globalized populist responses to climate change. China's conditional participation in international action on climate change has been less antagonistic than its responses to COVID-19, but nonetheless evinced populist resistance to the rules-based international order.

Appendix 4A
PRC Climate Change Policy Documents

Document	Measurement (macro-/ micro-data)[1]	Distribution (business enterprises/civic actors)[2]	Autonomy (state/ market)[3]
NDRC, National Plan on Adaptation to Climate Change, 2007[4]	Macro national/ regional data	• Business enterprises	• Plan – 28 (计划 – 8; 规划 – 20) • Market (市场 – 13)
NDRC, 11th Five-Year Plan, 2006–10[5]	Macro national/ regional data	• Business enterprises (Chapters II and III) • Indirect social benefit (Chapter I)	• Market (市场 – 88) • Plan – 78 (计划 – 17; 规划 – 61)
SCIO, Climate White Paper, 2011 (English)[6]	Macro national/ regional data	• Business enterprises (Sections I.1, I.2) • Indirect social benefit (Foreword, Section II)	• Plan – 63 • Market – 10
State Council, National Environmental Protection "12th Five-Year Plan," 2011[7]	Macro national/ regional data	• Business enterprises (Sections II.2, IV, V) • Indirect social benefit (Section II.2, IV-Box 2)	• Plan – 21 (计划 – 2; 规划 – 19) • Market (市场 – 5)
CPC, Decision of 3rd Plenum of 18th CPC Congress on Deepening Reform, 2014 (English)[8]	Macro national/ regional data	• "Institutions and mechanisms" (Section I.2) • Social benefit through "people first" approach (Section I.4)	• Market – 18 • Plan – 3
NDRC, 12th Five-Year Plan (FYP), 2011–15[9]	Macro national/ regional data	• Business enterprises (Chapters 4, 9) • Indirect social benefit (Chapter 2)	• Market (市场 – 107) • Plan – 97 (计划 – 16; 规划 – 81)
NDRC, National Climate Change Adaptation Strategy, 2013[10]	Macro national/ regional data	• Business (Section 5.3) • Indirect social benefit (Section 2.1)	• Plan – 25 (计划 – 0; 规划 – 25) • Market (市场 – 5)

▸

◄

Document	Measurement (macro-/ micro-data)[1]	Distribution (business enterprises/civic actors)[2]	Autonomy (state/ market)[3]
NDRC, National Plan on Adaptation to Climate Change, 2014[11]	Macro national/ regional data	• Business (Section 2.4) • Indirect social benefits (Preface, Sections II.1, II.3)	• Plan – 52 (计划 – 4; 规划 – 48) • Market (市场 – 28)
NDRC, NDC Submission to COP21 (Paris), 2015[12]	Macro national/ regional data	• Business (Section II.12) • Indirect social benefit (Section I)	• Plan – 12 (计划 – 4; 规划 – 8) • Market – (市场 – 3)
NDRC, 13th FYP, 2016–20 (English)[13]	Macro national/ regional data	• Business enterprises (Chapter 4) • Indirect social benefit (Chapter X)	• Plan – 87 • Market – 87
CPC CC and State Council, Opinion on Environment and Pollution, June 24, 2018[14]	Macro national/ regional data	• Business enterprises (Sections IV.2, V.2.1, X.1) • Indirect social benefit (Introduction, Sections I, II)	• Plan – 19 (计划 – 9; (规划 – 10) • Market (市场 – 3)
MEE, China's Policies and Actions for Addressing Climate Change, 2019 (English)[15]	Macro national/ regional data	• Business (Section III.2) • Indirect social benefit (Foreword)	• Plan – 65 • Market – 24
SCIO, White Paper: Energy in China's New Era, December 2020 (English)[16]	Macro national/ regional data	• Business (Section I, V) • Social benefit from "people first" approach (Sections I.2, II.6)	• Market – 80 • Plan – 42
NDRC, 14th FYP, 2021–26[17]	Macro national/ regional data	• Business (Part III) • Social benefit from "new development concept" (Section II.1)	• Plan – 129 (计划 – 20; 规划 – 109) • Market (市场 – 113)
NDRC, NDC Submission to COP26 (Glasgow), 2021 (English)[18]	Macro national/ regional data	• Business (Sections II.4.2, III.3) • Social benefit from "people centred approach" (Introduction, p. 2)	• Plan – 112 • Market – 37

Document	Measurement (macro-/ micro-data)[1]	Distribution (business enterprises/civic actors)[2]	Autonomy (state/ market)[3]
MEE, Guiding Opinion on Integrating and Strengthening Climate Action, January 2021[19]	Macro national/ regional data	• Business enterprises (Section I.1: "environmental governance") • Social benefit from "new development philosophy" (Section I.1)	• Plan – 14 (计划 – 1; 规划 – 13) • Market (市场 – 6)
MEE, China's Policies and Actions for Addressing Climate Change, June 2021 (English)[20]	Macro national/ regional data	• Business (Sections II.1, II.2, II.4, II.6) • Social benefit from "people first" approach (Section I.3)	• Plan – 52 • Market – 12
CPC CC and State Council, Opinion on the Complete, Accurate, and Comprehensive Implementation of the New Development Concept to Achieve Carbon Neutrality, 2021[21]	Macro	• Private • Public ("new development philosophy" – "common prosperity")	• Plan – 12 (计划 – 0; 规划 – 12) • Market (市场 – 20)
SCIO, White Paper: Responding to Climate Change, October 2021 (English)[22]	Macro national/ regional data	• Business enterprises (Sections II.2, II.6) • Social benefit through "people first" approach (Section I.3)	• Plan – 43 • Market – 31
NDRC, Working Guidance for Carbon Dioxide Peaking and Carbon Neutrality, October 2021 (English)[23]	Macro national/ regional data	• Business enterprises (Sections II.2, II. 6) • Social benefit from "new development philosophy" (Section I.1)	• Market – 21 • Plan – 21
NDRC, Action Plan for Carbon Dioxide Peaking Before 2030, October 2021 (English)[24]	Macro national/ regional data	• Business enterprises (Sections II.3.e and II.3.f, II.6, II.7) • Social benefit from "new development philosophy" (Section I.1)	• Plan – 41 • Market – 15

▸

◄

Notes: The documents listed in column 1 are in Chinese unless otherwise stated. NDRC = National Development and Reform Commission; MEE = Ministry of Ecology and Environment; SCIO = State Council Information Office; CPC CC = Communist Party of China Central Committee.

1 Content and discourse analysis was applied to the texts of the documents listed, yielding conclusions regarding relative priorities related to reliance on macro-/micro-data in measuring prosperity. "Content Analysis," Columbia University Mailman School of Public Health, https://www.publichealth.columbia.edu/research/population-health-methods/content-analysis.

2 Content and discourse analysis was applied to the texts of the documents listed, yielding conclusions regarding relative priorities related to distribution of prosperity through business enterprises/civic actors. "Content Analysis," Columbia University Mailman School of Public Health.

3 The relative orientation toward planning and markets as the dominant force in economic activity, and thereby the obverse of autonomy from state intrusion or market discipline, is indicated by the relative frequency of use of the terms "plan" (*guihua* // 规划 and *jihua* // 计划) and "market" (*shichang* // 市场) in the selected documents. Sage, "Word Frequency Counts," https://methods.sagepub.com/methods-map/word-frequency-counts.

4 NDRC, "Zhongguo yingdui qihou bianhua guojia fangan" [China national plan for adapting to climate change], June 2007, http://www.ccchina.org.cn/WebSite/CCChina/UpFile/File189.pdf.

5 NDRC, "CHINA: 11th Five Year Plan (2006–2010) for National Economic and Social Development," 2006, https://policy.asiapacificenergy.org/node/115.

6 SCIO, "China's Policies and Actions for Addressing Climate Change," November 2011, http://english.www.gov.cn/archive/white_paper/2014/09/09/content_281474986284685.htm.

7 State Council, "National Environmental Protection 'Twelfth Five-Year' Plan (Chinese Text)," December 15, 2011, https://www.cecc.gov/resources/legal-provisions/national-environmental-protection-twelfth-five-year-plan-chinese-text.

8 "Decision of the Central Committee of the Communist Party of China on Some Major Issues Concerning Comprehensively Deepening the Reform (Adopted November 12, 2013)," January 16, 2014, http://www.china.org.cn/china/third_plenary_session/2014-01/16/content_31212602.htm.

9 NDRC, "CHINA: 12th Five Year Plan (2011–2015) for National Economic and Social Development," 2011, https://policy.asiapacificenergy.org/node/37.

10 NDRC, "Guojia shiying qihou bianhua zhanlue" [National climate adaptation strategy], December 9, 2013, https://www.gov.cn/gzdt/att/att/site1/20131209/001e3741a2cc140f6a8701.pdf.

11 NDRC, "Guojia yingdui qihou bianhua guihua" (2014–2020 nian) [National plan on adaptation to climate change (2014–2020], September 2014, https://www.ndrc.gov.cn/xxgk/zcfb/tz/201411/W020190905507100475236.pdf.

12 NDRC, "Qianghua ying dui qihou bianhua xingdong – Zhongguo guojia zizhu gongxian" [Enhanced actions on climate change: China's intended nationally determined contributions], June 30, 2015, http://www.xinhuanet.com//politics/2015-06/30/c_1115774759.htm.

13 NDRC, "The13th Five-Year Plan for Economic and Social Development of the People's Republic of China (2016–2020)," https://en.ndrc.gov.cn/policies/202105/P020210527785800103339.pdf.

14 CPC CC and State Council, "Zhonggong zhongyang, Guowuyuan guanyu quanmian jiaqiang shengtao huanjing baohu jianjue dahao wuran fangzhi gongjian zhan de yijian" [Opinion of the CPC Central Committee and the State Council on comprehensively strengthening ecological and environmental protection and resolutely fighting the tough battle of pollution prevention and control], June 24, 2018, http://www.gov.cn/zhengce/2018-06/24/content_5300953.htm.

15 MEE, "China's Policies and Actions for Addressing Climate Change (2019)," November 2019, https://english.mee.gov.cn/Resources/Reports/reports/201912/P020191204495763994956.pdf.

16 SCIO, "Full Text: Energy in China's New Era," December 2020, http://english.scio.gov.cn/whitepapers/2020-12/21/content_77035604.htm.

17 NDRC, "Zhonghua renmin gongheguo guomin jingji he shehui fazhan de shisige wunian guihua he 2035 nian yuanjing mubiao gangyao" [PRC 14th five-year plan for national economic and social development and outline of long-range goals for 2035], March 13, 2021, http://www.gov.cn/xinwen/2021-03/13/content_5592681.htm. For an English translation, see "Outline of the People's Republic of China 14th Five-Year Plan for National Economic and Social Development and Long-Range Objectives for 2035," March 12, 2021, https://cset.georgetown.edu/publication/china-14th-five-year-plan/. Also see Jiang Yifan, "14th Five Year Plan: China's Carbon-Centred Environmental Blueprint," Dialogue Earth, March 25, 2021, https://chinadialogue.net/en/climate/14th-five-year-plan-china-carbon-centred-environmental-blueprint/.

18 Nationally Determined Contributions Registry, "China's Achievements, New Goals and New Measures for Nationally Determined Contributions," 2021, https://unfccc.int/sites/default/files/NDC/2022-06/China's%20Achievements%2C%20New%20Goals%20and%20New%20Measures%20for%20Nationally%20Determined%20Contributions.pdf.

19 MEE, "Guanyu tongchou he jiaqiang yingdui qihou bianhua yu shengtai huanjing baohu xiangguan gongzuo de zhidai yijian" [Guiding opinion on integrating and strengthening efforts in climate action and ecological and environmental protection], January 11, 2021, https://www.mee.gov.cn/xxgk2018/xxgk/xxgk03/202101/t20210113_817221.html. For an English translation, see https://www.clientearth.org/media/00tnkuc5/guiding-opinions-on-integrating-and-strengthening-efforts-in-climate-action-and-ecological-and-environmental-protection.pdf.

20 MEE, "China's Policies and Actions for Addressing Climate Change (2020)," June 2021, http://www.ncsc.org.cn/yjcg/cbw/202111/P020211117418821628432.pdf.,

21 CPC CC and State Council, "Zhonggong zhongyang guowuyuan guanyu wanzheng zhunque quanmian guanche xinfazhan linian zuohao tadafeng tanzhonghe gongzuo de yijian" [Opinions of the CPC Central Committee and the State Council on the complete, accurate and comprehensive implementation of the new development concept to do a good job in carbon peaking and carbon neutrality], September 22, 2021, http://www.gov.cn/zhengce/2021-10/24/content_5644613.htm.

22 SCIO, "Full Text: Responding to Climate Change: China's Policies and Actions," October 2021, http://english.scio.gov.cn/whitepapers/2021-10/27/content_77836502_4.htm.

23 NDRC, "Working Guidance for Carbon Dioxide Peaking and Carbon Neutrality in Full and Faithful Implementation of the New Development Philosophy," October 24, 2021, https://en.ndrc.gov.cn/policies/202110/t20211024_1300725.html.

24 NDRC, "Action Plan for Carbon Dioxide Peaking Before 2030," October 27, 2021, https://en.ndrc.gov.cn/policies/202110/t20211027_1301020.html.

5 Involuntary Migration
Passive Populism

THIS CHAPTER EXAMINES PRC responses to the global crisis of involuntary migration as a further example of China's globalized populism. We begin with a review of China's conventional domestic measures and tentative international cooperation on migration, followed by an examination of China's engagement with the international migration policy system in light of conditions of inequality and of complexity. The chapter then examines China's populist response involving opposition to global elites associated with international migration systems and justification through grievance against pressure on China to accept migrants despite its claimed limitations as a developing country. We turn next to the third element of China's populist response, involving practical resistance through alternative law and policy practice related to community identity, diversity, and mobility. China's refugee policy has consistently depicted the country's response in terms of socio-cultural relations,[1] underscoring the relevance of "community" as a standard for assessment. The chapter then addresses rhetorical markers of sovereignty, development, and human rights that lend resilience to China's populist responses to the international crisis of involuntary migration. China's policy and practice on migration have involved largely passive resistance to the standards of the rules-based international order, somewhat less active than the participatory populism of China's climate change response and quite distinct from the antagonistic populism characterizing its response to the COVID-19 crisis.

China and the Crisis of Involuntary Migration

China's increased stature in global affairs has led to calls for greater involvement in responding to the global crisis of involuntary migration.[2] As with the long-running climate change crisis but distinct from the shorter-term COVID-19 crisis, the crisis of involuntary migration has been ongoing for many years, inviting discussion of China's early responses through conventional domestic measures and international cooperation on international migration.

Conventional Domestic Measures

Initially, China's conventional domestic measures related to involuntary migration included basic provisions on nationality in the PRC Constitution and Nationality Law, coupled with legal and policy guidance on refugees. As exemplified by its handling of Indo-Chinese migrants fleeing conflict in Southeast Asia from the late 1970s to early 1980s, China's initial response to involuntary migration relied on administrative discretion enabled by a general lack of domestic legal and policy provisions. Refugees coming to China from Vietnam, Laos, and Cambodia were granted refugee status on a prima facie basis and were de facto integrated into society with the same rights as Chinese nationals.[3] However, little was done to establish broader legal standards and processes for treatment of involuntary migrants generally.

The general absence of clear and comprehensive legal standards has remained a challenge for China. While the 2013 report of the Office of the United Nations High Commissioner for Refugees (UNHCR) to the United Nations Human Rights Council (UNHRC) Universal Periodic Review (UPR) process on China's performance acknowledged the importance of China's 2013 Exit and Entry Administration Law permitting refugee applicants to remain in China while their claims are assessed, the report also noted the absence of specific laws on rights of refugees.[4] At the G20 2016 summit in Hangzhou, the members recognized the challenges posed by the "worldwide massive forced displacement of people, unprecedented since the Second World War, especially those generated from violent conflicts," and pledged to address root causes, strengthen humanitarian assistance for refugees and refugee resettlement, and find durable solutions to the crisis.[5] China's responses were assessed as "partially" in compliance with commitments of financial aid, but deemed a failure in "develop[ing] new concrete actions."[6]

Tentative International Cooperation

In light of the gaps in domestic law and policy, China's tentative engagement with international standards had particular significance. International standards on involuntary migration extend to issues of refugees and forced migrants.[7] Under the 1951 UN Convention Relating to the Status of Refugees (1951 Refugee Convention), refugees are defined as persons "unable or unwilling to return to their country of origin owing to a well-founded fear of being persecuted for reasons of race, religion, nationality, membership of a particular social group, or political opinion."[8] The Organization for African Unity (OAU) Convention Governing Specific Aspects of Refugee Problems in Africa (adopted September 10, 1969, entered into force June 20, 1974) expanded the definition of refugees to include persons compelled to leave their country "owing to external aggression, occupation, foreign domination or events seriously disturbing public order in either part or the whole of his country or origin or nationality."[9] These definitions were augmented yet further pursuant to the 1984 Cartagena Declaration on Refugees to include "persons who have fled their country because their lives, safety or freedom have been threatened by generalized violence, foreign aggression, internal conflicts, massive violation of human rights or other circumstances which have seriously disturbed public order."[10] Thus, involuntary migration includes not only movement by refugees but also forced movement of people not classified as refugees under the 1951 Refugee Convention and its 1967 Protocol, who are fleeing such drivers as natural disaster, environmental destruction, and poverty.

China's tentative international engagement has included participation in international treaties and organizations. China is a party to the 1951 Refugee Convention and its 1967 Protocol.[11] It joined the New York Declaration for Refugees and Migrants, adopted at the UN General Assembly Summit for Refugees and Migrants in September 2016.[12] The declaration called for work toward adoption of "global compacts" on refugees and migration.[13] The Global Compact for Safe, Orderly and Regular Migration (GCM) was endorsed by the General Assembly in December 2018,[14] along with the Global Compact on Refugees (GCR) incorporating the Comprehensive Refugee Response Framework (CRRF) proposed in the New York Declaration.[15] Participation in these international arrangements added important substantive and procedural content to China's responses to the crisis of involuntary migration. Yet, because China's treaties are mostly dependent on local administrative action and legislation to take effect as domestic law,[16] their application is impeded by the general absence of local law and regulation on the rights of refugees.

China's tentative engagement with the international system has reflected the effects of increased migration both into and out of China.[17] China has promoted linkages between migration and development, accepting the mandate of the Sustainable Development Goals (SDG) to facilitate "orderly, safe, regular and responsible migration and mobility of people."[18] China became a member state of the International Organization for Migration (IOM) in June 2016 after having held observer status since 2001.[19] A joint IOM–Ministry of Foreign Affairs (MFA) workshop on migration and development held in June 2019 called for planned and well-managed migration policies, and introduced key policy instruments and best practices, including a Chinese-language version of the IOM's basic text on the issue.[20] Although not listed as a participant in the First Global Refugee Forum in December 2019 or among the countries making pledges on refugees in connection with the forum, China was credited with co-sponsoring a dialogue on jobs and livelihoods at which partners from the Hong Kong private sector pledged to enhance labour opportunities and legal aid for persons of concern.[21] Outmigration from China has long attracted attention as a proxy for critiques of China's authoritarian governance. This has taken on greater significance recently in the context of claims regarding migrants from the PRC travelling through Mexico to cross into the United States at a time when the US southern border has been the focus of political and policy debates over immigration controls.[22]

China's Relationship with Global Migration Systems: Inequality and Complexity

The MFA's 2004 summary of China's ties with the UNHCR claimed that the relationship was "friendly" and "good," noting China's membership on the High Commission's Executive Committee (ExCom), assumed after the UN seat formerly held by the Republic of China (ROC) was terminated in favour of the PRC.[23] Nonetheless, respected observers have noted tensions in China's relations with the UNHCR.[24] As with its experience with COVID-19 and climate change, China's involvement with international institutions and standards on migration reflects underlying conditions of inequality and complexity.

Factors of inequality in China's relationship with established international policy systems on refugees and migration are grounded in history. China's historical role as a source of involuntary migrants led initially to isolation from world migration policy.[25] While the ROC government had made efforts to receive and resettle Jewish refugees fleeing Nazi Germany in the late 1930s,[26] the PRC's relationships with the international refugee policy establishment have been more conflicted. The seemingly endless stream of migrants fleeing Mao's revolution, the famine of the early 1960s, and later the Cultural Revolution undermined China's international legitimacy and pleas for diplomatic recognition.[27] Despite China's re-engagement with the world community through the post-Mao economic and legal reforms, its relationship with the world policy system on involuntary migration continued to reflect the impacts of history.

Issues of inequality also arise in the context of China's policy positions asserting the need for international standards on migration to defer to local conditions in recipient countries. The theme of "common but differentiated responsibilities and respective capabilities" requested for international responses to COVID-19 and climate change resonated in calls that international cooperation on migration should account for "different national realities, capacities and levels of development."[28] Inequality is also evident in China's financial contributions to the UNHCR, which remain modest in comparison with other donors and in light of the size of China's economy. While its contributions to the UNHCR (excluding "private donors") have grown from US$941,841 in 2015 (ranked fifty-first) to US$1,765,630 in 2020 (ranked fifty-sixth),[29] China still lags well behind the top ten donors – the United States, the European Union, Germany, the United Kingdom, Japan, Sweden, Denmark, Netherlands, Norway, and Canada.

Conditions of complexity and alienation have also played a role. China's alienation from the complexities of the international refugee migration system includes ambivalence regarding the complex relationships and practices among liberal states that dominate global migration discourse. While China presents itself as a multi-ethnic state, its law and policy practices suggest deep ambivalence over the equality and complexity aspects of standards on inclusion that inform international systems on involuntary migration.[30] Resentment over inequality and alienation from complexity has also been evident in the range of bilateral conflicts over issues such as trade, security, and human rights with key state actors supporting the international migration system.[31] Not unlike the circumstances around China's responses to the COVID-19 pandemic and climate change, tensions over inequality and complexity have complicated Beijing's relations with the UNHCR and the international migration policy community.[32] While China has sought to influence policy positions of UNHCR, most notably by focusing on improving conditions in source countries and recognizing different responsibilities for developed and developing countries in responding to the crisis of involuntary migration, its success has been modest as these proposals were well embedded in the international discourse on involuntary migration without China's interventions.[33]

China's Populist Response to the Migration Crisis

As with COVID-19 and climate change, China's populist responses to the global migration crisis have involved opposition to elites, justification through grievance ideology, and practical resistance. Unlike China's antagonistic stance on COVID-19 and conditional participation in international climate change efforts, however, China's engagement with international migration systems has mainly involved a passive populism through inaction in adopting international standards and processes for accepting and resettling migrants.

Opposition to Elites: Challenging the Global Migration System

China has resisted calls from the international migration policy community to strengthen its standards and processes for handling involuntary migrants. Speaking at a worldwide consultation session on refugee policy in May 2001, its former UN ambassador, Qin Huasheng, "spoke against the idea and practice of pressurizing the asylum country to have refugees naturalized in the name of permanently resolving the refugee problem."[34] Such reluctance reflected the influences of international political relations, as well as concerns around stability and development.[35] In contrast with China's treatment of migrants fleeing the Vietnam War, the China-Vietnam border war, and local conflicts in Laos, Myanmar, and elsewhere in the late 1970s, its more recent treatment of asylum seekers from North Korea and Myanmar has been less welcoming.[36] China's response to migrants from North Korea has been challenged as being out of step with its obligations under the 1951 Refugee Convention and its 1967 Protocol.[37] China's response to the crisis of Rohingya refugees from Myanmar has been similarly resistant to international calls for refugee reception and resettlement.[38]

While supporting migration of skilled workers and professionals, China has resisted "irregular migration" in response to economic deprivation in developing countries.[39] Speaking at a 2018 intergovernmental conference on adoption of the GCM, the leader of China's delegation noted the need to address "irregular migration."[40] China's 2020 position paper issued for the seventy-fifth anniversary of the United Nations noted that "unbalanced development is the main underlying cause of migration" and called for more attention to development issues "that lie at the heart of irregular migration."[41]

Opposition to global elites embodied in the UN migration system has also been evident in China's partial implementation of UNHCR-termed "durable solutions" to the international refugee crisis: (1) voluntary repatriation and return, (2) integration and other local solutions, and (3) resettlement and complementary pathways.[42] China's support for integration and resettlement of involuntary migrants has been limited to its acceptance of the recommendation of the third human rights Universal Periodic Review in 2019 that "all children, especially those of asylum seekers and refugees have access to education," which was consistent with the PRC's Education Law providing for universal education.[43] China's enactment of its Exit and Entry Administration Law (2013), with Article 46 on residence rights for refugee claimants, was an important step toward clarifying the status of involuntary migrants in China.[44] Nonetheless, other legal measures on voluntary return, integration, and resettlement of involuntary migrants in China have been slow to emerge. The COVID-19 crisis has created additional challenges, highlighting China's resistance to receiving migrants from abroad.[45]

China's resistance to the international refugee system has been compounded by unease over refugee applicants from China itself. Asylum seekers from China increased dramatically under Xi Jinping's rule, from 12,362 in 2012 to 176,239 in 2024.[46] Many of these flee human rights abuses, ethnic abuse in Xinjiang and Tibet, and more recently political repression in Hong Kong.[47]

Grievance: Resisting Pressure to Accept Migrants

China's responses to the international migration system have included expressions of grievance around pressure on developing countries to accept migrants. Ambivalence in supporting global programs for involuntary migrants has been driven by assertions that developed countries – primarily liberal democracies – bear primary responsibility for conditions leading to involuntary migration and so should bear the cost.[48] The focus on development enables China to treat its own development and stability as a sufficient response to the global crisis of involuntary migration while calling on developed countries to do more.[49] The MFA summary on relations with the UNHCR quoted remarks by China's UN ambassador, Qiao Zhonghuai, at the 2000 UNHCR ExCom session in Geneva to the effect that "developed countries should shoulder more responsibility in providing assistance and protection to refugees."[50] China's position paper on the occasion of the United Nations' seventy-fifth anniversary reaffirmed the point by relying on the discourse of "common but differentiated responsibilities" (CBDR).[51]

China's concerns related to development include its own claims to developing country status as well as the priority it gives to resolving conditions in source countries that lead to involuntary migration. China's submission to the October 2021 UNHCR ExCom session noted the importance of development disparities in allocating responsibilities for refugees – "the allocation of responsibilities in responding to the refugee issues is seriously out of alignment (*yanzhong bu pipei* // 严重不匹配) with levels of national economic development" – while calling for attention to development in resolving the root causes of involuntary migration: "We must dedicate ourselves to addressing development and other root issues and assist refugee source countries' long-standing governance and peace in order to create conditions for refugees returning."[52] Priorities related to development were also evident in the PRC's 2004 regulations on determining permanent residence, which prioritize applications linked with contributions to China's development.[53]

Thus, China's responses to the global migration crisis involved populist expressions of anti-elitism and grievance in the wake of conditions of inequality and complexity. Dynamics of opposition to international elites associated with global migration standards and justification through grievances over systemic pressures to accept migrants were integral to China's populist response to the international migration crisis. As discussed below, such response has also included practical resistance through legal and regulatory standards and practice presenting alternatives to established arrangements.

Practical Resistance in China's Responses to Involuntary Migration

As with its responses to COVID-19 and climate change, China's response to the crisis of involuntary migration has included practical resistance through law and policy measures offering alternative approaches to migration in furtherance of PRC policy needs.[54] Mindful of links between migration policy and socio-cultural relations,[55] China's practical resistance to the international migration system may be assessed in terms of law and policy practices on community identity, diversity, and mobility, which may in turn be compared with corresponding standards of the rules-based international order.

Context: Managing Community in China

As discussed in Chapter 1, operational norms and law and policy practices related to community involve standards on identity (particularly the distinction between inherent and acquired identity), processes on diversity (particularly questions about conditions of integration and segregation), and mobility of people (involving questions about opportunity and threat in the context of both socio-economic status mobility and geographic mobility). These issues have informed discourses on community in China.

Identity: From Class Struggle to Citizenship

Perspectives on identity in China were expressed early on through notions of class struggle associated with Maoist goals of revolutionary transformation.[56] Identity was determined by class, which itself was a product of material conditions over which the affected individual had little if any control. As class struggle became a rubric of governance threatening ever-widening segments of society along with Mao's political opponents, the relatively broad social and political consensus built in the early years after 1949 eroded.[57] The ideology of class struggle as a foundation for identity not only affected the mainstream of Chinese society but also extended to ethnic minorities, whose traditions and practices were attacked during the Cultural Revolution as feudal and backward.[58] The post-Mao reform period heralded at the 3rd Plenum of the 11th Central Committee in November–December 1978 called for a re-examination of class struggle:

> We must not relax our class struggle against them, nor can we weaken the dictatorship of the proletariat. But as Comrade Mao Tse-tung pointed out, the large-scale turbulent class struggles of a mass character have in the main come to an end. Class struggle in socialist society should be carried out on the principle of strictly differentiating the two different types of contradictions and correctly handling them in accordance with the procedures prescribed by the Constitution and the law.[59]

At the 13th National Communist Party of China (CPC) Congress in 1987, General Secretary Zhao Ziyang asserted that China was in the "preliminary stage of socialism," affirming the turn away from class struggle.[60] Successive decades saw class struggle devolve from questions of socio-economic and political status to classifications based on behaviour, as anti-crime and anti-corruption campaigns adopted the vernacular of class struggle to define and legitimate their objectives.[61] The CPC's 2021 resolution on Party history confirmed that the Party had "decisively abandoned the policy of taking class struggle as the key link" at the 1978 3rd Plenum.[62]

With the decline of class struggle, approaches to community identity in PRC governance saw a transition from class to citizenship as the basis for socio-economic and political identity.[63] Principles of equality of citizens before the law were articulated specifically as a riposte to the ideology of class struggle that had characterized the Maoist period.[64] While movement from one class designation to another was difficult if not impossible (the post-Mao reforms treating intellectuals as mental workers, for example, required considerable massaging of ideological boundaries[65]), such barriers faded as class gave way to citizenship as the basis for social classification.[66] Citizenship in turn depends on nationality (*guoji* // 国籍), which under the PRC Constitution and the Nationality Law of the PRC is determined by reference to ethnicity.[67] The PRC Constitution provides in Article 33: "All persons holding the nationality of the People's Republic of China are citizens (公民) of the People's Republic of China."[68] The Nationality Law reifies the distinction between members of China's recognized ethnic groups and others:[69]

> Article 2. The People's Republic of China is a unitary multiethnic state (*duo minzu de guojia* // 多民族的国家; persons belonging to any of the ethnicities (*minzu* // 民族) in China shall have Chinese nationality (*guoji* // 国籍).
>
> Article 4. Any person born in China whose parents are both Chinese nationals or one of whose parents is a Chinese national shall have Chinese nationality.
>
> Article 7. Foreign nationals or stateless persons who are willing to abide by China's Constitution and other laws and who meet one of the following conditions may be naturalized upon approval of their applications:
>
> (1) they are near relatives of Chinese nationals;
> (2) they have settled (*dingzhu* // 定住) in China; or
> (3) they have other legitimate reasons.

No longer classified by class, citizens were classified by their ethnicity (*minzu* // 民族) as a precondition for nationality (*guoji* // 国籍).[70] The Nationality Law's reliance on the doctrine of *jus sanguinis* (nationality based on blood lineage) over *jus soli* (nationality based on birthplace), underscored the ethnic foundations for nationality in the PRC.[71] Official observers have termed this as the principle of "lineage as the mainstay, birthplace as supplementary" (*yi xuetong zhuyi weizhu, yi chushengdi zhuyi wei fu* // 以血统主义为主以出生地主义为辅).[72]

Diversity and Ethnic Relations

Law and policy practices related to community identity have important implications for social diversity, particularly in relations between the dominant Han and minority nationalities (*shaoshu minzu* // 少数民族).[73] Traditional PRC practice included segregation of minority nationalities in ethnic-centred "autonomous" areas where minorities were to live and practise their culture separated from mainstream Han society.[74] Such arrangements were formalized in the Law of the PRC on Regional National Autonomy (LRNA). Enacted initially in 1984, the LRNA was amended in 2001 to account primarily for issues related to economic development.[75] Echoing a familiar trope of "separate but equal," China's minority policies hinge on assertions of formal equality among different ethnic groups affirmed in the PRC Constitution and two government white papers on ethnic affairs.[76] Yet political and socio-economic practices, including the effects of "great Han chauvinism" (*da Han zhuyi* // 大汉主义), undermine genuine equality for minority nationalities.[77]

Against this background, themes of national unity and assimilation have come to the fore in China's minorities policy.[78] As suggested by the government's 2009 white paper, China's ethnic policy reinforced minority nationality "allegiance to the central government and their identification with Chinese culture" pursuant to ideals of "unification and diversity."[79] Under Xi Jinping, PRC policy on ethnic minorities has shifted sharply toward assimilation under the rubric of "Sinicization" (*Zhongguohua* // 中国化).[80] The theme of community (*gongtongti* // 共同体) has been used as a proxy for Sinicization, emphasizing the need for unity among minority groups around Chinese culture.[81] Xi's report to the 19th CPC Congress in 2017 emphasized the unity of *all* ethnic groups (Han and minority) under the Party's leadership:

> We must conscientiously safeguard the solidarity and unity of the Party, maintain the Party's deep bond with the people, and strengthen the great unity of the Chinese people of all ethnic groups and the great unity of all the sons and daughters of the Chinese nation at home and abroad. We must unite all the forces that can be united and work as one to progress toward the brilliant future of national rejuvenation ... We, the entire Party and the Chinese people of all ethnic groups, should rally closely around the Party

> Central Committee, and hold high the banner of socialism with Chinese characteristics.[82]

Similarly, Xi's speech to the Central Nationalities Work Conference in 2021 underscored links between community and assimilation of minority nationality cultures:

> We must take forging a strong sense of community of the Chinese nation as the main line of the party's ethnic work in the new era, promote all ethnic groups to firmly identify with the great motherland, the Chinese nation, Chinese culture, the Communist Party of China, and socialism with Chinese characteristics, and continuously promote the construction of a community of the Chinese nation.[83]

PRC law and policy practice related to minority nationalities has particular relevance for China's responses to involuntary migration, as both involve dilemmas of segregation and integration in managing relations between different socio-cultural groups.

Local and International Mobility

The transition from class to citizenship as the basis for social identity and the continuing priority given to segregation of different ethnic groups in China call attention to questions concerning socio-economic and geographic mobility. The partial opening of the economy to entrepreneurship and accumulation widened the possibilities for mobility in socio-economic circumstances, while possibilities for geographic mobility expanded as people moved from rural areas to seek employment and prosperity in China's cities.[84] For decades, internal migration was inhibited by China's household registration (*hukou* // 户口) system, which bound people to their registered places of residence.[85] In an effort to bolster economic growth, initiatives continue to reform and ultimately to abolish the *hukou* system, facilitating greater mobility.[86] China's "social credit system" (*shehui xinyong tixi* // 社会信用体系) collects information on citizens to ward off unorthodox thinking and behaviour, using artificial intelligence and multiple imaging and tracking technologies to ensure that supervision is not affected by internal migration.[87] Inequalities in socio-economic position continue to affect internal migration even in the wake of diminution of the *hukou* restrictions.[88] This has contributed to international migration as well.[89]

Conventional discourses on community mobility in China have also included perspectives on foreigners. Foreigners resident in China have long known both the direct and the more subtle measures that insulate local society from the purported influence of foreigners.[90] Identity standards around ethnicity are applied to differentiate between Han overseas Chinese visitors and foreigners. Diversity standards around segregation are applied in the context of *she-wai* (涉外) distinctions between foreigners and local people. While many of these have faded as China's increased globalization in investment, trade, and social relations have made the distinction less compelling, the distinction remains in sectors such as dispute resolution, education, and civil relations such as marriage and inheritance.[91] Local attitudes about foreigners have been mixed, but in any case have tended to reinforce the sense of separation between the foreign and the local, and the barriers to integration of the two.[92]

Mobility standards have also been applied to the general question of foreigners accessing PRC travel visas and permits. China's COVID-19 control policies further dampened local treatment of foreigners.[93] Concerns about arbitrary detention, particularly in the aftermath of China's detention of Canadians Michael Spavor and Michael Kovrig, revealed doubts about the treatment of foreigners by the PRC regime.[94] The crisis involving the "Two Michaels" revealed yet further the distinctions between the foreign and the local, as their treatment was in many ways more lenient than that meted out to prisoners of Chinese nationality.[95] China does not recognize "dual nationality," which inhibits efforts by foreigners working and living in China to obtain PRC nationality and also facilitates the government's efforts to repatriate Chinese nationals who have taken citizenship abroad but whose activities offend the PRC regime.[96]

Implications for PRC Responses to Involuntary Migration

PRC discourses on community have implications for China's response to the crisis of involuntary migration by setting the parameters for law and policy practice on community identity, diversity, and mobility. Focused primarily on relations between the Han majority and multiple national minorities, PRC policy standards on identity have tended to focus on ethnicity. To the extent that identity might also entail acquired traits, PRC law and policy have tended to focus on the need to instill Han-oriented features in non-Han people. While nominally supportive of China's multi-ethnic social conditions, PRC standards on diversity have tended toward segregation of different ethnic groups through enforcement of the minority autonomous region system. Mobility standards have focused primarily on control of internal migration through the *hukou* system, while also differentiating between local people and foreigners along ethnic lines. Each of these has significance for China's response to the crisis of involuntary migration.

Law and Policy Practice Related to Community: Responding to Involuntary Migration

As discussed in Chapter 1, social community involves operational norms on identity, diversity, and mobility and associated law and policy practices. Law and policy practice related to identity vary between preferences for inherent or acquired identity. Practices related to diversity involve competing preferences between integration and segregation of individuals and groups of different ethnicities. Practices related to mobility involve questions around treating socio-economic and geographic mobility as an opportunity or a threat to affected societies. Each of these is evident in China's responses to the crisis of involuntary migration.

Community Identity: Inherent/Acquired

PRC law and policy practice related to social community has tended to prioritize inherent identity based on ethnicity. Chinese nationality has come to depend primarily on being a member of a recognized PRC ethnic group. Language hegemony favouring Mandarin Chinese over minority languages has contributed to the dominance of Han Chinese over other ethnic groups.[97] The Nationality Law allows Chinese nationality to be granted to foreign nationals and stateless persons who are "near relatives" of Chinese nationals or who have "settled" (*dingzhu* // 定住) in China or otherwise have "other legitimate reasons" to acquire Chinese nationality.[98]

The ethnicity-based determinations of Chinese nationality were reflected in the Passport Law of the PRC (2006): "The passport of the People's Republic of China is a document certifying the nationality and identity of a citizen of the People's Republic of China when he [sic] leaves and enters the territory of the People's Republic of China or when he [sic] is abroad."[99] China's regulations on resident identity cards affirm this orientation by requiring such cards (required of all Chinese citizens) to include confirmation of ethnicity (*minzhu* // 民族).[100] Such ethnicity-based classifications of identity affect not only Han people dominant in China but also those of the fifty-five officially recognized minority nationalities.[101] Minority nationalities face restrictions in obtaining passports for travel abroad.[102]

Links between identity and ethnicity are also evident in China's immigration law and regulations distinguishing between foreigners and Chinese nationals. Entry to and exit from the PRC by Chinese nationals and foreigners are governed by separate sets of regulations. Following enactment of the Exit and Entry Administration Law (2013),[103] which purports to offer a comprehensive framework for handling immigration and emigration, China issued national regulations on entry and exit of foreigners to replace earlier regulations (enacted in 1986 and revised in 1994 and 2010) on entry and exit of aliens.[104] The new regulations involved cooperation between the Public Security Ministry for services and administration and the Ministry of Foreign Affairs for visa matters (Articles 3, 5). The regulations made clear that entry and stay of foreigners is conditional and dependent on visa compliance subject to oversight and inspection by local public security departments (Articles 21, 25). While China recently eased visa requirements for business, tourism, and family visits,[105] the Exit and Entry Administration Law and associated regulations on foreign entry and exit still distinguish foreigners from Chinese nationals, underscoring the largely ethnic criteria for assessing identity.

Whereas criteria for citizenship have tended toward ethnicity, requirements for permanent residence have tended toward acquired attributes. China's 2004 regulations on determining permanent residence allowed applications from foreigners who were direct investors with three years' operation and tax compliance, senior managers, professionals and academics, or those who have made outstanding contributions to China, together with their spouses and unmarried children.[106] These categories were retained in a draft regulation circulated in 2020, which added provisions for wealth, education, and experience as criteria for obtaining permanent residence in China.[107] The 2023 Guidelines on permanent residence approvals echoed the 2004 regulations but placed the requirement for "remarkable contributions to the economic and social development of China" as a first precondition of eligibility for permanent residence status.[108] While permanent residence may well be required to satisfy the "settled in" requirement for naturalization for foreign nationals and stateless persons into PRC nationality under Article 7 of the Nationality Law, the focus on material attributes such as wealth, education, and contributions to China suggested an effort to separate permanent residence based on acquired attributes from ethnicity-based nationality. Differentiation between nationality and permanent residence underscored distinctions between classifying local people based on ethnicity and foreigners based on acquired capacity to assist in China's development.

China's approach to identity in the context of involuntary migration from Indochina and North Korea revealed similar perspectives. In connection with the China's second UPR (2013), the UNHCR submitted concerns over differences in the treatment of migrants from Indochina, who had generally received refugee status and integration in China,[109] and migrants from North Korea, who were being treated as economic migrants without the legal protections offered refugees.[110] In early 2024, some two thousand Korean workers at a factory in Helong City, Yanbian Korean Autonomous Prefecture, along the PRC–North Korea border, reportedly rioted over unpaid wages and abusive working conditions.[111] The veracity of this reporting has been challenged, but not the long-standing pattern of unpaid wages and abusive conditions in China for migrants from North Korea.[112] China's differential treatment of migrants from Indochina and North Korea reveals distinctions related to identity that conflate dimensions of geostrategy and ethnicity.[113] The migrants from Indochina are almost universally ethnically Han Chinese, while those from North Korea are not (although Koreans are one of China's fifty-five officially recognized minority nationalities[114]). China intensified repatriation of North Korean migrants beginning in 2021.[115] To the extent that law and policy practices related to identity hinge on expectations about inherency based on ethnicity, the distinction between ethnic Chinese refugee claimants and migrants of other ethnicities speaks to the primacy of ethnicity in PRC determinations of refugee status and willingness to support entry and integration in Chinese society.

China's law and policy practices related to community identity operate against the background of international standards. The International Covenant on Economic, Social and Cultural Rights (ICESCR)[116] underscores ideals of fundamental equality that transcend ethnicity:

> Article 1.1. All peoples have the right of self-determination. By virtue of that right they freely determine their political status and freely pursue their economic, social and cultural development.
>
> Article 2.2. The States Parties to the present Covenant undertake to guarantee that the rights enunciated in the present Covenant will be exercised without discrimination of any kind as to race, colour, sex, language, religion,

> political or other opinion, national or social origin, property, birth or other status.

Similarly the International Covenant on Civil and Political Rights (ICCPR, signed by China and awaiting ratification), in addition to reiterating rights to self-determination and non-discrimination (Articles 1.1, 2.1, and 26), affirms the principle of human equality regardless of ethnicity and nationality, thereby accepting that identity is not inherent and immutable but rather derived from circumstances.[117] While ICCPR Article 27 protects the rights of ethnic minorities to practise their culture, this does not authorize determinations of social identity based on ethnicity. Thus, international standards tend to consider identity in the context of fluidity and change, rather than in terms of immutable inherency. This contrasts with PRC law and policy practice on inherency of community identity.

Community Diversity: Integration/Segregation

Long-standing PRC law and policy have couched integration and segregation of disparate ethnic groups on the needs of stability for development:

> This correct ethnic policy in line with China's actual situation has fostered the unity and harmonious coexistence of all ethnic groups who are striving with one mind for economic development, political stability, cultural prosperity and social harmony ...
>
> The unity of all ethnic groups is an important guarantee for the development of all social endeavors. Only unity can concentrate the strength of all the ethnic groups for the construction and development of the country, promote economic and social progress and improve the Chinese people's lives.[118]

Development and stability concerns continue to inform policies on assimilation and stability in managing China's disparate ethnic groups under the theme of "community" (*gongtongti* // 共同体).[119] While this has potential implications for the reception and resettlement of involuntary migrants, assimilation of domestic minorities who are already educated and to some degree socialized under the PRC is quite different from the challenge of integrating foreign-born, educated, and socialized migrants.

The orientation toward assimilation in China's minority nationalities policy has not been evident in the context of reception and resettlement of refugees. Indeed, China has taken few steps to integrate migrants into local society – its number of foreign-born permanent residents (the lowest worldwide) suggests ongoing resistance to integration.[120] While China's policies emphasizing assimilation of minority nationalities[121] suggests potential openness to greater integration of refugees and other involuntary migrants, so far this potential remains unfulfilled. Admission of refugees to China has shown only a modest increase from 2000 (294,109) to 2020 (303,436), with a sharp drop-off in 2023 to 296.[122] Popular reactions to recent expansion of provisions on permanent residence for foreigners have often been couched in terms rejecting the value of integration and diversity.[123]

Augmenting general barriers to foreigners obtaining Chinese nationality, PRC law and regulation on permanent residence entrench segregation of foreign migrants from local society. In contrast to the largely ethnic criteria for nationality under the Nationality Law, criteria for obtaining permanent residence hinge largely on benefits to China under the PRC's 2004 regulations on administration of permanent residence as reiterated and expanded in the 2020 draft revisions and the 2023 Guidelines for Approval of Foreign Nationals' Eligibility for Permanent Residence in China.[124] And in contrast to provisions of the Nationality Law (Articles 9–10) that allow only for voluntary renunciation of Chinese nationality, China's 2004 regulations on administration of permanent residence and the 2023 guidelines provide that such status may be withdrawn under circumstances of a person's (1) being a potential threat to national security or interests; (2) being sentenced to deportation by a People's Court; (3) having obtained permanent residence through false materials or by other illegal means; or (4) having stayed in China without approval for a period of less than three cumulative months in a year or less than a cumulative year in five years.[125] Thus, foreigners' permanent residence in China depends on compliance with legal and unspecified national security requirements. Such distinctions between nationals and permanent residents underscore the contingency of foreigners' residency in China, and contribute to the segregation of foreigners from local society.

Law and policy practices related to diversity are also evident in the establishment of China's National Immigration Administration (NIA) in 2018. The NIA's policy entrenches distinctions between foreigners and travellers of Chinese nationality but offers little guidance on treatment of refugees and involuntary migrants, suggesting further barriers to integration of involuntary migrants.[126] As immigration matters were long the province of China's public security bureaucracy, the NIA continues to maintain close ties with the public security regime.[127] This public security dimension was evident in the NIA's leadership in a major illegal immigration case in late 2021 (focused mainly on Chinese migrants).[128] Its guidance on categories of foreigners entering China distinguished ordinary visa holders from those entering China under residence permits for "work, personal matters, or reunion purposes," while saying nothing about irregular immigration by asylum seekers and refugees.[129] Despite official PRC orthodoxy that China is a "unitary multinational state" (Nationality Law, Article 2) in which all ethnic groups are equal (Constitution, Article 4), the NIA classifies migrants to China separately from Chinese nationals, suggesting barriers to their integration into Chinese society. This is a particular challenge for involuntary migrants who are unable or unwilling to return home.

China's law and policy practices related to community diversity stand in comparison with international standards. The Universal Declaration on Cultural Diversity of the United Nations Educational, Scientific and Cultural Organization (UNESCO) treats social diversity as a human right enjoyed equally by all, and champions positive links between diversity and development:

> Article 3. Cultural diversity as a factor in development
> Cultural diversity widens the range of options open to everyone; it is one of the roots of development, understood not simply in terms of economic growth, but also as a means to achieve a more satisfactory intellectual, emotional, moral and spiritual existence.
>
> Article 4. Human rights as guarantees of cultural diversity
> The defence of cultural diversity is an ethical imperative, inseparable from respect for human dignity. It implies a commitment to human rights and fundamental freedoms, in particular the rights of persons belonging to minorities and those of indigenous peoples. No one may invoke cultural diversity to infringe upon human rights guaranteed by international law, nor to limit their scope.[130]

Underscoring the link between development and human rights in diversity, international human rights standards deny states the right to abridge human rights in the name of development.[131] Moreover, the International Covenant on the Elimination of All Forms of Racial Discrimination (ICERD) prohibits segregationist policies.[132] Thus, international standards tend to challenge segregation as intruding on the human right to equality in diversity. These contrast with PRC preferences on segregation in response to diversity.

Community Mobility: Opportunity/Threat

PRC law and policy practice related to international migration has tended toward viewing mobility as driven by opportunism even while raising concerns about threats to local security and stability.[133] Experience with migrant labor in China has shown the importance of economic need as an important driver.[134] Not surprisingly, China's caution about offering refugee status to economic migrants is informed by similar conclusions. Speaking to the UN General Assembly on the UNHCR's 2007 report on refugees, PRC delegation adviser Ke Yousheng stressed the importance of protecting genuine refugees while preventing the UNHCR regime from being abused:

> The Chinese Government welcomes the efforts made by the UNHCR to ensure prompt and effective protection of refugees who are genuinely eligible. Furthermore, the Chinese Government believes that effective improvement of the efficiency of refugee protection also calls for effective measures to keep the protection regime from being abused by various illegal migrants and criminals. We call on all the parties concerned to strictly abide by the provisions of the Convention on Refugees and prevent the refugee protection regime from being abused.[135]

The distinction between refugees and economic migrants was further evidenced in China's response to recommendations from Canada and the Netherlands to the first human rights UPR (2009) on implementation of principles of non-refoulement to refugees from North Korea:

> Concerning the illegal immigrants and protection of refugees and the policies practiced the delegation noted that China has acceded to the 1951 Convention on the Status of Refugees and its Additional Protocol. It followed the principle of non-refoulement in accordance with the convention. Since 1978, China has provided effective refuge for 300,000 refugees from Indochina. China is working on refugee legislation which will clarify further the screening procedures for refugees. Some people who illegally entered China because of economic reasons are not "refugees," but illegal immigrants. With regard to illegal immigrants, China has always handled properly specific cases.[136]

China's proposed governing principles for the 2018 GCM, underscored the distinction between regular and irregular migration in application of the non-refoulement principle:

> Second, achieving safe, orderly and regular migration flows. China advocates regularization of migration flows and active efforts to meet the legitimate aspirations of regular immigrants for employment, education and health care, among others, to protect the legitimate rights and interests of vulnerable migrant groups, and eliminate the discrimination and exclusion of migrants. Countries should, in accordance with their domestic laws, relevant international law and humanitarian principles, properly address the issue of irregular migration and bolster cross-border law enforcement and security cooperation against smuggling and human trafficking. Since migrants and refugees fall under different legal categories, the non-refoulement principle should not be applied to migration issues.[137]

Caution over the impact of migration on local security and stability was also evident in China's 2021 Land Border Law.[138] The law authorizes cooperation between the NIA and China's public security and customs departments in curbing illegal immigration:

> Article 52. Departments such as for public security, customs, and immigration may establish cooperation mechanisms with relevant departments of neighboring land countries, exchange information, carry out law enforcement cooperation, and jointly prevent and combat cross-border illegal and criminal activities.

By empowering the NIA to coordinate immigration control activities with public security units, the new law entrenched a perspective on immigration focused on protecting security and stability in China. Speaking to the NIA's responses to international migration, the director of the NIA's policy and law department explained: "Since the beginning of this year, the National Immigration Administration has resolutely implemented the decision-making and deployment of the Party Central Committee and the State Council, firmly defended the country's political security, coordinated the work of maintaining the stability of the port border, preventing the import of overseas epidemics, and serving economic and social development."[139]

PRC law and policy practices related to community mobility stand in comparison with international standards. While the latter acknowledge the role of state sovereignty, rights to migration are recognized in the Universal Declaration of Human Rights (UDHR), which underscores equality in their application and admits to the complexities involved in enforcement:

> Article 13.2. Everyone has a right to leave any country, including his own, and to return to his country.
>
> Article 14.1. Everyone has the right to seek and to enjoy in other countries asylum from persecution.[140]

The UDHR also offers human rights guarantees for mobility within states (Article 13.1). Thus, international law standards tend to treat mobility not so much as a threat but rather as a matter of opportunity and benefit for receiving communities. These contrast with PRC practices.

THUS, PRC LAW and policy practice related to operational norms on identity, diversity, and mobility has tended toward restrictions against migration that contrast with the ideals associated with the rules-based international order. Practices related to identity have tended to favour inherent criteria such as ethnicity and, when accepting the capacity for acquired identity, have focused on instilling Han cultural attributes in non-Han people. PRC law and policy practices related to diversity have tended to lean toward segregation rather than integration in response to involuntary migration. Informed by traditional policies on ethnic minorities but not yet taking up recently emerging themes on assimilation, China's response to foreign migrants – especially involuntary migrants unlikely to be returning home unless forced – has remained oriented toward segregation. China's law and policy practices related to mobility have tended to focus on threats to stability and security, even while recognizing the role of opportunity in driving migration.

These areas of law and policy practice contrast with the standards associated with the rules-based international order favouring acquired identity, integration in support of diversity, and mobility as a source of opportunity for recipient countries. China's law and policy practices related to social community exemplify its globalized populist resistance to global systems and communities managing the crisis of involuntary migration.

Aside from their substantive differences with corresponding international law standards, PRC law and policy practice on community reflected tensions with international ideals on equality and complexity. As suggested in Chapter 1 and illustrated in Figure 6, international standards on acquired identity, integration in response to diversity, and opportunity in socio-economic and geographic mobility, reflect policy orientations favouring equality and accepting diversity. These contrast with the acceptance of inequality and resistance to complexity bound up in China's approaches

TABLE 6 Community: Comparing China standards with rules-based international order (RBIO) standards

	Identity	Diversity	Mobility	Migrant Integration Policy Index score[1]
China standards	Inherent	Segregation	Threat	32/100
RBIO standards	Acquired	Integration	Opportunity	N/A

1 Migrant Integration Policy Index 2020, https://www.mipex.eu/key-findings.

favouring inherency of identity, segregation of diversity, and threat perception on mobility. As with the examples of COVID-19 and climate change, although China's opposition to elites and embrace of grievance ideology spoke to resentments over inequality, the PRC's alternative law and policy practices related to community identity, diversity, and mobility often embrace inequality. Table 6 depicts PRC law and policy practices related to community in the context of China's global Migrant Integration Policy Index (MIPEX) ranking compared with international standards.

Rhetorical Markers of China's Globalized Populism in Response to Migration

China's engagement with the international migration policy system includes rhetorical markers on sovereignty, development, and human rights that lend resilience to China's populist policy priorities. As with the role of rhetorical markers in China's responses to COVID-19 and climate change, PRC discourses on sovereignty work to insulate PRC migration law and policy from international scrutiny, discourses on development serve to justify PRC practices on migration, and discourses on human rights provide alternatives to international human rights standards on migration as a condition for accepting refugees in the face of international disregard, and in practical resistance through China's challenges to UN human rights standards on migration.

Sovereignty: Safeguarding PRC Policy Choices on Migration

Sovereignty issues have long been a key dimension of international law and policy on refugees.[141] The PRC extols state sovereignty as a fundamental condition for migration policy.[142] Sovereignty concerns were given priority in China's 2013 Exit and Entry Administration Law,[143] which noted its primary purpose as the protection of sovereignty, security, and social order (Article 1). China's 2021 Land Border Law states: "The sovereignty and territorial integrity of the People's Republic of China shall be sacred and inviolable."[144]

Priorities concerning sovereignty have been evident in China's general reluctance to enact comprehensive legislation on migration, despite international pressure to do so.[145] A 2004 Ministry of Foreign Affairs summary on China's relations with the UNHCR noted concerns over sovereignty as grounds for China's resistance to international direction on treatment of involuntary migrants:

> The Chinese delegate [to the Sixth Asia-Pacific Inter-governmental Consultation on Refugee, Displaced and Migrants in December 2001] pointed out that sovereign countries should shoulder the primary responsibility in the protection of refugees and the displaced as well as the prevention of illegal immigrants whereas UNHCR and IOM play a vital, but not leading role in assisting countries in question to settle the issue.[146]

While China's engagement with globalization has seen calls for relaxation in the country's treatment of exit and entry procedures,[147] expansive changes have not been forthcoming. China's Exit and Entry Administration Law was the first to provide even modest detail on treatment of refugees:

> Article 46. Foreigners applying for refugee status may, during the screening process, stay in China on the strength of temporary identity certificates issued by public security organs; foreigners who are recognized as refugees may stay or reside in China on the strength of refugee identity certificates issued by public security organs.[148]

Despite its detailed provisions on different types of visas and residency permits and addressing issues of repatriation, the implementing regulations for the Exit and Entry law contained no provisions elaborating specifically on the treatment of refugees.[149] Defending his country's election to avoid extensive legislative detail on involuntary migration as an exercise of state sovereignty, Chinese ambassador Li Li noted at the 2018 launch of the GCM that "each country has the right to develop its own laws and policies on migration."[150] Li went further to assert state sovereignty as a precondition for accepting responsibility for involuntary migrants.

> First, upholding the principle of respect for national sovereignty. The principle of sovereignty of states should form the basis of migration governance. The migration issue is closely linked with border control and societal governance. Just as countries vary greatly in the stages of their economic and social development, they face different situations in migration as well. Global migration governance should be based on full respect for national sovereignty.[151]

Echoing the point, China's 2020 position paper to the United Nations called for implementation of the GCM to be based on respect for national sovereignty and account for local conditions: "The implementation of the Compact must be based on respect for national sovereignty, take into full account conditions of different countries, and accommodate the interests of all parties."[152]

Revealing concerns over the possibility of UNHCR intrusion on China's sovereignty in making refugee determinations and arranging resettlement, China's support for the GCR adopted by extension the compact's principle on the primacy of state sovereignty:

> While recognizing the primary responsibility and sovereignty of States, a multi-stakeholder and partnership approach will be pursued, in line with relevant legal frameworks and in close coordination with national institutions. In addition to the exercise of its mandate responsibilities, UNHCR will play a supportive and catalytic role.[153]

China's suggested revisions to the GCR consistently proposed removing language on sharing responsibilities and substituting instead language on cooperation, emphasizing the voluntariness of cooperation over the language of responsibilities that has implications for diminution of sovereignty.[154]

As with its reliance on sovereignty in its responses to COVID-19 and climate change, China has deployed the rhetoric of sovereignty to insulate its migration and refugee policies from intrusion by international elites and the policy systems they purportedly control. Thus, the rhetorical marker of sovereignty serves as a mechanism of resilience supporting China's resistance to international elites.

Development: Conditions for Accepting Migrants

The rhetorical marker of development lends resilience to China's migration policies. China's preoccupation with its purported status as a developing country has been combined with complaints over perceived inattention on the part of the international migration policy system to local conditions in international refugee standards – including conditions in both source and destination countries. This was evident in China's position on governing principles presented at the 2018 intergovernmental conference accepting the GCM:

> Third, strengthening governance by persisting in tackling the root causes. Underdevelopment and unbalanced development are the main drivers of migration. Ultimately, solutions to the problems resulting from underdevelopment can only be achieved through development. The international community should comprehensively implement the 2030 Agenda for Sustainable Development, including the target of promoting orderly, safe, regular and responsible migration and population movement. China supports strengthening international cooperation for development to help origin countries of migration to develop their economies, improve people's livelihoods and enhance capacity building in areas such as immigration administration, disaster relief and mitigation, and response to climate change. The Member States should promote the in-depth participation of migrants in inclusive socio-economic development and give full play to their positive role in promoting development.[155]

China's preference for focusing refugee policy on supporting development in countries of origin supported its claims to developing country status (despite growing prosperity) even while limiting its own responsibility to accept refugees as a destination country, which seems out of step with international standards.[156]

China's support for countries of origin has been closely linked with its Belt and Road Initiative (BRI), enabling investments in developing economies where China has economic and strategic interests.[157] This is an integral component of China's "South-South cooperation" (*nan-nan hezuo //* 南南合作) strategy.[158] The UNHCR has apparently endorsed this approach.[159] Thus, while China has increased its donations to countries of origin – particularly Syria – it made only modest strides toward strengthening the legal protections for refugee claimants arriving in China.[160] China also noted that the countries responsible for conditions in Afghanistan should assume most of the burden of addressing the needs of the Afghan people, once again defending its own reluctance to accept refugee claimants from Afghanistan (or other war-torn regions such as Syria).[161]

China's focus on resolving conditions in source countries was evident in its response to relief programs organized to assist refugees fleeing Syria's civil war.[162] Foreign Minister Wang Yi's remarks to the 2016 Syria Donors Conference co-chaired by the United Kingdom, Germany, Norway, and Kuwait focused not on refugee support but rather on promoting the political process in Syria as the fundamental way to resolve the humanitarian crisis.[163] China's pledge of US$35 million for Syrian refugee relief was quite modest in comparison with other donors (ranking twentieth out of forty-seven donors).[164] Conjoining challenges of migration and refugees, Premier Li Keqiang's speech to the 2016 UN General Assembly Summit for Refugees and Migrants noted the impacts not only on source and destination countries but also on regional peace and stability, global economic recovery, the international order, and terrorism, and called for more attention to be paid to development in source countries.[165] Following reports on its modest contributions following a 2017 Brussels conference on Syrian refugee aid (of its US$29 million pledged, China had disbursed US$5 million, or 17 percent, in 2017), China was not listed among donors at the subsequent Brussels conferences in in 2018 and 2020.[166] The rhetorical marker of development thus serves to justify China's resistance to the international migration policy system. The migration crisis is presented as a result of a failure by international elites to assist developing countries, while China's reluctance to accept migrants is premised on conditions of China's own development. As a mechanism for resilience, China's development rhetoric insulates PRC migration policy and practice from international critique and calls for reform.

Human Rights: Contrary Treatment of Refugees

Human rights have long been associated with the treatment of refugees and asylum seekers in destination countries.[167] Both the GCM and the GCR emphasize their reliance on principles of international human rights law.[168] Yet China's human rights orthodoxy has empowered its disregard of migrant rights, lending resilience to PRC migration policy.[169] The UN Human Rights Council's UPR process has underscored the human rights implications of China's handling of involuntary migrants.[170] The first UPR cycle (2009) saw the UNHRC express concerns that non-citizens, including asylum seekers, refugees, and stateless persons, are excluded for PRC constitutional guarantees to the rights and freedoms enshrined in the UN Convention on the Status of Refugees.[171]

The issue of forced repatriation (refoulement) has been particularly prominent. Practices of forced repatriation contradict provisions of the 1951

Refugee Convention prohibiting forced repatriation of refugees under the principle of non-refoulement:

> Article 33. Prohibition of Expulsion or Return ("Refoulement")
> 1 No Contracting State shall expel or return ("refouler") a refugee in any manner whatsoever to the frontiers of territories where his life or freedom would be threatened on account of his race, religion, nationality, membership of a particular social group or political opinion.
> 2 The benefit of the present provision may not, however, be claimed by a refugee whom there are reasonable grounds for regarding as a danger to the security of the country in which he is, or who, having been convicted by a final judgment of a particularly serious crime, constitutes a danger to the community of that country.[172]

The 2009 UPR report also noted concerns raised by the UN Committee on Economic, Social and Cultural Rights (CESCR) "that some asylum-seekers are excluded by the refugee determination procedure of China, in particular those coming from a neighbouring country, who are regarded as economic migrants, and are thus compelled to return to their countries."[173] China's practices of forced repatriation despite the international law principle of non-refoulement have been particularly evident in its interpretation of its treatment of refugees from North Korea.[174] Despite apparent inconsistencies with the non-refoulement principle, China has attempted to justify its forced repatriation of North Korean refugees on grounds that they were not genuine refugees but rather economic migrants.[175]

On this and other issues, the second human rights UPR (2013) for China included three recommendations on treatment of refugees:[176]

> 186.241. Protect North Korean refugees in accordance with international law, honouring the principle of non-refoulement (Czech Republic);
>
> 186.242. Accept the recommendations of UNHCR on refugee issues including the adoption of national asylum legislation (Republic of Korea);
>
> 186.243. Provide adequate protection to asylum seekers and cross-border refugees, including especially those from neighbouring countries, in accordance with humanitarian considerations and relevant international norms such as the principle of non-refoulement (Republic of Korea).

While clearly reflecting concerns over China's forced repatriation of refugee claimants from North Korea, the recommendations had broader application – particularly in calling for national asylum legislation and providing adequate protection for asylum seekers and cross-border refugees from neighbouring countries. China supported the call for national legislation, but simply "noted" the recommendations on North Korean refugees and on asylum seekers and refugees from neighbouring countries.

The second UPR also included reporting from UN agencies calling for more work on these issues:

> UNHCR recommended that China adopt national asylum legislation with technical support from UNHCR; establish a responsible government institution in charge of refugee matters; and accept UNHCR technical support in capacity-building for Government officials and in the development of a national refugee status determination procedure. UNHCR further recommended that China facilitate the naturalization of Indo-Chinese refugees.

As well, the UN Committee on the Elimination of Racial Discrimination reiterated its concern that asylum seekers from a neighbouring country continued to be systematically refused asylum and forcibly returned. The UNHCR "recommended that China take all measures to ensure viable and effective humanitarian space for those asylum seekers who might be determined to be in need of international protection, including issuing them identification and documentation to legally reside in China."[177]

The third UPR (2018) called again for China to expand legal provisions for protecting involuntary migrants:

> The Office of the United Nations High Commissioner for Refugees (UNHCR) noted that in 2016, there were 668 asylum seekers and 162 recognized refugees awaiting a durable solution. Despite possession of certificates confirming their registration and status with UNHCR, urban asylum seekers and refugees continued to face the risk of arrest and detention in China for violation of immigration offences if they entered the country unlawfully or overstayed their visas.[178]

Following up on the third human rights UPR, the UNHRC called for China to take steps "ceasing the forcible repatriation of nationals of the

Democratic People's Republic of Korea and allowing those nationals unimpeded access to UNHCR for a determination of their international protection needs."[179] All three UPR reports called for the application of the 1951 Refugee Convention to Hong Kong. Contributions by UNHCR and other agencies to the Human Rights Council's UPR process highlighted the contradictions between PRC law and policy on involuntary migrants and China's international human rights obligations. Conflicts with human rights were evident in the 2022 Land Border Law's mandate for "effective measures to resolutely safeguard territorial sovereignty and the security of the land borders and to prevent and combat any acts that undermine territorial sovereignty and undermine the land borders," which used a national security discourse to overcome the human rights principle of non-refoulement and other matters involving involuntary migrants.[180]

China's efforts to refocus international human rights standards concerning migration on conditions in source counties have also been evident. China's foreign relations and diplomacy priorities in source counties such as Syria, North Korea, and Myanmar have militated in favour of deference to local governance.[181] China's response to the challenge of involuntary migrants from Syria raised sensitive issues around its deference to the Assad regime, tolerating the widespread human rights abuses that generated much of the Syrian involuntary migration abroad. China's claim that migrants from North Korea are not genuine refugees but rather economic migrants supported its diplomatic and strategic relations with the Democratic People's Republic of Korea premised on denial of that regime's use of food security as a tool of political repression.[182] China's positions on human rights issues were evident as well in the Rohingya refugee crisis of 2015.[183] Here again, China's policy response focused less on accepting and resettling refugees than on local political solutions and the repatriation of displaced persons.[184] Even as UN Secretary-General António Guterres emphasized the need to create conditions for the "voluntary, dignified and safe return" of Rohingya refugees to Rakhine State pursuant to a joint memorandum of understanding between the UNHCR, the UN Development Programme (UNDP), and Myanmar, China emphasized the need to accelerate repatriation even while downplaying local conditions facing repatriated Rohingya migrants.[185] China opposed a decision by the UN Human Rights Council supporting establishment of the Independent Investigative Mechanism for Myanmar (IIMM), an international body to prepare case files for criminal prosecution over human rights abuses against the Rohingya.[186]

China's human rights conflicts with the intentional migration policy system have extended to people fleeing abuse in Xinjiang, Tibet, and other areas of China, as evidenced in Beijing's pressure on local governments in neighbouring destination countries like Turkey and Afghanistan to repatriate them.[187] By terming refugees fleeing repression in China as criminals or terrorists, China sought to evade the provisions of the 1951 Refugee Convention prohibiting forced repatriation of refugees under the principle of non-refoulement.[188] China has also failed to implement the terms of Article 9 of its own Nationality Law, to the effect that a citizen of China loses that citizenship when taking citizenship in another country – as attested by the examples of Huseyin Celil and Xiao Jianhua, who were repatriated to China and imprisoned despite their having secured foreign citizenship.[189] China has also rejected the rights of destination countries to grant refugee status and asylum to refugees fleeing human rights abuses in Hong Kong under its newly enacted National Security Law.[190] Throughout these processes and debates the PRC has drawn on the rhetorical marker of human rights, emphasizing its own preferences to build resilience for its migration practices against international standards.

Thus, China's resistance to the international migration policy system has been bolstered by rhetorical markers of sovereignty, development, and human rights. The rhetorical marker of sovereignty has been evident in the regime's resistance to imposition of international standards on China's acceptance of migrants. The marker of development has been evident in PRC positions on respective duties of source and destination countries. The rhetorical marker of human rights highlights China's efforts to redraw international standards on migration such as non-refoulement and the legal status of refugees, so as to support China's political and policy preferences. These rhetorical markers of China's globalized populism reinforce tensions between China's policy preferences and the standards of the rules-based international order. Taken together, China's rhetorical markers of sovereignty in assertions of unfettered state control over immigration, development as justification to resist pressure to accept migrants, and restricted human rights for involuntary migrants provide resilience for China's globalized populism in resistance to the international migration policy system. The resilience provided by China's rhetorical markers on sovereignty, development, and human rights for PRC law and policy practice on involuntary migration may impede the possibilities for change, with implications for reform in China's ongoing approaches to community in society generally.

Conclusion

China's populist responses to the crisis of involuntary migration emerge from conditions of inequality and complexity in China's relationship with the international policy community on involuntary migration. Populist dynamics of opposition to global elites/systems, justification through grievance ideology, and practical resistance through alternative law and policy practice related to identity, diversity, and mobility in community infuse China's response to the crisis of involuntary migration. China's law and policy practices related to community identity have tended toward inherency and ethnic essentialism over international ideals extolling individual qualities and circumstances as the basis for identity. PRC law and policy practices on diversity in community have tended to favour segregation that contrast with international standards favouring integration. China's migration law and policy practices related to community mobility have tended to regard migration more as a threat to local socio-economic conditions than an opportunity, in contrast with international discourses favouring mobility as an opportunity for socio-economic development. China's law and policy practices related to operational norms of community identity, diversity, and mobility are supported by rhetorical markers on sovereignty in asserting China's right to determine its own migration policies, development as a condition for accepting migrants, and disregard of international standards on human rights of migrants. These in turn lend resilience to PRC policy and practice, diminishing the prospects for change. China's passive responses to the global crisis of involuntary migration contrast with the antagonism in its pandemic response and the conditional participation in its responses to climate change. Nonetheless, coupled with China's globalized populist responses to COVID-19 and climate change, PRC responses to the crisis of involuntary migration exemplify further the challenges China's globalized populism presents for the liberal international order.

Conclusion and Recommendations

THIS BOOK DEPICTS how discourses on populism help explain China's responses to the global crises of COVID-19, climate change, and involuntary migration, with implications for China's relationship with the rules-based international order. After introducing existing discourses on populism and explaining the concept of globalized populism and its application to China, we have reviewed the circumstances attendant to the global crises of COVID-19, climate change, and involuntary migration and responses from populist regimes that offer comparisons with China. We went on to show how China's handling of these global crises reflects responses to conditions of inequality and complexity that underpin populism generally, generating populist opposition to elites and associated systems of governance and regulation, justification through grievance ideology, and practical resistance through alternative law and policy practices around accountability, prosperity, and community. We have explored how rhetorical markers of sovereignty, development, and human rights are used to build resilience for China's globalized populism. We have suggested that understanding China's globalized populism can augment national interest analysis in explaining China's challenges to the rules-based international order.

This book's two analytical tracks – focusing first on the foundations of China's globalized populism and then on the details of PRC populist responses to the global crises of pandemic control, climate action, and involuntary migration – point to potential avenues for policy response from supporters of the rules-based international order. Such policy responses involve a fundamental question of whether the international order can accommodate China's greater participation. This involves a choice between adjusting international institutions and systems to accommodate China's populist resistance, or continuing with existing arrangements, with a possible consequence of emerging bipolarity in global governance and international relations.[1] Policy responses suggested here are premised on the need to continue encouraging China's participation in the international order to further the interests of both the proponents of that order and China itself.

Appreciation of underlying conditions of inequality and complexity invites policy responses focused on strengthening China's relationship with the existing international systems on public health, climate, and migration, and by extension with the rules-based international order more broadly. This would include proactive efforts by liberal democratic governments to build China's confidence that the equality and complexity dimensions of the rules-based international order do not threaten China but instead offer opportunities for greater participation and influence. This would extend to including PRC perspectives in public expressions of international policy priorities on pandemic control, climate action, and involuntary migration, while also avoiding granting China a veto over international policy initiatives that contradict its prerogatives. Institutional diplomacy with China by the World Health Organization (WHO), the United Nations Framework Convention on Climate Change (UNFCCC), and Office of the United Nations High Commissioner for Refugees (UNHCR), and equally importantly bilateral and multilateral diplomacy by dominant policy drivers like the United States and members of the European Union, can help strengthen China's confidence in the international rules-based order and its implementation through international policy systems on public health, climate, and migration.

As well, efforts to respond to rhetorical markers of China's globalized populism will be essential. The marker on *sovereignty* expresses China's diminished commitment to compliance with international standards, undermining the cooperation needed for effective responses to global crises. While acknowledging the principle of state sovereignty as expressed in the UN Charter and elsewhere, efforts are needed to temper China's expansive sovereignty claims even while encouraging it to honour the sovereignty of its bilateral partners. This would involve promoting global dialogue and revisiting limits on state sovereignty in light of the transnational reach of global policy crises of pandemic control, climate change, and involuntary migration. As international agreements generally involve the voluntary acceptance by states of diminution of their sovereignty, encouraging China to revisit its absolutist sovereignty discourse can be an important step toward improving its response to the aforementioned global crises. The International Law Commission (ILC) can play an important role on these issues.

The marker of *development* conditions China's international cooperation on local socio-economic conditions. This can be addressed by reviewing China's status as a developing country and pursuing efforts to build greater nuance and diversity into measures of development. While its large population supports per capita GDP indicators affirming China's developing country status, rising levels of wealth and development in the coastal and urban areas invite measures of prosperity that distinguish China from other developing economies. Accepting the principle of "common but differentiated responsibilities and respective capabilities" in allocating responsibilities between developed and developing countries on responding to pandemic response, climate change, and involuntary migration should be tempered by careful and rigorous assessment of what China's differentiated responsibilities should be in light of its already considerable national capacity. The United Nations Development Programme (UNDP) can be useful in adjusting measures of development to account for such differences.

The rhetorical marker of *human rights* expresses PRC orthodoxy subordinating individual interests to the collective interests of society as determined by the Party-state, diminishing the prospects for China's international cooperation around established human rights principles of universality and indivisibility. This can be addressed by acknowledging diversity in international human rights standards – particularly among civil and political rights and economic, social, and cultural rights. While challenging suggestions about hierarchies of rights or accepting enforcement timetables that call for achieving some rights before others, an approach to international human rights discourse that accepts conceptual diversity and material difference in local conditions would be useful. Equally important, considering China's ratification and/or signing of multiple international human rights agreements, China's human rights law and policy practice should be treated as a matter of treaty compliance not subject to derogation through broad claims about sovereignty, cultural difference, and/or stages of development. China's own human rights abuses should also be addressed in this way. The Universal Periodic Review (UPR) process of the United Nations Human Rights Council (UNHRC) can be useful in such efforts.

Aside from general efforts to induce greater compliance with international standards embedded in the numerous treaties China has signed and/or ratified, specific responses to its populist law and policy practices around COVID-19, climate change, and involuntary migration will be essential. Supporters of the rules-based international order should be modest in their expectations about the utility of sanctions, trade embargos, and other types of international pressure – the very activities from which China's globalized populism derives – in moving the PRC regime toward greater engagement. The recommendations provided below reflect the expectation that change in China must come from within, through local political actors and processes; academic and policy specialists and communities; nascent health, climate, and immigration interest groups in society; and other opinion and policy drivers. While the current climate of repression under Xi Jinping presents serious obstacles to open expression of political thought and policy reflection, analysts differ on whether Xi's grasp on power may be weakening.[2] In any event, Xi's rule will not last forever, and policy responses to China's global populism in practice should be pursued accordingly.

Accountability and Pandemic Control

Performance accountability. Responding to issues of performance accountability in China's COVID-19 response, efforts can be made to expand availability of empirical accounts of regime policy outcomes in public health. International assistance has already supported expansion of China's statistical research capacities.[3] While China's multiple interventions regarding COVID-19 have relied heavily on statistical reporting, the challenge is to encourage the transition from aspirational to empirical reporting in regime depictions of policy outcomes. International policy responses should include broader support for scholarly and policy research on empirical assessments of China's pandemic policies. Publication in Chinese- as well as English-language media would be useful, in the expectation that research approaches and results will gradually become available to researchers and policy-makers in China, with concomitant impacts on the availability and desirability of empirical analysis. This can have an important impact on the PRC regime's COVID-19 reporting and other policy challenges.

Process accountability. The close connection between process accountability and discourses on the rule of law offers opportunities and challenges. As has been evident for nearly fifty years, law-related exchange programming between Chinese and international legal institutions, including law schools and courts, has had important effects on legal thinking and practice in China.[4] This should continue with robust protections for freedom of thought and expression. Such programs should address head-on the challenge of comparing liberal rule of law standards with China's CPC-led socialist legal system, avoiding intellectual colonialism in presumptions about the superiority of Western models while also not legitimating rule through law policies that do not meet the basic requirements of the UN General Assembly's "delivering justice" standards.[5] This can have a significant effect on the socio-economic and political impacts of China's COVID-19 control programs, with likely spillover effects on other issues.

Information accountability. China's general orientation toward propaganda over transparency poses challenges for scholars, policy-makers, and politically informed citizens seeking accurate information on government policy actions. While China's censorship system (including the "great firewall" obstructing internet access) remains powerful, information dissemination in China still takes place through informal channels within discrete policy and civic communities. Distribution internationally and into China of information on regime policy action through all possible media channels (including social media, internet, TV, radio, and even print) would be useful, particularly if targeted toward policy communities where informal exchanges of information are centred. Ongoing efforts to strengthen transparency standards in China's regulatory and policy initiatives[6] should continue.

Prosperity and Climate Change

Measurement of prosperity. Responding to the continuing preference in PRC law and policy for reliance on aggregated national and regional macro-data, international policy responses should include support for reliance on locally informed micro-data in scholarly and policy discourses.[7] Supporting academic and policy research on the importance of micro-data in measuring climate change impacts in China and internationally will be important in establishing best practices for policy research generally.

Distribution of prosperity. In response to PRC law and policy practices around distribution of prosperity through subsidies and other incentives to the mostly state-controlled business sector, international policy response can focus on disseminating examples of the benefits of direct distribution to individuals and groups in society. As well, greater attention to anti-corruption efforts internationally and in China, and the highlighting of best practices in Corporate Social Responsibility (CSR)[8] will be useful in inhibiting abuses by business firms in the enforcement of climate policy.

Autonomy of prosperity. As the sustainability of Xi Jinping's "new development" discourse, with its implications for greater state control and autonomy from market discipline, remains uncertain, international policy responses can usefully support the social and economic justice dimensions of "common prosperity," while also publicizing potential costs of increased state control. Support for dissemination of operational best practices on balancing state control and market discipline[9] will be important for this effort.

Community and Involuntary Migration

Identity. The general orientation toward inherency of identity in China's responses to involuntary migration invites policy responses supporting research on the dangers of ethnic essentialism and its effects on social stability.[10] Support for academic and policy research on the benefits of considering identity as a matter of acquired attributes will also be important in furthering reception and resettlement of refugees and other involuntary migrants.

Diversity. International responses to China's law and policy practices around diversity can usefully emphasize the harmful effects that segregation of minorities has for social cohesion and stability.[11] Academic and policy studies on the effectiveness of integration over segregation in building social cohesion and stability can influence China's policies on community. This can have particular benefits for informing China's response to reception and resettlement of involuntary migrants.

Mobility. China's past practices of restricting domestic mobility through the *hukou* system and restricting in-migration invite international responses supporting research and programming on the opportunities presented by migration.[12] Efforts to orient the discourse on international mobility from threat to opportunity will be an essential step and can have beneficial effects on mobility within China.

EVEN WHILE ATTENDING to immediate issues of national security, economic competition, and geo-strategic positioning, supporters of the rules-based international order should also adopt longer-term strategies for managing China's globalized populism. International policy responses to China's globalized populism should address both the foundations and operational expressions of China's populist responses to international policy systems on public health, climate, and migration, and by extension the rules-based international order itself. The foundations of China's globalized populism in conditions of inequality and complexity invite efforts to overcome China's resistance to the liberal international order through greater engagement, mutual education, and confidence building. Efforts to respond to

China's operational norms and law and policy practices around themes of accountability in COVID-19, prosperity in climate change, and community in involuntary migration will be useful in encouraging China's international cooperation on these global crises and forthcoming ones as well. While many of the measures suggested here have been tried in the past with some success, too often they have been discontinued or downgraded in frustration over the pace of change. Instead, policy responses to the foundations and expressions of China's populist resistance to the rules-based international order and the international policy systems for public health, climate action, and involuntary migration that derive from it should continue and even expand. Encouraging China's responsible and constructive participation in global affairs is a long-term project requiring long-term commitments. These should proceed with full awareness of the potential impacts this may have on the character of the international system and should include commitments to ensure continuity of basic principles regarding effective political accountability, equitable economic prosperity, and cohesive social community. As the alternative of exclusion seems untoward in light of China's continued importance to the international system, robust engagement through responses to the foundations and expressions of China's globalized populism offers an effective way forward. For despite China's growing power and international influence, the PRC's embrace of globalized populism seems likely to continue.

Notes

INTRODUCTION

1 Nien-chung Chang-Liao, "China's New Foreign Policy Under Xi Jinping," *Asian Security* 12, 2 (2019), https://www.tandfonline.com/doi/abs/10.1080/14799855.2016.1183195; Michael D. Swaine, "The 19th Party Congress and Chinese Foreign Policy," Carnegie Endowment for International Peace, October 16, 2017, https://carnegieendowment.org/2017/10/16/19th-party-congress-and-chinese-foreign-policy-pub-73432; Scott L. Kastner and Phillip C. Saunders, "Is China a Status Quo or Revisionist State? Leadership Travel as an Empirical Indicator of Foreign Policy Priorities," *International Studies Quarterly* 56, 1 (March 2012), https://academic.oup.com/isq/article/56/1/163/1936753?login=false.

2 Ching Kwan Lee, "Global China at 20: Why, How and So What?" *China Quarterly* 250 (June 2022): 313–31; Nadège Rolland, *China's Vision for a New World Order*, National Bureau of Asian Research Special Report No. 83 (Seattle: National Bureau of Asian Research, 2020), https://www.nbr.org/wp-content/uploads/pdfs/publications/sr83_chinasvision_jan2020.pdf; Jessica Chen Weiss, "A World Safe for Autocracy? China's Rise and the Future of Global Politics," *Foreign Affairs*, July/August 2019, https://www.foreignaffairs.com/articles/china/2019-06-11/world-safe-autocracy?cid=otr-july_august_authors-061119; Melanie Hart and Blaine Johnson, "Mapping China's Global Governance Ambitions," Center for American Progress, February 28 2019, https://www.americanprogress.org/issues/security/reports/2019/02/28/466768/mapping-chinas-global-governance-ambitions/; Chen Weitseng, ed., *The Beijing Consensus? How China Has Changed Western Ideas of Law and Economic Development* (Cambridge: Cambridge University Press, 2017).

3 Michael Schuman, "Xi Jinping Is Done with the Established World Order," *The Atlantic*, September 9, 2023, https://www.theatlantic.com/international/archive/2023/09/g20-summit-china-xi-absence/675267/#:~:text=The%20world%27s%20most%20powerful%20leaders,turn%20in%20China%27s%20foreign%20policy; Zachary Paikin, "Canada's Dilemma: China and the 'Rules-Based International Order,'" Institute for Peace and Diplomacy, June 14, 2022, https://peacediplomacy.org/2022/06/14/canadas-dilemma-china-and-the-rules-based-international-order/; Daniel F. Vukovich, *Illiberal China: The Ideological Challenge of the People's Republic of China* (Singapore: Palgrave Macmillan, 2019), https://link.springer.com/book/10.1007/978-981-13-0541-2.

4 M. Taylor Fravel, "China's Global Security Initiative at Two: A Journey, Not a Destination," *China Leadership Monitor* no. 80 (May 30, 2024), https://www.prcleader.org/post/china-s-global-security-initiative-at-two-a-journey-not-a-destination; Ministry of Foreign Affairs of

the People's Republic of China, "Following the Guidance of Xi Jinping Thought on Diplomacy and Advancing in All Respects Major-Country Diplomacy with Chinese Characteristics in the New Era," September 29, 2022, http://us.china-embassy.gov.cn/eng/zgyw/202209/t20220930_10774938.htm.

5 Global Affairs Canada, "Canada's Indo-Pacific Strategy," July 24, 2023, https://www.international.gc.ca/transparency-transparence/indo-pacific-indo-pacifique/index.aspx?lang=eng.

6 US Department of State. "Integrated Country Strategy: People's Republic of China," February 2, 2023, https://www.state.gov/wp-content/uploads/2023/03/ICS_EAP_China_02FEB2023_PUBLIC.pdf.

7 House of Lords International Relations and Defence Committee, "The UK and China's Security and Trade Relationship: A Strategic Void," September 10, 2021, https://committees.parliament.uk/publications/7214/documents/75842/default/.

8 Australian Government, Department of Foreign Affairs and Trade, "China Country Brief," July 2022, https://www.dfat.gov.au/geo/china/china-country-brief.

9 Stephen McDonell, Simon Fraser, and Kell Ng, "Qin Gang: China Foreign Minister's Removal Sparks Speculation," *BBC News,* July 26, 2023, https://www.bbc.com/news/world-asia-china-66299379. The recent appointment of Lu Shaye as Chinese ambassador to the European Union suggests, however, that the "wolf warrior" ethos is not dead. Joe Leahy and Henry Foy, "China Appoints 'Wolf Warrior' Ambassador to Manage Affairs with Europe: Selection of Blunt-Talking Lu Shaye Signals Hardening of Beijing's Stance Towards EU," *Financial Times,* February 6, 2025, https://www.ft.com/content/3b608fa8-1af7-41a2-bd71-31c2eda33dbf.

10 "Xi Orders Chinese Envoys to Create 'Diplomatic Iron Army,'" *Asahi Shimbun,* January 5, 2024, https://www.asahi.com/ajw/articles/15103238.

11 The "rules-based international order" is generally associated with liberal norms on democracy and rule of law, open markets, and human rights protections against state intrusion. Global Affairs Canada, "Departmental Plan 2022–23," March 23, 2022, https://www.international.gc.ca/transparency-transparence/departmental-plan-ministeriel/2022-2023.aspx?lang=eng; Chatham House, "Challenges to the Rules-Based International Order," London Conference, June 1–2, 2015, Session One, https://www.chathamhouse.org/sites/default/files/London%20Conference%202015%20-%20Background%20Papers.pdf.

12 Pitman B. Potter, *Assessing Treaty Performance in China: Trade and Human Rights* (Vancouver: UBC Press, 2014), 4–6, https://www.ubcpress.ca/assessing-treaty-performance-in-china.

13 See, e.g., Cas Mudde and Cristobal Rovira Kaltwasser, *Populism: A Very Short Introduction* (Oxford: Oxford University Press, 2017), https://global.oup.com/academic/product/populism-a-very-short-introduction-9780190234874?cc=ca&lang=en&#; Noam Gidron and Bart Bonikowski, "Varieties of Populism: Literature Review and Research Agenda," Weatherhead Center for International Affairs, Harvard University (2013), https://www.wcfia.harvard.edu/sites/g/files/omnuum8891/files/wcfia/files/gidron_bonikowski_populismlitreview_2013.pdf.

14 Whereas "global populism" may refer to the global phenomenon of populism, I understand "globalized populism" as aimed at global rather than domestic elites. Maria Hsia Chang and A. James Gregor, *Political Populism in the Twenty-First Century: We the People* (Cambridge: Cambridge Scholars Publishing, 2021), https://cambridgescholars.com/product/978-1-5275-6472-5/; Barrie Axford, *Populism Versus the New Globalization* (London: Sage Publications, 2021), https://uk.sagepub.com/en-gb/eur/populism-versus-the-new-globalization/book267825; Terry Flew and Petros Iosifidis, "Populism, Globalization and Social Media," *International Communication Gazette* 82, 1 (October 12, 2019), https://journals.sagepub.com/doi/full/10.1177/1748048519880721; Stanford University, "About the Global Populisms Project," https://fsi.stanford.edu/global-populisms/global-populism-about.

15 Xi Jinping, "Speech at a Ceremony Marking the Centenary of the Communist Party of China, July 1, 2021," https://en.wikisource.org/wiki/Speech_at_a_Ceremony_Marking_the_Centenary_of_the_Communist_Party_of_China.

16 Ministry of Foreign Affairs of the People's Republic of China, "Wang Yi: COVID-19 Needs Origin-Tracing and Political Virus Also Needs Origin-Tracking," July 25, 2021, https://www.fmprc.gov.cn/eng/gjhdq_665435/3265_665445/3286_664530/3288_664534/202406/t20240611_11420513.html.

17 Ding Yihui, Guoyu Ren, Shi Guangyu, and Gong Peng, *China's National Assessment Report on Climate Change (I): Climate Change in China and the Future Trend* (2007), https://www.researchgate.net/publication/242281068_China's_National_Assessment_Report_on_Climate_

Change_I_Climate_change_in_China_and_the_future_trend; "The People's Republic of China Initial National Communication on Climate Change: Executive Summary," October 2004, https://unfccc.int/resource/docs/natc/chnnc1exsum.pdf.

18 Lili Song, "China and the International Refugee Protection Regime: Past, Present, and Potentials," *Refugee Survey Quarterly* 37, 2 (2018): 139–61, https://academic.oup.com/rsq/article/37/2/139/4934135?login=true.

19 See, e.g., Michael D. Swaine, Ezra F. Vogel, Paul Heer, J. Stapleton Roy, Rachel Esplin Odell, Mike Mochizuki, Avery Goldstein, and Alice Miller; Aaron L. Friedberg replies, "The Overreach of the China Hawks: Aggression Is the Wrong Response to Beijing," *Foreign Affairs,* October 23, 2020, https://www.foreignaffairs.com/articles/china/2020-10-23/overreach-china-hawks#author-info; Kerry Dumbaugh, "China's Foreign Policy: What Does It Mean for U.S. Global Interests," US Defense Technical Information Center, July 18, 2006, https://apps.dtic.mil/sti/citations/ADA484838; Thomas W. Robinson and David Shambaugh, eds., *Chinese Foreign Policy: Theory and Practice* (Oxford: Clarendon Press, 1994), https://global.oup.com/academic/product/chinese-foreign-policy-9780198290162?cc=ca&lang=en&; G.W. Choudhury, *China in World Affairs: The Foreign Policy of the PRC Since 1970* (New York: Routledge, 1982), https://www.taylorfrancis.com/books/mono/10.4324/9780429048852/china-world-affairs-foreign-policy-prc-since-1970-choudhury.

20 Yu Jie and Lucy Ridout, "Who Decides China's Foreign Policy? The Role of Central Government, Provincial Level Authorities and State-Owned Enterprises," Chatham House Asia Pacific Programme Briefing Paper, November 2021; Linda Jakobson and Ryan Manuel, "How Are Foreign Policy Decisions Made in China?" *Asia and the Pacific Policy Studies* (Australian National University) 3, 1 (2016): 101–10, https://onlinelibrary.wiley.com/doi/full/10.1002/app5.121; Chih-yu Shih and Chiung-chiu Huang, "China's Quest for Grand Strategy: Power, National Interest, or Relational Security?" *Chinese Journal of International Politics* 8, 1 (2015): 1–26, https://academic.oup.com/cjip/article/8/1/1/2863861; Zongyi Liu, "The Concept of National Interests," in *China's Diplomacy: Theory and Practice,* ed. Jiemian Yang (Singapore: World Scientific, 2015), https://www.worldscientific.com/doi/10.1142/9781938134395_0003; Rukmani Gupta, "China's National Interests: Exploring the Domestic Discourse," *Strategic Analysis* 36, 5 (2012): 804–18, https://www.tandfonline.com/doi/abs/10.1080/09700161.2012.712391?journalCode=rsan20; Yong Deng, "The Chinese Conception of National Interests in International Relations," *China Quarterly* 154 (June 1998): 308–29, https://www.cambridge.org/core/journals/china-quarterly/article/abs/chinese-conception-of-national-interests-in-international-relations/A400D958CB5F8406B4E666196662CDDA.

21 See, e.g., Jerry Brown, "Washington's Crackpot Realism," *New York Review of Books,* March 24, 2022, https://www.nybooks.com/articles/2022/03/24/washingtons-crackpot-realism-jerry-brown/; Chris Alden, "Critiques of the Rational Actor Model and Foreign Policy Decision Making," in *Oxford Research Encyclopedia of Politics,* ed. William R. Thompson and Tereza Capelos (Oxford: Oxford University Press, 2017), https://eprints.lse.ac.uk/84466/1/Alden_Critiques%20of%20rational%20actor_2017.pdf; Brantly Womack, "China as a Normative Foreign Policy Actor," CEPS Working Document No. 282 (January 2008), http://aei.pitt.edu/11662/1/1607.pdf.

22 Timothy R. Heath, "Xi's Cautious Inching Towards the China Dream," *Lawfare,* August 7, 2023, https://www.lawfaremedia.org/article/xi-s-cautious-inching-towards-the-china-dream; Charles Parton, "China Watching in the 'New Era': A Guide," Council on Geostrategy Explainer No. GPE05, February 2022, https://www.geostrategy.org.uk/app/uploads/2022/02/Explainer-GPE05.pdf. For discussion of policy orthodoxy in the China context, see Pitman B. Potter, *Exporting Virtue? China's International Human Rights Activism in the Age of Xi Jinping* (Vancouver: UBC Press, 2021), 5–6.

23 Sarah Biddulph and Ljiljana Biuković, ed., *Good Governance in Economic Development: International Norms and Chinese Perspectives* (Vancouver: UBC Press, 2019), ch. 1.

24 Lisa Xing, "As Trump Moves to Withdraw from Global Commitments, China Is Waiting in the Wings," *CBC News,* January 23, 2024, https://www.cbc.ca/news/world/trump-us-china-relations-climate-health-1.7438632.

CHAPTER 1: CONSIDERING GLOBALIZED POPULISM

1 Michael Bernhard, Arnie Kreppel, and Carlos de la Torre, eds., *Still the Age of Populism? Re-examining Theories and Concepts* (Abingdon, UK: Routledge, 2024), https://www.routledge.com/Still-the-Age-of-Populism-Re-examining-Theories-and-Concepts/Bernhard-Kreppel

-delaTorre/p/book/9781032591407?srsltid=AfmBOoqy8Ns1ieJ3dVyIxAL3iw3yA18sUb3QIKs T9JrPK5471IYZwaui; Kristin M.S. Bezio and George R. Goethals, *Leadership, Populism and Resistance* (Cheltenham, UK: Edward Elgar, 2020), https://www.e-elgar.com/shop/usd/leadership-populism-and-resistance-9781788979252.html; Noam Gidron and Bart Bonikowski, "Varieties of Populism: Literature Review and Research Agenda," Weatherhead Center for International Affairs, Harvard University, Working Paper Series No. 13-0004, 2013, https://scholar.harvard.edu/files/gidron_bonikowski_populismlitreview_2013.pdf.

2 Pankaj Mishra, *Age of Anger: A History of the Present* (New York: Farrar, Straus and Giroux, 2017), Prologue, https://us.macmillan.com/books/9781250159304/ageofanger/.

3 William G. Shade, "Review: Know Nothing Populism and the Origins of the GOP," *Pennsylvania History: A Journal of Mid-Atlantic Studies* 71, 2 (Spring 2004); Ben Eklof and Tatiana Saburova, "In Pursuit of a Different Revolution: Russian Populists of the Seventies Generation and 1917," *Slavic Review* 76, Special Issue 3 (2017); Maurice Meisner, "Leninism and Maoism: Some Populist Perspectives on Marxism-Leninism in China," *China Quarterly* 45 (January–March 1971): 2–36, https://www.jstor.org/stable/651881?seq=1; "A Brief History of Populism," *The Week,* September 26, 2015, https://theweek.com/articles/579018/brief-history-populism; Marc Horger, "American Populism and the Persistence of the Paranoid Style," *Origins* 4, 7 (April 2011), https://origins.osu.edu/article/american-populism-and-persistence-paranoid-style.

4 World Bank, *Populism, Inequality, and Economic Growth: A European Perspective Fide* (Washington, DC: Fide Foundation, June 2023), https://thedocs.worldbank.org/en/doc/3316541d70a706fbca6c53932d1aa272-0370012023/original/Paper-POPULISM-INEQUALITY-AND-ECONOMIC-GROWTH.pdf; Yuki Fukuoka, "The Populism Surge in the West: Support for Left-Wing Populism Among Young People: Implications for Environmental Policies," *Mitsui and Co. Global Strategic Studies Institute Monthly Report,* February 2020, https://www.mitsui.com/mgssi/en/report/detail/__icsFiles/afieldfile/2020/05/28/2002c_fukuoka_e.pdf; Ambassador Stéphane Dion, "European Liberal Democracies Facing Populism: Reasons for Cautious Optimism" (speech delivered at Tübingen University, March 18, 2019), https://www.international.gc.ca/country_news-pays_nouvelles/2019-03-18-germany-allemagne.aspx?lang=eng; Arlie Russell Hochschild, *Strangers in Their Own Land: Anger and Mourning on the American Right* (New York: New Press, 2018), https://thenewpress.com/books/strangers-their-own-land.

5 Richard Hofstadter, *The Age of Reform: From Bryant to FDR* (New York: Alfred A. Knopf, 1955); Nils Gilman, "Revisiting Hofstadter's Populism," *American Interest* 14, 1 (2018), https://www.the-american-interest.com/2018/05/02/revisiting-hofstadters-populism/.

6 Thomas Picketty's classic work *Capital in the Twenty-First Century* (Cambridge, MA: Harvard University Press, 2014) depicts in significant detail the causes and effects of inequality on socio-economic conditions. Also see Joseph Stiglitz, "Salvaging Global Democratic Politics Requires Far-Reaching Economic Reforms," *The Guardian,* September 1, 2023, https://www.theguardian.com/business/2023/sep/01/global-democratic-politics-economic-reforms; Larry Elliott, "Global Inequality 'As Marked as It Was at the Peak of Western Imperialism,'" *The Guardian,* December 7, 2021, https://www.theguardian.com/business/2021/dec/07/global-inequality-western-imperialism-super-rich?CMP=Share_AndroidApp_Other.

7 Robert Kuttner, "Dividends of a Just Economy," *New York Review of Books,* April 29, 2021, 17, https://www.nybooks.com/articles/2021/04/29/dividends-of-a-just-economy/; Adam Sennott, "Former Labor Secretary Robert Reich Calls for 'Progressive Populism' to Tip the Scales for the Working Class," *Real Change: Jobs, Journalism, Justice,* January 24, 2018, https://www.realchangenews.org/news/2018/01/24/former-labor-secretary-robert-reich-calls-progressive-populism-tip-scales-working-class; Dustin Voss, "The Political Economy of European Populism: Labour Market Dualisation and Protest Voting in Germany and Spain," London School of Economics "Europe in Question" Discussion Paper Series No. 132/2018, March 2018, https://www.lse.ac.uk/european-institute/Assets/Documents/LEQS-Discussion-Papers/LEQSPaper132.pdf.

8 Robert Reich, "The American Economy Is Perilously Fragile. Concentration of Wealth Is to Blame," *The Guardian,* June 23, 2021, https://www.theguardian.com/commentisfree/2021/jun/23/american-economy-us-concentration-wealth-blame; Jana Manasce Horowitz, Ruth Igielnik, and Rakesh Kochhar, "Trends in Income and Wealth Inequality," Pew Research Center, January 9, 2020, https://www.pewresearch.org/social-trends/2020/01/09/trends-in-income-and-wealth-inequality/.

9 Simon Bornschier, "Interview #28: Responsiveness and Populism in Latin America," Political Observatory on Populism, August 6, 2018, https://populismobserver.com/2018/08/06/interview-28-responsiveness-and-populism-in-latin-america/#more-3946; Chantal Mouffe, "In Defense of Left-Wing Populism," *The Conversation,* April 29, 2016, https://theconversation.com/in-defence-of-left-wing-populism-55869.

10 Dion Roboulin, "Most Investors Now Say the Stock Market Is 'Rigged,'" *Axios,* March 23, 2021, https://www.axios.com/most-investors-say-stock-market-rigged-2713838b-1d29-43c5-9dc9-37dd4e466702.html.

11 Stéphane Dion, "Cultural Insecurity as the Main Root Cause of Populism" (introductory remarks at the 22nd Forum 2000 Conference, "Democracy: In need of a Critical Update?" Prague, October 8, 2018), https://www.international.gc.ca/country_news-pays_nouvelles/2019-10-08-germany-allemagne.aspx?lang=eng.

12 See, e.g., Chris Lehmann, "The Zombie Populism of Today's GOP," *The Nation,* April 24, 2023, https://www.thenation.com/article/politics/zombie-populism/; Robert A. Pape and Keven Ruby, "The Capitol Rioters Aren't Like Other Extremists," *The Atlantic,* February 2, 2021, https://www.theatlantic.com/ideas/archive/2021/02/the-capitol-rioters-arent-like-other-extremists/617895/; Bonnie Kristian, "Who Were the Capitol Rioters?" *The Week,* January 15, 2021, https://theweek.com/articles/960978/who-capitol-rioters; Adam Serwer, "The Capitol Rioters Weren't 'Low Class,'" *The Atlantic,* January 12, 2021, https://www.theatlantic.com/ideas/archive/2021/01/thoroughly-re-rioters/617644/; K.A. Dilday, "Progressive Populism Roared Back in 2018," *Bloomberg,* December 31, 2018, https://www.bloomberg.com/news/articles/2018-12-31/the-year-progressive-populism-roared-back-in-america.

13 Alissa Quart, "Meet the New Class Traitors Who Are Coming Out as Rich," *The Guardian,* October 16, 2017, https://www.theguardian.com/us-news/2017/oct/16/coming-out-as-wealthy-inequality-progressives; Trevor Harrison, "The Impact of Right-Wing Populism on Taxation Policy in the United States and Canada," International Public Policy Association, https://www.ippapublicpolicy.org/file/paper/1432230053.pdf.

14 Jared Wesley and Rissa Reist, "Three Deep-Seated Drivers of the Convoy, and What We Can Do About Them: Status Threat (Felt by Working-Class White Men), Tribalism and a Lack of Losers' Consent Are Three Elements Canadians Must Acknowledge and Resolve," Policy Options, February 18, 2022, https://policyoptions.irpp.org/magazines/february-2022/three-deep-seated-drivers-of-the-convoy-and-what-we-can-do-about-them/; Diana C. Mutz, "Status Threat, Not Economic Hardship, Explains the 2016 Presidential Vote," *Proceedings of the National Academy of Sciences of the USA* 115, 19 (2018): E4330–E4339, https://www.pnas.org/doi/10.1073/pnas.1718155115, and Stephen L. Morgan, "Status Threat, Material Interests, and the 2016 Presidential Vote," *Socius* 4 (2018), https://journals.sagepub.com/doi/full/10.1177/2378023118788217. Also see Alain de Botton, *Status Anxiety* (New York: Penguin Random House, 2005), https://www.penguinrandomhouse.com/books/38358/status-anxiety-by-alain-de-botton/.

15 "Palladium Podcast 62: Michael Zargham on Society as a Complex System," *Palladium,* August 4, 2021, https://palladiummag.com/2021/08/04/palladium-podcast-62-michael-zargham-on-society-as-a-complex-system/; Ipsos, *Global Trends 2020: Understanding Complexity* (Ipsos, 2020), https://www.ipsos.com/sites/default/files/ct/publication/documents/2020-02/ipsos-global-trends-2020-understanding-complexity.pdf; Miguel A. Centeno, Manish Nag, Thayer S. Patterson, Andrew Shaver, and A. Jason Windawi, "The Emergence of Global Systemic Risk," *Annual Review of Sociology* 42 (2015): 65–85, https://www.annualreviews.org/content/journals/10.1146/annurev-soc-073014-112317; Ben Ramalingam and Harry Jones with Toussaint Reba and John Young, "Exploring the Science of Complexity: Ideas and Implications for Development and Humanitarian Efforts," Overseas Development Institute Working Paper 285, 2nd ed., October 2008, https://odi.org/en/publications/exploring-the-science-of-complexity-ideas-and-implications-for-development-and-humanitarian-efforts/; Neil Johnson, *Simply Complexity: A Clear Guide to Complexity Theory* (Oxford: One World Publications, 2007), https://oneworld-publications.com/work/simply-complexity/; Helga Nowotny, "The Increase of Complexity and Its Reduction: Emergent Interfaces Between Natural Sciences, Humanities and Social Sciences," *Theory, Culture and Society* 22, 5 (October 1, 2005): 15–31, https://journals.sagepub.com/doi/10.1177/0263276405057189.

16 Robert D. Putnam, *Bowling Alone: The Collapse and Revival of American Community* (New York: Simon and Schuster, 2000), https://www.simonandschuster.com/books/Bowling-Alone/Robert-D-Putnam/9780743219037; Melissa Marschall, "Robert D. Putnam, *Bowling Alone: The*

Collapse and Revival of American Community: Empirical Foundations, Causal Mechanisms and Policy Implications," in *The Oxford Handbook of Classics in Public Policy and Administration,* ed. Martin Lodge, Edward C. Page, and Steven J. Balla (Oxford: Oxford University Press, 2015), https://www.oxfordhandbooks.com/view/10.1093/oxfordhb/9780199646135.001.0001/oxfordhb-9780199646135-e-9; Alexandra Hudson, "*Bowling Alone* at Twenty," *National Affairs* no. 46 (Winter 2021), https://www.nationalaffairs.com/publications/detail/bowling-alone-at-twenty.

17 John M. Planchon and William L. James, "Cognitive Complexity and Alienation: A Re-examination," *Journal of Business Research* 23, 2 (September 1991): 189–98, https://www.sciencedirect.com/science/article/abs/pii/014829639190028V#. For discussion of the impact of complexity in music and loss of audience interest, see Daniel Levitin, *This Is Your Brain on Music: Understanding a Human Obsession* (London: Penguin Random House UK, 2006), 240, https://www.penguin.co.uk/books/314/314695/this-is-your-brain-on-music/9780241987353.html.

18 Kristaan P.W. Kok, Anne M.C. Loeber, and John Grin, "Politics of Complexity: Conceptualizing Agency Power and Powering in the Transitional Dynamics of Complex Adaptive Systems," *Research Policy* 50, 3 (April 2021), https://www.sciencedirect.com/science/article/pii/S0048733320302572; Alex Williams, *Political Hegemony and Social Complexity: Mechanisms of Power After Gramsci* (London: Palgrave Macmillan, 2020), https://www.palgrave.com/gp/book/9783030197940. Non-linear approaches to complexity are discussed in Diana Richards, ed., *Political Complexity: Nonlinear Models of Politics* (Ann Arbor: University of Michigan Press, 2000), https://www.press.umich.edu/16428/political_complexity.

19 Organisation of Economic Co-operation and Development (OECD), *Debate the Issues: New Approaches to Economic Challenges* (Paris: OECD, 2016), https://www.oecd.org/en/publications/debate-the-issues-new-approaches-to-economic-challenges_9789264264687-en.html; Harvard Growth Lab, "The Atlas of Economic Complexity," https://atlas.cid.harvard.edu; Observatory of Economic Complexity (OEC), "Methods," https://oec.world/en/resources/methods; Cesar A. Hidalgo and Ricardo Hausmann, "The Building Blocks of Economic Complexity," *Proceedings of the National Academy of Sciences of the USA* 106, 26 (2009): 10570–75, https://www.pnas.org/content/106/26/10570.

20 Filippo Aureli and Gabriele Schino, "Social Complexity from Within: How Individuals Experience the Structure and Organization of Their Groups," *Behavioral Ecology and Sociobiology* 73, 6 (2019), https://link.springer.com/article/10.1007/s00265-018-2604-5; Peter M. Kappeler, Tim Clutton-Brock, Susanne Shultz, and Dieter Lukas, "Social Complexity: Patterns, Processes, and Evolution," *Behavioral Ecology and Sociobiology* 73, 5 (2019), https://link.springer.com/article/10.1007/s00265-018-2613-4; Todd R. La Porte, *Organized Social Complexity: Challenge to Politics and Policy* (Princeton, NJ: Princeton University Press, 1975), https://press.princeton.edu/books/hardcover/9780691644806/organized-social-complexity.

21 Lauren Langman and Devorah Kalekin-Fishman, eds., *The Evolution of Alienation: Trauma, Promise and the Millennium* (Lanham, MD: Rowman and Littlefield, 2006), https://www.bloomsbury.com/us/evolution-of-alienation-9780742518346/; Felix Geyer, "Alienation, Sociology of," in *International Encyclopedia of the Social and Behavioral Sciences,* ed. Neil J. Smelser and Paul B. Baltes (Pergamon, 2001), 388–92, https://www.sciencedirect.com/science/article/pii/B0080430767018246; Sidney Joe Jackson, "The Alienation of the Individual from Society: A Social-Psychological Theory and Cross-Cultural Comparison" (PhD diss., Iowa State University, 1983), https://pdfs.semanticscholar.org/2753/9e80afa71b92ecfb43e2aff5331c8a94dc71.pdf?_ga=2.93783325.162429827.1615060538-1785908520.1615060538; James E. Twining, "Alienation as a Social Process," *Sociological Quarterly* 21, 3 (1980): 417–28, https://www.jstor.org/stable/4106303.

22 Dominik Hartmann and Flavio L. Pinheiro, "Economic Complexity and Inequality at the National and Regional Level" in *Handbook of Complexity Economics,* ed. Ping Chen, Wolfram Elsner, and Andreas Pyka (Abingdon, UK: Routledge, 2024), https://arxiv.org/pdf/2206.00818.pdf; Sheri Berman, "Populism and the Embrace of Complexity," Social Europe, April 23, 2019, https://www.socialeurope.eu/populism-and-complexity; Geoffrey M. Hodgson, "Capitalism, Complexity, and Inequality," *Journal of Economic Issues* 37, 2 (June 2003), https://www.researchgate.net/publication/252466119_Capitalism_Complexity_and_Inequality.

23 David C. Schwartz, ed., *Political Alienation and Political Behavior* (Abingdon, UK: Routledge, 2007), https://www.routledge.com/Political-Alienation-and-Political-Behavior/Schwartz/p/book/

9780202309453; Maria Oskarson, "Social Risk, Policy Dissatisfaction, and Political Alienation," in *The Political Sociology of the Welfare State: Institutions, Social Cleavages, and Orientations*, ed. Stefan Svallfors (Stanford, CA: Stanford University Press, 2007), ch. 4, https://www.sup.org/books/cite/?id=10158.

24 Asger Sorensen, *Capitalism, Alienation and Critique* (Leiden: Brill, 2019), https://brill.com/view/title/36299; Anthony Giddens, *Capitalism and Modern Society: An Analysis of the Writings of Marx, Durkheim, and Max Weber* (Cambridge: Cambridge University Press, 1967), 9–16, 224–32.

25 "Community Spirit Prevails Despite Anxieties and Alienation in English White Working Class Neighborhoods," press release, Open Society Foundations, June 12, 2014, https://www.opensocietyfoundations.org/newsroom/community-spirit-prevails-despite-anxieties-and-alienation-english-white-working; Daniel Little, "Alienation and Subjectivity," *Understanding Society* (blog), January 29, 2008, https://undsoc.org/2008/01/19/alienation-and-subjectivity/; Felix Geyer, "Alienation, Participation and Increasing Social Complexity," *Kybernetes* 23, 2 (1994): 10–34, https://www.emerald.com/insight/content/doi/10.1108/03684929410054852/full/html?skipTracking=true; George De Vos, *Social Cohesion and Alienation: Minorities in the United States and Japan* (Boulder, CO: Westview Press, 1992), https://psycnet.apa.org/record/1992-97870-000, republished in 2019 by Routledge, https://www.routledge.com/Social-Cohesion-And-Alienation-Minorities-In-The-United-States-And-Japan/Vos/p/book/9780367287498.

26 Terri Mannarini and Sergio Salvatore, "The Politicization of Otherness and the Privatization of the Enemy: Cultural Hindrances and Assets for Active Citizenship," *Human Affairs* 30, 1 (2020): 86–95, https://www.degruyter.com/view/journals/humaff/30/1/article-p86.xml?language=en; John Powell, "Building Belonging in a Time of Othering" (PowerPoint presentation for Community Action Partnership and Haas Institute, August 28, 2019), https://communityactionpartnership.com/wp-content/uploads/2019/10/BuildingBelongingInATimeOfOthering_johnpowell.pdf.

27 David Klepper, "Some QAnon Supporters Checked by Reality Seek a Way Out," *Huffington Post,* January 28, 2021, https://www.huffpost.com/entry/qanon-supporters-seek-a-way-out_n_60134b1fc5b63b0fb27f57d0; "Populist Government and Democracy: An Impact Assessment Using the Global State of Democracy Indices," *Global State of Democracy in Focus* no. 9 (February 2020), https://www.idea.int/sites/default/files/publications/populist-government-and-democracy-impact-assessement-using-gsod-indices.pdf.

28 Pitman B. Potter, *Assessing Treaty Performance in China: Trade and Human Rights* (Vancouver: UBC Press, 2014), 4–6.

29 Paul Kenny, *Why Populism? Political Strategy from Ancient Greece to the Present* (Cambridge: Cambridge University Press, 2023); Bram Geurkink, Andrej Zaslove, Roderick Sluiter, and Kristof Jacobs, "Populist Attitudes, Political Trust and External Political Efficacy: Old Wine in New Bottles?" *Political Studies* 68, 1 (2020): 247–67, https://journals.sagepub.com/doi/pdf/10.1177/0032321719842768; Neil Robinson and Sarah Milne, "Populism and Political Development in Hybrid Regimes: Russia and the Development of Official Populism," *International Political Science Review* 38, 4 (2017): 412–25, https://journals.sagepub.com/doi/abs/10.1177/0192512117697705?journalCode=ipsa. This point was applied to China in Edward Friedman, "Post-Deng China's Right Populist Authoritarian Foreign Policy," *China Review* (2000): 1–25, https://www.jstor.org/stable/23453359?seq=1.

30 Benjamin Moffitt, *The Global Rise of Populism: Performance, Political Style and Representation* (Stanford, CA: Stanford University Press, 2026), https://www.sup.org/books/politics/global-rise-populism/excerpts.

31 Leslie Bethell, "Populism of the 21st Century" (lecture for the Wilson Center Latin America Program, October 8, 2009), https://www.wilsoncenter.org/event/populism-the-21st-century.

32 Jon Henley, "How Europe's Far Right Is Marching Steadily into the Mainstream," *The Guardian,* June 30, 2023, https://www.theguardian.com/world/2023/jun/30/far-right-on-the-march-europe-growing-taste-for-control-and-order?CMP=Share_AndroidApp_Other.

33 David Molloy, "What Is Populism, and What Does the Term Actually Mean?" *BBC News,* March 6, 2018, https://www.bbc.com/news/world-43301423; Yascha Mounk and Jordan Kyle, "What Populists Do to Democracies," *The Atlantic,* December 26, 2018, https://www.theatlantic.com/ideas/archive/2018/12/hard-data-populism-bolsonaro-trump/578878/; Marc Horger, Gregory Kupsky, and Zoltán Ádám, "Fear and Loathing Around the World: The Rise of the New

Populism," *Origins: Current Events in Historical Perspective,* July 2018, https://origins.osu.edu/article/fear-and-loathing-around-world-rise-new-populism.

34 Mohamed Matawe, "Populism and Domestic/International Politics: Theory and Practice," *Review of Economics and Political Science* 9, 3 (2024): 194–211, https://www.emerald.com/insight/content/doi/10.1108/REPS-11-2019-0146/full/html; Yasmeen Serhan, "Populism Is Morphing in Insidious Ways," *The Atlantic,* January 5, 2020, https://www.theatlantic.com/international/archive/2020/01/future-populism-2020s/604393/.

35 Lica Purcile and Normal Eisen, "The Populist Paradox," Brookings, October 28, 2020, https://www.brookings.edu/blog/order-from-chaos/2020/10/28/the-populist-paradox/; Daniel Cox, "Could Social Alienation Among Some Trump Supporters Help Explain Why Polls Underestimate Trump Again?" *FiveThirtyEight,* November 24, 2020, https://fivethirtyeight.com/features/could-social-alienation-among-some-trump-supporters-help-explain-why-polls-underestimated-trump-again/; Mark Rice-Oxley and Ammar Kalia, "How to Spot a Populist," *The Guardian,* December 3, 2018, https://www.theguardian.com/news/2018/dec/03/what-is-populism-trump-farage-orban-bolsonaro.

36 John S. Huntington, *Far-Right Vanguard* (Philadelphia: University of Pennsylvania Press, 2021), https://www.jstor.org/stable/j.ctv1f45qdr; Jose Juan Moreso and Pablo E. Navarro, "The Reception of Norms, and Open Legal Systems," in *Normativity and Norms: Critical Perspectives on Kelsenian Themes,* ed. Stanley L. Paulson and Bonnie Litschewski Paulson (Oxford: Clarendon Press, 1998), 272–91, https://oxford.universitypressscholarship.com/view/10.1093/acprof:oso/9780198763154.001.0001/acprof-9780198763154-chapter-15.

37 Anna Grzymala-Busse, Didi Kuo, Francis Fukuyama, and Michael McFaul, *Global Populisms and Their Challenges* (Freeman Spogli Institute for International Studies, Stanford University, March 2020), https://archive.org/details/global-populisms-and-their-challenges-stanford-university-mar.-2020; Nadia Urbinati, "Political Theory of Populism," *Annual Review of Political Science* 22 (May 2019): 111–27, https://www.annualreviews.org/doi/full/10.1146/annurev-polisci-050317-070753.

38 "Media Populism: How Media Populism and Inflating Fear Empowers Populist Politicians," *Frontiers in Communication,* 2020, https://www.frontiersin.org/research-topics/10026/media-populism-how-media-populism-and-inflating-fear-empowers-populist-politicians; Katy Brown and Aurelien Mondon, "Populism, the Media, and the Mainstreaming of the Far Right: *The Guardian*'s Coverage of Populism as a Case Study," *Politics* 41, 3 (2020): 279–95, https://journals.sagepub.com/doi/full/10.1177/0263395720955036; Gianpietro Mazzoleni, "Populism and the Media," in *Twenty-First Century Populism,* ed. Daniele Albertazzi and Duncan McDonnell (New York: Palgrave Macmillan, 2008), 49–64, https://link.springer.com/chapter/10.1057/9780230592100_4.

39 Jordan Kyle and Limor Cultchin, "Populists in Power Around the World," Tony Blair Institute for Global Change, November 7, 2018, https://institute.global/policy/populists-power-around-world; Gerry Stoker, "When Governance Meets Populism: An Emerging Crisis?" International Policy Association, 2017, https://www.ippapublicpolicy.org/file/paper/593f76c91c772.pdf.

40 Giorgos Venizelos, *Populism in Power: Discourse and Performativity in SYRIZA and Donald Trump* (Abingdon, UK: Routledge, 2023), https://www.routledge.com/Populism-in-Power-Discourse-and-Performativity-in-SYRIZA-and-Donald-Trump/Venizelos/p/book/9781032398402?srsltid=AfmBOor7PB4cyQHqn-vMWyL43oBJ8os_vViVQzjWq62UiNspflGFxbfH; Michael Cox, *Understanding the Global Rise of Populism,* LSE Ideas Strategic Update (London: London School of Economics, 2018), https://www.lse.ac.uk/ideas/Assets/Documents/updates/LSE-IDEAS-Understanding-Global-Rise-of-Populism.pdf.

41 See, e.g., Kristian Humble, "Populism and the Threat to International Law," *Laws* 11, 3 (2022): 50, https://www.mdpi.com/2075-471X/11/3/50.

42 Milada Anna Vachudova, "Populism, Democracy, and Party System Change in Europe," *Annual Review of Political Science* 24 (2021): 471–98, https://www.annualreviews.org/doi/pdf/10.1146/annurev-polisci-041719-102711; Markus Hadler, Anja Eder, and Christian Meyer, "An Overview of Attitudes and Opinions on the Role of Government: A Cross-National Comparison Covering the Period of 1985–2016," *International Journal of Sociology* 49, 3 (2019): 171–81, https://www.tandfonline.com/doi/full/10.1080/00207659.2019.1605027.

43 "U.S. Election 2024; Presidential Election Results: Trump Wins," *CBC News,* https://newsinteractives.cbc.ca/elections/us/2024/results/; Louis Jacobson, "The Size of Donald Trump's 2024

Election Victory, Explained in 5 Charts," *PBS News,* November 24, 2024, https://www.pbs.org/newshour/politics/the-size-of-donald-trumps-2024-election-victory-explained-in-5-charts. The 2020 US election saw approximately 75 million voters support Trump in his loss to Joe Biden. David Wasserman, Sophie Andrews, Leo Saenger, Lev Cohen, Ally Flinn, and Griff Tatarsky, "2020 National Popular Vote Tracker," *Cook Political Report,* https://cookpolitical.com/2020-national-popular-vote-tracker; "Joe Biden Has Been Declared the Winner, Toppling Donald Trump After Four Years of Upheaval at the White House," *Politico,* January 6, 2021, https://www.politico.com/2020-election/results/president/.

44 Although the US mid-term election in 2022 signalled a degree of popular unease about the potential impacts of right-wing populism, the electoral margins suggested that populism retains a noteworthy level of public support. Austin Ahlman, "Democrats Rediscover Populism – and Not a Moment Too Soon," *American Prospect,* November 28, 2022, https://prospect.org/politics/democrats-rediscover-populism-not-a-moment-too-soon/; "Analyzing the Results of the US Midterms," *LSE Government* (blog), London School of Economics, December 6, 2022, https://blogs.lse.ac.uk/government/2022/12/06/analysing-the-results-of-the-us-midterms/.

45 "U.S. Election 2024; Presidential Election Results: Trump Wins"; Jacobson, "The Size of Donald Trump's 2024 Election Victory, Explained in 5 Charts." In the 2020 election, even larger proportions than the 47 percent who backed Trump's 2020 re-election bid supported candidates in local congressional elections espousing similar notions. Nathaniel Rakich and Ryan Best, "There Wasn't *That* Much Split-Ticket Voting in 2020," *FiveThirtyEight,* December 2, 2020, https://fivethirtyeight.com/features/there-wasnt-that-much-split-ticket-voting-in-2020/.

46 "Right Wing Populism in Latin America" (David Rockefeller Center for Latin American Studies conference recording, December 1, 2020), https://drclas.harvard.edu/event/right-wing-populism-latin-america; Jon Lee Anderson, "Populists Inflame the Coronavirus Outbreak Across Latin America," *New Yorker,* July 2, 2020, https://www.newyorker.com/news/news-desk/populists-inflame-the-coronavirus-outbreak-across-latin-america; Katharina de Moura Hofmann, "The Global Footprint of Right-Wing Populists," *International Politics and Society Journal,* August 26, 2019, https://www.ips-journal.eu/regions/latin-america/the-global-footprint-of-right-wing-populists-3687/; Luisa Garcia and Claudio Vallejo, *The New Populism in Latin America, More Alive Than Ever* (Madrid: Llorente and Cuenca, September 2017), https://ideas.llorenteycuenca.com/wp-content/uploads/sites/5/2017/09/170914_Informe_Populismo_ENG_OK.pdf.

47 Gordon Brown, "There's a Hard-Right Tidal Wave About to Hit Europe – and It Will Only Make the Economic Crisis Worse," *The Guardian,* April 9, 2024, https://www.theguardian.com/commentisfree/2024/apr/29/hard-right-tidal-wave-europe-economic-crisis-worse; Counter Extremism Project, "European Ethno-Nationalist and White Supremacy Groups" (2021), https://www.counterextremism.com/european-white-supremacy-groups.

48 "EU Referendum Results," *BBC News,* 2020, https://www.bbc.co.uk/news/politics/eu_referendum/results. Also see National Centre for Social Research, "What UK Thinks: If There Was a Referendum on Britain's Membership of the EU, How Would You Vote? (Eurotrack)," https://www.whatukthinks.org/eu/questions/if-there-was-a-referendum-on-britains-membership-of-the-eu-how-would-you-vote-2/.

49 Jan-Werner Müller, "The American Right Is Whitewashing Hungary's Nasty Autocratic Regime," *The Guardian,* May 24, 2022, https://www.theguardian.com/commentisfree/2022/may/24/the-american-right-is-whitewashing-hungarys-nasty-autocratic-regime?CMP=Share_AndroidApp_Other; Cas Mudde, "Surprised to See US Republicans Cozying Up to the European Far Right? Don't Be," *The Guardian,* October 15, 2021, https://www.theguardian.com/commentisfree/2021/oct/15/us-republicans-european-far-right?CMP=Share_AndroidApp_Other.

50 Samir Gandesha, "Understanding Right and Left Populisms," *Open Democracy,* May 23, 2018, https://www.opendemocracy.net/en/can-europe-make-it/understanding-right-and-left-populisms/.

51 Ipsos Public Affairs, *Understanding Society: Beyond Populism* (London: Ipsos Public Affairs, 2017), https://www.ipsos.com/sites/default/files/2017-07/Understanding_society-beyond_populism-2017.pdf; Daniele Albertazzi and Duncan McDonnell, eds., *Twenty-First Century Populism* (New York: Palgrave Macmillan, 2008); George Monbiot, "It's Shocking to See So Many Left-wingers Lured to the Far Right by Conspiracy Theories," *The Guardian,* September 22, 2021,

https://www.theguardian.com/commentisfree/2021/sep/22/leftwingers-far-right-conspiracy-theories-anti-vaxxers-power?CMP=Share_AndroidApp_Other.

52 Ruth Milkman, Stephanie Luce, and Penny Lewis, "Did Occupy Wall Street Make a Difference?" *The Nation,* October 4–11, 2021, 14–17, https://www.thenation.com/article/society/ows-occupy-zuccotti-protest/; Thomas Frank, *The People, No: A Brief History of Anti-Populism* (New York: Henry Holt, 2020); Park MacDougald, "What's the Matter with Populism? Nothing," *New York Magazine,* September 2, 2020, https://nymag.com/intelligencer/2020/09/whats-the-matter-with-populism-nothing.html; Alvin B. Tillery, "Is #BlackLivesMatter a Populist Movement? The View from Black Public Opinion," *ResearchGate,* December 2019, https://www.researchgate.net/publication/337782943_Is_BlackLivesMatter_a_Populist_Movement_The_View_from_Black_Public_Opinion; Mark Beeson, *Environmental Populism: The Politics of Survival in the Anthropocene* (New York: Palgrave Macmillan, 2019).

53 Jonathan White, "Community, Transnationalism, and the Left-Right Metaphor," *European Journal of Social Theory* 15, 2 (2012): 197–219, http://eprints.lse.ac.uk/43691/1/White_Community_Transnationalism.pdf; Daniel Casasanto and Evangelia G. Chrysikou, "When Left Is 'Right': Motor Fluency Shapes Abstract Concepts," *Psychological Science* 22, 4 (2011): 419–22, https://journals.sagepub.com/doi/10.1177/0956797611401755.

54 Factors associated with progressive and regressive populism are identified in the Global Populism Database. Kirk A. Hawkins, Rosario Aguilar, Bruno Castanho Silva, Erin K. Jenne, Bojana Kocijan, and Cristóbal Rovira Kaltwasser, "Measuring Populist Discourse: The Global Populism Database" (paper presented at the EPSA Annual Conference in Belfast, UK, June 20–22, 2019), https://populism.byu.edu/0000017d-bf5d-d270-a1fd-ff5fcf750001/global-populism-database-paper-pdf.

55 See, e.g., "QAnon, Boogaloo, Proud Boys: What's Next for the U.S. Extreme Right?" *Toronto Star,* February 1, 2021, https://www.thestar.com/podcasts/thismatters/2021/02/01/qanon-boogaloo-proud-boys-whats-next-for-the-us-extreme-right.html; David. M. Ricci, *A Political Science Manifesto for the Age of Populism* (Cambridge: Cambridge University Press, 2020), esp. ch. 1; Annalisa Merelli, "The State of Global Right-Wing Populism in 2019," *Quartz,* December 30, 2019, https://qz.com/1774201/the-global-state-of-right-wing-populism-in-2019/; "Europe and Right-Wing Nationalism: A Country by Country Guide," *BBC News,* December 13, 2019, https://www.bbc.com/news/world-europe-36130006; Octavia Bryant and Benjamin Moffitt, "What Actually Is Populism and Why Does It Have a Bad Reputation?" *The Conversation,* February 5, 2019, https://theconversation.com/what-actually-is-populism-and-why-does-it-have-a-bad-reputation-109874; Nicola Lacey, "Populism and the Rule of Law," LSE International Inequalities Institute Working Paper 28, January 2019, http://eprints.lse.ac.uk/101867/1/Lacey_populism_and_the_rule_of_law_wp28.pdf; Michael A. Peters, "The End of Neoliberal Globalisation and the Rise of Authoritarian Populism," *Educational Philosophy and Theory* 50, 4 (2018): 323–25, https://www.tandfonline.com/doi/full/10.1080/00131857.2017.1305720; Gianpietro Mazzoleni, Julianne Stewart, and Bruce Horsefield, eds., *The Media and Neo-Populism: A Contemporary Comparative Analysis* (Westport: Praeger, 2003), https://books.google.ca/books?hl=en&lr=&id=YdG5cLc_Pi4C&oi=fnd&pg=PA1&dq=growth+of+populism&ots=fX_myuelYX&sig=ekPKlq31ilh8pxA2qXmYrCBuj7Y#v=onepage&q=growth%20of%20populism&f=false.

56 Oz Frankel, "Guest Editor's Introduction," *Social Research* 89, 3 (Fall 2022), https://muse.jhu.edu/issue/48924.

57 A. González-Ruibal, P.A. González, and F. Criado-Boado, "Against Reactionary Populism: Towards a New Public Archaeology," *Antiquity* 92, 362 (2018): 507–15, https://www.cambridge.org/core/journals/antiquity/article/abs/against-reactionary-populism-towards-a-new-public-archaeology/EF08B18317BB17A81BE9320BEA3FB100; Santiago Zabala, "The Difference Between Right and Left-Wing Populism," *Al Jazeera,* January 17, 2017, https://www.aljazeera.com/opinions/2017/1/17/the-difference-between-right-and-left-wing-populism.

58 Hal Weitzman, "The Populism Puzzle," *Chicago Booth Review,* March 2, 2020, https://review.chicagobooth.edu/economics/2020/article/populism-puzzle; John Holbo, "Epistemic Sunk Costs and the Extraordinary, Populist Delusions of Crowds," *Crooked Timber* (blog), June 13, 2018, https://crookedtimber.org/2018/06/13/epistemic-sunk-costs-and-the-extraordinary-populist-delusions-of-crowds/. For a transactions cost approach to populism, see Zoltan Adam, "Explaining Orbán: A Political Transactions Cost Theory of Authoritarian Populism," *Problems*

of Post-Communism 66, 6 (2019): 385–401, https://www.tandfonline.com/doi/full/10.1080/10758216.2019.1643249.

59 Cas Mudde, "The Problem with Populism," *The Guardian,* February 17, 2015, https://www.theguardian.com/commentisfree/2015/feb/17/problem-populism-syriza-podemos-dark-side-europe; Santiago Zabala, "In Europe, Not All Populist Parties Are the Same," *Al Jazeera,* December 2, 2014, https://archive.wikiwix.com/cache/index2.php?url=http%3A%2F%2Famerica.aljazeera.com%2Fopinions%2F2014%2F12%2Fpodemos-spain-politicspopulismeurope.html#federation=archive.wikiwix.com&tab=url; Andrej Zaslove, "Here to Stay? Populism as a New Party Type," *European Review* 16, 3 (June 2008): 319–36.

60 See, e.g., Oscar Garcia Agustin, *Left-Wing Populism: The Politics of the People* (Bingley, UK: Emerald Publishing, 2020), https://bookstore.emerald.com/media/preview/9781839092060-23-2.pdf; Steven Rosefielde and Daniel Quinn Mills, *Populists and Progressives: The New Forces in American Politics* (Singapore: World Scientific, 2020), https://www.worldscientific.com/worldscibooks/10.1142/11744; Sarah Smarsh, "In Defense of Populism," *Columbia Journalism Review,* August 27, 2020, https://www.cjr.org/opinion/populism-progressive-aoc-sanders-warren.php; Ed Broadbent, "Populism Isn't a Bad Word – and Progressives Should Take It Back," *Globe and Mail,* March 22, 2019, https://www.theglobeandmail.com/opinion/article-populism-isnt-a-bad-word-and-progressives-should-take-it-back/.

61 K.A. Dilday, "Progressive Populism Roars Back in 2018," *Bloomberg,* December 31, 2018, https://www.bloomberg.com/news/articles/2018-12-31/the-year-progressive-populism-roared-back-in-america; Will Marshall, *Unleashing Innovation and Growth: A Progressive Alternative to Populism* (Progressive Policy Institute, 2016), https://www.progressivepolicy.org/wp-content/uploads/2016/03/2016_PPI_Unleashing-Innovation-and-Growth_A-Progressive-Alternative-to-Populism.pdf.

62 Michael Edinger, "Fighting the Establishment: The Role of Anti-Elitism in Contemporary Populism" (panel presentation at the European Consortium for Political Research conference, Wrocław, Poland, September 4–7, 2019), https://ecpr.eu/Events/Event/PaperDetails/47655.

63 See, e.g., Andrew Arato and Jean L. Cohen, *Populism and Civil Society: The Challenge to Constitutional Democracy* (Cambridge: Cambridge University Press, 2021), https://academic.oup.com/book/41832; Jan-Werner Müller, *What Is Populism* (Philadelphia: University of Pennsylvania Press, 2016), https://www.pennpress.org/9780812248982/what-is-populism/; Carlos M. Vilas, "Latin American Populism: A Structural Approach," *Science and Society* 56, 4 (Winter 1992): 389–420.

64 Morits Ege and Johannes Springer, eds., *The Cultural Politics of Anti-Elitism* (Abingdon, UK: Routledge, 2023), https://www.routledge.com/The-Cultural-Politics-of-Anti-Elitism/Ege-Springer/p/book/9780367692612?srsltid=AfmBOorpcrSDBxCw38TS80vpTVd0DC12grAbfZSG2L4tZQKnnT5dYy-o.

65 European Center for Populism Studies, "Anti-Establishment Populism," https://www.populismstudies.org/Vocabulary/anti-establishment-populism/.

66 Alexander Hudson and Seema Shah, "Explainer: Populism – Left and Right, Progressive and Regressive," Institute for Democracy and Electoral Assistance (IDEA), November 21, 2022, https://www.idea.int/blog/explainer-populism-left-and-right-progressive-and-regressive.

67 Peter H. Ditto and Cristian G. Rodriguez, "Populism and the Social Psychology of Grievance 1," in *The Psychology of Populism: The Tribal Challenge to Liberal Democracy,* ed. Joseph P. Forgas, William D. Crano, and Klaus Fiedler (New York: Routledge, 2021), https://www.taylorfrancis.com/books/edit/10.4324/9781003057680/psychology-populism-joseph-forgas-william-crano-klaus-fiedler?refId=67c8ee84-8a30-49d8-969a-8d68762b8ea0&context=ubx.

68 Jane Mansbridge and Stephen Mecado, "Populism and Democratic Theory," *Annual Review of Law and Social Science* no. 15 (2019), https://www.annualreviews.org/content/journals/10.1146/annurev-lawsocsci-101518-042843; Ditto and Rodriguez, "Populism and the Social Psychology of Grievance 1," 23–41.

69 Edelman, *2025 Edelman Trust Barometer: Trust and the Crisis of Grievance* (2025), https://www.edelman.com/trust/2025/trust-barometer; Richard Edelman, "We Are on the Precipice of a Grievance-Based Society," *TIME,* January 15, 2025, https://time.com/7208097/the-precipice-of-a-grievance-based-society/; George E. Marcus, *The Rise of Populism: The Politics of Justice, Anger, and Grievance* (Abingdon, UK: Routledge, 2021), https://www.taylorfrancis.com/chapters/edit/10.4324/9781003057680-6/rise-populism-george-marcus.

70 Sheri Berman, "The Causes of Populism in the West," *Annual Review of Political Science* 24 (May 2021): 1–88, https://www.annualreviews.org/doi/full/10.1146/annurev-polisci-041719-102503.
71 Linda Bos, Christian Schemer, Nicoleta Corbu, Michael Hameleers, Ioannis Andreadis, Anne Schulz, et al., "The Effects of Populism as a Social Identity Frame on Persuasion and Mobilization: Evidence from a 15-Country Experiment," *European Journal of Political Research* 59, 1 (February 2020): 3–24, https://ejpr.onlinelibrary.wiley.com/doi/full/10.1111/1475-6765.12334.
72 William A. Galston, "The Populist Challenge to Liberal Democracy," *Journal of Democracy* 29, 2 (2018): 5–19, https://www.brookings.edu/articles/the-populist-challenge-to-liberal-democracy/; Katja Freistein, Frank Gadinger, and Christine Unrau, "*It Just Feels Right:* Visuality and Emotion Norms in Right-Wing Populist Storytelling," *International Political Sociology* 16, 4 (December 2022): olac017, https://academic.oup.com/ips/article/16/4/olac017/6762012.
73 Kurt Weyland, "Populism and Authoritarianism," in *The Routledge Handbook on Global Populism,* ed. Carlos De la Torre (Abingdon, UK: Routledge, 2019), ch. 21, https://www.taylorfrancis.com/chapters/edit/10.4324/9781315226446-26/populism-authoritarianism-kurt-weyland; Rosefielde and Mills, *Populists and Progressives.*
74 Barry Eichengreen, *The Populist Temptation: Economic Grievance and Political Reaction in the Modern Era* (Oxford: Oxford University Press, 2018), https://global.oup.com/academic/product/the-populist-temptation-9780190866280?cc=ca&lang=en&; William Van Lear, *A Populist Challenge to Corporate Capitalism* (Singapore: World Scientific, 2022), https://www.worldscientific.com/worldscibooks/10.1142/4868#t=aboutBook.
75 Mark Zwolinski and John Tomasi, *The Individualists: Radicals, Reactionaries, and the Struggle for the Soul of Liberalism* (Princeton, NJ: Princeton University Press, 2023), https://press.princeton.edu/books/hardcover/9780691155548/the-individualists; Ipsos Global Advisor, *Populist and Nativist Sentiment in 2019: A 27-Country Survey* (2019), https://www.ipsos.com/sites/default/files/ct/news/documents/2019-08/populism-and-nativism-2019_0.pdf; Ipsos, "Populist and Nativist Views Still Prevail," (2019), https://www.ipsos.com/en/populist-and-nativist-views-still-prevail.
76 Martha Finnemore and Kathryn Sikkink, "International Norm Dynamics and Political Change," in *International Organization* 52, 4 (*International Organization* at Fifty: Exploration and Contestation in the Study of World Politics) (1998): 887–917, https://www.jstor.org/stable/2601361?refreqid=excelsior%3Afa28ce0dc3f7d5b6ffeaa9a408db38f4&seq=1; Sheri Berman, "Review: Ideas, Norms, and Culture in Political Analysis," *Comparative Politics* 33, 2 (January 2001): 231–50, https://www.jstor.org/stable/422380?seq=1.
77 Nathan Stoltzfus and Christopher Osmar, eds., *The Power of Populism and People: Resistance and Protest in the Modern World* (New York: Bloomsbury Academic, 2021).
78 Bethell, "Populism of the 21st Century"; "Hybrid Regime," in *Dictionary of Populism* (European Center for Populism Studies), https://www.populismstudies.org/Vocabulary/hybrid-regime/.
79 Jeremy Webber, "Understanding Populism," *Social and Legal Studies* 32, 6 (December 2023): 849–76, https://journals.sagepub.com/doi/full/10.1177/09646639231156144.
80 Larry Diamond, "When Does Populism Become a Threat to Democracy" (speech at the Stanford FSI Conference on Global Populisms, November 3–4, 2017), https://diamond-democracy.stanford.edu/speaking/speeches/when-does-populism-become-threat-democracy.
81 Dani Rodrik, "Why Does Globalization Fuel Populism? Economics, Culture, and the Rise of Right-Wing Populism," *Annual Review of Economics* 13 (2021): 133–70, https://drodrik.scholars.harvard.edu/publications/why-does-globalization-fuel-populism-economics-culture-and-rise-right-wing; Uri Friedman, "What Is a Populist? And Is Donald Trump One?" *The Atlantic,* February 2, 2017, https://www.theatlantic.com/international/archive/2017/02/what-is-populist-trump/516525/.
82 Dani Rodrik, "Populism and the Economics of Globalization," *Journal of International Business Policy* (2018), https://drodrik.scholar.harvard.edu/files/dani-rodrik/files/populism_and_the_economics_of_globalization.pdf.
83 Useful examples involve debates around such matters as UN governance reform and issues of sustainable economic and social development. See, e.g., Jeremy Farrall, "The Populist Challenge and the Future of the United Nations Security Council," *Maryland Journal of International Law* 35, 1 (2021): 73–89, https://digitalcommons.law.umaryland.edu/cgi/viewcontent.cgi?article=1704&context=mjil; Varun Gauri, "Populism and Development Policy," *World Bank Blogs,*

December 8, 2017, https://blogs.worldbank.org/developmenttalk/populism-and-development-policy; Paul Marschall and Stephen Klingebiel, "Populism: Consequences for Global Sustainable Development" (Deutsches Institut für Entwicklungspolitik [DIE] Briefing Paper No. 8, 2019), https://www.idos-research.de/fileadmin/migratedNewsAssets/Files/BP_8.2019.pdf.

84 Matthieu Bellon and Matthias Gnewuch, "Blog: Building Resilience in Times of Inflation-Induced Inequality," European Stability Mechanism, August 31, 2023, https://www.esm.europa.eu/blog/building-resilience-times-inflation-induced-inequality; Angie Hart, Emily Gagnon, Suna Eryigit-Madzwamuse, Josh Cameron, Kay Aranda, Anne Rathbone, and Becky Heaver, "Uniting Resilience Research and Practice with an Inequalities Approach" *Sage Open* 6, 4 (2016), https://journals.sagepub.com/doi/full/10.1177/2158244016682477.

85 "Resilience," in *APA Dictionary of Psychology* (2018), https://dictionary.apa.org/resilience.

86 Cheongil Kim, Jaesun Yeom, Seunghoo Jeong, and Ji-Bum Chung, "Resilience and Social Change: Findings from Research Trends Using Association Rule Mining," *Heliyon* 9, 8 (August 2023): e18766, https://www.sciencedirect.com/science/article/pii/S2405844023059741#bib18; Rob Cross, Karen Dillon, and Danna Greenberg, "The Secret to Building Resilience," *Harvard Business Review,* January 29, 2021, https://hbr.org/2021/01/the-secret-to-building-resilience.

87 Aistė Diržytė, Ona Gražina Rakauskienė, and Vaida Servetkienė, "Evaluation of Resilience Impact on Socio-Economic Inequality," *Entrepreneurship and Sustainability Issues* 4, 4 (June 2017): 489–501, https://etalpykla.lituanistika.lt/object/LT-LDB-0001:J.04~2017~1542035197522/J.04~2017~1542035197522.pdf; A. Hart, E. Gagnon, S. Eryigit-Madzwamuse, J. Cameron, K. Aranda, A. Rathbone, and B. Heaver, "Uniting Resilience Research and Practice with an Inequalities Approach," *Sage Open* 6, 4 (2016), https://journals.sagepub.com/doi/full/10.1177/2158244016682477.

88 Rasmus Dahlberg, "Resilience and Complexity: Conjoining the Discourses of Two Contested Concepts," *Culture Unbound Journal of Current Cultural Research* 7, 3 (October 2015): 541–57, https://www.researchgate.net/publication/283445051_Resilience_and_Complexity_Conjoining_the_Discourses_of_Two_Contested_Concepts; Jonathan Pugh, "Resilience, Complexity and Post-Liberalism," *Area* 46, 3 (September 2014): 313–19, https://www.jstor.org/stable/24030001; David Chandler, *Resilience: The Governance of Complexity* (London: Routledge, 2014), https://www.taylorfrancis.com/books/mono/10.4324/9781315773810/resilience-david-chandler; Andreas Duit, Victor Galaz, Katarina Eckerberg, and Jonas Ebbesson, "Governance, Complexity and Resilience," *Global Environmental Change* 20, 3 (August 2010): 363–68, https://www.sciencedirect.com/science/article/abs/pii/S095937801000035X.

89 George Newth and Alessio Scopelliti, "Common Sense, Populism, and Reactionary Politics on Twitter: An Analysis of Far-Right Common Sense Narratives Between 2008 and 2022," *Party Politics* 31, 2 (December 28, 2023): 375–91, https://journals.sagepub.com/doi/10.1177/13540688231224319; Simon Brown, "The Rise of the Elite Anti-Intellectual," *Dissent,* August 20, 2021, https://www.dissentmagazine.org/online_articles/the-rise-of-the-elite-anti-intellectuals/.

90 Hank Johnson, Enrique Larana, and Joseph R. Gusfield. "Identities, Grievances, and New Social Movements," in *New Social Movements: From Ideology to Identity,* ed. Enrique Larana, Hank Johnson, and Joseph R. Gusfield (Philadelphia: Temple University Press, 1994), https://users.ssc.wisc.edu/~oliver/SOC924/Articles/JohnstonLaranaGusfieldIdentitiesgrievancesandnewsocialmovements.pdf.

91 Paul Blokker, "Populism as a Constitutional Project," *International Journal of Constitutional Law* 17, 2 (April 2019): 536–53, https://academic.oup.com/icon/article/17/2/536/5523745?login=false.

92 Kurt Weyland, *Democracy's Resilience to Populism's Threat* (New York: Cambridge University Press, 2024), https://www.cambridge.org/core/books/democracys-resilience-to-populisms-threat/B3D9E2C5F9316B2B71F0B6E93203818A; Ben Crum and Alvaro Oleart, *Populist Parties and Democratic Resilience: A Cross-National Analysis of Populist Parties' Impact on Democratic Pluralism in Europe* (Abingdon, UK: Routledge, 2023), https://www.routledge.com/Populist-Parties-and-Democratic-Resilience-A-Cross-National-Analysis-of/Crum-Oleart/p/book/9781032218908.

93 Jean François Drolet and Michael C. Williams, "The View from MARs: American Populism and the Liberal World Order," *CIPS Blog,* Centre for International Policy Studies, July 15, 2018, https://www.cips-cepi.ca/2018/07/15/the-view-from-mars-american-populism-and-the-liberal-world-order/; Samuel T. Francis, *Leviathan and Its Enemies* (Brooklyn, NY: Radix Media, 2016), https://www.abebooks.com/products/isbn/9781593680497?cm_sp=bdp-_-ISBN10-_-PLP.

94 See generally Michael Goodhart, "Democratic Accountability in Global Politics: Norms Not Agents," *Journal of Politics* 73, 1 (January 2011): 45–60, https://www.journals.uchicago.edu/doi/abs/10.1017/S002238161000085X?journalCode=jop; Rosaria Conte, Rino Falcone, and Giovanni Santor, "Introduction: Agents and Norms: How to Fill the Gap?" *Artificial Intelligence and the Law* 7, 1 (March 1999): 1–15, https://link.springer.com/article/10.1023/A:1008397328506; Robert Axelrod, *The Complexity of Cooperation: Agent-Based Models of Competition and Collaboration* (Princeton, NJ: Princeton University Press, 1997), https://press.princeton.edu/books/paperback/9780691015675/the-complexity-of-cooperation.

95 Benoit Guerin, Julian McCrae, and Marcus Shepheard, *Accountability in Modern Government: What Are the Issues? A Discussion Paper* (London: Institute for Government, 2018), https://www.instituteforgovernment.org.uk/sites/default/files/publications/IfG%20accountability%20discussion%20paper%20april%202018.pdf; Chul Kim, "A Sense of Alienation Towards Government: An Analytical Framework," *International Review of Public Administration* 9, 2 (2004): 55–64, https://www.tandfonline.com/doi/abs/10.1080/12294659.2005.10805049.

96 Carlos de la Torre, "Democracy and Autocracy in the Age of Populism," in *The New Handbook of Political Sociology,* ed. Thomas Janoski, Cedric De Leon, Joya Misra, and Isaac William Martin (Cambridge: Cambridge University Press, 2020), 1027–52, https://www.cambridge.org/core/books/new-handbook-of-political-sociology/democracy-and-autocracy-in-the-age-of-populism/555AA6E9CD10419CC82B8ADEE8472547; Marlies Glasius, "What Authoritarianism Is ... and Is Not: A Practice Perspective," *International Affairs* 94, 3 (May 2018): 515–33, https://academic.oup.com/ia/article/94/3/515/4992409; Steven Levitsky and Lucan Ahmad Way, "Elections Without Democracy: The Rise of Competitive Authoritarianism," *Journal of Democracy* 11, 3 (April 2002): 51–65, https://www.journalofdemocracy.org/articles/elections-without-democracy-the-rise-of-competitive-authoritarianism/; Michael Goodhart, "Human Rights and Global Democracy," *Ethics and International Affairs* 22, 4 (2008): 395–420, https://www.cambridge.org/core/journals/ethics-and-international-affairs/article/abs/human-rights-and-global-democracy/4FB432010C490E7B9AED5EB59161FB45; Charles Tilly, *Democracy* (New York: Cambridge University Press, 2007); David Held, *Models of Democracy* (Stanford, CA: Stanford University Press, 2006); Wolfgang Merkel, "Embedded and Defective Democracies," *Democratization* 11, 5 (2004): 33–58, https://www.tandfonline.com/doi/abs/10.1080/13510340412331304598.

97 Douglas A. Johnson, "In Defense of Democratic Populism," in *Human Rights in a Time of Populism,* ed. Gerald L. Neuman (Cambridge: Cambridge University Press, 2020), 192–217, https://www.cambridge.org/core/books/human-rights-in-a-time-of-populism/in-defense-of-democratic-populism/2CEAF9A196FA1A0EF9F670E8E91C9228; Andrew J. Nathan, "The Puzzle of Authoritarian Legitimacy," *Journal of Democracy* 31, 1 (January 2020): 158–68, https://www.journalofdemocracy.org/articles/the-puzzle-of-authoritarian-legitimacy/; Johannes Gerschewski, "Legitimacy in Autocracies: Oxymoron or Essential Feature?" *Perspectives on Politics* 16, 3 (2018): 652–65, https://www.cambridge.org/core/journals/perspectives-on-politics/article/abs/legitimacy-in-autocracies-oxymoron-or-essential-feature/ABFD028D0BF3A11BBF553D66D3993C8E; Sofya de Boulay, "Why Authoritarian Legitimation Matters?" Around the Caspian, January 10, 2019, http://caspianet.eu/2019/01/10/why-authoritarian-legitimation-matters/.

98 Patrick Liddiard, "Is Populism Really a Problem for Democracy?" Wilson Center for Scholars, August 2019, https://www.wilsoncenter.org/article/populism-really-problem-for-democracy; Dom Phillips, Jason Burke, and Paul Lewis, "How Brazil and South Africa Became the World's Most Populist Countries," *The Guardian,* May 1, 2019, https://www.theguardian.com/world/2019/may/01/how-brazil-and-south-africa-became-the-worlds-most-populist-countries; Mounk and Kyle, "What Populists Do to Democracies."

99 Melissa De Witte, "Populism Is a Political Problem That Is Putting Democracy at Risk, Stanford Scholars Say," *Stanford Report,* March 11, 2020, https://news.stanford.edu/2020/03/11/populism-jeopardizes-democracies-around-world/; Jeremiah Morelock, ed., *Critical Theory and Authoritarian Populism* (London: University of Westminster Press, 2018), https://library.oapen.org/bitstream/handle/20.500.12657/26034/UWP-030-REVISED.pdf?sequence=1&isAllowed=y.

100 Uri Friedman, "How Populism Helped Wreck Venezuela," *The Atlantic,* June 4, 2017, https://www.theatlantic.com/international/archive/2017/06/venezuela-populism-fail/525321/; "Populism in Brazil: How Liberalization and Austerity Led to the Rise of Lula and Bolsonaro," *The Conversation,* September 20, 2020, https://theconversation.com/populism-in-brazil-how-liberalisation-and-austerity-led-to-the-rise-of-lula-and-bolsonaro-146780.

101 See generally Yousueng Han and Mehmet Akif Demircioglu, "Accountability, Politics, and Power," in *Global Encyclopedia of Public Administration, Public Policy and Governance*, ed. Ali Farazmand (Cham, Switzerland: Springer, 2016), https://link.springer.com/referencework entry/10.1007/978-3-319-31816-5_2453-2; Goodhart, "Democratic Accountability in Global Politics"; Alicia Adsera, Carles Boix, and Mark Payne, "Are You Being Served? Political Accountability and Quality of Government," *Journal of Law, Economics and Organization* 19, 2 (2003): 445–90, https://www.princeton.edu/~adsera/JLEO.pdf.

102 Alois Stutzer and Thorsten Henne, "Aspiration Theory," in *Encyclopedia of Quality of Life and Well-Being*, ed. Alex C. Michalos (Dordrecht, Netherlands: Springer, 2014), https://link.springer.com/referenceworkentry/10.1007%2F978-94-007-0753-5_115; Sally Engle Merry, "Measuring the World: Indicators, Human Rights and Global Governance," *Current Anthropology* 52, S3 (2011): S83–S95, https://www.law.berkeley.edu/files/Merry-MeasuringtheWorld.pdf. Also see Sounman Hong, "A Behavioral Model of Public Organizations: Bounded Rationality, Performance Feedback, and Negativity Bias," *Journal of Public Administration Research and Theory* 29, 1 (January 2019): 1–17; Henrik Greve, "Performance, Aspirations, and Risky Organizational Change," *Administrative Science Quarterly* 43, 1 (1998): 58–86, https://www.researchgate.net/publication/272550286_Performance_Aspirations_and_Risky_Organizational_Change.

103 Jeremy Waldron, "The Rule of Law," in *The Stanford Encyclopedia of Philosophy*, ed. Edward N. Zalta and Uri Nodelman (2020), https://plato.stanford.edu/cgi-bin/encyclopedia/archinfo.cgi?entry=rule-of-law; Brian Z. Tamanaha, "How an Instrumental View of Law Corrodes the Rule of Law," *DePaul Law Review* 56, 2 (Winter 2007): 469–506, https://core.ac.uk/download/pdf/232966755.pdf.

104 Martin Krygler, "The Rule of Law and State Legitimacy," in *Legitimacy: The State and Beyond*, ed. Wojciech Sadurski, Michael Sevel, and Kevin Walton (Oxford: Oxford University Press, 2019), 106–36, https://oxford.universitypressscholarship.com/view/10.1093/oso/9780198825265.001.0001/oso-9780198825265-chapter-7; Iutisone Salevao, *Rule of Law, Legitimate Governance and Development in the Pacific* (Canberra: ANU Press, 2005), https://press.anu.edu.au/publications/rule-law-legitimate-governance-development-pacific.

105 "Fighting Corruption in the Age of 'Fake News,'" *Transparency International*, October 8, 2019, https://www.transparency.org/en/news/fighting-corruption-in-the-age-of-fake-news; Katleen Janssen, "Open Government Data and the Right to Information: Opportunities and Obstacles," *Journal of Community Informatics* 8, 2 (2012), https://openjournals.uwaterloo.ca/index.php/JoCI/article/view/3042; Gia B. Lee, "Persuasion, Transparency, and Government Speech," *Hastings Law Review* 56, 5 (2005): 983–1057, https://repository.uchastings.edu/cgi/view content.cgi?article=3591&context=hastings_law_journal.

106 Alexander Brown, *Ronald Dworkin's Theory of Equality: Domestic and Global Perspectives* (New York: Palgrave Macmillan, 2009), https://link.springer.com/content/pdf/bfm%3A978-0-230-24446-7%2F1.pdf; "Equality," *Stanford Encyclopedia of Philosophy*, March 27, 2001, https://plato.stanford.edu/entries/equality/; Anne Applebaum, *The Twilight of Democracy: The Seductive Lure of Authoritarianism* (New York: Penguin Random House: 2020).

107 Michael J. Sandel, *The Tyranny of Merit: What's Become of the Common Good?* (New York: Farrar, Straus and Giroux, 2020), https://us.macmillan.com/books/9780374289980. For an insightful review, see Elizabeth Anderson, "The Broken System: What Comes After Meritocracy?" *The Nation*, March 8–15, 2021, https://www.thenation.com/article/society/sandel-tyranny-merit/.

108 Peter Berkowitz, "Liberal Democracy vs Communism," *Defining Ideas* (Hoover Institution), February 27, 2020, https://www.hoover.org/research/liberal-democracy-vs-communism; Ed Rooksby, "The Relationship Between Liberalism and Socialism," *Science and Society* 76, 4 (October 2012): 495–520, https://www.jstor.org/stable/41714354?seq=1; Daniel A. Bell, *The China Model: Political Meritocracy and the Limits of Democracy* (Princeton, NJ: Princeton University Press, 2015).

109 World Population Review, "Democratic Socialist Countries 2021," https://worldpopulation review.com/country-rankings/democratic-socialist-countries.

110 Andrew A. Little and Thomas B. Pepinsky, "Simple and Formal Modals in Comparative Politics," *Chinese Political Science Review* 1, 3 (2016): 425–47, https://tompepinsky.files.wordpress.com/2017/06/cpsr2016.pdf; James F. Fairbank, Goce Andrevski, and Michael Parzen, "Striving Toward the Future: Aspiration-Performance Discrepancies and Planned Organizational Change," *Strategic Organization* 7, 4 (2009): 433–66, https://www.researchgate.

net/publication/253950620_Striving_toward_the_future_Aspiration-performance_discrepancies_and_planned_organizational_change.

111 Ronald J. Allen, "Taming Complexity: Rationality, the Law of Evidence and the Nature of the Legal System," *Law, Probability and Risk* 12, 2 (June 2013): 99–113, https://academic.oup.com/lpr/article/12/2/99/945305.

112 Richard T. Thakor and Robert C. Merton, "Trust, Transparency, and Complexity," *Review of Financial Studies* 36, 8 (August 2023): 3213–56, https://papers.ssrn.com/sol3/papers.cfm?abstract_id=4314920; Ullrich K.H. Ecker, Stephan Lewandowsky, John Cook, Philipp Schmid, Lisa K. Fazio, Nadia Brashier, Panayiota Kendeou, et al., "The Psychological Drivers of Misinformation Belief and Its Resistance to Correction," *Nature Reviews Psychology* 1 (2022): 13–29, https://www.nature.com/articles/s44159-021-00006-y#auth-Ullrich_K__H_-Ecker-Aff1; Dennis M. Murphy and James F. White, "Propaganda: Can a Word Decide a War?" *Parameters,* Autumn 2007, https://apps.dtic.mil/sti/pdfs/ADA486008.pdf.

113 Katharina Lima de Miranda and Denis J. Snower, "Recoupling Economic and Social Prosperity," IZA (Institute of Labor Economics), Discussion Paper No. 12998, February 2020, https://docs.iza.org/dp12998.pdf; James R. Otteson, "The Inhuman Alienation of Capitalism," *Society* 49 (2012): 139–43.

114 Heidi Learner, "The Economic Impact of Populism," Impacts, April 2019, https://www.savills.com/impacts/market-trends/the-economic-impact-of-populism.html; Dani Rodrik, "Is Populism Necessarily Bad Economics?" *AEA Papers and Proceedings* 108 (2018): 196–99, https://drodrik.scholars.harvard.edu/publications/populism-necessarily-bad-economics.

115 Henrietta Moore, "Beyond GDP: Here's a Better Way to Measure People's Prosperity," *The Conversation,* October 13, 2021, https://theconversation.com/beyond-gdp-heres-a-better-way-to-measure-peoples-prosperity-168023; Éloi Laurent, *Measuring Tomorrow: Accounting for Well-Being, Resilience, and Sustainability in the Twenty-First Century* (Princeton, NJ: Princeton University Press, 2018), https://press.princeton.edu/books/hardcover/9780691170695/measuring-tomorrow; "How to Measure Prosperity," *The Economist,* April 30, 2016, https://www.economist.com/leaders/2016/04/30/how-to-measure-prosperity.

116 Anna Chrysopoulou, "The Vision of a Well-Being Economy," *Stanford Social Innovation Review,* December 16, 2020, https://ssir.org/articles/entry/the_vision_of_a_well_being_economy; Romina Boarini, Fabrice Murtin, and Paul Schreyer, "Inclusive Growth: The OECD Measurement Framework," OECD, June 2015, https://www.oecd.org/content/dam/oecd/en/publications/reports/2015/11/inclusive-growth_g17a2715/5jrqppxjqhg4-en.pdf; "How Do We Measure Well-Being?" *The Conversation,* January 8, 2018, https://theconversation.com/how-do-we-measure-well-being-70967.

117 Sarah White and Chloe Blackmore, eds., *Cultures of Wellbeing: Method, Place, Policy* (New York: Palgrave Macmillan, 2016), https://www.palgrave.com/gp/book/9781137536440; OECD, *OECD Framework for Statistics on the Distribution of Household Income, Consumption and Wealth* (Paris: OECD Publishing, 2013), https://read.oecd-ilibrary.org/economics/framework-for-statistics-on-the-distribution-of-household-income-consumption-and-wealth_9789264194830-en#page4.

118 World Bank, "Inequality and Shared Prosperity," https://www.worldbank.org/en/topic/isp; Francisco H.G. Ferreira, Emanuela Galasso, and Mario Negre, "Shared Prosperity: Concepts, Data, and Some Policy Examples," World Bank Policy Research Working Paper No. 8451, May 23, 2018, https://papers.ssrn.com/sol3/papers.cfm?abstract_id=3183493.

119 The distinction between public and private goods is generally useful as a criterion for distribution of prosperity. Thomas Laudal, *A New Approach to the Economics of Public Goods* (Abingdon, UK: Routledge, 2020), https://www.routledge.com/A-New-Approach-to-the-Economics-of-Public-Goods/Laudal/p/book/9780367787776; UN Industrial Development Organization (UNIDO), *Public Goods for Economic Development* (UNIDO, 2008), https://www.unido.org/sites/default/files/2009-02/Public%20goods%20for%20economic%20development_sale_0.pdf. However, as corporate actors in populist regimes are often state-owned, the conventional distinction between public and private goods in the distribution of prosperity becomes blurred, inviting use of an alternative metric. For the purposes of this work, distribution of prosperity is assessed as between recipients in the business community and society.

120 Sustainable Development Goals, "UN Secretary-General's Strategy for Financing the 2030 Agenda," July 18, 2019, https://www.un.org/sustainabledevelopment/sg-finance-strategy/; World Business Council for Sustainable Development (WBCSD), *A Business Guide to Development*

Actors: Introducing Company Managers to the Development Community (Geneva: WBCSD, 2004), http://docs.wbcsd.org/2004/10/A-Business-Guide-To-Development-Actors.pdf.

121 Max Risch, "Trickle-Down Revisited," *Oxford Review of Economic Policy* 39, 2 (Autumn 2023): 498–512, https://academic.oup.com/oxrep/article-abstract/39/3/498/7245719; Sarah Kuypers, Francesco Figari, and Gerlinde Verbist, *Redistribution from a Joint Income-Wealth Perspective,* OECD Social, Employment and Migration Working Papers No. 257 (Paris: OECD Publishing, 2021), https://www.oecd.org/en/publications/redistribution-from-a-joint-income-wealth-perspective_22103c5e-en.html; Jan W. Rivkin, Karen G. Mills, and Michael E. Porter, *The Challenge of Shared Prosperity: Findings of Harvard Business School's 2015 Survey on U.S. Competitiveness* (Harvard Business School, September 2015), https://www.hbs.edu/competitiveness/Documents/challenge-of-shared-prosperity.pdf.

122 Melissa Leach, "Introduction: States, Markets and Society: Looking Back to Look Forward," *IDS Bulletin* 47, 2A (2016), https://bulletin.ids.ac.uk/index.php/idsbo/article/view/2805/ONLINE%20ARTICLE; Joseph E. Stiglitz, *The State, the Market, and Development,* WIDER Working Paper 2016/001 (Helsinki: World Institute for Development Economics Research, 2016), https://doi.org/10.35188/UNU-WIDER/2016/044-7.

123 Sheldon Richman, "Market, State, and Autonomy," Foundation for Economic Education, August 10, 2012, https://fee.org/articles/market-state-and-autonomy/; Alan Wolfe, *The Future of Liberalism* (New York: Penguin Random House, 2010), https://www.penguinrandomhouse.com/books/193105/the-future-of-liberalism-by-alan-wolfe/. Also see generally Ronald H. Coase, "The Problem of Social Cost," *Journal of Law and Economics* 3 (October 1960): 1–44.

124 On equality, see Augusto Lopez-Claros, "Equality of Opportunity as an Engine of Prosperity," *World Bank Blogs,* July 29, 2015, https://blogs.worldbank.org/developmenttalk/equality-opportunity-engine-prosperity; Antony Davies, James R. Harrigan, and Megan Teague, "Equality, Liberty, and Prosperity," *Social Philosophy and Policy* 31, 2 (Spring 2015): 180–203, https://www.cambridge.org/core/journals/social-philosophy-and-policy/article/abs/equality-liberty-and-prosperity/8A8C4AE31B7FC601C37EBCEB5982C9AE. On complexity, see Ricardo Hausmann, César A. Hidalgo, Sebastián Bustos, Michele Coscia, Alexander Simoes, and Muhammed A. Yildirim, *The Atlas of Economic Complexity: Mapping Paths to Prosperity,* 2nd ed. (Cambridge, MA: MIT Press, 2013).

125 Elizabeth Chambliss, "When Do Facts Persuade? Some Thoughts on the Market for 'Empirical Legal Studies,'" *Law and Contemporary Problems* 71 (Spring 2008): 17–39, https://scholarship.law.duke.edu/cgi/viewcontent.cgi?article=1463&context=lcp; David M. Trubek and John P. Esser, "'Critical Empiricism' in American Legal Studies: Paradox, Program, or Pandora's Box?" *Law and Social Inquiry* 14, 1 (January 1989): 3–52, https://onlinelibrary.wiley.com/doi/full/10.1111/j.1747-4469.1989.tb00577.x.

126 See, e.g., Cecilia Garcia-Peñalosa, "Inequality in Macroeconomic Models," *Revue de L'OFCE* 3, 157 (March 2018): 93–115, https://www.cairn.info/revue-de-l-ofce-2018-3-page-93.htm; European Central Bank, "Inequality and Macroeconomic Policies: Intervention by Vítor Constâncio, Vice-President of the ECB at the Annual Congress of the European Economic Association Lisbon, 22 August 2017," https://www.ecb.europa.eu/press/key/date/2017/html/ecb.sp170822.en.html.

127 Catherine Barnard and Bob Hepple, "Substantive Equality," *Cambridge Law Journal* 59, 3 (2000): 562–82, https://www.cambridge.org/core/journals/cambridge-law-journal/article/abs/substantive-equality/1AC13C0FF5C509808284AFDD1F2531A9; Sandra Fredman, "Substantive Equality Revisited," *International Journal of Constitutional Law* 14, 3 (July 2016): 712–38, https://academic.oup.com/icon/article/14/3/712/2404476.

128 See, e.g., Morris Pearl, "Why Are We Still Pretending 'Trickle-Down' Economics Work?" *The Guardian,* June 13, 2019, https://www.theguardian.com/commentisfree/2019/jun/12/why-are-we-still-pretending-trickle-down-economics-work; Neera Tanden, "Burying Supply-Side Once and for All," *Democracy: A Journal of Ideas* no. 29 (Summer 2013), https://democracyjournal.org/magazine/29/burying-supply-side-once-and-for-all/; Gene Sperling, "Rising-Tide Economics: In the Twenty-First Century, Growth and Equality Must Go Hand in Hand," *Democracy: A Journal of Ideas* no. 6 (Fall 2007), https://democracyjournal.org/magazine/6/rising-tide-economics/; Sylvia Bashevkin, "Rethinking Retrenchment: North American Social Policy During the Early Clinton and Chrétien Years," *Canadian Journal of Political Science* 33, 1 (2000): 7–36, https://www.cambridge.org/core/journals/canadian-journal-of-political-science-revue

-canadienne-de-science-politique/article/abs/rethinking-retrenchment-north-american-social-policy-during-the-early-clinton-and-chretien-years/40CC1E26316B77C60FE24FDBB6E096CD.

129 Daniel M. Hausman, "Equality of Autonomy," *Ethics* 199, 4 (July 2009): 742–56, https://www.journals.uchicago.edu/doi/abs/10.1086/605729?journalCode=et; Christine Helliwell, "Autonomy as Natural Equality: Inequality in 'Egalitarian' Societies," *Journal of the Royal Anthropological Society* 1, 2 (June 1995): 359–75, https://www.jstor.org/stable/3034693?seq=1.

130 Éloi Laurent, "Good and Bad Indicators: The Case of GDP," in *Measuring Tomorrow: Accounting for Well-Being, Resilience, and Sustainability in the Twenty-first Century* (Princeton, NJ: Princeton University Press, 2018), ch. 2, https://press.princeton.edu/books/hardcover/9780691170695/measuring-tomorrow?srsltid=AfmBOopUCOe2G5B__gzyj9EMdfwEC_yySLsaQJmZUq56HhkF3wwAqyqJ.

131 Donald J. Boudreaux, "Complexity in the Service of Simplicity," The Daily Economy, January 31, 2022, https://www.aier.org/article/complexity-in-the-service-of-simplicity/; Kimberly Amadeo, "Why Trickle-Down Economics Works in Theory but Not in Fact: The Shortcomings of Supply-Side Economics," *The Balance,* December 30, 2021, https://www.thebalancemoney.com/trickle-down-economics-theory-effect-does-it-work-3305572.

132 Michael Ellman, "Socialist Planning," in *Problems of the Planned Economy,* ed. John Eatwell, Murray Milgate, and Peter Newman (London: Palgrave Macmillan, 1990), 13–21, https://link.springer.com/chapter/10.1007/978-1-349-20863-0_2.

133 Harold Noonan and Ben Curtis, "Identity," in *The Stanford Encyclopedia of Philosophy,* ed. Edward N. Zalta (2018), https://plato.stanford.edu/archives/sum2018/entries/identity/; Michael Kalin and Nicholas Sambanis, "How to Think About Social Identity," *Annual Review of Political Science* 21 (May 2018): 239–57, https://www.annualreviews.org/doi/full/10.1146/annurev-polisci-042016-024408.

134 Hilary Silver, "The Contexts of Social Inclusion," United Nations Department of Economic and Social Affairs (DESA) Working Paper No. 144, December 6, 2016, https://papers.ssrn.com/sol3/papers.cfm?abstract_id=2879940; Global Diversity Practice, "What Is Diversity and Inclusion?" https://globaldiversitypractice.com/what-is-diversity-inclusion; Martin Papillon, "Immigration, Diversity and Social Inclusion in Canada's Cities," Canadian Policy Research Network Discussion Paper F/27, December 2002, https://d1wqtxts1xzle7.cloudfront.net/29887035/immigration__diversity___social_inclusion_in_canadas_cities_-_m_1_._papillon_%28_cprn_2002_%29-libre.pdf?1390878409=&response-content-disposition=inline%3B+filename%3DImmigration_diversity_and_social_inclusi.pdf&Expires=1764024073&Signature=HsbeuNmYGpr1IqkkeTje8~T8y6EqGS8RKHuO7NJCMtpi4EZAWNE0ydlla7yoQp1kII8qzkRBjEtdtNB5W9D2rDmCnrEvWQvPlQyAYh4YZr6Tv91UXizCu~TLdd2LVI2~NLRHCWBF5aR69Gnk5KhRG6jn3mz9Tf50IaZ0ISv99DqsRn2homxvLedF12p~piG8VeQRj~qfOfXDirBMmNjPkq4yLpswxT5D1GCuKr5kNlrZQQ~ijAXEyn5Wi2Kil3iYQXSQGZgriTJ5hZLOFfiSr0X7G1BcTQroSQg42mTVV3jzBmuKouUg6bGEWbtwtVacI11BT5ai4m0YsVENHLq1CA__&Key-Pair-Id=APKAJLOHF5GGSLRBV4ZA.

135 Peter Adey, *Mobility,* 2nd ed. (Abingdon, UK: Routledge, 2017), https://www.routledge.com/Mobility/Adey/p/book/9781138949010; Tim Cresswell, "Towards a Politics of Mobility," *Environment and Planning D: Society and Space* 28, 1 (January 1, 2010): 17–31, https://journals.sagepub.com/doi/abs/10.1068/d11407?id=d11407&journalCode=epda.

136 Stuart White, *Equality* (Cambridge: Polity Press, 2006), https://www.wiley.com/en-gy/Equality-p-9780745627731.

137 Nancy Foner, Kay Deaux, and Katharine M. Donato, "Introduction: Immigration and Changing Identities," *Russell Sage Foundation Journal of the Social Sciences* 4, 5 (August 2018), https://www.researchgate.net/publication/327663210_Introduction_Immigration_and_Changing_Identities.

138 See, e.g., Derek Thompson, "How Globalization Saved the World and Damned the West," *The Atlantic,* February 7, 2019; Chiara Oldani and Jan Wouters eds., *The G7, Anti-Globalism and the Governance of Globalization* (Abingdon, UK: Routledge, 2018), https://www.routledge.com/The-G7-Anti-Globalism-and-the-Governance-of-Globalization/Oldani-Wouters/p/book/9781032094748; Joseph Nye, "Globalism Versus Globalization," *The Globalist,* April 15, 2002, https://www.theglobalist.com/globalism-versus-globalization/.

139 See, e.g., Nenad Miscevic, *Nationalism and Beyond: Introducing Moral Debate About Values* (Budapest: Central European University Press, 2013), https://books.openedition.org/ceup/440; David Miller, "Nationalism," in *The Stanford Encyclopedia of Philosophy* (June 19, 2025), https://plato.stanford.edu/entries/nationalism/.
140 Elena A. Korosteleva and Irina Petrova, "What Makes Communities Resilient in Times of Complexity and Change?" *Cambridge Review of International Affairs* 5, 2 (2021): 137–57, https://www.tandfonline.com/doi/full/10.1080/09557571.2021.2024145; U.A. Segal, "Globalization, Migration, and Ethnicity," *Public Health* 172 (July 2019): 135–42, https://www.sciencedirect.com/science/article/abs/pii/S0033350619301349.
141 Gil S. Epstein and Odelia Heizleer, "Ethnic Identity: A Theoretical Framework," *IZA Journal of Migration* 4, 1 (2015): 1–11, https://izajodm.springeropen.com/articles/10.1186/s40176-015-0033-z; Sonia Roccas and Marilynn B. Brewer, "Social Identity Complexity," *Personality and Social Psychology Review* 6, 2 (2002): 88–106, https://journals.sagepub.com/doi/abs/10.1207/S15327957PSPR0602_01.
142 Scott E. Page, *Diversity and Complexity* (Princeton, NJ: Princeton University Press, 2011), https://press.princeton.edu/books/paperback/9780691137674/diversity-and-complexity; Ted Brader, Nicolas A. Falentino, and Elizabeth Suhay, "What Triggers Public Opposition to Immigration? Anxiety, Group Cues, and Immigration Threat," *American Journal of Political Science* 52, 4 (October 2008): 959–78, https://onlinelibrary.wiley.com/doi/abs/10.1111/j.1540-5907.2008.00353.x.
143 Cristina Bicchieri, Ryan Muldoon, and Alessandro Sontuoso, "Social Norms," in *The Stanford Encyclopedia of Philosophy* (2018), https://www.sas.upenn.edu/ppe-repec/ppc/wpaper/0015.pdf; Katie Williamson, "Building Blocks: What's in a Norm?" *Medium,* October 25, 2018, https://medium.com/in-rare-form/building-blocks-whats-in-a-norm-436180fad1ab; Ingolfur Bluhdorn and Felix Butzlaff, "Rethinking Populism: Peak Democracy, Liquid Identity and the Performance of Sovereignty," *European Journal of Social Theory* 22, 2 (February 7, 2018): 191–211, https://journals.sagepub.com/doi/full/10.1177/1368431017754057; Robert B. Cialdini, Carl A. Kallgren, and Raymond R. Reno, "A Focus Theory of Normative Conduct: A Theoretical Refinement and Re-evaluation of the Role of Norms in Human Behavior," *Advances in Experimental Social Psychology* 24 (1991): 201–34, https://www.sciencedirect.com/science/article/pii/S0065260108603305#!.
144 John H. Jackson, "Sovereignty – Modern: A New Approach to an Outdated Concept," *American Journal of International Law* 97 (2003): 782–802, https://scholarship.law.georgetown.edu/cgi/viewcontent.cgi?article=1108&context=facpub.
145 See "Goal 10: Reduced Inequalities," in United Nations Commission on International Trade Law (UNCITRAL), "Sustainable Development Goals," https://uncitral.un.org/en/about/sdg; World Trade Organization, "Principles of the Trading System," https://www.wto.org/english/thewto_e/whatis_e/tif_e/fact2_e.htm.
146 United Nations, "The Foundation of International Human Rights Law," https://www.un.org/en/about-us/udhr/foundation-of-international-human-rights-law; Office of the High Commissioner for Human Rights (OHCHR), *Human Rights in the Administration of Justice: A Manual on Human Rights for Judges, Prosecutors and Lawyers,* OHCHR Training Series No. 9 (2003), Chapter 13, https://www.ohchr.org/sites/default/files/Documents/Publications/training9chapter13en.pdf.
147 Martha A. Fineman, "Equality Across Legal Cultures – The Role for International Human Rights," Vulnerability and the Human Condition, September 21 2020, https://scholarblogs.emory.edu/vulnerability/2020/09/21/equality-across-legal-cultures-the-role-for-international human-rights/#:~:text=Formal%20equality%20is%20the%20circumstance,%2C%20however%2C%20guarantee%20equal%20outcomes.
148 Paul C. Szasz, "The Complexification of the United Nation System," *Max Planck Yearbook of United Nations Law* 3 (1999): 1–57, https://www.mpil.de/files/pdf2/mpunyb_szasz_3.pdf; John H. Jackson, "International Economic Law: Complexity and Puzzles," in *Journal of International Economic Law* 10, 1 (2007): 3–12, https://academic.oup.com/jiel/article-abstract/10/1/3/818525; Steven Wheatley, "Complexity as Methodology in International Law," in *The Idea of International Human Rights Law* (Oxford: Oxford University Press 2019), 37–64, https://academic.oup.com/book/4999/chapter-abstract/147484725?redirectedFrom=fulltext.

CHAPTER 2: CHINA'S GLOBALIZED POPULISM AND GLOBAL CRISES

1 Kun He, Scott A. Eldridge II, and Marcel Broersma, "Conceptualizing Populism: A Comparative Study Between China and Liberal Democratic Countries," *International Journal of Communication* 15 (2021): 3006–24, https://ijoc.org/index.php/ijoc/article/view/16563; Mark Chou, Benjamin Moffett, and Octavia Bryant, *Political Meritocracy and Populism: Cure or Curse?* (London and New York: Routledge, 2020), https://www.routledge.com/Political-Meritocracy-and-Populism-Cure-or-Curse/Chou-Moffitt-Bryant/p/book/9780367271022; Chenchen Zhang, "Right-Wing Populism with Chinese Characteristics? Identity, Otherness and Global Imaginaries in Debating World Politics Online," *European Journal of International Relations* 26, 1 (2019): 88–115, https://journals.sagepub.com/doi/abs/10.1177/1354066119850253; Salvatore Babones, "Xi Jinping: Communist China's First Populist President," *Forbes*, October 20, 2017, https://www.forbes.com/sites/salvatorebabones/2017/10/20/populism-chinese-style-xi-jinping-cements-his-status-as-chinas-first-populist-president/?sh=4a6f97de152e; James R. Townsend, "Chinese Populism and the Legacy of Mao Tse-tung," *Asian Survey* 17, 11 (November 1977): 1003–15, https://online.ucpress.edu/as/article-abstract/17/11/1003/21225/Chinese-Populism-and-the-Legacy-of-Mao-Tse-Tung?redirectedFrom=fulltext.

2 Lucien Bianco, *Origins of the Chinese Revolution 1915–1949* (Stanford, CA: Stanford University Press, 1971).

3 Yang Kuisong, "Reconsidering the Campaign to Suppress Counterrevolutionaries," *China Quarterly* 193 (March 2008): 102–21, https://www.cambridge.org/core/journals/china-quarterly/article/abs/reconsidering-the-campaign-to-suppress-counterrevolutionaries/00F0246FA6A1448DCCC9888104694908; Wen-hui Tsai, "Mass Mobilization Campaigns in Mao's China," *American Journal of Chinese Studies* 6, 1 (April 1999): 21–48, https://www.jstor.org/stable/44288599.

4 Michael Schoenhals, ed., *China's Cultural Revolution: Not a Dinner Party* (Abingdon, UK: Routledge, 2015).

5 Tang Tsou and Morton H. Halperin, "Mao Tse-tung's Revolutionary Strategy and Peking's International Behavior," *American Political Science Review* 59, 1 (March 1965): 80–99, https://www.cambridge.org/core/journals/american-political-science-review/article/abs/mao-tsetungs-revolutionary-strategy-and-pekings-international-behavior/45BA74C75DE3FF399F01EC01B6BCB005.

6 Julia Lovell, *Maoism: A Global History* (New York: Alfred A. Knopf, 2019), https://www.penguinrandomhouse.com/books/602335/maoism-by-julia-lovell/; Lawrence R. Sullivan, "Assault on the Reforms: Conservative Critics of Political and Economic Liberalization in China 1985–1986, *China Quarterly* 114 (June 1988): 198–222, https://www.cambridge.org/core/journals/china-quarterly/article/abs/assault-on-the-reforms-conservative-criticism-of-political-and-economic-liberalization-in-china-198586/13A74ECF8A5DEA136B2976CC90EBC4B0.

7 Teresa Wright, ed., *Handbook on Dissent and Protest in China* (Cheltenham, UK: Edward Elgar, 2019); Christian Gobel and Lynette Ong, "Social Unrest in China," in *China and the EU in Context: Insights for Business and Investors*, ed. Kerry Brown (London: Palgrave Macmillan, 2014), Chapter 5, 178–213, https://link.springer.com/book/10.1057/9781137351869. On environmental protest, see Samantha Hoffman and Jonathan Sullivan, "Environmental Protests Expose Weaknesses in China's Leadership," *Forbes Asia*, June 22, 2015, http://www.forbes.com/sites/forbesasia/2015/06/22/environmental-protests-expose-weakness-in-chinas-leadership/#901e2d72f091; Yanhua Deng and Guobin Yang, "Pollution and Protest in China: Environmental Mobilization in Context," *China Quarterly* 214 (June 2013): 321–36. On labour protests, see Aaron Halegna, "Who Will Represent China's Workers? Lawyers, Legal Aid, and the Enforcement of Labor Rights," US-Asia Law Institute (October 2016), https://papers.ssrn.com/sol3/papers.cfm?abstract_id=2845977; Manfred Elfstrom and Sarosh Kuruvilla, "The Changing Nature of Labor Unrest in China," *ILR Review* 67, 2 (April 2014): 453–80, https://journals.sagepub.com/doi/10.1177/001979391406700207; Fang Lee Cooke, "The Changing Dynamics of Employment Relations in China: An Evaluation of the Rising Level of Labour Disputes," *Journal of Industrial Relations* 50 (February 2008): 111–38.

8 John Garnaut, *The Rise and Fall of the House of Bo* (New York: Penguin, 2012), https://www.penguin.com.au/books/the-rise-and-fall-of-the-house-of-bo-penguin-special-9781742538808; Jamil Anderlini, "Bo Xilai: Power, Death, and Politics," *Financial Times*, July 20, 2012, https://www.ft.com/content/d67b90f0-d140-11e1-8957-00144feabdc0.

9 Michael Schuman, "The End of Optimism in China: Young People Should Learn to 'Eat Bitterness,' Says Xi Jinping," *The Atlantic*, June 29, 2023, https://www.theatlantic.com/international/archive/2023/06/-china-pessimism-economy-censorship/674556/; Grace Tsoi, "Kong Yiji: The Memes That Lay Bare China's Youth Disillusionment," *BBC News*, June 10, 2023, https://www.bbc.com/news/world-asia-china-65425941; "Why Has a Hundred-Year-Old Short Story Gone Viral Among China's Graduates?" *The Economist*, May 1, 2023, https://www.economist.com/podcasts/2023/05/02/why-has-a-hundred-year-old-short-story-gone-viral-among-chinas-graduates; Andrew Methven, "'Kong Yiji Literature' – Phrase of the Week," The China Project, March 31, 2023, https://thechinaproject.com/2023/03/31/kong-yiji-literature-phrase-of-the-week/; Bert Hofman, "Commentary: Xi Jinping's 'Common Prosperity' Looks More Like Populism Than Socialism," *Channel News Asia*, September 10, 2021, https://www.channelnewsasia.com/commentary/china-xi-jinping-cpc-socialist-reform-deng-mao-2166641.

10 Ilaria Mazzocco and Scott Kennedy, "Is It Me or the Economic System? Changing Evaluations of Inequality in China," *Big Data China*, July 9, 2024, https://bigdatachina.csis.org/is-it-me-or-the-economic-system-changing-evaluations-of-inequality-in-china/.

11 Chenchen Zhang, "Right-Wing Populism with Chinese Characteristics? Identity, Otherness and Global Imaginaries in Debating World Politics Online," *European Journal of International Relations* 26, 1 (May 20, 2019): 88–115, https://journals.sagepub.com/doi/abs/10.1177/1354066119850253?journalCode=ejta; Edward Friedman, "Post-Deng China's Right Populist Authoritarian Foreign Policy," *China Review* (2000): 1–25, https://www.jstor.org/stable/23453359?seq=1.

12 US Department of State Policy Planning Staff, *The Elements of the China Challenge* (November 2020; rev. December 2020), https://www.state.gov/wp-content/uploads/2020/11/20-02832-Elements-of-China-Challenge-508.pdf; Jessica Chen Weiss, "A World Safe for Autocracy? China's Rise and the Future of Global Politics," *Foreign Affairs*, July/August 2019, https://www.foreignaffairs.com/articles/china/2019-06-11/world-safe-autocracy?cid=otr-july_august_authors-061119; Melanie Hart and Blaine Johnson, "Mapping China's Global Governance Ambitions," Center for American Progress, February 28 2019, https://www.americanprogress.org/issues/security/reports/2019/02/28/466768/mapping-chinas-global-governance-ambitions/.

13 Chris Horton, "The World Is Fed Up with China's Belligerence," *The Atlantic*, November 8, 2021, https://www.theatlantic.com/international/archive/2021/11/china-taiwan-democracy/620647/; Jiang Shigong, "Meng Wanzhou Surely Won't Be the Last: The Hidden Logic of the American Handover," Reading the China Dream, https://www.readingthechinadream.com/jiang-shigong-on-meng-wanzhou.html; Tessa Wong and BBC Chinese, "China: The Patriotic 'Ziganwu' Bloggers Who Attack the West," *BBC News*, October 21, 2021, https://www.bbc.com/news/world-asia-china-58922011.

14 "Guojia Anquanbu fabu 2021 nian di yi hao ling 'Fan wendie anquan fangfan gongzuo guiding'" [Ministry of State Security issues document no. 1 for 2021, regulations on the work of opposing espionage and protecting security], April 26, 2021, http://legal.people.com.cn/n1/2021/0426/c205462-32088423.html; "Foreign Hostile Forces," *China Digital Times*, 2025, https://chinadigitaltimes.net/china/foreign-hostile-forces/; Sarah McKune, "Foreign Hostile Forces: The Human Rights Dimension of China's Cyber Campaigns," in *China and Cyber Security: Espionage, Strategy, and Politics in the Digital Domain*, ed. Jon R. Lindsay, Tai Ming Cheung, and Derek S. Reveron (Oxford: Oxford University Press, 2015), ch. 11, https://oxford.universitypressscholarship.com/view/10.1093/acprof:oso/9780190201265.001.0001/acprof-9780190201265-chapter-11.

15 Mercy A. Guo, "China's Alternative Global Trade System; Insights from Henry Gao," *The Diplomat*, April 29, 2024, https://thediplomat.com/2024/04/chinas-alternative-global-trade-system/; Anthony M. Cordesman, *China's Emergence as a Superpower* (Washington, DC: Center for Strategic and International Studies, 2023), https://www.csis.org/analysis/chinas-emergence-superpower; Yuwa Hedrick-Wong, "China, Populism, and the Demise of the Liberal Global Economic Order," *Forbes*, November 3, 2019, https://www.forbes.com/sites/yuwahedrickwong/2019/11/03/china-populism-and-the-demise-of-the-liberal-global-economic-order/.

16 Hu Weijia, "'Scientific Superpower' or Not, China Won't Stop Walking the Road of Innovation," *Global Times*, June 20, 2024, https://www.globaltimes.cn/page/202406/1314550.shtml; "China Has Become a Scientific Superpower," *The Economist*, June 12, 2024, https://www.economist.

com/science-and-technology/2024/06/12/china-has-become-a-scientific-superpower?ppccampaignID=18798097116&ppcadID=.

17 Loren Thomson, "Why China's Bid to Become a Superpower Is Doomed to Failure," *Forbes,* August 25, 2023, https://www.forbes.com/sites/lorenthompson/2023/08/25/why-chinas-bid-to-become-a-superpower-is-doomed-to-failure/; Jake Sullivan and Hal Brands, "China Has Two Paths to Global Domination," Carnegie Endowment for International Peace, May 22, 2020, https://carnegieendowment.org/posts/2020/05/china-has-two-paths-to-global-domination?lang=en.

18 "Chairman of Everything," in *The China Story, Yearbook 2014: Shared Destiny,* https://www.thechinastory.org/yearbooks/yearbook-2014/introduction-under-one-heaven/chairman-of-everything/.

19 Xi Jinping, "Speech at a Ceremony Marking the Centenary of the Communist Party of China, July 1, 2021," https://en.wikisource.org/wiki/Speech_at_a_Ceremony_Marking_the_Centenary_of_the_Communist_Party_of_China. For discussion of China's culture of grievance, see Jessica Chan Weiss, "'Ours Will No Longer Be a Nation Subject to Insult and Humiliation,'" *New York Times,* September 28, 2019, https://www.nytimes.com/2019/09/28/opinion/sunday/china-xi-foreign-policy.html.

20 Recent survey data suggest that while many people in China support ideals of engagement with the international system, many also endorse the regime's efforts to become more assertive of China's interests internationally, particularly including resistance to US influence. Tsinghua University Center for International Security and Strategy, "2023 Public Opinion Polls: Chinese Outlook on International Security," May 26, 2023, https://ciss.tsinghua.edu.cn/info/banner/6145.

21 Michael Schuman, "Why China Won't Win the Global South," Atlantic Council, October 16, 2023, https://www.atlanticcouncil.org/in-depth-research-reports/report/why-china-wont-win-the-global-south/; Amy Hawkins, "Xi Jinping's [sic] Wants a 'Multipolar World,' as China Accelerates Its Shift Away from the West," *The Guardian,* October 9, 2023, https://www.theguardian.com/world/2023/oct/09/xi-jinpings-wants-a-multipolar-world-as-china-accelerates-its-shift-away-from-the-west; "China Wants to Be the Leader of the Global South," *The Economist,* September 21, 2023, https://www.economist.com/china/2023/09/21/china-wants-to-be-the-leader-of-the-global-south; Dawn C. Murphy, *China's Rise in the Global South: The Middle East, Africa, and Beijing's Alternative World Order* (Stanford, CA: Stanford University Press, 2021), https://www.sup.org/books/title/?id=33516.

22 Xi Jinping, "Hold High the Great Banner of Socialism with Chinese Characteristics and Strive in Unity to Build a Modern Socialist Country in All Respects" (full text of the report to the 20th National Congress of the Communist Party of China, October 16, 2022), https://www.idcpc.org.cn/english2023/tjzl/cpcjj/20thPartyCongrssReport/; Xi Jinping, "Speech at a Ceremony Marking the Centenary of the Communist Party of China."

23 Jerker Hellström, "Sovereignty," in *The Decoding China Dictionary,* ed. The Decoding China Project (Berlin: The Decoding China Project, 2025), https://decodingchina.eu/sovereignty/; Wim Muller, "China's Sovereignty in International Law: From Historical Grievance to Pragmatic Tool," *China-EU Law Journal* 1 (2013): 35–59, https://link.springer.com/article/10.1007/s12689-012-0011-3. China's new Foreign State Immunity Law adopts many international standards to clarify circumstances under which foreign states may or may not claim sovereign immunity. China Law Translate, "Foreign State Immunity Law of the People's Republic of China," September 1, 2023, https://www.chinalawtranslate.com/en/foreign-immunities-law/. The law aims to support reciprocal protections for PRC government entities and state firms abroad but does little to temper China's expansive claims of sovereign immunity to insulate the PRC regime from international criticism or sanctions. Anushka Saxena, "Restricting Foreign State Immunity: China's New Law and What It Means," *The Diplomat,* September 7, 2023, https://thediplomat.com/2023/09/restricting-foreign-state-immunity-chinas-new-law-and-what-it-means/.

24 Xi Jinping, "Speech at a Ceremony Marking the Centenary of the Communist Party of China."

25 "Full Text of Xi Jinping's Report at 19th CPC National Congress," *China Daily,* November 14, 2017, Section I.9, http://www.chinadaily.com.cn/china/19thcpcnationalcongress/2017-11/04/content_34115212.htm; Yang Jiechi, "Study and Implement General Secretary Xi Jinping's Thought on Diplomacy in a Deep-Going Way and Keep Writing New Chapters of Major Country Diplomacy with Distinctive Chinese Features" (full text of Chinese state councillor's

article on Xi Jinping's diplomacy thought), *Xinhuanet,* July 19, 2019, http://www.xinhuanet.com/english/2017-07/19/c_136456009.htm. For an in-depth account of the role of sovereignty in China's international affairs, see Jeremy Paltiel, *The Empire's New Clothes: Cultural Particularism and Universal Value in China's Quest for Global Status* (New York: Palgrave Macmillan, 2007), https://link.springer.com/book/10.1057/9780230605121.

26 Paul Charon and Jean-Baptiste Jeangène Vilnmer, *Chinese Influence Operations: A Machiavellian Moment* (Paris: Institute for Strategic Research [IRSEM], Ministry for the Armed Forces, October 2021), https://www.irsem.fr/report.html; Alliance Canada HK, "In Plain Sight: Beijing's Unrestricted Network of Foreign Influence in Canada," May 2021, https://alliancecanadahk.com/wp-content/uploads/2022/06/ACHK_InPlainSight.pdf.

27 Xi Jinping, "Hold High the Great Banner of Socialism," 9–10. Many of these themes were presaged in Foreign Minister Wang Yi's speech to the UN General Assembly in September 2022. Phelim Kine, "China Faces Skeptics with UNGA Pitch for Global Leader Status," *Politico,* September 23, 2022, https://www.politico.com/news/2022/09/23/china-united-nations-global-leader-skeptics-00058556.

28 Joe McDonald, "Xi Accuses U.S. of Attempting to Block China's Development," *PBS News,* March 8, 2023, https://www.pbs.org/newshour/world/xi-accuses-u-s-of-attempting-to-block-chinas-development; Karson Yiu, "China's Xi Blames US for 'Containment and Suppression' Amid Tensions," *ABC News,* March 7, 2023, https://abcnews.go.com/International/chinas-xi-blames-us-containment-suppression-amid-tensions/story?id=97676556; Zongyuan Zoe Liu, "China Is Hardening Itself for Economic War," *Foreign Policy,* June 16, 2022, https://foreignpolicy.com/2022/06/16/china-economic-war-decoupling-united-states-containment/.

29 Chris Buckley, "Behind Public Assurances, Xi Jinping Has Spread Grim Views on U.S.," *New York Times,* November 13, 2023, https://www.nytimes.com/2023/11/13/world/asia/china-xi-asia-pacific-summit.html.

30 "Wang Yi: Meifang weibei bugao xin lengzhan xuanshi, paozhi Angelu-Sakexun 'xiaoyuanzi'" [Wang Yi: the US violates declaration against starting a new Cold War, concocts Anglo-Saxon clique], *Caixin,* September 29, 2021, https://international.caixin.com/2021-09-29/101782207.html; "Wang Yi: U.S.-Britain-Australia Nuclear Submarine Cooperation Poses Three Hidden Dangers," Embassy of the People's Republic of China in the United States of America, September 28, 2021, https://www.fmprc.gov.cn/eng/wjb/zzjg_663340/xos_664404/xwlb_664406/202406/t20240606_11404302.html.

31 State Council Information Office (SCIO), "China's International Development Cooperation in the New Era," white paper, January 10, 2021, Sections 1.2, 1.3, http://english.www.gov.cn/archive/whitepaper/202101/10/content_WS5ffa6bbbc6d0f72576943922.html; SCIO, "China and the World in the New Era," white paper, September 27, 2019, Section III.3, http://english.www.gov.cn/archive/whitepaper/201909/27/content_WS5d8d80f9c6d0bcf8c4c142ef.html.

32 Amy Hawkins, "China Woos Global South and Embraces Putin at Belt and Road Beijing Summit," *The Guardian,* October 16, 2023, https://www.theguardian.com/world/2023/oct/16/china-woos-global-south-and-embraces-putin-at-belt-and-road-beijing-summit; China International Development Cooperation Agency, "Global Development and South-South Cooperation Assistance Fund," 2018, http://en.cidca.gov.cn/southsouthcooperationfund.html; Martin Khor, "China's Boost to South-South Cooperation," *South Bulletin* 90 (May 16, 2016), https://www.southcentre.int/question/chinas-boost-to-south-south-cooperation/; Molly Elgin-Cossart and Melanie Hart, "China's New International Finance Institutions," Center for American Progress, September 22, 2015, https://www.americanprogress.org/issues/security/reports/2015/09/22/121668/chinas-new-international-financing-institutions/.

33 "Full Text: Proposal of the People's Republic of China on the Reform and Development of Global Governance," *Xinhua,* September 13, 2023, https://english.news.cn/20230913/edf2514b79a34bf6812a1c372dcdfc1b/c.html?utm_source=substack&utm_medium=email.

34 Xi Jinping, "Speech at a Ceremony Marking the Centenary of the Communist Party of China," 8.

35 Li Haidong, "Why a Prospering China Frightens the West," *Global Times,* September 15, 2021, https://www.globaltimes.cn/page/202109/1234367.shtml; "Foreign Ministry Spokesperson Geng Shuang's Regular Press Conference on February 18, 2019," February 18, 2019, https://govt.chinadaily.com.cn/s/201902/18/WS5cc7eebd498e079e6801f638/foreign-ministry-spokesperson-geng-shuangs-regular-press-conference-on-february-18-2019.html.

36 Charles Mok and Dennis Kwok, "China's Neo-Nationalism Poses Risks for International Business," *The Diplomat,* November 2, 2021, https://thediplomat.com/2021/11/chinas-neo-nationalism-poses-risks-for-international-businesses/.

37 Xi Jinping, "Hold High the Great Banner of Socialism," 18.

38 See, e.g., Pitman B. Potter, *Exporting Virtue? China's International Human Rights Activism in the Age of Xi Jinping* (Vancouver: UBC Press, 2021).

39 SCIO, "Seeking Happiness for People: 70 Years of Progress on Human Rights in China," white paper, September 2019, http://english.www.gov.cn/archive/whitepaper/201909/22/content_WS5d87752fc6d0bcf8c4c13d32.html; Ministry of Foreign Affairs of the People's Republic of China (MFA), "China and the United Nations: Position Paper of the People's Republic of China for the 74th Session of the United Nations General Assembly," September 18, 2019, https://www.mfa.gov.cn/eng/zy/gb/202405/t20240531_11367393.html; SCIO, "National Human Rights Action Plan of China (2012–2015)," June 11, 2012, Introduction, http://www.china.org.cn/government/whitepaper/2012-06/11/content_25619560.htm.

40 "Shehui zhuyi hexin jiazhiguan jiben neirong" [The basic content of the core values of socialism], *Renmin ribao* [*People's Daily*], February 12, 2014, http://theory.people.com.cn/n/2014/0212/c40531-24330538.html; Guo Jianming, *Shehui zhuyi hexin jiazhiguan jiben neirong jieyi* [Interpretation of the basic content of the core values of socialism] (Beijing: Renmin chubanshe [People's Publishing House], 2014), http://theory.people.com.cn/GB/68294/384764/; Ying Miao, "Romanticisng the Past: Core Socialist Values and the China Dream as Legitimisation Strategy," *Journal of Current Chinese Affairs* 49, 2 (January 4, 2021): 162–84, https://journals.sagepub.com/doi/full/10.1177/1868102620981963; Delia Lin and Susan Trevaskes, "Creating a Virtuous Leviathan: The Party, Law, and Socialist Core Values," *Asian Journal of Law and Society* 6, 1 (2019): 41–66, https://www.cambridge.org/core/journals/asian-journal-of-law-and-society/article/creating-a-virtuous-leviathan-the-party-law-and-socialist-core-values/EA7DF40DB0F70D9305D1E557F8A1ACAA; Michael Gow, "The Core Socialist Values of the Chinese Dream: Towards a Chinese Integral State," *Critical Asian Studies* 49, 1 (2016): 92–116 https://dx.doi.org/10.1080/14672715.2016.1263803.

41 China Heritage, "Red Allure & the Crimson Blindfold," July 13, 2021, n. 35, https://chinaheritage.net/journal/red-allure-the-crimson-blindfold/.

42 Deng Yuwen, "Jiepou 'Shehui zhuyi hexin jiazhi,'" [Dissection of core socialist values] *FT Zhongwenwang* [*Financial Times* Chinese website], February 23, 2014, https://www.ftchinese.com/story/001054925?archive. A related effort is evident in a report from by the New China Research think tank associated with the official New China News Agency attempting to explain China's approach to democracy, freedom, and human rights as consistent with global values. New China Research, "Pursuing Common Values of Humanity – China's Approach to Democracy, Freedom and Human Rights," December 7, 2021, http://english.www.gov.cn/archive/whitepaper/202112/07/content_WS61af46cdc6d09c94e48a1e49.html.

43 "Constitution of the People's Republic of China," rev. 2018, http://www.lawinfochina.com/display.aspx?lib=law&id=3437&CGid=, Article 33.4: "Every citizen enjoys the rights prescribed by the Constitution and other laws and at the same time must perform the duties prescribed by the Constitution and other laws." Recent efforts to term China's governance regime a matter of "whole process democracy" (*quan guocheng minzhu* // 全过程民主), exemplify efforts to appropriate liberal terminology for PRC regime needs. Stella Chen, "Whole-Process Democracy," China Media Project, November 23, 2021, https://chinamediaproject.org/the_ccp_dictionary/whole-process-democracy/.

44 National People's Congress of the People's Republic of China, "Zhongyang Xuanchuanbu, Zhongyang Zhengfawei, Quanguo Renda Changweihui Bangongting, Sifabu yinfa 'yijian' Jianli shehui zhuyi hexin jiazhiguan rufa rugui xietiao jizhi" [Central Propaganda Department, Central Politics and Law Committee, NPC Standing Committee Office, Ministry of Justice opinion, establish mechanisms for coordinating insertion of core socialist values in law and regulation], September 28, 2021, http://politics.people.com.cn/n1/2021/0928/c1001-32239145.html; "Zhonggong Zhongyang yinfa 'Shehui zhuyi hexin jiazhiguan rongru fazhi jianshe lifa xiufa guihua'" [Party centre releases plan for assimilating core socialist values in legal system construction, legislation and legal amendments], *Xinhuanet,* May 7, 2018, http://www.xinhuanet.com/politics/2018-05/07/c_1122796215.htm.

45 Li Yuan, "'Reversing Gears': China Increasingly Rejects English and the World," *New York Times*, September 9, 2021, https://www.nytimes.com/2021/09/09/business/china-english.html?smid=em-share.
46 "Foreign Ministry Spokesperson Lu Kang's Remarks," August 14, 2018, https://ch.china-embassy.gov.cn/ger/fyrth/201808/t20180814_3192736.htm; Human Rights in China (HRIC), "Follow-Up Letter Sent to the State Party by the Committee (November 24, 2020)" in HRIC "International Convention on the Elimination of All Forms of Racial Discrimination (CERD), sidebar, https://www.hrichina.org/en/international-convention-elimination-all-forms-racial-discrimination-cerd (sidebar link was disabled). Also see OHCHR, "Committee on the Elimination of Racial Discrimination Reviews the Report of China," press release, August 13, 2018, https://www.ohchr.org/en/NewsEvents/Pages/DisplayNews.aspx?NewsID=23452&LangID=E; Committee on the Elimination of Racial Discrimination (CERD), "Concluding Observations on the Combined Fourteenth to Seventeenth Periodic Reports of China (Including Hong Kong, China and Macao, China)," August 30, 2018, CERD/C/CHN/CO/14-17, https://docs.un.org/en/cerd/c/chn/co/14-17; "UN Rights Panel Grills China over Mass Detention of Uyghurs," *Radio Free Asia*, August 10, 2018, https://www.rfa.org/english/news/uyghur/panel-08102018165922.html.
47 Xi Jinping, "Speech at a Ceremony Marking the Centenary of the Communist Party of China," 9.
48 See generally Sonya Sceats and Shaun Breslin, *China and the International Human Rights System* (London: Chatham House, 2012), https://www.chathamhouse.org/sites/default/files/public/Research/International%20Law/r1012_sceatsbreslin.pdf.
49 Xi Jinping, "Hold High the Great Banner of Socialism," Section VI.1, 31–32.
50 For discussion of similar tactics by authoritarian leaders elsewhere, see Ruth Ben-Ghiat, *Strongmen: Mussolini to the Present* (New York: W.W. Norton, 2021). The legitimating effects of China's populist rhetoric seem to be working, as public support for the ruling regime's populist authoritarianism under Xi Jinping continues. See Vincent Ni, "Alt-Right Finds New Partners in Hate on China's Internet," *The Guardian*, September 11, 2021, https://www.theguardian.com/world/2021/sep/11/alt-right-finds-new-partners-in-hate-on-chinas-internet?CMP=Share_iOSApp_Other; Wenfang Tang, *Populist Authoritarianism: Chinese Political Culture and Regime Sustainability* (Oxford: Oxford University Press, 2016), https://oxford.universitypressscholarship.com/view/10.1093/acprof:oso/9780190205782.001.0001/acprof-9780190205782.
51 See, e.g., Suisheng Zhao, *The Dragon Roars Back: Transformational Leaders and Dynamics of Chinese Foreign Policy* (Stanford, CA: Stanford University Press, 2022).
52 Benjamin Tze Ern Ho, *China's Political Worldview and Chinese Exceptionalism: International Order and Global Leadership* (Amsterdam: Amsterdam University Press, 2021). This is consistent with Edward Friedman, "Post-Deng China's Right Populist Authoritarian Foreign Policy," *China Review* (2000): 1–25, https://www.jstor.org/stable/23453359?seq=1.
53 World Health Organization (WHO), "Coronavirus Disease (COVID-19) Pandemic," https://www.who.int/europe/emergencies/situations/covid-19; Centers for Disease Control and Prevention (CDC), "CDC Museum COVID-19 Timeline," https://www.cdc.gov/museum/timeline/covid19.html.
54 "WHO Chief Declares End to COVID-19 as Global Health Emergency," *UN News*, May 5, 2023, https://news.un.org/en/story/2023/05/1136367; WHO, "WHO Director-General's Opening Remarks at the Media Briefing – 5 May 2023," May 5, 2023, https://www.who.int/news-room/speeches/item/who-director-general-s-opening-remarks-at-the-media-briefing---5-may-2023.
55 WHO, "WHO COVID-19 Dashboard," https://covid19.who.int; "Covid-19: The Story of a Pandemic," *New Scientist*, March 10, 2021, https://www.newscientist.com/article/2270361-covid-19-the-story-of-a-pandemic/.
56 Kathy Katella, "Omicron and Its Subvariants: A Guide to What We Know," *Yale Medicine*, September 1, 2023, https://www.yalemedicine.org/news/5-things-to-know-omicron.
57 Dante Disparte, "Preparing for the Next Pandemic: Early Lessons from COVID-19," Brookings, February 16, 2021, https://www.brookings.edu/research/preparing-for-the-next-pandemic-early-lessons-from-covid-19/; "The COVID-19 Pandemic in 2023: Far from Over," *The Lancet* 401, 10371 (January 14, 2023): 79, https://www.thelancet.com/journals/lancet/article/PIIS0140-6736(23)00050-8/fulltext.

58 Suyin Haynes, "We Now Need to Do the Impossible: How Greta Thunberg Is Fighting for a Greener Post-Pandemic World," *TIME,* September 8, 2020; Justin Rowlatt, "Greta Thunberg: Climate Change 'As Urgent' as Coronavirus," *BBC News,* June 19, 2020, https://www.bbc.com/news/science-environment-53100800.

59 Intergovernmental Panel on Climate Change (IPCC), "Climate Change Widespread, Rapid, and Intensifying – IPCC," August 9, 2021, https://www.ipcc.ch/2021/08/09/ar6-wg1-20210809-pr/; IPCC, "Global Warming of 1.5°C," October 8, 2018, https://www.ipcc.ch/sr15/.

60 Involuntary migration includes not only migrants who meet specific treaty requirements for refugee status but also asylum seekers, displaced persons, and other migrants whose movement is compelled by political, economic, and/or social conditions. Amnesty International, "Refugees, Asylum Seekers and Migrants," https://www.amnesty.org/en/what-we-do/refugees-asylum-seekers-and-migrants/.

61 Office of the UN High Commissioner for Refugees (UNHCR), "Operational Data Portal: Ukraine Refugee Situation," https://data.unhcr.org/en/situations/ukraine; UNHCR, "Refugee Data Finder," https://www.unhcr.org/refugee-statistics.

62 "United Nations Refugee Chief, Briefing Security Council, Appeals for Ceasefire to Halt 'Spiral of Death' as Humanitarian Crisis Grips Gaza," press release, October 31, 2023, SC/15477, https://press.un.org/en/2023/sc15477.doc.htm; Sigal Samuel, "Palestinians Fear They're Being Displaced Permanently. Here's Why That's Logical," *Vox,* October 27, 2023, https://www.vox.com/world-politics/23933707/israel-palestine-hamas-gaza-nakba-displacement-refugees-history.

63 OHCHR, "Lebanon: UN Experts Deplore Israel's Increasing Disregard for International Law," press release, October 4, 2024, https://www.ohchr.org/en/press-releases/2024/10/lebanon-un-experts-deplore-israels-increasing-disregard-international-law; Also see United Nations Relief and Works Agency for Palestine Refugees in the Near East (UNRWA), "UNRWA Situation Report #12 on the Lebanon Emergency Response," November 7, 2024, https://www.unrwa.org/resources/reports/unrwa-situation-report-12-lebanon-emergency-response#.

64 UNHCR, "Refugee Data Finder."

65 Our World (United Nations University), "Migration, Climate Change, and COVID-19," https://ourworld.unu.edu/en/migration-climate-change-and-covid19.

66 Colin J. Carlson, Gregory F. Albery, Cory Merow, Christopher H. Trisos, Casey M. Zipfel, Evan A. Eskew, Kevin J. Olival, et al., "Climate Change Increases Cross-Species Viral Transmission Risk," *Nature* 607 (2022): 555–62, https://www.nature.com/articles/s41586-022-04788-w; White House, "Report on the Impact of Climate Change on Migration," October 2021, https://bidenwhitehouse.archives.gov/wp-content/uploads/2021/10/Report-on-the-Impact-of-Climate-Change-on-Migration.pdf.

67 Migration Data Portal, "Migration Data Relevant for the COVID-19 Pandemic," https://migrationdataportal.org/themes/migration-data-relevant-covid-19-pandemic; Bryan Walsh, "Why the Climate Crisis Will Intensify the Border Crisis," *Axios,* March 27, 2021, https://www.axios.com/climate-change-immigration-border-crisis-07aab997-e7e5-42eb-ac81-f711dd8ca54b.html; Alex de Sherbinin, "Climate Impacts as Drivers of Migration," Migration Policy Institute, October 23, 2020, https://www.migrationpolicy.org/article/impacts-climate-change-drivers-migration; John Podesta, "The Climate Crisis, Migration, and Refugees," Brookings Policy Brief, July 25, 2019, https://www.brookings.edu/research/the-climate-crisis-migration-and-refugees/; Lucile Maertens and Alice Baillat, "The Partial Climatisation of Migration, Security and Conflict," in *Globalising the Climate: COP21 and the Climatization of Global Debates,* ed. Stefan C. Aykut, Jean Foyer, and Edouard Morena (Abingdon, UK: Routledge, 2017), 116–34, https://www.routledge.com/Globalising-the-Climate-COP21-and-the-climatisation-of-global-debates/Aykut-Foyer-Morena/p/book/9780367026790.

68 Ingrid Robeyns and Morten Byskov, "The Capability Approach," in *The Stanford Encyclopedia of Philosophy* (April 17, 2025), https://plato.stanford.edu/entries/capability-approach/.

69 Joel Millward-Hopkins and Yannick Oswald, "Reducing Global Inequality to Secure Human Wellbeing and Climate Safety: A Modelling Study," *Lancet Planetary Health* 7, 2 (February 2023): e147–e154, https://www.thelancet.com/journals/lanplh/article/PIIS2542-5196(23)00004-9/fulltext; Lucas Chancel, Thomas Piketty, Emmanuel Saez, and Gabriel Zucman, eds., *World Inequality Report 2022* (World Inequality Lab, 2021), https://wir2022.wid.world/www-site/uploads/2023/03/D_FINAL_WIL_RIM_RAPPORT_2303.pdf; Suzanne Egan and Anna Chadwick, eds., *Poverty and Human Rights: Multidisciplinary Perspectives* (London: Edward Elgar,

2021), https://www.e-elgar.com/shop/usd/poverty-and-human-rights-9781839102103.html; Richard Barichello, Arianto A. Patunru, and Richard Schwindt, eds., *Globalization, Poverty, and Income Inequality: Insights from Indonesia* (Vancouver: UBC Press, 2021), https://www.ubcpress.ca/globalization-poverty-and-income-inequality; Organization for Economic Co-operation and Development (OECD), "Income Inequality," https://www.oecd.org/en/data/indicators/income-inequality.html#:~:text=The%20OECD's%20Social%20Benefit%20Recipients,All%20Topics.

70 United Nations Department of Economic and Social Affairs (DESA), *World Social Report 2020: Inequality in a Rapidly Changing World* (New York: United Nations 2020), https://www.un.org/development/desa/dspd/wp-content/uploads/sites/22/2020/02/World-Social-Report2020-FullReport.pdf; Augustin Kwasi Fosu, "Growth, Inequality and Poverty Reduction in Developing Countries: Recent Global Evidence," Brooks World Poverty Institute Working Paper 147, April 18, 2011, https://ssrn.com/abstract=1813968.

71 See generally *Global Governance* 19, 1 (Special Focus: Regime Complexity) (January–March 2013), https://www.jstor.org/stable/i24526234. Such challenges are made more acute by wavering support from developed economies, as exemplified by the second Trump administration's withdrawal of the United States from the WHO in 2025 and suspension of foreign aid. White House, "Withdrawing the United States from the World Health Organization," Executive Order, January 20, 2025, https://www.whitehouse.gov/presidential-actions/2025/01/withdrawing-the-united-states-from-the-worldhealth-organization/; White House, "Reevaluating and Realigning United States Foreign Aid," January 20, 2025, https://www.whitehouse.gov/presidential-actions/2025/01/reevaluating-and-realigning-united-states-foreign-aid/.

72 Lawrence O. Gostin, *Global Health Security: A Blueprint for the Future* (Cambridge, MA: Harvard University Pres, 2021), https://www.hup.harvard.edu/catalog.php?isbn=9780674976610; Pablo Gutierrez and Ashley Kirk, "Vaccine Inequality: How Rich Countries Cut Covid Deaths as Poorer Fall Behind," *The Guardian,* June 28, 2021, https://www.theguardian.com/world/ng-interactive/2021/jun/28/vaccine-inequality-how-rich-countries-cut-covid-deaths-as-poorer-fall-behind?CMP=Share_AndroidApp_Other; "Notes from the Editors," *Monthly Review,* April 1, 2021, https://monthlyreview.org/2021/04/01/mr-072-11-2021-04_0/; "WHO Chief Warns Against 'Catastrophic Moral Failure' in COVID-19 Vaccine Access," *UN News,* January 18, 2021, https://news.un.org/en/story/2021/01/1082362; Nishant Yonzan, Christoph Lakner, Gerszon Mahler, R. Andres Castañeda Aguilar, and Haiyu Wu, "Impact of COVID-19 on Global Poverty Under Worsening Growth and Inequality," *World Bank Blogs,* November 9, 2020, https://blogs.worldbank.org/opendata/impact-covid-19-global-poverty-under-worsening-growth-and-inequality.

73 WHO, "World Bank and WHO: Half the World Lacks Access to Essential Health Services, 100 Million Still Pushed into Extreme Poverty Because of Health Expenses," news release, December 13, 2017, https://www.who.int/news/item/13-12-2017-world-bank-and-who-half-the-world-lacks-access-to-essential-health-services-100-million-still-pushed-into-extreme-poverty-because-of-health-expenses.

74 McKinsey Sustainability, *The Net-Zero Transition: What It Would Cost, What It Could Bring* (Chicago: McKinsey and Co., 2022), https://www.mckinsey.com/business-functions/sustainability/our-insights/the-net-zero-transition-what-it-would-cost-what-it-could-bring; Lucas Chancel, "The Richest 10% Produce Half of Greenhouse Gas Emissions. They Should Pay to Fix the Climate," *The Guardian,* December 7, 2021, https://www.theguardian.com/commentisfree/2021/dec/07/we-cant-address-the-climate-crisis-unless-we-also-take-on-global-inequality?CMP=Share_AndroidApp_Other; "Inequality and Climate Change: The Rich Must Step Up," *The Conversation,* June 23, 2019, https://theconversation.com/inequality-and-climate-change-the-rich-must-step-up-119074; Josie Garthwaite, "Climate Change Has Worsened Global Economic Inequality," Stanford Doerr School of Sustainability, April 22, 2019, https://earth.stanford.edu/news/climate-change-has-worsened-global-economic-inequality#gs.101t777; S. Nazrul Islam and John Winkel, "Climate Change and Social Inequality," DESA Working Paper No. 152, October 2017, ST/ESA/2017/DWP/152, https://www.un.org/esa/desa/papers/2017/wp152_2017.pdf; Gian Carlo Delgado-Ramos, ed., *Inequality and Climate Change: Perspectives from the South* (Dakar: CODESRIA, 2015); J. Timmons Roberts, "Global Inequality and Climate Change," *Society and Natural Resources* 14, 6 (2001): 501–9, https://www.tandfonline.com/doi/abs/10.1080/08941920118490?journalCode=usnr20.

75 Joern Birkmann, Emma Liwenga, Rajiv Pandey, Emily Boyd, Riyanti Djalante, François Gemenne, Walter Leal Filho, et al., "Poverty, Livelihoods and Sustainable Development," in *Climate Change 2022: Impacts, Adaptation and Vulnerability,* Contribution of Working Group II to the Sixth Assessment Report of the Intergovernmental Panel on Climate Change (Cambridge: Cambridge University Press, 2022), 1171–1274, https://www.ipcc.ch/report/ar6/wg2/chapter/chapter-8/. The decision by the second Trump administration to withdraw the United States from the Paris Agreement, along with the decision to cut all foreign aid, would appear to compound the problem. White House, "Putting America First in International Environmental Agreements," Executive Order, January 20, 2025, https://www.whitehouse.gov/presidential-actions/2025/01/putting-america-first-in-international-environmental-agreements/; White House, "Reevaluating and Realigning United States Foreign Aid."

76 Rachel M. Gisselquist, "Involuntary Migration, Inequality and Integration: Vietnamese and Afghan Migrants in Canada, Germany, the UK, and the US," *Journal of Ethnic and Migration Studies* 47, 21 (Special Issue) (2021), https://www.wider.unu.edu/publication/involuntary-migration-inequality-and-integration-0; David McKenzie, "Poverty, Inequality, and International Migration: Insights from 10 Years of Migration and Development Conferences," *Revue d'économie du développement* 25, 3 (2017): 13–28, https://www.cairn.info/revue-d-economie-du-developpement-2017-3-page-13.htm; Michael Clemens, "Why Today's Migration Crisis Is an Issue of Global Economic Inequality," Center for Global Development, August 2, 2016, https://www.cgdev.org/blog/why-todays-migration-crisis-issue-global-economic-inequality.

77 Jeff Crisp, "As the World Abandons Refugees, UNHCR's Constraints Are Exposed," *New Humanitarian,* September 13, 2018, https://deeply.thenewhumanitarian.org/refugees/community/2018/09/13/as-the-world-abandons-refugees-unhcrs-constraints-are-exposed#:~:text=The%20U.N.,refugee%20policy%20expert%20Jeff%20Crisp; Alexander Betts, "Regime Complexity and International Organizations: UNHCR as a Challenged Institution," *Global Governance* 19, 1 (January–March 2013): 69–81, https://www.jstor.org/stable/24526241.

78 Mark Fischetti, "Climate Change Hastened Syria's Civil War," *Scientific American,* March 2, 2015, https://www.scientificamerican.com/article/climate-change-hastened-the-syrian-war/.

79 UNHCR, "Resettlement," 2021–23, https://www.unhcr.org/what-we-do/build-better-futures/solutions/resettlement; Refugee Sponsorship Training Program, "RAP (Resettlement Assistance Program) Rates," 2023, https://www.rstp.ca/en/bvor/rap-rates/; MOSAIC, "MOSAIC's Private Refugee Sponsorship Program," https://mosaicbc.org/our-services/refugee-resettlement/.

80 WHO, "Timeline: WHO's COVID-19 Response," https://www.who.int/emergencies/diseases/novel-coronavirus-2019/interactive-timeline.

81 Lisa Schlein, "WHO Urges Nations to Prepare for Future Pandemics," *VOA News,* December 27, 2020, https://www.voanews.com/science-health/who-urges-nations-prepare-future-pandemics; WHO, "The Best Time to Prevent the Next Pandemic Is Now: Countries Join Voices for Better Emergency Preparedness," news release, October 1, 2020, https://www.who.int/news/item/01-10-2020-the-best-time-to-prevent-the-next-pandemic-is-now-countries-join-voices-for-better-emergency-preparedness.

82 "A Timeline of COVID-19 Vaccine Developments in 2021," *American Journal of Managed Care,* June 3, 2021, https://www.ajmc.com/view/a-timeline-of-covid-19-vaccine-developments-in-2021.

83 White House, "Withdrawing the United States from the World Health Organization"; White House, "Reevaluating and Realigning United States Foreign Aid."

84 White House, "Withdrawing the United States from International Organizations, Conventions, and Treaties That Are Contrary to the Interests of the United States," January 7, 2026, https://www.whitehouse.gov/presidential-actions/2026/01/withdrawing-the-united-states-from-international-organizations-conventions-and-treaties-that-are-contrary-to-the-interests-of-the-united-states/; Nate Perez and Rachel Waldholz, "Trump Is Withdrawing from the Paris Agreement (Again), Reversing U.S. Climate Policy," *NPR,* January 21, 2025, https://www.npr.org/2025/01/21/nx-s1-5266207/trump-paris-agreement-biden-climate-change; US Department of State, "The United States Officially Rejoins the Paris Agreement," February 19, 2021, https://2021-2025.state.gov/the-united-states-officially-rejoins-the-paris-agreement/; US Department of State, "On the U.S. Withdrawal from the Paris Agreement," press statement, November 4, 2019, https://2017-2021.state.gov/on-the-u-s-withdrawal-from-the-paris-agreement/; "Statement by President Trump on the Paris Climate Accord," June 1, 2017, https://trumpwhitehouse.archives.gov/briefings-statements/statement-president-trump-paris-climate-accord/.

Also see United Nations Climate Action, "COP 26: Together for Our Planet," https://www.un.org/en/climatechange/cop26.

85 Emma Carmel, Katharina Lenner, and Regine Paul, eds., *Handbook on Governance and Politics of Migration* (London: Edward Elgar, 2021), https://www.elgaronline.com/view/edcoll/9781788117227/9781788117227.00006.xml; Catherine Dauvergne, ed., *Research Handbook on the Law and Politics of Migration* (London: Edward Elgar, 2021), https://www.e-elgar.com/shop/usd/research-handbook-on-the-law-and-politics-of-migration-9781789902259.html; Satvinder Singh Juss, ed., *Research Handbook on International Refugee Law* (London: Edward Elgar, 2019), https://www.e-elgar.com/shop/usd/research-handbook-on-international-refugee-law-9780857932808.html.

86 International Organization for Migration (IOM), *World Migration Report 2024* (Geneva: IOM, 2024), https://worldmigrationreport.iom.int; UNHCR, "The 1951 Refugee Convention," https://www.unhcr.org/1951-refugee-convention.html.

87 "Global Compact for Safe, Orderly and Regular Migration," Resolution adopted by the UN General Assembly on December 19, 2018, A/RES/73/195, https://documents-dds-ny.un.org/doc/UNDOC/GEN/N18/451/99/PDF/N1845199.pdf?OpenElement; OHCHR, "Global Compact for Safe, Orderly and Regular Migration (GCM)," https://www.ohchr.org/en/migration/global-compact-safe-orderly-and-regular-migration-gcm.

88 UNHCR, *Global Compact on Refugees* (New York: United Nations, 2018), https://www.unhcr.org/5c658aed4; UNHCR, "Report of the United Nations High Commissioner for Refugees, Part II: Global Compact for Refugees," September 13, 2018, A/73/12 (Part II), https://documents-dds-ny.un.org/doc/UNDOC/GEN/G18/238/37/PDF/G1823837.pdf?OpenElement; UNHCR, "The Global Compact on Refugees," https://www.unhcr.org/the-global-compact-on-refugees.html.

89 Dominique Vervoort and Hloni Bookholane, "Covid-19 Isn't Political, It's Response Shouldn't Be Politicized," Global Health Now, January 25, 2021, https://www.globalhealthnow.org/2021-01/covid-19-isnt-political-its-response-shouldnt-be-politicized.

90 Karl Mathiesen, "Populists vs. the Planet: How Climate Became the New Culture War Front Line," *Politico,* November 6, 2022, https://www.politico.eu/article/populists-vs-the-planet-the-rights-new-playbook-on-climate-change-cop27-egypt-sharm-el-sheikh-donald-trump-midterms-republicans-meloni/; Jason Hickel, "The Limits of Clean Energy," *Foreign Policy,* September 6, 2019, https://foreignpolicy.com/2019/09/06/the-path-to-clean-energy-will-be-very-dirty-climate-change-renewables/; Matthew J. Burke and Jennie C. Stephens, "Political Power and Renewable Energy Futures: A Critical Review," *Energy Research and Social Science* 35 (January 2018): 78–93, https://www.sciencedirect.com/science/article/pii/S2214629617303468.

91 Cas Mudde, "Putting Our Own People First," *Foreign Policy,* September 29, 2019, https://foreignpolicy.com/2019/09/29/putting-our-own-people-first-nativism-us-vs-them-far-right-parties-lega-fpo-kkk-europe-usa/; Kristin Bakkaer Simonsen, "'Us' or 'Them'? How Policies, Public Opinion, and Political Rhetoric Affect Immigrants' Sense of Belonging," Migration Policy Institute, April 18, 2019, https://www.migrationpolicy.org/article/policies-public-opinion-rhetoric-immigrants-sense-belonging; Felix Geyer, *Alienation, Ethnicity, and Postmodernism* (Santa Barbara, CA: Praeger Press, 1996), https://products.abc-clio.com/ABC-CLIOCorporate/product.aspx?pc=C1606C.

92 Ulrike M. Vieten, "The 'New Normal' and 'Pandemic Populism': The COVID-19 Crisis and Anti-Hygienic Mobilisation of the Far-Right," *Social Sciences* 9, 9 (September 2020): 1–14, https://ideas.repec.org/a/gam/jscscx/v9y2020i9p165-d417371.html; Jay J. Van Bavel, Katherine Baiker, Paulo S. Boggio, Valerio Capraro, et al., "Using Social and Behavioural Science to Support COVID-19 Pandemic Response," *Nature Human Behaviour* 4 (2020): 460–71, https://www.nature.com/articles/s41562-020-0884-z.

93 Matthew Lockwood, "Right-Wing Populism and the Climate Change Agenda: Exploring the Linkages," *Environmental Politics* 27, 4 (2018), https://www.tandfonline.com/doi/full/10.1080/09644016.2018.1458411.

94 Peter Scholten, "Mainstreaming versus Alienation: Conceptualizing the Role of Complexity in Migration and Diversity Policymaking," *Journal of Ethnic and Migration Studies* 26, 1 (2020): 108–26, https://doi.org/10.1080/1369183X.2019.1625758.

95 Pew Research Center, "Coronavirus (COVID-19)," https://www.pewresearch.org/topics/coronavirus-disease-2019-covid-19/.

96 Moira Fagen and Christine Huang, "Many Globally Are as Concerned About Climate Change as About the Spread of Infectious Diseases," Pew Research Center, October 16, 2020, https://www.pewresearch.org/fact-tank/2020/10/16/many-globally-are-as-concerned-about-climate-change-as-about-the-spread-of-infectious-diseases/.
97 Pew Research Center, "Migration Issues," https://www.pewresearch.org/topic/international-affairs/international-issues/migration-issues/.
98 Alasdair Fotheringham, "In the Pandemic, Are Europeans More Attracted to the Far Right?" *Al Jazeera,* February 3, 2021, https://www.aljazeera.com/features/2021/2/3/far-right-europe-pandemic; Human Rights Watch, "European Union: Events of 2020," https://www.hrw.org/world-report/2021/country-chapters/european-union#.
99 Kevin Sheives and Ryan Arick, "Authoritarian States Are Using COVID Vaccines to Subvert Democracy," *Nikkei Asia,* May 8, 2021, https://asia.nikkei.com/Opinion/Authoritarian-states-are-using-COVID-vaccines-to-subvert-democracy.
100 Sara Gottenhuber and Eric Mulholland, "Implementing the Sustainable Development Goals in Times of Rising Right-Wing Populism in Europe," *Sustainability* 12 (October 14, 2020): 8465, https://www.mdpi.com/2071-1050/12/20/8465; Beth Gardiner, "For Europe's Far-Right Parties, Climate Is a New Battleground," *Yale Environment 360,* October 29, 2019, https://e360.yale.edu/features/for-europes-far-right-parties-climate-is-a-new-battleground.
101 Neil Vowles, "The Threat Posed to Climate Change Policies by the Rise of the Populist Right," University of Sussex, *Broadcast: News Items,* April 14, 2022, https://sussex.ac.uk/broadcast/read/57813; Climate Investigations Center, "The Global Climate Coalition: Big Business Funds Climate Change Denial and Regulatory Delay," March 25, 1919, https://climateinvestigations.org/wp-content/uploads/2019/04/The-Global-Climate-Coalition-Denial-and-Delay.pdf; Lockwood, "Right-Wing Populism and Climate Change."
102 Rebeca Hamlin, *Crossing: How We Label and React to People on the Move* (Stanford, CA: Stanford University Press, 2021), https://searchworks.stanford.edu/view/13864228; Oliviero Angeli, "Migration and the Rise of Populism: How Closely Related Are They?" *European Insights,* 2018, https://www.vuesdeurope.eu/en/news/migration-and-the-rise-of-populism-how-closely-related-are-they/.
103 Stef W. Kight, "Record Migration Sparks Backlash in Wealthy Nations," *Axios,* July 16, 2023, https://www.axios.com/2023/07/16/record-migration-backlash-us-europe; Cas Mudde, "Why Copying the Populist Right Isn't Going to Save the Left," *The Guardian,* May 14, 2019, https://www.theguardian.com/news/2019/may/14/why-copying-the-populist-right-isnt-going-to-save-the-left; Michelle Mittelstadt, "Pushing Migration to the Forefront: Populists Make New Strides," Migration Policy Institute, December 20, 2018, https://www.migrationpolicy.org/article/top-10-2018-issue-2-populists-make-new-strides.
104 UNHCR, "UNHCR Warns Asylum Under Attack at Europe's Borders, Urges End to Pushbacks and Violence Against Refugees," press release, January 28, 2021, https://www.unhcr.org/news/press/2021/1/601121344/unhcr-warns-asylum-under-attack-europes-borders-urges-end-pushbacks-violence.html; Jeffrey Gedmin, "Right-Wing Populism in Germany: Muslims and Minorities After the 2015 Refugee Crisis," Brookings, July 24, 2019, https://www.brookings.edu/research/right-wing-populism-in-germany-muslims-and-minorities-after-the-2015-refugee-crisis/; Bernd Riegert, "Migration Problems Strengthen Populists' Hand in Europe," Deutsche Welle, June 19, 2018, https://www.dw.com/en/world-refugee-day-migration-problems-help-populists-prosper-in-europe/a-44263784.
105 Jon Henley, "EU Reaches Asylum Deal That Rights Groups Say Will Create 'Cruel System,'" *The Guardian,* December 20, 2023, https://www.theguardian.com/world/2023/dec/20/eu-reaches-asylum-deal-human-rights-groups-cruel-system.
106 Bruce Newbold, "COVID-19 Has Hardened Canadian Views on Immigration," *The Conversation,* October 1, 2020, https://theconversation.com/covid-19-has-hardened-canadian-views-on-immigration-146512.
107 United Nations Economic and Social Commission for Asia and the Pacific (ESCAP), ed., *Asia Pacific Migration Report 2020: Assessing Implementation of the Global Compact for Migration* (United Nations, 2020), https://www.unescap.org/sites/default/files/APMR2020_FullReport.pdf; Thomas Pepinsky, "Migrants, Minorities, and Populism in Southeast Asia," *Pacific Affairs* 93, 3 (June 5, 2019), https://pacificaffairs.ubc.ca/perspectives/migrants-minorities-and-populism-in-southeast-asia/.

108 The relative progressive and regressive features of particular governing regimes may be ascertained by reference to Freedom House, *Freedom in the World 2025: The Uphill Battle to Safeguard Rights,* https://freedomhouse.org/report/freedom-world, and Economist Intelligence Unit, *Democracy Index 2023* (2024), https://www.eiu.com/n/campaigns/democracy-index-2023/.

109 Jeffery R. Webber, "A Great Little Man: The Shadow of Jair Bolsonaro," *Historical Materialism* 28, 1 (March 13, 2020): 3–49, https://brill.com/view/journals/hima/28/1/article-p3_1.xml; Wendy Hunter and Timothy J. Power, "Bolsonaro and Brazil's Illiberal Backlash," *Journal of Democracy* 30, 1 (January 2019): 68–82, https://muse.jhu.edu/article/713723/summary; Marcella Ayres and Lisandra Paraguassu, "Brazil Unveils Reform Package to Tackle Huge Fiscal Deficit," *Reuters,* November 5, 2019, https://www.reuters.com/article/us-brazil-politics-idUSKBN1XF1Y9; "Brazil Pensions, Victory for Jair Bolsonaro as Reform Passes," *BBC News,* October 24, 2019, https://www.bbc.com/news/world-latin-america-50151327; "Brazil's Bolsonaro Vows No New Taxes or CPMF Return in Tax Reform Agenda," *Reuters,* July 19, 2019, https://www.reuters.com/article/us-brazil-economy-tax-idUSKCN1UE1YI.

110 Diane Jeantet and Carla Bridi, "Brazil's Brash President Bolsonaro Mum After Election Loss," *Associated Press,* October 31, 2022, https://apnews.com/article/lula-elected-president-brazil-election-24a50c4820a8a1ae38210407a499ef3d; Yascha Mounk, "What Bolsonaro's Loss Reveals About the Limits of Populism," *The Atlantic,* November 4, 2022, https://www.theatlantic.com/ideas/archive/2022/11/brazil-election-results-lula-wins-bolsonaro-democracy/671989/.

111 Tom Phillips, "Lula Suspects Pro-Bolsonaro Staff Helped Mob Enter Presidential Palace," *The Guardian,* January 12, 2023, https://www.theguardian.com/world/2023/jan/12/lula-bolsonaro-brazil-mob-presidential-palace?CMP=Share_AndroidApp_Other; Jenna Benchetrit, "How Brazil's Political Unrest Reached a Violent Crescendo Months After a Contentious Election," *CBC News,* January 10, 2023, https://www.cbc.ca/news/world/brazil-political-violence-lookback-1.6709387; Meridith McGraw, "Bannon on Brazil Riots: 'I'm Not Backing Off 1 Inch,'" *Politico,* January 9, 2023, https://www.politico.com/news/2023/01/09/bannon-brazil-riots-trump-00077155; "Brazil Congress Attack: What We Know So Far," *The Guardian,* January 9, 2023, https://www.theguardian.com/world/2023/jan/09/brazil-congress-attack-stormed-invasion-jair-bolsonaro-supporters-what-we-know-so-far.

112 Tom Phillips, "Judges Ban Bolsonaro from Running for Office for Eight Years over 'Appalling Lies,'" *The Guardian,* June 30, 2023, https://www.theguardian.com/world/2023/jun/30/jair-bolsonaro-judges-vote-ban-running-for-office?CMP=Share_AndroidApp_Other.

113 Tom Phillips, "Bolsonaro Was Engineer of 'Wilful Coup Attempt,' Brazil Congress Inquiry Alleges," *The Guardian,* October 17, 2023, https://www.theguardian.com/world/2023/oct/17/bolsonaro-brazil-coup-report. Also see Constance Malleret, "Bolsonaro Laid Out Plan for Brazil Coup After Defeat by Lula, Ex-Commanders Say," *The Guardian,* March 15, 2024, https://www.theguardian.com/world/2024/mar/15/bolsonaro-brazil-coup-lula-testimony, and "Jair Bolsonaro Surrenders Passport in Coup Attempt Investigation," *The Guardian,* February 8, 2024, https://www.theguardian.com/world/2024/feb/08/jair-bolsonaro-asked-passport-brazil-coup-attempt-investigation.

114 "Former Brazilian President Jair Bolsonaro Begins Serving 27-Year Sentence," *CBC News,* November 25, 2025, https://www.cbc.ca/news/world/bolsonaro-27-year-sentence-9.6992044.

115 The draft Program and Principles of Maduro's United Socialist Party of Venezuela (PSUV) express progressive ideals around socio-economic equality. "Venezuela: Draft Program and Principles of the United Socialist Party of Venezuela (PSUV)" and "Draft Declaration of Principles of the United Socialist Party of Venezuela (PSUV)," *Links: International Journal of Socialist Renewal,* n.d., https://links.org.au/venezuela-draft-program-and-principles-united-socialist-party-venezuela-psuv.

Under Maduro, however, illiberalism in governance has become a norm. Maria Pilar Garcia-Guadilla and Ana Mallen, "Polarization, Participatory Democracy, and Democratic Erosion in Venezuela's Twenty-First Century Socialism," *Annals of the American Academy of Political and Social Science* 681, 1 (2018): 62–77, https://journals.sagepub.com/doi/full/10.1177/0002716218817733. Under him, Venezuela's rule of law ranking was 113 – last among the countries surveyed. World Justice Project, *Rule of Law Index 2017–2018* (Washington, DC: World Justice Project, 2018), https://worldjusticeproject.org/sites/default/files/documents/WJP-ROLI-2018-June-Online-Edition_0.pdf.

116 Rahina Nasa, "Timeline: How the Crisis in Venezuela Unfolded," *Frontline,* February 22, 2019, https://www.pbs.org/wgbh/frontline/article/timeline-how-the-crisis-in-venezuela-unfolded/; Steve Ellner, "Venezuela's Fragile Revolution: From Chávez to Maduro," *Monthly Review* 69, 5 (October 2017): 1–14, https://search.proquest.com/openview/88d41527cede654c516dd87bf77f21a0/1.pdf?pq-origsite=gscholar&cbl=48155.

117 The Lima Group was formed in 2017 to address the crisis in Venezuela, and comprises multiple Latin American countries along with Canada. Member countries include Belize, Bolivia, Brazil, Chile, Colombia, Costa Rica, Guatemala, Guyana, Haiti, Honduras, Mexico, Panama, Paraguay, Peru, and Saint Lucia. Argentina was originally a member but departed the organization in March 2021. Government of Canada, "Canada's Response to the Venezuela Crisis," March 3, 2021, https://www.international.gc.ca/world-monde/issues_development-enjeux_developpement/response_conflict-reponse_conflits/crisis-crises/venezuela.aspx?lang=eng.

118 Rebecca Falconer, "U.S. Eases Oil Sanctions on Venezuela After Maduro Election Deal," *Axios,* October 8, 2023, https://www.axios.com/2023/10/19/us-eases-venezuela-oil-sanctions-maduro-2024-election-deal; "Venezuela Takes First Step Out of Political Stalemate," *BBC News,* November 27, 2022, https://www.bbc.com/news/world-latin-america-63771107; Oriana Gonzales, "U.S. to Ease Some Economic Sanctions on Venezuela," *Axios,* May 17, 2022, https://www.axios.com/2022/05/17/us-sanctions-venezuela-nicolas-maduro.

119 Ione Wells and Thomas Mackintosh, "Overwhelming Evidence Venezuela Opposition Won Election – Blinken," *BBC News,* August 2, 2024, https://www.bbc.com/news/articles/cd1d10453zno; Astrid Galvan, "Venezuela's Maduro and Opposition Both Claim Election Win," *Axios,* July 29, 2024, https://www.axios.com/2024/07/29/venezuela-election-maduro-opposition-gonzalez; Sam Jones, "'Hard to Believe': Venezuela Election Result Met with Suspicion Abroad," *The Guardian,* July 29, 2024, https://www.theguardian.com/world/article/2024/jul/29/venezuela-election-result-suspicion-abroad-nicolas-maduro.

120 Robert Tait, "Trump's Full-Throttle Threats Suggest No Backing Down from Aims to Topple Maduro's Regime," *The Guardian,* December 2, 2025, https://www.theguardian.com/world/2025/dec/02/trump-nicolas-maduro-venezuela; Mariel Ferragamo, "A Guide to Maduro's Capture and Venezuela's Uncertain Future," Council on Foreign Relations, January 8, 2026, https://www.cfr.org/article/guide-maduros-capture-and-venezuelas-uncertain-future.

121 Péter Krekó and Zsolt Enyedi, "Explaining Eastern Europe: Orbán's Laboratory of Illiberalism," *Journal of Democracy* 29, 3 (July 2018): 39–51, https://www.journalofdemocracy.org/articles/explaining-eastern-europe-orbans-laboratory-of-illiberalism/; Paul Lendval, *Orbán: Hungary's Strongman* (New York: Oxford University Press, 2017).

122 Jennifer Rankin, "Hungary Is No Longer a Full Democracy, Says European Parliament," *The Guardian,* September 15, 2022, https://www.theguardian.com/world/2022/sep/15/hungary-is-no-longer-a-full-democracy-says-european-parliament?CMP=Share_AndroidApp_Other; Zsuzsanna Szelényi, "Eyewitness to History: Viktor Orbán, Fidesz, and Me," *American Interest,* September 30, 2019, https://www.the-american-interest.com/v/zsuzsanna-szelenyi/; Patrick Kingsley, "How a Liberal Dissident Became a Far-Right Hero, in Hungary and Beyond," *New York Times,* April 6, 2018, https://www.nytimes.com/2018/04/06/world/europe/viktor-orban-hungary-politics.html.

123 Yiannis Baboulias, "Alexis Tsipras Is Smarter Than You Think," *Foreign Policy,* January 25, 2019, https://foreignpolicy.com/2019/01/25/alexis-tsipras-is-smarter-than-he-looks/; Jean Chapman, "'Our Time Has Come': Syriza's Rise to Power," *Social Scientist* 43, 11/12 (November–December 2015): 37–48, https://www.jstor.org/stable/24642384?seq=1.

124 Aristedes N. Hatzis, "Has Greece Found the Formula for Defeating Populism?" *Washington Post,* July 16, 2019, https://www.washingtonpost.com/opinions/2019/07/16/has-greece-found-formula-defeating-populism/.

125 Helena Smith, "Alexis Tsipras Steps Down as Syriza Leader After Greek Election Rout," *The Guardian,* June 29, 2023, https://www.theguardian.com/world/2023/jun/29/alexis-tsipras-step-down-syriza-leader-greece-election-rout?CMP=Share_AndroidApp_Other.

126 Oliver Laughland and Matthew Weaver, "Indian Election Result: 2014 Is Modi's Year as BJP Secures Victory," *The Guardian,* May 16, 2014, https://www.theguardian.com/world/2014/may/16/india-election-2014-results-live. Nahlah Ayed and Stephanie Jenzer, "How Modi's Populist Message Won the Indian PM a Second Term," *CBC News,* May 22, 2019, https://www.cbc.ca/news/world/india-modi-election-bjp-1.5142961.

127 Anisha Dutta, "India Secretly Works to Preserve Reputation on Global Democracy Index," *The Guardian,* June 22, 2023, https://www.theguardian.com/world/2023/jun/22/india-democracy-index-flawed-preserve-reputation-narendra-modi?CMP=Share_AndroidApp_Other; Azeem Ibrahim, "Modi's Slide Toward Autocracy," *Foreign Policy,* July 13, 2020, https://foreignpolicy.com/2020/07/13/modi-india-hindutva-hindu-nationalism-autocracy/. On judicial independence, see Saraphin Dhanani, "India's Justice System Is No Longer Independent: Part I," *Lawfare,* September 21, 2023, https://www.lawfaremedia.org/article/india-s-justice-system-is-no-longer-independent-part-i; Part II, September 22, 2023, https://www.lawfaremedia.org/article/india-s-justice-system-is-no-longer-independent-part-ii; Part III, September 25, 2023, https://www.lawfaremedia.org/article/india-s-justice-system-is-no-longer-independent-part-iii.

128 Salimah Shivji, "Popularity Crumbles for Indian PM Modi as Devastating COVID-19 Surge Continues," *CBC News,* May 15, 2021, https://www.cbc.ca/news/world/modi-india-coronavirus-1.6027346; Vidya Krishnan, "India Is What Happens When Rich People Do Nothing," *The Atlantic,* April 26, 2021, https://www.theatlantic.com/international/archive/2021/04/india-covid19-moral-failure/618702/.

129 Simon Fraser and Robert Greenall, "India's Modi Claims Victory as He Heads for Reduced Majority," *BBC News,* June 4, 2024, https://www.bbc.com/news/articles/c0vv93pz14zo; Soutik Biswas, "Why India's Modi Failed to Win Outright Majority," *BBC News,* June 4, 2024, https://www.bbc.com/news/articles/c977g8gl5q2o.

130 Lisandra Paraguassu and Richard Brito, "Bolsonaro Threatens WHO Exit as COVID-19 Kills 'a Brazilian a Minute,'" *Reuters,* June 5, 2020, https://www.reuters.com/article/us-health-coronavirus-brazil-idUSKBN23C1TF.

131 Glenn Greenwald, "Why Brazil Still Matters," *The Nation,* April 19–26, 2021, 20–27, https://www.thenation.com/article/world/brazil-lula-bolsonaro-amazon/.

132 "Venezuela Makes Second COVAX Payment for Vaccines as Official Visits," *Reuters,* April 18, 2021, https://www.reuters.com/world/americas/venezuela-makes-second-covax-payment-vaccines-un-official-visits-2021-04-19/.

133 Tom Phillips, "Maduro Starts New Venezuelan Term by Accusing US of Imperialist 'World War,'" *The Guardian,* January 10, 2019, https://www.theguardian.com/world/2019/jan/10/venezuela-president-nicolas-maduro-begins-second-term.

134 Zack Beauchamp, "The American Right's Favorite Strongman," *Vox,* August 10, 2020, https://www.vox.com/2020/5/21/21256324/viktor-orban-hungary-american-conservatives.

135 Gal Kirn, "European Progressive Future? Neither Yesterday's Tsipras nor Today's Greens," *The Bullet,* June 5, 2019, https://socialistproject.ca/2019/06/european-progressive-future/; "Alexis Tsipras: Leader Who Risked Greece's Euro Future," *BBC News,* September 21, 2015, https://www.bbc.com/news/world-europe-33243579; Luke Hurst, "Greece Signs Reform Deal with OECD to Avoid Troika 'Blackmail,'" *Newsweek,* March 12, 2015, https://www.newsweek.com/greece-signs-reform-deal-oecd-troika-blackmail-313399.

136 Amrita Narlikar, "India's Role in Global Governance: A Modi-fication?" *International Affairs* 93, 1 (January, 2017): 102–5, https://www.chathamhouse.org/sites/default/files/publications/ia/INTA93_1_06_Narlikar.pdf. For comparisons with China, see Haiyun Ma, "Why China and India's Populism Threatens the World Order," *NOĒMA,* October 19, 2023, https://www.noemamag.com/why-china-and-indias-populism-threaten-the-world-order/.

137 See, e.g., Kilian Spandler and Fredrik Söderbaum, "Populist (De)legitimation of International Organizations," *International Affairs* 99, 1 (May 2023): 1023–41, https://academic.oup.com/ia/article/99/3/1023/7147399; Kenneth Roth, "The Dangerous Rise of Populism: Global Attacks on Human Rights Values," *Journal of International Affairs* Special Issue (2017): 79–84, https://jia.sipa.columbia.edu/news/dangerous-rise-populism-global-attacks-human-rights-values.

138 Mauricio Savarese and Debora Alvares, "Bolsonaro Under Fire as Brazil Hits 300,000 Virus Deaths," *Associated Press,* March 25, 2021, https://apnews.com/article/brazil-jair-bolsonaro-coronavirus-pandemic-9eeadec9835665c5937ffac507a42b9a.

139 Clara Nugent, "Why the Threat of U.S. Intervention in Venezuela Revives Historical Tensions in the Region," *TIME,* January 25, 2019, https://time.com/5512005/venezuela-us-intervention-history-latin-america/.

140 "Venezuelan President Maduro Proposed New UN Fund to Support Countries Facing Discrimination," *UN News*, September 23, 2020, https://news.un.org/en/story/2020/09/1073382.

141 Bálint Mikola, "Hungary's Rule of Law Backsliding Continues Amidst the COVID-19 Crisis," *Transparency International* (blog), February 18, 2021, https://www.transparency.org/en/blog/

hungarys-rule-of-law-backsliding-continues-amidst-the-covid-19-crisis; "Orbán Orwellian Law Paves Way for 'Information Police State' in Hungary," Reporters Without Borders, April 1, 2020, https://rsf.org/en/news/orbans-orwellian-law-paves-way-information-police-state-hungary.

142 DEMOS, "Orbán's Handling of the Coronavirus Shows How Populists Exercise Power," November 20, 2020, https://cordis.europa.eu/article/id/421744-orban-s-handling-of-the-coronavirus-shows-how-populists-exercise-power; Lydia Gall, "Hungary's Orbán Uses Pandemic to Seize Unlimited Power," Human Rights Watch, March 23, 2020, https://www.hrw.org/news/2020/03/23/hungarys-orban-uses-pandemic-seize-unlimited-power.

143 Gabor Tanacs and Natalie Huet, "Hungary Ends Emergency Powers, but New Law Opens Up Potential to Re-apply Them," *Euronews,* June 16, 2020, https://www.euronews.com/2020/06/16/hungary-debates-end-to-emergency-powers-but-new-law-opens-up-potential-to-re-apply-them.

144 Sarantis Michalapoulos, "Tsipras Backs AstraZeneca, Slams Europe's 'One Industry' Approach," *Euractiv,* April 28, 2021, https://www.euractiv.com/section/coronavirus/news/tsipras-backs-astrazeneca-slams-europes-one-industry-approach/.

145 "PM Narendra Modi Shares His Ayurvedic Formulae to Increase Immunity," *Times of India,* April 1, 2020, https://timesofindia.indiatimes.com/life-style/food-news/pm-narendra-modi-shares-his-ayurvedic-formulae-to-increase-immunity/articleshow/74945873.cms; "India's Traditional Medicine Boosted Immunity to COVID-19: PM Modi," *the quint,* November 13, 2020, https://www.thequint.com/news/breaking-news/indias-traditional-medicine-helped-boost-immunity-in-corona-crisis.

146 Sadanand Dhume, "Modi Declared Victory, Then Covid Struck Back with a Vengeance," *Wall Street Journal,* May 13, 2021, https://www.wsj.com/articles/modi-declared-victory-then-covid-struck-back-with-a-vengeance-11620922164.

147 Philip M. Fearnside, "Will President Bolsonaro Withdraw Brazil from the Paris Agreement? (Commentary)" *Mongabay,* January 31, 2019, https://news.mongabay.com/2019/01/commentary-will-president-bolsonaro-withdraw-brazil-from-the-paris-agreement/.

148 "Orban's Verdict," May 25, 2021 5:09 p.m., in "As It Happened: EU Summit on Belarus, COVID-19 and Climate," *Politico,* May 24, 2021, https://www.politico.eu/article/european-council-summit-live-blog-belarus-plane-hijack-coronavirus-climate-change/#id_1285509.

149 "India Didn't Cause Climate Change: Prakash Javadekar," *Indian Express,* December12, 2020, https://indianexpress.com/article/india/india-didnt-cause-climate-change-prakash-javadekar-7101545/; Anjali Jaiswal and Madhura Joshi, "Climate Action: All Eyes on India," *Natural Resources Defense Council (NRDC) Expert Blog,* December 12, 2020, https://www.nrdc.org/experts/anjali-jaiswal/climate-action-all-eyes-india.

150 "UN Affirms 'Historic' Global Compact to Support World Refugees," *UN News,* December 17, 2018, https://news.un.org/en/story/2018/12/1028791; Megan Specia, "Hungary Pulls Out of U.N. Global Migration Agreement," *New York Times,* July 18, 2018, https://www.nytimes.com/2018/07/18/world/europe/hungary-migration-united-nations.html; Shaun Walker, "Viktor Orbán Trumpets Hungary's 'Procreation, Not Immigration,' Policy," *The Guardian,* September 6, 2019, https://www.theguardian.com/world/2019/sep/06/viktor-orban-trumpets-far-right-procreation-anti-immigration-policy.

151 "Tsipras Underlines Greek Solidarity to Refugees at Migration Summit," *Ekathimerini,* December 10, 2018, https://www.ekathimerini.com/news/235524/tsipras-underlines-greek-solidarity-to-refugees-at-migration-summit/; Helena Smith, "Greece's Refugee Crisis: PM Says Country Is Overwhelmed," *The Guardian,* March 1, 2018, https://www.theguardian.com/world/2016/mar/01/greeces-refugee-crisis-pm-says-country-is-overwhelmed.

152 "'Not in My Backyard' Attitude Will Not Resolve Crises – Greek Prime Minister," *UN News,* September 28, 2018, https://news.un.org/en/story/2018/09/1021482; Salomi Boukala and Dimitra Dimitrakopoulo, "Absurdity and the 'Blame Game' Within the Schengen Area: Analyzing Greek (Social) Media Discourses on the Refugee Crisis," *Journal of Immigrant and Refugee Studies* 16, 1–2 (2018): 179–97, https://www.tandfonline.com/doi/abs/10.1080/15562948.2017.1303560.

153 See, e.g., Immanuel Wallerstein, "The Rise and Future Demise of the World Capitalist System; Concepts for Comparative Analysis," *Comparative Studies in Society and History* 16, 4 (1974): 387–415, http://bev.berkeley.edu/ipe/readings/Wallerstein.pdf. Wallerstein's theory was summarized and updated in Wallerstein, *World Systems Analysis: An Introduction* (Durham, NC: Duke University Press, 2004), https://www.dukeupress.edu/world-systems-analysis.

154 See, e.g., Heike Krieger, "Populist Governments and International Law," *European Journal of International Law* 30, 3 (2019): 971–96, http://www.ejil.org/pdfs/30/3/2990.pdf; Erik Voeten, "Populism and Backlashes Against International Courts," *Perspectives in Politics* 18, 2 (2019): 407–22, https://www.cambridge.org/core/journals/perspectives-on-politics/article/populism-and-backlashes-against-international-courts/22D6468FD3316BB74A63BAD7BBAE8E5C; Human Rights Watch, "The Dangerous Rise of Populism: Global Attacks on Human Rights Values," World Report 2017, https://www.hrw.org/world-report/2017/country-chapters/global-4.

155 Sergei Guriev and Elias Papaioannou, "The Political Economy of Populism," *Journal of Economic Literature* 60, 3 (2022): 753–832, https://www.aeaweb.org/articles?id=10.1257/jel.20201595; Patricia Justino and Bruno Martorano, "Populism in Brazil: How Liberalization and Austerity Led to the Rise of Lula and Bolsonaro," *The Conversation,* September 30 2020, https://theconversation.com/populism-in-brazil-how-liberalisation-and-austerity-led-to-the-rise-of-lula-and-bolsonaro-146780; Dom Phillips, Jason Burke, and Paul Lewis, "How Brazil and South Africa Became the World's Most Populist Countries," *The Guardian,* May 1, 2019, https://www.theguardian.com/world/2019/may/01/how-brazil-and-south-africa-became-the-worlds-most-populist-countries; Uri Friedman, "What Is a Populist? And Is Donald Trump One?" *The Atlantic,* February 2, 2017, https://www.theatlantic.com/international/archive/2017/02/what-is-populist-trump/516525/; Antonis Galanopopulos, "Populism in Greece and Why the Theory of the Two Extremes Is Wrong," *Euro Crisis in the Press* (blog), September 30, 2013, https://blogs.lse.ac.uk/eurocrisispress/2013/09/20/1846/.

156 William A. Galston, "The Populist Challenge to Liberal Democracy," *Journal of Democracy* 29, 2 (2018): 5–19, https://www.brookings.edu/articles/the-populist-challenge-to-liberal-democracy/.

157 Ibrahim Ozturk, "Populist Attacks on Institutions as a Reaction to Hyper-Globalization," *Populism and Politics,* May 21, 2021, https://www.populismstudies.org/populist-attacks-on-institutions-as-a-reaction-to-the-hyper-globalization/; Paul Marschall and Stephan Klingebiel, "Populism: Consequences for Global Sustainable Development," Deutsches Institut für Entwicklungspolitik (DIE) Briefing Paper No. 8/2019, 2019, https://www.econstor.eu/handle/10419/199843.

158 Caroline Nagel, "Populism, Immigration and the Trump Phenomenon in the U.S.," *Environment and Planning C: Politics and Space* 37, 1 (2019): 12–16, https://journals.sagepub.com/doi/10.1177/0263774X18811923c; European Commission Against Racism and Intolerance (ECRI), "Unrelenting Rise in Xenophobic Populism, Resentment, Hate Speech in Europe in 2017," Council of Europe *News 2018,* https://www.coe.int/en/web/portal/-/unrelenting-rise-in-xenophobic-populism-resentment-hate-speech-in-europe-in-2017.

159 Francesca Paris, "Brazilian President Bolsonaro Withdraws from U.N. Compact on Migration," *NPR News,* January 9, 2019, https://www.npr.org/2019/01/09/683634412/brazilian-president-bolsonaro-withdraws-from-u-n-compact-on-migration.

160 "Venezuelan President Maduro Proposed New UN Fund to Support Countries Facing Discrimination."

161 Nikoletta Nagy, "Orban's Opportunistic Record Belies Hungary's New Pro-Climate Rethoric [sic]," *Clean Energy Wire,* July 4, 2024, https://www.cleanenergywire.org/news/orbans-opportunistic-record-belies-hungarys-new-pro-climate-rethoric; "Climate Protection: PM Orbán Holds Propaganda Speeches Instead of Acting," *Daily News Hungary,* May 26, 2021, https://dailynewshungary.com/climate-protection-pm-orban-holds-propaganda-speeches-instead-of-acting/.

162 Jamie Dettmer, "COVID-19 Prompts Rethink of European Populist Tactics," *Voice of America,* April 8, 2021, https://www.voanews.com/europe/covid-19-prompts-rethink-european-populist-tactics.

163 "Greece's Syriza Party Calls for Pandemic Debt Forgiveness for Small Business," *Reuters,* April 13, 2021, https://www.reuters.com/article/health-coronavirus-greece-opposition-idUSL8N2M64IQ; Alexis Tsipras, "Vaccines Are a Public Good, Not a Corporate Product," *Politico,* January 28, 2021, https://www.politico.eu/article/coronavirus-vaccines-public-good-not-corporate-product/; "Tsipras: We Must Support the People on the Frontline, as the Pandemic Is Not Over," *ANA-MPA News,* December 23, 2020, https://www.amna.gr/en/article/515438/Tsipras-We-must-support-the-people-on-the-frontline-as-the-pandemic-is-not-over.

164 Nikhila Henry and Kathryn Armstrong, "CAA: India to Enforce Migrant Law That Excludes Muslims," *BBC News,* March 11 2024, https://www.bbc.com/news/world-asia-68538260; Bansari Kamdar, "Indian Refugee Policy: From Strategic Ambiguity to Exclusion?" *The Diplomat,* February 3, 2020, https://thediplomat.com/2020/02/indian-refugee-policy-from-strategic-ambiguity

-to-exclusion/; Jayshree Bajoria, "'Shoot the Traitors': Discrimination Against Muslims Under India's New Citizenship Policy," Human Rights Watch, April 9, 2020, https://www.hrw.org/report/2020/04/09/shoot-traitors/discrimination-against-muslims-under-indias-new-citizenship-policy.

165 Miguel Polares Maduro and Paul W. Kahn, eds., *Democracy in Times of Pandemic: Different Futures Imagined* (Cambridge: Cambridge University Press, 2020), https://www.cambridge.org/core/books/democracy-in-times-of-pandemic/959F17CB35A00C057DCBC46FA930CDC1.

166 Yasmeen Serhan, "The Pandemic Isn't a Death Knell for Populism," *The Atlantic,* August 22, 2020, https://www.theatlantic.com/international/archive/2020/08/populism-will-survive-the-pandemic/615358/; Brett Meyer, "Pandemic Populism: An Analysis of Populist Leaders' Responses to Covid-19," Tony Blair Institute for Global Change, August 17, 2020, https://institute.global/policy/pandemic-populism-analysis-populist-leaders-responses-covid-19.

167 Walter Bruchhausen, "Global Health in the Colonial Era: The Expansion of European Medicine," European History on Line, May 15, 2020, http://ieg-ego.eu/en/threads/theories-and-methods/knowledge-transfer/walter-bruchhausen-global-health-in-the-colonial-era-the-expansion-of-european-medicine#section_10.

168 Giorgos Katsambekis and Yannis Stavrakakis, *Populism and the Pandemic: A Collaborative Report,* Populismus Interventions 7, June 2020, https://populismus.gr/wp-content/uploads/2020/06/interventions-7-populism-pandemic-UPLOAD.pdf; Francis Fukuyama, "The Thing That Determines a Country's Resistance to the Coronavirus," *The Atlantic,* March 20, 2020, https://www.theatlantic.com/ideas/archive/2020/03/thing-determines-how-well-countries-respond-coronavirus/609025/.

169 Alexandre Zouev, "COVID and the Rule of Law: A Dangerous Balancing Act," UN COVID-19 Response, June 22, 2020, https://www.un.org/en/coronavirus/covid-and-rule-law-dangerous-balancing-act; Council of Europe Directorate General for Human Rights and the Rule of Law, "The Impact of COVID-19 on Human Rights and the Rule of Law – Our Action," https://www.coe.int/en/web/human-rights-rule-of-law/covid19.

170 Peter G. Danchin, Jeremy Farrall, Shruti Rana, and Imogen Saunders, "The Pandemic Paradox in International Law," *American Journal of International Law* 114 (2020), https://papers.ssrn.com/sol3/papers.cfm?abstract_id=3675519; Ted Piccone, "The Rule of Law Is Under Duress Everywhere," Brookings, March 17, 2020, https://www.brookings.edu/blog/order-from-chaos/2020/03/17/the-rule-of-law-is-under-duress-everywhere/.

171 Sarah Repucci and Amy Slipowitz, *Democracy Under Lockdown: The Impact of COVID-19 on the Global Struggle for Freedom* (Washington, DC: Freedom House, 2020), https://freedomhouse.org/report/special-report/2020/democracy-under-lockdown; John Daniszawski, "In Struggle Against Pandemic, Populist Leaders Fare Poorly," *Associated Press,* July 23, 2020, https://apnews.com/article/brazil-u-s-news-ap-top-news-understanding-the-outbreak-mexico-2a4b5159e9c8b1510973801297243c3d.

172 Caitlin Williams, Jocelyn Getgen Kestenbaum, and Benjamin Mason Meier, "Populist Nationalism Threatens Health and Human Rights in COVID-19 Response," *American Journal of Public Health* 110 (November 12, 2020): 1766–68, https://ajph.aphapublications.org/doi/10.2105/AJPH.2020.305952; Lydia Khalil, "Digital Authoritarianism, China and COVID," Lowy Institute, November 2, 2020, https://www.lowyinstitute.org/publications/digital-authoritarianism-china-and-covid; Haifeng Huang, "The Pathology of Hard Propaganda," *Journal of Politics* 80, 3 (July 2018), https://www.journals.uchicago.edu/doi/abs/10.1086/696863.

173 Heather J. Williams and Caitlin McCulloch, "Truth Decay and National Security," *Lawfare,* August 1, 2023, https://www.lawfaremedia.org/article/truth-decay-and-national-security; Jonathan Rauch, *The Constitution of Knowledge: A Defense of Truth* (Washington, DC: Brookings Institution Press, 2021), https://www.brookings.edu/book/the-constitution-of-knowledge/; Lee McIntyre, *Post-Truth* (Cambridge, MA: MIT Press, 2018), https://mitpress.mit.edu/books/post-truth. On the relevance of Gnosticism, see Timothy Pettipiece, "History Repeats Itself: From the New Testament to QAnon," *The Conversation,* March 21, 2021, https://theconversation.com/history-repeats-itself-from-the-new-testament-to-qanon-156915; Morgan Lee, "What the Bible Says About QAnon," *Christianity Today,* May 20, 2020, https://www.christianitytoday.com/ct/podcasts/quick-to-listen/conspiracy-theories-qanon-bible-christians-jesus.html.

174 Council of Europe, *Democratic Governance and COVID-19: Report* (Strasbourg: Council of Europe, 2020), https://rm.coe.int/cddg-2020-20e-final-reportdemocraticgovernancecovid19-for-publication-/1680a0beed.
175 Guriev and Papaioannou, "The Political Economy of Populism."
176 Jeremy Ko, James Downes, and Wai-Kit Ming, "Populism vs. the Planet: How Leaders Undermine Climate Adaptation (1995–20)," *Research and Politics* September 19, 2025, https://journals.sagepub.com/doi/10.1177/20531680251378563?int.sj-full-text.similar-articles.4; Sebastian Keicker, "The Politics of Populism and Climate Action," *E3G*, December 16, 2024, https://www.e3g.org/news/the-politics-of-populism-and-climate-action/#:~:text=Populism%2C%20particularly%20on%20the%20right,priorities%20of%20"the%20people.
177 Ernest Gnan and Donato Masciandaro, "Populism, Economic Policies and Central Banking: An Overview," European Money and Finance Forum, SUERF Policy Note No. 131, February 2020, https://www.suerf.org/policynotes/9985/populism-economic-policies-and-central-banking-an-overview.
178 Refugee Research Online, "TAG Identity Transformation," https://refugeeresearchonline.org/tag/identity-transformation/; Ilias Louis Hatzis, "The Refugee Crisis Is an Identity Crisis," *The Leap of Faith,* February 23, 2025, https://iliashatzis.substack.com/p/the-refugee-crisis-and-blockchain?utm_campaign=post&utm_medium=web; "Identity and the Refugee Crisis," *Sphere Identity,* May 16, 2019, https://medium.com/sphere-identity/identity-and-the-refugee-crisis-fd7981880746; Kari Burnett, "Feeling Like an Outsider: A Case Study of Refugee Identity in the Czech Republic," UNHCR Research Paper No. 251, January 2013, https://www.unhcr.org/research/working/510947989/feeling-outsider-case-study-refugee-identity-czech-republic-kari-burnett.html.
179 Yvonne Donders, "Diversity in Europe: From Pluralism to Populism?" in *European Populism and Human Rights,* ed. Jure Vidmar (Leiden: Brill, 2020), 52–71, https://brill.com/view/title/56233; Peter Scholten, *Mainstreaming Versus Alienation; A Complexity Approach to the Governance of Migration and Diversity* (New York: Palgrave Macmillan, 2020), https://www.palgrave.com/gp/book/9783030422370; Ilona van Breugel, "Towards a Typology of Local Migration Diversity Policies," *Comparative Migration Studies* 8, 23 (2020), https://comparativemigrationstudies.springeropen.com/articles/10.1186/s40878-020-00179-0.
180 Seth Zimmerman, "Immigration and Economic Mobility," Urban Institute, https://www.urban.org/sites/default/files/publication/31186/1001162-immigration-and-economic-mobility.pdf; Zolberg Institute on Migration and Mobility, https://zolberginstitute.org.
181 Beatriz Martinez Saavedra, "Trump, Bolsonaro, Modi: Anti-Migration, Ecocide, and Conflict Escalation: The Agenda of the Global Right," Open Democracy, September 20, 2019, https://www.opendemocracy.net/en/democraciaabierta/trump-bolsonaro-modi-anti-migración-ecocidio-y-escalada-de-conflictos-aspectos-en-la-agenda-de-la-derecha-global-en/; Stéphane Dion, "Cultural Insecurity as the Main Root Cause of Populism" (introductory remarks at the 22nd Forum 2000 Conference, "Democracy: In Need of a Critical Update?" Prague, October 8, 2018), https://www.international.gc.ca/country_news-pays_nouvelles/2019-10-08-germany-allemagne.aspx?lang=eng; Susi Meret and Birte Slim, "Multiculturalism, Right-Wing Populism and the Crisis of Social Democracy," in *The Crisis of Social Democracy in Europe,* ed. Michael Keating (Cambridge: Cambridge University Press, 2013), 125–39.
182 Will Kymlicka, "Defending Diversity in an Era of Populism," in *Multiculturalism and Interculturalism: Debating the Dividing Lines,* ed. Nasar Meer, Tariq Modood, and Ricard Zapata-Barero (Edinburgh: Edinburgh University Press, 2016), ch. 7, https://edinburgh.universitypressscholarship.com/view/10.3366/edinburgh/9781474407083.001.0001/upso-9781474407083.

CHAPTER 3: COVID-19

1 An abbreviated version of an earlier draft of this chapter appears as Pitman B. Potter, "China and COVID-19: Alienation and Its Discontents," *Asia Pacific Issues* (East-West Center) 151 (January 2022), https://www.eastwestcenter.org/publications/china-and-covid-19-alienation-and-its-discontents.
2 Michael R. Reich, "The Core Roles of Transparency and Accountability in the Governance of Global Health Public-Private Partnerships," *Health Systems and Reform* 4, 3 (2018): 239–48, https://www.tandfonline.com/doi/full/10.1080/23288604.2018.1465880#abstract; Sameen Siddiqi, Tayyeb I. Masud, Sania Nishtar, David H. Peters, Belgacem Sabri, Khalif M. Bile, and Mohamed A. Jama, "Framework for Assessing Governance of Health System in Developing

Countries: Gateway to Good Governance," *Health Policy* 90, 1 (April 2009): 13–25, https://www.sciencedirect.com/science/article/abs/pii/S0168851008002005.

3 Centers for Disease Control and Prevention (CDC), "CDC Museum COVID-19 Timeline," https://www.cdc.gov/museum/timeline/covid19.html; Congressional Research Service (CRS), "COVID-19 and China: A Chronology of Events (December 2019–January 2020)," https://www.congress.gov/crs-product/R46354.

4 John Dotson, "The CCP's New Leading Small Group for Countering the Coronavirus Epidemic – and the Mysterious Absence of Xi Jinping," *China Brief* 20, 3 (February 5, 2020), https://jamestown.org/program/the-ccps-new-leading-small-group-for-countering-the-coronavirus-epidemic-and-the-mysterious-absence-of-xi-jinping/. For discussion of Leading Small Groups under Xi Jinping, see Christopher K. Johnson, Scott Kennedy, and Mingda Qiu, "Xi's Signature Governance Innovation: The Rise of Leading Small Groups," Center for Strategic and International Studies, October 17, 2017, https://www.csis.org/analysis/xis-signature-governance-innovation-rise-leading-small-groups. Also see Alice Miller, "The CCP Central Committee's Leading Small Groups," *China Leadership Monitor* no. 26 (Fall 2008), https://www.hoover.org/sites/default/files/uploads/documents/CLM26AM.pdf.

5 "Wuhan Lockdown: A Year of China's Fight Against the Covid Pandemic," *BBC News,* January 22, 2021, https://www.bbc.com/news/world-asia-china-55628488; Fang Fang, *Wuhan Diary: Dispatches from a Quarantined City,* trans. Michael Berry (Toronto: HarperCollins Canada, 2020), https://www.harpercollins.ca/9780063052642/wuhan-diary/; Fan Wang and Grace Tsoi, "Fang Fang: Author Vilified for Wuhan Diary Speaks Out a Year On," *BBC News,* January 19, 2021, https://www.bbc.com/news/world-asia-54987675.

6 Tracy Wen Liu, "'We're Hardly Heroic': Wuhan Medical Workers Look Back in Anger," ChinaFile, April 3, 2020, https://www.chinafile.com/reporting-opinion/viewpoint/were-hardly-heroic; Gao Yu, Peng Yanfeng, Yang Rui, Ma Danmeng, Flynn Murphy, Han Wei, and Timmy Shen, "In Depth: How Early Coronavirus Signs Were Spotted and Throttled," *Caixin,* February 29, 2020, https://www.caixinglobal.com/2020-02-29/in-depth-how-early-signs-of-a-sars-like-virus-were-spotted-spread-and-throttled-101521745.html.

7 Xiaohu Wang, Hanyu Xiao, Bo Yan, and Jingyuan Xu, "New Development: Administrative Accountability and Early Responses During Public Health Crises – Lessons from Covid-19 in China," *Public Money and Management* 41, 1 (2021): 73–76, https://www.tandfonline.com/doi/full/10.1080/09540962.2020.1819012.

8 Zhang Wei, Zhang Diyang, Jing Yibu, Li Zailei, Zheng Yiling, and Wu Chao, "Si ren xunzhi, si ren binwei, Wuhan Zhongxin Yiyuan 'zhian shike'" [Four people died in the line of duty and four are endangered: Wuhan Central Hospital's dark moment], *Southern Weekend* // 南方周末, March 11, 2020, https://www.infzm.com/content/178912; Stephanie Hegarty, "The Chinese Doctor Who Tried to Warn Others About Coronavirus," *BBC News,* February 6, 2020, https://www.bbc.com/news/world-asia-china-51364382.

9 Gao Wenqian, "Xi Jinping Is the Culprit of the Wuhan Epidemic," Human Rights in China, February 27, 2020, https://www.hrichina.org/en/press-work/hric-commentary/xi-jinping-culprit-wuhan-epidemic.

10 Jasmine Wright and Chandelis Duster, "Blinken Criticizes China's Failure to 'Provide Real Transparency' Earlier in Pandemic," *CNN,* April 11, 2021, https://www.cnn.com/2021/04/11/politics/blinken-taiwan-china-coronavirus/index.html.

11 Helen Davidson, "Beijing School Pupils in Lockdown After Staff Tests Positive for Covid," *The Guardian,* November 3, 2021, https://www.theguardian.com/world/2021/nov/03/beijing-school-pupils-lockdown-staff-tests-positive-covid-china?CMP=Share_AndroidApp_Other; "Nanjing: New Virus Outbreak Worst Since Wuhan, Say Chinese State Media," *BBC News,* July 30, 2021, https://www.bbc.com/news/world-asia-china-58021911; Barbie Latza Nadeau, "China Thought They'd Beaten COVID, Now the Indian Variant Is Surging," *Daily Beast,* June 1, 2021, https://www.thedailybeast.com/china-thought-theyd-beaten-covid-now-the-indian-variant-is-surging?source=email&via=desktop.

12 Jaime Metzl, "Open Letter to the World Health Organization and the Members of Its Executive Board," April 30, 2021, https://jamiemetzl.com/wp-content/uploads/2021/04/Open-Letter-to-the-World-Health-Organization-and-the-Members-of-its-Executive-Board-1.pdf; Zhao Shili, "An Urgent Call Regarding the Pandemic" (translation), *China Digital Times,* March 16, 2020, https://chinadigitaltimes.net/2020/03/translation-an-urgent-call-regarding-the-epidemic/.

13 World Health Organization (WHO), "WHO Calls for Further Studies, Data on Origin of SARS-CoV-2 Virus, Reiterates That All Hypotheses Remain Open," press release, March 30, 2021, https://worldhealthorganization.cmail19.com/t/ViewEmail/d/39A4023639DBA9B0254 0EF23F30FEDED/1076FE65EB5EBEA4DCC9454293137CA2; Caitlin Owens and Zachary Basu, "Long-Awaited WHO-China Report Inconclusive on Coronavirus Origins," *Axios,* March 29, 2021, https://www.axios.com/who-china-report-coronavirus-origins-e1a0b917-6302-437d -956c-aa7df7cb8f42.html; Jamey Keaten and Ken Moritsugu, "WHO Report: COVID likely 1st Jumped into Humans from Animals," *Associated Press,* March 29, 2021, https://apnews.com/ article/who-report-animals-source-covid-19-coronavirus-8a839c179c330c56fa46a76 3b7286a7f?utm_source=Twitter&utm_campaign=SocialFlow&utm_medium=AP.

14 Kristian G. Andersen, Andrew Rambaut, W. Ian Lipkin, Edward C. Holmes, and Robert F. Gerry, "The Proximal Origin of SARS-CoV-2," *Nature Medicine* 26 (2020): 450–52, https:// www.nature.com/articles/s41591-020-0820-9; Jimmy Tobias, "Evolution of a Theory: Unredacted NIH Emails Show Efforts to Rule Out Lab Origin of Covid," *The Intercept,* January 19, 2023, https://theintercept.com/2023/01/19/covid-origin-nih-emails/.

15 Francesca Gillett, "German Spy Agency 'Believed Covid Likely Started in Lab,'" *BBC News,* March 13, 2025, https://www.bbc.com/news/articles/cz7vypq31z7o.

16 WHO, "WHO-Convened Global Study of Origins of SARS-CoV-2: China Part – Joint WHO-China Study Team Report, 14 January–10 February 2021," March 30, 2021, https://www.who. int/publications/i/item/who-convened-global-study-of-origins-of-sars-cov-2-china-part; Yanzhong Huang, "What the WHO Investigation Reveals About the Origins of COVID-19," *Foreign Affairs,* March 31, 2021, https://www.foreignaffairs.com/articles/china/2021-03-31/ what-who-investigation-reveals-about-origins-covid-19; WHO, *Report of the WHO-China Joint Mission on Coronavirus Disease 2019 (COVID-19)* (February 16–24, 2020), https://www. who.int/docs/default-source/coronaviruse/who-china-joint-mission-on-covid-19-final -report.pdf; Kai Kepferschmidt and Jon Cohen, "China's Aggressive Measures Have Slowed the Coronavirus. They May Not Work in Other Countries," *ScienceInsider,* March 2, 2020, https://www.sciencemag.org/news/2020/03/china-s-aggressive-measures-have-slowed -coronavirus-they-may-not-work-other-countries.

17 WHO, "WHO-Convened Global Study of the Origins of SARS-CoV-2: China Part." Subsequent analysis by a member of the WHO team concluded that the first case of COVID-19 involved a seafood vendor at the Wuhan live animal market, suggesting that zoonotic transfer was indeed the cause. Daniel Engber, "The Lab-Leak Theory Meets Its Perfect Match," *The Atlantic,* November 24, 2021, https://www.theatlantic.com/ideas/archive/2021/11/lab-leak -covid-origin-coincidence-wet-market/620794/; Hannah Devlin, "First Known Covid Case Was Wuhan Market Vendor, Says Scientist," *The Guardian,* November 19, 2021, https://www. theguardian.com/world/2021/nov/19/first-covid-patient-in-wuhan-was-at-animal-market -study-finds?CMP=Share_AndroidApp_Other.

18 Jon Cohen, "With Call for 'Raw Data' and Lab Audits, WHO Chief Pressures China on Pandemic Origin Probe," *ScienceInsider,* July 17, 2021, https://www.sciencemag.org/news/ 2021/07/who-chief-sharpens-call-china-further-help-probe-origin-pandemic; "A Joint WHO-China Study of Covid's Origins Leaves Much Unclear," *The Economist,* March 31, 2021, https:// www.economist.com/china/2021/04/03/a-joint-who-china-study-of-covid-19s-origins -leaves-much-unclear.

19 Office of the Director of National Intelligence (DNI), "Origins: Intelligence Community Assessment," August 27, 2021, https://www.dni.gov/files/ODNI/documents/assessments/Unclassified -Summary-of-Assessment-on-COVID-19-Origins.pdf; Christina Larson and Nomaan Merchant, "EXPLAINER: The US Investigation into COVID-19 Origins," *Associated Press,* June 8, 2021, https://apnews.com/article/investigation-covid-origins-wuhan-lab-nature-850b7a6ee 1005596bb0f8b2bc6b79dd5. Additional details have emerged on China's coronavirus research facilities that involve not only the Wuhan Institute of Virology but also the Wuhan University Center for Animal Experimentation. Sharon Lerner and Mara Hvistendahl, "New Details Emerge About Coronavirus Research at Chinese Lab," *The Intercept,* September 6, 2021, https://theintercept.com/2021/09/06/new-details-emerge-about-coronavirus-research -at-chinese-lab/.

20 DNI, "Updated Assessment on COVID-19 Origins," October 29, 2021, https://www.dni.gov/ files/ODNI/documents/assessments/Declassified-Assessment-on-COVID-19-Origins.pdf.

21 John Sudworth, "Toxic Debate Over Lab Leak Theory Hampers Search for Covid Origins," *BBC News*, March 2, 2023, https://www.bbc.com/news/world-us-canada-64819965; Michael R. Gordon and Warren P. Strobel, "Lab Leak Most Likely Origin of Covid-19 Pandemic, Energy Department Now Says," *Wall Street Journal*, February 26, 2023, https://www.wsj.com/articles/covid-origin-china-lab-leak-807b7b0a; David Gitter, Sandy Lu, and Brock Erdahl, "China Will Do Anything to Deflect Coronavirus Blame," *Foreign Policy*, March 30, 2020, https://foreignpolicy.com/2020/03/30/beijing-coronavirus-response-see-what-sticks-propaganda-blame-ccp-xi-jinping/.

22 Philip Ball, "Three Years On, Covid Lab-Leak Theories Aren't Going Away. This Is Why," *Prospect*, January 25, 2023, https://www.prospectmagazine.co.uk/politics/60415/three-years-on-covid-lab-leak-theories-arent-going-away.-this-is-why; Carolyn Korman, "The Mysterious Case of the Covid-19 Lab Leak Theory," *New Yorker*, October 12, 2021, https://www.newyorker.com/science/elements/the-mysterious-case-of-the-covid-19-lab-leak-theory; Ainsley Hawthorn, "Germ Warfare: Weaponizing an Illness Is Older Than You Might Think," *CBC News*, June 6, 2021, https://www.cbc.ca/news/canada/newfoundland-labrador/apocalypse-then-germ-warfare-1.6052178; Amy Maxmen and Smirti Mallapaty, "The COVID Lab-Leak Hypothesis: What Scientists Do and Don't Know," *Nature*, June 8, 2021, https://www.nature.com/articles/d41586-021-01529-3; John Ruwitch, "Theory that COVID Came From a Chinese Lab Takes On New Life in Wake of WHO Report," *NPR News*, March 31, 2021, https://www.npr.org/2021/03/31/983156340/theory-that-covid-came-from-a-chinese-lab-takes-on-new-life-in-wake-of-who-repor.

23 Compare DNI, "(U) Potential Links Between the Wuhan Institute of Virology and the Origin of the COVID-19 Pandemic," June 2023, https://www.dni.gov/files/ODNI/documents/assessments/Report-on-Potential-Links-Between-the-Wuhan-Institute-of-Virology-and-the-Origins-of-COVID-19-20230623.pdf, with John Ratcliffe and Cliff Sims, "The CIA Politicizes Intelligence on China and Covid: A Whistleblower Says That Analysis Who Favored The Lab-Leak Theory Were Paid to Change Positions," *Wall Street Journal*, September 28, 2023, https://www.wsj.com/articles/the-cia-politicizes-intelligence-on-china-whistleblower-covid-election-interference-trump-f74806c3, and Michael R. Gordon, "U.S.-Funded Scientist Among Three Chinese Researchers Who Fell Ill amid Early Covid-19 Outbreak: Identification of Three Who Worked at Wuhan Institute of Virology Fuels Suspicion for Proponents of Lab-Leak Theory," *Wall Street Journal*, June 20, 2023, https://www.wsj.com/articles/u-s-funded-scientist-among-three-chinese-researchers-who-fell-ill-amid-early-covid-19-outbreak-3f919567?st=oxvsxxumanans8w&reflink=desktopwebshare_permalink.

24 Amy Hawkins, "Covid Lab Leak Theory Should Not Be Ruled Out, Top Chinese Scientist Says," *The Guardian*, May 30, 2023, https://www.theguardian.com/world/2023/may/30/covid-lab-leak-theory-should-not-be-ruled-out-chinese-scientist?CMP=Share_AndroidApp_Other; John Sudworth and Simon Maybin, "Covid: Top Chinese Scientist Says Don't Rule Out Lab Leak," *BBC News*, May 29, 2023, https://www.bbc.com/news/world-asia-65708746.

25 Compare Neil L. Harrison and Jeffrey D. Sachs, "A Call for an Independent Inquiry into the Origin of the SARS-CoV-2 Virus," *Proceedings of the National Academy of Sciences*, May 19, 2022, https://www.pnas.org/doi/10.1073/pnas.2202769119; and Michael Worobey, Joshua I. Levy, Lorena Malpica Serrano, Alexander Crits-Christoph, Jonathan E. Pekar, Stephen A. Goldstein, Angela L. Rasmussen, et al., "The Huanan Seafood Wholesale Market in Wuhan Was the Early Epicenter of the COVID-19 Pandemic," *Science*, July 20, 2022, https://www.science.org/doi/10.1126/science.abp8715. Also see Jamie Matzl and Matt Pottinger, "We Still Don't Know the Truth About Covid: Congress Should Establish a Bipartisan National Commission of Inquiry into the Pandemic's Origins," *Wall Street Journal*, February 8, 2023, https://www.wsj.com/articles/we-still-dont-know-the-truth-about-covid-wuhan-lab-virology-pandemic-source-gain-of-function-who-research-accountability-china-congress-11675893326?mod=opinion_lead_pos5.

26 Claire Klobucista, "Will the World Ever Solve the Mystery of COVID-19's Origin?" backgrounder, Council on Foreign Relations, November 3, 2021, https://www.cfr.org/backgrounder/will-world-ever-solve-mystery-covid-19s-origin; Jamie P. Horsley, "Let's End the COVID-19 Blame Game: Reconsidering China's Role in the Pandemic," Brookings, August 20, 2020, https://www.brookings.edu/blog/order-from-chaos/2020/08/19/lets-end-the-covid-19-blame-game-reconsidering-chinas-role-in-the-pandemic/.

27 Katherine Eban, "'This Shouldn't Happen': Inside the Virus-Hunting Nonprofit at the Center of the Lab Leak Controversy," *Vanity Fair,* March 31, 2022, https://www.vanityfair.com/news/2022/03/the-virus-hunting-nonprofit-at-the-center-of-the-lab-leak-controversy?utm_source=China+Leadership+Monitor+new+issue+alert&utm_campaign=379549f837-EMAIL_CAMPAIGN_2019_09_05_04_36_COPY_01&utm_medium=email&utm_term=0_4ca9bcd56f-379549f837-74126902. Compare "Testimony of Dr. Kristian G. Andersen PhD, Professor Scripps Research Before the Select Subcommittee on the Coronavirus Pandemic," July 11, 2023, https://oversight.house.gov/wp-content/uploads/2023/07/Testimony-of-Dr.-Kristian-Andersen.pdf; Jonathan E. Pekar, Andrew Magee, Edyth Parker, Niema Moshiri, Katherine Izhikevich, Jennifer L. Havens, et al., "SARS-CoV-2 Emergence Very Likely Resulted from At Least Two Zoonotic Events," *Zenodo,* February 26, 2022, https://zenodo.org/record/6291628#.YiZmWS-cbkI; and Michael Worobey, Joshua I. Levy, Lorena Malpica Serrano, Alexander Crits-Christoph, Jonathan E. Pekar, Stephen A. Goldstein, Angela L. Rasmussen, et al., "The Huanan Market Was the Epicenter of SARS-CoV-2 Emergence," *Zenodo,* February 26, 2022, https://zenodo.org/record/6299600#.YiZmyC-cbkI, with Xu Luyi and Wan An, "Yanjiu: Huanan haixian shichang de xinguan bingdu huolai ziren er fei dongwu" [Research: the coronavirus at the Huanan seafood market may have come from humans, not animals], *Caixin,* March 3, 2022, https://webcache.googleusercontent.com/search?q=cache:h3MceTV4j7QJ:https://www.caixin.com/2022-03-03/101849956.html+&cd=1&hl=en&ct=clnk&gl=us (accessed December 7, 2023, and subsequently removed).

28 Michael Safi and Eli Block, "'Being Truthful Is Essential': Scientist Who Stumbled Upon Wuhan Covid Data Speaks Out," *The Guardian,* March 28, 2023, https://www.theguardian.com/world/2023/mar/28/being-truthful-is-essential-scientist-who-stumbled-upon-wuhan-covid-data-speaks-out?CMP=Share_AndroidApp_Other; Katherine J. Wu, "A Major Clue to COVID's Origins Is Just Out of Reach," *The Atlantic,* March 21, 2023, https://www.theatlantic.com/science/archive/2023/03/covid-pandemic-origins-missing-evidence-debate/673460/; Katherine J. Wu, "The Strongest Evidence Yet That an Animal Started the Pandemic," *The Atlantic,* March 16, 2023, https://www.theatlantic.com/science/archive/2023/03/covid-origins-research-raccoon-dogs-wuhan-market-lab-leak/673390/.

29 Bryan Walsh, "The Key to Covid's Origins Lies in Beijing, Not Wuhan," *Vox,* March 18, 2023, https://www.vox.com/future-perfect/2023/3/18/23644776/covid-origin-raccoon-dog-beijing-wuhan-coronavirus-zoonotic-lab-leak-sars; Jon Cohen, "'It's Inexcusable.' WHO Blasts China for Not Disclosing Potential Data on COVID-19's Origins," *ScienceInsider,* March 17, 2023, https://www.science.org/content/article/it-s-inexcusable-who-blasts-china-not-disclosing-potential-data-covid-19-s-origin; Caitlin Owens and Alison Snyder, "The Missing Evidence in the COVID Origins Debate," *Axios,* March 3, 3023, https://www.axios.com/2023/03/02/missing-evidence-covid-origins.

30 Compare Alexandre Silberman, "Where Did COVID-19 Originate? Saskatoon Lab Helps with Genetic Analysis That Points to Animal Market," *CBC News,* November 20, 2024, https://www.cbc.ca/news/canada/saskatoon/where-did-covid-19-originate-saskatoon-lab-helps-with-genetic-analysis-that-points-to-animal-market-1.7386847, with Michael R. Gordon and Warren P. Strobel, "Behind Closed Doors: The Spy-World Scientists Who Argued Covid Was a Lab Leak," *Wall Street Journal,* December 26, 2024, https://www.wsj.com/politics/national-security/fbi-covid-19-pandemic-lab-leak-theory-dfbd8a51?st=bh65Yq&reflink=desktopwebshare_permalink, and "Lab Leak Most Likely Origin of Covid-19 Pandemic, Energy Department Now Says."

31 Lee Kyung-tak, "Biden Directs Agencies to Re-investigate COVID-19 Origins Before Retirement," *Chosun Biz,* January 18, 2025, https://biz.chosun.com/en/en-international/2025/01/18/G3E5RYMSC5GYNFRKMF5GDFZBDA/; "White House Commissions Review of Coronavirus Origins Ahead of Trump's Arrival," January 17, 2025, https://www.washingtonpost.com/health/2025/01/17/covid-origin-biden-commission-jake-sullivan/.

32 David Klepper, "The CIA Believes COVID Most Likely Originated from a Lab but Has Low Confidence in Its Own Finding," *Associated Press,* January 26, 2025, https://apnews.com/article/covid-cia-trump-china-pandemic-lab-leak-9ab7e84c626fed68ca13c8d2e453dde1; Holly Honderich, "CIA Says Lab Leak Most Likely Source of Covid Outbreak," *BBC News,* January 25, 2025, https://www.bbc.com/news/articles/cd9qjjj4zy5o.

33 Daniel Engber, "Trump Thinks He Knows What Started the Pandemic," *The Atlantic,* May 20, 2025, https://www.theatlantic.com/science/archive/2025/05/lab-leak-pandemic-trump-maga/

682854/; White House, "Lab Leak: The True Origins of Covid-19," April 18, 2025, https://www.whitehouse.gov/lab-leak-true-origins-of-covid-19/.

34 WHO, "WHO Scientific Advisory Group Issues Report on Origins of COVID-19," news release, June 27, 2025, https://www.who.int/news/item/27-06-2025-who-scientific-advisory-group-issues-report-on-origins-of-covid-19; "Origins of Covid-19 Still Unclear, According to Final Report from WHO Expert Group," *CBC News,* June 27, 2025, https://www.cbc.ca/news/health/covid-19-origins-report-1.7572830.

35 Austin Ramzy, "China's Zero-Covid Approach Explained," *New York Times,* September 8, 2022, https://www.nytimes.com/2022/09/08/world/asia/china-zero-covid-explainer.html; Bill Bishop, "Standing Committee Doubles Down on 'Dynamic Zero-Covid' and Calls for Struggle Against Doubters," *Sinocism* (blog), May 5, 2022, https://sinocism.com/p/standing-committee-doubles-down-on; "EXPLAINER: Why Are China's Covid Rules So Strict?" *Associated Press,* November 29, 2022, https://apnews.com/article/why-china-covid-rules-so-strict-bba6e93e5e5ef8b47fc2251a95a6b2a5; "China Covid: The Politics Driving the Hellish Lockdowns," *BBC News,* October 20, 2022, https://www.bbc.com/news/world-asia-china-63310524.

36 "Zhonghua renmin gongheguo guojia weisheng jiankang weiyuanhui gonggao 2020 nian di yi hao" [Notice from the People's Republic of China State Health Commission, 2020, no. 1], January 20, 2020, https://www.gov.cn/zhengce/zhengceku/2020-01/21/content_5471164.htm. Congressional Executive Commission on China (CECC), "Zhonghua renmin gongheguo zhuanranbing fangzhi fa" [Law on prevention and control of infectious diseases of the People's Republic of China], August 28, 2004, Articles 3, 4, 41–42, https://www.cecc.gov/resources/legal-provisions/law-on-the-prevention-and-control-of-infectious-diseases-chinese-text. English translation appears at http://www.npc.gov.cn/zgrdw/englishnpc/Law/2007-12/12/content_1383919.htm.

37 WHO, "COVID-19. Ukraine & Other Global Health Issues Virtual Press Conference Transcript – 10 May 2022," especially at minute 00:46:40, https://www.who.int/publications/m/item/covid-19--ukraine---other-global-health-issues-virtual-press-conference-transcript---10-may-2022.

38 Bethany Allen-Ebrahimian, "China's COVID Storm," *Axios,* November 26, 2022, https://www.axios.com/2022/11/26/china-covid-outbreak-lockdown-economy; Frances Mao and Patrick Jackson, "China Covid: Record Number of Cases of Virus Surges Nationwide," *BBC News,* November 24, 2022, https://www.bbc.com/news/world-asia-china-63739617.

39 "Covid in China: Chengdu Lockdown After Outbreak," *BBC News,* September 1, 2022, https://www.bbc.com/news/world-asia-china-62751295; Helen Davidson and Vincent Ni, "Shanghai's Full Covid Lockdown Ends After Two Months," *The Guardian,* May 31, 2022, https://www.theguardian.com/world/2022/may/31/shanghai-starts-to-dismantle-fences-as-covid-lockdown-due-to-end.

40 "Beijing in Lockdown as China Hits COVID-19 Case Record," *CBC News,* November 24, 2022, https://www.cbc.ca/news/world/china-coronavirus-lockdown-beijing-1.6662651; Rebecca Falconer, "China Locks Down Key iPhone City as Daily COVID Cases Hit Record High," *Axios,* November 24, 2022, https://www.axios.com/2022/11/24/china-iphone-city-lockdown-covid-record.

41 Wang Xiangwei, "Xian's Covid-19 Chaos Exposes Dark Side of China's Top-Down Governing Approach," *South China Morning Post,* January 15 2022, https://www.scmp.com/week-asia/opinion/article/3163443/xians-covid-19-chaos-exposes-dark-side-chinas-top-down-governing?utm_source=email&utm_medium=share_widget&utm_campaign=3163443; "Chinese Officials Punished Over COVID Outbreak That Led to Xian Lockdown," *Reuters,* December 24, 2021, https://www.reuters.com/world/china/china-reports-87-new-covid-19-cases-dec-23-vs-100-day-earlier-2021-12-24/; "Xi'an: Chinese City Under Lockdown as Covid Cases Rise," *BBC News,* December 22, 2021, https://www.bbc.com/news/world-asia-china-59743487.

42 "China Locks Down Shenzhen, Province of 24 Million Over Covid," *Bloomberg,* March 14, 2022, https://www.bloomberg.com/news/articles/2022-03-13/china-places-all-shenzhen-residents-under-lockdown-afp.

43 Helen Davidson, "China Locks Down Province of 24m as New Covid Infections Rise," *The Guardian,* March 14, 2022, https://www.theguardian.com/world/2022/mar/14/china-locks-down-province-of-24m-as-new-covid-infections-rise.

44 Bethany Allen-Ebrahimian, "A Modern City Starves," *Axios,* April 22, 2022, https://www.axios.com/shanghai-china-covid-lockdowns-1a3c4bb0-c76d-4a60-bf35-f997dd880ad6.html;

"Shanghai Lockdown Tests China's 'Zero-COVID' Limits," *CBC News*, March 29, 2022, https://www.cbc.ca/news/world/china-shanghai-covid-pandemic-lockdown-1.6400881.

45 Jonathan Guyer, "What Happens When Omicron Hits China," *Vox*, December 24, 2021, https://www.vox.com/22850441/covid-omicron-china-lockdown-olympics-travel-ban; Yuan Zhang, Chong You, Xin Gai, and Xiaohua Zhou, "Perspectives: On Coexistence with COVID-19: Estimations and Perspectives," *CCDC Weekly* 3, 50 (2021): 1057–61, http://weekly.chinacdc.cn/en/article/doi/10.46234/ccdcw2021.245; Donald Low, "Beijing's Insistence on Zero-Covid Strategy Challenged Long-Held Assumptions About China," *South China Morning Post*, October 22, 2021, https://www.scmp.com/week-asia/opinion/article/3153262/beijings-insistence-zero-covid-strategy-challenges-long-held; Yanzhong Huang, "China's Immunity Gap: The Zero-COVID Strategy Leaves the Country Vulnerable to an Omicron Tsunami," *Foreign Affairs*, January 26, 2022, https://www.foreignaffairs.com/articles/china/2022-01-26/chinas-immunity-gap.

46 "'Voices of April': China's Internet Erupts in Protest Against Censorship of Shanghai Lockdown Video," *CTV News*, April 25, 2022, https://www.ctvnews.ca/world/article/voices-of-april-chinas-internet-erupts-in-protest-against-censorship-of-shanghai-lockdown-video/; "2022: Chinese Law Prof's Lament and Encouragement," *David Cowhig's Translation Blog*, January 29, 2022, https://gaodawei.wordpress.com/2022/01/29/2022-chinese-law-profs-lament-and-encouragement/; Bart W. Édes and Danielle Goldfarb, "China Has Hit an Inflection Point in Its Zero-Covid Policies," Asia Pacific Foundation of Canada, November 10, 2021, https://www.asiapacific.ca/publication/china-has-hit-inflection-point-its-zero-covid-policies; Helen Davidson and Vincent Ni, "'People Are Starting to Wane': China's Zero-Covid Policy Takes Toll," *The Guardian*, October 30, 2021, https://www.theguardian.com/world/2021/oct/30/people-are-starting-to-wane-china-zero-covid-policy-takes-toll?CMP=Share_AndroidApp_Other.

47 Larry Elliott, "Rise in Covid Cases Slows Manufacturing in China to Weakest in Two Years," *The Guardian*, January 31, 2022, https://www.theguardian.com/world/2022/jan/31/rise-in-covid-cases-slows-manufacturing-in-china-to-weakest-in-two-years?CMP=Share_AndroidApp_Other; Phelim Kine, "China's 'Zero Covid Strategy' Chokes U.S.-China Ties," *Politico*, December 7, 2021, https://www.politico.com/news/2021/12/07/us-china-covid-strategy-523843; K. Oanh Ha and Jack Wittels, "China's Covid Zero Policy Towards Seafarers Escalates Supply Chain Crisis," *gCaptain*, November 24, 2021, https://gcaptain.com/chinas-covid-zero-policy-seafarers-escalates-supply-chain-crisis/.

48 "China Study Warns of 'Colossal' COVID Outbreak if It Opens Up Like U.S., France," *Reuters*, November 28, 2021, https://www.reuters.com/world/china/china-study-warns-colossal-covid-outbreak-if-it-opens-up-like-us-france-2021-11-28/.

49 Editorial Board, "Opinion: In Hong Kong, China's 'Covid Zero' Strategy Is Falling Apart," *Washington Post*, February 19, 2022, https://www.washingtonpost.com/opinions/2022/02/19/china-covid-zero-strategy-falling-apart-hong-kong/; Tony Cheung, Lillian Cheng, and Gary Cheung, "Coronavirus Hong Kong: Xi Jinping Puts City Government on Notice, Instructs It to Bear 'Main Responsibility' to Contain Spiralling Health Crisis, Focus on Social Stability," *South China Morning Post*, February 16, 2022, https://www.scmp.com/news/hong-kong/health-environment/article/3167192/coronavirus-hong-kong-xi-jinping-says-stabilising?module=inline&pgtype=article.

50 Courtney Brown, "China's Economy Grows at Slowest Pace Since 2020 as Lockdowns Bite," *Axios*, July 14, 2022, https://www.axios.com/2022/07/15/china-economy-pandemic-lockdown; Asia Pacific Foundation of Canada, "COVID-19 Outbreaks and Responses Rattle Zero-Tolerant China," *Asia Watch*, May 12, 2022, https://www.asiapacific.ca/asia-watch/covid-19-outbreaks-and-responses-rattle-zero-tolerant-china: Jeremy Mark and Michael Schuman, *China's Faltering "Zero COVID" Policy: Politics in Command, Economy in Reverse* (Washington, DC: Atlantic Council, 2022), https://www.atlanticcouncil.org/in-depth-research-reports/report/chinas-faltering-zero-covid-policy-politics-in-command-economy-in-reverse/?mkt_tok=NjU5LVdaWC0wNzUAAAGEd8gx-1NDAx66bWxF52EFsu7Ezwm98P_Oe1WLp-tNzvZoYQMVZwF09CNq9hK1cKyIC-fGtm4k2uIPuVCEiF0f1Niqpsnxw8ZakNQq4eSgkg; Vincent Ni, "'Do Whatever It Takes': Beijing Urged to Act as China's Economy Falters," *The Guardian*, May 20, 2022, https://www.theguardian.com/world/2022/may/20/do-whatever-it-takes-beijing-urged-to-act-as-china-economy-falters.

51 "Li Keqiang dui quanguo wenjiuye gongzuo dianshi dianhua hui zuochu zhongyao pishi" [Li Keqiang gave important instructions on the national video and telephone conference on

stabilizing employment], May 7, 2022, http://www.gov.cn/xinwen/2022-05/07/content_5689087.htm.

52 "Li Keqiang zai quanguo wenzhu jingji dapan dianshi dianhua he shang zuo zhongyao jianghua Han Zheng zhuchi" [Li Keqiang delivered an important speech at the national video and telephone conference on stabilizing the economy, Han Zheng chairs], May 25, 2022, http://www.gov.cn/xinwen/2022-05/25/content_5692298.htm.

53 State Council of the People's Republic of China, "China Holds Central Economic Work Conference to Plan for 2023," December 17, 2022, https://english.www.gov.cn/news/topnews/202212/17/content_WS639d0051c6d0a757729e4885.html.

54 Yanzhong Huang, "Can Xi Jinping Reopen China? Ending the Havoc of Zero COVID – Without Causing a Crisis," *Foreign Affairs,* October 7, 2022, https://www.foreignaffairs.com/china/can-xi-jinping-reopen-china; Steve McDonell, "Zero Covid Holds Danger for China's Xi," *BBC News,* July 8, 2022, https://www.bbc.com/news/world-asia-china-62046521; Helen Davidson, "As China Looks On at a World Opening Up, Can Xi Jinping Survive Zero-Covid?" *The Guardian,* April 29, 2022, https://www.theguardian.com/world/2022/apr/29/china-xi-jinping-zero-covid-lockdown-vaccination?CMP=Share_AndroidApp_Other.

55 Xi Jinping, "Hold High the Great Banner of Socialism with Chinese Characteristics and Strive in Unity to Build a Modern Socialist Country in All Respects" (full text of the report to the 20th National Congress of the Communist Party of China, October 16, 2022), https://www.idcpc.org.cn/english2023/tjzl/cpcjj/20thPartyCongrssReport/; Yvette Tan, Tessa Wong, and Stephen McDonell, "China Congress: Xi Doubles Down on Zero-Covid as Meeting Opens," *BBC News,* October 16, 2022, https://www.bbc.com/news/world-asia-china-63226230; Stephen McDonell, "Xi Jinping Speech: Zero-Covid and Zero Solutions," *BBC News,* October 16, 2022, https://www.bbc.com/news/world-asia-china-63274391.

56 Herb Scribner, "China's COVID Frustration Boils Over, Protestors Call for Xi to Resign," *Axios,* November 27, 2022, https://www.axios.com/2022/11/26/china-protests-covid-lockdowns; Stephen McDonell, "China Zero Covid: Violent Protests in Guangzhou Put Curbs Under Strain," *BBC News,* November 15, 2022, https://www.bbc.com/news/world-asia-china-63633109.

57 Tessa Wong and Nathan Williams, "China Covid: Protests Continue in Major Cities Across the Country," *BBC News,* November 27, 2022, https://www.bbc.com/news/world-asia-63771109; Eddy Wax, "Protests Against Zero-COVID Policy Spread Across China in Challenge to Beijing," *Politico,* November 27, 2022, https://www.politico.eu/article/anti-lockdown-coronavirus-protests-spread-across-china-zero-covid/; "Protesters Call for Xi to Resign amid Unprecedented Unrest Over China's COVID-19 Measures," *CBC News,* November 27, 2022, https://www.cbc.ca/news/world/china-protest-covid-1.6665822; James FitzGerald and Sophie Williams, "China Xinjiang: Urumqi Rocked by Covid Lockdown Protests After Deadly Fire," *BBC News,* November 26, 2022, https://www.bbc.com/news/world-asia-china-63766125.

58 Matt Murphy, "China's Protests: Blank Paper Becomes the Symbol of Rare Demonstrations," *BBC News,* November 28, 2022, https://www.bbc.com/news/world-asia-china-63778871.

59 Evan Dyer, "China Eases 'Zero-COVID' Rules Following Protests – but Xi May Have Painted Himself into a Corner," *CBC News,* December 3, 2022, https://www.cbc.ca/news/politics/china-zero-covid-xi-1.6672804; Michael Shuman, "China's Zero Tolerance for Xi's COVID Restrictions," *The Atlantic,* November 28, 2022, https://www.theatlantic.com/international/archive/2022/11/china-zero-covid-protests-xi-jinping-shanghai-beijing/672278/; Dake Kang, "China's Xi Faces Threat from Public Anger over 'Zero Covid,'" *Associated Press,* November 28, 2022, https://apnews.com/article/health-china-arrests-beijing-xi-jinping-1596604782d165d268d1dbc137034749; Terril Yue Jones, "What the Tiananmen Protest Can Tell Us About China's Zero-Covid Unrest," *Politico,* November 27, 2022, https://www.politico.com/news/magazine/2022/12/06/tiananmen-protest-china-zero-covid-00072430. The calls for Xi to step down (*Xi Jinping xia tai* // 习近平下台) echoed with striking precision calls made during the 1989 Tiananmen protests for the Politburo to step down (*Zhengzhi ju xiatai* // 政治局下台).

60 Ivana Saris and Han Chen, "China Entering 'New Stage' of COVID Response, Senior Official Says," *Axios,* December 1 2022, https://www.axios.com/2022/12/01/china-covid-protests-new-stage; Helen Davidson, "Rumours of Zero-Covid Easing Spread in China amid Anger at Restrictions," *The Guardian,* November 4, 2022, https://www.theguardian.com/world/2022/nov/04/rumours-of-zero-covid-easing-spread-in-china-amid-anger-at-restrictions?CMP=Share_AndroidApp_Other; Katherine J. Wu, "China's COVID Wave Is Coming," *The*

Atlantic, December 6, 2022, https://www.theatlantic.com/health/archive/2022/12/china-zero-covid-wave-immunity-vaccines/672375/.

61 Herb Scribner, "China Begins Loosening Covid Restrictions After Massive Protests," *Axios,* December 3, 2022, https://www.axios.com/2022/12/03/china-covid-restrictions-end-zero-covid-protests; "China Eases Some Anti-Virus Restrictions amid Public Anger," *CBC News,* December 1, 2022, https://www.cbc.ca/news/world/china-protests-covid-restrictions-1.6670469.

62 "Guanyu jinyibu youhua luoshi xinguan feiyan yiqing fankong cuosho de tongzhi: Lianfang liankong jizhi zongfa [2022] 113 hao" [Notice on further optimizing the implementation of prevention and control measures of the novel corona pneumonia epidemic, document (2022) #113 issued by the Joint Prevention and Control Mechanism, December 7, 2022], https://www.gov.cn/xinwen/2022-12/07/content_5730443.htm.

63 Compare "Guanyu jinyibu youhua luoshi xinguan feiyan yiqing fankong cuosho de tongzhi: Lianfang liakong jizji zongfa [2022] 113 hao" [Notice on further optimizing the implementation of prevention and control measures of the novel corona pneumonia epidemic, document (2022) #113 issued by the Joint Prevention and Control Mechanism, December 7, 2022] with "Zhonggong zhongyang zhengzhiju changwu weiyuanhui zhaokai huiyi, tingqu xinguan feiyan yiqing fangkong gongzuo huibao, yanjiu bushu jinyibu youhua fangkong gonzuo de ershi tiao cuoshi, Zhonggon zhangyang shuji Xi Jinping zhuchi huiyi" [CPC Politburo Standing Committee meets, hears report on COVID-19 prevention and control work, study and deploy the twenty measures on further optimizing prevention and control work, CPC Politburo General Secretary Xi Jinping chairs meeting], November 20, 2022, http://www.news.cn/politics/2022-11/10/c_1129118595.htm.

64 Emma Graham-Harrison, "Fears of Deadly Infection Surge as China Abandons Zero-Covid Policy," *The Guardian,* December 4, 2022, https://www.theguardian.com/world/2022/dec/04/fears-of-deadly-infection-surge-as-china-abandons-zero-covid-policy?CMP=Share_Android App_Other.

65 Yanzhong Huang, "China's Hidden COVID Catastrophe: How Xi Obscured a Lethal Viral Wave – and What It Means for the Future of His Regime," *Foreign Affairs,* February 16, 2023, https://www.foreignaffairs.com/china/chinas-hidden-covid-catastrophe; Isabel Hinton, "Xi Jinping's Reputation in China and His Standing in the World May Not Survive This Covid Disaster," *The Guardian,* January 1, 2023, https://www.theguardian.com/commentisfree/2023/jan/01/xi-jinpings-reputation-in-china-and-his-standing-in-the-world-may-not-survive-this-covid-disaster?CMP=Share_AndroidApp_Other; Edward White, "Xi Jinping's Credibility 'Badly Wounded' as China's Covid Death Toll Mounts," *Financial Times,* December 31, 2022, https://www.ft.com/content/fb879510-c2bb-4a04-8e36-182078ae15ec; Michael Schuman, "Zero Covid's Failure Is Xi's Failure," *The Atlantic,* December 10, 2022, https://www.theatlantic.com/international/archive/2022/12/zero-covids-failure-is-xi-jinpings-failure/672422/.

66 Richard Baum, *Burying Mao: Chinese Politics in the Age of Deng Xiaoping* (Princeton, NJ: Princeton University Press, 1994), chs. 1 and 12.

67 Frank Dikötter, *Mao's Great Famine: The History of China's Most Devastating Catastrophe, 1958–62* (New York: Walker, 2010); Roderick MacFarquhar, *The Origins of the Cultural Revolution, Book 2: The Great Leap Forward (1958–1960)* (New York: Columbia University Press, 1983), and *The Origins of the Cultural Revolution, Book 3: The Coming of the Cataclysm 1961–1966* (Oxford/New York: Oxford University Press/Columbia University Press, 1997).

68 Helen Davidson, "Eight in 10 People in China Caught Covid Since Early December, Say Officials," *The Guardian,* January 23, 2023, https://www.theguardian.com/world/2023/jan/23/80-of-people-in-china-caught-covid-since-early-december-say-officials?CMP=Share_AndroidApp_Other; "WHO 'Very Concerned' About Reports of Severe COVID in China," *Associated Press,* December 21, 2022, https://apnews.com/article/health-china-covid-world-organization-ecea4b11f845070554ba832390fb6561; Michaeleen Doucleff and A. Martinez, "COVID Spreading Faster Than Ever in China, 800 Million Could Be Infected This Winter," *NPR,* December 15, 2022, https://www.npr.org/sections/goatsandsoda/2022/12/15/1143002538/china-appears-to-be-facing-what-could-be-the-world-s-largest-coronavirus-outbrea.

69 Stephen McDonell, "China Covid: Coffins Sell Out as Rural Losses Mount," *BBC News,* January 26, 2023, https://www.bbc.com/news/world-asia-china-64347085; Samuel Oakford, Lily Kuo, Vic Chiang, and Lyric Li, "Satellite Images Show Crowds at China's Crematoriums as Covid Surges," *Washington Post,* January 9, 2023, https://www.washingtonpost.com/investigations/

2023/01/09/china-crematorium-covid-deaths/; Dake Kang, "Packed ICUs, Crowded Crematoriums: COVID Roils Chinese Towns," *Associated Press,* December 26, 2022, https://apnews.com/article/health-china-beijing-covid-d0718b53ded7fb1a70c2db8e564ed072; Asia Pacific Foundation of Canada, "China's Health-Care System on the Brink as COVID-19 Patients Flood Hospitals," *Asia Watch,* December 22, 2022, https://www.asiapacific.ca/publication/chinas-health-care-system-brink-covid-19-patients-flood; Gu Ting, "Funeral Homes Operating Around the Clock in COVID-Hit Beijing: Employees," *Radio Free Asia,* December 4, 2022, https://www.rfa.org/english/news/china/china-covid-update-12142022134038.html.

70 Dezan Shira and Associates Staff, "China Reopening After COVID: Latest Developments and Business Advisory," *China Briefing,* January 9, 2023, https://www.china-briefing.com/news/china-coronavirus-updates-latest-developments-business-advisory-part-2; Virginia Harrison, Carly Earl, and Michael Wade, "From Zero-Tolerance into the Unknown – a Visual Guide to Three Years of Covid in China," *The Guardian,* December 15, 2022, https://www.theguardian.com/world/2022/dec/15/from-zero-tolerance-into-the-unknown-a-visual-guide-to-three-years-of-covid-in-china?CMP=Share_AndroidApp_Other.

71 Helen Davidson, "Chinese Warned Not to Visit Elderly Relatives as Covid Spreads from Cities," *The Guardian,* January 12, 2023, https://www.theguardian.com/world/2023/jan/12/chinese-warned-not-visit-elderly-relatives-covid-spreads-cities?CMP=Share_AndroidApp_Other; Wenxin Fan, "China Reopens to the World as International Travel Restrictions End," *Wall Street Journal,* January 8, 2023, https://www.wsj.com/articles/china-reopens-to-the-world-as-international-travel-restrictions-end-11673154181; Frances Mao and Fan Wang, "China Ends Covid Quarantine for Travellers in January," *BBC News,* December 27, 2022, https://www.bbc.com/news/world-asia-china-64097497.

72 Graham-Harrison, "Fears of Deadly Infection Surge as China Abandons Zero-Covid Policy"; Dennis Normile, "China Is Flying Blind as Pandemic Rages," *ScienceInsider,* January 3, 2023, https://www.science.org/content/article/china-flying-blind-pandemic-rages#.

73 Donna Lu, "Newly Identified Langya Virus Tracked After China Reports Dozens of Cases," *The Guardian,* August 10, 2022, https://www.theguardian.com/science/2022/aug/10/newly-identified-langya-virus-tracked-after-china-reports-dozens-of-cases.

74 "China Says a Surge in Respiratory Illnesses Is Caused by Flu and Other Known Pathogens," *Associated Press,* November 26, 2023, https://apnews.com/article/china-respiratory-illnesses-who-ff6da613bf15d6848f12095b8e0d8fd1; Amy Hawkins, "China Supplies Data to WHO About Clusters of Respiratory Illness," *The Guardian,* November 23 2023, https://www.theguardian.com/world/2023/nov/23/china-respiratory-illness-spike-children-who.

75 Wenxian Liu, Linwei Lu, Cheng Ma, Chen Yan, Zhengxiao Zhao, Nabijan Mohammadtursun, Lingli Hu, et al., "The Evolution of Traditional Chinese Medicine as a Disciplinary Concept and Its Essence Throughout History," *Traditional Medicine and Modern Medicine* 1, 3 (2018): 171–80, https://www.worldscientific.com/doi/pdf/10.1142/S257590001810002X.

76 Abraar Karan and Mishal Khan, "Opinion: The Ghosts of Colonialism Are Haunting the World's Response to the Pandemic," *NPR,* May 29, 2020, https://www.npr.org/sections/goatsandsoda/2020/05/29/862602058/opinion-the-ghosts-of-colonialism-are-haunting-the-worlds-response-to-the-pandem; Walter Bruchhausen, "Global Health in the Colonial Era: The Expansion of European Medicine," *European History Online,* May 15, 2020, http://ieg-ego.eu/en/threads/theories-and-methods/knowledge-transfer/walter-bruchhausen-global-health-in-the-colonial-era-the-expansion-of-european-medicine#section_10.

77 Aurelia Dochnal, "120th Anniversary of Yale-China: Pioneering Equal Partnership in Medicine," *China Hands,* March 7, 2021, https://chinahandsmagazine.org/2021/03/07/120th-anniversary-of-yale-china-the-beginnings-2/; Xiaoping Fang, *Barefoot Doctors and Western Medicine in China* (Rochester, NY: University of Rochester Press, 2012); David Luesink, "Review of *Barefoot Doctors and Western Medicine in China* by Xiaoping Fang," *Pacific Affairs* 87, 30 (September 2014), https://pacificaffairs.ubc.ca/book-reviews/barefoot-doctors-and-western-medicine-in-china-by-xiaoping-fang/.

78 WHO, "Thirteenth General Program of Work 2019–2023: Promote Health, Keep the World Safe, Serve the Vulnerable," 2019, https://iris.who.int/server/api/core/bitstreams/f35461a5-91b1-41b0-8ef8-b4bd66e08449/content.

79 United Nations China, "Our Work on the Sustainable Development Goals in China," 2021, https://china.un.org/en/sdgs.

80 Lawrence O. Gostin et al., "The World Health Organization Was Born as a Normative Agency: Seventy-Five Years of Global Health Law Under WHO Governance," *PLOS Global Public Health* 4. 4 (April 11, 2024), https://pmc.ncbi.nlm.nih.gov/articles/PMC11008771/.
81 Lowy Institute, "Covid Performance Index," January 9, 2021, https://interactives.lowyinstitute.org/features/covid- performance/.
82 Srinivas Mazumdaru, "What Influence Does China Have over the WHO?" *Deutsche Welle,* April 17, 2020, https://www.dw.com/en/what-influence-does-china-have-over-the-who/a-53161220.
83 WHO, "Voluntary Contributions by Fund and by Contributor, 2017," 71st World Health Assembly, Provisional agenda item 15.1, April 19, 2018, A71/INF./2, https://apps.who.int/gb/ebwha/pdf_files/WHA71/A71_INF2-en.pdf; WHO, "Our Contributors: Partnering for a Healthier World," https://www.who.int/about/funding/contributors; HowMuch.net, "World Health Organization Funding in One Map: How Much Each Country Contributes," April 28, 2020, https://howmuch.net/articles/who-contribution.
84 "Top Twenty Contributors," WHO, "WHO Results Report – Programme Budget 2018–2019," https://www.who.int/about/accountability/results/2018-2019.
85 "Top WHO Contributors," WHO, "Our Contributors: Partnering for a Healthier World," https://www.who.int/about/funding/contributors.
86 White House, "Withdrawing the United States from the World Health Organization," Executive Order, January 20, 2025, https://www.whitehouse.gov/presidential-actions/2025/01/withdrawing-the-united-states-from-the-worldhealth-organization/; Ana Faguy and Dominic Hughes, "US Exit from WHO Could See Fifth of Budget Disappear," *BBC News,* January 20, 2025, https://www.bbc.com/news/articles/c391j738rm3o.
87 Hematology Advisor, "China Donates $500M to WHO as U.S. Pulls Back Support," June 2, 2025, https://www.hematologyadvisor.com/news/china-donates-500m-to-who-as-u-s-pulls-back-support/#:~:text=(HealthDay%20News)%20—%20China%20has,become%20the%20group's%20top%20donor.
88 David Dollar, "Reluctant Player: China's Approach to International Economic Institutions," Brookings, September 14, 2020, https://www.brookings.edu/articles/reluctant-player-chinas-approach-to-international-economic-institutions/; Philip Anstren, "The Case for Greater US-EU Collaboration on Taiwan," Atlantic Council, June 30, 2021, https://www.atlanticcouncil.org/blogs/new-atlanticist/the-case-for-greater-us-eu-collaboration-on-taiwan/; Human Rights Watch, "39 Countries at UN Express 'Grave Concerns' About China's Abuses," October 6, 2020, https://www.hrw.org/news/2020/10/06/39-countries-un-express-grave-concerns-about-chinas-abuses.
89 Barbara S. Romzek and Melvin J. Dubnick, "Accountability," in *Defining Public Administration,* ed. Jay M. Shafritz (New York: Routledge, 2020), https://www.taylorfrancis.com/chapters/edit/10.4324/9780429501074-39/accountability-barbara-romzek-melvin-dubnick; Mark Philp, "Delimiting Democratic Accountability," *Political Studies* 57, 1 (2009): 28–53, https://journals.sagepub.com/doi/abs/10.1111/j.1467-9248.2008.00720.x; Andreas Duit and Victor Galaz, "Governance and Complexity: Emerging Issues for Governance Theory," *Governance* 21, 3 (July 9, 2008): 311–35, https://www.stockholmresilience.org/download/18.39aa239f11a8dd8de6b800026687/1459560200739/DuitGalaz_Governance_2008.pdf; Philip G. Cerny, "Globalization, Governance, and Complexity," in *Globalization and Governance,* ed. Jeffrey A. Hart and Aseem Prakash (Abingdon, UK: Routledge, 1999), 188–212, https://www.taylorfrancis.com/books/mono/10.4324/9780203478790/globalization-governance-jeffrey-hart-aseem-prakash.
90 "China Is Firmly Committed to a Path of Human Rights Development That Suits Its National Conditions," September 26, 2021, https://www.fmprc.gov.cn/mfa_eng/wjb/zygy/hd/202406/t20240603_11374881.html.
91 WHO, "Human Rights," December 1, 2023, https://www.who.int/news-room/fact-sheets/detail/human-rights-and-health.
92 Winston Wen-yi Chen, "China's Exclusion of Taiwan from the World Health Assembly Is Detrimental to World Health – Especially During a Pandemic," *iPolitics,* September 30, 2020, https://ipolitics.ca/2020/12/30/chinas-exclusion-of-taiwan-from-the-world-health-assembly-is-detrimental-to-world-health-especially-during-a-pandemic/; Jo Kim, "Taiwan's Success Is the Bane of Beijing's Global Coronavirus Propaganda," *The Diplomat,* April 8, 2020, https://thediplomat.com/2020/04/taiwans-success-is-the-bane-of-beijings-global-coronavirus-propaganda/; Tom Miles, "Shut Out of U.N. Forum, Taiwan Slams China's 'Coercion and

Threats,'" *Reuters,* May 20, 2017, https://www.reuters.com/article/us-taiwan-china-idUS KCN18G0X2.
93 Lowy Institute, "Covid Performance Index."
94 Nathan Vanderklippe, "Margaret Chan Reshaped the WHO and Brought It Closer to CHINA," *Globe and Mail,* June 12, 2020, https://www.theglobeandmail.com/world/article-margaret-chan-reshaped-the-who-and-brought-it-closer-to-china/; Simon Shen, "Borrowing the Hong Kong Identity for Chinese Diplomacy: Implications of Margaret Chan's World Health Organization Campaign," *Pacific Affairs* 81, 3 (2008), https://pacificaffairs.ubc.ca/articles/borrowing-the-hong-kong-identity-for-chinese-diplomacy-implications-of-margaret-chans-world-health-organization-campaign/.
95 WHO, *Leading the Realization of Human Rights to Health and Through Health: Report of the High-Level Working Group on the Health and Human Rights of Women, Children and Adolescents* (Geneva: WHO, 2017), https://www.ohchr.org/Documents/Issues/Women/WRGS/Health/ReportHLWG-humanrights-health.pdf.
96 Geoffrey York, "Questions Surfacing About History of WHO's Director Tedros Adhanom Ghebreyesus," *Globe and Mail,* April 24, 2020, https://www.theglobeandmail.com/world/article-questions-surfacing-about-history-of-whos-director-tedros-adhanom/.
97 "WHO and China: A Healthy Relationship?" *France 24,* March 29, 2021, https://www.france24.com/en/live-news/20210329-who-and-china-a-healthy-relationship; James Palmer, "The WHO Investigation Shows Beijing Still Pulls the Strings," *Foreign Policy,* February 10, 2021, https://foreignpolicy.com/2021/02/10/world-health-organization-investigation-coronavirus-origins-china-propaganda/; Michael Collins, "The WHO and China: Dereliction of Duty," Council on Foreign Relations, February 27, 2020, https://www.cfr.org/blog/who-and-china-dereliction-duty; Hinnerk Feldwisch-Drentrup, "How WHO Became China's Coronavirus Accomplice," *Foreign Policy,* April 2, 2020, https://foreignpolicy.com/2020/04/02/china-coronavirus-who-health-soft-power/.
98 Zhang Hui, "WHO Chief Succumbs to US-Led West's Pressure in Virus Origins Remarks," *Global Times,* July 16, 2021, https://www.globaltimes.cn/page/202107/1228863.shtml.
99 Ian Johnson, "Chinese Medicine in the Covid Wards," *New York Review of Books,* November 4, 2021, https://www.nybooks.com/articles/2021/11/04/traditional-chinese-medicine-covid-wards/; Pratik Jakhar, "Covid-19: China Pushes Traditional Remedies amid Outbreak," *BBC News,* June 29, 2020, https://www.bbc.com/news/world-asia-53094603.
100 Editorial, "The World Health Organization's Decision About Traditional Chinese Medicine Could Backfire," *Nature,* June 5, 2019, https://www.nature.com/articles/d41586-019-01726-1; Editorial, "The World Health Organization Gives the Nod to Chinese Traditional Medicine. Bad Idea," *Scientific American,* April 1, 2019, https://www.scientificamerican.com/article/the-world-health-organization-gives-the-nod-to-traditional-chinese-medicine-bad-idea/.
101 Yanzhong Huang, "The SARS Epidemic and Its Aftermath In China: A Political Perspective," in *Learning from SARS: Preparing for the Next Disease Outbreak: Workshop Summary,* ed. S. Knobler, A. Mahmoud, S. Lemon, et al. (Washington, DC: National Academies Press, 2004), https://www.ncbi.nlm.nih.gov/books/NBK92479/; Thomas Crampton, "W.H.O. Criticizes China over Handling of Mystery Disease," *New York Times,* April 7, 2003, https://www.nytimes.com/2003/04/07/international/asia/who-criticizes-china-over-handling-of-mystery-disease.html; Maria Cheng, "WHO Experts Say Search for COVID-19 Origins Stalled," *Globe and Mail,* August 25, 2021, https://www.theglobeandmail.com/world/article-who-experts-say-search-for-covid-19-origins-has-stalled/; Nicholas West, "How COVID-19's Origins Were Obscured, by the East and the West," *Bulletin of the Atomic Scientists,* August 17, 2021, https://thebulletin.org/2021/08/how-covid-19s-origins-were-obscured-by-the-east-and-the-west/.
102 Florian Schneider, "COVID-19 Nationalism and the Visual Construction of Sovereignty During China's Coronavirus Crisis," *China Information* 35, 3 (2021): 301–24, https://journals.sagepub.com/doi/full/10.1177/0920203X211034692.
103 Priyanka Boghani, "A Timeline of China's Response in the First Days of COVID-19," *Frontline,* February 2, 2021, https://www.pbs.org/wgbh/frontline/article/a-timeline-of-chinas-response-in-the-first-days-of-covid-19/; "A Timeline of COVID-19 Developments in 2020," *AJMC,* January 1, 2021, https://www.ajmc.com/view/a-timeline-of-covid19-developments-in-2020; WHO, "Listings of WHO's Response to COVID-19," June 29, 2020, https://www.who.int/news/item/29-06-2020-covidtimeline; Zunyou Wu and Jennifer McGoogan, "Characteristics of and Important Lessons from the Coronavirus Disease 2019 (COVID-19) Outbreak in China,"

JAMA 323, 13 (February 24, 2020): 1239–42, https://jamanetwork.com/journals/jama/fullarticle/2762130; WHO, "Statement on the Second Meeting of the International Health Regulations (2005) Emergency Committee Regarding the Outbreak of Novel Coronavirus (2019-nCoV)," January 30, 2020, https://www.who.int/news/item/30-01-2020-statement-on-the-second-meeting-of-the-international-health-regulations-(2005)-emergency-committee-regarding-the-outbreak-of-novel-coronavirus-(2019-ncov).

104 WHO, "Report of the WHO-China Joint Mission on Coronavirus Disease (COVID-19)," February 28, 2020, https://www.who.int/publications/i/item/report-of-the-who-china-joint-mission-on-coronavirus-disease-2019-(covid-19).

105 "Premier Li Keqiang Meets the Press: Full Transcript of Questions and Answers," State Council of the People's Republic of China, May 29, 2020, http://english.www.gov.cn/premier/news/202005/29/content_WS5ed058d2c6d0b3f0e9498f21.html.

106 State Council Information Office (SCIO), "Full Text: Fighting COVID-19: China in Action," white paper, June 7, 2020, http://english.scio.gov.cn/whitepapers/2020-06/07/content_76135269.htm.

107 Jeremy Page and Natasha Khan, "On the Ground in Wuhan: Signs of China Stalling Probe of Coronavirus Origins," *Wall Street Journal,* May 12, 2020, https://www.wsj.com/articles/china-stalls-global-search-for-coronavirus-origins-wuhan-markets-investigation-11589300842.

108 Emily Rauhala, Teo Armus, and Gerry Shih, "With Ultimatum, Trump Deepens Crisis with the World Health Organization," *Washington Post,* May 19, 2020, https://www.washingtonpost.com/world/with-ultimatum-trump-deepens-crisis-with-the-world-health-organization/2020/05/19/c037be08-99cf-11ea-ad79-eef7cd734641_story.html.

109 Luca D'Urbino, "Where Did the Novel Coronavirus Come From? China's Opacity Has Allowed Dangerous Conspiracy Theories to Flourish," *The Economist,* May 2, 2020, https://www.economist.com/leaders/2020/05/02/where-did-the-novel-coronavirus-come-from.

110 Verma Patel, "How Omicron, the New Covid-19 Variant, Got Its Name," *New York Times,* November 27, 2021, https://www.nytimes.com/2021/11/27/world/africa/omicron-covid-greek-alphabet.html.

111 Xi Jinping, "Bolstering Confidence and Jointly Overcoming Difficulties to Build a Better World," Ministry of Foreign Affairs of the People's Republic of China (MFA), September 21, 2021, https://www.mfa.gov.cn/eng/xw/zyjh/202405/t20240530_11341561.html.

112 Wang Yi, "China's Diplomacy in 2021: Embracing a Global Vision and Serving the Nation and Its People," address to Symposium on the International Situation and China's Foreign Relations, December 20, 2021, https://www.ciis.org.cn/english/NEWS_183/202112/t20211228_8347.html; MFA, "Ministry of Foreign Affairs Holds Briefing on COVID-19 Origin-Tracing for Diplomatic Envoys in China," August 13, 2021, https://www.mfa.gov.cn/eng/wjb/zygy/hd/202406/t20240603_11374867.html.

113 "Xi Calls for Concerted APEC Efforts to Combat Virus, Accelerate Green Growth, but Avert Forming 'Small Circles,'" *Global Times,* November 11, 2021, https://www.globaltimes.cn/page/202111/1238708.shtml.

114 "China Berates WHO Chief for 'Irresponsible' Remarks on Its Zero-Covid Policy," *The Standard (HK),* May 11, 2022, https://www.thestandard.com.hk/china-news/article/190053/China-berates-WHO-chief-for-irresponsible-remarks-on-its-zero-Covid-policy; Jennifer Rigby and Josephine Mason, "WHO Chief Says China's Zero-COVID Policy Not 'Sustainable,'" *Reuters,* May 10, 2022, https://www.reuters.com/world/china/who-chief-says-chinas-zero-covid-policy-not-sustainable-2022-05-10/.

115 WHO Scientific Advisory Group for the Origins of Novel Pathogens (SAGO), "Preliminary Report of the SAGO," June 9, 2022, https://cdn.who.int/media/docs/default-source/scientific-advisory-group-on-the-origins-of-novel-pathogens/sago-report-09062022.pdf?sfvrsn=42b55bbc_1&download=true; Vincent Ni, "China Calls Theory That Covid Originated in Chinese Lab 'Politically Motivated Lie,'" *The Guardian,* June 10, 2022, https://www.theguardian.com/world/2022/jun/10/china-calls-theory-that-covid-originated-in-chinese-lab-politically-motivated-lie.

116 Xi Jinping, "Hold High the Great Banner of Socialism with Chinese Characteristics and Strive in Unity to Build a Modern Socialist Country in All Respects" (full text of the report to the 20th National Congress of the Communist Party of China, October 16, 2022), https://www.idcpc.org.cn/english2023/tjzl/cpcjj/20thPartyCongrssReport/. But see "Covid Is Complicating China's Efforts to Re-engage with the World," *The Economist,* January 10, 2023, https://www.economist.com/china/2023/01/10/covid-is-complicating-chinas-efforts-to-re-engage-with

-the-world; Nicholas Ross Smith and Tracey Fallon, "An Epochal Moment? The COVID-19 Pandemic and China's International Order Building," *World Affairs* 183, 3 (September 2020): 235–55, https://www.ncbi.nlm.nih.gov/pmc/articles/PMC8263375/.

117 Neil L. Harrison and Jeffrey D. Sachs, "A Call for an Independent Inquiry into the Origin of the SARS-CoV-2 Virus," *Proceedings of the National Academy of Sciences,* May 19, 2022, https://www.pnas.org/doi/10.1073/pnas.2202769119.

118 Kim Sengupta, "China Deliberately Destroyed Evidence About Start of Coronavirus, Report Says," *The Independent,* May 2, 2020, https://www.independent.co.uk/news/world/asia/coronavirus-cause-china-research-evidence-destroyed-a9495856.html; "China Didn't Warn Public of Likely Pandemic for 6 Key Days," *Politico,* April 15, 2020, https://www.politico.com/news/2020/04/15/china-didnt-warn-public-of-likely-pandemic-for-6-key-days-187614; Gao Yu, Peng Yanfeng, Yang Rui, Ma Danmeng, Flynn Murphy, Han Wei, and Timmy Shen, "In Depth: How Early Coronavirus Signs Were Spotted and Throttled," *Caixin,* February 29, 2020, https://www.caixinglobal.com/2020-02-29/in-depth-how-early-signs-of-a-sars-like-virus-were-spotted-spread-and-throttled-101521745.html.

119 Erika Kinetz, "Anatomy of a Conspiracy: With COVID, China Took Leading Role," *Associated Press,* February 14, 2021, https://apnews.com/article/pandemics-beijing-only-on-ap-epidemics-media-122b73e134b780919cc1808f3f6f16e8; Emma Graham-Harrison and Robin McKie, "A Year After the Wuhan Alarm, China Seeks to Change Covid Origin Story," *The Guardian,* November 29, 2020, https://www.theguardian.com/world/2020/nov/29/a-year-after-wuhan-alarm-china-seeks-to-change-covid-origin-story.

120 Stephanie Nebehay, "WHO Proposes Fresh Coronavirus Mission to China and Lab Audits," *Reuters,* July 16, 2021, https://www.reuters.com/world/asia-pacific/who-proposes-fresh-mission-china-lab-audits-diplomats-2021-07-16/; Frank Jordans and Maria Cheng, "WHO Chief Says It Was 'Premature' to Rule Out COVID Lab Leak," *Associated Press,* July 15, 2021, https://apnews.com/article/joe-biden-world-news-health-science-coronavirus-pandemic-c0c594f9060f676c0ea48c2d1c69daec.

121 MFA, "Wang Yi: COVID-19 Needs Origin-Tracing and Political Virus Also Needs Origin-Tracking," July 25, 2021, https://www.fmprc.gov.cn/eng/gjhdq_665435/3265_665445/3286_664530/3288_664534/202406/t20240611_11420513.html.

122 Mark Gollom, "The WHO Hopes Its New Panel Can Determine the Origin of COVID-19. Some Experts Are Skeptical," *CBC News,* October 19, 2021, https://www.cbc.ca/news/health/who-panel-covid-lab-leak-1.6210964; "Covid: New WHO Group May Be Last Chance to Find Virus Origins," *BBC News,* October 13, 2021, https://www.bbc.com/news/health-58905945; Drew Hinshaw and Betsy McKay, "WHO Seeks to Revive Stalled Inquiry into Origins of Covid-19 with New Team," *Wall Street Journal,* September 26, 2021, https://www.wsj.com/articles/who-seeks-to-revive-stalled-inquiry-into-origins-of-covid-19-with-new-team-11632657603.

123 Carlo Martuscelli, "China Hits Back After EU Official Joins Calls for Cooperation on Pandemic Origins Probe," *Politico,* July 28, 2021, https://www.politico.eu/article/china-hits-back-after-eu-official-joins-call-for-cooperation-on-pandemic-origins-probe/.

124 Kathryn Armstrong, "China Covid: EU Officials 'Strongly' Urge Testing for Travel," *BBC News,* January 4, 2023, https://www.bbc.com/news/world-europe-64167061; US Department of State, "Department Press Briefing," January 3, 2023, https://2021-2025.state.gov/briefings/department-press-briefing-january-3-2023/; Ezekiel J. Emanuel, "China's Let-It-Rip Covid Reopening," *Wall Street Journal,* December 22, 2022, https://www.wsj.com/articles/china-goes-from-zero-to-epidemic-in-no-time-covid-vaccines-spread-180-mrna-pfizer-new-year-11671716102.

125 Ken Moritsugu, "Beijing Threatens Response to 'Unacceptable' Virus Measures," *Associated Press,* January 3, 2023, https://apnews.com/article/politics-sports-health-china-beijing-d9b5f0e1520c899ffe6b614135be73a8; "Beijing Condemns Newly Reimposed COVID-19 Travel Requirements for Chinese Travellers," *CBC News,* January 3, 2023, https://www.cbc.ca/news/world/china-who-covid-meeting-1.6702005.

126 Ashleigh Furlong, "How Countries Are Throwing Away Their Best Chance to Prevent the Next Pandemic," *Politico,* May 19, 2023, https://www.politico.eu/article/how-countries-are-throwing-away-their-best-chance-to-prevent-the-next-pandemic-covid-coronavirus/.

127 See generally "A Timeline of the Coronavirus Pandemic," *New York Times,* March 17, 2021, https://www.nytimes.com/article/coronavirus-timeline.html; Boghani, "A Timeline of China's

Response in the First Days of COVID-19"; Robin Muccari, Denise Chow, and Joe Murphy, "Coronavirus Timeline: Tracking the Critical Moments of Covid-19," *NBC News,* January 1, 2021, https://www.nbcnews.com/health/health-news/coronavirus-timeline-tracking-critical-moments-covid-19-n1154341; Alyn Woodward and Susie Neilson, "A Comprehensive Timeline of the Coronavirus Pandemic at 1 Year, from China's First Case to the Present," *Business Insider,* December 24, 2020, https://www.businessinsider.com/coronavirus-pandemic-timeline-history-major-events-2020-3; D. Taylor, "What Did China Do About Early Outbreak," *BBC News,* June 9, 2020, https://www.bbc.com/news/world-52573137; Liwei Zhang, Huijie Li, and Kelin Chen, "Effective Risk Communication for Public Health Emergency: Reflection on the COVID-19 (2019-nCoV) Outbreak in Wuhan, China," *Healthcare* 8, 64 (March 21, 2020), https://www.mdpi.com/2227-9032/8/1/64/pdf; Yoel Kornreich, "China's Response to the Coronavirus Outbreak: From Concealment to 'All-Out-War,'" Asia Pacific Foundation of Canada, February 20, 2020, https://www.asiapacific.ca/publication/chinas-response-coronavirus-outbreak-concealment-all-out-war/.

128 Huang, "The Myth of Authoritarian Superiority." Also see John Nkengasong, "China's Response to the Novel Coronavirus Stands in Stark Contrast to the 2002 SARS Outbreak Response," *Nature Medicine* 26 (2020): 310–11, https://www.nature.com/articles/s41591-020-0771-1; Keyuan Zou, "SARS and the Rule of Law in China," in *The SARS Epidemic: Challenges to China's Crisis Management,* ed. John Wong (Singapore: World Scientific, 2004), 99–122, https://www.worldscientific.com/doi/abs/10.1142/9789812565556_0005.

129 "Zhonghua renmin gongheguo zhuanranbing fangzhi fa" [Law on prevention and control of infectious diseases of the People's Republic of China].

130 "Tufa gonggong weisheng shijian yingji tiaoli" [Regulations on responding to public health emergencies], May 9, 2003, http://www.gov.cn/zwgk/2005-05/20/content_145.htm.

131 "Guojia tufa gonggong weisheng shijian yingji yu'an" [National contingency plan for public health emergencies], January 10, 2006, https://www.nhc.gov.cn/yjb/c100058/200601/c511ded8a67546d0973e482d7ff42f72.shtml.

132 Li Enshen, Lin Xinfen, and Liu Shihong, "'Special Times Call for Special Measures': China's Regulation of COVID-19 Through Criminal Justice Innovation," *China: An International Journal* 21, 1 (February 2023): 1–23, https://muse.jhu.edu/article/884127; Wang Chenguang, "Legal Tools Used in China in the COVID-19 Emergency," *Bill of Health* (blog), May 12, 2020, https://blog.petrieflom.law.harvard.edu/2020/05/12/china-global-responses-covid19/; Qian Jiwei, "China's Health Initiatives in the COVID-19 Outbreak," EAI Background Brief 1511, March 5, 2020, https://research.nus.edu.sg/eai/wp-content/uploads/sites/2/2020/04/EAIBB-No.-1511-Chinas-health-initiatives-in-the-COVID-19-outbreak.pdf.

133 Vaccine Administration Law of the People's Republic of China, June 29, 2019, http://www.lawinfochina.com/display.aspx?id=30707&lib=law.

134 Chris Baraniuk, "What Do We Know About China's Covid-19 Vaccines?" *BMJ* 373, 912 (April 9, 2021), https://www.bmj.com/content/373/bmj.n912; "White Paper Presser: China Is Racing to Develop COVID-19 Vaccines," *China Global Television Network* (*CGTN*), June 7, 2020, https://news.cgtn.com/news/2020-06-07/White-paper-presser-China-is-racing-to-develop-COVID-19-vaccines-R7Jj6fQpcA/index.html.

135 Scott Anderson, Rachel Ward, and Bob McKeown, "How a Failed Deal with China to Produce a Made-in-Canada COVID-19 Vaccine Wasted Months and Millions," *CBC News,* October 14, 2021, https://www.cbc.ca/news/canada/cansino-deal-canada-nrc-fifth-estate-1.6208241.

136 Maria Cheng, "WHO Asks Western Countries to Recognize China's COVID-19 Vaccines," *Global News,* July 1, 2021, https://globalnews.ca/news/7996100/who-decision-covid-vaccines/; Smriti Mallapaty, "China's COVID Vaccines Are Going Global – but Questions Remain," *Nature,* May 12, 2021, https://www.nature.com/articles/d41586-021-01146-0; Sui-Lee Wee, "China Wanted to Show Off Its Vaccines. It's Backfiring," *New York Times,* April 1, 2021, https://www.nytimes.com/2021/01/25/business/china-covid-19-vaccine-backlash.html.

137 Law of the People's Republic of China on Basic Medical and Health Care and the Promotion of Health, December 28, 2019, http://en.moj.gov.cn/2021-06/26/c_636455.htm.

138 SCIO, "China Publishes White Paper on COVID-19 Fight," June 8, 2020, http://english.scio.gov.cn/pressroom/2020-06/08/content_76137321.htm.

139 "Guanyu tuidong yange guifan gongzheng wenming zhifa wei yiqing fangkong gongzuo tigong youli fazhi baozhang de yijian" [Opinion on promoting strictly regulated, just, and civilized law enforcement to provide forceful legal safeguards for epidemic prevention and control work],

February 24, 2020, http://www.gov.cn/zhengce/zhengceku/2020-02/25/content_5483027.htm; English translation at https://www.chinalawtranslate.com/en/just-and-civilized-law-enforcement/.

140 Sarah Biddulph and Ljiljana Biuković, eds., *Good Governance in Economic Development: International Norms and Chinese Perspectives* (Vancouver: UBC Press, 2020), https://www.ubcpress.ca/good-governance-in-economic-development.

141 Pitman B. Potter, *Exporting Virtue? China's International Human Rights Activism in the Age of Xi Jinping* (Vancouver: UBC Press, 2021), 9, 35–36.

142 Paul F. Scotchmer, "Is China Headed for a Clash of Cultures as Xi Jinping Fuses Confucianism and Marx?" *South China Morning Post,* July 27, 2019, https://www.scmp.com/comment/opinion/article/3017929/china-headed-clash-cultures-xi-jinping-fuses-confucius-and-marx; "Xinhua Insight: Drawing on Confucian Wisdom for Better Governance," *Xinhua,* May 1, 2016, http://www.china.org.cn/china/Off_the_Wire/2016-01/05/content_37468802.htm; Jeremy Page, "Why China Is Turning Back to Confucius," *Wall Street Journal,* September 20, 2015, http://www.wsj.com/articles/why-china-is-turning-back-to-confucius-1442754000.

143 Deng Xiaoping, "Jianchi sixiang jiben yuanze" [Uphold the four cardinal principles], Zhongguo gaige xinxi ku [China reform database], March 30, 1979, http://www.reformdata.org/1979/0330/5172.shtml.

144 Xi Jinping, "Secure a Decisive Victory in Building a Moderately Prosperous Society in All Respects and Strive for the Great Success of Socialism with Chinese Characteristics for a New Era" (speech delivered at the 19th National Congress of the CPC, October 18, 2017), 17, https://www.neac.gov.cn/seac/c103372/202201/1156519.shtml.

145 Jerome A. Cohen, "'Rule of Law' with Chinese Characteristics: Evolution and Manipulation," *International Journal of Constitutional Law* 19, 5 (September 7, 2021): 1882–87, https://academic.oup.com/icon/advance-article-abstract/doi/10.1093/icon/moab085/6365813?redirectedFrom=fulltext; Rogier Creemers and Susan Trevaskes, eds., *Law and the Party in China: Ideology and Organization* (Cambridge: Cambridge University Press, 2020), https://www.cambridge.org/core/books/law-and-the-party-in-china/52DF088170800D47194526F8E6681DC9; Eleanor Albert, "Is China Committed to Rule of Law?" (interviewing Elizabeth Economy, October 28, 2014), https://www.cfr.org/interview/china-committed-rule-law; Stanley B. Lubman, "Riding the Tiger: China's Struggle with Rule of Law," *Wall Street Journal,* December 18, 2013, http://blogs.wsj.com/chinarealtime/2013/12/18/riding-the-tiger-chinas-struggle-with-rule-of-law/; Jamie P. Horsley, "Rule of Law: Pushing the Limits of Party Rule," in *China Today, China Tomorrow: Domestic Politics, Economy, and Society,* ed. Joseph Fewsmith (Lanham, MD: Rowman and Littlefield, 2010), 51–70.

146 Mark De Wilde, "The Dark Side of Institutionalism; Carl Schmitt Reading Santi Romano," *Ethics and Global Politics* 11, 2 (2018): 12–24, https://www.tandfonline.com/doi/full/10.1080/16544951.2018.1498700 (Schmitt's theories have found significant support in China's legal regulatory discourse); Addis Goldman, "Why Carl Schmitt Matters to China: Uncovering the Pathology of Schmitt Fever," *Hedgehog Review,* October 21, 2021, https://hedgehogreview.com/web-features/thr/posts/why-carl-schmitt-matters-to-china; Jackson T. Reinhardt, "Totalitarian Friendship: Carl Schmitt in Contemporary China," *Inquiries* 12, 7 (2020), http://www.inquiriesjournal.com/articles/1784/totalitarian-friendship-carl-schmitt-in-contemporary-china; Sebastian Veg, "The 'Restructuring' of Hong Kong and the Rise of Neostatism," *Tocqueville 21,* June 27, 2020, https://tocqueville21.com/le-club/the-restructuring-of-hong-kong-and-the-rise-of-neostatism/.

147 CPC dominance over the PRC legal system was confirmed and formalized at the 4th Plenum of the 18th CPC Central Committee in October 2014. "Communiqué of the 4th Plenary Session of the 18th Central Committee of the Communist Party of China, October 23, 2014," China.org, December 2, 2014, http://www.china.org.cn/china/fourth_plenary_session/2014-12/02/content_34208801.htm. A recent example of the regime's assertion of Party leadership requirements in legal education and research is found in "Zhonggong Zhongyang bangongting Guowuyuan bangongting yifa 'Guanyu jiaqiang xinshidai faxue jiaoyu he faxue lilun yanjiu de yijian'" [The General Office of the CPC Central Committee and the General Office of the State Council issue opinions on strengthening legal education and legal theory research in the new era], February 26 2023, https://www.gov.cn/zhengce/2023-02/26/content_5743383.htm. Also see "China Releases Key Guidelines on Legal Education, Stresses Firm Stand to Oppose Western Erroneous Views," *Global Times,* February 27, 2023, https://www.globaltimes.cn/page/202302/1286308.shtml.

148 "Guowuyuan gongzuo guize" [Rules on the work of the State Council], March 17, 2023, https://www.gov.cn/zhengce/content/2023-03/24/content_5748128.htm.

149 "Zhonggong zhongyang bangongting yinfa 'Zhongguo Gongchandang jilü jiancha jiguan jiandu zhiji gongzuo guice'" [CPC Central Committee General Office issues regulations on discipline inspection organs supervising discipline enforcement work], *Xinhuanet,* January 6, 2019, https://www.gov.cn/zhengce/2019-01/06/content_5355392.htm; "Zhongguo Gongchandang jilü jiancha jiguan jiandu zhiji gongzuo guice (shixing)" [CPC provisional regulations on discipline inspection organs supervising discipline enforcement work], *Xinhuanet,* January 20, 2017, http://www.xinhuanet.com/politics/2017-01/20/c_1120352829.htm.

150 "Zhongguo gongchandang jilu chufen tiaoli" [Regulations on disciplinary measures of the Communist Party of China], December 23, 2023, https://www.ccdi.gov.cn/fgk/law_display/71035.

151 "Central Inspection Group Gives Feedback to the Supreme People's Court (2020 Edition)," *Supreme People's Court Monitor,* January 12, 2020, https://supremepeoplescourtmonitor.com/2020/01/12/central-inspection-group-gives-feedback-to-the-supreme-peoples-court-2020-edition/. Also see Holly Snapes, "The Rise of Party Law: Rewiring the Party, Recalibrating the Party-State Relationship," *China Journal* 92 (July 2024): 1–26, https://www.journals.uchicago.edu/doi/10.1086/730530.

152 CECC, "Administrative Procedure [sic] Law of the People's Republic of China (Chinese and English Text)," April 4 1989, https://www.cecc.gov/resources/legal-provisions/administrative-procedure-law-chinese-and-english-text; Kevin J. O'Brien and Lianjiang Li, "Suing the Local State: Administrative Litigation in Rural China," *China Journal* 51 (January 2004): 75–96; Minxin Pei, "Citizens v. Mandarins: Administrative Litigation in China," *China Quarterly* 152 (December 1997): 832–62.

153 China Law Translate, "Administrative Litigation Law 2015," October 1, 2015, https://www.chinalawtranslate.com/en/Administrative-Litigation-Law-(2015)/#gsc.tab=0; He Haibo, "How Much Progress Can Legislation Bring? The 2014 Amendment of the Administrative Litigation Law of PRC," *University of Pennsylvania Asian Law Review* 13 (2018): 137–90, https://scholarship.law.upenn.edu/cgi/viewcontent.cgi?article=1033&context=alr; Chinalawinfo Database, "The Administrative Litigation Law of the People's Republic of China," 2017 revision, June 27, 2017, http://www.lawinfochina.com/display.aspx?lib=law&id=23600; China Law Translate, "Supreme People's Court Interpretation on the Application of the 'Administrative Litigation Law of the P.R.C.,'" February 6, 2018, https://www.chinalawtranslate.com/en/supreme-peoples-court-interpretation-on-the-application-of-the-administrative-litigation-law-of-the-p-r-c/; Wei Cui, Jie Cheng, and Dominika Wiesner, "Judicial Review of Administrative Action," *China Perspectives* no. 2019/1 (2019), https://journals.openedition.org/chinaperspectives/pdf/8703.

154 China Law Translate, "Supervision Law of the PPRC," March 20, 2018, https://www.chinalawtranslate.com/en/supervision-law-of-the-prc-2018/#gsc.tab=0; Jiaming Zhang and Na Jiang, "Changes After Enforcement of Supervision Law in China," *Chinese Studies* 8, 4 (November 2019), https://www.scirp.org/journal/paperinformation.aspx?paperid=96765.

155 "State Compensation Law of the People's Republic of China 1994," http://www.lehmanlaw.com/resource-centre/laws-and-regulations/general/state-compensation-law-of-the-peoples-republic-of-china-1994.html; "State Compensation Law of the PRC (Revised in 2010)," http://www.china.org.cn/china/LegislationsForm2001-2010/2011-02/12/content_21905705.htm; Chinalawinfo Database, "State Compensation Law of the People's Republic of China (2012 Amendment)," October 26, 2012, http://www.lawinfochina.com/display.aspx?id=12606&lib=law&EncodingName=big5; Keith Hand, "Watching the Watchdog: China's State Compensation Law as a Remedy for Procuratorial Misconduct," *Pacific Rim Law and Policy Journal* 9, 1 (2000): 95–138, https://digitalcommons.law.uw.edu/cgi/viewcontent.cgi?article=1233&context=wilj.

156 Jamie P. Horsley, "China's Central Government Seeks to Rein In Regulatory Documents," Brookings, June 28, 2019, https://www.brookings.edu/opinions/chinas-central-government-seeks-to-rein-in-regulatory-documents/.

157 World Justice Project, 2024 Rule of Law Index, https://worldjusticeproject.org/rule-of-law-index/global/2024.

158 SCIO, "China Publishes White Paper on COVID-19 Fight"; "Guanyu tuidong yange guifan gongzheng wenming zhifa wei yiqing fangkong gongzuo tigong youli fazhi baozhang de yijian" [Opinion on promoting strictly regulated, just, and civilized law enforcement to provide forceful legal safeguards for epidemic prevention and control work], February 24, 2020, http://

www.gov.cn/zhengce/zhengceku/2020-02/25/content_5483027.htm; English translation at https://www.chinalawtranslate.com/en/just-and-civilized-law-enforcement/.

159 See generally Hongxing Yang and Dingxin Zhao, "Performance Legitimacy, State Autonomy and China's Economic Miracle," *Journal of Contemporary China* 24, 91 (2015): 64–82, https://www.tandfonline.com/doi/abs/10.1080/10670564.2014.918403; Heike Holbig and Bruce Gilley, "Reclaiming Legitimacy in China," *Politics and Policy* 38, 2 (June 2010): 395–422, https://onlinelibrary.wiley.com/doi/abs/10.1111/j.1747-1346.2010.00241.x; Mark C. Suchman, "Managing Legitimacy: Strategic and Institutional Approaches," *Academy of Management Review* 20 (July 1995): 577–85.

160 SCIO, "Full Text: Fighting COVID-19: China in Action."

161 "Full Text of Xi Jinping's Speech at the Opening of the 73rd World Health Assembly," *China Daily*, May 18, 2020, https://www.chinadaily.com.cn/a/202005/18/WS5ec273d1a310a8b2411568f1.html.

162 "'Guanyu jinyibu youhua luoshi xinguan feiyan yiqing fankong cuoshi de tongzhi' jiedu wenda" [Reading Q&A on the notice on further optimizing the implementation of prevention and control measures of the novel corona pneumonia epidemic], December 7, 2022, https://www.gov.cn/zhengce/2022-12/07/content_5730449.htm.

163 WHO, "Thirteenth General Programme of Work 2019–2023."

164 WHO, "Constitution of World Health Organization" (1946 as amended), Preamble, https://apps.who.int/gb/bd/PDF/bd47/EN/constitution-en.pdf?ua=1.

165 "Guanyu tuidong yange guifan gongzheng wenming zhifa wei yiqing fangkong gongzuo tigong youli fazhi baozhang de yijian" [Opinion on promoting strictly regulated, just, and civilized law enforcement to provide forceful legal safeguards for epidemic prevention and control work], February 24, 2020, http://www.gov.cn/zhengce/zhengceku/2020-02/25/content_5483027.htm. English translation at https://www.chinalawtranslate.com/en/just-and-civilized-law-enforcement/.

166 "Guanyu tuidong yange guifan gongzheng wenming zhifa wei yiqing fangkong gongzuo tigong youli fazhi baozhang de yijian" [Opinion on promoting strictly regulated, just, and civilized law enforcement to provide forceful legal safeguards for epidemic prevention and control work].

167 "Yanjiu jiaqiang xinxing guanzhuang bingdu ganran xianzhuan de feiyan yiqing fangkong gongzuo" [Study how to strengthen work in the prevention and control of COVID-19 pneumonia epidemic], February 4, 2020, http://politics.people.com.cn/n1/2020/0204/c1024-31569333.html; Josephine Ma and Mimi Lau, "Xi Jinping 'Told China's Top Echelon' to Control Coronavirus Outbreak in Early Days," *South China Morning Post*, February 15, 2020, https://www.scmp.com/news/china/politics/article/3050815/xi-jinping-put-chinas-top-echelon-notice-early-days-coronavirus?module=perpetual_scroll&pgtype=article&campaign=3050815.

168 "Highlights: Chairman Xi Recounts Early Role in Coronavirus Battle," *Reuters*, February 17, 2020, https://www.reuters.com/article/us-china-health-xi-highlights/highlights-chinas-xi-recounts-early-role-in-coronavirus-battle-idUSKBN20B1MC.

169 Yun Jiang, "Neican: 17 May 2020," *The China Story* (blog), May 17, 2020, https://www.thechinastory.org/neican-17-may-2020/.

170 "Zhongyang zhengfawei: Jianjue yifa daji didui shili shentou puohuai huodong" [Central Politics and Law Commission: resolutely attack hostile forces infiltrating harmful activities], *Sina caijing* [*Sina Finance*], November 30, 2022, https://finance.sina.com.cn/china/2022-11-30/doc-imqmmthc6475837.shtml; "China Vows Crackdown on 'Hostile Forces' as Public Tests Xi," *Associated Press*, November 30, 2022, https://apnews.com/article/health-china-beijing-shanghai-covid-9a702c3794b5beaa13608484b8397e6d.

171 "Guanyu jinyibu youhua luoshi xinguan feiyan yiqing fankong cuosho de tongzhi: Lianfang liankong jizhi zongfa [2022] 113 hao" [Notice on further optimizing the implementation of prevention and control measures of the novel corona pneumonia epidemic, document (2022) #113 issued by the Joint Prevention and Control Mechanism, December 7, 2022], https://www.gov.cn/xinwen/2022-12/07/content_5730443.htm.

172 "Guanyu jinyibu youhua luoshi xinguan feiyan yiqing fankong cuosho de tongzhi: Lianfang liakong jizji zongfa [2022] 113 hao" [Notice on further optimizing the implementation of prevention and control measures of the novel corona pneumonia epidemic, document (2022) #113 issued by the Joint Prevention and Control Mechanism], paragraph 2; "'Guanyu jinyibu youhua luoshi xinguan feiyan yiqing fankong cuosho de tongzhi' jiedu wenda" [Reading Q&A on the

notice on further optimizing the implementation of prevention and control measures of the novel corona pneumonia epidemic], Section 1.

173 Kathy Huang and Mengyu Han, "Did China's Street Protests End Harsh COVID Policies?" Council on Foreign Relations, December 14, 2022, https://www.cfr.org/blog/did-chinas-street-protests-end-harsh-covid-policies.

174 Compare "Guanyu jinyibu youhua luoshi xinguan feiyan yiqing fankong cuosho de tongzhi: Lianfang liakong jizji zongfa [2022] 113 hao" [Notice on further optimizing the implementation of prevention and control measures of the novel corona pneumonia epidemic, document (2022) #113 issued by the Joint Prevention and Control Mechanism] with "Zhonggong zhongyang zhengzhiju changwu weiyuanhui zhaokai huiyi, tingqu xinguan feiyan yiqing fangkong gongzuo huibao, yanjiu bushu jinyibu youhua fangkong gonzuo de ershi tiao cuoshi, Zhonggon zhangyang shuji Xi Jinping zhuchi huiyi" [CPC Politburo Standing Committee meets, hears report on COVID-19 prevention and control work, study and deploy the twenty measures on further optimizing prevention and control work, CPC Politburo General Secretary Xi Jinping chairs meeting].

175 "Guanyu jinyibu youhua luoshi xinguan feiyan yiqing fankong cuosho de tongzhi: Lianfang liakong jizji zongfa [2022] 113 hao" [Notice on further optimizing the implementation of prevention and control measures of the novel corona pneumonia epidemic, document (2022) #113 issued by the Joint Prevention and Control Mechanism].

176 Emily Chan and Hwang Chun-mei, "Two Changsha Funeng Activists Jailed for Two, Three Years," *Radio Free Asia,* July 22, 2021, https://www.rfa.org/english/news/china/jailed-07222021140802.html; Frontline Defenders, "Open Letter to Chinese Officials on the Status of the Changsha Funeng 3," November 9, 2020, https://www.frontlinedefenders.org/en/statement-report/open-letter-chinese-officials-status-changsha-funeng-3; Changsha Funeng Jigou [Changsha Funeng Institute], "Gongyi jigou yiwu xiezhu xinfei ganranzhe jiating suopei gonggao" [Public interest institution announcement on duty to assist families of those deceased from the new lung infection to file claims for compensation], February 27, 2020, https://www.rfa.org/cantonese/news/sue-02272020060606.html; Emily Feng, "Inside China's Crackdown on Human Rights Advocates," *NPR,* September 6, 2019, https://www.npr.org/2019/09/06/753478775/inside-chinas-crackdown-on-human-rights-advocates.

177 UNDP, "2021 Annual Report – Rule of Law and Human Rights," August 15, 2022, Rule of Law and Human Rights Programme, *Annual Report,* 2021, https://www.undp.org/rolhr/publications/2021-annual-report-rule-law-and-human-rights; Stephanie Beaulac, "The Rule of Law in International Law Today," in *Relocating the Rule of Law,* ed. Gianluigi Palombella and Neil Walker (New York: Bloomsbury Publishing/Hart, 2014), ch. 9, https://www.bloomsbury.com/ca/relocating-the-rule-of-law-9781841135977/; *International Covenant on Civil and Political Rights,* UNGA Res. 2200A (XXI), 1966, Art. 14, https://www.ohchr.org/en/instruments-mechanisms/instruments/international-covenant-civil-and-political-rights#:~:text=Article%2017-,1.,against%20such%20interference%20or%20attacks.

178 United Nations and the Rule of Law, "Equality and Non-Discrimination," https://www.un.org/ruleoflaw/thematic-areas/human-rights/equality-and-non-discrimination/.

179 He Qinglian, *The Fog of Censorship: Media Control in China,* trans. Paul Frank (New York: Human Rights in China, 2008), http://yangl3.sg-host.com/wp-content/uploads/2013/01/Fog-of-Censorship.pdf.

180 Beina Xu and Eleanor Albert, "Media Censorship in China," backgrounder, Council on Foreign Relations, February 17, 2017, https://www.cfr.org/backgrounder/media-censorship-china; "Document 9: A ChinaFile Translation: How Much Is a Hardline Party Directive Shaping China's Current Political Climate?" April 22, 2013, http://www.chinafile.com/document-9-chinafile-translation.

181 Alexander Boyd, "Administrative Proceedings – 'People Suing Government' – Removed from Chinese Legal Database in New Blow to Transparency," *China Digital Times,* March 24, 2023, https://chinadigitaltimes.net/2023/03/administrative-proceedings-removed-from-chinese-legal-database-in-blow-to-transparency/.

182 China Law Translate, "National Security Law of the People's Republic of China," July 1, 2015, Article 29, https://www.chinalawtranslate.com/en/2015nsl/#gsc.tab=0.

183 "Zhonghua renmin gongheguo baocun guojia mimi fa" [State secrets protection law of the People's Republic of China], https://www.gov.cn/yaowen/liebiao/202402/content_6934648.htm; CECC, "State Secrets Protection Law of the People's Republic of China," https://www.

cecc.gov/resources/legal-provisions/law-on-the-protection-of-state-secrets-cecc-partial-translation-and; Human Rights in China (HRIC), *State Secrets: China's Legal Labyrinth* (New York: Human Rights in China, 2007), https://www.hrichina.org/en/publications/hric-report/state-secrets-chinas-legal-labyrinth.

184 "Zhonghua renmin gongheguo baocun guojia mimi shishi tiaoli" [Implementing regulations for the state secrets protection law of the People's Republic of China], January 17, 2014, http://www.gov.cn/zwgk/2014-02/03/content_2579949.htm.

185 SCIO, "Building of Political Democracy in China," white paper, October 2005, http://www.china.org.cn/english/features/book/145877.htm.

186 Walter Lohman and Justin Rhee, *2021 China Transparency Report* (Washington, DC: Heritage Foundation, 2021), http://static.heritage.org/2021/China_Transparency_Report.pdf. China is ranked 177th of 180 countries in the World Press Freedom Indexes for 2019, 2020, and 2021, prepared by Reporters Without Borders, https://rsf.org/en/ranking.

187 "Zhonghua renmin gongheguo zhengfu xinxi gongkai tiaoli" [Regulations of the People's Republic of China on disclosure of government information], April 5, 2007, http://www.gov.cn/zwgk/2007-04/24/content_592937.htm, Article 3.

188 "Zhonghua renmin gongheguo zhuanranbing fangzhi fa" [Law on prevention and control of infectious diseases of the People's Republic of China].

189 "Tufa gonggong weisheng shijian yingji tiaoli" [Regulations on responding to public health emergencies].

190 "Guojia tufa gonggong weisheng shijian yingji yu'an" [National contingency plan for public health emergencies].

191 "Zhonghua renmin gongheguo jiben yiliao weisheng yu jiankang cujin fa" [Law of the People's Republic of China on basic health care and health promotion].

192 SCIO, "Fighting COVID-19: China in Action."

193 Lotus Ruan, Jeffrey Knockel, and Masashi Crete-Nishihata, *Censored Contagion: How Information on the Coronavirus Is Managed on Chinese Social Media,* Citizen Lab Research Report No. 125 (Toronto: University of Toronto, March 2020), https://citizenlab.ca/2020/03/censored-contagion-how-information-on-the-coronavirus-is-managed-on-chinese-social-media/.

194 Shawna Chen, "Meta Removes Accounts Linked to COVID Disinformation Effort by China," *Axios,* December 1, 2021, https://www.axios.com/covid-chinese-disinformation-facebook-instagram-752d24ad-0671-4271-baa7-1693a412c78b.html; Erika Kinetz, "Anatomy of a Conspiracy: With COVID, China Took Leading Role," *Associated Press,* February 14, 2021, https://apnews.com/article/pandemics-beijing-only-on-ap-epidemics-media-122b73e134b780919cc1808f3f6f16e8; Kaiping Chen, "COVID-19 Misinformation on Chinese Social Media – Lessons for Countering Conspiracy Theories," *The Conversation,* January 28, 2021, https://theconversation.com/covid-19-misinformation-on-chinese-social-media-lessons-for-countering-conspiracy-theories-150718.

195 Helen Davidson, "Detained, Missing, Close to Death: The Toll of Reporting on Covid in China," *The Guardian,* January 4, 2022, https://www.theguardian.com/world/2022/jan/04/detained-missing-close-to-death-toll-reporting-covid-china?CMP=Share_AndroidApp_Other.

196 Lily Kuo, "'They're Chasing Me': The Journalist Who Wouldn't Stay Quiet on Covid-19," *The Guardian,* March 1, 2020, https://www.theguardian.com/world/2020/mar/01/li-zehuajournalist-wouldnt-stay-quiet-covid-19-coronavirus, and "Missing Wuhan Citizen Journalist Reappears After Two Months," *The Guardian,* April 22, 2020, https://www.theguardian.com/world/2020/apr/22/missing-wuhan-citizen-journalist-reappears-after-two-months.

197 Office of the High Commissioner for Human Rights (OHCHR), "Comment by UN Human Rights Office Spokesperson Marta Hurtado on China," press briefing notes, November 19, 2021, https://www.ohchr.org/EN/NewsEvents/Pages/DisplayNews.aspx?NewsID=27833&LangID=E; Agence France-Presse, "Chinese Journalist Jailed over Covid Reporting Is 'Close to Death,' Family Say," *The Guardian,* November 5, 2021, https://www.theguardian.com/world/2021/nov/05/chinese-journalist-jailed-over-covid-reporting-is-close-to-death-family-say?CMP=Share_AndroidApp_Other; "Picking quarrels and provoking trouble" is a catch-all provision in Article 293 of the Criminal Law of the People's Republic of China used to suppress protest and dissent. Guo Rui, "Explainer: 'Picking Quarrels and Provoking Trouble': How China's Catch-All Crime Muzzles Dissent," *South China Morning Post,* August 25, 2021, https://www.scmp.com/news/china/politics/article/3146188/picking-quarrels-and-provoking-trouble-how-chinas-catch-all.

198 Grace Tsoi, "Fang Bin: China Covid Whistleblower Returns Home to Wuhan After Jail," *BBC News,* May 2, 2023, https://www.bbc.com/news/world-asia-china-65454824.
199 William Zheng, "China Coronavirus Critic Ren Zhiqiang Under Investigation, Communist Party Disciplinary Committee Says," *South China Morning Post,* April 7, 2020, https://www.scmp.com/news/china/politics/article/3078858/chinese-critic-ren-zhiqiang-under-investigation-communist-party.
200 Verna Yu and Emma Graham-Harrison, "'This May Be the Last Piece I Write': Prominent Xi Critic Has Internet Cut After House Arrest," *The Guardian,* February 16, 2020, https://www.theguardian.com/world/2020/feb/15/xi-critic-professor-this-may-be-last-piece-i-write-words-ring-true; Xu Zhangrun, "Viral Alarm: When Fury Overcomes Fear," trans. Geremie R. Barmé, ChinaFile, February 10, 2020, https://www.chinafile.com/reporting-opinion/viewpoint/viral-alarm-when-fury-overcomes-fear.
201 Xu Zhiyong, "Dear Chairman Xi, It's Time for You to Go," trans. Geremie R. Barmé, ChinaFile, February 26, 2020, https://www.chinafile.com/reporting-opinion/viewpoint/dear-chairman-xi-its-time-you-go; Emily Feng, "Rights Activist Xu Zhiyong Arrested in China amid Crackdown on Dissent," *NPR,* February 17, 2020, https://www.npr.org/2020/02/17/806584471/rights-activist-xu-zhiyong-arrested-in-china-amid-crackdown-on-dissent.
202 China Change, "Indictment of Citizens Movement Advocate Xu Zhiyong – a Full Translation," 2021, https://chinachange.org/2021/10/06/indictment-of-citizens-movement-advocate-xu-zhiyong-a-full-translation/; Amnesty International, "China: Further Information: Activist Subjected to Torture and Charged with Subversion: Xu Zhiyong," February 26, 2021, https://www.amnesty.org/en/documents/asa17/3753/2021/en/; CECC, "Criminal Law of the People's Republic of China," https://www.cecc.gov/resources/legal-provisions/criminal-law-of-the-peoples-republic-of-china#Chapter%20II.1.
203 "Chinese Police Search People's Phones After Anti-Lockdown Protests Erupt Across Country," *CBC News,* November 28, 2022, https://www.cbc.ca/news/world/china-protest-covid-measures-1.6666287; Susannah Savage, "Beijing Clamps Down on Social Media Critics of COVID Policies," *Politico,* January 7, 2023, https://www.politico.eu/article/china-zero-covid-policy-coronavirus-social-media-critics-sina-weibo/.
204 Mara Hvistendahl and Benjamin Mueller, "Chinese Censorship Is Quietly Rewriting the Covid-19 Story," *New York Times,* April 23, 2023, https://www.nytimes.com/2023/04/23/world/europe/chinese-censorship-covid.html; Nicole Hong and Zixu Wang, "China Moves to Erase Vestiges of 'Zero Covid' to Deter Dissent," *New York Times,* February 28, 2023, https://www.nytimes.com/2023/02/28/world/asia/china-covid-lab-leak.html; Maya Wang, "Opinion: The Chinese Have Long Faced State Secrecy and Stonewalling, Now the World Is Seeing That with Covid-19," *Washington Post,* September 9, 2021, https://www.washingtonpost.com/opinions/2021/09/09/china-covid-19-investigations-secrecy-human-rights-stonewalling/?utm_medium=email&utm_source=newsletter&wpisrc=nl_opinions&utm_campaign=wp_opinions; Li Yuan, "How Beijing Turned China's Covid-19 Tragedy to Its Advantage," *New York Times,* June 9, 2021, https://www.nytimes.com/2021/01/22/business/china-covid-19-beijing.html; Wang Yaqiu, "Zhongguo kang bing chenggong de beihou shi yi yang renquan beiju" [Behind China's success in controlling COVID-19 lies a human rights tragedy], Human Rights Watch, January 26, 2021, https://www.hrw.org/zh-hans/news/2021/01/26/377695.
205 "'Guanyu jinyibu youhua luoshi xinguan feiyan yiqing fankong cuosho de tongzhi' jiedu wenda" [Reading Q&A on the notice on further optimizing the implementation of prevention and control measures of the novel corona pneumonia epidemic]. The CPC's 2014 Document No. 9 proscribed so-called Western notions of freedom of expression and the press. "Zhonggong Zhongyang bangongting yinfa 'Guanyu dangqian yishi xingtai lingyu qingkuang de tongbao'" [Communiqué on the current state of the ideological sphere: a notice from the Central Committee of the Communist Party of China's General Office], May 8, 2014, https://www.bannedbook.org/forum34/topic3971.html; ChinaFile, "Document No. 9: A ChinaFile Translation," April 22, 2013, http://www.chinafile.com/document-9-chinafile-translation.
206 Ken Moritsugu and Huizhong Wu, "Lack of Info on China's Covid-19 Surge Stirs Global Concern," *Associated Press,* December 29, 2022, https://apnews.com/article/health-china-disease-outbreaks-covid-19-pandemic-guangzhou-01318eb4fc58a0515d8e8bd1577e385d.
207 Joe McDonald, "China Reports 60,000 COVID-Related Deaths, Says Peak Passed," *Associated Press,* January 14, 2023, https://apnews.com/article/health-china-beijing-covid-425a5de577126b042d4eea915c174bc0; "China Coronavirus: 60,000 Covid-Related Deaths in Just over a

Month," *BBC News,* January 14, 2023, https://www.bbc.com/news/world-asia-china-64276608; "China Covid: How Many Cases and Deaths Are There?" *BBC News,* December 29, 2022, https://www.bbc.com/news/59882774.

208 George Wright, "Covid in China: Officials Must Share Data on Its Impact, Says WHO," *BBC News,* December 30, 2022, https://www.bbc.com/news/world-asia-64131713.

209 Dake Kang, "Ignoring Experts, China Sudden Zero-COVID Exit Cost Lives," *Associated Press,* March 24, 2023, https://apnews.com/article/zero-covid-exit-china-reopening-investigation-05e1bf6d14e3b77ade26b719093ac43b.

210 United Nations Educational, Scientific and Cultural Organization (UNESCO), "UNESCO Sets Ambitious International Standards for Open Science," press release, November 26, 2021, https://www.unesco.org/en/articles/unesco-sets-ambitious-international-standards-open-science?TSPD_101_R0=080713870fab2000e41583d40c4ed5cd84b3e6e510fd3ef09441a62434185f3642c48ca7370312830865f1e49c143000df20a4fcf2a7b331d25518c8fd109dce418f4b3b84ef8936dcb156a6030852709935fdc437b42818835bd82be93ae0d2.

211 WHO, "Thirteenth General Programme of Work 2019–2023."

212 Jinghua Gao and Pengfei Zhang, "China's Public Health Policies in Response to Covid-19: From an 'Authoritarian' Perspective," *Public Health* 9 (December 15, 2021), https://www.frontiersin.org/articles/10.3389/fpubh.2021.756677/full.

213 SCIO, "China Democracy That Works," white paper, December 4, 2021, http://www.scio.gov.cn/zfbps/ndhf/2021n_2242/202207/t20220704_130720.html; Yanzhong Huang, "The Myth of Authoritarian Superiority: China's Response to Covid-19 Revisited," *China Leadership Monitor* no. 68 (June 1, 2021), https://www.prcleader.org/yanzhong-huang.

214 SCIO, "Fighting COVID-19: China in Action."

215 "Full Text of Xi Jinping's Speech at the Opening of the 73rd World Health Assembly."

216 MFA, "Position Paper of the People's Republic of China for the 77th Session of the United Nations General Assembly," September 17, 2022, https://www.fmprc.gov.cn/eng/zy/wjzc/202405/t20240531_11367524.html.

217 Difeng Ding and Ruilian Zhang, "China's COVID-19 Control Strategy and Its Impact on the Global Pandemic," *Frontiers in Public Health* 10 (March 14, 2022): 857003, https://www.ncbi.nlm.nih.gov/pmc/articles/PMC8964044/.

218 "China Urges US to Stop Politicizing COVID-19 Origins-Tracing," *Global Times,* June 26, 2023, https://www.globaltimes.cn/page/202306/1293184.shtml.

219 SCIO, "Fighting COVID-19: China in Action."

220 "Communiqué of the 4th Plenary Session of the 18th Central Committee of the Communist Party of China, October 23, 2014."

221 SCIO, "Full Text: Development of China's Public Health as an Essential Element of Human Rights," white paper, September 29, 2017, http://english.www.gov.cn/archive/white_paper/2017/09/29/content_281475894089810.htm.

222 Potter, *Exporting Virtue?,* 43–44.

223 SCIO, "Fighting COVID-19: China in Action," Section III.

224 United Nations and the Rule of Law, "Freedom of Information," https://www.un.org/ruleoflaw/thematic-areas/governance/freedom-of-information/.

225 SCIO, "Fighting COVID-19: China in Action."

226 David P. Goldman, "China Suppressed Covid-19 with AI and Big Data," *Asia Times,* March 3, 2020, https://asiatimes.com/2020/03/china-suppressed-covid-19-with-ai-and-big-data/.

227 Dake Kang, "China Will Stop Reporting Asymptomatic COVID Cases After Dropping Mass Testing Requirements," *PBS News,* December 14, 2022, https://www.pbs.org/newshour/world/china-will-stop-reporting-asymptomatic-covid-cases-after-dropping-mass-testing-requirements.

228 Potter, *Exporting Virtue?,* Introduction, and ch. 2. Relevant citations are: "Full Text of Xi Jinping's Report at 19th CPC National Congress," *China Daily,* November 14, 2017, Section I.9, http://www.chinadaily.com.cn/china/19thcpcnationalcongress/2017-11/04/content_34115212.htm. In October 2019, the 4th Plenum of the CPC's 19th Central Committee reiterated the themes of taking an active part in global governance and disseminating Xi Jinping's thoughts on building a community with a shared future for humanity. "19th CPC Central Committee Concludes Fourth Plenary Session, Releases Communiqué," *Xinhuanet,* October 31, 2019, http://www.xinhuanet.com/english/2019-10/31/c_138518832.htm.

229 Collins, "The WHO and China: Dereliction of Duty"; Feldwisch-Drentrup, "How WHO Became China's Coronavirus Accomplice."

230 HRIC, *State Secrets.*
231 "10 Questions for Zhao Lijian," *Jamie Metzel* (blog), April 13, 2021, https://jamiemetzl.com/10-questions-for-zhao-lijian/.
232 US Department of State Policy Planning Staff, *The Elements of the China Challenge* (Washington, DC: Department of State, 2020), https://www.state.gov/wp-content/uploads/2020/11/20-02832-Elements-of-China-Challenge-508.pdf; Gao Wenqian, "Xi Jinping Is the Culprit of the Wuhan Epidemic," Human Rights in China, February 27, 2020, https://www.hrichina.org/en/press-work/hric-commentary/xi-jinping-culprit-wuhan-epidemic; Xu Zhiyong: "Dear Chairman Xi, It's Time for You to Go."
233 See, e.g., April A. Herlevi, "Fighting the Battle for Pandemic Narrative: The PRC White Paper on Its COVID-19 Response," *China Brief* 20, 11 (June 24, 2020), https://jamestown.org/program/fighting-the-battle-for-the-pandemic-narrative-the-prc-white-paper-on-its-covid-19-response/.
234 Yanzhong Huang, "The Myth of Authoritarian Superiority"; Caitlin Dearing Scott and Adam George, "As China Promotes Authoritarian Model, the Resilience of Its Democratic Targets Is Key," Just Security, December 28, 2020, https://www.justsecurity.org/73925/as-china-promotes-authoritarian-model-the-resilience-of-its-democratic-targets-is-key/; Zach Beauchamp, "The Myth of Authoritarian Coronavirus Supremacy," *Vox,* March 26, 2020, https://www.vox.com/2020/3/26/21184238/coronavirus-china-authoritarian-system-democracy.
235 Maria Cheng, "WHO Experts Say Search for COVID-19 Origins Stalled"; West, "How COVID-19's Origins Were Obscured, by the East and the West"; Patrice Taddonio, "In Public, the World Health Organization Praised China's Early COVID Response. In Private They Had Concerns," *Frontline,* January 26, 2021, https://www.pbs.org/wgbh/frontline/article/in-public-the-world-health-organization-praised-chinas-early-covid-response-in-private-they-had-concerns/; "China Covid-19: How State Media and Censorship Took on Coronavirus," *BBC News,* December 29, 2020, https://www.bbc.com/news/world-asia-china-55355401; Kathy Gilsinan, "How China Deceived the WHO," *The Atlantic,* April 12, 2020, https://www.theatlantic.com/politics/archive/2020/04/world-health-organization-blame-pandemic-coronavirus/609820/.
236 "Zhonghua renmin gongheguo zhengfu xinxi gongkai tiaoli" [Regulations of the People's Republic of China on disclosure of government information].
237 Lohman and Rhee, *2021 China Transparency Report.*
238 HRIC, *State Secrets.*
239 "Zhonghua renmin gongheguo zhengfu xinxi gongkai tiaoli" [Regulations of the People's Republic of China on disclosure of government information]; "Zhonghua renmin gongheguo baocun guojia mimi shishi tiaoli" [Implementing regulations for the state secrets protection law of the People's Republic of China].
240 Chonglong Gu and Rebecca Tipton, "(Re-)voicing Beijing's Discourse Through Self-Referentiality: A Corpus-Based CDA Analysis of Government Interpreters' Discursive Mediation at China's Political Press Conferences (1998–2017)," *Studies in Translation Theory and Practice* 28, 3 (2020): 406–23, https://www.tandfonline.com/doi/full/10.1080/0907676X.2020.1717558. As a distinguished observer has noted, "transparency is more than press conferences." Ben S. Bernanke and Peter Olsen, "China's Transparency Challenges," Brookings, March 8, 2016, https://www.brookings.edu/blog/ben-bernanke/2016/03/08/chinas-transparency-challenges/.
241 Ken Moritsugu, "How Accurate Are China's Virus Numbers?" *PBS News,* April 1, 2020, https://www.pbs.org/newshour/world/how-accurate-are-chinas-virus-numbers; Scott N. Romaniuk and Tobias Burgers, "Can China's COVID-19 Statistics Be Trusted?," *The Diplomat,* March 26, 2020, https://thediplomat.com/2020/03/can-chinas-covid-19-statistics-be-trusted/.
242 Larry Diamond, "Democracy Versus the Pandemic," *Foreign Affairs,* June 13, 2020, https://www.foreignaffairs.com/articles/world/2020-06-13/democracy-versus-pandemic. For a critical view, see Eugénie Mérieau, "COVID-19, Authoritarianism vs. Democracy: What the Epidemic Reveals About the Orientalism of Our Categories of Thought," *SciencesPo,* August 28, 2020, https://www.sciencespo.fr/ceri/en/content/covid-19-authoritarianism-vs-democracy-what-epidemic-reveals-about-orientalism-our-categorie.
243 "Full Text of Xi Jinping's Speech at the Opening of the 73rd World Health Assembly"; Valerie Niquet, "Decoding Xi Jinping's Speech at the World Health Assembly," *The Diplomat,* May 19, 2020, https://thediplomat.com/2020/05/decoding-xi-jinpings-speech-at-the-world-health-assembly/; Isha Verma, "Analysing President Xi Jinping's Speech at the World Health Assembly," *Asia Power Watch,* May 21, 2020, https://asiapowerwatch.com/analysing-president

-xi-jinpings-speech-at-the-world-health-assembly/; Yuliya Talmazan, Keir Simmons, and Laura Saravia, "China's Xi Announces $2B for Coronavirus Response as WHO Faces Calls for Investigation," *NBC News,* May 18, 2020, https://www.nbcnews.com/news/world/coronavirus-who-faces-global-call-investigation-general-assembly-n1209061.

244 Jeremy Page and Drew Hinshaw, "China Says Covid-19 Origin Probe Should Shift Focus to Other Countries," *Wall Street Journal,* March 31, 2021, https://www.wsj.com/articles/china-says-covid-19-origin-probe-should-shift-focus-to-other-countries-11617186625.

245 David H. Shinn, "The Environmental Impact of China's Investment in Africa," *Cornell International Law Journal* 49, 1 (2016): 25–67, http://www.lawschool.cornell.edu/research/ILJ/upload/Shinn-final.pdf; Uche Ofodile, "Aid and Human Rights: China's Africa Policy in Perspective," *Journal of International Commercial Law and Technology* 4, 2 (2009): 86–99, https://www.researchgate.net/publication/26595005_Trade_Aid_and_Human_Rights_China's_Africa_Policy_in_Perspective.

246 In October 2019, the 4th Plenum of the CPC's 19th Central Committee reiterated calls for taking an active part in global governance and disseminating Xi Jinping's thoughts on building a community with a shared future for humanity. "19th CPC Central Committee Concludes Fourth Plenary Session, Releases Communiqué," *Xinhuanet,* October 31, 2019, http://www.xinhuanet.com/english/2019-10/31/c_138518832.htm. Also see Nadège Rolland, *China's Vision for a New World Order,* National Bureau of Asian Research Special Report No. 83 (Seattle: National Bureau of Asian Research, 2020), https://www.nbr.org/wp-content/uploads/pdfs/publications/sr83_chinasvision_jan2020.pdf.

247 "Guanyu tuidong yange guifan gongzheng wenming zhifa wei yiqing fangkong gongzuo tigong youli fazhi baozhang de yijian" [Opinion on promoting strictly regulated, just, and civilized law enforcement to provide forceful legal safeguards for epidemic prevention and control work].

248 "Yanjiu jiaqiang xinxing guanzhuang bingdu ganran xianzhuan de feiyan yiqing fangkong gongzuo" [Study how to strengthen work in the prevention and control of COVID-19 pneumonia epidemic].

249 "Communiqué of the 4th Plenary Session of the 18th Central Committee of the Communist Party of China, October 23, 2014."

250 "Zhonggong Zhongyang yinfa 'Fazhi Zhongguo jianshe guihua (2020–2025 nian),'" [The CPC Central Committee issues plan for establishment of legal rule in China (2020–2025)], January 10, 2021, http://www.gov.cn/zhengce/2021-01/10/content_5578659.htm.

251 "Xi Jinping zhuchi zhaokai Zhongyang quanmian yifa zhiguo weiyhuanhui de yici huiyi" [Xi Jinping convenes the first session of the Central Commission on comprehensively ruling the country according to law], *Xinwen,* August 24, 2018, http://www.gov.cn/xinwen/2018-08/24/content_5316286.htm.

252 "Guowuyuan guanyu gongan jiguan zhifa guifanhua jianshe gongzuo qingkuang de baogao (2020 nian)" [Report of the State Council on the situation of work on construction of law enforcement standardization in public security organs (2020)], August 10, 2020, https://zh.wikisource.org/zh-hans/国务院关于公安机关执法规范化建设工作情况的报告_(2020年).

253 Straton Papagianneas and Nino Junius, "Fairness and Justice Through Automation in China's Smart Courts," *Computer Law and Security Review* 51 (November 2023), https://www.sciencedirect.com/science/article/pii/S0267364923001073; Li Yang, "Time to Tighten Screws to Ensure Fairness in Law," *China Daily,* January 13, 2021, https://www.chinadaily.com.cn/a/202101/13/WS5ffe3a5aa31024ad0baa2297.html.

254 Zhang Honghao, "Yifa zhifa jiushi zuihao de wenming zhifa" [Law enforcement according to law is the best civilized law enforcement], *China Courts,* July 30, 2018, https://www.chinacourt.org/article/detail/2018/07/id/3435419.shtml.

255 "Guowuyuan bangongting guanyu quanmian tuixing xingzheng zhifa gongshi zhidu zhifa quan guocheng jilü zhidu zhongda zhifa jueding fazhi shenke zhidu de zhidao yijian" [Guiding opinion of the State Council on all-round practice of the administrative law enforcement publicity system, the general process and record-keeping system, and the legal system and verification system for major law enforcement decisions], *Guobanfa* no. 118 (December 5, 2018), http://www.gov.cn/zhengce/content/2019-01/03/content_5354528.htm. These in turn are drawn from the CPC Central Committee and State Council's "Implementation Outline on Building the Government Under Rule of Law (2015–2020)," December 27, 2015, https://law.yale.edu/sites/default/files/area/center/china/document/2015-12_rol_govt_constructn_outline_en_2015-20202.pdf.

256 "Zhonggong Zhongyang Guowuyuan yinfa 'Fazhi zhengfu jianshe shishi gangyao (2021–2025)'" [CPC Central Committee/State Council issue provisional outline on establishment of lawful governance (2021–2025)], August 11, 2021, Section 16, http://www.gov.cn/zhengce/2021-08/11/content_5630802.htm. For discussion of the use of "guiding cases" by the Supreme People's Court, see Stanford Law School's "China Guiding Cases Project," https://law.stanford.edu/china-guiding-cases-project/#slsnav-the-team.

257 MOJ, "Sifabu xingzheng zhifa xietiao jiandu ju" [Administrative Law Enforcement Coordination and Supervision Bureau], https://www.moj.gov.cn/jgsz/jgszjgtj/jgtjxzzfxtjdj/.

258 China Law Translate, "Supervision Law of the PRC (2018)," March 21, 2018, https://www.chinalawtranslate.com/en/supervision-law-of-the-prc-2018/; Jamie P. Horsley, "What's So Controversial About China's New Anti-Corruption Body: Digging into the National Supervision Commission," Brookings, May 30, 2018, https://www.brookings.edu/opinions/whats-so-controversial-about-chinas-new-anti-corruption-body/.

259 Jiayuan Li, Xing Ni, and Rui Wang, "Blame Avoidance in China's Cadre Responsibility System," *China Quarterly* 247 (February 22, 2021): 1–22; Yan Zhang, "Police Discretion and Restorative Justice in China: Stories from the Street-Level Police," *International Journal of Offender Therapy and Comparative Criminology* 65, 4 (March 2020): 498–520, https://journals.sagepub.com/doi/10.1177/0306624X20944686?url_ver=Z39.88-2003&rfr_id=ori:rid:crossref.org&rfr_dat=cr_pub%20%200pubmed; Michael Dutton, "Toward a Government of the Contract," in *Crime, Punishment, and Policing in China,* ed. Borge Bakken (Lanham, MD: Rowman and Littlefield, 2005), 206–7, https://www.bloomsbury.com/us/crime-punishment-and-policing-in-china-9780742535749/.

260 Wang Qingbin, "Lun zhifa baozhang yu xingzheng zhifa nengli de tigao" [On safeguarding law enforcement and raising the effectiveness of administrative law enforcement], *Fazhi zhengfu wang* [Rule of law government network/website], May 30, 2012, http://fzzfyjy.cupl.edu.cn/info/1145/3793.htm.

CHAPTER 4: CLIMATE CHANGE

1 Nationally Determined Contributions Registry, "China's Achievements, New Goals and New Measures for Nationally Determined Contributions," https://www.preventionweb.net/publication/chinas-achievements-new-goals-and-new-measures-nationally-determined-contributions; State Council Information Office (SCIO), "China's Policies and Actions for Addressing Climate Change," white paper, November 22, 2011, http://english.www.gov.cn/archive/white_paper/2014/09/09/content_281474986284685.htm; National Development and Reform Commission (NDRC), "China's National Climate Change Programme," June 2007, http://www.ccchina.org.cn/WebSite/CCChina/UpFile/File188.pdf.

2 Alex Wang, "Climate Change Policy and Law in China," in *The Oxford Handbook of International Climate Change Law,* ed. Kevin R. Gray, Richard Tarasofsky, and Cinnamon Carlarne (Oxford: Oxford University Press, 2016), https://www.oxfordhandbooks.com/view/10.1093/law/9780199684601.001.0001/oxfordhb-9780199684601. Also see "United Nations Framework Convention on Climate Change" (UNFCCC), 1992, https://unfccc.int/files/essential_background/background_publications_htmlpdf/application/pdf/conveng.pdf; "Paris Agreement," 2015, https://unfccc.int/sites/default/files/english_paris_agreement.pdf; "Decisions Adopted by the Conference of the Parties," January 26, 2016, FCCC/CP/2015/10/Add.1, https://unfccc.int/resource/docs/2015/cop21/eng/10a01.pdf.

3 Lindsay Maizland, "China's Fight Against Climate Change and Environmental Degradation," backgrounder, Council on Foreign Relations, May 19, 2021, https://www.cfr.org/backgrounder/china-climate-change-policies-environmental-degradation.

4 David Sandalow, Michal Meidan, Philip Andrews-Speed, Anders Hove, Sally Yue Qiu, and Edmund Downie, *Guide to Chinese Climate Policy 2022* (Oxford: Oxford Institute for Energy Studies, October 2022), ch. 3, https://chineseclimatepolicy.oxfordenergy.org.

5 SCIO, "China's Policies and Actions for Addressing Climate Change."

6 Fan Gang, Nicholas Stern, Ottmar Edenhofer, Xu Shanda, Klas Eklund, Frank Ackerman, et al., eds., *The Economics of Climate Change in China: Towards a Low-Carbon Economy* (Abingdon, UK: Routledge, 2011), https://www.taylorfrancis.com/books/edit/10.4324/9781315067209/economics-climate-change-china-fan-gang-nicholas-stern-ottmar-edenhofer-xu-shanda-klas-eklund-frank-ackerman-lailai-li-karl-hallding.

7 NDRC, "CHINA: 11th Five-Year Plan (2006–2010) for National Economic and Social Development," 2006, https://policy.asiapacificenergy.org/node/115; Jing Cao, Richard Garbaccio, and Mun S. Ho, "China's 11th Five Year Plan and the Environment: Reducing SO_2 Emissions," *Review of Environmental Economics and Policy* 3, 2 (2009): 1–20, https://www.gtap.agecon.purdue.edu/resources/download/5509.pdf.
8 Ding Yihui et al., "China's National Assessment Report on Climate Change (I): Climate Change in China and the Future Trend," *Advances in Climate Change Research* 2, 1 (January 2006), https://www.academia.edu/15602018/National_Assessment_Report_of_Climate_Change_I_Climate_change_in_China_and_its_future_trend.
9 NDRC, "Zhongguo yingdui qihou bianhua guojia fangan" [China national plan for adapting to climate change], June 2007, http://www.ccchina.org.cn/WebSite/CCChina/UpFile/File189.pdf. For an English translation, see "China's National Climate Change Programme," June 2007, https://www.ccchina.org.cn/WebSite/CCChina/UpFile/File188.pdf.
10 NDRC, "CHINA: 12th Five-Year Plan (2011–2015) for National Economic and Social Development," 2011, https://policy.asiapacificenergy.org/node/37; Joseph Casey and Katherine Koleski, *Backgrounder: China's 12th Five-Year Plan* (US-China Economic and Security Review Commission, June 24, 2011), https://www.uscc.gov/sites/default/files/Research/12th-FiveYearPlan_062811.pdf.
11 NDRC, "Guojia shiying qihou bianhua zhanlue" [National climate adaptation strategy], November, 2013, https://www.gov.cn/gzdt/att/att/site1/20131209/001e3741a2cc140f6a8701.pdf.
12 NDRC, "Guojia yingdui qihou bianhua guihua" [National plan in response to climate change], September 2014, https://www.ndrc.gov.cn/xxgk/zcfb/tz/201411/W020190905507100475236.pdf. English text available at "CHINA: National Plan on Climate Change 2014–2020," https://policy.asiapacificenergy.org/node/3011.
13 NDRC, "The 13th Five-Year Plan for Economic and Social Development of the People's Republic of China (2016–2020)," https://en.ndrc.gov.cn/policies/202105/P020210527785800103339.pdf; Katherine Koleski, *The 13th Five-Year Plan* (US-China Economic and Security Review Commission, February 14, 2013), https://www.uscc.gov/sites/default/files/Research/The%2013th%20Five-Year%20Plan_Final_2.14.17_Updated%20(002).pdf.
14 NDRC, "Zhonghua renmin gongheguo guomin jingji he shehui fazhan de shisige wunian guihua he 2035 nian yuanjing mubiao gangyao" [People's Republic of China 14th five-year plan for national economic and social development and outline of long-range goals for 2035], March 13, 2021, http://www.gov.cn/xinwen/2021-03/13/content_5592681.htm. For an English translation, see "Outline of the People's Republic of China 14th Five-Year Plan for National Economic and Social Development and Long-Range Objectives for 2035," March 12, 2021, https://cset.georgetown.edu/publication/china-14th-five-year-plan/.
15 "Q&A: What Does China's 14th 'Five Year Plan' Mean for Climate Change?" *CarbonBrief*, December 3, 2021, https://www.carbonbrief.org/qa-what-does-chinas-14th-five-year-plan-mean-for-climate-change; Jiang Yifan, "14th Five Year Plan: China's Carbon-Centred Environmental Blueprint," Dialogue Earth, March 26, 2021, https://chinadialogue.net/en/climate/14th-five-year-plan-china-carbon-centred-environmental-blueprint/.
16 The focus on carbon intensity over general carbon emissions has been challenged as potentially allowing actual emissions to grow as China's GDP grows. Fiona Harvey, "China's Five-Year Plan Could Push Emissions Higher Unless Action Is Taken," *The Guardian*, March 5, 2021, https://www.theguardian.com/world/2021/mar/05/china-five-year-plan-emissions?CMP=Share_AndroidApp_Other.
17 Tony Han, "China's Emissions May Be Falling – Here's What You Should Know," *BBC News*, July 8, 2025, https://www.bbc.com/news/articles/c4gdd6jdm42o.
18 Jianwei Zhang, Xiaoyi Jiang, and Xiaobin Pan, "Regional Legislation to Address Climate Change in China: Necessity and Feasibility," *International Journal on Climate Change Studies and Management* 11, 4 (June 21, 2019): 536–51, https://www.sciencedirect.com/org/science/article/pii/S1756869219000115; Zhang Zitai, "Zhongguo qihou bianhua yingdui fa kuangjia tixi chutan" [Inquiry into the framework for China's climate change adaptation law], *Nanjing daxue xuebao: Zhexue, renwen kexue, shehui kexue* [*Nanjing University Journal: Philosophy, Humanities and Social Science*] 5 (2010), http://dianda.cqvip.com/Qikan/Article/Detail?id=35470863.
19 Huang Shumao, "Zhongguo 'Qihou bianhua yingdui fa' cao'an wancheng" [China's draft climate change adaptation law draft completed], Dialogue Earth, August 6, 2014, https://

chinadialogue.net/zh/3/42416/; "Zhongguo qicao wancheng 'Qihou bianhua yingdui fa' cao'an" [China has drafted a complete climate change adaptation law draft], *Caixin,* July 23, 2014, https://china.caixin.com/2014-07-23/100707692.html; "Zhonghua renmin gongheguo qihou bianhua yingdui fa" [Climate change adaptation law of the People's Republic of China], https://baike.baidu.com/item/中华人民共和国气候变化应对法/19521242.

20 Cao Mingde, "Wanshan Zhongguo qihou bianhua fa shiyingxing lifa de sikao" [Considering China's climate change adaptation legislation], *Zhongzhou xuekan* [*Academic Journal of Zhongzhou*] (August 2018), https://www.pkulaw.com/qikan/026ffea136743313a7d0b8ce3696 34a2bdfb.html.

21 See, e.g., NDRC, "Guojia yingdui qihou bianhua guihua" [National plan in response to climate change].

22 Chang Ji-wen and Tian Dan-yu, "Yingdui qihou bianhua fa de lifa tanjiu" [Legislative inquiry into climate change law], *Zhongguo huanjing guanli* [*Chinese Journal of Environmental Management*] 13, 2 (2021): 16–19, http://zghjgl.ijournal.cn/html/zghjgl/2021/2/20210203.htm. Also see Climate Change Laws of the World, "China," https://climate-laws.org/geographies/china.

23 Xiangbai He, Hao Zhang, Alexander Zahar, eds., *Climate Change Law in China in Global Context* (London: Routledge, 2020), https://www.routledge.com/Climate-Change-Law-in-China-in-Global-Context/He-Zhang-Zahar/p/book/9781138742536; Peter C. Pang, "China: China's Evolving Environmental Protection Laws," *Mondaq,* June 18, 2020, https://www.mondaq.com/china/clean-air-pollution/955486/china39s-evolving-environmental-protection-laws.

24 Environmental Protection Law of the People's Republic of China, 2015, http://www.lawinfochina.com/Display.aspx?lib=law&Cgid=223979.

25 "Zhonggong zhongyang, Guowuyuan guanyu quanmian jiaqiang shengtao huanjing baohu jianjue dahao wuran fangzhi gongjian zhan de yijian" [Opinion of the CPC Central Committee and the State Council on comprehensively strengthening ecological and environmental protection and resolutely fighting the tough battle of pollution prevention and control], June 24, 2018, Section III, https://www.gov.cn/zhengce/2018-06/24/content_5300953.htm.

26 World Bank, "China: Fighting Air Pollution and Climate Change Through Clean Financing," June 21, 2020, https://www.worldbank.org/en/results/2020/06/21/china-fighting-air-pollution-and-climate-change-through-clean-energy-financing; Chan Yang, "Policies, Regulatory Framework and Enforcement for Air Quality Management: The Case of China," OECD Environment Working Paper No. 157, March 13, 2020, https://www.oecd-ilibrary.org/environment/policies-regulatory-framework-and-enforcement-for-air-quality-management-the-case-of-china_7d1d1a82-en.

27 Laney Zhang, "China: 2020 Air Pollution Action Plan Released," Library of Congress, August 16, 2018, https://www.loc.gov/item/global-legal-monitor/2018-08-16/china-2020-air-pollution-action-plan-released/; Clean Air Alliance of China, *State Council Air Pollution Prevention and Control Action Plan* (October 2013), https://policy.asiapacificenergy.org/sites/default/files/Air%20Pollution%20Prevention%20and%20Control%20Action%20Plan%20%28EN%29.pdf.

28 State Council, "National Environmental Protection 'Twelfth Five-Year' Plan (Chinese Text)," December 15, 2011, https://www.cecc.gov/resources/legal-provisions/national-environmental-protection-twelfth-five-year-plan-chinese-text.

29 See, e.g., Yifei Liu and Judith Shapiro, *China Goes Green: Coercive Environmentalism for a Troubled Planet* (Cambridge: Polity Press, 2020), https://politybooks.com/bookdetail/?isbn=9781509543113; Mark Gilley, "Authoritarian Environmentalism and China's Response to Climate Change," *Environmental Politics* 21, 2 (March 2012): 287–307, https://www.tandfonline.com/doi/abs/10.1080/09644016.2012.651904; Lisa Williams, "China's Climate Change Policies: Actors and Drivers," Lowy Institute, July 2014, https://www.lowyinstitute.org/sites/default/files/chinas-climate-change-policies.pdf.

30 Ma Tianjie and Liu Qin, "China Reshapes Ministry to Better Protect Environment," Dialogue Earth, March 14, 2018, https://www.chinadialogue.net/article/show/single/en/10502-China-reshapes-ministries-to-better-protect-environment. For the Ministry of Ecology and Environment (MEE) website, see http://english.mee.gov.cn.

31 MEE, "China's Policies and Actions for Addressing Climate Change (2019)," November 2019, https://english.mee.gov.cn/Resources/Reports/reports/201912/P020191204495763994956.pdf.

32 MEE, "China's Policies and Actions for Addressing Climate Change (2020)," June 2021, http://www.ncsc.org.cn/yjcg/cbw/202111/P020211117418821628432.pdf.
33 David Sandalow, *Guide to Chinese Climate Change Policy 2019* (New York: SIPA Center on Global Energy Policy, Columbia University, September 2019), 30–32, https://energypolicy.columbia.edu/sites/default/files/file-uploads/Guide%20to%20Chinese%20Climate%20Policy_2019.pdf.
34 "Guowuyuan guanyu chengli guojia yingdui qihou bianhua ji jieneng jianpai gongzuo lingdao xiaozu de tongzhi" [State Council note on establishment of the national leading small group on adaptation to climate change and energy conservation and emissions reduction work], June 12, 2007, https://www.ccchina.org.cn/Detail.aspx?newsId=28014&TId=60%22%20title=%22. A key distinction between "coordinating committees" and "Leading Small Groups" is that LSGs have authority to issue "red-headed documents" (*hongtou wenjian* // 红头文件) and to compel attendance at meetings. See generally George G. Chen and Matthias Stepan, "Ruling the Country by Red-Letterhead Documents?" Asia Dialogue (University of Nottingham), September 19, 2017, https://www.researchgate.net/publication/365703262_Ruling_the_Country_by_Red-letterhead_Documents.
35 "Guowuyuan guanyu chengli guojia yingdui qihou bianhua ji jieneng jianpai gongzuo lingdao xiaozu de tongzhi" [State Council note on establishment of the national leading small group on adaptation to climate change and energy conservation and emissions reduction work], June 12, 2007, https://www.ccchina.org.cn/Detail.aspx?newsId=28014&TId=60%22%20title=%22.
36 "Guowuyuan bangingting guanyu tiaozheng guojia yingdui qihou bianhua ji jieneng jianpai gongzuo lingdao xiaozu chengrenyuan de tongzhi – guobanhan (2019) 99 hao" [Notice of the State Council general office on adjustment of the membership of the national leading small group on climate change adaptation, energy conservation, and emissions reduction work – general office letter no. 99 of 2019], October 7, 2019, https://www.gov.cn/zhengce/content/2019-10/12/content_5438830.htm. Under the MEE organizational chart, the Office for Climate Change Response had responsibility for "undertaking the work of the national leading group on climate change, energy conservation, and emissions reduction." MEE, "Department of Climate Change," 2025, https://english.mee.gov.cn/About_MEE/Internal_Departments/202501/t20250106_1100027.shtml#:~:text=Functions,Energy%20Conservation%20and%20Emissions%20Reduction.
37 MEE, "China's Policies and Actions for Addressing Climate Change (2020)," 9.
38 MEE, "Guanyu tongchou he jiaqiang yingdui qihou bianhua yu shengtai huanjing baohu xiangguan gongzuo de zhidai yijian" [Guiding opinions on integrating and strengthening efforts in climate action and ecological and environmental protection], January 11, 2021, https://www.mee.gov.cn/xxgk2018/xxgk/xxgk03/202101/t20210113_817221.html. English text available at https://www.clientearth.org/media/00tnkuc5/guiding-opinions-on-integrating-and-strengthening-efforts-in-climate-action-and-ecological-and-environmental-protection.pdf.
39 Xiaoying You, "Explainer: China Created New 'Leaders Group' to Help Deliver Its Climate Goals," *CarbonBrief*, June 3, 2021, https://www.carbonbrief.org/explainer-china-creates-new-leaders-group-to-help-deliver-its-climate-goals.
40 "Zhonggong zhongyang guowuyuan guanyu wanzheng zhunque quanmian guanche xinfazhan linian zuohao tandafeng tanzhonghe gongzuo de yijian" [Opinions of the CPC Central Committee and the State Council on the complete, accurate and comprehensive implementation of the new development concept to do a good job in carbon peaking and carbon neutrality], September 22, 2021, http://www.gov.cn/zhengce/2021-10/24/content_5644613.htm.
41 NDRC, "Action Plan for Carbon Dioxide Peaking Before 2030," October 27, 2021, https://en.ndrc.gov.cn/policies/202110/t20211027_1301020.html; NDRC, "Working Guidance for Carbon Dioxide Peaking and Carbon Neutrality in Full and Faithful Implementation of the New Development Philosophy," October 24, 2021, https://en.ndrc.gov.cn/policies/202110/t20211024_1300725.html.
42 Compare "China's Achievements, New Goals and New Measures for Nationally Determined Contributions" with NDRC, "Qianghua ying dui qihou bianhua xingdong – Zhongguo guojia zizhu gongxian" [Enhanced actions on climate change: China's intended nationally determined contributions], June 30, 2015, http://www.xinhuanet.com//politics/2015-06/30/c_1115774759.htm.
43 Compare "Zhonghua renmin gongheguo guomin jingji he shehui fazhan de shisige wunian guihua he 2035 nian yuanjing mubiao gangyao" [People's Republic of China 14th five-year plan

for national economic and social development and outline of long-range goals for 2035] with Nationally Determined Contributions Registry, "China's Achievements, New Goals and New Measures for Nationally Determined Contributions."

44 "Guojia Fazhan Gaige Wei deng bumen guanyu tuijin gongjian 'yidai yilu' lüse fazhan de yijian" [Opinion of NDRC and other departments on promoting common development of green development in the one belt, one road], *Fagai kaifang* [*Reform and Opening Up*] no. 408 (March 16, 2022), https://www.ndrc.gov.cn/xxgk/zcfb/tz/202203/t20220328_1320629.html?code=&state=123.

45 "Guojia Fazhangaigewei, Caizhengbu, Zhongguo Renmin Yinhan, Guojia Shuiwu Zongju lianhe zhaokai xinwen fabuhui jieshao 'Dahao congguan zengce hequan tuiji jingji gao zhiliang fazhan youguan qingkuan' yuanda" [The National Development and Reform Commission, the Ministry of Finance, the People's Bank of China, and the State Administration of Taxation jointly held a press conference to introduce the relevant situation of playing a good macro policy combination to promote high-quality economic development], August 3, 2023, https://www.ndrc.gov.cn/xwdt/wszb/dtdjjgzlfz/wzsl/202308/t20230804_1359141.html and https://www.ndrc.gov.cn/xwdt/wszb/dtdjjgzlfz/.

46 Yang Liu, "Reading Between the Lines of the CEWC Report," *Pekingnology* (blog), December 21, 2023, https://www.pekingnology.com/cp/139983662.

47 Adam Vaughn, "China Must Act Fast to Avoid Breaching the World's 1.5°C Climate Goal," *New Scientist,* April 22, 2021, https://www.newscientist.com/article/2275172-china-must-act-fast-to-avoid-breaching-the-worlds-1-5c-climate-goal/; Climate Action Tracker, "China," September 15, 2021, https://climateactiontracker.org/countries/china/.

48 Helen Davidson, "China Continues Coal Spree Despite Climate Goals," *The Guardian,* August 29, 2023, https://www.theguardian.com/world/2023/aug/29/china-coal-plants-climate-goals-carbon; Lauri Myllyvirta, "Analysis: China's Carbon Emissions Grow at Fastest Rate for More Than a Decade," *CarbonBrief,* May 20, 2021, https://www.carbonbrief.org/analysis-chinas-carbon-emissions-grow-at-fastest-rate-for-more-than-a-decade.

49 Helen Davidson, "Chinese Premier Calls for More Coal Production as Electricity Demand Soars," *The Guardian,* June 24, 2022, https://www.theguardian.com/world/2022/jun/24/chinese-premier-calls-for-more-coal-production-as-electricity-demand-soars?CMP=Share_AndroidApp_Other; "China to Step Up Support for Industrial and Services Sectors in Special Difficulty," *People's Daily,* February 16, 2022, http://en.people.cn/n3/2022/0216/c90000-9958540.html. Also see Joe Lo, "After Blackouts, China's Green Goals Take Back Seat to Energy Security," *Climate Home News,* March 24, 2022, https://www.climatechangenews.com/2022/03/24/after-blackouts-chinas-green-goals-take-back-seat-to-energy-security/?utm_campaign=Daily%20Briefing&utm_content=20220325&utm_medium=email&utm_source=Revue%20newsletter.

50 Helen Davidson, "China Drought Causes Yangtze to Dry Up, Sparking Shortage of Hydropower," *The Guardian,* August 22, 2022, https://www.theguardian.com/world/2022/aug/22/china-drought-causes-yangtze-river-to-dry-up-sparking-shortage-of-hydropower; Ryan Woo, "Heatwaves to Menace China as Almanac's 'Bug Heat' Day Looms," *Reuters,* July 22, 2022, https://www.reuters.com/world/china/heatwaves-hit-china-east-west-almanacs-big-heat-day-looms-2022-07-21/.

51 "Iron Ore Smashes $150 After China Eases Steel's Green Targets," *Bloomberg,* February 8, 2022, https://www.bloomberg.com/news/articles/2022-02-08/iron-ore-smashes-150-after-beijing-eases-steel-s-green-targets.

52 Sam Giall, "China, Climate Politics, and COP26," Lowy Institute, October 25, 2021, https://www.lowyinstitute.org/publications/china-climate-politics-and-cop26.

53 Xiaoying You, "China Issues New 'Single Game' Instructions to Guide Its Climate Action," *CarbonBrief,* August 4, 2021, https://www.carbonbrief.org/china-issues-new-single-game-instructions-to-guide-its-climate-action.

54 United Nations Climate Change, "China," https://unfccc.int/node/180417.

55 "The People's Republic of China Fourth National Communication on Climate Change," December 2023, https://unfccc.int/sites/default/files/resource/China_NC4_English.pdf; MEE, "The People's Republic of China Third National Communication on Climate Change," December 2018, https://english.mee.gov.cn/Resources/Reports/reports/201907/P020190702566752327206.pdf; "Second National Communication on Climate Change of the People's Republic of China," 2012, https://unfccc.int/resource/docs/natc/chnnc2e.pdf; "The People's

Republic of China Initial National Communication on Climate Change," October 2004, https://unfccc.int/resource/docs/natc/chnnc1exsum.pdf.

56 United Nations Environment Programme (UNEP), "Partnership with China," https://www.unep.org/explore-topics/green-economy/what-we-do/economic-and-fiscal-policy/partnership-china.

57 Tu Ruihe, "UNEP and China: A Shared Green Dream," *China Global Television Network (CGTN)*, October 11, 2021, https://news.cgtn.com/news/2021-10-11/UNEP-and-China-A-shared-green-dream-148FNL3bSLe/index.html.

58 SCIO, "Full Text: China's International Development Cooperation in the New Era," white paper, January 2021, http://english.scio.gov.cn/whitepapers/2021-01/10/content_77099782.htm. Some suggest that in light of China's self-interested positions on climate and its efforts to win influence with the G7, India was a more legitimate representative of the Global South. Sreeram Chaulia, "Modi Articulated the Global South's Position at CoP-26," *Mint*, November 3, 3021, https://www.livemint.com/opinion/online-views/modi-articulated-the-global-south-s-position-at-cop26-11635872441232.html.

59 UNEP, "China and UN Environment Strengthen Cooperation," January 8, 2018, https://www.unep.org/news-and-stories/story/china-and-un-environment-strengthen-cooperation; UNEP, "China Trust Fund," 2015, https://www.unep.org/about-un-environment/funding/china-trust-fund.

60 National Intelligence Council, "National Intelligence Estimate: Climate Change and International Responses Increasing Challenges to US National Security Through 2040," October 21, 2021, https://nsarchive.gwu.edu/document/32888-document-3-national-intelligence-council-national-intelligence-estimate-climate.

61 Scott Moore and Michelle Melton, "China's Pivot on Climate Change and National Security," *Lawfare*, April 2, 2019, https://www.lawfareblog.com/chinas-pivot-climate-change-and-national-security.

62 US Department of State, "U.S.-China Joint Statement Addressing the Climate Crisis," April 17, 2021, https://2021-2025.state.gov/u-s-china-joint-statement-addressing-the-climate-crisis/.

63 "Full Text: Remarks by Chinese President Xi Jinping at Leaders Summit on Climate," *Xinhuanet*, April 26, 2021, https://english.mee.gov.cn/News_service/media_news/202104/t20210426_830358.shtml; White House, "Leaders Summit on Climate Change: Summary of Proceedings," April 23, 2021, https://bidenwhitehouse.archives.gov/briefing-room/statements-releases/2021/04/23/leaders-summit-on-climate-summary-of-proceedings/.

64 "Full Text of Xi's Statement at the General Debate of the 76th Session of the United Nations General Assembly," *Xinhuanet*, September 22, 2021, https://english.www.gov.cn/news/topnews/202109/22/content_WS614a9d11c6d0df57f98e0a81.html.

65 Government of Canada, "G20 Rome Leaders' Declaration," November 1, 2021, https://www.international.gc.ca/world-monde/international_relations-relations_internationales/g20/2021-10-31-g20-rome.aspx?lang=eng.

66 Zachary Basu, "Biden: China's Xi Made a 'Big Mistake' Not Showing Up to COP26," *Axios*, November 2, 2021, https://www.axios.com/biden-china-cop26-xi-mistake-675d4be3-de16-4bc8-be02-af7e83fd1656.html. Former president Barack Obama, closely associated with achievements of the 2015 Paris Agreement, also weighed in against China's (and Russia's) "absence of urgency" at COP26. Ellen Knickmeyer, Anirudda Ghosal, and Seth Borenstein, "Obama Faults Russia, China for 'Lack of Urgency' on Climate," *Associated Press*, November 7, 2021, https://apnews.com/article/climate-donald-trump-joe-biden-united-nations-barack-obama-33aacb939b5ee0b8aa1add7688cb267a.

67 Heidi Wang-Kaeding, *China's Environmental Foreign Relations* (Milton Park, UK: Routledge, 2021), https://www.routledge.com/Chinas-Environmental-Foreign-Relations/Wang-Kaeding/p/book/9780367712327.

68 UNFCCC, Article 3, https://unfccc.int/files/essential_background/background_publications_htmlpdf/application/pdf/conveng.pdf; UN Climate Change, "Introduction to Climate Finance," https://unfccc.int/topics/introduction-to-climate-finance.

69 Earth.org, "Explainer: What Is the Kyoto Protocol?" August 10, 2021, https://earth.org/the-kyoto-protocol/.

70 Jonathan Watts, Damian Carrington, and Suzanne Goldenberg, "China's Fears of Rich Nation 'Climate Conspiracy' at Copenhagen Revealed," *The Guardian*, February 11, 2010, https://www.theguardian.com/environment/2010/feb/11/chinese-thinktank-copenhagen-document;

"'Common but Differentiated Responsibilities' Must Never Be Compromised: Premier," *Xinhua*, December 18, 2009, http://www.china.org.cn/environment/Copenhagen/2009-12/18/content_19094598.htm.

71 Paris Agreement, Article 2.2, https://unfccc.int/sites/default/files/english_paris_agreement.pdf.

72 Gideon Rachman, "China's Self-Isolation Is a Global Concern," *Financial Times*, November 8, 2021, https://www.ft.com/content/1d00bff4-ac9d-486a-9a50-ae819e106d4c.

73 Paul Dragos Aligica, Peter J. Boettke, and Vlad Tarko, eds., *Public Governance and the Classical-Liberal Perspective: Political Economy Foundations* (New York: Oxford University Press, 2019), https://oxford.universitypressscholarship.com/view/10.1093/oso/9780190267032.001.0001/oso-9780190267032; Patrick Love and Julia Stockdale-Otarola, eds., *Debate the Issues: Complexity and Policy Making* (Paris: OECD, 2017), https://www.oecd.org/en/publications/2017/06/debate-the-issues-complexity-and-policy-making_g1g75dd8.html.

74 See, e.g., Haig Patapan and Yi Wang, "The Hidden Ruler: Wang Huning and the Making of Contemporary China," *Journal of Contemporary China* 27, 109 (2018): 47–60, https://www.tandfonline.com/doi/full/10.1080/10670564.2017.1363018; Liu He, "Overcoming the Great Recession: Lessons from China," Harvard Kennedy School, M-RCBG Associate Working Paper Series No. 33, July 2014, https://www.hks.harvard.edu/sites/default/files/centers/mrcbg/files/summers_foreword_AWP.pdf.

75 United Nations Climate Change, "Glasgow Climate Pact. Proposal by the President," November 13, 2021, https://unfccc.int/documents/311127; Mark Nevitt, "Key Takeaways from the Glasgow Climate Summit," *Lawfare*, November 17, 2021, https://www.lawfareblog.com/key-takeaways-glasgow-climate-pact.

76 "Glasgow Climate Pact," November 13, 2021, paragraphs 20–21, https://unfccc.int/sites/default/files/resource/cma2021_L16E.pdf.

77 Asia Pacific Foundation of Canada, "COP27 Highlights Differing Climate Priorities Across Asia-Pacific," *Asia Watch*, November 17, 2022, https://www.asiapacific.ca/asia-watch/cop27-highlights-differing-climate-priorities-across-asia; Damien Carrington, "What Is 'Loss and Damage' and Why Is It Critical for Success at Cop26," *The Guardian*, November 13, 2021, https://www.theguardian.com/environment/2021/nov/13/what-is-loss-and-damage-and-why-is-it-critical-for-success-at-cop26?CMP=Share_AndroidApp_Other; United Nations Climate Change, "Warsaw International Mechanism for Loss and Damage Associated with Climate Change Impacts (WIM)," 2013, https://unfccc.int/topics/adaptation-and-resilience/workstreams/loss-and-damage/warsaw-international-mechanism.

78 UNEP, "What You Need to Know About the COP 27 Loss and Damage Fund," November 29, 2022, https://www.unep.org/news-and-stories/story/what-you-need-know-about-cop27-loss-and-damage-fund#:~:text=The%20establishment%20of%20a%20Loss,the%20effects%20of%20climate%20change; Zia Weise, Sara Schonhardt, and Karl Mathiesen, "The Money Fight That Could 'Break' the Climate Summit," *Politico*, October 30, 2023, https://www.politico.com/news/2023/10/30/climate-disaster-fund-dubai-un-summit-00124038; Zack Colman, "'A Lot of Anger': U.S. Faces Flak as It Pushes for World Bank to Run Climate Fund," *Politico*, October 19, 2023, https://www.politico.com/news/2023/10/19/biden-climate-fund-fight-un-summit-00121772; Karen Sokol, "What Comes After the Loss and Damage Fund for Responsibility and Repair in a Climate-Disrupted World?" *Lawfare*, December 14, 2022, https://www.lawfareblog.com/what-comes-after-loss-and-damage-fund-responsibility-and-repair-climate-disrupted-world.

79 Zia Weise and Sara Schonhardt, "Eye-Catching Climate Donations Put Spotlight on China at COP Talks," *Politico*, November 30, 2023, https://www.politico.eu/article/climate-donations-spotlight-china-un-cop28-talks/; Andrew Freedman, "Climate Aid Fund Established on First Day of COP28 After 30-Year Controversy," *Axios*, November 28, 2023, https://www.axios.com/2023/11/30/cop-28-climate-impacts-damage-fund-passes.

80 Fiona Harvey, "Cop29 Gave Us a Putin-Friendly Deal – and a Glimpse of the Dark Future of Climate Talks," *The Guardian*, December 3, 2024, https://www.theguardian.com/commentisfree/2024/dec/03/cop-climate-baku-talks-division; Adam Morton, Fiona Harvey, Patrick Greenfield, Dharna Noor, and Damian Carrington, "Cop29: Wealthy Countries Agree to Raise Climate Finance Offer to $300bn a Year," *The Guardian*, November 23, 2024, https://www.theguardian.com/environment/2024/nov/23/cop29-wealthy-countries-agree-to-raise-climate-finance-offer-to-300bn-a-year; "COP Climate Talks Aren't Working and Need an Overhaul,

Climate Leaders Say in Letter," *CBC News,* November 15, 2024, https://www.cbc.ca/news/climate/cop29-open-letter-1.7384602.

81 Patrick Greenfield and Fiona Harvey, "China and India Should Not Be Called Developing Countries, Several Cop29 Delegates Say," *The Guardian,* November 19, 2024, https://www.theguardian.com/environment/2024/nov/19/china-india-developing-countries-cop29-climate-talks.

82 Chris Brown, "Why Climate-Shaming China at COP26 Likely Won't Work," *CBC News,* November 10, 2021, https://www.cbc.ca/news/world/china-cop26-summit-1.6242275; Angel Hsu, "Don't Be So Quick to Doubt China's Climate Change Dedication," *New York Times,* November 7, 2021, https://www.nytimes.com/2021/11/07/opinion/cop26-china-climate.html.

83 Ken Moritsugu, "Analysis: US-China Friction Complicates Progress on Climate," *Associated Press,* September 3, 2021, https://apnews.com/article/europe-business-china-climate-environment-and-nature-7b451066c440bdb301009dfd7bdc0aa4; "China Warns Kerry That Bad Ties Could Set Back Climate Talks," *Associated Press,* September 1, 2021, https://apnews.com/article/business-climate-environment-and-nature-256e47a2abcaace17370c78ef200bd95/.

84 Eileen Claussen and Elliot Diringer, "A New Climate Treaty: US Leadership After Kyoto," Center for Climate and Energy Solutions, March 2007, https://www.c2es.org/document/a-new-climate-treaty-us-leadership-after-kyoto/.

85 Yasuo Takeuchi, "US Paris Accord Exit Moves China to Center of Climate Change Fight," *Nikkei Asia,* November 6, 2021, https://asia.nikkei.com/Spotlight/Environment/US-Paris-accord-exit-moves-China-to-center-of-climate-change-fight.

86 Karl Mathiesen and Zack Colman, "Newest Cause for Climate Optimism? The U.S. Rivalry with China," *Axios,* August 20, 2022, https://www.politico.com/news/2022/08/20/china-clean-energy-ira-climate-00052684; Scott Moore, "China's New Climate Pledge: Is Geopolitical Competition Good for the Climate?" *Lawfare,* October 4, 2021, https://www.lawfareblog.com/chinas-new-climate-pledge-geopolitical-competition-good-climate; Pew Center on Global Climate Change and Asia Society, *Common Challenge, Collaborative Response: A Roadmap of U.S.-China Cooperation on Energy and Climate Change* (New York: Asia Society, January 2009), https://e360.yale.edu/assets/site/features/us-china-roadmap.pdf.

87 Bethany Allen-Ebrahimian, "The China Quandary for U.S. Climate Policy," *Axios,* November 2, 2021, https://www.axios.com/the-china-quandary-for-us-climate-policy-b34a43a9-29a4-477a-b27f-41ab6343b3b6.html; Jacob Helberg, "A Green Deal at COP26 Can't Be a Green Light for China," *Foreign Policy,* November 1, 2021, https://foreignpolicy.com/2021/11/01/china-climate-appeasement-democracy-cop26/; Phelim Kine, "The U.S.-China COP26 Cliffhanger," *Politico,* October 28, 2021, https://www.politico.com/newsletters/politico-china-watcher/2021/10/28/the-us-china-cop26-cliffhanger-494872; Gabriel Collins and Andrew S. Erickson, "China's Climate Cooperation Smokescreen: A Roadmap for Seeing Through the Trap and Countering the Competition," Baker Institute for Public Policy (Rice University), August 31, 2021, https://www.bakerinstitute.org/media/files/files/0f95cafa/ces-pub-china-climate-083121.pdf.

88 US Department of State, "China's Environmental Abuses Fact Sheet," September 25, 2020, https://2017-2021.state.gov/chinas-environmental-abuses-fact-sheet/index.html; Steven Mufsen, "China Delivers Diatribe Against U.S. Climate Policies," *Washington Post,* October 19, 2020, https://www.washingtonpost.com/climate-environment/2020/10/19/china-delivers-diatribe-against-us-climate-policies/.

89 Matt McGrath, "Climate Change: US Pushes China to Make Faster Carbon Cuts," *BBC News,* July 20, 2021, https://www.bbc.com/news/science-environment-57904042.

90 Shannon Tiezzi, "In China, Kerry Faces Uphill Battle for Climate Change Cooperation," *The Diplomat,* September 4, 2021, https://thediplomat.com/2021/09/in-china-kerry-faces-uphill-battle-for-climate-change-cooperation/; Catherine Wong, "China 'Tells US Envoy John Kerry It Will Follow Its Own Climate Road Map,'" *South China Morning Post,* September 3, 2021, https://www.scmp.com/news/china/diplomacy/article/3147540/china-tells-us-envoy-john-kerry-it-will-follow-its-own-climate.

91 US Department of State, "U.S.-China Joint Glasgow Declaration on Enhancing Climate Action in the 2020s," November 10, 2021, https://2021-2025.state.gov/u-s-china-joint-glasgow-declaration-on-enhancing-climate-action-in-the-2020s/.

92 Oliver Milman, "What Does the US-China Row Mean for Climate Change?" *The Guardian,* August 5 2022, https://www.theguardian.com/environment/2022/aug/05/what-does-the-us-china-row-mean-for-climate-change-taiwan?CMP=Share_AndroidApp_Other; Peter Prengaman,

"At Davos, Kerry Cites Progress on China-US Climate Group," *Associated Press,* May 24, 2022, https://apnews.com/article/russia-ukraine-world-economic-forum-climate-politics-technology-f783a29f3f1a54e6dc78f5efc0210e15.

93 Fiona Harvey, "China's Top Climate Official Urges US to 'Clear Barriers' to Talks," *The Guardian,* November 9, 2022, https://www.theguardian.com/world/2022/nov/09/cop7-china-us-climate-talks-taiwan?CMP=Share_AndroidApp_Other; Fiona Harvey, "'We Need to Get China': John Kerry Calls for Return to Bilateral Climate Talks," *The Guardian,* October 25, 2022, https://www.theguardian.com/us-news/2022/oct/25/john-kerry-china-return-climate-talks?CMP=Share_AndroidApp_Other.

94 Sara Schonhardt and Phelim Kine, "'It's Just Crazy': How the U.S.-China Energy Race Imperils the Climate Fight," *Politico,* May 18, 2023, https://www.politico.com/news/2023/05/18/us-china-energy-fossil-fuels-00097207; Bethany Allen-Ebrahimian, "The U.S. and China Hold the World's Climate Future in Their Hands," *Axios,* November 22, 2022, https://www.axios.com/2022/11/22/us-china-climate-change; "US and China Restart Climate Talks," *CarbonBrief,* November 15, 2022, https://www.carbonbrief.org/daily-brief/us-and-china-restart-climate-talks/.

95 Tessa Wong, "John Kerry in Beijing: Can US and China Set Aside Rivalry for Climate Action?" *BBC News,* July 15, 2023, https://www.bbc.com/news/world-asia-china-66185535; Andrew Freedman, "Exclusive: Kerry, China Envoy to Co-Chair 1st Local Climate Summit," *Axios,* September 19, 2023, https://www.axios.com/2023/09/19/cop28-kerry-china-local-climate-summit.

96 US Department of State, "Sunnylands Statement on Enhancing Cooperation to Address the Climate Crisis," November 14, 2023, https://2021-2025.state.gov/sunnylands-statement-on-enhancing-cooperation-to-address-the-climate-crisis/; David Cohen, "China Should Be Pressured on Climate Issues, Jake Sullivan Says," *Politico,* July 16, 2023, https://www.politico.com/news/2023/07/16/china-sullivan-climate-change-00106494.

97 White House, "Putting America First in International Environmental Agreements," Executive Order, January 20, 2025, https://www.whitehouse.gov/presidential-actions/2025/01/putting-america-first-in-international-environmental-agreements/; Andrew Freedman, "Trump Signs Order to Pull U.S. Out of Paris Agreement," *Axios,* January 20, 2025; Nina Lakhani, "US Exits Fund That Compensates Poorer Countries for Global Heating," *The Guardian,* March 7, 2025, https://www.theguardian.com/us-news/2025/mar/07/us-exits-fund-that-compensates-poorer-countries-for-global-heating; United Nations Climate Change, "COP28 Agreement Signals 'Beginning of the End' of the Fossil Fuel Era," press release, December 13, 2023, https://unfccc.int/news/cop28-agreement-signals-beginning-of-the-end-of-the-fossil-fuel-era.

98 Jordan Wolman, "Collision Course at COP," *Politico,* November 12, 2024, https://www.politico.com/newsletters/the-long-game/2024/11/12/collision-course-at-cop-00188991; Zoë Schlanger, "Trump Is Handing China a Golden Opportunity on Climate," *The Atlantic,* November 11, 2024, https://www.theatlantic.com/science/archive/2024/11/trump-cop-china-climate/680611/.

99 European Commission, "Joint Press Communique Following the Second EU-China High Level Environment and Climate Dialogue," October 10, 2021, https://climate.ec.europa.eu/news-your-voice/news/joint-press-communique-following-second-eu-china-high-level-environment-and-climate-dialogue-2021-10-10_en#:~:text=This%20would%20aim%20at%20reversing,regular%20basis%2C%20at%20least%20annually. A series of joint European Union, Canada, and China ministerial climate meetings tended to underscore hopes for cooperation. European Commission, "China, the EU and Canada Co-convene the 5th Ministerial on Climate Action," March 23, 2021, https://ec.europa.eu/clima/news-your-voice/news/china-eu-and-canada-co-convene-5th-ministerial-climate-action-2021-03-23_en.

100 The methane pledge was co-initiated by the United States and the European Union at the "Major Economies Forum" (MEF) convened in September 2021 as a follow-up to the April Leaders Summit, and adopted as a deliverable for the COP26 meetings. Sara Schonhardt, "More Countries Join Global Methane Pledge," *Scientific American,* October 12, 2021, https://www.scientificamerican.com/article/more-countries-join-global-pledge-to-cut-methane-emissions/; White House, "Meeting of the Major Economies on Energy and Climate September 17, 2021: Chair's Summary," September 17, 2021, https://bidenwhitehouse.archives.gov/briefing-room/statements-releases/2021/09/17/meeting-of-the-major-economies-on-energy-and-climate-september-17-2021-chairs-summary/.

101 Vincent Ni, "Chinese Leader Xi Jinping to Attend Cop26 by Video Link – Report," *The Guardian,* October 29, 2021, https://www.theguardian.com/world/2021/oct/29/chinese-leader-xi-jinping-to-attend-cop26-by-video-link?CMP=Share_AndroidApp_Other.

102 "Full Text: Written Statement by Xi Jinping at the World Leaders Summit," *Qiushi,* November 2, 2021, https://en.qstheory.cn/2021-11/02/c_676248.htm.
103 Nationally Determined Contributions Registry, "China's Achievements, New Goals and New Measures for Nationally Determined Contributions," 2021, https://unfccc.int/sites/default/files/NDC/2022-06/China's%20Achievements%2C%20New%20Goals%20and%20New%20Measures%20for%20Nationally%20Determined%20Contributions.pdf; UNEP, "Emissions Gap Report 2021," October 26, 2021, https://www.unep.org/resources/emissions-gap-report-2021.
104 "LMDC Ministerial Statement," October 2021, https://static.pib.gov.in/WriteReadData/specificdocs/documents/2021/oct/doc2021101821.pdf.
105 SCIO, "Full Text: Responding to Climate Change: China's Policies and Actions," October 2021, http://english.scio.gov.cn/whitepapers/2021-10/27/content_77836502_4.htm.
106 "Zhonggong zhongyang guowuyuan guanyu wanzheng zhunque quanmian guanche xinfazhan linian zuohao tandafeng tanzhonghe gongzuo de yijian" [Opinions of the CPC Central Committee and the State Council on the complete, accurate and comprehensive implementation of the new development concept to do a good job in carbon peaking and carbon neutrality], September 22, 2021, http://www.gov.cn/zhengce/2021-10/24/content_5644613.htm.
107 Fiona Harvey, "China's Top Cop26 Delegate Says It Is Taking 'Real Action' on Climate Targets," *The Guardian,* November 10, 2021, https://www.theguardian.com/environment/2021/nov/10/chinas-top-cop26-delegate-says-it-is-taking-real-action-on-climate-targets?CMP=Share_AndroidApp_Other.
108 Dave Lawler, "Top EU Negotiator Expects Tensions with China as COP26 Talks Heat Up," *Axios,* November 4, 2021, https://www.axios.com/eu-negotiator-china-cop26-tensions-9bbef09c-7f25-40b0-84fc-91e3e35b4c30.html.
109 Karl Mathiesen, "The Last-Minute Coal Demand That Almost Sunk the Glasgow Climate Deal," *Politico,* November 13, 2021, https://www.politico.com/news/2021/11/13/coalglasgow-climate-deal-521802. The "phase down" wording echoed provisions in China's 2021 submission on Nationally Determined Contributions (NDC), as well as the Kigali Amendment (2016) to the Montreal Protocol (1987) on ozone depletion calling for a phase down of hydrofluorocarbon production and consumption. See Nationally Determined Contributions Registry, "China's Achievements, New Goals and New Measures for Nationally Determined Contributions," Introduction 2 and Section I.III 2–3, https://unfccc.int/sites/default/files/NDC/2022-06/China's%20Achievements%2C%20New%20Goals%20and%20New%20Measures%20for%20Nationally%20Determined%20Contributions.pdf; United Nations Industrial Development Organization, "The Montreal Protocol Evolves to Fight Climate Change," https://www.unido.org/sites/default/files/2017-07/UNIDO_leaflet_07_MontrealProtocolEvolves_170126_0.pdf.
110 Andrew Freedman, "Top Emitter China Says No to Fossil Fuel 'Phase Out' Language at COP28," *Axios,* September 25, 2023, https://www.axios.com/2023/09/25/china-us-climate-talks-cop28.
111 Inger Andersen, "Green Prosperity Through Energy Transitions and Renewables," (speech at Open Forum: Synergizing the Efforts on Climate Change and Forging a Path to Green Prosperity, Beijing, August 29, 2023), https://www.unep.org/news-and-stories/speech/green-prosperity-through-energy-transitions-and-renewables.
112 The rich academic literature on PRC economic policy includes, e.g., David Dollar, Yiping Huang, and Yang Yao, eds., *China 2049: Economic Challenges of a Rising Global Power* (Washington, DC: Brookings Institution Press, 2020), https://www.brookings.edu/book/china-2049/; Fang Cai, Ross Garnaut, and Ligang Song, eds., *China's 40 Years of Reform and Development: 1978–2018* (Canberra: Australian National University Press, 2018), https://press-files.anu.edu.au/downloads/press/n4267/pdf/book.pdf; Bert Hofman, "Reflections on Forty Years of China's Reforms" (speech at the Fudan University's Fanhai School of International Finance, January 2018), https://thedocs.worldbank.org/en/doc/934911517472447837-0070022018/original/Reflectionson40yearsofreformsfinal.pdf; Congressional Research Service, "China's Economic Rise: History, Trends, Challenges, and Implications for the United States," CRS Report RL33534, June 25, 2019, https://crsreports.congress.gov/product/pdf/RL/RL33534/96; Dwight H. Perkins, *The Economic Transformation of China* (Singapore: World Scientific, 2015), https://www.worldscientific.com/worldscibooks/10.1142/9201; Roselyn Hsueh, *China's Regulatory State: A New Strategy for Globalization* (Ithaca, NY: Cornell University Press, 2011), https://cornell.universitypressscholarship.com/view/10.7591/cornell/9780801449956.001.0001/upso-9780801449956; Loren Brandt and Thomas G. Rawski, *China's Great Economic Transformation* (Cambridge: Cambridge University Press, 2010), https://www.cambridge.org/

core/books/chinas-great-economic-transformation/BD126A197B16634501EA12F594D528DF; Barry Naughton, *The Chinese Economy: Transitions and Growth* (Cambridge, MA: MIT Press, 2007), https://mitpress.mit.edu/books/chinese-economy.

113 Dwight H. Perkins, "The Economy, 1949–1978," *Oxford Bibliographies*, October 28, 2020, https://www.oxfordbibliographies.com/view/document/obo-9780199920082/obo-9780199920082-0016.xml; Graham Young, "Mao Zedong and the Class Struggle in Socialist Society," *Australian Journal of Chinese Affairs* 16 (July 1986): 41–80, https://www.journals.uchicago.edu/doi/10.2307/2158775.

114 "Communiqué of the Third Plenary Session of the 11th Central Committee of the Communist Party of China," *Beijing Review*, December 29, 1978, http://www.bjreview.com/Special_Reports/2018/40th_Anniversary_of_Reform_and_Opening_up/Timeline/201806/t20180626_800133641.html.

115 Wei Liu, "Combining Marxism and China's Practices for the Development of a Socialist Political Economy with Chinese Characteristics," *Chinese Political Economy* 1, 1 (2018): 30–44, https://www.emerald.com/insight/content/doi/10.1108/CPE-09-2018-001/full/pdf?title=combining-marxism-and-chinas-practices-for-the-development-of-a-socialist-political-economy-with-chinese-characteristics.

116 Yingyi Qian, *How Reform Worked in China: The Transition from Plan to Market* (Cambridge, MA: MIT Press, 2017), https://mitpress.mit.edu/books/how-reform-worked-china.

117 Jacques deLisle and Avery Goldstein, "China's Economic Reform and Opening Up at Forty: Past Accomplishments and Future Challengers," in *To Get Rich Is Glorious: Challenges Facing China's Economic Reforms and Opening at Forty*, ed. Jacques deLisle and Avery Goldstein (Washington, DC: Brookings Institution Press, 2019), https://www.brookings.edu/book/to-get-rich-is-glorious/.

118 Yongnian Zheng, *Globalization and State Transformation in China* (Cambridge: Cambridge University Press, 2004), https://www.cambridge.org/core/books/globalization-and-state-transformation-in-china/303EF635F36782883E682160AD6440A7.

119 Barry Naughton, "The Impact of the Tiananmen Crisis on China's Economic Transformation," *China Perspectives* (January 1, 2009): 63–78, https://journals.openedition.org/chinaperspectives/4807.

120 Craig A. Smith, "Datong and Xiaokang," in *Afterlives of Chinese Communism: Political Concepts from Mao to Xi*, ed. Christian Sorace, Ivan Franceschini, and Nicholas Loubere (Sydney: ANU Press, 2019), 63–66, https://press.anu.edu.au/publications/afterlives-chinese-communism.

121 Alice Miller, "Hu Jintao and the 6th Plenum," *China Leadership Monitor* no. 20 (January 1, 2007), https://www.hoover.org/sites/default/files/uploads/documents/clm20am.pdf; Joseph Fewsmith, "Promoting the Scientific Development Concept," *China Leadership Monitor* no. 11 (July 30, 2004), https://www.hoover.org/research/promoting-scientific-development-concept.

122 "Decision of the Central Committee of the Communist Party of China on Some Major Issues Concerning Comprehensively Deepening the Reform," January 16, 2014, http://www.china.org.cn/china/third_plenary_session/2014-01/16/content_31212602.htm.

123 Scott Kennedy and Ilaria Mazzocco, "Can Chinese Firms Be Truly Private?" Big Data China, February 7, 2023, https://bigdatachina.csis.org/can-chinese-firms-be-truly-private/; Barry Naughton and Briana Boland, "CCP Inc.: The Reshaping of China's State Capitalist System," Center for Strategic and International Studies, January 2023, https://www.csis.org/analysis/ccp-inc-reshaping-chinas-state-capitalist-system?utm_source=substack&utm_medium=email. The PRC ambassador to the World Trade Organization averred in 2018 that China considered the socialist market economy as a market economy under the leadership of the Communist Party of China. Henry Gao, "What Is 'Socialist Market Economy?'" *International Economic Law and Policy Blog*, July 29, 2018, https://ielp.worldtradelaw.net/2018/07/what-is-socialist-market-economy/.

124 "Communiqué of the Fifth Plenary Meeting of the 18th Central Committee of the Chinese Communist Party," November 2, 2015, https://chinacopyrightandmedia.wordpress.com/2015/10/29/communique-of-the-fifth-plenary-meeting-of-the-18th-central-committee-of-the-chinese-communist-party; Nathaniel Taplin and Jacky Wong, "Common Prosperity: Decoding China's New Populism," *Wall Street Journal*, August 28, 2021, https://www.wsj.com/articles/common-prosperity-decoding-chinas-new-populism-11630159381; Minxin Pei, "The Origins and Implications of Xi Jinping's 'Common Prosperity' Agenda," *China Leadership Monitor* no. 70 (December 1, 2021), https://www.prcleader.org/pei-4; Alexander Chipman Koty, "How to

Understand China's Common Prosperity Policy," *China Briefing,* March 21, 2022, https://www.china-briefing.com/news/china-common-prosperity-what-does-it-mean-for-foreign-investors/.

125 Mary Gallagher, "China's Struggle for Common Prosperity," *China Leadership Monitor* no. 75, March 1, 2023, https://www.prcleader.org/post/china-s-struggle-for-common-prosperity.

126 Ilaria Mazzocco, "How Inequality Is Undermining China's Prosperity," Big Data China, May 28, 2022, https://www.csis.org/analysis/how-inequality-undermining-chinas-prosperity; Dexter Tiff Roberts, *The Domestic Challenges That Threaten China's Superpower Future* (Washington, DC: Atlantic Council, 2021), https://www.atlanticcouncil.org/wp-content/uploads/2021/12/The_Domestic_Challenges_that_Threaten_Chinas_Superpower_Future.pdf.

127 Xibai Xu, Jude Blanchette, Maya Wang, and Fergus Ryan, "Tightening Up: A ChinaFile Conversation," ChinaFile, October 20, 2021, https://www.chinafile.com/conversation/china-regulatory-crackdown.

128 "Zhonggong Zhongyang Guowuyuan yinfa 'Fazhi zhengfu jianshe shishi gangyao' (2021–2025)" [CPC Central Committee/State Council issue provisional outline on establishment of lawful governance (2021–2025)], Section 16, August 11, 2021, http://www.gov.cn/zhengce/2021-08/11/content_5630802.htm. Increased state ownership of high-tech firms was exemplified by the regime's taking controlling interests in Alibaba and Tencent in early 2023 through mandated acquisition of "special management shares" (also known as "golden shares"). Mark Sweney, "China to Take 'Golden Shares' in Tech Firms Alibaba and Tencent," *The Guardian,* January 13, 2023, https://www.theguardian.com/world/2023/jan/13/china-to-take-golden-shares-in-tech-firms-alibaba-and-tencent?CMP=Share_AndroidApp_Other.

129 Renewed attention to anti-monopoly efforts and protection of enterprises and individuals participating in the economy, referred to as "market subjects" (*shichang zhuti* // 市场主体), echoed the 2019 regulations on optimizing the business environment. "Youhua shangye huanjing tiaoli" [Regulations on optimizing the business environment], October 22, 2019, https://www.gov.cn/zhengce/content/2019-10/23/content_5443963.htm.

130 "Full Text of Xi Jinping's Report at 19th CPC National Congress," *China Daily,* November 4, 2017, https://www.chinadaily.com.cn/china/19thcpcnationalcongress/2017-11/04/content_34115212.htm.

131 "Zhonggong shijiujie wuzhong quanhui gongbao (quanwen)" [Communiqué of the fifth plenum of the 19th CPC Central Committee (full text)], October 29, 2020, https://wap.peopleapp.com/article/rmh17257967/rmh17257967.

132 Xi Jinping, "Understanding the New Development Stage, Applying the New Development Philosophy, and Creating a New Development Dynamic," *China Daily,* July 12, 2021, https://www.chinadaily.com.cn/a/202107/12/WS60ec3e56a310efa1bd6614fb.html.

133 "Xi Jinping zhuchi zhaokai zhongyang caijing weiyuanhui di shici huiyi" [Xi Jinping chairs the 10th meeting of the Central Finance and Economic Commission], *Xinhuanet,* August 18, 2021, https://www.mee.gov.cn/ywdt/szyw/202108/t20210818_858115.shtml; "Xi Jinping zhuchi zhaokai Zhongyang Caijing Weiyuanhui di shici huiyi qiangdiao zai gao zhiliang fazhan zhong cujin gongtong fuyu tongchou zuoha zhongda jinrong fengxian fangfan huajie gongzuo – Li Keqiang, Wang Yang, Hu Huning, Han Zheng chuxi" [Xi Jinping chairs 10th meeting of the Central Commission on Finance and Economics called to emphasize promoting common prosperity in high-quality development and to do a good job in preventing and resolving major financial risks – Li Keqiang, Wang Yang, Wang Huning, Han Zheng in attendance], August 17, 2021, http://www.xinhuanet.com/politics/leaders/2021-08/17/c_1127770343.htm.

134 "Xi Stresses Promoting Common Prosperity Amid High-Quality Development, Forestalling Major Financial Risks," *Beijing Review,* August 2021, http://www.bjreview.com/CHINA_INSIGHT_2021/Special_Issue_on_Promoting_Common_Prosperity_Amid_High_Quality_Development/202109/t20210930_800259600.html.

135 SCIO, "Full Text: China's Epic Journey from Poverty to Prosperity," white paper, September 28, 2021, http://english.scio.gov.cn/whitepapers/2021-09/28/content_77779569.htm.

136 "Zhongguo fazhan yanjiu jijinhui fabu gongtong fuyu baogao" [China Development Research Foundation releases report on common prosperity], September 19, 2022, https://www.cdrf.org.cn/jjhdt/6371.htm.

137 "'Zhongguo fazhan baogao 2021–2022: Zou gongtong fuyu zhi lu' hui ying le naxie guanjian wenti?" [What are the key issues raised by 'China development report 2021–2022: taking the path of common prosperity'?), https://www.cdrf.org.cn/jjhdt/6373.htm; "Honggujo fazhan

hyanjiu jijinhui fabu gongtong fuyu baogao: Wanshan zhongdeng shouru fahaoxing zhengce, guojian shenghuo zhiliang lingjia kuangjia" [China Development Research Foundation releases common prosperity report: improving middle-income–friendly policies and building a framework for assessing quality of life], *21 Caijing,* September 19, 2022, https://m.21jingji.com/article/20220919/herald/967d9fe609842752992b58a0c840ee2c.html.

138 "Full Text: Resolution of the CPC Central Committee on the Major Achievements and Historical Experience of the Party over the Past Century," *Xinhua,* November 16, 2021, https://english.www.gov.cn/policies/latestreleases/202111/16/content_WS6193a935c6d0df57f98e50b0.html.

139 Zichen Wang and Nathan Zheng, "Central Economic Work Conference Readout & Notes: A Near-Full Translation with Analysis," *Pekingnology* (blog), December 10, 2021, https://pekingnology.substack.com/p/central-economic-work-conference. Offering a foretaste of Xi's remarks, an SCIO white paper issued in August 2021 had lauded China's achievement of moderate prosperity. SCIO, "Full Text: Moderate Prosperity in All Respects: Another Milestone Achieved in China's Human Rights," white paper, August 2021, http://english.www.gov.cn/archive/whitepaper/202108/12/content_WS611492b4c6d0df57f98de5ac.html.

140 Xi Jinping, "Zhengque renshi he ba wo woguo fazhan zhongda lilun he shixian wenti" [Correctly understand and master major issues of theory and practice in our country's development], *Qiushi* [*Truth*], October 2022, http://www.qstheory.cn/dukan/qs/2022-05/15/c_1128649331.htm.

141 Xi Jinping, "Hold High the Great Banner of Socialism with Chinese Characteristics and Strive in Unity to Build a Modern Socialist Country in All Respects" (full text of the report to the 20th National Congress of the Communist Party of China, October 16, 2022, 18, https://www.idcpc.org.cn/english2023/tjzl/cpcjj/20thPartyCongrssReport/. Speaking to Xi's efforts to install loyalists in the CPC Politburo and removing potential critics like former general secretary Hu Jintao from the final public meeting of the 20th CPC Congress, respected observers suggested Xi was embracing "common prosperity" as a solution to difficult times ahead – to the point of terming the 20th CPC Politburo a "common prosperity cabinet." Ken Moriyasu, "Xi's Removal of Hu Points to 'Common Prosperity,' Not Taiwan Invasion," *Nikkei Asia,* November 4, 2022, https://asia.nikkei.com/Spotlight/Comment/Xi-s-removal-of-Hu-points-to-common-prosperity-not-Taiwan-invasion.

142 "Zhonggong Zhongyang Guowuyuan yinfa 'Kuoda neixu zhanlue guihua gangyao (2022–2035nian)'" [CPC Central Committee and State Council issue strategic plan for 2022–2035 on expanding domestic demand], December 14, 2022, http://www.gov.cn/zhengce/2022-12/14/content_5732067.htm.

143 "Xi Jinping zai xuexi guanche Dang de ershi da jingshen yantao bankai banshi shang fabiao zhongyao jianghua qiangdiao zhengque lijie he dali tuidong Zhongguo shixiandaihua" [Xi Jinping delivers important speech at the opening ceremony of the seminar to study and implement the spirit of the CPC 20th National Congress emphasizing correctly understanding and vigorously promoting Chinese-style modernization], http://paper.people.com.cn/rmrb/html/2023-02/08/nw.D110000renmrb_20230208_1-01.htm; Hu Zimo, "Xi Jinping Launches His 'Non-Western' Model of Modernization," *Bitter Winter,* February 20, 2023, https://bitterwinter.org/xi-jinping-non-western-model-of-modernization/. Also see Xi Jinping, "Uphold and Develop Socialism with Chinese Characteristics," *Qiushi,* January 5, 2013, https://en.qstheory.cn/2020-08/11/c_607578.htm.

144 "'Shuzi jingji cujin gongtong fuyu shishi fang an' chutai, tuijin quanti renmin gongtong fuyu shuzi shidai fazhan hongli" [Implementation plan for promoting common prosperity through the digital economy was promulgated to promote all people to share the dividends of development in the digital era], *CCTV News,* December 26, 2023, https://news.cri.cn/20231226/41e49012-78df-fa63-a948-2e4ba5a23bf5.html.

145 Matt Phillips and Bethany Allen-Ebrahimian, "China's Economy Is Sputtering," *Axios,* April 19, 2022, https://www.axios.com/china-economy-covid-lockdowns-6baf86ed-1a84-4a54-ba44-184e16e28972.html; "China Suspends Promotion of 'Common Prosperity' Amid Economic Slump," *Kyodo News,* April 18, 2022, https://english.kyodonews.net/news/2022/04/316dcc-ce0e13-china-suspends-promotion-of-common-prosperity-amid-economic-slump.html; Andrew Collier, "China's 'Common Prosperity' Campaign Is Going to Be Tough Going," *The Diplomat,* September 18, 2021, https://thediplomat.com/2021/09/chinas-common-prosperity-campaign-is-going-to-be-tough-going.

146 "2022 nian Zhongyang jingji gongzuo huiyi ceji: 'Wei quanmian jianshe shehuizhuyi xiandaihua guojia kaihao juqi haobu'" [Side note to the 2022 Central Economic Work Conference: a good step toward all-round construction of a modern socialist country], December 18, 2022, http://www.gov.cn/xinwen/2022-12/18/content_5732562.htm. Compare with "2022 Zhongyang jingji gongzuo huiyi gongbao quanwen" [Full text of the communiqué for the 2022 Central Economic Work Conference], December 16, 2022, http://www.china-cer.com.cn/guwen/2022121622596.html.

147 George Magnus, "The Chinese Economy: Troubled Times Ahead," Council on Geostrategy, October 2022, https://www.geostrategy.org.uk/research/the-chinese-economy-troubled-times-ahead/; Katsuji Nakazawa, "Analysis: Xi's 'Common Prosperity' Puts Cake Debate Back in Oven" *Nikkei Asia,* November 3, 2021, https://asia.nikkei.com/Editor-s-Picks/China-up-close/Analysis-Xi-s-common-prosperity-puts-cake-debate-back-in-oven; Willie Wo-Lap Lam, "Early Warning Brief: Xi Jinping Issues Tough Warnings to Enemies Within the Party," *China Brief* 21, 15 (July 23, 2021), https://jamestown.org/program/early-warning-brief-xi-jinping-issues-tough-warnings-to-enemies-within-the-party/.

148 Anne Stevenson-Yang, "'Common Prosperity': The Graft That Is Actually Powering Chinese Politics," *Forbes,* November 11, 2021, https://www.forbes.com/sites/annestevenson-yang/2021/11/11/common-prosperity-the-graft-that-is-actually-powering-chinas-politics/?sh=2d6e59c86a4b.

149 Zongyuan Zoe Liu, "Xi's Policies Have Shortened the Fuse on China's Economic Time Bomb," *Foreign Policy,* September 6, 2023, https://foreignpolicy.com/2023/09/06/china-xi-jinping-economic-uncertainty-deflation-policy-mistakes/; Zongyuan Zoe Liu and Ben Steil, "Xi's Plan for China's Economy Is Doomed to Fail," *Foreign Affairs,* June 29, 2023, https://www.foreignaffairs.com/china/xis-plan-chinas-economy-doomed-fail.

150 Xi Jinping, "Understanding the New Development Stage, Applying the New Development Philosophy, and Creating a New Development Dynamic," *Qiushi* [*Truth*], November 9, 2021, http://en.qstheory.cn/2021-07/08/c_641137.htm; "New Development Concept" [*Xin fazhan linian*], Center for Strategic Translation, 2022, https://chinaopensourceobservatory.org/glossary/new-development-concept; Xi Jinping, "Fostering a New Development Paradigm and Pursuing Mutual Benefit and Win-Win Cooperation," November 19, 2020, https://www.mfa.gov.cn/eng/xw/zyjh/202405/t20240530_11341479.html#:~:text=The%20new%20development%20paradigm%20is,changes%20in%20the%20external%20environment; "New Development Pattern" [*Xin fazhan geju*], Center for Strategic Translation, 2022, https://www.strategictranslation.org/glossary/new-development-pattern.

151 Dai Xiaohe, "Wenzi dangtou, wenzhong qiujin, zai gao zhiliang fazhan lu shang qianding qianxing – Han Wenxiu jie du 2021 nian zhongyang jingji gongzuo huiyi jingshen" [Putting stability first, seeking progress while maintaining stability, and moving forward firmly on the road of high-quality development – Han Wenxiu interprets the spirit of the 2021 Central Economic Work Conference], Xinhua wang [New China News], December 11, 2021, http://www.xinhuanet.com/fortune/2021-12/11/c_1128154822.htm.

152 "China Holds Central Economic Work Conference to Plan for 2023," *Xinhua,* December 17, 2022, https://english.www.gov.cn/news/topnews/202212/17/content_WS639d0051c6d0a757729e4885.html; "2022 zhongyang jingji gongzuo huiyi gongbao quanwen" [Full text of the communiqué for the 2022 Central Economic Work Conference]. Links between "common prosperity" and the "new development philosophy" are articulated in Xi Jinping, "Understanding the New Development Stage, Applying the New Development Philosophy, and Creating a New Development Dynamic."

153 Neil Thomas, "Xi Signals More Growth but Same Strategy at China's Central Economic Work Conference," Asia Society Policy Institute, December 14, 2023, https://asiasociety.org/policy-institute/xi-signals-more-growth-same-strategy-chinas-central-economic-work-conference.

154 "Xi Delivers Important Speech at Central Economic Work Conference," *Xinhua,* December 4, 2023, https://english.www.gov.cn/news/202312/14/content_WS657aacdec6d0868f4e8e22a5.html; Xi Jinping, "Hold High the Great Banner of Socialism with Chinese Characteristics and Strive in Unity to Build a Modern Socialist Country in All Respects." Also see Giulia Interesse, "China's Central Economic Work Conference Outlines Key Priorities for 2024," *China Briefing,* December 21, 2023, https://www.china-briefing.com/news/chinas-central-economic-work-conference-outlines-key-priorities-for-2024/.

155 Andrew Peaple, "Barry Naughton on the State of the Xi Jinping Economy," *Wire China*, January 5, 2025, https://www.thewirechina.com/2025/01/05/barry-naughton-on-the-state-of-the-xi-jinping-economy/; "Xi Delivers Important Speech at Central Economic Work Conference," *Xinhua*, December 17, 2024, https://english.www.gov.cn/news/202412/17/content_WS6760b3e6c6d0868f4e8ee061.html; Giulia Interesse, "China's Central Economic Work Conference (CEWC): Key Takeaways and Priorities for 2025," *China Briefing*, December 16, 2024, https://www.china-briefing.com/news/chinas-central-economic-work-conference-cewc-key-takeaways-and-priorities-for-2025/.

156 Bill Bishop, "December Politburo Meeting Ahead of the Central Economic Work Conference (CEWC)," *Sinocism* (blog), December 9, 2024, https://sinocism.com/p/december-politburo-meeting-ahead.

157 Jeremy Mark and Michael Schuman, *China's Faltering "Zero COVID" Policy: Politics in Command, Economy in Reverse* (Washington, DC: Atlantic Council, 2022), https://www.atlanticcouncil.org/wp-content/uploads/2022/05/Chinas-Faltering-Zero-COVID-Policy-Politics-in-Command-Economy-in-Reverse.pdf.

158 Asia Pacific Foundation of Canada, "China's Snowballing Mortgage Crisis," *Asia Watch*, July 21, 2022, https://www.asiapacific.ca/asia-watch/chinas-snowballing-mortgage-crisis.

159 Michael Shuman, "The China Model Is Dead," *The Atlantic*, September 7, 2023, https://www.theatlantic.com/international/archive/2023/09/china-economy-slowdown-xi-jinping/675236/; Graeme Wearden, "Chinese Economy Slips into Deflation as Recovery Falters and Demand Slows," *The Guardian*, August 9, 2023, https://www.theguardian.com/world/2023/aug/08/chinese-economy-expected-to-have-slipped-into-deflation-as-recovery-falters.

160 Annabelle Liang, "China Congress: Beijing Delays Key Economic Figures as Leaders Meet," *BBC News*, October 18, 2022, https://www.bbc.com/news/business-63295495.

161 "Xi Delivers Important Speech at Central Economic Work Conference," *Xinhua*, December 4, 2023.

162 Phillip Inman, "Moody's Cuts China Credit Outlook to Negative as Economy Slows," *The Guardian*, December 5, 2023, https://www.theguardian.com/business/2023/dec/05/moodys-china-credit-outlook-negative-economy.

163 "Official Data, Other Signs Hint at Bad State of China's Economy," *SinoInsider*, August 25, 2024, https://sinoinsider.com/2024/08/official-data-other-signs-hint-at-bad-state-of-chinas-economy/; International Monetary Fund (IMF), *People's Republic of China: 2024, IMF Staff Country Reports 2024 Article IV Consultation–Press Release; Staff Report; and Statement by the Executive Director for the People's Republic of China*, IMF Country Reports 24/258 (Washington, DC: IMF, 2024), https://www.elibrary.imf.org/view/journals/002/2024/258/002.2024.issue-258-en.xml?cid=552803-com-dsp-crossref; Courtney Brown, "China's Broken Recovery: New Data Shows Drag on Its Economy," *Axios*, June 17, 2024, https://www.axios.com/2024/06/17/china-economy-housing-crisis; Daniel H. Rosen and Logan Wright, "China's Economic Collision Course: As Growth Slows, Beijing's Moves Are Drawing a Global Backlash," *Foreign Affairs*, March 27, 2024; George Magnus, "China's Many Systemic Problems Dominate Its Outlook for 2024," *The Guardian*, January 1, 2024, https://www.theguardian.com/business/2024/jan/01/chinas-many-systemic-problems-dominate-its-outlook-for-2024.

164 "CPC to Convene 3d Plenary Session of 20th Central Committee on July 15," *China Daily*, June 28, 2024, https://www.chinadaily.com.cn/a/202406/28/WS667e09aea31095c51c50b437.html; João da Silva, "Xi Tackles Slow Growth as Economy 'Hits the Brakes,'" *BBC News*, July 14, 2024, https://www.bbc.com/news/articles/cl4y6mexgz8o.

165 "China Unveils Fresh Stimulus to Boost High-Quality Economic Development," *China Daily*, September 25, 2024, https://english.www.gov.cn/news/202409/25/content_WS66f3602ec6d0868f4e8eb3c0.html; Phillip Inman, "China Unleashes Boldest Stimulus in Years to Boost Ailing Economy," *The Guardian*, September 24, 2024, https://www.theguardian.com/world/2024/sep/24/china-economy-stimulus-package-measures-yuan-pbc; Jason Douglas, "China Tries to Jolt Ailing Economy," *Wall Street Journal*, September 24, 2024, https://www.wsj.com/world/china/china-central-bank-takes-more-steps-to-boost-flagging-economy-b43e8aef?mod=hp_lead_pos2.

166 Suranjana Tewari, "Three Reasons Trump Tariffs Aren't China's Only Problem," *BBC News*, January 16, 2025, https://www.bbc.com/news/articles/ceq9lxlg811o; George Magnus, "China's Plan to Boost Flagging Economy Is the Very Definition of Economic Insanity," *The Guardian*,

October 13, 2024, https://www.theguardian.com/business/2024/oct/13/chinas-plan-to-boost-flagging-growth-is-the-very-definition-of-economic-insanity.

167 He Yiting, "Zhongguo shi xiandaihua shi quanti renmin gongtong fuyu de shehui zhuyi xiandaihua" [Chinese-style modernization is socialist modernization with common prosperity for all people], *Ai sixiang* [*Loving Ideas*], May 20, 2025, https://www.aisixiang.com/data/162837.html; Martin K. Whyte, "Xi Jinping Confronts Inequality: Bold Leadership or Modest Steps?" in *The Xi Jinping Effect*, ed. Ashley Esarey and Rongbin Han (Seattle: University of Washington Press, 2024), 93–128, https://library.oapen.org/handle/20.500.12657/92972.

168 Amy Hawkins, "China Cracks Down on Negativity over Economy in Bid to Boost Confidence," *The Guardian*, December 29, 2023, https://www.theguardian.com/world/2023/dec/29/china-cracks-down-on-negativity-over-economy-in-bid-to-boost-confidence.

169 "At Third Plenum, CCP Opts for Political Control over Economic Liberalization," *SinoInsider*, July 24, 2024, https://sinoinsider.com/2024/07/at-third-plenum-ccp-opts-for-political-control-over-economic-liberalization/.

170 Phillip Inman, "Xi Says China's Economy on Course to Expand by 5% Despite Trump Concerns," *The Guardian*, December 31, 2024, https://www.theguardian.com/world/2024/dec/31/xi-china-economy-trump-tariffs; Lingling Wei, "Xi Jinping Muzzles Chinese Economist Who Dared to Doubt GDP Numbers," *Wall Street Journal*, January 8, 2025, https://www.wsj.com/world/china/xi-jinping-muzzles-chinese-economist-who-dared-to-doubt-gdp-numbers-2a2468ef?mod=hp_lead_pos10.

171 "China's Economy Meets Official Growth Target, but Many Feel Worse Off," *Reuters*, January 21, 2025, https://www.reuters.com/world/china/chinas-economic-growth-surpasses-forecasts-stimulus-push-2025-01-17/.

172 Heather Stewart, "China's Economy Hits 5% Growth Target but Rate Among Slowest in Decades," *The Guardian*, January 17, 2025, https://www.theguardian.com/business/2025/jan/17/china-economy-hits-growth-target-but-rate-among-slowest-in-decades; Daniel H. Rosen, Logan Wright, Jeremy Smith, Matthew Mingey, and Rogan Quinn "After the Fall: China's Economy in 2025," Rhodium Group, December 31, 2024, https://rhg.com/research/after-the-fall-chinas-economy-in-2025/.

173 "Meituan: China Tech Giant's Shares Slide over Ancient Poem," *BBC News*, May 11 2021, https://www.bbc.com/news/business-57066908.

174 "Zhonggong Zongyang Guowuyuan guanyu cujin minying jingji fazhan zhangda de yijian" [CPC Central Committee and State Council opinion on promoting growth in the private economy], *Xinhua*, July 29, 2023, https://www.gov.cn/zhengce/202307/content_6893055.htm; "China Vows to Spur Growth of Private Economy," *Xinhua*, July 29, 2023, https://english.www.gov.cn/policies/latestreleases/202307/19/content_WS64b7e139c6d0868f4e8ddf20.html; Jane Cai, "China Has 31-Point Plan for Private Sector to Kick-Start Economy. But Are Bruised Businesses Buying It?" *South China Morning Post*, August 9, 2023, https://www.scmp.com/news/china/politics/article/3229706/china-has-31-point-plan-private-sector-kick-start-economy-are-bruised-business-owners-buying-it.

175 "Zhonghua renmin gongheguo minying jingji cujin fa (cao'an zhengqiu jiangao)" [Law of the People's Republic of China on the promotion of the private economy (draft for solicitation of comments)], *NPC Observer*, https://npcobserver.com/wp-content/uploads/2024/10/Private-Economy-Promotion-Law-2024-Draft.pdf; "Sifabu Guojia fazhan gaige wei guanyu 'Zhonghua renmin gongheguo minying jingji cujin fa (cao'an zhengqiu jiangao)' gongkai zhengqiu yijian de Tongzhi" [Notice of the Ministry of Justice and the National Development and Reform Commission on the "law of the People's Republic of China on the promotion of the private economy (draft for solicitation of comments)" for public solicitation of comments], October 10, 2024, https://www.moj.gov.cn/pub/sfbgw/lfyjzj/lflfyjzj/202410/t20241010_507325.html; Ministry of Justice (MOJ) and NDRC, "Minying jingji cujinfa cao'an xiang shehui gongkai zhengqiu yijian" [The draft law on the economic promotion of the people's police is open to the public to solicit opinions], October 10, 2024, https://www.moj.gov.cn/pub/sfbgw/gwxw/xwyw/202410/t20241010_507314.html. Also see "Opinion: Grasping the Essence of the Private Economy Promotion Law," *Caixin*, October 28, 2024, https://www.caixinglobal.com/2024-10-28/opinion-grasping-the-essence-of-the-private-economy-promotion-law-102250379.html; Ouyang Shijia, "China Issues Draft Law to Foster a Healthier Private Economy," *China Daily*, October 10, 2024, https://www.chinadaily.com.cn/a/202410/10/WS6707bbd5a310f1265a1c6eda.html.

176 Vanessa Cai, "Xi Jinping 'Personally' Steering China's Reform Process, State Media Report Says," *South China Morning Post,* December 18, 2023, https://www.scmp.com/news/china/politics/article/3245488/xi-jinping-personally-steering-chinas-reform-process-state-media-report-says.

177 See generally National Bureau of Statistics of the People's Republic of China, "Classifications and Methods," February 23, 2022, http://www.stats.gov.cn/english/ClassificationsMethods/Classifications/; Asian Development Bank (ADB), "Inclusive and Sustainable Growth Assessment," 2021, https://www.adb.org/sites/default/files/linked-documents/prc-cps-2021-2025-ld01.pdf; Josh Lipski, "The 2021 Economic Scorecard: How China Stacks Up with the US and Its Allies," Atlantic Council, 2021, https://www.atlanticcouncil.org/content-series/the-big-story/the-2021-economic-scorecard-how-china-stacks-up-with-the-us-and-its-allies/; Congressional Research Service, "China's Economic Rise."

178 Ken Wills, "Seeking Balance: China Strives to Adapt Social Protection to the Needs of a Market Economy," *Finance and Development* (IMF), December 2018, https://www.imf.org/external/pubs/ft/fandd/2018/12/social-protection-in-china-wills.htm; Stein Ringen and Kinglun Ngok, "What Kind of Welfare State Is Emerging in China?" UN Research Institute for Social Development (UNRISD) Working Paper 2013-2, September 2013, https://www.researchgate.net/publication/314160044_What_Kind_of_Welfare_State_Is_Emerging_in_China.

179 University of Alberta China Institute, *State-Owned Enterprises in the Chinese Economy Today: Role, Reform, and Evolution* (Edmonton: University of Alberta, 2018), https://www.ualberta.ca/china-institute/media-library/media-gallery/research/policy-papers/soepaper1-2018.pdf; Barry Naughton, "The Transformation of the State Sector: SASAC, the Market Economy, and the New National Champions," in *State Capitalism, Institutional Adaptation, and the Chinese Miracle,* ed. Barry Naughton and Kellee S. Tsai (Cambridge: Cambridge University Press, 2015), ch. 3, https://www.cambridge.org/core/books/abs/state-capitalism-institutional-adaptation-and-the-chinese-miracle/transformation-of-the-state-sector-sasac-the-market-economy-and-the-new-national-champions/2C3428F4C7A565BB7222B820E3FBC522.

180 Nicolas Borst, "Has China Given Up on State-Owned Enterprise Reform?" *The Interpreter* (Lowy Institute), April 15, 2021, https://www.lowyinstitute.org/the-interpreter/has-china-given-state-owned-enterprise-reform; Karen Jingrong Lin, Xiaoyan Lu, Junsheng Zhang, and Ying Zheng, "State-Owned Enterprises in China: A Review of 40 Years of Research and Practice," *China Journal of Accounting Research* 13, 1 (March 2020): 31–55, https://www.sciencedirect.com/science/article/abs/pii/S1755309119300437#!; Amir Guluzade, "The Role of China's State-Owned Companies Explained," World Economic Forum, May 7, 2019, https://www.weforum.org/agenda/2019/05/why-chinas-state-owned-companies-still-have-a-key-role-to-play/.

181 Zhiqiang Dong, Zijin Huo, and Xiahai Wei, "Social Insurance with Chinese Characteristics: The Role of the Communist Party in Private Firms," *China Economic Review* 37, 6 (February 2016): 40–51, https://www.sciencedirect.com/science/article/pii/S1043951X15001212; "Zhonggong zhongyang guowuyuan guanyu yingzao genghaofazhan huanjing zhichi minying qiye gaige fazhan de yijian" [Opinion of the CPC Central Committee and the State Council on building a better development environment to support the development of reform in private enterprises], *Xinhua,* December 22, 2019, http://www.gov.cn/zhengce/2019-12/22/content_5463137.htm.

182 Yi-min Lin, *Between Politics and Markets: Firms, Competition, and Institutional Change in Post-Mao China* (Cambridge: Cambridge University Press, 2004), https://assets.cambridge.org/97805217/71306/frontmatter/9780521771306_frontmatter.pdf.

183 See generally Guoguang Wu, *China's Common Prosperity Program: Causes, Challenges and Implications* (Washington, DC: Asia Society Policy Institute, 2022), https://asiasociety.org/sites/default/files/2022-03/ASPI_ChinaCommonProsp_report_fin.pdf.

184 Binbin Wang and Qinnan Zhou, "Climate Change in the Chinese Mind: An Overview of Public Perceptions at Macro and Micro Levels," *WIREs Climate Change* 11, 3 (2020), https://wires.onlinelibrary.wiley.com/doi/full/10.1002/wcc.639.

185 Yasheng Huang, *Capitalism with Chinese Characteristics: Entrepreneurship and the State* (Cambridge: Cambridge University Press, 2008), https://www.cambridge.org/core/books/capitalism-with-chinese-characteristics/CECD36DB2C3623DEE4670F7897BAA3CB; "'The Long and Winding Road': Sorting Out the Puzzle of Growth – the Macro and the Micro of It," Centre for International Governance Innovation, https://www.cigionline.org/articles/long-and-winding

-road-sorting-out-puzzle-growth-macro-and-micro-it/. Also see Wangyue Li and Ting Dai, "The Differences of Micro Data and Macro Data Used in Statistical Analysis: C-D Production Function," Statistics Hong Kong, https://www.statistics.gov.hk/wsc/CPS111-P3-S.pdf.

186 Northwestern University Kellogg School of Management, "Global Poverty Research Lab – China Cluster," https://www.kellogg.northwestern.edu/academics-research/global-poverty-research-lab/geographical-clusters/china/; OECD, *Data and Meta Data Reporting and Presentation Handbook* (2007), https://www.oecd.org/content/dam/oecd/en/publications/reports/2007/06/data-and-metadata-reporting-and-presentation-handbook_g1gh7b15/9789264030336-en.pdf.

187 Casey and Koleski, "Backgrounder: China's 12th Five-Year Plan."

188 NDRC, "The13th Five-Year Plan for Economic and Social Development of the People's Republic of China (2016–2020)."

189 Tucker Van Aken and Orion A. Lewis, "The Political Economy of Noncompliance in China: The Case of Industrial Energy Policy," *Journal of Contemporary China* 24, 95 (2015): 798–822, https://www.tandfonline.com/doi/full/10.1080/10670564.2015.1013374.

190 NDRC, "Zhongguo yingdui qihou bianhua guojia fangan" [China national plan for adapting to climate change].

191 MEE, "China's Policies and Actions for Addressing Climate Change (2020)," 55–58; Bing Wang, Ge Hong, Chao-Qun Cui, Hao Yu, and Tad Murty, et al., "Comprehensive Analysis of China's National Climate Change Assessment Reports: Action and Emphasis," *Frontiers in Engineering Management* 6 (2019): 52–61, https://link.springer.com/article/10.1007/s42524-019-0002-y; Yun Gao, "China's Response to Climate Change Issues After Paris Climate Change Conference," *Advances in Climate Change Research* 7, 4 (December 2016): 235–40, https://www.sciencedirect.com/science/article/pii/S1674927816300727#bib4.

192 Sandalow, *Guide to Chinese Climate Change Policy 2019.*

193 SCIO, "China's Policies and Actions for Addressing Climate Change," Section III.

194 NDRC, "Guojia shiying qihou bianhua zhanlue" [National climate adaptation strategy]; NDRC, "Guojia yingdui qihou bianhua guihua" [National plan in response to climate change]; Ye Qi et al., "Translating a Global Issue into Local Priority: China's Local Government Response to Climate Change," *Journal of Environment and Development* 17, 4 (2008): 379–400, https://journals.sagepub.com/doi/abs/10.1177/1070496508326123.

195 NDRC, "Qianghua ying dui qihou bianhua xingdong – Zhongguo guojia zizhu gongxian" [Enhanced actions on climate change: China's intended nationally determined contributions].

196 Nationally Determined Contributions Registry, "China's Achievements, New Goals and New Measures for Nationally Determined Contributions."

197 MEE, "China's Policies and Actions for Addressing Climate Change (2019)"; MEE, "China's Policies and Actions for Addressing Climate Change (2020)."

198 MEE, "Guanyu tongchou he jiaqiang yingdui qihou bianhua yu shengtai huanjing baohu xiangguan gongzuo de zhidai yijian" [Guiding opinions on integrating and strengthening efforts in climate action and ecological and environmental protection].

199 SCIO, "Full Text: Responding to Climate Change: China's Policies and Actions."

200 SCIO, "Full Text: Energy in China's New Era," white paper, December 2020, http://english.scio.gov.cn/whitepapers/2020-12/21/content_77035604.htm.

201 NDRC, "Working Guidance for Carbon Dioxide Peaking and Carbon Neutrality in Full and Faithful Implementation of the New Development Philosophy."

202 NDRC, "Action Plan for Carbon Dioxide Peaking Before 2030."

203 NDRC, "Full Text: Report on China's National Economic, Social Development Plan," March 16, 2023, http://www.china.org.cn/china/2023-03/16/content_85171202.htm.

204 See generally Xi Jinping, "Understanding the New Development Stage, Applying the New Development Philosophy, and Creating a New Development Dynamic."

205 China Meteorological Administration, "2021 nian Zhongguo qihou bianhua lanpishu fabu: Zhuanjia cong qihou xitong duoyuanceng jiexi pishu" [China's 2021 blue book on climate change released: experts from multiple climate circles analyze the blue book], August 5, 2021, http://www.cma.gov.cn/2011xwzx/2011xqxxw/2011xqxyw/202108/t20210805_582404.html, and "'Zhongguo qihou bianhuo lanpishu (2021)' fabu: Qihou xitong renzai texu bianai" [China's blue book on climate change (2021) was released: the climate system continues to warm], August 4, 2021, http://finance.people.com.cn/n1/2021/0804/c1004-32181132.html.

206 "Guanyu zhichi xiaowei qiye rongzi youguan shuishou zhengce de gongbao" [Announcement on tax policies related to supporting financing for small and micro enterprises], Ministry of

Finance State Administration of Taxation Announcement No. 2023/13, August 2, 2023, https://www.gov.cn/zhengce/zhengceku/202308/content_6896295.htm.

207 "Transforming Our World: The 2030 Agenda for Sustainable Development," Resolution adopted by the UN General Assembly on September 25, 2015, A/Res/70/1, paragraph 48, https://documents-dds-ny.un.org/doc/UNDOC/GEN/N15/291/89/PDF/N1529189.pdf?OpenElement.

208 NDRC, "Qianghua ying dui qihou bianhua xingdong – Zhongguo guojia zizhu gongxian" [Enhanced actions on climate change: China's intended nationally determined contributions].

209 NDRC, "Guojia shiying qihou bianhua zhanlue" [National climate adaptation strategy].

210 SCIO, "Guojia yingdui qihou bianhua guihua" [National plan in response to climate change].

211 MEE, "China's Policies and Actions for Addressing Climate Change (2019)."

212 MEE, "China's Policies and Actions for Addressing Climate Change (2019)."

213 "Zhonggong zhongyang, Guowuyuan guanyu quanmian jiaqiang shengtao huanjing baohu jianjue dahao wuran fangzhi gongjian zhan de yijian" [Opinion of the CPC Central Committee and the State Council on comprehensively strengthening ecological and environmental protection and resolutely fighting the tough battle of pollution prevention and control].

214 SCIO, "Full Text; Energy in China's New Era."

215 Nationally Determined Contributions Registry, "China's Achievements, New Goals and New Measures for Nationally Determined Contributions."

216 SCIO, "China's Policies and Actions for Addressing Climate Change," Section II.

217 State Council, "National Environmental Protection 'Twelfth Five-Year' Plan (Chinese Text)."

218 NDRC, "Guojia shiying qihou bianhua zhanlue" [National climate adaptation strategy], 7.

219 NDRC, "Qianghua ying dui qihou bianhua xingdong – Zhongguo guojia zizhu gongxian" [Enhanced actions on climate change: China's intended nationally determined contributions].

220 New China Research, *People First: Political Commitment of the Century-Old Communist Party of China Xinhua* (June 2021), http://www.xinhuanet.com/english/download/2021-6-29/PeopleFirst.pdf.

221 MEE, "China's Policies and Actions for Addressing Climate Change (2019)."

222 SCIO, "Full Text: Energy in China's New Era."

223 SCIO, "Full Text: Responding to Climate Change: China's Policies and Actions."

224 Nationally Determined Contributions Registry, "China's Achievements, New Goals and New Measures for Nationally Determined Contributions."

225 NDRC, "Full Text: Report on China's National Economic, Social Development Plan."

226 European Commission, "Social Climate Fund," https://climate.ec.europa.eu/eu-action/european-green-deal/delivering-european-green-deal/social-climate-fund_en#key-elements; Government of Canada, "Environment and Climate Change Canada Funding Programs," https://www.canada.ca/en/environment-climate-change/services/environmental-funding.html.

227 Office of the High Commissioner for Human Rights (OHCHR), *Guiding Principles on Business and Human Rights* (New York/Geneva: United Nations, 2011), Section I.A.1 Commentary, https://www.ohchr.org/sites/default/files/documents/publications/guidingprinciples businesshr_en.pdf.

228 "Decision of the Central Committee of the Communist Party of China on Some Major Issues Concerning Comprehensively Deepening the Reform."

229 Atlantic Council and Rhodium Group, *China Pathfinder: Annual Scorecard* (October 2021), https://www.atlanticcouncil.org/wp-content/uploads/2021/10/China-Pathfinder-Annual-Scorecard-2021.pdf.

230 NDRC, "CHINA: 11th Five-Year Plan (2006–2010) for National Economic and Social Development"; NDRC, "CHINA: 12th Five-Year Plan (2011–2015) for National Economic and Social Development."

231 NDRC, "The 13th Five-Year Plan for Economic and Social Development of the People's Republic of China (2016–2020)."

232 NDRC, "Zhonghua renmin gongheguo guomin jingji he shehui fazhan de shisige wunian guihua he 2035 nian yuanjing mubiao gangyao" [People's Republic of China 14th five-year plan for national economic and social development and outline of long-range goals for 2035]. Also see Jiang Yifan, "14th Five Year Plan: China's Carbon-Centred Environmental Blueprint."

233 SCIO, "Full Text: Responding to Climate Change: China's Policies and Actions."

234 State Council, "National Environmental Protection 'Twelfth Five-Year' Plan (Chinese Text)."

235 NDRC, "Guojia shiying qihou bianhua zhanlue" [National climate adaptation strategy].

236 SCIO, "Guojia yingdui qihou bianhua guihua" [National plan in response to climate change].

237 SCIO, "Full Text: Energy in China's New Era," Section VI.
238 SCIO, "Full Text: Responding to Climate Change: China's Policies and Actions," Section II.4.
239 Nationally Determined Contributions Registry, "China's Achievements, New Goals and New Measures for Nationally Determined Contributions."
240 "Zhonggong zhongyang, Guowuyuan guanyu quanmian jiaqiang shengtao huanjing baohu jianjue dahao wuran fangzhi gongjian zhan de yijian" [Opinion of the CPC Central Committee and the State Council on comprehensively strengthening ecological and environmental protection and resolutely fighting the tough battle of pollution prevention and control].
241 MEE, "China's Policies and Actions for Addressing Climate Change (2019)," Section III.3.
242 MEE, "Guanyu tongchou he jiaqiang yingdui qihou bianhua yu shengtai huanjing baohu xiangguan gongzuo de zhidai yijian" [Guiding opinions on integrating and strengthening efforts in climate action and ecological and environmental protection].
243 François Godement, "China's Third Plenum: Great Expectations," European Council on Foreign Relations, November 12, 2013, https://ecfr.eu/article/commentary_chinas_third_plenum_great_expectations/; Dexter Roberts, "China's Economic Policy Factory: The NDRC," *Bloomberg Businessweek,* June 20, 2013, http://www.bloomberg.com/news/articles/2013-06-20/chinas-economic-policy-factory-the-ndrc.
244 NDRC, "Guojia shiying qihou bianhua zhanlue" [National climate adaptation strategy].
245 NDRC, "Guojia yingdui qihou bianhua guihua" [National plan in response to climate change].
246 NDRC, "Working Guidance for Carbon Dioxide Peaking and Carbon Neutrality in Full and Faithful Implementation of the New Development Philosophy."
247 NDRC, "Action Plan for Carbon Dioxide Peaking Before 2030."
248 Asian Development Bank, *Asia's Journey to Prosperity: Policy, Market, and Technology over 50 Years* (Manila: Asian Development Bank, 2020), ch. 2, https://www.adb.org/sites/default/files/publication/549191/asias-journey-prosperity.pdf; Alexander S. Kritikos et al., *The Socio-Ecological Market Economy in Germany* (GIZ, 2018) https://www.reformgestaltung.de/fileadmin/user_upload/Dokumente/GIZ_Standard_A4_hoch_en_DIW_web.pdf.
249 "Paris Agreement," Article 6, paragraph 8.
250 Bill Hayton, "China's Vision of Sovereignty for the Next World Order," *The Interpreter* (Lowy Institute), October 9, 2020, https://www.lowyinstitute.org/the-interpreter/china-s-vision-sovereignty-next-world-order.
251 MEE, "China's Policies and Actions for Addressing Climate Change (2020)."
252 Nationally Determined Contributions Registry, "China's Achievements, New Goals and New Measures for Nationally Determined Contributions."
253 "2021 nian 10 yue 14 ri waijiaobu faxin Zhao Lijian jianzhu chilixing jizhehui" [MFA spokesperson Zhao Lijian chairs regular press conference], October 14, 2021, http://mu.china-embassy.gov.cn/fyrth/202110/t20211014_9544432.htm.
254 Sanna Kopra, *China and Great Power Responsibility for Climate Change* (London/New York: Routledge, 2019), https://www.researchgate.net/publication/326838256_China_and_Great_Power_Responsibility_for_Climate_Change; David Held, Eva-Maria Nag, and Charles Roger, "The Governance of Climate Change in China: Preliminary Report, LSE-AFD Climate Governance Programme," LSE Global Governance Working Paper WP 01/2011, January 2011, https://www.files.ethz.ch/isn/129031/Held%20Nag%20%20Roger%20-%20The%20Governance%20of%20Climate%20Change%20in%20China%20_3_.pdf.
255 "United Nations Framework Convention on Climate Change," Preamble.
256 "Joint Statement of the 20th EU-China Summit," paragraph 2, July 16, 2018, https://www.consilium.europa.eu/media/36165/final-eu-cn-joint-statement-consolidated-text-with-climate-change-clean-energy-annex.pdf.
257 Ryan Martinez Mitchell, "China's Engagement with the ITLOS Climate Change Advisory Proceedings and Its Strategic Formalism in International Law," National University of Singapore Centre for International Law, February 6, 2024, https://cil.nus.edu.sg/blogs/chinas-engagement-with-the-itlos-climate-change-advisory-proceedings-and-its-strategic-formalism-in-international-law/. China has steadily worked to erode territorial and sovereignty standards set forth in the United Nations Convention on the Law of the Sea (UNCLOS), to which China is a party. Alan Dutton, "Oceans Under Pressure: China's Challenge to the Maritime Order," *Britain's World,* January 23, 2024, https://www.geostrategy.org.uk/britains-world/oceans-under-pressure-chinas-challenge-to-the-maritime-order/. China rejected the award by the Permanent Court of Arbitration refuting China's sovereignty claims in the South China Sea, despite

being bound to accept the arbitration decision due to its ratification of UNCLOS. See "Full Text of Statement of China's Foreign Ministry on Award of South China Sea Arbitration Initiated by the Philippines," *China Daily,* July 12, 2016, http://www.chinadaily.com.cn/world/2016scsi/2016-07/12/content_26062029.htm; Permanent Court of Arbitration, "PCA Press Release: The South China Sea Arbitration (The Republic of the Philippines v. the People's Republic of China)," July 12, 2016, https://pca-cpa.org/en/news/pca-press-release-the-south-china-sea-arbitration-the-republic-of-the-philippines-v-the-peoples-republic-of-china/.

258 Karl Hallding, Guoyi Han, and Marie Olsson, *A Balancing Act: China's Role in Climate Change* (New York: United Nations Commission on Sustainable Development, 2009), 23, 36, 81, https://mediamanager.sei.org/documents/Publications/china-cluster/chinacluster_abalancingact.pdf.

259 "Xi Calls for 'Unprecedented Ambition, Action' to Build Community of Life," April 23, 2021, https://en.chinadiplomacy.org.cn/2021-04/23/content_77433176.shtml.

260 Nationally Determined Contributions Registry, "China's Achievements, New Goals and New Measures for Nationally Determined Contributions," Chapter II.1.

261 NDRC, "Working Guidance for Carbon Dioxide Peaking and Carbon Neutrality in Full and Faithful Implementation of the New Development Philosophy."

262 MEE, "China's Policies and Actions for Addressing Climate Change (2019)."

263 NDRC, "Qianghua ying dui qihou bianhua xingdong – Zhongguo guojia zizhu gongxian" [Enhanced actions on climate change: China's intended nationally determined contributions]; Nationally Determined Contributions Registry, "China's Achievements, New Goals and New Measures for Nationally Determined Contributions."

264 SCIO, "Guojia yingdui qihou bianhua guihua" [National plan in response to climate change].

265 NDRC, "Qianghua ying dui qihou bianhua xingdong – Zhongguo guojia zizhu gongxian" [Enhanced actions on climate change: China's intended nationally determined contributions], Introduction; NDRC, "China's National Climate Change Programme."

266 Wang Yi, "Pursuing a Country-Specific Path to Human Rights Advancement and Jointly Promoting Worldwide Progress in Human Rights," *Qiushi*, December 7, 2023, https://subsites.chinadaily.com.cn/Qiushi/2023-12/07/c_945584.htm.

267 SCIO, "Full Text: Moderate Prosperity in All Respects," Sections II.4.2 and III.3.

268 United Nations, "With 161 Votes in Favour, 8 Abstentions, General Assembly Adopts Landmark Resolution Recognizing Clean, Health, Sustainable Environment as Human Right," press release, July 28, 2022, GA/12437, https://press.un.org/en/2022/ga12437.doc.htm; Zhu Mingzhe, "Environmental Rights Are Now Human Rights. What Does This Mean for Climate Litigation?" Dialogue Earth, September 26 2022, https://chinadialogue.net/en/climate/environmental-rights-human-rights-climate-litigation/.

269 Nationally Determined Contributions Registry, "China's Achievements, New Goals and New Measures for Nationally Determined Contributions."

270 Céline Guivarch, Nicolas Taconet, and Aurélie Méjean, "Linking Climate and Inequality," *Finance and Development* (IMF), September 2021, https://www.imf.org/en/Publications/fandd/issues/2021/09/climate-change-and-inequality-guivarch-mejean-taconet; Raymond A. Atuguba," Equality, Non-Discrimination and Fair Distribution of the Benefits of Development," in OHCHR, *Realizing the Right to Development* (New York/Geneva: United Nations, 2013), Chapter 7, https://www.ohchr.org/sites/default/files/Documents/Issues/Development/RTDBook/PartIIChapter7.pdf.

271 Andrew Varah Cooper, "Climate Governance After 2020: A European and Global Perspective – A Contribution to the UNFCCC COP 24," (July 2018), https://unfccc.int/sites/default/files/resource/296_COR-2018-00923-00-01-AC-TRA-EN%20%281%29.pdf.

CHAPTER 5: INVOLUNTARY MIGRATION

1 See Office of the United Nations High Commissioner for Refugees (UNHCR), "Suggestions and Amendments of China: Global Compact on Refugees," July 7, 2016, https://www.un.org/en/development/desa/population/migration/events/ga/documents/2016/07July2016/China_07July2016_GlobalCompact.pdf, in which China's comments on the draft Global Compact on Refugees (GCR) focused on "national conditions" as a key limit on acceptance of refugees by host countries; "Chinese Premier Delivers Keynote Speech at UN General Assembly," *CCTV,* September 20, 2016, http://english.cctv.com/2016/09/20/VIDEC7MT5Hjjfq27vTGFevyp160920.shtml, in which Premier Li Keqiang noted that China's assistance on refugee matters would

be conditional: "We are committed to shouldering our responsibilities compatible with our abilities."

2 Lili Song, "China and the International Refugee Protection Regime: Past, Present, and Potentials," *Refugee Survey Quarterly* 37, 2 (2018): 139–61, https://academic.oup.com/rsq/article/37/2/139/4934135?login=true.

3 UNHCR, "Submission by the United Nations High Commissioner for Refugees for the Office of the High Commissioner for Human Rights' Compilation Report – Universal Periodic Review: People's Republic of China," March 2013, Section I and Section III Issue 2, https://www.refworld.org/pdfid/5135b0cb2.pdf.

4 UNHCR, "Submission by the United Nations High Commissioner for Refugees for the Office of the High Commissioner for Human Rights' Compilation Report – Universal Periodic Review: People's Republic of China."

5 G20 Research Group (University of Toronto), "2016 G20 Hangzhou Summit Interim Compliance Report," April 8, 2017, http://www.g20.utoronto.ca/compliance/2016hangzhou-interim/11-2016-g20-compliance-interim-migration.pdf.

6 G20 Research Group (University of Toronto), "2016 G20 Hangzhou Summit Interim Compliance Report."

7 Migration Data Portal, "Forced Migration or Displacement," March 4, 2022, https://www.migrationdataportal.org/themes/forced-migration-or-displacement; Rachel M. Gisselquist, "Involuntary Migration, Inequality, and Integration: National and Subnational Influences," *Journal of Ethnic and Migration Studies* 47, 21 (2021): 4779–96, https://www.tandfonline.com/doi/full/10.1080/1369183X.2020.1724409; International Organization for Migration (IOM), *Glossary on Migration* (Geneva: IOM, 2019), https://publications.iom.int/system/files/pdf/iml_34_glossary.pdf.

8 Office of the High Commissioner for Human Rights (OHCHR), "Convention Relating to the Status of Refugees," July 28, 1951, Article I.A.2, https://www.ohchr.org/en/instruments-mechanisms/instruments/convention-relating-status-refugees.

9 UNHCR, "OAU Convention Governing Specific Aspects of Refugee Problems in Africa, Adopted by the Assembly of Heads of State and Government at Its Sixth Ordinary Session, Addis Ababa, 10 September 1969," Article 1(2), https://treaties.un.org/pages/showDetails.aspx?objid=080000028010432f.

10 "Cartagena Declaration on Refugees: Colloquium on the International Protection of Refugees in Central America, Mexico, and Panama," November 22, 1984, https://www.oas.org/dil/1984_cartagena_declaration_on_refugees.pdf. As a result, UNHCR distinguishes refugees from Venezuelans who have fled their homes and are covered by the Cartagena definition. Cecile Blouin, Isabel Berganza, and Louis Feline Freier, "The Spirit of Cartagena? Applying the Extended Refugee Definition to Venezuelans in Latin America," *Forced Migration Review* no. 63 (February 2020), https://www.fmreview.org/cities/blouin-berganza-freier.

11 UNHCR, "Fact Sheet: People's Republic of China," February 2023, https://reliefweb.int/report/china/peoples-republic-china-factsheet-february-2023.

12 UNHCR, "New York Declaration for Refugees and Migrants A71/L.1," October 3, 2016, A/RES/71/1, https://www.unhcr.org/57e39d987; UNHCR, "New York Declaration for Refugees and Migrants," https://www.unhcr.org/new-york-declaration-for-refugees-and-migrants.html.

13 Madalina Chesoi and Brendan Naef, "Primer on the Global Compact for Refugees and the Global Compact for Safe, Orderly and Regular Migration," background paper, Library of Parliament, May 30, 2019, https://lop.parl.ca/staticfiles/PublicWebsite/Home/ResearchPublications/BackgroundPapers/PDF/2019-21-e.pdf.

14 United Nations General Assembly (UNGA), "Resolution 73/195: Global Compact for Safe, Orderly and Regular Migration," December 19, 2018, A/RES/73/195, https://documents-dds-ny.un.org/doc/UNDOC/GEN/N18/451/99/PDF/N1845199.pdf?OpenElement.

15 United Nations (UN), "Global Compact on Refugees" (New York: United Nations, 2018), https://www.unhcr.org/5c658aed4; United Nations (UN), "Report of the United Nations High Commissioner for Refugees: Part II: Global Compact on Refugees," September 13, 2018, A/73/12 (Part II), https://documents-dds-ny.un.org/doc/UNDOC/GEN/G18/238/37/PDF/G1823837.pdf?OpenElement; UNHCR, "The Global Compact on Refugees," https://www.unhcr.org/the-global-compact-on-refugees.html.

16 "Law of the People's Republic of China on the Procedure of the Conclusion of Treaties," 1990, http://www.npc.gov.cn/zgrdw/englishnpc/Law/2007-12/12/content_1383893.htm; Hanqin Xue

and Qian Jin, "International Treaties in the Chinese Domestic Legal System," *Chinese Journal of International Law* 8, 2 (2009): 299–322, https://academic.oup.com/chinesejil/article/8/2/299/310810.

17 Heidi Ostbo Haugen and Tabitha Speelman, "China's Rapid Development Has Transformed Its Migration Trends," Migration Policy Institute, January 28, 2022, https://www.migrationpolicy.org/article/china-development-transformed-migration; Frank N. Pieke, "How Immigration Is Shaping Chinese Society," MERICS, November 27, 2019, https://merics.org/en/report/how-immigration-shaping-chinese-society; Shen Haimei, "Inflow of International Immigrants Challenges China's Migration Policy," Brookings, September 8, 2011, https://www.brookings.edu/opinions/inflow-of-international-immigrants-challenges-chinas-migration-policy/; Xiang Biao, "Emigration from China: A Sending Country Perspective," *International Migration* 41, 2 (2003): 21–48, https://library.fes.de/libalt/journals/swetsfulltext/17507186.pdf.

18 IOM, "China, UN's Migration Agency Advance Sustainable Development Agenda," June 28, 2019, https://www.iom.int/news/china-uns-migration-agency-advance-sustainable-development-agenda.

19 IOM, "IOM in China," https://china.iom.int/en/iom-china.

20 IOM, *Yimin yu "2030 nian kechixu fazhan yicheng": Yige gei shijianzhe de zhinan* [Migrants and the 2030 sustainable development agenda: a guide for implementers] (Geneva: IOM, 2018), https://www.iom.int/sites/g/files/tmzbdl486/files/press_release/file/migration-and-2030-agenda-practitioners-guide-zh.pdf.

21 Global Compact on Refugees, "Global Refugee Forum," https://globalcompactrefugees.org/article/global-refugee-forum; UNHCR, "Global Refugee Forum 2019," https://www.unhcr.org/programme-and-practical-information.html; UNHCR, "Jobs and Livelihoods," December 16, 2019, https://www.unhcr.org/events/conferences/5d1a11267/jobs-and-livelihoods.html; UNHCR, "Fact Sheet: People's Republic of China," February 2023, https://reliefweb.int/report/china/peoples-republic-china-factsheet-february-2023.

22 Peter Yeung, "'Disillusioned About China,' More Chinese Aim for US via Risky Darien Gap," *Al Jazeera*, February 22, 2024, https://www.aljazeera.com/economy/2024/2/22/disillusioned-about-china-more-chinese-aim-for-us-via-risky-darien-gap; "2023: PRC Outmigration 1960–2020," *David Cowhig's Translation Blog*, December 18, 2023, https://gaodawei.wordpress.com/2023/12/18/2023-prc-outmigration-1960-2020/.

23 MFA, "China's Relation with UNHCR," September 27, 2003, https://www.mfa.gov.cn/eng/wjb/zzjg_663340/gjs_665170/gjzzyhy_665174/2594_665176/2600_665188/202406/t20240606_11404354.html.

24 Song, "China and the International Refugee Protection Regime," Section 4; Fengshi Wu, "China and the Global Refugee Crisis," Centre for Contemporary Chinese Studies, Research Brief No. 13, May 2018, https://arts.unimelb.edu.au/__data/assets/pdf_file/0003/2780670/Research-Brief-No-13.pdf.

25 Glen Peterson, "Sovereignty, International Law, and the Uneven Development of the International Refugee Regime," *Modern Asian Studies* 49, 2 (March 2015): 439–68, https://www.cambridge.org/core/journals/modern-asian-studies/article/abs/sovereignty-international-law-and-the-uneven-development-of-the-international-refugee-regime/24EF7308A6BD7FE2BCEC1DDBAD9B3AE3.

26 Irene Eber, *Jewish Refugees in Shanghai 1933–1947: A Selection of Documents* (Gottingen: Vandenhoeck and Ruprecht, 2018), https://www.vr-elibrary.de/doi/abs/10.13109/9783666301957; Gao Bei, *Shanghai Sanctuary: Chinese and Japanese Policy Toward European Jewish Refugees During World War II* (Oxford: Oxford University Press, 2013), https://oxford.universitypressscholarship.com/view/10.1093/acprof:oso/9780199840908.001.0001/acprof-9780199840908.

27 Ronald Skeldon, "Migration from China," *Journal of International Affairs* 49, 2 (Winter 1996): 434–55, https://www.jstor.org/stable/24357566.

28 Xiaohui Wu, "Chronology of Practice: Chinese Practice in Public International Law in 2017," *Chinese Journal of International Law* 17, 4 (December 2018): 1017–99, https://academic.oup.com/chinesejil/article/17/4/1017/5231504. On China's application of "common but differentiated responsibilities" (CBDR) to climate change, see "'Common but Differentiated Responsibilities' Must Never Be Compromised: Premier," *Xinhua*, December 18, 2009, http://

www.china.org.cn/environment/Copenhagen/2009-12/18/content_19094598.htm. On potential application to COVID-19, see Abhinav Verma, "Adapting Common but Differentiated Responsibilities to the Global Cooperation for COVID-19 Response," *Columbia Journal of International Affairs* 73, 3 (2020): 215–22, https://jia.sipa.columbia.edu/news/adapting-common-differentiated-responsibility-global-cooperation-covid-19-response.

29 UNHCR, "Contributions to UNHCR for Budget Year 2015, as at 31 December 2015," https://www.unhcr.org/558a639f9.pdf; Executive Committee of the High Commissioner's Programme, "Update on Budgets and Funding (2020–2021)," March 4, 2021, EC/72/SC/CRP.7, Annex V, https://www.unhcr.org/605c429d4.pdf.

30 Compare UNHCR, "Promoting Welcoming and Inclusive Societies," March 9, 2024, https://www.unhcr.org/handbooks/ih/welcoming-inclusive-societies/promoting-welcoming-and-inclusive-societies, and Sara de Jong, "Converging Logics? Managing Migration and Managing Diversity," *Journal of Ethnic and Migration Studies* 42, 3 (2016): 341–58, https://www.tandfonline.com/doi/abs/10.1080/1369183X.2015.1074857 with Hu Lianhe and Hu An'gang, "How the Nationalities Question Is Handled Outside of China (Introduction and Translation by David Ownby)," Reading the China Dream, https://www.readingthechinadream.com/hu-and-hu-nationalities-question.html.

31 European Union, "EU China Relations," April 2022, https://www.eeas.europa.eu/sites/default/files/documents/EU-China_Factsheet_01Apr2022.pdf; John Kirton, "Canada-China Relations Remain on the Rocks," *East Asia Forum,* October 5, 2019, https://www.eastasiaforum.org/2019/10/05/canada-china-relations-remain-on-the-rocks/; US Department of State, "China's Disregard for Human Rights," https://2017-2021.state.gov/chinas-disregard-for-human-rights/.

32 David Dollar, "Reluctant Player: China's Approach to International Economic Institutions," Brookings, September 14, 2020, https://www.brookings.edu/articles/reluctant-player-chinas-approach-to-international-economic-institutions/; Philip Anstrén, "The Case for Greater US-EU Collaboration on Taiwan," Atlantic Council, June 30, 2021, https://www.atlanticcouncil.org/blogs/new-atlanticist/the-case-for-greater-us-eu-collaboration-on-taiwan/; Louis Charbonneau, "39 Countries at UN Express 'Grave Concerns' About China's Abuses," Human Rights Watch, October 6, 2020, https://www.hrw.org/news/2020/10/06/39-countries-un-express-grave-concerns-about-chinas-abuses.

33 Compare MFA, "China's Relation with UNHCR," September 27, 2003 https://www.mfa.gov.cn/eng/wjb/zzjg_663340/gjs_665170/gjzzyhy_665174/2594_665176/2600_665188/202406/t20240606_11404354.html with UN, "Report of the High Commissioner for Refugees Part II: Global Compact on Refugees," paragraphs 4 and 88. Also see UNHCR, "ExCom Plenary Sessions," 2021–22, https://www.unhcr.org/excom-plenary-sessions.html.

34 MFA, "China's Relationship with the United Nations High Commissioner for Refugees (UNHCR)."

35 Jasmine Lam, "Refugee Policy and Foreign Policy: Examining Policy Linkage in Chinese Relations with North Korea, Myanmar, and Vietnam," *Inquiries* 5, 10 (2013): 2–6, http://www.inquiriesjournal.com/articles/771/2/refugee-policy-and-foreign-policy-examining-policy-linkage-in-chinese-relations-with-north-korea-myanmar-and-vietnam.

36 Jessica Meyers, "China Once Welcomed Refugees, but Its Policies Now Make Trump Look Lenient," *Los Angeles Times,* October 18, 2017, https://www.latimes.com/world/asia/la-fg-china-forgotten-refugees-2017108-story.html; US Committee for Refugees and Immigrants, "U.S. Committee for Refugees World Refugee Survey 2000 – China," June 1, 2000, https://www.refworld.org/docid/3ae6a8cc4.html.

37 Russell Aldrich, "An Examination of China's Treatment of North Korean Asylum Seekers," *North Korean Review* 7, 1 (Spring 2011): 36–48, https://www.jstor.org/stable/43908831; US Committee for Refugees and Immigrants, "World Refugee Survey 2008 – China," June 19, 2008, https://www.refworld.org/publisherUSCRI,ANNUALREPORT,CHN,485f50ca7b,0.html; Rhoda Margesson, Emma Chanlett-Avery, and Andorra Bruno, "North Korean Refugees in China and Human Rights Issues: International Response and U.S. Policy Options," Congressional Research Service, CRS Report for Congress, September 27, 2007, https://sgp.fas.org/crs/row/RL34189.pdf; Elim Chan and Andreas Schloenhardt, "North Korean Refugees and International Law," *International Journal of Refugee Law* 19, 2 (July 4, 2007): 215–45, https://academic.oup.com/ijrl/article-abstract/19/2/215/1582300.

38 Poppy McPherson, Ruma Paul, and Shoon Naing, "China Struggles in New Diplomatic Role, Trying to Return Rohingya to Myanmar," *Reuters,* January 20, 2022, https://www.reuters.com/article/us-myanmar-rohingya-china-insight-idUSKBN1ZJ0SY; Rachel Lambert, "Hidden Parallels: The Impact of Beijing's Policies on the Rohingya Crisis," *Asia Dispatches* (Wilson Center blog), January 18, 2022, https://www.wilsoncenter.org/blog-post/hidden-parallels-impact-beijings-policies-rohingya-crisis.
39 Centre for China and Globalization (CCG), *Attracting Skilled International Migrants to China: A Review and Comparison of Policies and Practices* (International Labour Organization/International Organization for Migration, 2017), https://www.iom.int/sites/g/files/tmzbdl486/files/country/docs/china/r1_attracting_skilled_international_migrants_to_china_en.pdf. China has used the irregular economic migrant discourse to justify forced return of refugees from North Korea. Lina Yoon, "China Restarts Forced Return of Refugees to North Korea," Human Rights Watch, July 22, 2021, https://www.hrw.org/news/2021/07/22/china-restarts-forced-returns-refugees-north-korea.
40 "Statement of Ambassador Li Li, Leader of the Chinese Delegation and Chinese Ambassador to the Kingdom of Morocco, at the Intergovernmental Conference to Adopt the Global Compact for Safe, Orderly and Regular Migration," December 11, 2018, https://www.un.org/en/conf/migration/assets/pdf/GCM-Statements/china.pdf.
41 "Full Text of China's Position Paper on the UN's 75th Anniversary," September 10, 2020, Section III, paragraph 11, http://www.china.org.cn/world/2020-09/10/content_76690893.htm.
42 UNGA, "Report of the United Nations High Commissioner for Refugees. Covering the Period 1 July 2020 – 30 June 2021," August 20, 2021, A/76/12, Section V, https://www.unhcr.org/615eb32c4.pdf.
43 "Annex to Letter to PRC Foreign Minister Wang Yi from Michelle Bachelet, UN High Commissioner for Human Rights," April 29, 2019, 7, https://www.ohchr.org/sites/default/files/lib-docs/HRBodies/UPR/Documents/Session31/CN/LetterChina.pdf. Also see "Education Law of the People's Republic of China," Article 18, 1995, http://www.china.org.cn/english/education/184669.htm.
44 National Immigration Administration of the People's Republic of China (NIA), "Exit and Entry Administration Law of the People's Republic of China," adopted June 30, 2012, entered into force July 1, 2013, https://www.nia.gov.cn/n741440/n741547/c757592/content.html.
45 Lili Song, "Anywhere but Here? China's Response to Refugee Protection During COVID-19," *Open Democracy,* March 19, 2021, https://www.opendemocracy.net/en/pandemic-border/anywhere-but-here-chinas-response-to-refugee-protection-during-covid-19/.
46 "China's Mass Exodus: Number of Asylum Seekers Surpasses One Million Under Xi," Safeguard Defenders, January 6, 2025, https://safeguarddefenders.com/en/blog/chinas-mass-exodus-number-asylum-seekers-surpasses-one-million-under-xi.
47 Natalie Wong, "Goodbye, Hong Kong: Protesters Seeking Asylum Abroad from National Security Law Vow to Fight On but Feel 'Survivor's Guilt,'" *South China Morning Post,* June 22, 2021, https://www.scmp.com/news/hong-kong/politics/article/3138186/goodbye-hong-kong-protesters-seeking-asylum-abroad-national; Melissa Chan, "I Never Thought China Could Ever Be This Dark," *The Atlantic,* April 8, 2021, https://www.theatlantic.com/international/archive/2021/04/uyghur-women-china-xinjiang/618531/; "Chinese Asylum," Political Asylum USA, 2013, https://www.politicalasylumusa.com/countries/chinese-asylum/; Seonaigh MacPherson, Anne-Sophie Bentz, and Dawa Bhuti Ghoso, "Global Nomads: The Emergence of the Tibetan Diaspora (Part I)," Migration Policy Institute, September 2, 2008, https://www.migrationpolicy.org/article/global-nomads-emergence-tibetan-diaspora-part-i.
48 Ai Jun, "China Won't Play by US Playbook in Terms of Afghan Refugee Issue," *Global Times,* September 3, 2021, https://www.globaltimes.cn/page/202109/1233289.shtml; Liang Pan, "Why China Isn't Hosting Syrian Refugees," *Foreign Policy,* February 26, 2016, https://foreignpolicy.com/2016/02/26/china-host-syrian-islam-refugee-crisis-migrant/.
49 Merriden Varrall, "How China Views the Plight of Refugees," *The Interpreter* (Lowy Institute), July 5, 2017, https://www.lowyinstitute.org/the-interpreter/how-china-views-plight-refugees.
50 MFA, "China's Relationship with the United Nations High Commissioner for Refugees (UNHCR)."
51 "Full text of China's Position Paper on the UN's 75th Anniversary," Section III, paragraph 11.
52 UNHCR, "China," statement at the 72nd session of the UNHCR Executive Committee, October 6, 2021, https://www.unhcr.org/615dab634.

53 Laws of the People's Republic of China, "Measures for the Administration of Examination and Approval of Foreigner's Permanent Residence in China," December 13, 2003, Article 6, http://www.asianlii.org/cn/legis/cen/laws/mftaoeaaofpric899/; Dorcas Wong and Fuki Fu, "Foreign Permanent Residency in China: New Draft Regulations Released," *China Briefing,* March 5, 2020, https://www.china-briefing.com/news/foreign-permanent-residency-china-new-regulations-exposure-draft-released/.

54 See generally Lili Song, *Chinese Refugee Law and Policy* (Cambridge: Cambridge University Press, 2020), https://www.cambridge.org/core/books/abs/chinese-refugee-law-and-policy/mainland-china/BDF950E41358EA66B5C8DC8D57FFDC4B; Guofu Liu, *Chinese Refugee Law* (Leiden, Netherlands: Brill, 2020), https://brill.com/view/title/55970.

55 Graeme Hugo, "Migrants in Society: Diversity and Cohesion," Global Commission on International Migration, September 2005, https://www.iom.int/sites/g/files/tmzbdl2616/files/2018-07/TP6.pdf.

56 See generally Marc Blecher, David S.G. Goodman, Yingjie Guo, Jean-Louis Rocca, and Tony Saich, *Class and the Communist Party of China, 1921–1978* (Abingdon, UK: Routledge, 2022), https://www.routledge.com/Class-and-the-Communist-Party-of-China-1921-1978-Revolution-and-Social/Blecher-Goodman-Guo-Rocca-Saich/p/book/9781032185095; Yingjie Guo, ed., *Handbook on Class and Social Stratification in China* (Cheltenham, UK: Edward Elgar, 2016), https://www.e-elgar.com/shop/gbp/handbook-on-class-and-social-stratification-in-china-9781783470631.html.

57 William A. Joseph, ed., *Politics in China: An Introduction,* 3rd ed. (Oxford: Oxford University Press, 2019), https://global.oup.com/academic/product/politics-in-china-9780190870713?cc=ca&lang=en&#;ndrew; Andrew G. Walder, *China Under Mao: A Revolution Derailed* (Cambridge, MA: Harvard University Press, 2015), https://www.hup.harvard.edu/catalog.php?isbn=9780674975491; Suijian Guo, *Chinese Politics and Government: Power, Ideology and Organization* (London: Routledge, 2012), chs. 15 and 16, https://www.taylorfrancis.com/books/mono/10.4324/9780203106167/chinese-politics-government-sujian-guo?refId=60888ed2-bd3b-461e-9a54-ccfe3dc5e8d1&context=ubx.

58 Tsering Woeser, *Forbidden Memory: Tibet During the Cultural Revolution,* ed. Robert Barnett, trans. Susan T. Chen (Dulles, VA: Potomac Books, 2020), https://www.nebraskapress.unl.edu/potomac-books/9781612349695/; Thomas Heberer, *China and Its National Minorities: Autonomy or Assimilation?* (Abingdon, UK: Routledge, 1989), ch. 2, https://www.taylorfrancis.com/books/mono/10.4324/9781315171876/china-andits-national-minorities-thomas-heberer.

59 "Communique of the Third Plenary Session of the 11th Central Committee of the Communist Party of China," *Beijing Review,* December 29, 1978, http://www.bjreview.com/Special_Reports/2018/40th_Anniversary_of_Reform_and_Opening_up/Timeline/201806/t20180626_800133641.html. The reference to "two different kinds of contradictions" speaks to Mao's distinction between antagonistic contradictions between "ourselves and the enemy" and non-antagonistic contradictions among the people, as laid out in Mao Zedong, "On the Correct Handling of Contradictions Among the People," *People's Daily,* June 19, 1957, https://www.marxists.org/reference/archive/mao/selected-works/volume-5/mswv5_58.htm.

60 Wu Guoguang, "Democracy and Rule of Law in Zhao Ziyang's Political Reform," in *Zhao Ziyang and China's Political Future,* ed. Wu Guoguang and Helen Lansdowne (London: Routledge, 2013), 34–36.

61 Simon Gilbert, "Class and Class Struggle in China Today," *International Socialism,* June 29, 2017, http://isj.org.uk/class-and-class-struggle-in-china-today/; M. Scott Tanner, "Ideological Struggle over Police Reform," in *Transition from Communism in China: Institutional and Comparative Analysis,* ed. Edwin A. Winkler (Boulder, CO: Lynne Rienner, 1999), 113–15, https://www.degruyterbrill.com/document/doi/10.1515/9781685858407-005/html; Keith Forster, "The 1982 Campaign Against Economic Crime in China," *Australian Journal of Chinese Affairs* 14 (July 1985): 1–19, https://www.journals.uchicago.edu/doi/10.2307/2159024.

62 "Full Text: Resolution of the CPC Central Committee on the Major Achievements and Historical Experience of the Party over the Past Century," November 16, 2021, https://english.www.gov.cn/policies/latestreleases/202111/16/content_WS6193a935c6d0df57f98e50b0.html.

63 Sophia Woodman and Zhonghua Guo, "Introduction: Practising Citizenship in Contemporary China," in *Citizenship Studies* 21, 7 (2017), https://www.tandfonline.com/toc/ccst20/21/7;

Michael Keane, "Redefining Chinese Citizenship," *Economy and Society* 30, 1 (2001): 1–17, https://www.tandfonline.com/doi/abs/10.1080/03085140020019061; Merle Goldman and Elizabeth J. Perry, eds., *Changing Meaning of Citizenship in China* (Cambridge, MA: Harvard University Press, 2002), https://www.hup.harvard.edu/catalog.php?isbn=9780674008434.

64 Wu Guoguang, "Democracy and Rule of Law in Zhao Ziyang's Political Reform," 34–36; Pitman B. Potter, *From Leninist Discipline to Socialist Legalism: Peng Zhen on Law and Political Authority in the PRC* (Stanford, CA: Stanford University Press, 2003), 137–40.

65 "Public Intellectuals in China: Roundtable," Congressional Executive Commission on China (CECC), March 10, 2005, https://catalog.hathitrust.org/Record/005024199; Ellen R. Judd, "Working Class Intellectuals in China," *Journal of Contemporary Asia* 14, 2 (1984): 156–70, https://www.tandfonline.com/doi/abs/10.1080/00472338485390121.

66 Zhonghua Guo, ed., *The Routledge Handbook of Chinese Citizenship* (Abingdon, UK: Routledge, 2022), https://www.routledge.com/The-Routledge-Handbook-of-Chinese-Citizenship/Guo/p/book/9781032126913.

67 "Zhonghua renmin gongheguo guoji fa" [Nationality law of the People's Republic of China], https://data.globalcit.eu/NationalDB/docs/04_CHN_1980_NationalityLaw_PRC%20%5BORIGINAL%20LANGUAGE%5D.pdf0; "Nationality Law of the People's Republic of China," http://www.npc.gov.cn/zgrdw/englishnpc/Law/2007-12/13/content_1384056.htm.

68 "Zhonghua renmin gongheguo xianfa" [Constitution of the People's Republic of China], Article 33, http://www.gov.cn/guoqing/2018-03/22/content_5276318.htm; "Constitution of the People's Republic of China," Article 33, https://english.www.gov.cn/archive/lawsregulations/201911/20/content_WS5ed8856ec6d0b3f0e9499913.html.

69 "Zhonghua renmin gongheguo guoji fa" [Nationality law of the People's Republic of China]; "Nationality Law of the People's Republic of China."

70 Hyun Choe, "National Identity and Citizenship in the People's Republic of China and the Republic of Korea," *Journal of Historical Sociology* 19, 1 (March 2006): 84–188, https://onlinelibrary.wiley.com/doi/10.1111/j.1467-6443.2006.00270.x.

71 Shao Dan, "Chinese by Definition: Nationality Law, Jus Sanguinis, and State Succession, 1909–1980" *Twentieth Century China* 35, 1 (2009): 4–28, https://www.tandfonline.com/doi/abs/10.1179/tcc.2009.35.1.4. The Nationality Law of the People's Republic of China includes provision for children born in China having PRC nationality (Article 6), thus accepting limited application of *jus soli,* although *jus sanguinis* remains the main criterion for determining nationality. Sanzhuan Guo, "Unblocking Access to Citizenship in the Global South: Should the Process Be Decentralized?" Global Citizenship Observatory, November 16, 2020, https://globalcit.eu/unblocking-access-to-citizenship-in-the-global-south-should-the-process-be-decentralised/5/; Tung-Pi Chen, "The Nationality Law of the People's Republic of China and the Overseas Chinese in Hong Kong, Macao and Southeast Asia," *NYLS Journal of International and Comparative Law* 5, 2 (1984): 281–340, https://digitalcommons.nyls.edu/cgi/viewcontent.cgi?article=1190&context=journal_of_international_and_comparative_law.

72 Ma Zhendong, Zhou Haimin, Lou Pengying, and Ke Wei, "Woguo 'Guoji fa' zhuyao neirong de juedu ji xiangguan wenti de sikao" [Analysis of the main contents of our nationality law and reflections on related issues], *Journal of Shanghai Public Security Academy* 14, 6 (December 2004): 63–68, http://www.ims.sdu.edu.cn/__local/5/A8/B9/1559CDD7D869A425C88BB3F5C4D_0E59C2AE_B29BA.pdf?e=.pdf.

73 See generally Christopher J. Smith, *China in the Post-Utopian Age* (Abingdon, UK: Routledge: 2020), ch. 12, https://www.routledge.com/China-In-The-Post-utopian-Age/Smith/p/book/9780367159337#toc; Xiaowei Zang, ed., *Handbook on Ethnic Minorities in China* (Cheltenham, UK: Edward Elgar, 2015), https://www.e-elgar.com/shop/usd/handbook-on-ethnic-minorities-in-china-9781784717353.html.

74 Haiting Zhang, "The Laws on the Ethnic Minority Autonomous Regions in China: Legal Norms and Practices," *Loyola University Chicago International Law Review* 9, 2 (Spring/Summer 2012): 249–64, https://lawecommons.luc.edu/cgi/viewcontent.cgi?article=1002&context=lucilr.

75 "Law of the People's Republic of China on Regional National Autonomy," 1984, http://www.lawinfochina.com/display.aspx?id=43&lib=law; "Law of the People's Republic of China on Regional National Autonomy (2001 Amendment)," February 28, 2001, http://www.lawinfochina.com/display.aspx?id=6211&lib=law.

76 "Zhonghua renmin gongheguo xianfa" [Constitution of the People's Republic of China], Article 4; "Constitution of the People's Republic of China," Article 4; SCIO, "China's Ethnic Policy and Common Prosperity and Development of All Ethnic Groups," white paper, September 27, 2009, Section II, http://www.china.org.cn/government/whitepaper/node_7078073.htm; SCIO, "National Minorities Policy and Its Practice in China," September 1, 1999, Section II, http://www.lawinfochina.com/display.aspx?lib=dbref&id=20.
77 Patrik Meyer, "Could Han Chauvinism Turn the 'Chinese Dream' into 'Chinese Nightmare'?" *The Diplomat,* June 14, 2016, https://thediplomat.com/2016/06/could-han-chauvinism-turn-the-chinese-dream-into-a-chinese-nightmare/; James Leibold, "More Than a Category: Han Supremacism on the Chinese Internet," *China Quarterly* 203 (September 2010): 539–59, https://www.cambridge.org/core/journals/china-quarterly/article/abs/more-than-a-category-han-supremacism-on-the-chinese-internet/10DDFA7B3E9EC93372EE10201C994790.
78 Greg Caskey and Alia Murtazashvili, "The Predatory State and Coercive Assimilation of the Uyghurs in Xinjiang," *SSRN,* November 8, 2021, https://papers.ssrn.com/sol3/papers.cfm?abstract_id=3878514; Ju-Han Zoe Wang and Gerald Roche, "Urbanizing Minority *Minzu* in the PRC: Insights from the Literature on Settler Colonialism," *Modern China* 48, 3 (2021): 593–616, https://journals.sagepub.com/doi/abs/10.1177/0097700421995135. For discussion of earlier policies of accommodation, see Xiaohui Wu, "From Assimilation to Autonomy: Realizing Ethnic Minority Rights in China's National Autonomous Regions," *Chinese Journal of International Law* 13, 1 (March 2014): 55–90; Heberer, *China And Its National Minorities.*
79 "PRC State Council White Paper, China's Ethnic Policy and Common Prosperity and Development of All Ethnic Groups."
80 Congressional Research Service, "Human Rights in China and U.S. Policy: Issues for the 117th Congress," March 31, 2021, 6, 9–16, https://crsreports.congress.gov/product/pdf/R/R46750; Khalid Jamel and Wiam Lena, "Made in China – Assimilating Ethnic Minorities in the 21st Century: An Examination of Xi Jinping's Efforts to Sinicise Ethnic Minorities in China Through Framing" (MA thesis, Stockholm University, January 25, 2021), https://www.diva-portal.org/smash/record.jsf?pid=diva2%3A1521444&dswid=-610; Eva Xiao, Jonathan Cheng, and Liza Lin, "China Accelerates Campaign of Ethnic Assimilation," *Wall Street Journal,* December 31, 2020, https://www.wsj.com/articles/beijing-accelerates-campaign-of-ethnic-assimilation-11609431781; James Leibold, *Ethnic Policy in China: Is Reform Inevitable?* (Honolulu: East-West Center, 2013), https://www.eastwestcenter.org/sites/default/files/private/ps068.pdf.
81 "Zhulao zhonghua minzu gongtong ti yijian" [Realize the unity of Chinese ethnic groups], *people.cn/人民网*, September 30, 2024, http://opinion.people.com.cn/n1/2024/0930/c1003-40331198.html.
82 Xi Jinping, "Secure a Decisive Victory in Building a Moderately Prosperous Society in All Respects and Strive for the Great Success of Socialism with Chinese Characteristics for a New Era" (speech delivered at the 19th National Congress of the CPC, October 18, 2017), 64, http://www.xinhuanet.com/english/download/Xi_Jinping's_report_at_19th_CPC_National_Congress.pdf.
83 "Xi Jinping zai zhongyang minzu gongzuo huiyi shang qiangdiao yi zhulao zhonghua minzu gongtongti yizhi wei zhuxian tuidong xin shidai dang de minzu gongzuo gao zhiliang fazhan" [Xi Jinping at the Central Nationalities Work Conference: emphasized casting the unity of Chinese nationalities as the main line, promote high quality development of the Party's nationalities work in the new period], August 28, 2021, http://www.news.cn/politics/leaders/2021-08/28/c_1127804776.htm.
84 "Internal Migration and Stability in China," *Migration News* 3, 10 (October 1996), https://migration.ucdavis.edu/mn/more.php?id=1058_0_3_0.
85 Kam Wing Chan and Li Zhang, "The *Hukou* System and Rural-Urban Migration in China: Processes and Challenges," *China Quarterly* 160 (December 1999): 818–55, https://www.cambridge.org/core/journals/china-quarterly/article/abs/hukou-system-and-ruralurban-migration-in-china-processes-and-changes/64180F68ABC54EDF984DEB31EFFE7A64; Tiejun Cheng and Mark Selden, "The Origins and Social Consequences of China's *Hukou* System," *China Quarterly* 139 (September 1994): 644–68, https://www.jstor.org/stable/655134.
86 Amy Hawkins, "China to Relax Internal Migration Rules to Kickstart Economy," *The Guardian,* August 4, 2023, https://www.theguardian.com/world/2023/aug/04/china-to-relax-internal

-migration-rules-to-kickstart-economy?CMP=Share_AndroidApp_Other; Zhuoran Li and Gavin Xu, "CSR Blog: How Hukou Reform Can Liberate China's Economic Growth Potential," *SAIS China Studies Review,* November 1, 2021, https://saiscsr.org/2021/11/01/how-hukou-reform-can-liberate-chinas-growth-potential/; Cai Xuejiao, "China's Yangtze Delta Eases Habitat Rules to Lure Big-City Talent," *Nikkei Asia,* July 17, 2021, https://asia.nikkei.com/Spotlight/Caixin/China-s-Yangtze-Delta-eases-habitat-rules-to-lure-big-city-talent; Priyanka Juneja, "China's Hukou System: An Interview with Fei-ling Wang," *The Diplomat,* July 14, 2017, https://thediplomat.com/2017/07/chinas-hukou-system/; Immigration and Refugee Board of Canada, "China: 2014 Hukou Reform Policy and Its Local Implementation; Security Features and Other Physical Characteristics of Hukou [Household Registry] Documents Issued in 2013–2014; Anti-Fraud Measures Introduced for Hukou Documents; Whether Features Are Standardized Across the Country," December 23, 2015, https://www.refworld.org/docid/57551d0c4.html.

87 "China's Social Credit System in 2021: From Fragmentation Towards Integration," MERICS, March 3, 2021, https://merics.org/en/report/chinas-social-credit-system-2021-fragmentation-towards-integration; Rogier Creemers, "China's Social Credit System: An Evolving Practice of Control," *SSRN,* May 9, 2018, https://papers.ssrn.com/sol3/papers.cfm?abstract_id=3175792.

88 Max Masuda-Farkas, "China's Hukou System and the Urban-Rural Divide," *Regulatory Review,* August 18, 2021, https://www.theregreview.org/2021/08/18/masuda-farkas-china-hukou-system-urban-rural-divide/; "Changes to China's Hukou System Are Creating New Divides," *The Economist,* August 9, 2020, https://www.economist.com/china/2020/08/19/changes-to-chinas-hukou-system-are-creating-new-divides.

89 "China Millionaire Exodus to Continue This Year: Report," *Nikkei Asia,* June 13, 2023, https://asia.nikkei.com/economy/china-millionaire-exodus-to-continue-this-year-report#https://bens.org/china-millionaire-exodus-to-continue-this-year-report/; Haugen and Speelman, "China's Rapid Development Has Transformed Migration Trends."

90 Anne Stevenson-Yang, "Keeping the Flies Out," ChinaFile, February 3, 2022, https://www.chinafile.com/reporting-opinion/viewpoint/keeping-flies-out; Anne-Marie Brady, *Making the Foreign Serve China: Managing Foreigners in the People's Republic* (Lanham, MD: Rowman and Littlefield, 2003), https://www.bloomsbury.com/uk/making-the-foreign-serve-china-9781461704751/. For a general collection of articles on foreigners in China, see "Foreigners in China," *South China Morning Post,* https://www.scmp.com/topics/foreigners-china.

91 See, e.g., Supreme People's Court of the People's Republic of China (SPC), "Foreign-Related Trials," 2025, https://english.court.gov.cn/foreigntrials.html; Ministry of Education of the People's Republic of China, " Regulations of the People's Republic of China on Chinese-Foreign Cooperation in Running Schools," September 1, 2003, https://www.crs.jsj.edu.cn/news/index/3; SPC, "Law of the People's Republic of China on the Law Applicable to Foreign-Related Civil Relationships (Excerpts)," July 19, 2022, https://english.court.gov.cn/2022-07/19/c_790717.htm; Ministry of Civil Affairs of the People's Republic of China, "Shewai shehui zuzhi" [Foreign-related social organizations], https://www.gov.cn/c16813/ztfw_forthcommon.htm.

92 Tabitha Speelman, "Chinese Attitudes Toward Immigrants; Emerging, Divided Views," *The Diplomat,* December 21, 2020, https://thediplomat.com/2020/12/chinese-attitudes-toward-immigrants-emerging-divided-views/.

93 Edward White, Primrose Riordan, and Demetri Sevastopulo, "Departing US Business Chiefs Warn of Expat Exodus from China," *Financial Times,* November 1, 2021, https://www.ft.com/content/53e5c1eb-83ed-468f-a055-dc08f7ede2ca; Nathan Vanderklippe, "'Stay Away from Here': In China Foreigners Have Become a Target for Coronavirus Discrimination," *Globe and Mail,* April 10, 2021, https://www.theglobeandmail.com/world/article-stay-away-from-here-in-china-foreigners-have-become-a-target-for/.

94 Jenni Marsh, "Westerners Are Increasingly Scared of Traveling to China as Threat of Detention Rises," *CNN,* March 9, 2021, https://www.cnn.com/2021/03/09/china/china-travel-foreigners-arbitrary-detention-hnk-dst-intl/index.html.

95 Among the many excellent reviews of the ordeal suffered by the Two Michaels, see in particular Fen Hampson and Mike Blanchfield, *The Two Michaels: Innocent Canadian Captives and High Stakes Espionage in the US-China Cyber War* (Toronto: Sutherland House, 2021), and Clive Ansley, David Kilgour, and Pater Lamont, "Opinion: Two Michaels and 'Trials' in China," *Toronto Sun,* March 22, 2021, https://torontosun.com/opinion/opinion-two-michaels-and-trials-in-china.

96 Jasper Habicht and Eva Lena Richter, "De Facto Dual Nationality in Chinese Law and Practice," *China: An International Journal* 20, 1 (2022): 24–45, https://papers.ssrn.com/sol3/papers.cfm?abstract_id=4043945. This may be changing, as China seemed to recognize the Canadian citizenship of former Chinese nationals executed in China for drug offences in March 2025. Koh Ewe, "China Executed Four Canadians for Drug Crimes, Says Ottawa," *BBC News,* March 20, 2025, https://www.bbc.com/news/articles/c204ywyl4kvo.

97 Gina Anne Tam, "China's Language Police: Why Beijing Seeks to Extend the Hegemony of Mandarin," *Foreign Affairs,* September 19, 2023, https://www.foreignaffairs.com/china/chinas-language-police.

98 "Zhonghua renmin gongheguo guoji fa" [Nationality law of the People's Republic of China]; "Nationality Law of the People's Republic of China."

99 "Passport Law of the People's Republic of China," 2006, Article 2, http://www.npc.gov.cn/zgrdw/englishnpc/Law/2008-01/02/content_1388000.htm.

100 "Zhonghua renmin gongheguo jumin shenfenzheng fa" [Law of the People's Republic of China on residential identity cards], rev. 2011, Article 3, http://www.npc.gov.cn/zgrdw/npc/xinwen/2011-10/31/content_1678466_2.htm.

101 Debasish Chaudhuri, *Xinjiang and the Chinese State: Violence in the Reform Era* (Abingdon, UK: Routledge, 2018), https://www.routledge.com/Xinjiang-and-the-Chinese-State-Violence-in-the-Reform-Era/Chaudhuri/p/book/9780367345112; Enze Han, *Contestation and Adaptation: The Politics of National Identity in China* (Oxford: Oxford University Press, 2013), https://oxford.universitypressscholarship.com/view/10.1093/acprof:oso/9780199936298.001.0001/acprof-9780199936298; Thomas Mullaney, *Coming to Terms with the Nation: Ethnic Classification in Modern China* (Berkeley: University of California Press, 2010), https://www.ucpress.edu/book/9780520272743/coming-to-terms-with-the-nation.

102 Human Rights Watch, "One Passport, Two Systems: China's Restrictions on Foreign Travel by Tibetans and Others," 2015, https://www.hrw.org/report/2015/07/13/one-passport-two-systems/chinas-restrictions-foreign-travel-tibetans-and-others.

103 NIA, "Exit and Entry Administration Law of the People's Republic of China."

104 NIA, "Regulations of the People's Republic of China on Administration of the Entry and Exit of Foreigners," September 1, 2013, https://en.nia.gov.cn/n147418/n147458/c155970/content.html.

105 Helen Davidson, "China's Economic Need and Soft Diplomacy Spur About-Face on Visa-Free Entry," *The Guardian,* January 22, 2025, https://www.theguardian.com/world/2025/jan/22/china-visa-free-entry-travel-eligible-countries.

106 "Regulations on Examination and Approval of Permanent Residence of Aliens in China," 2004, Article 6, https://en.nia.gov.cn/n147418/n147458/c155972/content.html.

107 Wong and Fu, "Foreign Permanent Residency in China: New Draft Regulations Released."

108 "Guidelines for Approval of Foreign Nationals' Eligibility for Permanent Residence in China," 2023, Article IV, https://en.nia.gov.cn/n147423/n147478/n147715/c158291/content.html.

109 UNHCR, "Submission by the United Nations High Commissioner for Refugees for the Office of the High Commissioner for Human Rights' Compilation Report – Universal Periodic Review: People's Republic of China," Section I, Section III Issue 2.

110 UNHCR, "Submission by the United Nations High Commissioner for Refugees for the Office of the High Commissioner for Human Rights' Compilation Report – Universal Periodic Review: People's Republic of China," Section I, Section III Issue 3. An oblique reference to this issue is made in the first UPR report on China (2009), which noted concerns "that some asylum-seekers are excluded by the refugee determination procedure of China, in particular those coming from a neighbouring country, who are regarded as economic migrants, and are thus compelled to return to their countries." United Nations Human Rights Council (UNHRC), "Compilation Prepared by the Office of the High Commissioner for Human Rights, in Accordance with Paragraph 15(B) of the Annex to Human Rights Council Resolution 5/1 – People's Republic of China (Including Hong Kong and Macao Special Administrative Regions (HKSAR) and (MSAR))," February 2–13, 2009, Section II.B.9.41, https://digitallibrary.un.org/record/645995?v=pdf.

111 Junichi Toyoura, "North Korean Workers in China Riot over Unpaid Wages; 2,000 Occupy Factory, Kill Plant Manager," *Japan News,* February 17, 2024, https://japannews.yomiuri.co.jp/world/asia-pacific/20240217-169463/.

112 Ifang Bremer and Lina Park, "Deciphering Reports of North Korea Workers' Strike in Chinese Textile Factories," *NK News,* January 29, 2024, https://www.nknews.org/2024/01/deciphering

-reports-of-north-korean-workers-strike-in-chinese-textile-factories/; Aadil Brar, "North Korean Official Killed in China After 'Violent Protests,'" *Newsweek,* January 31, 2024, https://www.newsweek.com/north-korea-china-official-killed-workers-strike-wages-1865115.

113 Elaine Lynn-Ee Ho, "'Refugee' or 'Returnee'? The Ethnic Geopolitics of Diasporic Resettlement in China and Intergenerational Change," *Transactions* 38, 4 (October 2013): 599–611, https://rgs-ibg.onlinelibrary.wiley.com/doi/10.1111/j.1475-5661.2012.00548.x.

114 "Culture and Feelings of China's Korean Ethnic Minority Should Be Respected and So-Called 'Cultural Appropriation' Is Groundless: Chinese Embassy in Seoul," *Global Times,* February 8, 2022, https://www.globaltimes.cn/page/202202/1251791.shtml.

115 Lina Yoon, "China Forcibly Returns More Than 500 to North Korea," Human Rights Watch, October 12, 2023, https://www.hrw.org/news/2023/10/12/china-forcibly-returns-more-500-north-korea; Lina Yoon, "China Restarts Forced Return of Refugees to North Korea," Human Rights Watch, July 22, 2021, https://www.hrw.org/news/2021/07/22/china-restarts-forced-returns-refugees-north-korea.

116 OHCHR, "International Covenant on Economic, Social and Cultural Rights" (ICESCR), https://www.ohchr.org/en/instruments-mechanisms/instruments/international-covenant-economic-social-and-cultural-rights.

117 OHCHR, "International Covenant on Civil and Political Rights" (ICCPR), https://www.ohchr.org/en/instruments-mechanisms/instruments/international-covenant-civil-and-political-rights; OHCHR, "About Minorities and Human Rights," https://www.ohchr.org/en/minorities/about-minorities-and-human-rights; International Human Rights Law Clinic, University of California, Berkeley School of Law, "Right to Identity," November 2007, http://scm.oas.org/pdfs/2007/cp19277.pDF, which defines identity as "an individual's significant and knowable personal attributes and social relationships."

118 State Council Information Office (SCIO), "China's Ethnic Policy and Common Prosperity and Development of All Ethnic Groups," white paper, September 27, 2009, Preface, Section III, http://www.china.org.cn/government/whitepaper/node_7078073.htm.

119 "Zhulao zhonghua minzu gongtong ti yijian" [Realize the unity of Chinese ethnic groups], *people.cn/人民网,* September 30, 2024, http://opinion.people.com.cn/n1/2024/0930/c1003-40331198.html.

120 Dan Kopf, "In One Metric of Diversity, China Comes in Dead Last," *Quartz,* December 27, 2017, https://qz.com/1163632/china-still-has-the-smallest-share-of-incoming-migrants-in-the-world/.

121 Xiao, Cheng, and Lin, "China Accelerates Campaign of Ethnic Assimilation"; Willie Wo-Lap Lam, "The CCP Extends Its Policies of Forced Ethnic Assimilation to Inner Mongolia," *China Brief* 20, 17 (2020), https://jamestown.org/program/the-ccp-extends-its-policies-of-forced-ethnic-assimilation-to-inner-mongolia/.

122 World Bank, "Refugee Population by Country or Territory of Asylum for China," https://fred.stlouisfed.org/series/SMPOPREFGCHN#:~:text=Markets%20%3E%20Population%20%3E%20Migration-,Refugee%20Population%20by%20Country%20or%20Territory%20of%20Asylum%20for%20China,Need%20help.

123 Arjun Kharpal, "China's Plans to Ease Its 'Green Card' Rule for Foreigners Spark Racist Backlash Online," *CNBC,* March 13, 2020, https://www.cnbc.com/2020/03/13/china-permanent-residency-proposal-racist-backlash-spills-onto-twitter.html; Wong and Fu, "Foreign Permanent Residency in China: New Draft Regulations Released."

124 "Regulations on Examination and Approval of Permanent Residence of Aliens in China"; Wong and Fu, "Foreign Permanent Residency in China: New Draft Regulations Released"; "Guidelines for Approval of Foreign Nationals' Eligibility for Permanent Residence in China."

125 "Regulations on Examination and Approval of Permanent Residence of Aliens in China," Article 24; "Guidelines for Approval of Foreign Nationals' Eligibility for Permanent Residence in China," Article V.

126 NIA, https://en.nia.gov.cn.

127 Tabitha Speelman, "Establishing the National Immigration Administration: Change and Continuity in China's Immigration Reforms," *China Perspectives* 2020, 4 (2020): 7–16, https://journals.openedition.org/chinaperspectives/11103.

128 NIA, "Over 1200 Suspects Arrested! NIA Directs the Cracking of a Major Illegal Immigration Case," November 10, 2021, https://en.nia.gov.cn/n147413/c160359/content.html.

129 NIA, "Interpretation; Three Categories of Foreign Nationals Allowed Entering China from September 28," March 29, 2021, https://en.nia.gov.cn/n147418/n147463/c155990/content.html.
130 OHCHR, "Universal Declaration on Cultural Diversity," November 2, 2001, Articles 3, 4, https://www.ohchr.org/en/instruments-mechanisms/instruments/universal-declaration-cultural-diversity#:~:text=The%20defence%20of%20cultural%20diversity,and%20those%20of%20indigenous%20peoples. Also see Yvonne Donders, "Do Cultural Diversity and Human Rights Make a Good Match?" *International Social Science Journal* 61, 199 (March 2010): 15–35, https://onlinelibrary.wiley.com/doi/abs/10.1111/j.1468-2451.2010.01746.x.
131 "Vienna Declaration and Programme of Action," June 25, 1993, A/CONF.157/23, Article 10, http://www.ohchr.org/EN/ProfessionalInterest/Pages/Vienna.aspx.
132 *International Convention on the Elimination of All Forms of Racial Discrimination,* UNGA Res. 2106 (XX), December 21, 1965, Article 3, https://www.ohchr.org/en/instruments-mechanisms/instruments/international-convention-elimination-all-forms-racial.
133 Haugen and Speelman, "China's Rapid Development Has Transformed Its Migration Trends."
134 Cai Xuejiao, "China's Yangtze Delta Eases Habitat Rules to Lure Big-City Talent"; "Internal Migration and Stability in China."
135 "Statement by Mr. Ke Yousheng, Adviser of the Chinese Delegation, at the Third Committee of the 62nd Session of the General Assembly, on the Report of UNHCR (Item 42)," November 8, 2007, https://un.china-mission.gov.cn/eng/hyyfy/200711/t20071108_8399179.htm.
136 UNHRC, "Report of the Working Group on the Universal Periodic Review – China," October 5, 2009, A/HRC/11/25, paragraphs 28, 30, and 112, https://documents-dds-ny.un.org/doc/UNDOC/GEN/G09/162/99/PDF/G0916299.pdf?OpenElement.
137 "Statement of Ambassador Li Li, Leader of the Chinese Delegation and Chinese Ambassador to the Kingdom of Morocco, at the Intergovernmental Conference to Adopt the Global Compact for Safe, Orderly and Regular Migration."
138 "Zhonghua renmin gongheguo ludi guojie fa" [Land border law of the People's Republic of China], adopted October 23, 2021, entered into force January 2, 2022, http://www.lawinfochina.com/display.aspx?id=36689&lib=law; Shuxian Luo, "China's Land Border Law: A Preliminary Assessment," Brookings, November 4, 2021, https://www.brookings.edu/blog/order-from-chaos/2021/11/04/chinas-land-border-law-a-preliminary-assessment/.
139 Chen Jie, "Guojia yimin guanli ju xinwen fabuhui" [Press conference of the National Migration Administration] (summarizing NIA activities January–June 2021), July 30, 2021, https://www.nia.gov.cn/n741435/n1194535/n1431602/index.html.
140 OHCHR, "Universal Declaration of Human Rights," December 10, 1948, https://www.ohchr.org/en/universal-declaration-of-human-rights#:~:text=The%20Universal%20Declaration%20of%20Human%20Rights%20(UDHR)%20is%20a%20milestone,rights%20to%20be%20universally%20protected. Also see Tanya Golash-Boza and Cecilia Menjivar, "Causes and Consequences of International Migration: Sociological Evidence for the Right to Mobility," *International Journal of Human Rights* 16, 8 (November 22, 2012): 1213–27, https://www.tandfonline.com/doi/abs/10.1080/13642987.2012.727802; Stefanie Grant, "International Migration and Human Rights," Global Commission on International Migration, September 2005, https://www.iom.int/sites/g/files/tmzbdl486/files/jahia/webdav/site/myjahiasite/shared/shared/mainsite/policy_and_research/gcim/tp/TP7.pdf.
141 Vanja Petricevic, "Unwanted Immigration: Has the Concept of State Sovereignty Become Obsolete?" Canadian Global Affairs Institute, October 2018, https://www.cgai.ca/unwanted_immigration_has_the_concept_of_state_sovereignty_become_obsolete; Catherine Dauvergne, "Challenges to Sovereignty: Migration Laws for the 21st Century," New Issues in Refugee Research Working Paper 92, UNHCR, July 2003, https://www.refworld.org/pdfid/4ff2b0b82.pdf.
142 NIA, "Exit and Entry Administration Law of the People's Republic of China," Article 1.
143 NIA, "Exit and Entry Administration Law of the People's Republic of China."
144 "Zhonghua renmin gongheguo ludi guojie fa" [Land border law of the People's Republic of China]; Shuxian Luo, "China's Land Border Law: A Preliminary Assessment."
145 Lili Song, "Who Shall We Help? The Refugee Definition in Chinese Context," *Refugee Survey Quarterly* 33, 1 (March 2014): 44–58, https://academic.oup.com/rsq/article-abstract/33/1/44/1570418; UNHRC, "Compilation Prepared by the Office of the High Commissioner for Human Rights, in Accordance with Paragraph 15(B) of the Annex to Human Rights Council Resolution 5/1 – People's Republic of China."

146 MFA, "China's Relationship with the United Nations High Commissioner for Refugees (UNHCR)."
147 Guofu Liu, "Changing Chinese Migration Law: From Restriction to Relaxation," *International Migration and Integration,* 2009, https://link.springer.com/article/10.1007/s12134-009-0105-0.
148 NIA, "Exit and Entry Administration Law of the People's Republic of China."
149 NIA, "Regulations of the People's Republic of China on Administration of the Entry and Exit of Foreigners."
150 "Statement of Ambassador Li Li, Leader of the Chinese Delegation and Chinese Ambassador to the Kingdom of Morocco, at the Intergovernmental Conference to Adopt the Global Compact for Safe, Orderly and Regular Migration."
151 "Statement of Ambassador Li Li, Leader of the Chinese Delegation and Chinese Ambassador to the Kingdom of Morocco, at the Intergovernmental Conference to Adopt the Global Compact for Safe, Orderly and Regular Migration."
152 MFA, "Position Paper of the People's Republic of China on the 75th Anniversary of the United Nations," Section III.11.
153 UN, "Report of the High Commissioner for Refugees Part II: Global Compact on Refugees," paragraph 33.
154 UNHCR, "Suggestions and Amendments of China: Global Compact on Refugees."
155 "Statement of Ambassador Li Li, Leader of the Chinese Delegation and Chinese Ambassador to the Kingdom of Morocco, at the Intergovernmental Conference to Adopt the Global Compact for Safe, Orderly and Regular Migration."
156 Compare State Council of the People's Republic of China, "Premier Li Addresses UN General Assembly," September 20, 2016, http://english.www.gov.cn/premier/news/2016/09/20/content_281475446293659.htm with Danish Refugee Council, International Rescue Committee, and Norwegian Refugee Council, *The Global Compact on Refugees Three Years On: Navigating Barriers and Maximising Incentives in Support of Refugees and Host Countries* (September 2021), https://www.rescue.org/sites/default/files/document/6324/ircdrcnrcjointreportv4final.pdf.
157 Vivian Tan, "China Can Play Key Role in Solving Refugee Crisis – UNHCR Chief," UNHCR, June 8, 2017, https://www.unhcr.org/news/latest/2017/6/593946b64/china-play-key-role-solving-refugee-crises-unhcr-chief.html.
158 UNHCR, "China."
159 UNHCR Canada, "UN Refugee Chief Connects with Chinese Companies at Boao Forum," May 29, 2019, https://www.unhcr.ca/news/un-refugee-chief-connects-chinese-companies-boao-forum/.
160 Song Lili, "The Power of Giving: China Deepens Involvement in Refugee Affairs," *The China Story, Yearbook 2018: Power,* https://www.thechinastory.org/yearbooks/yearbook-2018-power/forum-with-great-power-comes-great-responsibility/the-power-of-giving-china-deepens-involvement-in-refugee-affairs/.
161 Ai Jun, "China Won't Play by US Playbook in Terms of Afghan Refugee Issue"; Liang Pan, "Why China Isn't Hosting Syrian Refugees."
162 John Calabrese, "China and Syria: In War and Reconstruction," Middle East Institute, July 9, 2019, https://www.mei.edu/publications/china-and-syria-war-and-reconstruction; Samy Akii and Karam Shaar, "The Red Dragon in the Land of Jasmine: An Overview of China's Role in the Syrian Conflict," Operations and Policy Center, March 24, 2021, https://opc.center/an-overview-of-chinas-role-in-the-syrian-conflict/.
163 "China Backs Political Process in Syria: Chinese FM," *Xinhua,* February 5, 2016, http://www.china.org.cn/world/Off_the_Wire/2016-02/05/content_37744839.htm; UK Government, "Syria Donors Conference 2016: Joint Announcement," press release, November 16, 2015, https://www.gov.uk/government/news/syria-donors-conference-2016-joint-announcement; Moritz Rudolf and Angela Stanzel, "China Should Do More to Solve the Syrian Refugee Crisis," *The Diplomat,* February 2, 2016, https://thediplomat.com/2016/02/china-should-do-more-to-solve-to-syrian-refugee-crisis/.
164 "Supporting Syria and the Region: Co-host's Statement Annex: Fundraising," *Supporting Syria and the Region: London 2016,* February 8, 2016, https://webarchive.nationalarchives.gov.uk/ukgwa/20180601145806/https://www.supportingsyria2016.com/news/co-hosts-statement-annex-fundraising/.
165 UN, "General Assembly Adopts Declaration for Refugees and Migrants, as United Nations, International Organization for Migration Sign Key Agreement," press release, September 19,

2016, GA/11820, https://www.un.org/press/en/2016/ga11820.doc.htm; "Chinese Premier Delivers Keynote Speech at UN General Assembly."

166 Compare European Commission, "Supporting Syria and the Region: Post-Brussels Conference Financial Tracking Report 4," October 2017, 10–11, with European Commission, "Supporting Syria and the Region: Post-Brussels Conference Financial Tracking Report 6," September 2018, 12–15, https://www.consilium.europa.eu/media/36437/syria-report-six.pdf, and European Commission, "Supporting Syria and the Region: Post-Brussels Conference Financial Tracking Report 10," September 2020, 5–8, https://www.consilium.europa.eu/media/46336/financial-tracking-report-no10.pdf.

167 Jacqueline Bhabha, "Internationalist Gatekeepers? The Tension Between Asylum Advocacy and Human Rights," *Harvard Human Rights Journal* 15 (Spring 2002): 155–81, http://www.mcrg.ac.in/AddReading/2008/C_Bhaba.pdf.

168 UNGA, "Resolution 73/195: Global Compact for Safe, Orderly and Regular Migration," Preamble; UN, *Global Compact on Refugees,* Section B (General Principles), paragraph 5; and UN, "Report of the High Commissioner for Refugees Part II: Global Compact on Refugees."

169 MFA, "China and the United Nations: Position Paper of the People's Republic of China for the 74th Session of the United Nations General Assembly," September 18, 2019, Section VIII, https://www.mfa.gov.cn/eng/zy/gb/202405/t20240531_11367393.html; SCIO, "The Right to Development: China's Philosophy, Practice and Contribution," white paper, December 2, 2016, http://english.www.gov.cn/archive/white_paper/2016/12/01/content_281475505407672.htm.

170 UNHRC, "Universal Periodic Review – China," https://www.ohchr.org/EN/HRBodies/UPR/Pages/CNindex.aspx.

171 UNHRC, "Compilation Prepared by the Office of the High Commissioner for Human Rights, in Accordance with Paragraph 15(B) of the Annex to Human Rights Council Resolution 5/1 – People's Republic of China," Sections I.A.1 and I.B.4; UN, "Convention Relating to the Status of Refugees," July 28, 1951, https://www.ohchr.org/en/instruments-mechanisms/instruments/convention-relating-status-refugees.

172 UNHCR, "The 1951 Refugee Convention and 1967 Protocol Relating to the Status of Refugees," https://www.unhcr.org/3b66c2aa10.

173 UNHCR, "The 1951 Refugee Convention and 1967 Protocol Relating to the Status of Refugees," Section II.B.9.41.

174 Jason Bartlett, "China's New Land Borders Law Is a Nightmare for North Korean Refugees," *The Diplomat,* October 28, 2021, https://thediplomat.com/2021/10/chinas-new-land-borders-law-is-a-nightmare-for-north-korean-refugees/; Roberta Cohen, "Legal Grounds for Protection of North Korean Refugees," Brookings, September 13, 2010, https://www.brookings.edu/opinions/legal-grounds-for-protection-of-north-korean-refugees/; Joel R. Charny, "North Koreans in China: A Human Rights Analysis," *International Journal of Korean Unification Studies* 13, 2 (2004): 75–97, https://www.refworld.org/reference/countryrep/ri/2004/en/53240.

175 UNHRC, "Report of the Working Group on the Universal Periodic Review – China," paragraphs 28, 30, and 112.

176 UNHRC, "Report of the Working Group on the Universal Periodic Review – China (Including Hong Kong, China and Macao, China)," December 4, 2013, A/HRC/25/5, paragraphs 186.240–186.243, and "Matrix of Recommendations" Theme G5 Refugees and Asylum Seekers, in UNHRC, "Universal Periodic Review – China," Second Cycle, Outcome of the Review, https://www.ohchr.org/en/hr-bodies/upr/cn-index.

177 UNHRC, "Compilation Prepared by the Office of the High Commissioner for Human Rights in Accordance with Paragraph 15(b) of the Annex to Human Rights Council Resolution 5/1 and Paragraph 5 of the Annex to Council Resolution 16/21 – China (Including Hong Kong, China and Macao, China)," August 7, 2013, A/HRC/WG.6/17/CHN/2, https://documents-dds-ny.un.org/doc/UNDOC/GEN/G13/161/90/PDF/G1316190.pdf?OpenElement.

178 UNHRC, "Compilation on China: Report of the Office of the United Nations High Commissioner for Human Rights," August 27, 2018, A/HRC/WG.6/31/CHN/2, https://documents-dds-ny.un.org/doc/UNDOC/GEN/G18/259/12/PDF/G1825912.pdf?OpenElement.

179 Office of the High Commissioner for Human Rights (OHCHR), "Annex to Letter to PRC Foreign Minister Wang Yi from Michelle Bachelet, UN High Commissioner for Human Rights," April 29, 2019, https://www.ohchr.org/sites/default/files/lib-docs/HRBodies/UPR/Documents/Session31/CN/LetterChina.pdf. China's forcible repatriation of migrants from North Korea

appears to violate the international law principle of non-refoulement, which "prohibits States from transferring or removing individuals from their jurisdiction or effective control when there are substantial grounds for believing that the person would be at risk of irreparable harm upon return, including persecution, torture, ill-treatment or other serious human rights violations." OHCHR, "The Principle of *Non-refoulement* Under International Human Rights Law," https://www.ohchr.org/Documents/Issues/Migration/GlobalCompactMigration/ThePrincipleNon-RefoulementUnderInternationalHumanRightsLaw.pdf.

180 "Zhonghua renmin gongheguo ludi guojie fa" [Land border law of the People's Republic of China], Article 4.

181 David Volodzko, "How China Helped Cause the Syrian Refugee Crisis," *The Diplomat,* September 14, 2015, https://thediplomat.com/2015/09/how-china-helped-cause-the-syrian-refugee-crisis/; Jasmine Lam, "Refugee Policy and Foreign Policy: Examining Policy Linkage in Chinese Relations with Korea, Myanmar, and Vietnam," *Inquiries* 5, 10 (2013), http://www.inquiriesjournal.com/articles/771/2/refugee-policy-and-foreign-policy-examining-policy-linkage-in-chinese-relations-with-north-korea-myanmar-and-vietnam.

182 UNHRC, "Report of the Working Group on the Universal Periodic Review – China," paragraphs 28, 30, and 112.

183 Jacob Kurtzer, Sana Vaidya, and Imrul Islam, "Aspirations to Action: Making the Refugee Compact Work for the Rohingya," Center for Strategic and International Studies, December 16, 2021, https://www.csis.org/analysis/aspirations-action-making-refugee-compact-work-rohingya.

184 Government of the People's Republic of China, "China, Myanmar and Bangladesh Reach Positive Consensus on Accelerating the Repatriation of Rohingya Refugees," press release, January 21, 2021, https://reliefweb.int/report/bangladesh/china-myanmar-and-bangladesh-reach-positive-consensus-accelerating-repatriation.

185 "Zhongguo zai lianheguo zongbu zhuchi zhaokai youguan luozingya nanmin huiyi lianheguo mishuzhang guteleisi huyu mianmi mengjialaguo kaizhan hezuo" [China hosts a meeting on Rohingya refugees at UN headquarters, UN Secretary-General António Guterres called for Myanmar and Bangladesh cooperation], *UN News,* September 27, 2018, https://news.un.org/zh/story/2018/09/1018962; UNHCR, "UNHCR and UNDP Agree on Text of MoU with Myanmar to Support the Creation of Conditions for the Return of Rohingya Refugees," press release, May 31, 2018, https://www.unhcr.org/news/press-releases/unhcr-and-undp-agree-text-mou-myanmar-support-creation-conditions-return.

186 "China Says Rohingya Issue Should Not Be 'Internationalised,'" *Reuters,* September 27, 2018, https://www.reuters.com/article/us-myanmar-rohingya-china-idUSKCN1M8062; UNHRC, "Situation of Human Rights of Rohingya Muslims and Other Minorities in Myanmar," September 27, 2018, A/HRC/RES/39/2, https://ap.ohchr.org/documents/dpage_e.aspx?si=A/HRC/RES/39/2; UNHRC, "Independent Investigative Mechanism for Myanmar," https://www.ohchr.org/EN/HRBodies/HRC/IIMM/Pages/Index.aspx; Human Rights Watch, "Myanmar: UN Rights Council Backs Atrocity Victims," news release, September 27, 2018, https://www.hrw.org/news/2018/09/27/myanmar-un-rights-council-backs-atrocity-victims.

187 Joel Gunter, "Afghanistan's Uyghurs Fear the Taliban, and Now China Too," *BBC News,* August 27, 2021, https://www.bbc.com/news/world-asia-58342790; Gopal Sharma, "Nepal Detains Tibetan Refugees in Crackdown as China's Influence Grows," *Reuters,* November 15, 2016, https://www.reuters.com/article/us-nepal-tibet-refugees-idUSKBN13A2BQ. On abuses in Xinjiang, see Lindsay Maizland, "China's Repression of Uyghurs in Xinjiang," Council on Foreign Relations, March 1, 2021, https://www.cfr.org/backgrounder/chinas-repression-uyghurs-xinjiang. On abuses in Tibet, see Kelsang Dolma, "Tibet Was China's First Laboratory of Repression," *Foreign Policy,* August 31, 2020, https://foreignpolicy.com/2020/08/31/tibet-china-repression-xinjiang-sinicization/.

188 UNHCR, "The 1951 Refugee Convention and 1967 Protocol Relating to the Status of Refugees."

189 On Huseyin Celil, see Amnesty International, "Huseyin Celil," 2022, https://www.amnesty.ca/huseyin-celil/. The non-refoulement provision is contained in UNHCR, *Recommended Principles and Guidelines on Human Rights at International Borders* (Geneva: UNHCR), https://www.ohchr.org/Documents/Issues/Migration/OHCHR_Recommended_Principles_Guidelines.pdf. On Xiao Jianhua, see James Griffiths, "Canadian-Chinese Billionaire Xiao Jianhua Sentenced to 13 Years in Prison in Secret Trial in Shanghai," *Globe and Mail,* August 19, 2022, https://www.theglobeandmail.com/world/article-canadian-chinese-billionaire-xiao

-jianhua-prison/; Alexandra Stevenson, "Chinese Canadian Billionaire Sentenced to 13 Years for Financial Crimes," *New York Times*, August 19, 2022, https://www.nytimes.com/2022/08/19/business/chinese-canadian-billionaire-xiao-jianhua-sentenced.html.

190 Mike Blanchfield, "China Warns Canada Not to Grant Asylum to Hong Kong Protesters," *Global News*, October 15, 2020, https://globalnews.ca/news/7399654/hong-kong-china-canada-asylum/.

CONCLUSION AND RECOMMENDATIONS

1 See, e.g., Cliff Kupchan, "Bipolarity Is Back: Why It Matters," *Washington Quarterly* 44, 4 (2021): 123–39, https://www.tandfonline.com/doi/full/10.1080/0163660X.2021.2020457; Øystein Tunsjø, *The Return of Bipolarity in World Politics: China, the United States, and Geostructural Realism* (New York: Columbia University Press, 2018), https://cup.columbia.edu/book/the-return-of-bipolarity-in-world-politics/9780231176545. Also see Andrew J. Nathan's review of Tunsjø's book in *Foreign Affairs*, May/June 2018, https://www.foreignaffairs.com/reviews/capsule-review/2018-04-16/return-bipolarity-world-politics-china-united-states-and.

2 Compare David Badurski and Alex Colville, "Is Xi's Grip Holding?" China Media Project, June 25, 2025, https://chinamediaproject.org/2025/06/26/is-xis-grip-holding/, and "Xi Is 'Losing Power.' Or Is He?" *SinoInsider*, June 25, 2025, https://sinoinsider.com/2025/06/xi-is-losing-power-or-is-he/, with Vanessa Cai and Xinyu Liang, "New Communist Party Rules Hint China's Xi Jinping Is Delegating More Power to Deputies," *South China Morning Post*, July 6, 2025, https://www.scmp.com/news/china/politics/article/3317101/new-communist-party-rules-hint-chinas-xi-jinping-delegating-more-power-deputies.

3 See, e.g., Bela Prigly, "The Achievements of the Canada-China Statistical Cooperation Program," November 30, 2004, https://www.stats.gov.cn/english/SpecialTopics/IntSymposium/200411/t20041130_52293.html.

4 See, e.g., US-Asia Institute, "Rule of Law Exchange Program," https://www.usasiainstitute.org/ruleoflaw; "Legal Briefs: US Training Programs for Chinese Legal Professionals," *China Exchange News* 22, 4 (Winter 1994): 31–35, https://www.google.ca/books/edition/China_Exchange_News/K75AVNKx5nwC?hl=en&gbpv=1&dq=CLEEC+China+law+exchange+programs&printsec=frontcover.

5 United Nations General Assembly (UNGA), "Delivering Justice: Programme of Action to Strengthen the Rule of Law at the National and International Levels: Report of the Secretary-General," March 16, 2012, A/66/749, http://archive.ipu.org/splz-e/unbrief12/sg-report.pdf.

6 See, e.g., Yipeng Xi, Anfan Chen, and Aaron Ng, "Conditional Transparency: Differentiated News Framings of COVID-19 Severity in the Pre-Crisis Stage in China," *PLoS ONE* 16, 5 (2001): e0252062, https://journals.plos.org/plosone/article?id=10.1371/journal.pone.0252062.

7 See, e.g., Binbin Wang and Qinnan Zhou, "Climate Change in the Chinese Mind: An Overview of Public Perceptions at Macro and Micro Levels," *WIREs Climate Change* 11 (2020): e639, https://wires.onlinelibrary.wiley.com/doi/pdf/10.1002/wcc.639.

8 See, e.g., Shouhao Li, Weiquan Cheng, Jingjing Li, and Hao Shen, "Corporate Social Responsibility Development and Climate Change: Regional Evidence of China," *Sustainability* 13, 21 (2021): 11859, https://www.mdpi.com/2071-1050/13/21/11859.

9 See, e.g., United Nations Department of Economic and Social Affairs (DESA), Division for Sustainable Development, "International Cooperation to Accelerate Sustainable Development in Developing Countries & Related Domestic Policies," in *AGENDA 21: The Report of the United Nations Conference on Environment and Development (Earth Summit) in Rio* (1992), ch. 2, http://www.un-documents.net/a21-02.htm; Arun Ghosh, "Planning Versus Market in Developing Economies – Discussions in Honour of the Late Amiya Dasgupta," *Economic and Political Weekly* 30, 17 (April 29, 1995): 99–923, https://www.epw.in/journal/1995/17/columns-random-reflections/planning-versus-market-developing-economies-discussions.

10 See, e.g., Irini Kadianaki and Eleni Andreouli, "Essentialism in Social Representation of Citizenship; An Analysis of Greeks' and Migrants' Discourse," *Political Psychology* 38, 5 (October 2017): 833–48, https://onlinelibrary.wiley.com/doi/abs/10.1111/pops.12271; Raymond U. Scupin, "Ethnic Essentialism or Conciliatory Multiculturalism? The People's Republic of China," *Journal of Cognition and Culture* 20 (2020): 458–80, https://brill.com/downloadpdf/journals/jocc/20/5/article-p458_4.xml.

11 See, e.g., Deborah Phillips, "Minority Ethnic Segregation, Integration and Citizenship: A Euro-

pean Perspective," in *Linking Integration and Residential Segregation,* ed. Gideon Bolt, A. Sule Ozuekren, and Deborah Phillips (London: Routledge, 2012), ch. 3, https://www.routledge.com/Linking-Integration-and-Residential-Segregation/Bolt-Ozuekren-Phillips/p/book/9781138110083.

12 Lara Sansus, David Ramiro Troitiño, and Tanel Kerikmäe, "Migration to Europe: A Threat or Opportunity?" in *The EU in the 21st Century: Challenges and Opportunities for the European Integration Process,* ed. David Ramiro Troitiño, Tanel Kerikmäe, Ricardo Martín de la Guardia, and Guillermo Á. Pérez Sánchez (Cham, Switzerland: Springer Nature, 2020), 59–84, https://link.springer.com/chapter/10.1007/978-3-030-38399-2_5; Michele Bruni, "The World at the Crossroad: Demographic Polarization and Mass Migration. Global Threat or Global Opportunity," Global Labor Organization Discussion Paper 301, 2019, https://www.econstor.eu/bitstream/10419/191049/1/GLO-DP-0301.pdf.

Authorities Cited

CONSTITUTION AND LEGISLATION

Administrative Litigation Law of the People's Republic of China, June 27, 2017, http://www.lawinfochina.com/display.aspx?lib=law&id=23600.

Administrative Procedure Law of the People's Republic of China (Chinese and English text), April 4, 1989, https://www.cecc.gov/resources/legal-provisions/administrative-procedure-law-chinese-and-english-text.

Constitution of the People's Republic of China (rev. 2018), https://english.www.gov.cn/archive/lawsregulations/201911/20/content_WS5ed8856ec6d0b3f0e9499913.html.

Environmental Protection Law of the People's Republic of China, 2015, http://www.lawinfochina.com/Display.aspx?lib=law&Cgid=223979.

Exit and Entry Administration Law of the People's Republic of China (adopted June 30, 2012, entered into force July 1, 2013), https://www.nia.gov.cn/n741440/n741547/c757592/content.html.

Foreign State Immunity Law of the People's Republic of China, September 1, 2023, https://www.chinalawtranslate.com/en/foreign-immunities-law/.

Law of the People's Republic of China on Basic Medical and Health Care and the Promotion of Health, December 28, 2019, http://en.moj.gov.cn/2021-06/26/c_636455.htm.

Law of the People's Republic of China on the Law Applicable to Foreign-Related Civil Relationships (Excerpts), July 19, 2022, https://english.court.gov.cn/2022-07/19/c_790717.htm.

Law of the People's Republic of China on Promotion of the Private Economy (draft for solicitation of comments), 2024, https://npcobserver.com/wp-content/uploads/2024/10/Private-Economy-Promotion-Law-2024-Draft.pdf.

Law of the People's Republic of China on Regional National Autonomy, 1984, http://www.lawinfochina.com/display.aspx?id=43&lib=law.

Law of the People's Republic of China on Regional National Autonomy (2001 amendment), February 28, 2001, http://www.lawinfochina.com/display.aspx?id=6211&lib=law.

National Land Boundary Law of the People's Republic of China (adopted October 23, 2021, entered into force January 1, 2022), http://www.lawinfochina.com/display.aspx?id=36689&lib=law.

National Security Law of the People's Republic of China, July 2, 2015, https://www.chinalawtranslate.com/en/2015nsl/#gsc.tab=0.

Nationality Law of the People's Republic of China, September 10, 1980, http://www.npc.gov.cn/zgrdw/englishnpc/Law/2007-12/13/content_1384056.htm.
Passport Law of the People's Republic of China, 2006, http://www.npc.gov.cn/zgrdw/englishnpc/Law/2008-01/02/content_1388000.htm.
State Compensation Law of the People's Republic of China, 1994, http://www.lehmanlaw.com/resource-centre/laws-and-regulations/general/state-compensation-law-of-the-peoples-republic-of-china-1994.html.
State Compensation Law of the People's Republic of China (2012 amendment), October 26, 2012, http://www.lawinfochina.com/display.aspx?id=12606&lib=law&EncodingName=big5.
State Compensation Law of the People's Republic of China (rev. 2010), http://www.china.org.cn/china/LegislationsForm2001-2010/2011-02/12/content_21905705.htm.
State Secrets Protection Law of the People's Republic of China, 2010, https://www.cecc.gov/resources/legal-provisions/law-on-the-protection-of-state-secrets-cecc-partial-translation-and.
Supervision Law of the People's Republic of China, March 20, 2018, https://www.chinalawtranslate.com/en/supervision-law-of-the-prc-2018/.
Supreme People's Court Interpretation on the Application of the "Administrative Litigation Law of the P.R.C.," February 6, 2018, https://www.chinalawtranslate.com/en/supreme-peoples-court-interpretation-on-the-application-of-the-administrative-litigation-law-of-the-p-r-c/.
Vaccine Administration Law of the People's Republic of China, June 29, 2019, http://www.lawinfochina.com/display.aspx?id=30707&lib=law.
"Zhongguo qicao wancheng 'Qihou bianhua yingdui fa' cao'an" [China has drafted a complete climate change adaptation law draft], *Caixin,* July 23, 2014, https://china.caixin.com/2014-07-23/100707692.html.
"Zhonghua renmin gongheguo baocun guojia mimi fa" [State secrets protection law of the People's Republic of China], February 27, 2024, https://www.gov.cn/yaowen/liebiao/202402/content_6934648.htm.
"Zhonghua renmin gongheguo guoji fa" [Nationality law of the People's Republic of China], September 10, 1980, https://data.globalcit.eu/NationalDB/docs/04_CHN_1980_NationalityLaw_PRC%20%5BORIGINAL%20LANGUAGE%5D.pdf0.
"Zhonghua renmin gongheguo jumin shenfenzheng fa" [Law of the People's Republic of China on residential identity cards] (rev. 2011), http://www.npc.gov.cn/zgrdw/npc/xinwen/2011-10/31/content_1678466_2.htm.
"Zhonghua renmin gongheguo qihou bianhua yingdui fa" [Climate change adaptation law of the People's Republic of China], https://baike.baidu.com/item/中华人民共和国气候变化应对法/19521242.
"Zhonghua renmin gongheguo xianfa" [Constitution of the People's Republic of China], http://www.gov.cn/guoqing/2018-03/22/content_5276318.htm.
"Zhonghua renmin gongheguo zhuanranbing fangzhi fa [Law on prevention and control of infectious diseases of the People's Republic of China], August 28, 2004, Articles 3, 4, 41–42, https://www.cecc.gov/resources/legal-provisions/law-on-the-prevention-and-control-of-infectious-diseases-chinese-text. English translation at http://www.npc.gov.cn/zgrdw/englishnpc/Law/2007-12/12/content_1383919.htm.

POLICIES, PLANS, AND REPORTS

"2022 nian Zhongyang jingji gongzuo huiyi ceji: 'Wei quanmian jianshe shehuizhuyi xiandaihua guojia kaihao juqi haobu'" [Side note to the 2022 Central Economic Work Conference: a good step toward all-round construction of a modern socialist country], December 18, 2022, http://www.gov.cn/xinwen/2022-12/18/content_5732562.htm.
"2022 Zhongyang jingji gongzuo huiyi gongbao quanwen" [Full text of the communiqué for the 2022 Central Economic Work Conference], December 16, 2022, http://www.china-cer.com.cn/guwen/2022121622596.html.
"Central Inspection Group Gives Feedback to the Supreme People's Court (2020 Edition)," *Supreme People's Court Monitor,* January 12, 2020, https://supremepeoplescourtmonitor.com/2020/01/12/central-inspection-group-gives-feedback-to-the-supreme-peoples-court-2020-edition/.

China International Development Cooperation Agency, "Global Development and South-South Cooperation Assistance Fund," 2018, http://en.cidca.gov.cn/southsouthcooperation fund.html.

Clean Air Alliance of China, *State Council Air Pollution Prevention and Control Action Plan* (October 2013), https://policy.asiapacificenergy.org/sites/default/files/Air%20Pollution%20Prevention%20and%20Control%20Action%20Plan%20%28EN%29.pdf.

"Communiqué of the 4th Plenary Session of the 18th Central Committee of the Communist Party of China, October 23, 2014," December 2, 2014, http://www.china.org.cn/china/fourth_plenary_session/2014-12/02/content_34208801.htm.

"Communiqué of the Fifth Plenary Meeting of the 18th Central Committee of the Chinese Communist Party," November 2, 2015, https://chinacopyrightandmedia.wordpress.com/2015/10/29/communique-of-the-fifth-plenary-meeting-of-the-18th-central-committee-of-the-chinese-communist-party.

"Communiqué of the Third Plenary Session of the 11th Central Committee of the Communist Party of China," *Beijing Review,* December 29, 1978, http://www.bjreview.com/Special_Reports/2018/40th_Anniversary_of_Reform_and_Opening_up/Timeline/201806/t20180626_800133641.html.

CPC Central Committee and State Council, "Implementation Outline on Building the Government Under Rule of Law (2015–2020)," December 27, 2015, https://law.yale.edu/sites/default/files/area/center/china/document/2015-12_rol_govt_constructn_outline_en_2015-20202.pdf,.

"Decision of the Central Committee of the Communist Party of China on Some Major Issues Concerning Comprehensively Deepening the Reform," January 16, 2014, http://www.china.org.cn/china/third_plenary_session/2014-01/16/content_31212602.htm.

Ding Yihui, Guoyu Ren, Shi Guangyu, and Gong Peng, *China's National Assessment Report on Climate Change (I): Climate Change in China and the Future Trend* (2007), https://www.researchgate.net/publication/242281068_China's_National_Assessment_Report_on_Climate_Change_I_Climate_change_in_China_and_the_future_trend.

"Document No. 9: A ChinaFile Translation," April 22, 2013, http://www.chinafile.com/document-9-chinafile-translation.

"'Guanyu jinyibu youhua luoshi xinguan feiyan yiqing fankong cuosho de tongzhi' jiedu wenda" [Reading Q&A on the notice on further optimizing the implementation of prevention and control measures of the novel corona pneumonia epidemic], December 7, 2022, https://www.gov.cn/zhengce/2022-12/07/content_5730449.htm.

"Guanyu tuidong yange guifan gongzheng wenming zhifa wei yiqing fangkong gongzuo tigong youli fazhi baozhang de yijian" [Opinion on promoting strictly regulated, just, and civilized law enforcement to provide forceful legal safeguards for epidemic prevention and control work], February 24, 2020, http://www.gov.cn/zhengce/zhengceku/2020-02/25/content_5483027.htm. English translation at https://www.chinalawtranslate.com/en/just-and-civilized-law-enforcement/.

Guo Jianming, *Shehui zhuyi hexin jiazhiguan jiben neirong jieyi* [Interpretation of the basic content of the core values of socialism] (Beijing: Renmin chubanshe [People's Publishing House], 2008), http://theory.people.com.cn/GB/68294/384764/.

"Guojia Fazhan Gaige Wei deng bumen guanyu tuijin gongjian 'yidai yilu' lüse fazhan de yijian" [Opinion of NDRC and other departments on promoting common development of green development in the one belt, one road], *Fagai kaifang* [*Reform and Opening Up*] no. 408 (March 16, 2022), https://www.ndrc.gov.cn/xxgk/zcfb/tz/202203/t20220328_1320629.html?code=&state=123.

"Guowuyuan bangongting guanyu quanmian tuixing xingzheng zhifa gongshi zhidu zhifa quan guocheng jilü zhidu zhongda zhifa jueding fazhi shenke zhidu de zhidao yijian" [Guiding opinion of the State Council on all-round practice of the administrative law enforcement publicity system, the general process and record-keeping system, and the legal system and verification system for major law enforcement decisions], *Guobanfa* no. 118 (December 5, 2018), http://www.gov.cn/zhengce/content/2019-01/03/content_5354528.htm.

"Guowuyuan guanyu chengli guojia yingdui qihou bianhua ji jieneng jianpai gongzuo lingdao xiaozu de tongzhi" [State Council note on establishment of the national leading small group on adaptation to climate change and energy conservation and emissions reduction

work], June 12, 2007, https://www.ccchina.org.cn/Detail.aspx?newsId=28014&TId=60%22%20title=%22.
"Guowuyuan guanyu gongan jiguan zhifa guifanhua jianshe gongzuo qingkuang de baogao," [Report of the State Council on the situation of work on construction of law enforcement standardization in public security organs], August 10, 2020, https://zh.wikisource.org/zh-hans/国务院关于公安机关执法规范化建设工作情况的报告_(2020年)%20.
Ministry of Civil Affairs of the People's Republic of China (MCA), "Shewai shehui zuzhi" [Foreign-related social organizations], https://www.gov.cn/c16813/ztfw_forthcommon.htm.
Ministry of Ecology and Environment of the People's Republic of China (MEE), "China's Policies and Actions for Addressing Climate Change (2019)," November 2019, https://english.mee.gov.cn/Resources/Reports/reports/201912/P020191204495763994956.pdf.
Ministry of Ecology and Environment of the People's Republic of China (MEE), "China's Policies and Actions for Addressing Climate Change (2020)," June 2021, http://www.ncsc.org.cn/yjcg/cbw/202111/P020211117418821628432.pdf.
Ministry of Ecology and Environment of the People's Republic of China (MEE), "Guanyu tongchou he jiaqiang yingdui qihou bianhua yu shengtai huanjing baohu xiangguan gongzuo de zhidai yijian" [Guiding opinions on integrating and strengthening efforts in climate action and ecological and environmental protection], January 11, 2021, https://www.mee.gov.cn/xxgk2018/xxgk/xxgk03/202101/t20210113_817221.html. English text available at https://www.clientearth.org/media/00tnkuc5/guiding-opinions-on-integrating-and-strengthening-efforts-in-climate-action-and-ecological-and-environmental-protection.pdf.
Ministry of Ecology and Environment of the People's Republic of China (MEE), "The People's Republic of China Third National Communication on Climate Change," December 2018, https://english.mee.gov.cn/Resources/Reports/reports/201907/P020190702566752327206.pdf.
Ministry of Education of the People's Republic of China, "Regulations of the People's Republic of China on Chinese-Foreign Cooperation in Running Schools," September 1, 2003, https://www.crs.jsj.edu.cn/news/index/3.
National Bureau of Statistics of the People's Republic of China, "Classifications and Methods," February 23, 2022, http://www.stats.gov.cn/english/ClassificationsMethods/Classifications.
National Development and Reform Commission (NDRC), "The 13th Five-Year Plan for Economic and Social Development of the People's Republic of China (2016–2020)," https://en.ndrc.gov.cn/policies/202105/P020210527785800103339.pdf.
National Development and Reform Commission (NDRC), "Action Plan for Carbon Dioxide Peaking Before 2030," October 27, 2021, https://en.ndrc.gov.cn/policies/202110/t20211027_1301020.html.
National Development and Reform Commission (NDRC), "CHINA: 11th Five-Year Plan (2006–2010) for National Economic and Social Development," 2006, https://policy.asiapacificenergy.org/node/115.
National Development and Reform Commission (NDRC), "CHINA: 12th Five-Year Plan (2011–2015) for National Economic and Social Development," 2011, https://policy.asiapacificenergy.org/node/37.
National Development and Reform Commission (NDRC), "China's National Climate Change Programme," June 2007, http://www.ccchina.org.cn/WebSite/CCChina/UpFile/File188.pdf.
National Development and Reform Commission (NDRC), "Guojia shiying qihou bianhua zhanlue" [National climate adaptation strategy], November 2013, https://www.gov.cn/gzdt/att/att/site1/20131209/001e3741a2cc140f6a8701.pdf.
National Development and Reform Commission (NDRC), "Guojia yingdui qihou bianhua guihua" [National plan in response to climate change], September 2014, https://www.ndrc.gov.cn/xxgk/zcfb/tz/201411/W020190905507100475236.pdf. English text available at "CHINA: National Plan on Climate Change 2014–2020," https://policy.asiapacificenergy.org/node/3011.
National Development and Reform Commission (NDRC), "Qianghua ying dui qihou bianhua xingdong – Zhongguo guojia zizhu gongxian" [Enhanced actions on climate change: China's intended nationally determined contributions], June 30, 2015, http://www.xinhuanet.com//politics/2015-06/30/c_1115774759.htm.

National Development and Reform Commission (NDRC), "Report on China's National Economic, Social Development Plan," March 16, 2023, http://www.china.org.cn/china/2023-03/16/content_85171202.htm.

National Development and Reform Commission (NDRC), "Working Guidance for Carbon Dioxide Peaking and Carbon Neutrality in Full and Faithful Implementation of the New Development Philosophy," October 24, 2021, https://en.ndrc.gov.cn/policies/202110/t20211024_1300725.html.

National Development and Reform Commission (NDRC), "Zhongguo yingdui qihou bianhua guojia fangan" [China national plan for adapting to climate change], June 2007, http://www.ccchina.org.cn/WebSite/CCChina/UpFile/File189.pdf. For an English translation, see https://www.ccchina.org.cn/WebSite/CCChina/UpFile/File188.pdf.

National Development and Reform Commission (NDRC), "Zhonghua renmin gongheguo guomin jingji he shehui fazhan de shisige wunian guihua he 2035 nian yuanjing mubiao gangyao" [People's Republic of China 14th five-year plan for national economic and social development and outline of long-range goals for 2035], March 13, 2021, http://www.gov.cn/xinwen/2021-03/13/content_5592681.htm. For an English translation, see "Outline of the People's Republic of China 14th Five-Year Plan for National Economic and Social Development and Long-Range Objectives for 2035," March 12, 2021, https://cset.georgetown.edu/publication/china-14th-five-year-plan/.

National Immigration Administration of the People's Republic of China (NIA), "Interpretation; Three Categories of Foreign Nationals Allowed Entering China from September 28," March 29, 2021, https://en.nia.gov.cn/n147418/n147463/c155990/content.html.

National People's Congress of the People's Republic of China, "Zhongyang Xuanchuanbu, Zhongyang Zhengfawei, Quanguo Renda Changweihui Bangongting, Sifabu yinfa 'yijian' Jianli shehui zhuyi hexin jiazhiguan rufa rugui xietiao jizhi" [Central Propaganda Department, Central Politics and Law Committee, NPC Standing Committee Office, Ministry of Justice opinion, establish mechanisms for coordinating insertion of core socialist values in law and regulation], September 28, 2021, http://politics.people.com.cn/n1/2021/0928/c1001-32239145.html.

Nationally Determined Contributions Registry, "China's Achievements, New Goals and New Measures for Nationally Determined Contributions," https://www.preventionweb.net/publication/chinas-achievements-new-goals-and-new-measures-nationally-determined-contributions.

"The People's Republic of China Initial National Communication on Climate Change," October 2004, https://unfccc.int/resource/docs/natc/chnnc1exsum.pdf.

"Proposal of the People's Republic of China on the Reform and Development of Global Governance," *Xinhua*, September 13, 2023, https://english.news.cn/20230913/edf2514b79a34bf6812a1c372dcdfc1b/c.html?utm_source=substack&utm_medium=email.

"Resolution of the CPC Central Committee on the Major Achievements and Historical Experience of the Party over the Past Century," *Xinhua*, November 16, 2021, https://english.www.gov.cn/policies/latestreleases/202111/16/content_WS6193a935c6d0df57f98e50b0.html.

"Second National Communication on Climate Change of the People's Republic of China," 2012, https://unfccc.int/resource/docs/natc/chnnc2e.pdf.

"Shehui zhuyi hexin jiazhiguan jiben neirong" [The basic content of the core values of socialism], *Renmin ribao* [*People's Daily*], February 12, 2014, http://theory.people.com.cn/n/2014/0212/c40531-24330538.html.

State Council, "National Environmental Protection 'Twelfth Five-Year' Plan (Chinese Text)," December 15, 2011, https://www.cecc.gov/resources/legal-provisions/national-environmental-protection-twelfth-five-year-plan-chinese-text.

State Council Information Office (SCIO), "Building of Political Democracy in China," white paper, October 2005, http://www.china.org.cn/english/features/book/145877.htm.

State Council Information Office (SCIO), "China and the World in the New Era," white paper, September 27, 2019, http://english.www.gov.cn/archive/whitepaper/201909/27/content_WS5d8d80f9c6d0bcf8c4c142ef.html.

State Council Information Office (SCIO), "China Democracy That Works," white paper, December 4, 2021, http://www.scio.gov.cn/zfbps/ndhf/2021n_2242/202207/t20220704_130720.html.

State Council Information Office (SCIO), "China's Epic Journey from Poverty to Prosperity," white paper, September 28, 2021, http://english.scio.gov.cn/whitepapers/2021-09/28/content_77779569.htm.

State Council Information Office (SCIO), "China's Ethnic Policy and Common Prosperity and Development of All Ethnic Groups," white paper, September 27, 2009, http://www.china.org.cn/government/whitepaper/node_7078073.htm.

State Council Information Office (SCIO), "China's International Development Cooperation in the New Era," white paper, January 10, 2021, http://english.www.gov.cn/archive/whitepaper/202101/10/content_WS5ffa6bbbc6d0f72576943922.html.

State Council Information Office (SCIO), "China's Policies and Actions for Addressing Climate Change," white paper, November 22, 2011, http://english.www.gov.cn/archive/white_paper/2014/09/09/content_281474986284685.htm.

State Council Information Office (SCIO), "Development of China's Public Health as an Essential Element of Human Rights," white paper, September 29, 2017, http://english.www.gov.cn/archive/white_paper/2017/09/29/content_281475894089810.htm.

State Council Information Office (SCIO), "Energy in China's New Era," white paper, December 2020, http://english.scio.gov.cn/whitepapers/2020-12/21/content_77035604.htm.

State Council Information Office (SCIO), "Fighting COVID-19: China in Action," white paper, June 7, 2020, http://english.scio.gov.cn/whitepapers/2020-06/07/content_76135269.htm.

State Council Information Office (SCIO), "Moderate Prosperity in All Respects: Another Milestone Achieved in China's Human Rights," white paper, August 2021, http://english.www.gov.cn/archive/whitepaper/202108/12/content_WS611492b4c6d0df57f98de5ac.html.

State Council Information Office (SCIO), "National Human Rights Action Plan of China (2012–2015)," June 11, 2012, Introduction, http://www.china.org.cn/government/whitepaper/2012-06/11/content_25619560.htm.

State Council Information Office (SCIO), "Full Text: Responding to Climate Change: China's Policies and Actions," October 2021, http://english.scio.gov.cn/whitepapers/2021-10/27/content_77836502_4.htm.

State Council Information Office (SCIO), "The Right to Development: China's Philosophy, Practice and Contribution," white paper, December 2, 2016, http://english.www.gov.cn/archive/white_paper/2016/12/01/content_281475505407672.htm.

State Council Information Office (SCIO), "Seeking Happiness for People: 70 Years of Progress on Human Rights in China," white paper, September 2019, http://english.www.gov.cn/archive/whitepaper/201909/22/content_WS5d87752fc6d0bcf8c4c13d32.html.

Supreme People's Court of the People's Republic of China (SPC), "Foreign-Related Trials," 2025, https://english.court.gov.cn/foreigntrials.html.

"Zhonggong shijiujie wuzhong quanhui gongbao (quanwen)" [Communiqué of the fifth plenum of the 19th CPC Central Committee (full text)], October 29, 2020, https://wap.peopleapp.com/article/rmh17257967/rmh17257967.

"Zhonggong Zhongyang bangongting Guowuyuan bangongting yifa 'Guanyu jiaqiang xinshidai faxue jiaoyu he faxue lilun yanjiiu to yijian'" [The General Office of the CPC Central Committee and the General Office of the State Council Issue opinions on strengthening legal education and legal theory research in the new era], February 26, 2023, https://www.gov.cn/zhengce/2023-02/26/content_5743383.htm.

"Zhonggong zhongyang bangongting yinfa 'Guanyu dangqian yishi xingtai lingyu qingkuang de tongbao'" [Communiqué on the current state of the ideological sphere: a notice from the Central Committee of the Communist Party of China's General Office], May 8, 2014, https://www.bannedbook.org/forum34/topic3971.html.

"Zhonggong zhongyang, Guowuyuan guanyu quanmian jiaqiang shengtao huanjing baohu jianjue dahao wuran fangzhi gongjian zhan de yijian" [Opinion of the CPC Central Committee and the State Council on comprehensively strengthening ecological and environmental protection and resolutely fighting the tough battle of pollution prevention and control], June 24, 2018, https://www.gov.cn/zhengce/2018-06/24/content_5300953.htm.

"Zhonggong zhongyang guowuyuan guanyu wanzheng zhunque quanmian guanche xinfazhan linian zuohao tadafeng tanzhonghe gongzuo de yijian" [Opinions of the CPC Central Committee and the State Council on the complete, accurate and comprehensive implementation of the new development concept to do a good job in carbon peaking and carbon neutrality], September 22, 2021, http://www.gov.cn/zhengce/2021-10/24/content_5644613.htm.

"Zhonggong zhongyang guowuyuan guanyu yingzao genghaofazhan huanjing zhichi minying qiye gaige fazhan de yijian" [Opinion of the CPC Central Committee and the State Council on building a better development environment to support the development of reform in private enterprises], *Xinhua*, December 22, 2019, http://www.gov.cn/zhengce/2019-12/22/content_5463137.htm.

"Zhonggong Zhongyang Guowuyuan yinfa 'Fazhi zhengfu jianshe shishi gangyao (2021–2025)'" [CPC Central Committee/State Council issue provisional outline on establishment of lawful governance (2021–2025)], August 11, 2021, http://www.gov.cn/zhengce/2021-08/11/content_5630802.htm.

"Zhonggong Zhongyang Guowuyuan yinfa 'Kuoda neixu zhanlue guihua gangyao (2022–2035nian)'" [CPC Central Committee and State Council issue strategic plan for 2022–2035 on expanding domestic demand], December 14, 2022, http://www.gov.cn/zhengce/2022-12/14/content_5732067.htm.

"Zhonggong Zhongyang yinfa 'Fazhi Zhongguo jianshe guihua (2020–2025 nian)'" [The CPC Central Committee issues plan for establishment of legal rule in China (2020–2025)], January 10, 2021, http://www.gov.cn/zhengce/2021-01/10/content_5578659.htm.

"Zhonggong Zhongyang yinfa 'Shehui zhuyi hexin jiazhiguan rongru fazhi jianshe lifa xiufa guihua'" [Party centre releases plan for assimilating core socialist values in legal system construction, legislation and legal amendments], *Xinhuanet,* May 7, 2018, http://www.xinhuanet.com/politics/2018-05/07/c_1122796215.htm.

"Zhonggong zhongyang zhengzhiju changwu weiyuanhui zhaokai huiyi, tingqu xinguan feiyan yiqing fangkong gongzuo huibao, yanjiu bushu jinyibu youhua fangkong gonzuo de ershi tiao cuoshi, Zhonggon zhangyang shuji Xi Jinping zhuchi huiyi" [CPC Politburo Standing Committee meets, hears report on COVID-19 prevention and control work, study and deploy the twenty measures on further optimizing prevention and control work, CPC Politburo General Secretary Xi Jinping chairs meeting], November 20, 2022, http://www.news.cn/politics/2022-11/10/c_1129118595.htm.

"'Zhongguo fazhan baogao 2021–2022: Zou gongtong fuyu zhi lu' hui ying le naxie guanjian wenti?" [What are the key issues raised by 'China development report 2021–2022: taking the path of common prosperity'?], https://www.cdrf.org.cn/jjhdt/6373.htm.

"Zhongguo fazhan yanjiu jijinhui fabu gongtong fuyu baogao" [China Development Research Foundation releases report on common prosperity], September 19, 2022, https://www.cdrf.org.cn/jjhdt/6371.htm.

"Zhonghua renmin gongheguo guojia weisheng jiankang weiyuanhui gonggao 2020 nian di yi hao" [Notice from the People's Republic of China State Health Commission 2020, no. 1], January 20, 2020, https://www.gov.cn/zhengce/zhengceku/2020-01/21/content_5471164.htm.

"Zhongyang zhengfawei: Jianjue yifa daji didui shili shentou puohuai huodong" [Central Politics and Law Commission: resolutely attack hostile forces infiltrating harmful activities], *Sina caijing* [*Sina Finance*], November 30, 2022, https://finance.sina.com.cn/china/2022-11-30/doc-imqmmthc6475837.shtml.

REGULATIONS

"Guanyu jinyibu youhua luoshi xinguan feiyan yiqing fankong cuosho de tongzhi: Lianfang liakong jizji zongfa [2022] 113 hao" [Notice on further optimizing the implementation of prevention and control measures of the novel corona pneumonia epidemic, document (2022) #113 issued by the Joint Prevention and Control Mechanism, December 7, 2022], https://www.gov.cn/xinwen/2022-12/07/content_5730443.htm.

"Guojia Anquanbu fabu 2021 nian di yi hao ling 'Fan wendie anquan fangfan gongzuo guiding'" [Ministry of State Security issues document no. 1 for 2021, regulations on the work of opposing espionage and protecting security], April 26, 2021, http://legal.people.com.cn/n1/2021/0426/c205462-32088423.html.

"Guojia tufa gonggong weisheng shijian yingji yu'an" [National contingency plan for public health emergencies], January 10, 2006, https://www.nhc.gov.cn/yjb/c100058/200601/c511ded8a67546d0973e482d7ff42f72.shtml.

"Guowuyuan gongzuo guize" [Rules on the work of the State Council], March 17, 2023, https://www.gov.cn/zhengce/content/2023-03/24/content_5748128.htm.
"Measures for the Administration of Examination and Approval of Foreigner's Permanent Residence in China," December 13, 2003, http://www.asianlii.org/cn/legis/cen/laws/mftaoeaaofpric899/.
"Regulations of the People's Republic of China on Administration of the Entry and Exit of Foreigners," September 1, 2013, https://en.nia.gov.cn/n147418/n147458/c155970/content.html.
"Tufa gonggong weisheng shijian yingji tiaoli" [Regulations on responding to public health emergencies], May 9, 2003, http://www.gov.cn/zwgk/2005-05/20/content_145.htm.
"Youhua shangye huanjing tiaoli" [Regulations on optimizing the business environment], October 22, 2019, https://www.gov.cn/zhengce/content/2019-10/23/content_5443963.htm.
"Zhonggong zhongyang bangongting yinfa 'Zhongguo Gongchandang jilü jiancha jiguan jiandu zhiji gongzuo guice'" [CPC Central Committee General Office issues regulations on discipline inspection organs supervising discipline enforcement work], *Xinhuanet,* January 6, 2019, http://www.xinhuanet.com/politics/2019-01/06/c_1123953624.htm.
"Zhonggong zhongyang bangongting yinfa 'Zhongguo Gongchandang jilü jiancha jiguan jiandu zhiji gongzuo guice'" [CPC Central Committee General Office issues regulations on discipline inspection organs supervising discipline enforcement work], *Xinhuanet,* January 6, 2019, https://www.gov.cn/zhengce/2019-01/06/content_5355392.htm.
"Zhongguo Gongchandang jilü jiancha jiguan jiandu zhiji gongzuo guice (shixing)" [CPC provisional regulations on discipline inspection organs supervising discipline enforcement work), *Xinhuanet,* January 20, 2017, http://www.xinhuanet.com/politics/2017-01/20/c_1120352829.htm.
"Zhonghua renmin gongheguo baocun guojia mimi shishi tiaoli" [Implementing regulations for the state secrets protection law of the People's Republic of China], January 17, 2014, http://www.gov.cn/zwgk/2014-02/03/content_2579949.htm.
"Zhonghua renmin gongheguo zhengfu xinxi gongkai tiaoli" [Regulations of the People's Republic of China on disclosure of government information], April 5, 2007, http://www.gov.cn/zwgk/2007-04/24/content_592937.htm.

SPEECHES AND STATEMENTS

Chen Jie, "Guojia yimin guanli ju xinwen fabuhui" [Press conference of the National Migration Administration] (summarizing National Immigration Administration activities January–June 2021), July 30, 2021, https://www.nia.gov.cn/n741435/n1194535/n1431602/index.html.
"China Is Firmly Committed to a Path of Human Rights Development That Suits Its National Conditions," September 26, 2021, https://www.fmprc.gov.cn/mfa_eng/wjb/zygy/hd/202406/t20240603_11374881.html.
"'Common but Differentiated Responsibilities' Must Never Be Compromised: Premier," *Xinhua,* December 18, 2009, http://www.china.org.cn/environment/Copenhagen/2009-12/18/content_19094598.htm.
Deng Xiaoping, "Jianchi sixiang jiben yuanze" [Uphold the four cardinal principles], March 30, 1979, Zhongguo gaige xinxi ku [China reform database], http://www.reformdata.org/1979/0330/5172.shtml.
"Full Text of Xi Jinping's Report at 19th CPC National Congress," *China Daily,* November 4, 2017, Section I.9, http://www.chinadaily.com.cn/china/19thcpcnationalcongress/2017-11/04/content_34115212.htm.
"Full Text of Xi Jinping's Speech at the Opening of the 73rd World Health Assembly," *China Daily,* May 18, 2020, https://www.chinadaily.com.cn/a/202005/18/WS5ec273d1a310a8b2411568f1.html.
"Full Text of Xi's Statement at the General Debate of the 76th Session of the United Nations General Assembly," *Xinhuanet,* September 22, 2021, https://english.www.gov.cn/news/topnews/202109/22/content_WS614a9d11c6d0df57f98e0a81.html.
"Full Text: Written Statement by Xi Jinping at the World Leaders Summit," *Qiushi,* November 2, 2021, https://en.qstheory.cn/2021-11/02/c_676248.htm.
"Greece Signs Reform Deal with OECD to Avoid Troika 'Blackmail,'" *Newsweek,* March 12, 2015, https://www.newsweek.com/greece-signs-reform-deal-oecd-troika-blackmail-313399.

"Highlights: Chairman Xi Recounts Early Role in Coronavirus Battle," *Reuters,* February 17, 2020, https://www.reuters.com/article/us-china-health-xi-highlights/highlights-chinas-xi-recounts-early-role-in-coronavirus-battle-idUSKBN20B1MC.

"Li Keqiang dui quanguo wenjiuye gongzuo dianshi dianhua hui zuochu zhongyao pishi" [Li Keqiang gave important instructions on the national video and telephone conference on stabilizing employment], May 7, 2022, http://www.gov.cn/xinwen/2022-05/07/content_5689087.htm.

"Li Keqiang zai quanguo wenzhu jingji dapan dianshi dianhua he shang zuo zhongyao jianghua Han Zheng zhuchi" [Li Keqiang delivered an important speech at the national video and telephone conference on stabilizing the economy, Han Zheng chairs], May 25, 2022, http://www.gov.cn/xinwen/2022-05/25/content_5692298.htm.

Mao Zedong, "On the Correct Handling of Contradictions Among the People," *People's Daily,* June 19, 1957, https://www.marxists.org/reference/archive/mao/selected-works/volume-5/mswv5_58.htm.

Ministry of Foreign Affairs of the People's Republic of China (MFA), "China and the United Nations: Position Paper of the People's Republic of China for the 74th Session of the United Nations General Assembly," September 18, 2019, https://www.mfa.gov.cn/eng/zy/gb/202405/t20240531_11367393.html.

Ministry of Foreign Affairs of the People's Republic of China (MFA), "China's Relation with UNHCR," September 27, 2003, https://www.mfa.gov.cn/eng/wjb/zzjg_663340/gjs_665170/gjzzyhy_665174/2594_665176/2600_665188/202406/t20240606_11404354.html.

Ministry of Foreign Affairs of the People's Republic of China (MFA), "Following the Guidance of Xi Jinping Thought on Diplomacy and Advancing in All Respects Major-Country Diplomacy with Chinese Characteristics in the New Era," September 29, 2022, http://us.china-embassy.gov.cn/eng/zgyw/202209/t20220930_10774938.htm.

Ministry of Foreign Affairs of the People's Republic of China (MFA), "Full Text of China's Position Paper on the UN's 75th Anniversary," September 10, 2020, Section III, paragraph 11, http://www.china.org.cn/world/2020-09/10/content_76690893.htm.

State Council of the People's Republic of China, "Premier Li Addresses UN General Assembly," September 20, 2016, http://english.www.gov.cn/premier/news/2016/09/20/content_281475446293659.htm.

"Statement by Mr. Ke Yousheng, Adviser of the Chinese Delegation, at the Third Committee of the 62nd Session of the General Assembly, on the Report of UNHCR (Item 42)," November 8, 2007, https://un.china-mission.gov.cn/eng/hyyfy/200711/t20071108_8399179.htm.

"Statement of Ambassador Li Li, Leader of the Chinese Delegation and Chinese Ambassador to the Kingdom of Morocco, at the Intergovernmental Conference to Adopt the Global Compact for Safe, Orderly and Regular Migration," December 11, 2018, https://www.un.org/en/conf/migration/assets/pdf/GCM-Statements/china.pdf.

Wang Yi, "China's Diplomacy in 2021: Embracing a Global Vision and Serving the Nation and its People," address to Symposium on the International Situation and China's Foreign Relations, December 20, 2021, https://www.ciis.org.cn/english/NEWS_183/202112/t20211228_8347.html.

Wang Yi, "Pursuing a Country-Specific Path to Human Rights Advancement and Jointly Promoting Worldwide Progress in Human Rights," December 5, 2023, https://subsites.chinadaily.com.cn/Qiushi/2023-12/07/c_945584.htm.

Xi Jinping, "Bolstering Confidence and Jointly Overcoming Difficulties to Build a Better World," September 21, 2021, https://www.mfa.gov.cn/eng/xw/zyjh/202405/t20240530_11341561.html.

Xi Jinping, "Fostering a New Development Paradigm and Pursuing Mutual Benefit and Win-Win Cooperation," November 19, 2020, https://www.mfa.gov.cn/eng/xw/zyjh/202405/t20240530_11341479.html#:~:text=The%20new%20development%20paradigm%20is,changes%20in%20the%20external%20environment.

Xi Jinping, "Hold High the Great Banner of Socialism with Chinese Characteristics and Strive in Unity to Build a Modern Socialist Country in All Respects" (full text of the report to the 20th National Congress of the Communist Party of China, October 16, 2022), https://www.idcpc.org.cn/english2023/tjzl/cpcjj/20thPartyCongrssReport/.

Xi Jinping, "Secure a Decisive Victory in Building a Moderately Prosperous Society in All Respects and Strive for the Great Success of Socialism with Chinese Characteristics for a New Era" (speech delivered at the 19th National Congress of the CPC, October 18, 2017), https://www.neac.gov.cn/seac/c103372/202201/1156519.shtml.

Xi Jinping, "Speech at a Ceremony Marking the Centenary of the Communist Party of China, July 1, 2021," https://en.wikisource.org/wiki/Speech_at_a_Ceremony_Marking_the_Centenary_of_the_Communist_Party_of_China.

Xi Jinping, "Understanding the New Development Stage, Applying the New Development Philosophy, and Creating a New Development Dynamic," *China Daily,* July 12, 2021, https://www.chinadaily.com.cn/a/202107/12/WS60ec3e56a310efa1bd6614fb.html; *Qiushi* [*Truth*], November 9, 2021, http://en.qstheory.cn/2021-07/08/c_641137.htm.

Xi Jinping, "Uphold and Develop Socialism with Chinese Characteristics," *Qiushi,* January 5, 2013, https://en.qstheory.cn/2020-08/11/c_607578.htm.

Xi Jinping, "Zhengque renshi he ba wo woguo fazhan zhongda lilun he shixian wenti [Correctly understand and master major issues of theory and practice in our country's development], *Qiushi* [*Truth*], October 2022, http://www.qstheory.cn/dukan/qs/2022-05/15/c_1128649331.htm.

"Xi Jinping zai xuexi guanche Dang de ershi da jingshen yantao bankai banshi shang fabiao zhongyao jianghua qiangdiao zhengque lijie he dali tuidong Zhongguo shixiandaihua" [Xi Jinping delivers important speech at the opening ceremony of the seminar to study and implement the spirit of the CPC 20th National Congress emphasizing correctly understanding and vigorously promoting Chinese-style modernization], http://paper.people.com.cn/rmrb/html/2023-02/08/nw.D110000renmrb_20230208_1-01.htm.

"Xi Jinping zhuchi zhaokai Zhongyang Caijing Weiyuanhui di shici huiyi qiangdiao zai gao zhiliang fazhan zhong cujin gongtong fuyu tongchou zuoha zhongda jinrong fengxian fangfan huajie gongzuo – Li Keqiang, Wang Yang, Hu Huning, Han Zheng chuxi" [Xi Jinping chairs 10th meeting of the Central Commission on Finance and Economics called to emphasize promoting common prosperity in high-quality development and to do a good job in preventing and resolving major financial risks – Li Keqiang, Wang Yang, Wang Huning, Han Zheng in attendance], August 17, 2021, http://www.xinhuanet.com/politics/leaders/2021-08/17/c_1127770343.htm.

"Xi Jinping zhuchi zhaokai Zhongyang caijing weiyuanhui di shici huiyi" [Xi Jinping chairs the 10th meeting of the Central Finance and Economic Commission], *Xinhuanet,* August 18, 2021, https://www.mee.gov.cn/ywdt/szyw/202108/t20210818_858115.shtml.

"Xi Jinping zhuchi zhaokai Zhongyang quanmian yifa zhiguo weiyhuanhui de yici huiyi" [Xi Jinping convenes the first session of the Central Commission on comprehensively ruling the country according to law], *Xinwen,* August 24, 2018, http://www.gov.cn/xinwen/2018-08/24/content_5316286.htm.

"Xi Stresses Promoting Common Prosperity Amid High-Quality Development, Forestalling Major Financial Risks," *Beijing Review,* August, 2021, http://www.bjreview.com/CHINA_INSIGHT_2021/Special_Issue_on_Promoting_Common_Prosperity_Amid_High_Quality_Development/202109/t20210930_800259600.html.

"Zhulao zhonghua minzu gongtong ti yijian" [Realize the unity of Chinese ethnic groups], *people.cn/人民网*, September 30, 2024, http://opinion.people.com.cn/n1/2024/0930/c1003-40331198.html.

INTERNATIONAL MATERIALS

Australian Government, Department of Foreign Affairs and Trade, "China Country Brief," July 2022, https://www.dfat.gov.au/geo/china/china-country-brief.

"Cartagena Declaration on Refugees: Colloquium on the International Protection of Refugees in Central America, Mexico, and Panama," November 22, 1984, https://www.oas.org/dil/1984_cartagena_declaration_on_refugees.pdf.

Congressional Research Service, "Human Rights in China and U.S. Policy: Issues for the 117th Congress," March 31, 2021, https://crsreports.congress.gov/product/pdf/R/R46750.

"Decisions Adopted by the Conference of the Parties," January 26, 2016, FCCC/CP/2015/10/add.1, https://unfccc.int/resource/docs/2015/cop21/eng/10a01.pdf.

European Commission (EC), "Joint Press Communique Following the Second EU-China High Level Environment and Climate Dialogue," October 10, 2021, https://climate.ec.europa.

eu/news-your-voice/news/joint-press-communique-following-second-eu-china-high-level-environment-and-climate-dialogue-2021-10-10_en#:~:text=This%20would%20aim%20at%20reversing,regular%20basis%2C%20at%20least%20annually.
European Commission (EC), "Social Climate Fund," https://climate.ec.europa.eu/eu-action/eurean-green-deal/delivering-european-green-deal/social-climate-fund_en#key-elements.
European Commission (EC), "Supporting Syria and the Region: Post-Brussels Conference Financial Tracking Report 10," September 2020, https://www.consilium.europa.eu/media/46336/financial-tracking-report-no10.pdf.
European Commission (EC), "Supporting Syria and the Region: Post-Brussels Conference Financial Tracking Report 4," October 2017.
European Commission (EC), "Supporting Syria and the Region: Post-Brussels Conference Financial Tracking Report 6," September 2018, https://www.consilium.europa.eu/media/36437/syria-report-six.pdf.
European Union (EU), "EU China Relations," April 2022, https://www.eeas.europa.eu/sites/default/files/documents/EU-China_Factsheet_01Apr2022.pdf.
"Glasgow Climate Pact," November 13, 2021, https://unfccc.int/sites/default/files/resource/cma2021_L16E.pdf.
Global Affairs Canada, "Canada's Indo-Pacific Strategy," July 24, 2023, https://www.international.gc.ca/transparency-transparence/indo-pacific-indo-pacifique/index.aspx?lang=eng.
"Global Compact for Safe, Orderly and Regular Migration," Resolution adopted by the UN General Assembly on December 19, 2018, A/RES/73/195, https://documents-dds-ny.un.org/doc/UNDOC/GEN/N18/451/99/PDF/N1845199.pdf?OpenElement.
Global Compact on Refugees, "Global Refugee Forum," https://globalcompactrefugees.org/article/global-refugee-forum.
Government of Canada, "Environment and Climate Change Canada Funding Programs," https://www.canada.ca/en/environment-climate-change/services/environmental-funding.html.
Government of Canada, "G20 Rome Leaders' Declaration," November 1, 2021, https://www.international.gc.ca/world-monde/international_relations-relations_internationales/g20/2021-10-31-g20-rome.aspx?lang=eng.
House of Lords International Relations and Defence Committee, "The UK and China's Security and Trade Relationship: A Strategic Void," September 10, 2021, https://committees.parliament.uk/publications/7214/documents/75842/default/.
Immigration and Refugee Board of Canada, "China: 2014 Hukou Reform Policy and Its Local Implementation; Security Features and Other Physical Characteristics of Hukou [Household Registry] Documents Issued in 2013–2014; Anti-Fraud Measures Introduced for Hukou Documents; Whether Features Are Standardized Across the Country," December 23 2015, https://www.refworld.org/docid/57551d0c4.html.
International Covenant on Civil and Political Rights, UNGA Res. 2200A (XXI), 1966, https://www.ohchr.org/en/instruments-mechanisms/instruments/international-covenant-civil-and-political-rights#:~:text=Article%2017-,1.,against%20such%20interference%20or%20attacks.
International Covenant on the Elimination of All Forms of Racial Discrimination, UNGA Res. 2106 (XX), December 21, 1965, https://www.ohchr.org/en/instruments-mechanisms/instruments/international-convention-elimination-all-forms-racial.
International Organization for Migration (IOM), "IOM in China," 2022, https://china.iom.int/en/iom-china.
International Organization for Migration (IOM), "China, UN's Migration Agency Advance Sustainable Development Agenda," June 28, 2019, https://www.iom.int/news/china-uns-migration-agency-advance-sustainable-development-agenda.
International Organization for Migration (IOM), *Yimin yu "2030 nian kechixu fazhan yicheng": Yige gei shijianzhe de zhinan* [Migrants and the 2030 sustainable development agenda: a guide for implementers] (Geneva: IOM, 2018), https://www.iom.int/sites/g/files/tmzbdl486/files/press_release/file/migration-and-2030-agenda-practitioners-guide-zh.pdf.
Islam, S. Nazrul, and John Winkel, "Climate Change and Social Inequality," DESA Working Paper No. 152, October 2017, ST/ESA/2017/DWP/152, https://www.un.org/esa/desa/papers/2017/wp152_2017.pdf.

"LMDC Ministerial Statement," October 2021, https://static.pib.gov.in/WriteReadData/specificdocs/documents/2021/oct/doc2021101821.pdf.

Northwestern University Kellogg School of Management, "Global Poverty Research Lab – China Cluster," https://www.kellogg.northwestern.edu/academics-research/global-poverty-research-lab/geographical-clusters/china/.

OECD, *Data and Meta Data Reporting and Presentation Handbook* (2007), https://www.oecd.org/content/dam/oecd/en/publications/reports/2007/06/data-and-metadata-reporting-and-presentation-handbook_g1gh7b15/9789264030336-en.pdf.

Office of the Director of National Intelligence (DNI), "National Intelligence Estimate: Climate Change and International Responses Increasing Challenges to US National Security Through 2040," October 21, 2021, https://nsarchive.gwu.edu/document/32888-document-3-national-intelligence-council-national-intelligence-estimate-climate.

Office of the Director of National Intelligence (DNI), "(U) Potential Links Between the Wuhan Institute of Virology and the Origin of the COVID-19 Pandemic," June 2023, https://www.dni.gov/files/ODNI/documents/assessments/Report-on-Potential-Links-Between-the-Wuhan-Institute-of-Virology-and-the-Origins-of-COVID-19-20230623.pdf.

Office of the Director of National Intelligence (DNI), "Unclassified Summary of Assessment on COVID-19 Origins: Intelligence Community Assessment," August 27, 2021, https://www.dni.gov/files/ODNI/documents/assessments/Unclassified-Summary-of-Assessment-on-COVID-19-Origins.pdf.

Office of the Director of National Intelligence (DNI), "Updated Assessment on COVID-19 Origins," October 29, 2021, https://www.dni.gov/files/ODNI/documents/assessments/Declassified-Assessment-on-COVID-19-Origins.pdf.

Office of the High Commissioner for Human Rights (OHCHR), "Comment by UN Human Rights Office Spokesperson Marta Hurtado on China," press briefing notes, November 19, 2021, https://www.ohchr.org/EN/NewsEvents/Pages/DisplayNews.aspx?NewsID=27833&LangID=E.

Office of the High Commissioner for Human Rights (OHCHR), *Guiding Principles on Business and Human Rights* (New York/Geneva: United Nations, 2011), https://www.ohchr.org/sites/default/files/documents/publications/guidingprinciplesbusinesshr_en.pdf.

Office of the High Commissioner for Human Rights (OHCHR), "International Covenant on Civil and Political Rights," https://www.ohchr.org/en/instruments-mechanisms/instruments/international-covenant-civil-and-political-rights.

Office of the High Commissioner for Human Rights (OHCHR), "International Covenant on Economic, Social and Cultural Rights," https://www.ohchr.org/en/instruments-mechanisms/instruments/international-covenant-economic-social-and-cultural-rights.

Office of the High Commissioner for Human Rights (OHCHR), "The Principle of *Non-refoulement* Under International Human Rights Law," https://www.ohchr.org/Documents/Issues/Migration/GlobalCompactMigration/ThePrincipleNon-RefoulementUnderInternationalHumanRightsLaw.pdf.

Office of the High Commissioner for Human Rights (OHCHR), "Universal Declaration of Human Rights," December 10, 1948, https://www.ohchr.org/en/universal-declaration-of-human-rights#:~:text=The%20Universal%20Declaration%20of%20Human%20Rights%20(UDHR)%20is%20a%20milestone,rights%20to%20be%20universally%20protected.

Office of the High Commissioner for Human Rights (OHCHR), "Universal Declaration on Cultural Diversity," November 2, 2001, https://www.ohchr.org/en/instruments-mechanisms/instruments/universal-declaration-cultural-diversity#:~:text=The%20defence%20of%20cultural%20diversity,and%20those%20of%20indigenous%20peoples.

Office of the United Nations High Commissioner for Refugees (UNHCR), "The 1951 Refugee Convention and the 1967 Protocol Relating to the Status of Refugees," https://www.unhcr.org/3b66c2aa10.

Office of the United Nations High Commissioner for Refugees (UNHCR), "2019 Global Refugee Forum," https://www.unhcr.org/programme-and-practical-information.html.

Office of the United Nations High Commissioner for Refugees (UNHCR), "About Minorities and Human Rights," https://www.ohchr.org/en/minorities/about-minorities-and-human-rights.

Office of the United Nations High Commissioner for Refugees (UNHCR), "Convention Relating to the Status of Refugees," July 28, 1951, https://www.ohchr.org/en/instruments-mechanisms/instruments/convention-relating-status-refugees.
Office of the United Nations High Commissioner for Refugees (UNHCR), "Fact Sheet: People's Republic of China," February 2023, https://reliefweb.int/report/china/peoples-republic-china-factsheet-february-2023.
Office of the United Nations High Commissioner for Refugees (UNHCR), *Global Compact on Refugees* (New York: United Nations, 2018), https://www.unhcr.org/5c658aed4.
Office of the United Nations High Commissioner for Refugees (UNHCR), "The Global Compact on Refugees," https://www.unhcr.org/the-global-compact-on-refugees.html.
Office of the United Nations High Commissioner for Refugees (UNHCR), "The Global Compact on Refugees," https://www.unhcr.org/the-global-compact-on-refugees.html.
Office of the United Nations High Commissioner for Refugees (UNHCR), "Jobs and Livelihoods," December 16, 2019, https://www.unhcr.org/events/conferences/5d1a11267/jobs-and-livelihoods.html.
Office of the United Nations High Commissioner for Refugees (UNHCR), "New York Declaration for Refugees and Migrants," https://www.unhcr.org/new-york-declaration-for-refugees-and-migrants.html.
Office of the United Nations High Commissioner for Refugees (UNHCR), "New York Declaration for Refugees and Migrants, A71/L.1," October 3, 2016, A/RES/71/1, https://www.unhcr.org/57e39d987.
Office of the United Nations High Commissioner for Refugees (UNHCR), "OAU Convention Governing Specific Aspects of Refugee Problems in Africa, Adopted by the Assembly of Heads of State and Government at Its Sixth Ordinary Session, Addis Ababa, 10 September 1969," Article 1(2), https://treaties.un.org/pages/showDetails.aspx?objid=080000028010432f.
Office of the United Nations High Commissioner for Refugees (UNHCR), "Operational Data Portal: Ukraine Refugee Situation," https://data.unhcr.org/en/situations/ukraine.
Office of the United Nations High Commissioner for Refugees (UNHCR), "Refugee Data Finder," 2025, https://www.unhcr.org/refugee-statistics.
Office of the United Nations High Commissioner for Refugees (UNHCR), "Report of the High Commissioner for Refugees Part II: Global Compact for Refugees," September 13, 2018, A/73/12 (Part II), https://documents-dds-ny.un.org/doc/UNDOC/GEN/G18/238/37/PDF/G1823837.pdf?OpenElement.
Office of the United Nations High Commissioner for Refugees (UNHCR), "Resettlement," 2021–23, https://www.unhcr.org/what-we-do/build-better-futures/solutions/resettlement.
Office of the United Nations High Commissioner for Refugees (UNHCR), "Submission by the United Nations High Commissioner for Refugees for the Office of the High Commissioner for Human Rights' Compilation Report – Universal Periodic Review: People's Republic of China," March 2013, https://www.refworld.org/pdfid/5135b0cb2.pdf.
Office of the United Nations High Commissioner for Refugees (UNHCR), "Suggestions and Amendments of China: Global Compact on Refugees," July 7, 2016, https://www.un.org/en/development/desa/population/migration/events/ga/documents/2016/07July2016/China_07July2016_GlobalCompact.pdf.
Office of the United Nations High Commissioner for Refugees (UNHCR), "UNHCR and UNDP Agree on Text of MOU with Myanmar to Support the Creation of Conditions for the Return of Rohingya Refugees," press release, May 31, 2018, https://www.unhcr.org/news/press/2018/5/5b0fff7b4/unhcr-undp-agree-text-mou-myanmar-support-creation-conditions-return-rohingya.html. The text of the memorandum of understanding is available at https://media.un.org/unifeed/en/asset/d216/d2169723.
"Paris Agreement," 2015, https://unfccc.int/sites/default/files/english_paris_agreement.pdf.
Refugee Sponsorship Training Program (Canada), "RAP (Resettlement Assistance Program) Rates," 2023, https://www.rstp.ca/en/bvor/rap-rates/.
UK Government, "Syria Donors Conference 2016: Joint Announcement," November 16, 2015, https://www.gov.uk/government/news/syria-donors-conference-2016-joint-announcement.
United Nations, "The Foundation of International Human Rights Law," https://www.un.org/en/about-us/udhr/foundation-of-international-human-rights-law.

United Nations, "General Assembly Adopts Declaration for Refugees and Migrants, as United Nations, International Organization for Migration Sign Key Agreement," press release, September 19, 2016, https://www.un.org/press/en/2016/ga11820.doc.htm.

United Nations and the Rule of Law, "Freedom of Information," https://www.un.org/ruleoflaw/thematic-areas/governance/freedom-of-information/.

United Nations Climate Change, "Glasgow Climate Pact. Proposal by the President," November 13, 2021, https://unfccc.int/documents/311127.

United Nations Climate Change, "China," https://unfccc.int/node/180417.

United Nations Climate Change, "Warsaw International Mechanism for Loss and Damage Associated with Climate Change Impacts (WIM)," 2013, https://unfccc.int/topics/adaptation-and-resilience/workstreams/loss-and-damage/warsaw-international-mechanism.

United Nations Commission on International Trade Law (UNCITRAL), "Sustainable Development Goals," https://uncitral.un.org/en/about/sdg.

United Nations Department of Economic and Social Affairs (DESA), *World Social Report 2020: Inequality in a Rapidly Changing World* (New York: United Nations 2020), https://www.un.org/development/desa/dspd/wp-content/uploads/sites/22/2020/02/World-Social-Report2020-FullReport.pdf.

United Nations Department of Economic and Social Affairs (DESA), Division for Sustainable Development, "International Cooperation to Accelerate Sustainable Development in Developing Countries & Related Domestic Policies," in *AGENDA 21: The Report of the United Nations Conference on Environment and Development (Earth Summit) in Rio* (1992), http://www.un-documents.net/a21-02.htm.

United Nations Development Programme (UNDP), "Our Work on the Sustainable Development Goals in China," 2021, https://china.un.org/en/sdgs.

United Nations Development Programme (UNDP) Rule of Law and Human Rights Programme, *Annual Report,* 2021, https://www.undp.org/rolhr/publications/2021-annual-report-rule-law-and-human-rights.

United Nations Economic and Social Commission for Asia and the Pacific (ESCAP), ed., *Asia Pacific Migration Report 2020: Assessing Implementation of the Global Compact for Migration* (United Nations, 2020), https://www.unescap.org/sites/default/files/APMR2020_FullReport.pdf.

United Nations Educational, Scientific and Cultural Organization (UNESCO), "UNESCO Sets Ambitious International Standards for Open Science," press release, November 26, 2021, https://www.unesco.org/en/articles/unesco-sets-ambitious-international-standards-open-science?TSPD_101_R0=080713870fab2000e41583d40c4ed5cd84b3e6e510fd3ef09441a62434185f3642c48ca7370312830865f1e49c143000df20a4fcf2a7b331d25518c8fd109dce418f4b3b84ef8936dcb156a6030852709935fdc437b42818835bd82be93ae0d2.

United Nations Environment Programme (UNEP), "Emissions Gap Report 2021," October 26, 2021, https://www.unep.org/resources/emissions-gap-report-2021.

United Nations Environment Programme (UNEP), "Partnership With China," https://www.unep.org/explore-topics/green-economy/what-we-do/economic-and-fiscal-policy/partnership-china.

"United Nations Framework Convention on Climate Change," 1992, https://unfccc.int/files/essential_background/background_publications_htmlpdf/application/pdf/conveng.pdf.

United Nations General Assembly (UNGA), "Delivering Justice: Programme of Action to Strengthen the Rule of Law at the National and International Levels: Report of the Secretary-General," March 16, 2012, A/66/749, http://archive.ipu.org/splz-e/unbrief12/sg-report.pdf.

United Nations General Assembly (UNGA), "Report of the United National High Commissioner for Refugees. Covering the Period 1 July 2020 – 30 June 2021," August 20, 2021, A/76/12, https://www.unhcr.org/615eb32c4.pdf.

United Nations General Assembly (UNGA), "Transforming Our World: The 2030 Agenda for Sustainable Development," Resolution adopted by the General Assembly on September 25, 2015, A/Res/70/1, https://documents-dds-ny.un.org/doc/UNDOC/GEN/N15/291/89/PDF/N1529189.pdf?OpenElement.

United Nations Human Rights Council (UNHRC), "Compilation on China: Report of the Office of the United Nations High Commissioners for Human Rights," August 27, 2018, A/HRC/

WG.6/31/CHN/2, https://documents-dds-ny.un.org/doc/UNDOC/GEN/G18/259/12/PDF/G1825912.pdf?OpenElement.

United Nations Human Rights Council (UNHRC), "Compilation Prepared by the Office of the High Commissioner for Human Rights in Accordance with Paragraph 15(b) of the Annex to Human Rights Council Resolution 5/1 and Paragraph 5 of the Annex to Council Resolution 16/21 – China (Including Hong Kong, China and Macao, China)," August 7, 2013, A/HRC/WG.6/17/CHN/2, https://documents-dds-ny.un.org/doc/UNDOC/GEN/G13/161/90/PDF/G1316190.pdf?OpenElement.

United Nations Human Rights Council (UNHRC), "Compilation Prepared by the Office of the High Commissioner for Human Rights, in Accordance with Paragraph 15(B) of the Annex to Human Rights Council Resolution 5/1 – People's Republic of China (Including Hong Kong and Macao Special Administrative Regions (HKSAR) and (MSAR))," January 6, 2009, https://digitallibrary.un.org/record/645995?v=pdf.

United Nations Human Rights Council (UNHRC), "Independent Investigative Mechanism for Myanmar," https://www.ohchr.org/EN/HRBodies/HRC/IIMM/Pages/Index.aspx.

United Nations Human Rights Council (UNHRC), "Report of the Working Group on the Universal Periodic Review – China," October 5, 2019, A/HRC/11/25, https://documents-dds-ny.un.org/doc/UNDOC/GEN/G09/162/99/PDF/G0916299.pdf?OpenElement.

United Nations Human Rights Council (UNHRC), "Report of the Working Group on the Universal Periodic Review – China (Including Hong Kong, China and Macao, China)," December 4, 2013, A/HRC/25/5, https://documents-dds-ny.un.org/doc/UNDOC/GEN/G13/188/55/PDF/G1318855.pdf?OpenElement.

United Nations Human Rights Council (UNHRC), "Universal Periodic Review – China," 2025, https://www.ohchr.org/EN/HRBodies/UPR/Pages/CNindex.aspx.

United Nations Relief and Works Agency for Palestine Refugees in the Near East (UNRWA), "UNRWA Situation Report #12 on the Lebanon Emergency Response," November 7, 2024, https://www.unrwa.org/resources/reports/unrwa-situation-report-12-lebanon-emergency-response#.

US-Asia Institute, "Rule of Law Exchange Program," https://www.usasiainstitute.org/ruleoflaw.

US Committee for Refugees and Immigrants, "U.S. Committee for Refugees World Refugee Survey 2000 – China," June 1, 2000, https://www.refworld.org/docid/3ae6a8cc4.html.

US Committee for Refugees and Immigrants, "World Refugee Survey 2008 – China," June 19, 2008, https://www.refworld.org/publisher,USCRI,ANNUALREPORT,CHN,485f50ca7b,0.html.

US Department of State, "China's Disregard for Human Rights," https://2017-2021.state.gov/chinas-disregard-for-human-rights/.

US Department of State, "China's Environmental Abuses Fact Sheet," September 25, 2020, https://2017-2021.state.gov/chinas-environmental-abuses-fact-sheet/index.html.

US Department of State, "Integrated Country Strategy: People's Republic of China," February 2, 2023, https://www.state.gov/wp-content/uploads/2023/03/ICS_EAP_China_02FEB2023_PUBLIC.pdf.

US Department of State, "On the U.S. Withdrawal from the Paris Agreement," press statement, November 4, 2019, https://2017-2021.state.gov/on-the-u-s-withdrawal-from-the-paris-agreement/.

US Department of State, "Sunnylands Statement on Enhancing Cooperation to Address the Climate Crisis," November 14, 2023, https://2021-2025.state.gov/sunnylands-statement-on-enhancing-cooperation-to-address-the-climate-crisis/.

US Department of State, "The United States Officially Rejoins the Paris Agreement," February 19, 2021, https://2021-2025.state.gov/the-united-states-officially-rejoins-the-paris-agreement/.

US Department of State, "U.S.-China Joint Glasgow Declaration on Enhancing Climate Action in the 2020s," November 10, 2021, https://2021-2025.state.gov/u-s-china-joint-glasgow-declaration-on-enhancing-climate-action-in-the-2020s/.

US Department of State, "U.S.-China Joint Statement Addressing the Climate Crisis," April 17, 2021,https://2021-2025.state.gov/u-s-china-joint-statement-addressing-the-climate-crisis/.

US Department of State Policy Planning Staff, *The Elements of the China Challenge* (November 2020, rev. December 2020), https://www.state.gov/wp-content/uploads/2020/11/20-02832-Elements-of-China-Challenge-508.pdf.

"Vienna Declaration and Programme of Action," June 25, 1993, A/CONF.157/23, http://www.ohchr.org/EN/ProfessionalInterest/Pages/Vienna.aspx.
White House, "Leaders Summit on Climate Change: Summary of Proceedings," April 23, 2021, https://bidenwhitehouse.archives.gov/briefing-room/statements-releases/2021/04/23/leaders-summit-on-climate-summary-of-proceedings/.
White House, "Meeting of the Major Economies on Energy and Climate September 17, 2021: Chair's Summary," September 17, 2021, https://bidenwhitehouse.archives.gov/briefing-room/statements-releases/2021/09/17/meeting-of-the-major-economies-on-energy-and-climate-september-17-2021-chairs-summary/.
White House, "Putting America First in International Environmental Agreements," Executive Order, January 20, 2025, https://www.whitehouse.gov/presidential-actions/2025/01/putting-america-first-in-international-environmental-agreements/.
White House, "Reevaluating and Realigning United States Foreign Aid," January 20, 2025, https://www.whitehouse.gov/presidential-actions/2025/01/reevaluating-and-realigning-united-states-foreign-aid/.
White House, "Report on the Impact of Climate Change on Migration," October 2021, https://bidenwhitehouse.archives.gov/wp-content/uploads/2021/10/Report-on-the-Impact-of-Climate-Change-on-Migration.pdf.
White House, "Statement by President Trump on the Paris Climate Accord," June 1, 2017, https://trumpwhitehouse.archives.gov/briefings-statements/statement-president-trump-paris-climate-accord/.
White House, "Withdrawing the United States from the World Health Organization," Executive Order, January 20, 2025, https://www.whitehouse.gov/presidential-actions/2025/01/withdrawing-the-united-states-from-the-worldhealth-organization/.
World Health Organization (WHO), "Constitution of World Health Organization" (1946 as amended), https://apps.who.int/gb/bd/PDF/bd47/EN/constitution-en.pdf?ua=1.
World Health Organization (WHO), "Human Rights and Health," December 29, 2017, https://www.who.int/news-room/fact-sheets/detail/human-rights-and-health.
World Health Organization (WHO), *Leading the Realization of Human Rights to Health and Through Health: Report of the High-Level Working Group on the Health and Human Rights of Women, Children and Adolescents* (Geneva: WHO, 2017), https://www.ohchr.org/Documents/Issues/Women/WRGS/Health/ReportHLWG-humanrights-health.pdf.
World Health Organization (WHO), "Thirteenth General Program of Work 2019–2023: Promote Health, Keep the World Safe, Serve the Vulnerable," 2019, https://iris.who.int/server/api/core/bitstreams/f35461a5-91b1-41b0-8ef8-b4bd66e08449/content.
WHO Scientific Advisory Group for the Origins of Novel Pathogens (SAGO), "Preliminary Report of the SAGO," June 9, 2022, https://cdn.who.int/media/docs/default-source/scientific-advisory-group-on-the-origins-of-novel-pathogens/sago-report-09062022.pdf?sfvrsn=42b55bbc_1&download=true.
World Bank, "Refugee Population by Country or Territory of Asylum – China," https://fred.stlouisfed.org/series/SMPOPREFGCHN#:~:text=Markets%20%3E%20Population%20%3E%20Migration-,Refugee%20Population%20by%20Country%20or%20Territory%20of%20Asylum%20for%20China,Need%20help?.

Index

(f) after a page number indicates a figure; (t) after a page number indicates a table

Set in Futura Condensed, SimSun, and Warnock
by Artegraphica Design Co. Ltd.

Copyeditor: Francis Chow

Proofreader: Alison Strobel

Indexer: Margaret de Boer

Cover designer: Alexa Love

Cover image: iStock/Yamko

Authorized Representative: Easy Access System Europe –
Mustamäe tee 50, 10621 Tallinn, Estonia,
gpsr.requests@easproject.com

MIX

Papier | Fördert gute Waldnutzung

FSC® C083411

Kolibri 360 GmbH
Ferdinand-Jühlke-Straße 7
99095 Erfurt, Deutschland
produktsicherheit@kolibri360.de